DATE DUE

No — 2'00			

DEMCO 38-296

Unbound Voices

Unbound Voices

A DOCUMENTARY HISTORY OF
CHINESE WOMEN IN SAN FRANCISCO

Judy Yung

UNIVERSITY OF CALIFORNIA PRESS
Berkeley • Los Angeles • London

University of California Press
Berkeley and Los Angeles, California

University of California Press, Ltd.
London, England

Library of Congress Cataloging-in-Publication Data

Yung, Judy.
    Unbound voices : a documentary history of Chinese women in San Francisco /
Judy Yung.
        p.   cm.
    Includes index.
    ISBN 0-520-20870-6 (alk. paper). — ISBN 0-520-21860-4 (pbk. : alk paper)
        1. Chinese American women—California—San Francisco—History Sources.
    2. Chinese American women—California—San Francisco—Social conditions
    Sources.   3. Women immigrants—California—San Francisco—History Sources.
    4. Chinese American women—California—San Francisco Biography.   5. San
    Francisco (Calif.)—Social conditions Sources.   6. San Francisco (Calif.)—Ethnic
    relations Sources.   I. Title.
    F869.S39C597   1999
    979.4'61004951'00922—dc21   99-31772
                                                                     CIP

Manufactured in the United States of America
08   07   06   05   04   03   02   01   00   99
10   9   8   7   6   5   4   3   2   1

To my sisters Sharon, Sandy, Virginia, and Patricia
and my brother Warren

Contents

Illustrations

Terminology and Transliterations

Although *Oriental* was the common term used to describe East Asians in America (Chinese, Japanese, and Korean Americans) until recent times, I choose to use *Asian American* for political reasons and not to hyphenate *Chinese American* even when used as an adjective. During the late 1960s, Chinese and Japanese American activists called attention to *Oriental* as a derogatory name that connotes exoticism and inferiority. The term *Asian American* became the preferred name in recognition of the group's common history of oppression, geographical origins, panethnic identity, and political destiny. The hyphen was eliminated because it inferred that Chinese Americans have split identities, that somehow they are not fully American like everyone else. For the same reasons and to be consistent, I do not use the hyphen when referring to any ethnic American group.

In regard to racial and ethnic terms, I use what is generally preferred by the groups themselves. *Black* and *African American* are used interchangeably; so are *Native American* and *American Indian*. Depending on the time period under discussion, I use either Latino, Hispanic, Mexican, or Chicano; minority women or women of color. In a racial context, I generally use *white* instead of *European American*. Otherwise, I try to be ethnic specific in identifying the group by using *Italian American, German American, Jewish American*, etc. I capitalize *Black* but not *white* in recognition of the distinctive history, cultural identity, and political legacy that the former but not the latter term encompasses. The term *America* should be understood as an abbreviated form of *United States of America*. To be *Americanized* is to become acculturated but not necessarily assimilated into American life. To avoid the trap of associating the dominant white group with everything that is American, *Western* is preferred over *American* when the reference is to cultural practices; thus, *Western* dress, not *American* dress.

I call the *first generation* those who were foreign-born and came to the United States as immigrants, and their children who were born in the United States *second generation* or *American-born Chinese*. When referring to both groups, I use either *Chinese in America* or *Chinese Americans*, especially when I need to differentiate them from the Chinese in China. For example, when comparing women in China and Chinese women in America, I use *Chinese women* for the former group and *Chinese American women* for the latter. *Overseas Chinese* is used instead of *Chinese Americans* when the reference point is in China.

Following standard practice, I use the *pinyin* romanization system for Chinese proper nouns, except in cases where the names have been commonly spelled in a different romanization system, such as Sun Yat-sen and Macao. For common words and phrases in the Cantonese dialect or direct quotes from Cantonese-speaking persons, I use the Cantonese spelling according to Sidney Lau's *A Practical Cantonese-English Dictionary* (Hong Kong: The Government Printer, 1977). Place-names in Cantonese are followed by the *pinyin* spelling whenever deemed helpful; for example, Chungshan (Zhongshan) District. All Chinese proper nouns and terms mentioned in this book are recorded in the Glossary in the appendix, together with their Chinese characters. In addition, Chinese terms are generally defined at their first appearance in the text.

When using a person's Chinese name, I follow Chinese practice by giving the surname (family name) first, followed by the given name (usually two characters), without an intervening comma. For example, in the name Tom Yip Jing, Tom is the surname and Yip Jing, the given name. Exceptions occur when a particular individual (e.g., Joe Shoong) chooses to reverse the order to conform with Western usage. Without meaning to be disrespectful, I generally use the person's given name instead of his or her last name whenever I refer to him or her more than once in the text. Since many Chinese Americans share the same surname, I adopted this practice to avoid confusion. The appearance of *Shee* in a woman's name indicates that she is married. For example, a woman with the maiden name of Law who married into the Low family would thenceforth be known as Law Shee Low.

Chinese dates prior to the adoption of the Western calendar in 1949 are rendered according to the Chinese lunar calendar, followed by the corresponding Western date in parentheses. Before the establishment of the Chinese Republic in 1912, Chinese dates were reckoned by the emperor's reign; for example, K.S. 33/10-13 meant in the 33d year of Emperor Kuang Su's reign, 10th month, 13th day (November 18, 1907). Beginning in 1912, Chinese dates went by the name of the new republic; for example, CR 26-1-20 meant in the 26th year of the Chinese Republic, 1st month, 20th day (March 2, 1937). In converting Chinese dates into Western dates I followed Liang Qi and Hua Chao, eds., *Zhongxi duizhao yinyang hebi wannianli* (Ten-thousand-year calendar: a comparison of Chinese and Western dates) (Hong Kong: Shanghai Book Store, 1984).

Finally, although it is standard practice to indicate spelling and grammatical errors in quoted passages by the use of "[*sic*]," I chose to forgo doing so in many instances in order to remain faithful to the exact wording and style of speech, and to avoid interrupting the flow of the conversation.

Introduction

As a second-generation Chinese American woman from San Francisco Chinatown, I grew up in the 1950s with very little understanding of my own historical background. My parents, who were immigrants from Doumen District in Guangdong Province, refused to answer any of my questions about our family history, so afraid were they of having their illegal immigration status exposed. Although the elementary school I attended was almost all Chinese, we were taught a very Eurocentric male version of American history. There was no mention of African Americans, American Indians, Mexican Americans, Asian Americans, or women for that matter. Every day after "American" school I attended St. Mary's Chinese Language School, where I was taught the Chinese classics, history, patriotic heroes such as Sun Yat-sen and Yue Fei, and made to feel proud of my cultural heritage. The only famous women who were mentioned were beauties like Yang Guifei, who was blamed for the downfall of the empire. Looking back at my upbringing and education, I now see why I knew so little about my own history as a Chinese American woman.

Upon graduation from college I entered the female-dominated profession of librarianship and was assigned to the Chinatown Branch Library, where I went as a child to read. I would have been content to stay there until I retired except that I became politically aware of the omission of Chinese American and women's history in the public record. After park ranger Alexander Weiss discovered Chinese poetry carved into the barrack walls of the abandoned Angel Island Immigration Station in 1970, I was drawn into my first research project, translating these poems and interviewing Chinese immigrants about what happened to them at Angel Island. Historian Him Mark Lai, poet Genny Lim, and I ended up self-publishing *Island: Poetry and History of Chinese Immigrants on Angel Island, 1910–1940,* since no publisher at the time believed the subject important enough to be marketable. Inspired by the civil rights and women's liberation movements, I turned my attention to recovering Chinese American women's history after *Island* was published. With a grant from the U.S. Department of Education (Women's Educational Equity Act), Genny Lim, Vincente Tang, and I embarked on the Chinese Women of America Research Project, which resulted in a traveling exhibit and my next book, *Chinese Women of America: A Pictorial History.* Given the absence of written accounts by Chinese American women themselves and the availability of only stereotypical works by missionaries and journalists, we looked for women's stories in primary sources such as immigration documents, Chinese-language newspapers, and the records of women's organizations. We also conducted oral history interviews with 274 women of diverse backgrounds in different parts of the United States.

My enthusiasm for researching and writing Chinese American history soared as a result of these two book projects. I decided to leave librarianship and return to graduate school to improve my skills as a historian and scholar. While pursuing a Ph.D. in ethnic studies at the University of California, Berkeley, I made Chinese American women's history the focus of my dissertation. I wanted to move beyond descriptive history and to delve deeper into the hows and whys of Chinese women's lives in a specific location during a period of great social ferment. I decided to look at social change for Chinese women in San Francisco from 1902 to 1945. The result was *Unbound Feet: A Social History of Chinese Women in San Francisco.* By then I had accumulated a vast amount of primary materials on Chinese American women, crammed into sixteen vertical file drawers in my study. Although I had quoted extensively from these sources in my published works, I felt that my selective use of them had not done them justice. The full range of the women's voices deserved to be heard.

Unbound Voices: A Documentary History of Chinese Women in San Francisco thus complements my earlier work, *Unbound Feet,* in that it lets Chinese women tell their own stories about how they made a home for themselves and their families in San Francisco from the gold rush years through World War II. Without interruption, we hear their testimonies as they were interrogated by immigration officials at Angel Island; their laments at being abandoned in China by Gold Mountain (U.S.) husbands; their sorrow over being sold into servitude and duped into prostitution; their dreams, struggles, and rewards as hardworking wives and mothers in America; the stories of their daughters in confronting cultural conflicts and racial discrimination; the myriad ways women coped with the Great Depression; and their contributions to the causes of women's emancipation, Chinese nationalism, workers' rights, and World War II. By itself, *Unbound Voices* can also be used and read as a collection of primary sources, an educational tool for researching and reclaiming women's history, as well as a feminist lesson on how one group of women overcame the legacy of bound feet and bound lives in America.

The symphony of voices presented here lends immediacy, urgency, and reality to the lives of Chinese American women. Contrary to popular stereotypes of Chinese women as exotic curios, sexual slaves, drudges, or passive victims, this anthology allows a diverse group of women to express themselves as active agents in the making of their own history. Despite attempts by Chinese patriarchy and the intersectionality of race, class, and gender in America to silence them, Chinese women did manage to leave behind a written and oral record of their lives, thoughts, and feelings. For example, I found full transcripts of my great-grandmother's and mother's immigration interrogations at the National Archives. My painstaking search through Chinese-language and English-language microfilmed newspapers yielded such gems as a speech in 1901 by Mai Zhouyi, a merchant's wife, condemning the mistreatment of Chinese immigrants detained in the "wooden shed," and numerous articles by feminists and reformers such as Sieh King King and Jane Kwong Lee on Chinese nationalism, women's issues, and the war effort. In the meticulous records kept by the Presbyterian Mission Home I found the testimony and letters of Wong Ah So, who was unwillingly sold into prostitution and later rescued by missionary worker Donaldina Cameron. Oral history interviews that I conducted with Chinese women of different generations and socioeconomic backgrounds, aside from providing personal recollections and stories, led me to private letters, unpublished autobiographies, scrapbooks of news clippings and memorabilia, and family photo albums. (For a fuller discussion of my oral history methodology, see the appendix, "Giving Voice to Chinese American Women.")

From this rich array of primary materials I selected for inclusion in *Unbound Voices* a representative sampling of government documents per-

tinent to the immigration experiences of Chinese women; unpublished
or relatively unknown writings by Chinese American women, including
poems, letters, essays, autobiographical accounts, speeches, and editorials; and oral history interviews conducted by staff of the Survey of Race
Relations research project in the 1920s, the Chinese Historical Society of
America in the 1970s, the Chinese Women of America Research Project
in the early 1980s, and more recently by myself for *Unbound Feet.* The
main criteria for inclusion in this volume were that the entry had to be a
primary source related to the history of Chinese American women and
cited in *Unbound Feet.* Taken together, the selections in *Unbound Voices*
provide readers with an intimate understanding of a diverse range of
women-centered experiences and perspectives. We hear the voices of prostitutes and *mui tsai* (domestic slavegirls), immigrant wives of merchants
and laborers, American-born daughters of working-class background as
well as those with education and professional training, Christians and pa-
gans, homemakers and social activists alike. Thus, while the stories stem
from singular experiences, they are at the same time representative of the
lived experiences of Chinese women in San Francisco from 1850 to 1945.

In keeping with *Unbound Feet,* I chose to arrange the selections in the
same chronological and topical order, which allows us to see how social
change occurred for Chinese American women when their individual personalities intersected with historical moments and socioeconomic circumstances. As I tried to show in *Unbound Feet,* Chinese women in San
Francisco came to unbind their feet (figuratively) and their socially restricted lives (literally) in the first half of the twentieth century because
of (1) Chinese nationalism and the women's emancipation movement in
China, which raised the political and social consciousness of Chinese
women in America; (2) Protestant missionary women in the Progressive
era who helped to eradicate Chinese prostitution and provide a safe space
in the public arena for Chinese American women; (3) economic opportunities that opened up for Chinese women outside the home in the 1920s
and through the Great Depression, and then outside Chinatown during
World War II; (4) the effects of acculturation on American-born daughters through public school, church, social organizations, and popular culture; and (5) a more favorable attitude toward Chinese Americans during World War II because of labor shortages and China's allied relationship
to the United States. These same points are reinforced in the introductions
to each of the six sections in *Unbound Voices* in an effort to lend organization, continuity, interpretation, and historical context to the women's
voices without essentializing their history or interrupting their stories. For

the same reasons, I strategically placed historical references, biographical information, cultural explanations, and any critique of the sources in the introductions and footnotes whenever helpful.

Also in keeping with *Unbound Feet,* I employed footbinding as a symbol of women's subjugation and subordination to organize the selections into six sections, beginning with my mother's immigration history as an introduction to my work ("Lessons from My Mother's Past"), then moving from the nineteenth century ("Bound Feet") to immigrant women ("Unbound Feet") and the second generation ("First Steps") in the early twentieth century, to the Great Depression ("Long Strides"), and finally to the advances made during World War II ("In Step"). Thus, I begin the book with my search for the "truth" in my mother's family history, which ultimately led me to research the history of Chinese American women.

In Part I, "Lessons from My Mother's Past: Researching Chinese Immigrant Women's History," I show how complicated the immigration process was for Chinese immigrants like my mother because of the Chinese Exclusion Act of 1882, which prohibited the immigration of Chinese laborers and their families for over sixty years. During this exclusion period, Chinese immigrants had to be inventive and resourceful in circumventing the restrictive policies. By comparing the official testimonies given by my great-grandparents and parents to immigration officials against the coaching book used by my mother in preparation for the immigration interrogation as well as oral history interviews I conducted with my mother, I tried to figure out how and why Chinese immigrants such as my mother had to lie in order to immigrate to this country. In the process, I came to understand the problems involved in using immigration documents to reclaim Chinese American women's and family history.

The selections in Part II, "Bound Feet: Chinese Women in the Nineteenth Century," confirm that most Chinese women led socially restricted lives in San Francisco. Sexist Chinese proverbs, the laments of a wife left behind in China, and the stories of prostitutes, *mui tsai,* and immigrant wives in America shed light on how women's lives were triply bound by racism and sexism in the larger society and by the patriarchal social structure within Chinatown. But even as these women appeared to comply with gender norms and expectations, they were engaged in strategies and activities that actually challenged these same norms. For example, while faithfully waiting for her Gold Mountain husband to return home, Kwong King You pursued an education and became a midwife in order to support herself and her children through the Sino-Japanese War years.

Most of the testimonies by Chinese prostitutes, as told through white missionary women who befriended them, speak of the horrible conditions of indentured prostitution, but also of the women's coping mechanisms and hope for escape from their misery. As reported in a San Francisco newspaper, Huey Sin, a madam and owner of seven slavegirls, decided to free all of them, but it is not clear whether she did this out of rebellion, compassion, or because of her recent conversion to Christianity. One thing is for sure, Mary Tape stands out as an outspoken woman when she publicly condemns the San Francisco Board of Education for stopping her daughter Mamie from attending school with white children.

In contrast, the selections in Part III, "Unbound Feet: Chinese Immigrant Women, 1902–1929," illustrate how women immigrating during a progressive era—in both China and the United States—found new opportunities to bring about social change in their lives. Chinese newspapers were full of speeches and articles by women denouncing the practice of footbinding and advocating women's rights and education, some of which are reprinted here. By profiling the stories of a Chinese prostitute, a hardworking wife and mother, and a foreign student who becomes a community worker, I try to compare the diverse work, family, and social lives of Chinese immigrant women and show how each in her own way accommodated race, class, and gender oppression. During this period Chinese immigrant women, encouraged by Chinese nationalist thoughts on women's emancipation and American progressive ideals of freedom and equality, began to unbind their lives by moving from the domestic sphere into the public arena, as exemplified by Jane Kwong Lee's story and the founding of the Chinese Women's Self-Reliance Association (1913) and the Chinese YWCA (1916).

The stories and writings in Part IV, "First Steps: The Second Generation, 1920s," are the richest of all because of the literacy and acculturation level of American-born Chinese women under the influences of public schooling, Christianity, and popular culture. Coming of age in the 1920s, many daughters found themselves caught in a cultural dilemma: How could they exercise their rights as freethinking individuals while at the same time playing the role of obedient and subservient daughters at home? As U.S. citizens with political rights, how should they deal with racism and sexism in the larger society? There is a wide range of responses. Some like Esther Wong acquiesced in an attempt to please their parents. Others like Rose Yuen Ow and Flora Belle Jan openly rebelled by becoming a cabaret dancer and pursuing a career in writing. The majority, however, accommodated the boundaries of race, class, and gender by creating a new bicultural niche for themselves. They held on to their cultural heritage even as they became modernized in their outlook, appearance, and lifestyle, albeit in a segregated setting, as they strove to overcome discrimination.

The Chinese in San Francisco experienced the Great Depression differently than the rest of the country. As the voices in Part V, "Long Strides: The Great Depression, 1930s," make clear, Chinese American women in particular stood to gain more than lose by the hard economic times and liberal politics. Immigrant women such as Wong See Chan and Law Shee Low talk about how they became the chief breadwinners after their husbands lost their jobs and about how they found ways to make ends meet. The changing political climate encouraged second-generation women, who were less affected by unemployment, to become social activists by advocating for and providing public assistance to the less fortunate in the community. With the New Deal in place, Chinese garment workers like Sue Ko Lee took the initiative to form the first Chinese chapter of the International Ladies' Garment Workers' Union and to stage and sustain one of the longest strikes in Chinese American history. Thanks to Sue Ko Lee's diligence in keeping a scrapbook of the strike and her willingness to be interviewed, we hear for the first time the workers' perspective on the 1938 strike against Joe Shoong's National Dollar Stores.

China's war of resistance against Japan and the United States' entry into World War II provided Chinese American women with unprecedented opportunities to improve their socioeconomic status and move into the public arena as they worked on behalf of the war effort. In Part VI, "In Step: The War Years, 1931–1945," we hear about the gathering of forces and about Chinese women falling in step with others in their community and the country to fight for the twin causes of Chinese nationalism and American democracy. Stories of women's important role in the war effort were well represented in the periodicals of the day. Included in this section are the editorials of Chinese women's organizations rousing women to action; autobiographical accounts by Jane Kwong Lee and Dr. Margaret Chung, two exemplary female commandos on the home front; and interviews with May Lew Gee, a shipyard worker, Corporal Ruth Chan Jang of the Women's Air Corps, and Lorena How, whose mother was active in the war effort. Inspired by Chinese nationalism, American patriotism, and Chinese American feminism, women gave according to their means and in so doing fell in step with the rest of the country, earning both the satisfaction of serving their country and the respect of fellow Americans.

Unbound Voices and my efforts to reclaim Chinese American women's history would not have been possible without the generous support and assistance of many individuals and institutions. For their research assistance, I wish to acknowledge Chester Chan, Eva Ng Chin, Kathy Chin, Ruth Chinn, Philip P. Choy, Arthur Dong, Marlon K. Hom, Madeline Hsu, Him Mark Lai, Ann Lane, Erika Lee, Sandy Lee, Sharon Lee, Wing Lew, Haiming Liu, Ruthanne Lum McCunn, Peggy Pascoe, Tom Ngun Dai, Guanghua Wang, Eddie Wong, Judy Wu, Henry Yu, Xiaojian Zhao, Wei Chi Poon of the Ethnic Studies Library at the University of California, Berkeley, staffs of the National Archives in San Bruno, San Francisco Public Library, Bancroft Library at the University of California, Berkeley, the Labor Archives and Research Center at San Francisco State University, McHenry Library at the University of California, Santa Cruz, and the Hoover Institution on War, Revolution, and Peace at Stanford University.

As oral history forms the core of this study, I am especially grateful to the many Chinese American women who entrusted me with their life stories and to the sons and daughters who were willing to talk to me about their mothers' lives: Jeanne Fong, Alice Sue Fun, May Lew Gee, Gladys Ng Gin, Lorena How, Penny Chan Huie, Portia Chan Huie, Bessie Hung, Ruth Chan Jang, Jew Law Ying, Jew Siu Ping, Florence Chinn Kwan, Kwong King You, Clara Lee, Jane Kwong Lee, Louise Schulze Lee, Sue Ko Lee, Verna Lee, Law Shee Low, Victor Low, Eva Lowe, Fred Schulze, Wong Shee Chan, Jessie Lee Yip, and Alice Fong Yu.

For their expert and technical assistance, I wish to acknowledge Chris Huie for the photo reproductions; Ellen Yeung and Marlon K. Hom for translations from Chinese into English; the staffs of the Word Processing Center, University of California, Santa Cruz, for scanning much of the material; Anne Canright for her fine copyediting; and the University of California Press for guiding the publication process.

I want to also thank Ramón Gutiérrez for suggesting that I collect the voices from *Unbound Feet* into a second volume; George Anthony Peffer for coming up with the title, *Unbound Voices;* Dorothy Ko, Him Mark Lai, Ruthanne Lum McCunn, Valerie Matsumoto, Alice Yang Murray, Peggy Pascoe, Vicki Ruiz, and Chris Shinn for their critical feedback on the text; and the Committee on Research at the University of California, Santa Cruz, for granting me faculty research funds to complete this book.

PART ONE

Lessons from My Mother's Past

Researching Chinese Women's Immigration History

For a long time I assumed that my mother, Jew Law Ying, was the first in her family to immigrate to the United States, arriving in 1941. Only after I began researching our family history did I realize that her grandfather Chin Lung came in 1882, her grandmother Leong Shee arrived in 1893, and her mother, Chin Suey Kum, was born in San Francisco in 1894. My mother, born in China, was thus a derivative U.S. citizen; yet the only way she could fulfill her dream of coming to America was by marrying a Gold Mountain man like my father, Yung Hin Sen, who had been in the United States since 1921. Here the story gets complicated, because not only was my father a "paper son," someone who had entered this country using a bogus identity, but he was also a laborer and according to American law not eligible to bring his wife and family to the United States at all. Yet he evidently found a way to do so. How I figured this all out in the process of reconstructing my mother's family history—by poring over immigration files at the National Archives in San Bruno, California, and interviewing relatives and my mother about her life story—is a lesson in the complications involved in researching Chinese women's immigration history. In short, I learned that no document—whether a legal affidavit, an immigration transcript, a letter, or an oral history interview—should be taken at face value; care must

An earlier version of this essay appeared in *Chinese America: History and Perspectives,* *1998* (San Francisco: Chinese Historical Society of America, 1998), pp. 25–56.

be taken to distinguish the truth from the lies in piecing together a family history.

Many of the complications stem from the Chinese Exclusion Act of 1882, which prohibited the further immigration of Chinese laborers.[1] Passed at the height of the anti-Chinese movement, the Exclusion Act initiated a new era of restrictive immigration policy. For the first time in U.S. history, an immigrant group was barred entry on the basis of race and nationality. The act paved the way for the exclusion of other Asian immigrant groups and for severe restrictions on the numbers of immigrants from southern and eastern Europe.[2] Renewed in 1892 and extended indefinitely in 1904, the Chinese Exclusion Act was not repealed until 1943. Thus for more than sixty years, immigration from China was limited to certain exempt classes, namely merchants, teachers, students, officials, tourists, and those who claimed U.S. citizenship under the Fourteenth Amendment. Taking advantage of these loopholes, the Chinese developed an intricate system of fraudulent entry. For example, upon returning from a visit to China a Chinese merchant would claim the birth of a son, thus creating a slot by which a kinsman could later immigrate to the United States as his paper son. A Chinese claiming to be a native-born citizen needed only to produce one Chinese witness to verify his identity. Once verified, he would be eligible to bring in his foreign-born wife and children, real or otherwise. Thus, for a certain amount of money (usually $100 per year of age), people like my father—a peasant—could buy papers and come posing as the son of a merchant or U.S. citizen.[3]

---

1. For historical background on the causes and impact of the Chinese Exclusion Act of 1882, see Elmer Clarence Sandmeyer, *The Anti-Chinese Movement in California* (Urbana: University of Illinois Press, 1973); Alexander Saxton, *The Indispensable Enemy: Labor and the Anti-Chinese Movement in California* (Berkeley: University of California Press, 1980); Stuart Creighton Miller, *The Unwelcome Immigrant: The American Image of the Chinese, 1785–1882* (Berkeley: University of California Press, 1969); and Sucheng Chan, ed., *Entry Denied: Exclusion and the Chinese Community in America, 1882–1943* (Philadelphia: Temple University Press, 1991).

2. See Lucy E. Salyer, *Laws Harsh as Tigers: Chinese Immigrants and the Shaping of Modern Immigration Law* (Chapel Hill: University of North Carolina Press, 1995); and Erika Lee, "At America's Gates: Chinese Immigration During the Exclusion Era, 1882–1943" (Ph.D. diss., University of California, Berkeley, 1998).

3. Aside from the "paper son" system, other ways in which the Chinese circumvented the exclusion laws included being smuggled across the border and establishing merchant status by being falsely listed as a business partner. See Erika Lee, "At America's Gates," chap. 5.

Chinese women also immigrated as "paper daughters," though in lower numbers than the men. Most, however, came as wives of U.S. citizens or merchants. Then, after the Immigration Act of 1924 prohibited the immigration of Chinese wives of U.S. citizens, women mainly came as daughters of U.S. citizens or wives of merchants.[4] Both my great-grandmother and my mother immigrated as merchant wives; but whereas my great-grandfather was truly a merchant, my father was not.

Immigration officials, aware of these efforts on the part of the Chinese to circumvent the Exclusion Act, set up an elaborate process by which to keep the Chinese out. The burden of proof rested on the immigrants to prove their legal right to enter the United States. They had to pass a grueling examination covering their family history, village life in China, and relatives in the United States; the latter were in turn asked the same questions for confirmation of identity and relationship. Any discrepancies could mean deportation. Official records were kept of all documents and proceedings pertaining to each immigration case, which was linked to file numbers of other related cases. In anticipation of the interrogation, prospective immigrants in China spent months studying "coaching books" that gave answers to questions immigration officials were likely to ask them.[5] If the immigrant or his or her relatives were paper sons or paper daughters, much of the coaching book would contain bogus information. Since my father's identity was false but my mother's was true, only half of her coaching book contained false information.

Aware of this immigration history and process, I began researching my mother's family history at the National Archives—Pacific Sierra Region in San Bruno, California, which houses Record Group 85, that is,

---

4. In response to growing nativism, Congress passed the Immigration Act of 1924, aimed at excluding undesirable immigrants, namely those from southern and eastern Europe, and all aliens ineligible for citizenship, specifically the Chinese, Japanese, and Koreans. Chinese merchant wives were still admissible because of treaty obligations, but Chinese wives of U.S. citizens, being themselves ineligible for citizenship, were not.

5. Based on a number of sources, I estimate that 90 percent of the Chinese immigrants were fraudulent, 25 percent failed the interrogation, and 70 to 80 percent of those ordered debarred managed to enter the United States by appealing their cases in federal court. For a fuller discussion of the Chinese immigration process during the exclusion period, see Him Mark Lai, Genny Lim, and Judy Yung, *Island: Poetry and History of Chinese Immigrants on Angel Island, 1910–1940* (Seattle: University of Washington Press, 1991); and Erika Lee, "At America's Gates."

documents of the Immigration and Naturalization Service (INS) relating to the enforcement of the Chinese Exclusion Act in the San Francisco and Honolulu districts.[6] Because my great-grandfather Chin Lung was a prosperous farmer and businessman who made a number of trips back to China, it was easy to find his file by his name and the names of his businesses, Sing Kee Company and Shanghai Trunk Company. His file led me to my great-grandmother Leong Shee's file as well as that of their children. Similarly, I located my mother's immigration file through my father's case file, which I found by providing staff at the National Archives with the name of the ship he came on and the date of arrival. Contained within each case file were applications, certificates of identity, INS interrogation transcripts and decisions, witness statements and affidavits, photographs, and exhibit letters. Keeping in mind that my father was a paper son, I used these materials judiciously. Only after interviewing my parents and relatives about their versions of "the truth" was I able to tell what in these files was fake and what was true. In the process, I came to understand how hard it was for Chinese like my parents to immigrate to this country during the exclusion period, how one lie grew into many, and how one paper son could complicate matters for others in the family.

I have selected a number of documents from the INS files of Leong Shee and Jew Law Ying to illustrate the complicated process of immigration for Chinese women as well as the deceit they had to employ in order to circumvent anti-Chinese immigration policies. Because both my great-grandmother and my mother came at times when the Chinese Exclusion Act was still enforced, the burden of proof was on them to show

---

6. Record Group 85, which contains all documents relating to the enforcement of the Chinese Exclusion Act from 1882 to 1943, can be found in most of the regional archives and the National Archives in Washington, D.C. The National Archives—Pacific Sierra Region has a microfilm copy of the index to INS case files of the San Francisco District Office for all immigrants to San Francisco. The Chinese files are grouped in three major categories: Chinese Arrival Case Files (1882–ca. 1950), which document first-time immigrant arrivals; Chinese Departure Case Files (1913–ca. 1950), which document the departure of Chinese Americans for China; and Chinese Partnership Files, which relate to individual merchants and merchant firms (1890–ca. 1940). There is also a partial index by name to certificates of identity that could lead to a specific file. Other ways to access a case file are by the name of the ship the immigrant came on and its date of arrival, or the names of any business firms the immigrant might have been connected to. See Waverly Lowell, "Chinese Immigration and Chinese in the United States: Records in the Regional Archives of the National Archives and Records Administration," National Archives and Records Administration, Reference Information Paper 99 (1996).

that they were indeed the wives of merchants and therefore exempt from exclusion. Prior to their journey across the seas, their husbands had to declare merchant status with the immigration service. An affidavit in the file of Sing Kee Company dated August 16, 1893, showed that Chin Lung swore before a notary public that he had been a resident of San Francisco for fourteen years and a merchant and member of "Sing Kee & Company, Dealers in General Merchandise" for eleven years, and "that the interest of each of the named members in said firm is $500.00 or more." Another affidavit, dated May 11, 1892, and signed by eight white witnesses, attested to Chin Lung's status as merchant.[7] A third affidavit, dated May 14, 1892, stated that Chin Lung was a merchant and, furthermore, that his wife, a resident of San Francisco, had departed for Hong Kong in 1889 with their four-year-old daughter, Ah Kum. This was not the case. Subsequent testimonies by Chin Lung to the immigration service and oral histories I conducted with relatives confirm that Great-Grandmother immigrated to the United States for the first time in 1893.[8]

For some reason, Leong Shee felt compelled to claim Ah Kum, the eight-year-old *mui tsai* who accompanied her from China, as her daughter, which meant she also had to lie about the place and date of her marriage in order to justify having an eight-year-old daughter (Leong Shee's testimony dated April 18, 1893). This fabrication would come back to haunt her thirty-seven years later when she prepared to leave for China for the second time. In Leong Shee's testimony dated July 24, 1929, she denied outright that she had ever said that she immigrated to the United States before 1893 and asserted that Ah Kum died soon after they arrived in 1893. Although this was a major discrepancy, the immigration inspector ignored it, decided that there was sufficient proof that she was a legal resident of the United States, and approved her application for a return certificate.

According to Leong Shee's file, the only other time she encountered the immigration service was when she returned from China in 1921 after a seventeen-year stay, accompanied by Chin Lung, who by then had

---

7. The language and conditions in Chin Lung's affidavit met the requirements of the Exclusion Act of September 13, 1888, in regard to Chinese persons leaving the United States temporarily. Only two white witnesses were required. The fact that Chin Lung had eight witnesses speaks to his conscientiousness—or to his wariness of immigration officials.

8. Leong Shee returned to China in 1904, remaining there until 1921 when she re-immigrated to the United States.

made a total of six trips back to China since he first immigrated to the United States in 1882. (Each time he left he had to reestablish his merchant status, and on each return he was subjected to an immigration interrogation.) To make it easier on her, Chin Lung had an attorney request that Leong Shee, because she was a "first cabin" passenger and because her status as wife to Chin Lung, a merchant, had been previously established, "be permitted to land immediately upon the arrival of the steamer and not be sent to the Angel Island Immigration Station."[9] The very next day the request was granted on the basis that there was indeed such proof in her immigration records and, as the immigration inspector noted, "her alleged husband, Chin Lung, is well known to the officers of this Service, having been a merchant of Stockton for many years and is reported to be one of the wealthiest Chinese merchants residing in that vicinity and is commonly known as the 'Potato King.'"[10] Here we see an example of how upper-class status accorded one better treatment on arrival in this country.

Because my great-grandmother Leong Shee decided to return to China with all her children in 1904 and then married off my grandmother, a native-born U.S. citizen, to a prominent herb doctor, my mother was born in China. Although my mother was a daughter of a U.S. citizen, immigration as a derivative citizen through the mother was not legally permissible. Thus, she could come to America only by being arranged in marriage to my father, a Gold Mountain man, and in 1941 found herself repeating the same immigration process her grandmother had experienced close to a half-century earlier. She immigrated as a merchant's wife.

Documents in my mother's file show that my father, Yung Hin Sen, who was actually a poor gardener, had found a way to establish merchant status. This he did by investing $1,000, which he borrowed from various relatives, in the Far East Company, a Chinatown import busi-

---

9. Attorneys Worley and Goldberg, letter to Commissioner of Immigration, Port of San Francisco, August 11, 1921 (Leong Shee, folder 12017/37232, Chinese Departure Case Files, San Francisco District Office, INS, Record Group 85, National Archives, San Bruno, California). From 1910 to 1940 Chinese immigrants upon arrival in San Francisco were detained at the Angel Island Immigration Station and subjected to physical examinations and interrogations to determine their legal right to enter this country. See Lai, Lim, and Yung, *Island*.

10. Memorandum dated August 12, 1921, from Immigrant Inspector L. A. Root of the Angel Island Station (Leong Shee, folder 12017/37232).

ness. He then had the manager of that company and two white witnesses (a drayman and an expressman who had dealings with the firm) sign affidavits attesting to his active membership in the firm for more than one year past. Next, he had to appear at the Angel Island Immigration Station with the manager. Both were interrogated about details regarding the firm's business and Yung Hin Sen's role as salesman and partner. Then my mother had to apply for a visa as "wife of a domiciled Chinese merchant" from the American consulate general in Hong Kong. Meanwhile, she memorized the information in the coaching book about my father's "paper" family and village, her own family and village background, and their marriage (Jew Law Ying's coaching book, given to me by my mother). Her departure was delayed when my sister Bak Heong, who was born in Macao a year after my parents' marriage, was diagnosed as having trachoma and my mother had to find a doctor to treat her.[11]

Finally, my mother and sister arrived in San Francisco on March 13, 1941, and were immediately detained at the temporary immigration station at 801 Silver Avenue (the Angel Island Immigration Station was destroyed in a fire in 1940). They appeared before the Board of Special Inquiry for interrogation on April 2, 1941. The close to one hundred detailed questions asked of her, contained in a transcript I found in my mother's immigration file at the National Archives–Pacific Sierra Region, struck me as intimidating, but in an interview I conducted with her fifty years later she remembered the interrogation as "easy."[12] Apparently her answers and my father's answers agreed. According to the immigration inspector's summary statement, "Testimony has now been taken from the alleged wife, applicant 11-13 and from YUNG HIN SEN concerning their marriage and subsequent stay together in CHINA. This testimony is [in] very good agreement, both principals testifying freely. No discrepancies worthy of mention were brought out by the testimony."

---

11. In an attempt to exclude Chinese immigrants, the U.S. government classified certain parasitic diseases as dangerously contagious and grounds for denying admisison. Arrivals with trachoma were deported in 1903, those with uncinariasis or hookworm in 1910, and those with clonorchiasis or liver fluke in 1917. After considerable protests by Chinatown leaders, some patients were allowed to stay for medical treatment.

12. In contrast, many other detainees whom I interviewed recall the interrogation as the worst part of the immigration process, in which they were grilled about minute details of their family background and daily life in China. Interrogations could last all day for several days, depending on the nature of the case.

Although I was unable to interview my great-grandmother or my grandmother, I did conduct two interviews with my mother in the 1980s. The first interview was in 1982 in conjunction with my book *Chinese Women of America: A Pictorial History*.[13] I asked her the same questions that were asked of 273 other Chinese American women, covering her life history and reflections on being a Chinese woman in the United States. The second interview, in 1987, was to gather specific information about her grandparents Chin Lung and Leong Shee for author Ruthanne Lum McCunn, who subsequently included Chin Lung's story in *Chinese American Portraits: Personal Histories, 1828–1988*.[14] More recently, as I worked on this essay, I went back to my mother a number of times with specific questions about her true family history, the bogus answers in her coaching book, and the official answers she gave in the immigration transcript. Although it had been over fifty years since she immigrated, she was still able to answer some of my questions in detail.

Despite the problems of bias and unreliable memory, I believe oral history offers me the best approach to the truth, especially when I corroborate her story with that of other relatives, including my father, whom I interviewed twice before he died in 1987. I have included my mother's interviews following the translation of her coaching book and the transcript of her immigration interrogation, so that we might compare the false, official, and true versions of my mother's family history and thereby come to a better understanding and appreciation of the complex process of immigration for Chinese women during the exclusion period.

---

13. Judy Yung, *Chinese Women of America: A Pictorial History* (Seattle: University of Washington Press, 1986).

14. Ruthanne Lum McCunn, "Chin Lung's Gold Mountain Promise," in *Chinese American Portraits: Personal Histories, 1828–1988* (San Francisco: Chronicle Books, 1988), pp. 88–97.

Chin Lung's Affidavit, May 14, 1892

My great-grandfather Chin Lung (a.k.a. Chin Hong Dai) immigrated to the United States for a better livelihood right before the Chinese Exclusion Act of 1882 was passed. He was hardworking and resourceful. Within six years he had learned to speak English and saved enough money—sacking rice at the Sing Kee store in San Francisco Chinatown and, later, engaging in tenant farming with fellow villagers in the Sacramento– San Joaquin Delta—to go home and be arranged in marriage to Leong Kum Kew (a.k.a. Leong Yee, her maiden name; and Leong Shee, her married name). But he could not bring her back with him to the United States because he was still considered a laborer, and the Exclusion Act did not allow family members of Chinese laborers to immigrate to this country. Upon his return, therefore, Chin Lung invested wisely in the Sing Kee store in order to establish merchant status; he was finally able to send for Leong Shee in 1892.[1]

---

1. Biographical information on Chin Lung is from Chin Gway, interview with author and Him Mark Lai, July 29, 1979, San Francisco; Chin Sou and John Chin, interview with author and Sucheng Chan, October 12, 1979, San Jose; Jew Law Ying, interview with author, September 7, 1982, and January 14, 1987, San Francisco; Sucheng Chan, "Chinese American Entrepreneur: The California Career of Chin Lung," *Chinese America: History and Perspectives 1987* (San Francisco: Chinese Historical Society of America, 1987), pp. 73–86; and Ruthanne Lum McCunn, "Chin Lung's Gold Mountain Promise," in *Chinese American Portraits: Personal Histories, 1828–1988* (San Francisco: Chronicle Books, 1988), pp. 88–97.

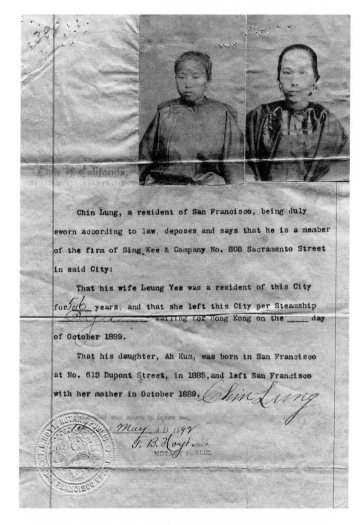

Chin Lung, a resident of San Francisco, being duly
sworn according to law, deposes and says that he is a member
of the firm of Sing Kee & Company No. 808 Sacramento Street
in said City:

That his wife Leung Yee was a resident of this City
for _5d/6_ years, and that she left this City per Steamship
_____ sailing for Hong Kong on the ____ day
of October 1889.

That his daughter, Ah Kum, was born in San Francisco
at No. 613 Dupont Street, in 1885, and left San Francisco
with her mother in October 1889.

(SOURCE: Leong Shee, case 12017/37232, Chinese Departure Case
Files, San Francisco District Office, Immigration and Naturalization
Service, Record Group 85, National Archives, San Bruno, California)

*This notarized affidavit, attesting to Chin Lung's merchant status, was
intended to pave the way for Leong Shee to immigrate as a merchant's
wife. Although Leong Shee had never lived in the United States, Chin
Lung for some reason stated that she had lived in San Francisco for five
or six years before leaving for Hong Kong in October 1889 with their
"daughter," Ah Kum, who supposedly was born in San Francisco Chi-*

natown in 1885. The photographs attached to the affidavit are of Leong Shee and seven-year-old Ah Kum.

From interviews with my mother and two of Chin Lung's sons, I learned that Ah Kum was really a mui tsai whom my great-grandmother wanted to bring to America. But why did Chin Lung and Leong Shee have to fabricate the story about Ah Kum's birth in San Francisco, when the treaty of 1880 stipulated that Chinese merchants could bring their household servants with them? I think it may be because they feared that slavegirls would not be permitted entry or that they might be accused of bringing in a potential prostitute, since there was a scarcity of Chinese women and Protestant missionary women like Donaldina Cameron were making an issue of Chinese prostitution. Whatever the reason, Leong Shee's testimony upon arrival (page 20–22) not only confirmed the story but elaborated on the fabrication.

Leong Shee's Testimony, April 18, 1893

This testimony was given by Leong Shee upon arrival in San Francisco. The original document was handwritten and in a narrative rather than a question-and-answer format. The cover sheet described Leong Shee as "female (small feet)," an important signifier of genteel or merchant class. However, descriptions of her in the immigration files of her family members after 1917 indicate that she had "natural feet." Also, whereas a 1904 photograph showed her with bound feet, photographs taken in the 1920s showed her with natural feet. I surmise that Great-Grandmother most likely unbound her feet after the 1911 Revolution in China, along with many other women who were encouraged to do so by the new government. By her signature mark, we know that Leong Shee was illiterate. In 1929, however, she told the immigration inspector that she could read and write Chinese, and indeed signed her own name on the document. Relatives told me that she converted to Christianity and learned to read and write at church after her return to China in 1904.

Leong Shee's testimony confirmed her husband's affidavit that she had lived in San Francisco before and had returned to China with their four-year-old daughter, Ah Kum, on October 17, 1889, on the vessel Belgic. *Probably in response to Interpreter Huff's questions, she elaborated on Chin Lung's story by saying that she first came to America with her parents and later married Chin Lung in San Francisco in 1885. After their marriage they lived above the Sang [Sing] Kee store at 808 Sacramento Street, where Ah Kum was born on December 28, 1886. (Chin Lung had*

said in his affidavit that Ah Kum was born at 613 Dupont Street in 1885,
but Interpreter Huff evidently did not catch this discrepancy.) She fur-
ther testified that she returned with her brother-in-law and daughter to
China in 1889. "Who else was on that ship?" she was probably asked.
In response she said that "Lee Moon's wife and child" were on the same
steamer with her. As to what she remembered of San Francisco China-
town, she ended with the statement that she did not know the city ex-
cept for a few street names "as I have small feet and never went out."
The immigration inspector evidently believed her story and landed her
and Ah Kum the next day. This testimony would come back to trouble
Great-Grandmother in 1929, when she appeared before immigration au-
thorities again, this time seeking permission to leave for China (see pp.
23–31).

San Francisco, April 18th, 1893.
Kind of Certificate, or Paper, Certificate of Identification *Ticket*
     No. 388.
Name of Passenger, Leong Yee & Ah Kum, child. *Sex,* Female.
Where born? China.
Here in U.S.? Yes. *Place of former residence in U.S.* San Francisco.
Date of departure from U.S.? Oct. 17/89.
Name of Vessel departed on, Belgic . . .
Do you speak English? No. *Destination,* San Francisco
Place of stopping in City, #808 Sacramento St.
Who bought your ticket to China? My brother-in-law.
With whom connected, Gurm Wo Jan—Jackson St., don't know
     number.
When did you first arrive in U.S.? 1879.

I was married in San Francisco on Dec. 15, 1885 to Chong [Chin] Lung
of the firm of Sang Kee wholesale dealers in tea & rice #808 Sac. St. San
Francisco. When I first came to this country I came with my father Leong
Hoong Wum and my mother Lee Shee and lived at #613 Dupont St. My
father was formerly connected with the firm of Sang Kee #808 Sac. St.
My father died in this city Nov. 25, 1887. My mother died in this city
1883 so long ago I have forgotten the date. I went home to China with
my brother-in-law Chun Gwun Dai and my daughter Ah Kum who was
4 years of age the time of departure. After I was married I lived on the
2nd floor over the store of Sang Kee #808 Sac. St where my daughter Ah

Kum was born on the 28 day of December 1886. My daughter is 8 years old now. My brother-in-law Chun Gwun Dai returned to S.F. in the later part of year 1891. Lee Moon's wife went home in the same steamer with me. I do not know her name. There was also a woman named Sam Moy and a child Ah Yuck on board. I do not speak English and do not know the city excepting the names of a few streets as I have small feet and never went out.

H. S. Huff, Interpreter

Leong X [her mark] Yee

(SOURCE: Leong Shee, case 12017/37232, Chinese Departure Case Files, San Francisco District Office, Immigration and Naturalization Service, Record Group 85, National Archives, San Bruno, California)

Leong Shee's Testimony, July 24, 1929

While Great-Grandfather Chin Lung farmed in the Sacramento Delta on hundreds of acres of leased land, amassing a fortune growing potatoes with borrowed credit and hired help, Great-Grandmother Leong Shee lived in San Francisco Chinatown, where she gave birth to five children, two girls and three boys. The oldest child was my grandmother Chin Suey Kum, born in 1894. Even though she had the means to live well and the help of a mui tsai, Leong Shee found life in America inconvenient, alienating, and harried. So unhappy was she that in 1904 she insisted that Chin Lung take the entire family back to China. Chin Lung returned to the United States alone and continued farming in the Sacramento Delta. Periodically he would visit the family in China, siring two more sons in the process.

Although Chin Lung's children all had the right to return to America, only the boys were encouraged to do so by their parents. The two girls—my grandmother Suey Kum and my grandaunt Mee Ngon—did not have a say in the matter. They were married into wealthy families in China. According to the Immigration Act of 1907, they automatically lost their U.S. citizenship by marrying foreigners. Mee Ngon's husband died soon after their wedding, and she was only able to return to America in 1920 by lying about her marital status. My grandmother ended up staying in China and having five daughters and two sons, the eldest being my mother, Jew Law Ying. In 1921 Chin Lung persuaded Leong Shee to return to the United States. This time she stayed for eight years before returning to China in 1929.

Under the exclusion laws, each time a Chinese person wanted to leave the country temporarily, he or she had to apply for a return certificate to ensure that he or she would be allowed back into the United States. In 1904, when the entire family returned to China, they were covered under Chin Lung's permit and Leong Shee did not have to make a separate application. But in 1929 Leong Shee was returning to China without Chin Lung, which necessitated her appearance and testimony before the immigration service at the Angel Island station. For some reason she departed as a laborer instead of a merchant's wife. Perhaps it was because her husband's merchant status was under investigation at the time and it was therefore easier for her to apply for a return certificate as a laborer than as a merchant's wife.[1] According to the Immigration Act of 1924, as a "laborer departing" she would be permitted reentry only if she had a relative who was a U.S. resident, such as her husband or one of her sons. And as the immigration officer further warned her, if she should be away for more than six months and her husband or child not be a resident of the United States, she must "be able to read in some language or dialect" in order to be readmitted (in accordance with the Immigration Act of 1917). In answer to an earlier question, "Can you read and write?" she had responded, "I can read and write Chinese, but not English." Unlike her affidavit of April 18, 1893, where she made an X mark as her signature, she was able to write her name, Leong Shee, in Chinese characters at the end of this document.

During the interrogation Leong Shee was confronted with earlier statements she had made in 1893 about her immigration history, her marriage, and her eldest daughter, Ah Kum. At first she stumbled and said that she had two daughters and that her eldest child, Chin Suey Kum (my grandmother, who was born in San Francisco in 1894), had died. She then

---

1. In order to discourage Chinese immigration, immigration officials chose to define the exempt class of merchant as narrowly as possible. In 1930 Chin Lung's application for a return certificate as a merchant was denied on the basis that his "Shanghai Trunk Company is an establishment whose main business is manufacturing and therefore this applicant is a manufacturer and not to be classed as a merchant under the Chinese Exclusion Law." Two years later, Chin Lung, age 69, joined his wife in Macao, departing the United States as a "lawfully domiciled Chinese laborer." He never returned. He retired comfortably in Macao and died there in 1942 at the age of 78.

changed her answer and said, "My oldest daughter is Chin Gum, who died shortly after she and I came to this country K.S. 19 (1893)."[2] (A family photograph taken in 1904 showed Chin Gum, or mui tsai Ah Kum, to be alive and well. My mother thinks Ah Kum was married off before Leong Shee returned to China in 1904. She would have been about eighteen years old, the right age for marriage.) Leong Shee also said that Chin Gum was born in China. The inspector then asked her to state again when she first arrived in the United States and where she was married. Leong Shee evidently forgot about her earlier testimony in 1893 and replied with the truth—she first came in 1893 and she was married in China. The inspector then cited the testimony she gave in 1893, that she had been in the United States "five or six years prior to October, 1889," and that her daughter Ah Kum was born in the United States. Leong Shee repeatedly denied ever giving such testimony, even after the inspector reminded her that she was making statements under oath. Fortunately for her, the inspector did not pursue the discrepancies or use them against her, probably because she was departing and not entering the country. As it turned out, Leong Shee never returned to the United States. She died in Macao in 1962 at the age of 94.

U.S. Immigration Service
Port of San Francisco

12017/37232   Angel Island Station
Leong Shee   July 24, 1929
Laborer Departing   Exam. Inspector, H. F. Hewitt
                                                Interpreter, Yong Kay

Applicant, sworn and admonished that if at any time she does not understand the interpreter to at once so state. Also advised of the crime of perjury and the penalty therefor. Speaks the Heung Shan dialect.

Q: What are all your names?
A: Leong Shee; Leong Yee was my maiden name.
Q: How old are you?
A: 61.
Q: Where were you born?

---

2. The reckoning of dates by the reign of Emperor Kuang Su (Guangxu, 1875–1908).

A: Kay Boo village, H.S.D.,[3] China.

Q: When did you first come to the U.S.?

A: K.S. 19/3 (1893, April) ss "China."

Q: Were you accompanied when you came to the U.S. in K.S. 19 (1893)?

A: By my daughter, Chin Kum, and a clansman, Leong Wai Kun, a clansman of mine.

Q: Under what status were you admitted to the U.S. at that time, K.S. 19 (1893)?

A: I do not know; I came here to join my husband, Chin Lung, who was a merchant of Sing Kee Co., San Francisco.

Q: Who is this (showing photo attached to affidavit of Chin Lung,[4] contained in file 20437/2-6, Leong Shee, Wife of Mer., "Shinyo Maru," 7/14/29—affidavit referred to attached to landing record April 18, 1893, Leong Yee & child, Ah Kum, ss "China")?

A: That is my photo.

Q: Who is represented in the photo of the child next attached to the photo which you claim is of yourself?

A: My daughter, Ah Kum.

Q: Have you ever left the U.S. since you arrived here in K.S. 19 (1893)?

A: Yes, one trip to China; departed K.S. 30/2 (1904, Mar.)? SS "China." I returned to the U.S. C.R. 10/7 (Aug. 1921),[5] ss "Shinyo Maru," at San Francisco, and was admitted as the wife of a merchant, wife of Chin Lung, who was then a merchant of Sing Kee Co., San Francisco.

Q: Have you a cer. of identity?

A: Yes. (There is contained in the present file CI No. 36086, Leong Shee, Mer. Wife returning, ss "Shinyo Maru," 20437/2-6, 8.14.21. Same is retained in file and contains photo of the present applicant.)

Q: Why do you appear here today?

A: I want to depart for China on a laborer's return certificate.

---

3. Heungshan (Xiangshan) District was renamed Chungshan (Zhongshan) District in 1925 in honor of Dr. Sun Yat-sen, who led the 1911 Revolution that overthrew the Qing dynasty and founded the Republic of China. In 1965 the Wong Leung Do area separated from Chungshan District to become Doumen District. Today, Doumen District is a part of Xiangzhou District of Zhuhai City. For a history of Wong Leung Do people in the United States, see Him Mark Lai, "Potato King and Film Producer, Flower Growers, Professionals, and Activists: The Huangliang Du Community in Northern California," in *Chinese America: History and Perspectives, 1998* (San Francisco: Chinese Historical Society of America, 1998), pp. 1–24.

4. See Chin Lung's affidavit of May 14, 1892 (pages 17–19).

5. The reckoning of dates since the establishment of the Chinese Republic in 1912.

Q: Are you married at this time?

A: Yes.

Q: How many times have you been married?

A: Once only.

Q: Will you name your husband?

A: Chin Lung—Chin Hong Dai.[6]

Q: Where is he at this time?

A: He is here today, with me.

Q: What is your present address?

A: 1210 Stockton St., S.F., Calif.

Q: With whom do you live there?

A: My husband and my children—one of my children lives there with me, a son, Chin Sow; also my husband lives there with me.

Q: What is your husband's occupation?

A: Merchant, Shang Hai Trunk Co., 1210 Stockton St., S.F., where I live.

Q: What is your present occupation?

A: Housewife.

Q: Do you follow any other occupation?

A: No.

Q: Can you read and write?

A: I can read and write Chinese, but not English.

Q: What will be your foreign address:

A: C/o Dok Jan Co., Macao, China; I don't remember the street or number. (Alleged husband states this applicant's address will be No. 16 Hung Shung San Street, Macao, China, Dok Jan Co.).

Q: Will anyone accompany you to China?

A: Yes, my son, Chin Sow, who lives with me in San Francisco (12017/37115).

Q: How many children have you ever had?

A: 5 sons and 2 daughters.

Q: Name all your children, their ages, date of birth and whereabouts.

A: My oldest child is Chin Suey Kum, who died (changes). My oldest daughter is Chin Gum, who died shortly after she and I came to this country K.S. 19 (1893).

Q: Is Chin Gum whom you have just mentioned as your oldest daughter, the child who accompanied you to the U.S. in K.S. 19 (1893)?

---

6. A Chinese person maintained the same surname throughout his life but usually adopted a different given name when he started school, entered business, or married. Chin Hong Dai was the name taken by Chin Lung when he married.

A: Yes.

Q: Was that daughter born in China?

A: Yes.

Q: How many daughters have you had born to you, altogether?

A: Three.

Q: Name your second daughter?

A: Chin Suey Kum, about 35 or 36; I don't remember her birth date; she is now in China; she was born in the U.S., at San Francisco. Chin Suey Kan, 29; she is now in San Francisco, living in the Yet Sin Building, Stockton St., near Broadway; she is not married; she was born in San Francisco; she works on Market St., I don't know for whom; she embroiders handkerchiefs. I don't remember the date of her birth.

Q: Name your sons, the ages, dates of birth and whereabouts and where born?

A: Chin Wing, 34 or 35; I don't remember the date of his birth; he was born in San Francisco. He is now in San Francisco, in my husband's store, he is a member of the firm; he lives on Powell Street, with his wife. Chin Wah, 32, he is in the East; he is in New York city; he was born in San Francisco. Chin Foo, 26; he was born in San Francisco; I don't remember the date of his birth; he is now in my husband's store; he is a member of the firm; he is married and lives in the Yet Sin Building; my daughter who lives in that building lives there with him. Chin Gway, 26, born K.S. 30/4-11 (May 25, 1904), in San Francisco, and is now a member of my husband's firm; he lives on Powell Street, with his wife. Chin Sow, 23, born K.S. 33/10-13 (1907, Nov. 17); he was born in China, in Nom Song village, China. He is not married; he lives with me in San Francisco.

Q: Are you the mother of any other children?

A: No.

Q: On what do you base your right to depart for China and to return to the U.S.?

A: On the ground that my son Chin Sow is a resident of the U.S. and that I can return to him in this country.

Q: When did Chin Sow come to the U.S.?

A: C.R. 13 (1924), ss "Korea," at San Francisco.

Q: Did you testify for him at that time?

A: Yes.

Q: Under what status was he admitted at that time?

A: As the son of a merchant.

Q: Did your husband testify for him at that time?

A: Yes.

Q: Did you state that Chin Sow will accompany you to China?

A: Yes.

Q: Is Chin Sow here today?

A: No.

Q: Have you a photograph of Chin Sow with you at this time?

A: No.

Q: Who is this (showing photo of applicant, Chin Sow, attached to affidavit contained in file 23303/12-7, Chin Sow, mer. Son, ss "Korea Maru," May 4, 1924)?

A: My son, Chin Sow.

Q: Who is this (showing photo attached to same affidavit next to that of applicant in above mentioned case)?

A: My husband, Chin Lung.

Q: Is your husband Chin Lung going to remain in the U.S.?

A: Yes.

Q: Do you expect that he will be a resident of the U.S. upon your return to this country?

A: Yes, I expect that if he is living he will be in the U.S.

Q: Will you again state when you first arrived in the U.S.?

A: K.S. 19/3 (1893, April).

Q: Where were you married?

A: I was married in Nom Song village, HSD, China.

Q: Do you remember the date of your marriage?

A: No, I can't remember that.

Q: Do you recognize this affidavit and the photos attached thereto (showing affidavit of Chin Lung, dated May 14, 1892, which contains photo of the present applicant, and which affidavit is attached to arrival record of Leong Yee and child, Ah Kum, ss "China," April 18, 1893)?

A: Yes, that is the paper I had when I first came to the U.S.

Q: You are advised that that affidavit sets forth that you had been in the U.S. five or six years prior to October, 1889—9th month, K.S. 15, and you now state that you first came to the U.S. in K.S. 19 (1893). Can you explain why that affidavit should set forth such information?

A: I first came to the U.S. in K.S. 19 (1893). I don't know why that information is in the affidavit that I was in this country before K.S. 19 (1893).[7]

---

7. Great-Grandmother obviously does not remember that she had to lie in 1893 in order to get *mui tsai* Ah Kum into the United States.

Q: Do you know that that affidavit also sets forth that your daughter, who accompanied you in K.S. 19 (1893) to the U.S., was born in the U.S., and you have stated today that she was born in China?

A: I don't know why; the fact is that that daughter was born in China.

Q: Had that daughter ever been in the U.S. before K.S. 19 (1893)?

A: No.

Q: Do you realize that you are making your statement today under oath?

A: Yes.

Q: Were you ever in the U.S. before K.S. 19 (1893)?

A: No.

Q: Do you ever recall being questioned by this Service, before, as to when you came to the U.S. the first time, and also that it was called to your attention that the affidavit just referred to sets forth that you were in the U.S. before K.S. 19 (1893)?

A: Yes, and I said that I had first come to the U.S. in K.S. 19 (1893).

Q: Do you remember when you testified to that effect?

A: Yes, in the case of Chin Sow.

Q: Do you remember being asked at that time where you were married?

A: Yes, and I said I had been married in China.

Q: You are advised that in order to permit your re-entry into the U.S. it will be necessary that your son, Chin Sow will have to return to the U.S. with you or prior thereto, in order that the grounds upon which you are basing your application shall then be existent. Do you understand?

A: Yes.

Q: You are further advised that should you remain away from the U.S. for a period longer than six months should your husband or your child not be a resident of the U.S. in the event of your reapplication for admission it would be necessary, in order to entitle you to admission to the U.S., that you be able to read in some language or dialect. Do you understand?

A: Yes.

Q: Who is this (showing photo of applicant, Chin Sow, 12017/37115, attached to Form 432)?

A: Chin Sow, my son.

Q: Have you anything further to state?

A: No.

Q: Who is this (indicating Chin Lung, alleged husband, who has been called into the room)?

A: My husband, Chin Lung.

Q: (to Chin Lung, alleged husband) Who is this woman?
A: My wife, Leong Shee. (Alleged husband dismissed.)
Q: Did you understand this interpreter (through interpreter J. Q. Moy)?
A: Yes.

Signed: [Leong Shee in Chinese characters] I certify that the foregoing is a true and correct record of testimony taken direct on the typewriter at the above described hearing.

H. F. HEWITT, typist

(SOURCE: Leong Shee, case 12017/37232, Chinese Departure Case Files, San Francisco District Office, Immigration and Naturalization Service, Record Group 85, National Archives, San Bruno, California)

Jew Law Ying's Coaching Book

As a result of Great-Grandmother Leong Shee's decision to return to China with all her children in 1904, my grandmother Chin Suey Kum, a native-born U.S. citizen, ended up marrying Jew Hin Gwin, an herb doctor in China, and forfeiting her right to return to the United States. My mother, Jew Law Ying, was thus born in Dai Chek Hom village, Heungshan District, Guangdong Province, in 1915. The eldest child and the favored grandchild of Chin Lung and Leong Shee, she lived with them in Macao from age seven until she was arranged in marriage to my father, Tom Yip Jing, in 1937. My father, born in Pai Shan village, Heungshan District, in 1903 had immigrated to the United States in 1921 as Yung Hin Sen, the paper son of Yung Ung of Sin Dung village, Sunwui District, which was adjacent to Heungshan District. At the age of thirty-three, he had finally saved enough money to come home to marry. The marriage to my mother was arranged by my great-grandfather Chin Lung, at the suggestion of his eldest daughter-in-law, Wong See Chan, who had befriended my father in San Francisco. As my mother later told me in an interview (see pp. 87–98), she agreed to the marriage only because it offered her a way to leave war-torn China and come to America.

After the wedding my father returned to the United States alone to make arrangements for my mother to immigrate as the wife of Yung Hin Sen, a bona fide merchant. In preparation for the immigration interrogation, my father sent her a coaching book to study. Hand-written in Chinese with blue ink on 8 × 11–inch thin paper folded in half and stapled *together, the book was fifteen pages long and contained 155 questions and answers about my mother's family history, my father's family history, their arranged marriage and wedding, where they lived together in China, their stay in Hong Kong before his departure to the United States, correspondence between them, mutual acquaintances, and a map of his home village. Like most other Chinese immigrants coming during the exclusion period, my father had multiple copies prepared by someone experienced in the business.[1] Father kept a carbon copy and sent the original to my mother to study. I would later inherit both copies.*

The point was that when interrogated by the immigration inspector my parents had to give the same information in answer to the same questions in order to prove their relationship as husband and wife. Answers also had to cross-check with answers given by relatives who had immigrated earlier. Moreover, as many of the old-timers I interviewed pointed out, one was never sure how many of the questions in the coaching book would be asked or precisely which ones. People spent months memorizing these coaching books. True sons were as likely to fail the examination as paper sons. In my mother's view, however, she had an easier time preparing for the interrogation because she kept her true identity. "I didn't have to study it too long," she told me. "I just read it through

---

1. In an interview conducted in 1977, a Mr. Yuen recounted how his uncle made a living writing coaching books: "He work with a lawyer, and he would certainly receive some compensation for it. The case is this: you got my case, then if you don't have a book already made, then uncle would help you to make them. He had enough of the basis to make a good book out of it, just by talking to you and your relatives, your father and mother, your grandfather. He might have to take a trip to Hong Kong. So make sure everything is recorded. Then also, he'll draw a house where you live in the village, showing every room, dimensions, bedroom, kitchen, where you cook. Maybe two, maybe three, and you better remember it. It's just fantastic. Just like an architect." See "Angel Island Immigration Station: Interviews with Chris Chow, Mr. Yuen, Ira and Ed Lee" (oral history conducted in 1977 by the Combined Asian American Resources Oral History Project, Bancroft Library, University of California, Berkeley), p. 21. According to my uncle Wing Lew, whose own coaching book was thirty-two pages long and contained 444 questions, his uncle had a Chinese American lawyer take care of the paperwork, including the coaching book. He thinks the lawyer obtained the information for the coaching book from the paper father, who updated the book each time he brought in another paper son. Immigration authorities knew that interrogation records of excluded cases which had been made available to attorneys for inspection were being used as models for coaching books. See letter dated January 15, 1925, from Commissioner John Nagle of the Angel Island Station to W. W. Husband, Commissioner-General of Immigration in Washington, D.C. (File 55452-385, Subject Correspondence, Immigration and Naturalization Service, National Archives). I am indebted to Erika Lee for sharing this letter with me.

and answered whatever question they asked me one by one. It was really quite simple." As it turned out, of the one hundred questions asked of my parents, only twenty-seven resembled those in my mother's coaching book.

Most immigrants I interviewed said they destroyed their coaching books before their arrival in San Francisco, but a few like my mother kept theirs. When asked why she did so, my mother replied, "For a souvenir." My father also kept his carbon copy through the years. In comparing the two copies, I can see that my father bothered to make changes and additions only to my mother's copy. I have thus translated my mother's copy in its entirety, inserting notes whenever necessary for clarification and to distinguish the lies from the truth. In general, because my father was a paper son but my mother's identity was true, the description of his family background in the coaching book is false, while my mother's family background is correct.

A few of the answers were written in my father's handwriting, probably because the compiler did not have all the answers at hand. At one point, my father teased my mother that she should be able to describe his appearance without his prompting. At other times, he warned her to omit certain information to avoid complications or contradictions in their stories. For example, he told her not to say that his mother and brother were at their wedding, since according to his paper identity his mother was deceased and his brother was in the United States at the time of the wedding. The section in the coaching book about witnesses was left blank, probably because he was not sure who they might be at the time. As it turned out, no other witnesses were called besides my father.

One major change my father made in the coaching book was the village where he and my mother supposedly got married. According to the coaching book, the wedding took place in Hin Bin village, a short distance south of Pai Shan village in Heungshan District, when by custom it should have taken place at his paper identity's birthplace, Sin Dung village in Sunwui District. In actuality, it took place in my father's true birthplace, Pai Shan village in Heungshan District. He probably set his wedding and their new home in Heungshan District because he and my mother were more familiar with the region. When I interviewed him in 1977, he told me that he was prepared to say that his family had had to move to Heungshan District because of the Sino-Japanese War in the 1930s. But why did he not use Pai Shan village if he was going to relocate to Heungshan District anyway? My mother thinks it may have been because there were more Yungs in Hin Bin village than in Pai Shan village. Indeed, that was the case, according to one of the answers given in the coaching book. Regardless of the reason, the decision to use Hin Bin village was evidently made after the coaching book was written, since my father had to change "Pai Shan village" to "Hin Bin village" throughout the book. The map, however, was the layout of Pai Shan village. Later, upon returning to the United States in 1937, he slipped and said that his wife was living in Sin Dung village instead of Hin Bin village. When confronted with this discrepancy in 1941, he replied, "I am a native of Sin Dung village and possibly I was thinking of my own home."

In a number of places the compiler gave helpful advice, an indication that he thoroughly understood the interrogation process. At one point he noted that it was important for my mother to say she was literate because then my father could produce letters she wrote him as evidence of their relationship.[2] As another example, the compiler advised my parents to pay close attention to questions about their living arrangements in Hin Bin village: "This is the most important part of the interrogation, so be careful with your answers." "When in doubt," he wrote in a number of places, "answer truthfully to avoid mistakes." He evidently also wanted to stay current of any changes that needed to be made in the coaching book, instructing all parties involved to notify him first of any changes.

According to my aunt Tom Ngun Dai, who lived in Pai Shan village from 1924 until 1948, the map that appears at the back of my mother's coaching book is a simplified version of the actual village as she remembered it: There were at least eighty houses, not just the ten shown on the map. There were many more children in the households than indicated. Missing from the map were a second ancestral hall, two watchtowers near the village gates, and an athletic field. She also said there were no bamboo groves to the west, no outhouse for the women, and my father's family actually owned two houses, not just the one given on the map. My father may have remembered certain things incorrectly, but most likely he wanted to keep things simple for my mother and himself.

---

2. In another case related to me by Haiming Liu, a husband told his wife to hide her literacy to better her chances of passing the interrogation. Liu's source is a collection of correspondence belonging to Sam Chang, a Chinese agribusinessman in southern California. See Haiming Liu, "The Trans-Pacific Family: A Case Study of Sam Chang's Family History," *Amerasia Journal* 18, no. 2 (1992): 1–34.

問汝姓也名也。可有別名否　答。我係姓趙名羅英又名趙氏。

問汝今年係有幾多歲　答。我今年係有二七歲。

問汝自己係何年何月何日出世　答。我係民國四年六月十三日出世。

問汝自己係在于何处出世　答。我係在于中國香山縣卯中山縣黃埔都大赤坎村处出世。

問汝自己可有嫁人否　答。我已經嫁人。

問汝係何時在于何处及係與何人結婚　答。我係民國廿六年正月廿日在于中國香山縣黃埔鄉村处與我丈夫楊庭順結婚。

問汝嫁過汝丈夫楊庭順之時可有人做媒人否　答。我聞得我母話係我外公陳康大做介紹人，今我嫁過我丈夫楊庭順。

問汝可有子女否　答。我係有一子女無子。

問汝女係姓也名也今年幾多歲現在于何处　答。我女係楊追鄉佢係今年四歲。現在同南我未金山。

問汝女楊追鄉佢係何年何月何日何時在于何处出世　答。我女楊追鄉佢係民國廿六年十一月初十日在于中國澳門白馬巷醫院处出世。我女係氏時出世。

First page of my mother Jew Law Ying's coaching book.

Q: What is your name? Do you have any other names?

A: My surname is Jew, name Law Ying. My other name is Jew Shee.

Q: How old are you?

A: I am twenty-seven years old.

Q: What is your birthdate?

A: I was born on C.R. 4th year [1915], 6th month, 13th day.

Q: Where were you born?

A: I was born in China, Heungshan District, Wong Leung Do section, Dai Cheuk Hom village.

Q: Are you married?

A: I am married.

Q: When, where, and to whom were you married?

A: I married my husband Yung Hin Sen on C.R. 26th year [1937], 1st month, 20th day, in China, Heungshan District, Wong Leung Do section, Hin Bin village.

Q: Who was the matchmaker?

A: My mother said that my maternal grandfather Chin Hong Dai was the matchmaker.

Q: Do you have any children?

A: I have one daughter, no son.

Q: What is your daughter's name, what is her age, and where is she now?

A: My daughter is Yung Bak Heong.[3] She is four years old. She came to the United States with me.

Q: What is your daughter Bak Heong's birthdate and birthplace?

A: My daughter Bak Heong was born on C.R. 26th year [1937], 11th month, 11th day, the *she* hour [between 7:00 and 9:00 P.M.], at the Bock Ma Hong Hospital in Macao, China.

Q: Was your husband present in China when your daughter Bak Heong was born?

A: My husband was not in China when our daughter was born. He had left for the United States three months before the birth of my daughter.

Q: How long was it after your daughter's birth before you wrote to inform your husband in the United States?

A: Two days after my daughter's birth I immediately sent a letter to inform my husband Yung Hin Sen in the United States.

Q: Did you or your husband name your daughter?

A: I named my daughter Yung Bak Heong and wrote my husband about it.

Q: Do you have any schooling? Can you read and write letters?

A: I went to school. I can read and write simple letters.

(NOTE: This is an important issue that will help shorten the interrogation and help the new immigrant Jew Shee get landed. Because if she

---

3. My eldest sister's true name is Tom Bak Heong, literally, "forced to leave the village."

knows how to write and send letters to her husband Yung Hin Sen in the United States, he can keep these letters and present them to the immigration inspector as evidence when Jew Shee arrives.)

Q: When and where did you marry your husband Yung Hin Sen and by what custom were you married?

A: I was married on C.R. 26th year [1937], 1st month, 20th day, in China, Heungshan District, Wong Leung Do section, Hin Bin village, according to the old Chinese custom of "riding the bright red sedan."[4]

Q: Can you describe the wedding ceremony?

A: (Be sure to describe the traditional ceremony as it happened, but do not mention that my [true] mother and brother were there.)[5]

Q: As a bride on the wedding day, what did you wear? Did you wear the red wedding skirt and veil?

A: (Describe the wedding as it happened and your husband should do the same.)

   (Do not say that my mother, brother, or relatives were there.)

Q: Who officiated at your wedding?

A: There was only one *seung tau gung*, older brother Hin Biew.[6]

Q: How many times did you see your husband before you married him?

A: I saw him twice before we married. Once in Nam San village and once at the Dow Moon Market.

Q: The two times that you saw one another, who introduced you and who was there with the two of you? What were the dates and times and how long did you talk?

A: (Reply as it happened to avoid mistakes.) The first time was at maternal Great-Grandfather's home in Nam Shan village. Great-Grandfather introduced us. Great-Grandfather and Great-Grandmother

---

4. This is the most honorable way for a woman to be married off in China. The "bright red bridal sedan," usually carried by four men, can only be occupied by a bride who is a virgin from a good family background.

5. My father's true mother, Lee Shee, and brother, Tom Yip Keung, were at the wedding. My father's paper mother, Wong Shee, was deceased and his paper brother, Yung Hin Biew, was in the United States at the time of the wedding.

6. *Seung tau gung* was an older married man who was responsible for combing the groom's hair and assisting him on his wedding day. The female counterpart, *seung tau poh*, was an older married woman who performed the ritual of combing the bride's hair and helping her dress before she left her parents' house for her husband's. My father made the mistake of writing in his paper brother's name, Hin Biew, as the *seung tau gung*, forgetting that he was in the United States at the time of the wedding.

were there, as well as a slavegirl. It was on C.R. 25th year [1936], 12th month, 25th day, about 10 A.M. We talked for about two hours. We had tea and lunch. The second time was on C.R. 26th year [1937], 1st month, 14th day, at 9:00 A.M. I met my husband in the Dow Moon Market, upstairs from Wong Jeet Mun [a distant relative of my mother's]. We talked for about an hour. There was no one there with us. My husband told me my grandfather had recommended me to him for a wife.

Q: The two times you met your husband before your marriage, what clothes did he and you have on?

A: (Reply as it happened to avoid mistakes.) At our meeting in Nam San, my husband wore a light red Chinese outfit. I wore a white dress with blue trim. At the Dow Moon Market meeting, he wore a black Western suit and I wore a light red *cheong saam* [Chinese dress]. (Note: Aside from the two of us, to prevent complications, don't mention there was a third person present.)

Q: How far is your native village Dai Chek Hom from the village where you were married? What bridges, rivers, and villages do you pass?

A: My village is about eight or nine miles from Hin Bin village. There is one bridge and no river near the village. You pass about six or seven villages of varying sizes. (If asked for the names of the villages, answer Lei Ok, Lik Kei, Sek Jue, Sum Tum, Dow Moon Market, See Ji Hou, Ngau Bing Tong, then you arrive at Hin Bin village.)

Q: How many people carried your bridal sedan chair?

A: Four people carried my sedan chair.

Q: When did you exchange engagement gifts? What was the bride-price? How many wedding cakes and roast pigs?

A: (Both of you should answer as it happened to avoid mistakes.) On C.R. 26th year [1937], 1st month, 16th day, we set the date for the 20th to exchange engagement gifts. The bride-price was $1,600. There were wedding cakes but no roast pigs.

Q: What dowry did you present to your husband?

A: (Both of you should answer as it happened to avoid mistakes.)

Q: What time did you arrive at your husband's home by sedan chair from your home?

A: (Both of you should answer as it happened to avoid mistakes.) It was approximately 6 P.M.

Q: What did your husband wear on the day of the wedding?

A: (Both of you should answer as it happened to avoid mistakes.) A black Western woolen suit.

Q: Did you invite three "fraternity brothers" for the wedding? Did you observe the custom of "knocking on the sedan door?"[7]

A: Yes, we observed the custom of "knocking on the sedan door" and invited three "fraternity brothers." Their names were Jun Hei, Ging Kau, and Wun Tong.

Q: What were their surnames, where were they from, and how old were they?

A: Yung surname, from Hin Bin village. Jun Hei was twenty-six years old, the second one was about twenty years old, and the third one was about thirty years old.

Q: How many days of celebration and how many wedding banquets?

A: Two days of celebration and one banquet.

Q: How many guests attended the wedding banquet?

A: About thirty people.

Q: Where was the wedding banquet held?

A: At the Yung ancestral hall in Hin Bin village.

Q: Did your husband put a gold wedding ring on your finger in the presence of the wedding guests?

A: No.

Q: Did your husband present you with any jewelry, clothes, or gifts before or after the wedding?

A: Nothing before. (Answer about after the wedding as it happened.)

Q: Did your husband put up a makeshift pavilion for the banquet on the day of the wedding?[8]

A: No.

Q: Were there any musicians hired for the wedding celebration?

A: Five musicians were hired.

Q: Were there any firecrackers and teasing of the bride?

A: Yes.

Q: Who served as *seung tau gung* at the wedding?

A: Yung Yip Ghin.[9]

---

7. Similar to ushers at a Western-style wedding, "fraternity brothers" were close friends of the groom who served as hosts at the wedding. They usually protected the groom from well-wishers who wanted to get him drunk. When the bride arrived at her husband's home, it was customary for the groom to knock on the door of the bridal sedan to claim his spouse.

8. It was customary for the women and children to eat in a separate area from the men, in this case in a makeshift pavilion built with bamboo poles and covered with palm leaves.

9. Here my father wrote in "Yung Yip Ghin" for the *seung tau gung* instead of "Yung Hin Biew," as he did earlier (see note 6).

Q: As the groom, did your husband wear a red sash?

A: I didn't see him with a red sash (in other words, you don't know).

Q: As the bride, did you kowtow to the ancestors, toast three cups of wine with the groom, and offer tea and betel nuts to the elders?

A: I kowtowed to the ancestors. Did not toast wine or offer tea. Offered betel nuts to the *seung tau gung* and *seung tau poh*. (If the interrogator asks you the ages of the *seung tau gung* and *seung tau poh*, say that the *seung tau gung* was about sixty years old and the *seung tau poh* Jew Shee was about sixty years old, had natural feet, and was from Dai Chek Hom.)

Q: Were the three "fraternity brothers" related to your husband?

A: No.

Q: Who owned the house in Hin Bin village that you and your husband lived in and was it an old or new house?

A: The house that we lived in was an old house belonging to Yung Yip Ghin. My husband rented it from him. The monthly rent was $10. My husband took care of paying the rent, so I didn't pay any attention to it.[10]

(NOTE: Be sure to agree on your answers regarding your living arrangements in Hin Bin village. This is the most important part of the interrogation, so be careful with your answers.)

Q: What was the house in which you and your husband lived made of and in what style?

A: (Answer according to the interior and exterior of my house. Do not say there were any livestock or ancestral tablets and pictures hanging inside.)[11]

Q: What is the floor of the house made of? How many bedrooms, balconies, parlors? How many entrances altogether? In which direction does the front entrance face?

A: (Both of you must describe the house in the village the same way to avoid mistakes.)

(Do not say there was livestock or ancestral tablets. Say that the ancestral picture was on red paper and hung on the altar.)

Q: Did anyone else live with the two of you?

---

10. According to what my mother told me, my parents lived with my father's mother, brother, sister-in-law, and nephew in my father's ancestral home after the wedding.

11. Here my father is instructing my mother to describe his house in Pai Shan village that they actually lived in after they married.

A: Just us one couple. No one else lived with us.[12]

Q: How long did the two of you live in Hin Bin village?

A: We lived there for three months.

Q: Did you follow the custom of returning to the bride's family three days after the wedding? Did your husband go with you to see your parents?

A: After the wedding, we did not follow the custom of returning to the bride's family together. I returned home alone to see my family four times after the wedding. The first time was on the one-month anniversary of the 2nd month, 5th day, when I stayed for four days. The second time was in the 3rd month, 11th day, and I stayed about ten days. The third time was in the 3rd month, 29th day, when I stayed only a few hours to talk before returning to my husband's home. The fourth time was in the 4th month, 20th day, when I stayed for three days. All four times I went home alone without my husband.

Q: Did your husband ever go visit your parents and family alone after you were married?

A: No.

Q: Where did you live after you left Hin Bin village?

A: We were married on C.R. 26th year [1937], 1st month, 20th day, in Hin Bin village and lived in our home there until the 5th month, 10th day of that same year, when my husband and I moved to Macao to live in the house of my maternal grandfather Chin Hong Dai.

Q: How long after you both moved to Macao to live with your maternal grandfather Chin Hong Dai before your husband returned to the United States?

A: After my husband accompanied me from Hin Bin village on C.R. 26th year [1937], 5th month, 10th day, to my maternal grandfather's home, my husband did not stay there because he had important business in Hong Kong. On the same day—5th month, 10th day—at 4:00 P.M. he took the boat from Macao to Hong Kong. Thus he never stayed overnight or had a meal at my family's home. He only had some tea. It wasn't until the 5th month, 5th or 6th day, that my husband returned alone from Hong Kong to Macao and took me from my grandfather's home to Hong Kong. We lived in Hong Kong until my husband returned by boat to the United States. Then I returned to live at

---

12. See note 10.

my maternal grandfather's home in the 8th month until I left for the United States with my daughter.[13]

Q: After you both left your maternal grandfather Chin Hong Dai's home for Hong Kong, where did you live and eat in Hong Kong? How long before your husband took a boat to return to the United States?

A: We lived at the Look Hoy Hung Hotel and ate at Wing Hung Cheong for about three months before my husband returned to the United States. (If you're asked about the Wing Hung Cheong Company, say that it belongs to your husband's friend, Tom Share Dew [a.k.a. Tom Yip Pooh].)

Q: What time did your husband leave to take the boat to the United States? What luggage did he take? Did he have anyone help him carry the luggage? Where did you and your husband part? Did you accompany your husband to the dock?

A: (Be sure that you both answer the above questions the same as it happened.)

(Note that besides you, all who came to say farewell were just friends. Be sure not to mention that Foo Wing is my true brother.)

Q: What furniture did you have in your home at Hin Bin village? Whose furniture was it?

A: There was a big bed and my dowry. Everything else belonged to the landlord.

Q: When you both lived in Hin Bin village, who did the cooking and who fetched the water?

A: I did it myself.

Q: When you both lived in Hin Bin village, were there occasions when you had a servant help with the housework or cooking?

A: No.

Q: When you both left Hin Bin village to go to your maternal grandfather Chin Hong Dai's home to live, what household furniture and bedding did you take with you?

A: When we went to Macao to my maternal grandfather's, we only brought three pieces of luggage. Everything else, including my bed, dresser, and chairs, we left to the landlord to take care of.

Q: Do you know which direction Hin Bin village faces? How many rows

---

13. According to what my mother told me, she returned to live with her mother-in-law for another three months. But her mother-in-law was so mean to her that she finally left and went to live in Macao.

of buildings are there? Is there a temple or ancestral hall? Any gates, fish ponds, village shrine, and wells?

A: I know that Hin Bin village faces east. The houses are arranged in six rows. There are five main lanes and one side lane, one ancestral hall, no temples or fish ponds. There are ten houses and one ancestral hall, making a total of eleven buildings. No fish ponds. There are two gates. One village shrine is on the left side of the village, to the left of the ancestral hall. There is a round well in front of the village.[14]

Q: Are there any walls, trees, or bamboo around Hin Bin village?

A: There are trees behind Hin Bin village, a wall in front, no bamboo.

Q: What is the predominant surname in Hin Bin village?

A: Mostly people with the surname Yung live in Hin Bin village.

Q: Do you know why your husband chose to get married and rent a house in Heungshan District, Hin Bin village?

A: My husband told me it was because his parents had passed away and he had no more relatives in Sunwui Sin Dung village. He was not planning to stay in China long and would be returning to the United States, so he rented that house.

Q: Do you know who are your husband's closest friends or relatives in Hin Bin village?

A: I don't know because my husband never talked about them.

Q: Do you know which families have members who have gone to the United States or have relatives there now?

A: I don't know aside from my husband what other villager has relatives in the United States.

Q: Which house in Hin Bin village did you both live in?

A: The second house, fourth row from the north.

Q: Do you know how many people live in Hin Bin village?

A: There are over thirty people.[15]

Q: Which room and on which side of the house did you sleep in, cook in, and dine in?

A: We slept in the north wing on the left side. The kitchen was to the left. The dining room was in the middle.

Q: During meal times, did the two of you eat together or did you eat after your husband?

A: We ate together at the same table at the same time.

---

14. This description corresponds to the simplified map of Pai Shan village at the back of the coaching book.

15. Aunt Tom Ngun Dai remembers that over one hundred people lived in the village.

Q: Do you know the age of your husband Yung Hin Sen and when he was born?

A: My husband is thirty-nine years old. He was born in K.S. 29th year [1903], 7th month, 15th day.[16]

Q: Do you know where your husband Yung Hin Sen was born?

A: My husband was born in China, Sunwui District, Sin Dung village.

Q: Do you know when your husband Yung Hin Sen first left China for the United States and after he came to the United States how many times he returned to China?

A: My husband first came to the United States when he was nineteen years old. He returned to China once, in C.R. 25th year [1936], the last month, to marry me. After that, he returned to the United States from Hong Kong in C.R. 26th year [1937], 8th month, 20th day. He has been in the United States since then.

Q: Do you know the names, ages, and present location of your husband's parents or your father-in-law and mother-in-law?

A: My husband's father is Yung Ung and his mother is Wong Shee. Both are dead. I don't know their ages.[17]

Q: Do you know when and where your father-in-law and mother-in-law passed away?

A: My father-in-law died in the United States eleven years ago and is buried in a cemetery in San Francisco. My mother-in-law died in Sunwui Sin Dung five years ago.[18]

Q: Do you know if your father-in-law and mother-in-law ever came to the United States?

A: My father-in-law was in the United States. My mother-in-law never came to the United States.

Q: Do you know what kind of work your father-in-law did when he was in the United States?

A: He was a businessman in the United States.[19]

---

16. My father was actually born in 1905 and was two years younger than his paper identity.

17. According to my interviews with my father, his true father was Tom Fat Kwong and his true mother was Lee Shee. Tom Fat Kwong was smuggled across the Mexican border sometime before 1911.

18. Tom Fat Kwong was killed in an automobile accident in Redwood City, California, around 1920. Lee Shee died in China in 1947.

19. According to my father, his true father, Tom Fat Kwong, was a farmworker in Redwood City and served in the U.S. Army during World War I.

Q: If you saw a picture of your father-in-law and mother-in-law, would
   you recognize them?
A: I've never seen a picture of them so I wouldn't be able to recognize them.
Q: Do you know if your husband Yung Hin Sen has any brothers and
   sisters?
A: My husband has an older brother in the United States.[20]
Q: Do you know the name, age, location, and work of your husband's
   siblings?
A: My husband has one older brother and no sisters. His name is Yung
   Hin Biew. He is forty years old and works in the United States.[21]
Q: Have you ever seen this brother in person or in a photograph?
A: I've never seen him before.
Q: Do you know if your husband visited Sunwui District, Sin Dung vil-
   lage, after the wedding?
A: He went before the wedding but not after the wedding.
Q: Do you know how far your husband's home village is from the vil-
   lage where you were married?
A: I have never been there so I do not know.
Q: Do you know which direction and how far Hin Bin village is from
   your ancestral village Dai Chek Hom? How far is it from Dow Moon
   Market and Macao?
A: From Hin Bin village to Dow Moon Market you go left to the north
   about three and a half miles. From Hin Bin village to my ancestral vil-
   lage Dai Chek Hom it is an eight- or nine-mile walk. To go to Dai Chek
   Hom you must pass Dow Moon Market, then from there it's a five-
   hour boat ride to Macao.
Q: Which direction does Dai Chek Hom face? How many rows of houses?
   How many houses?
A: (Answer according to the actual situation in Dai Chek Hom.)
   (If you are asked about your parents' house in Dai Chek Hom, answer
   according to what you know.)
Q: What is your father's name, age, residence, and line of work?
A: Jew Sun, also Hin Gwing, forty-eight years old, doctor.
Q: What is your mother's name and age? What kind of feet? Where is
   your mother now and what kind of work does she do?

---

20. My father actually had one older sister and one younger brother. Both remained in
China and farmed.

21. Yung Hin Biew was actually my father's cousin, Tom Hin Biew. The two immigrated to America posing as the sons of merchant Yung Ung in 1921.

A: My mother is Chin Shee. Her birth name is Chin Suey Kum. She is forty-eight years old. She has natural feet. She is in China living with her husband. She is a housewife.

Q: Do you know where your parents were born?

A: My father was born in China, Dai Chek Hom village. My mother Chin Shee was born in San Francisco, California, United States. My mother told me this.

Q: Do you know when your mother returned from the United States to China? Did she ever go back to the United States after she returned to China?

A: My mother came back to China when she was eleven years old to live. She has not returned to the United States since.

Q: Do you know the birthdate of your father Jew Sun?

A: (Answer according to the truth.)

Q: Has your father ever been to the United States or abroad?

A: No.

Q: Do you know when your mother Chin Shee or Chin Suey Kum was born?

A: (The new immigrant must find out what her mother reported to immigration as her birthdate when she returned to China.) She was born on February 13, 1894. She returned to China from the United States on March 23, 1904, by SS *Siberia*.

Q: Does your father Jew Sun or Hin Gwing have any brothers and sisters?

A: (Answer according to the truth.)

Q: Does your mother Chin Shee or Chin Suey Kum have any brothers or sisters?

A: My mother has five younger brothers and one younger sister.

Q: Does your mother have any brothers or sisters who died?

A: No.

Q: What are the names and ages of your mother's brothers and sisters? Where are they and what kind of work do they do?

A: My oldest uncle is Chin Wing, forty-six years old, married. His entire family is in the United States. I don't know how many children he has because we haven't corresponded. Second uncle Chin Wah is forty-three years old, unmarried, in the United States. Third uncle Chin Foo is thirty-nine years old, married, in the United States. He has children but I don't know their names or ages because we have not corresponded. Fourth uncle Chin Gway is thirty-seven years old, married, in the United States. His wife, Leong Jew Shee, who is twenty-three years old, is in Macao. They have one son named You Tien, who is four years old. Fifth uncle Chin Show is thirty-four years old, in the United States. His wife Lau Shee is thirty years old. They have two sons—Gwok Cheong, five years old, and Gwok Nam, four years old. Fifth aunt and their two sons are in Macao. I don't know where my uncles live or what work they do. Aunt Chin Mee Ngon is forty years old and is in the United States.

Q: Do your uncles have wives and children?

A: (See above.)

Q: Is your aunt married and where does she live now?

A: Unmarried, living in the United States but I don't know the address.[22]

Q: What are the names of your maternal grandfather and grandmother? Are they still alive?

A: My maternal grandfather is Chin Lung, also Chin Hong Dai. He is seventy-seven years old. My maternal grandmother Leong Shee is seventy-three years old, unbound feet. They both live in Macao, China, at 73 Haw Lon Yin Street.

Q: Do you know if your maternal grandfather Chin Hong Dai and maternal grandmother Leong Shee have ever been to the United States?

A: My maternal grandparents have been to the United States many times but I don't know exactly how many times.

Q: Do you know where they were born?

A: My maternal grandfather Chin Hong Dai was born in China, Heungshan District, Nam Shan village. My maternal grandmother Leong Shee was born in Heungshan, Kee Mo village.

Q: Did your maternal grandmother unbind her feet?

A: Yes.

Q: Do you know when your maternal grandfather Chin Lung or Chin Hong Dai made his last trip to the United States from China? When was his last trip to China from the United States?

A: (Ask maternal grandfather.)

Q: Do you know when your maternal grandmother Leong Shee made her last trip to the United States from China? When was her last trip to China from the United States?

A: (Ask maternal grandmother.)

---

22. Grandaunt Mee Ngon's husband died soon after their wedding. She was only able to return to the United States in 1920 by lying about her marital status.

Q: Do you know what kind of work your maternal grandfather Chin
   Lung or Chin Hong Dai did while in the United States?

A: When my maternal grandfather Chin Lung was in the United States,
   he did business at the Sang Kee rice store and, later, the Shanghai Trunk
   Company. He also grew potatoes.

Q: If you saw pictures of your maternal grandparents, your mother, your
   uncles and aunts, would you be able to recognize them?

A: I could recognize all of them.

Q: Who owned the house at 73 Haw Lon Yin Street in Macao in which
   your maternal grandfather Chin Lung or Chin Hong Dai and family
   lived?

A: It was my maternal grandfather Chin Hong Dai's property.

Q: What was this building made of? How many stories? Any garden?

A: (Answer according to the truth to avoid mistakes.)

Q: Did your husband Yung Hin Sen ever live or have a meal at your maternal grandfather Chin Lung's house?

A: He had a meal there and tea.

Q: Do you know if your maternal grandfather Chin Lung or Chin Hong
   Dai owned any other properties or land besides the house in which
   he and his family lived?

A: (You and your husband must answer according to the truth.)

(NOTE: Whenever the interrogator asks questions not in the coaching
book, you must both answer according to the truth to avoid mistakes.)

Q: When you married your husband Yung Hin Sen, did you exchange
   genealogies going back three generations?

A: We did not.

(NOTE: If you say you exchanged genealogies, then both of you must be
prepared to name the generations. It is best if the new immigrant could
bring her husband's genealogy to the United States and present it as evidence when interrogated. It will be easier if you said you did not exchange
genealogies. The two of you must agree on this answer to avoid mistakes.)

Q: During or after the wedding, did you take any pictures together?

A: (If you took a picture together, it is best that the new immigrant present the picture to the interrogator as evidence. If you didn't take any
   picture together, say you didn't.)[23]

---

23. See Exhibit A, page 68.

Q: When you were married in the village, did your husband change his name and post that name in the house?[24]

A: (Your and your husband's answers must agree.)

Q: Do you have any brothers and sisters?

A: Three younger sisters and three younger brothers, seven of us altogether. Sister Wun Jee is my same age. Third sister Jin Dai, twenty-five years old. Fourth sister Ngan Bun, twenty-three years old. Sing Haw, twelve years old.[25]

Q: Do you have any brothers and sisters who died?

A: No.

Q: Do you have any brothers or sisters who ever came to the United States?

A: No.

Q: What are the names of your brothers and sisters? Their ages, birthdates? Where do they live and what kind of work do they do?

A: (Answer according to the truth.) Two brothers Jew Sing Haw, twelve years old, and Jew Sing Lurt, nine years old, are in school. Third brother Sing Jun is seven years old.

Q: Has your husband Yung Hin Sen ever seen your brothers and sisters?

A: My husband saw my two sisters, Ah Dai and Ah Ngan, and younger brother Haw about five times in my husband's house.

Q: After your wedding, the three times that you went home to visit your family from your husband's village, did someone accompany you or did you go alone?

A: I went home to my family alone. When I returned to my husband's home, often I was accompanied by a brother or a sister.

(The last time Yung Ung returned to China was in C.R. 10th year [1921], 12th month, 10th day, on the SS *Golden State*. My father Yung Ung passed away in C.R. 18th year [1929], 7th month, at Chinese Hospital. Funeral services at Kwong Fook Sang. My mother Wong Shee passed away in C.R. 25th year, 1st month, 15th day, in Sunwui.)

---

24. My father's birth name was Tom Share Gow. When he married, he adopted the name Tom Yip Jing.

25. According to my mother's interview, she had three sisters and two brothers. She told me that my father wanted her to report an additional brother—Sing Jun—so that they could create a slot to bring over a relative later. She also lied that her sister Wun Jee was the same age as she, probably because my mother was really two years older than reported. At the time she was introduced to my father, she was actually twenty-five years old but said she was twenty-three. She had lied about her age to my father for fear of being considered "too old" for marriage.

Regarding correspondence and arrangements for the new immigrant to come to the United States.

Q: After your husband returned to the United States, how often and how much money did he send you for household expenses?

A: After my husband returned to the United States, he would send me about HK $200 four times a year, also ten or more letters.

Q: When he sent you money from the United States for household expenses, whom did he address it to and at what address?

A: He sent the money in my name Jew Law Ying to 73 Haw Lon Yin Street in Macao.

Q: When you sent letters to your husband in the United States, what address did you use?

A: In [C.R.] 26th, 27th year [1937, 1938], I sent letters to my husband at 1107 Stockton Street, care of Wah Ching.[26] After my husband said in his letters that he had become a partner in a Chinatown firm, Far East Company, I began sending my letters to him at 760 Sacramento Street.

Q: Do you have any schooling? Can you read and write letters?

A: I can read and write simple letters.

Q: Did you write the letters you sent your husband in the United States or did you have someone else write them for you?

A: All the letters I sent my husband I wrote myself. I did not have to ask anyone to write them for me.[27]

Q: Do you know what kind of work your husband does in the United States?

A: He is presently doing business at the Far East Company, located in San Francisco Chinatown at 760 Sacramento Street.[28]

---

26. Wah Ching (a.k.a. Wong See Chan), the eldest daughter-in-law of Chin Lung, was the person who recommended my father to Chin Lung as a prospective husband for my mother.

27. Many Chinese women in the villages were illiterate at this time and relied on professional letter writers to write for them. My mother was capable of writing her own letters, but she told me that she preferred having a professional letter writer compose the letter for her and then copying it in her own writing. She deliberately addressed all the letters to my father's paper name, Yung Hin Sen.

28. As I explained earlier, my father had to claim merchant status in order for my mother to immigrate to this country. This he did by investing $1,000 in the Far East Company. He told the INS that he worked there as a salesman, but he was actually working as a gardener on a private estate at the time.

Q: Do you know what your husband's position is at the Far East Company?

A: He is a salesman at the Far East Company.

Q: Do you know how long he has been with the Far East Company and how long he has held this position?

A: He has been there for over a year.

Q: Do you know what kind of work your husband did before he joined the Far East Company?

A: Before my husband joined the Far East Company, he worked for other people. (If you are asked where your husband worked, say you do not know.)

Q: Who financed your and your daughter's trip to the United States?

A: My husband sent the money to cover our traveling expenses to the United States.

Q: Whose decision was it for you and your daughter to come to the United States? Yours or your husband's?

A: It was my decision. I wrote and asked him to find a way for us to come to the United States.

Q: When did you write your husband to ask him to bring you two to the United States?

A: In C.R. 28th year [1939], the 9th month of the lunar calendar.

Q: When and who sent the photograph of you and your daughter to the United States to be used on the immigration documents?[29]

A: I sent the photograph of us to my husband in the 2nd month according to the lunar calendar.

Q: Aside from that photograph of you and your daughter for the application, what other photographs did you send your husband in the United States?

A: (You sent pictures four or five times. Best to give the dates you sent them. If not, just answer what really happened. Also mention that you sent them to me care of your uncle's address.)

Q: When did your husband Yung Hin Sen send you the visa papers and the money for the boat fare?

A: We were to leave on the 9th month, 18th day, on the SS *President Garfield*. He sent $800, care of Wing Hung Cheong Company.

Q: Whom did your husband write to in Hong Kong to arrange for your and your daughter's trip to Hong Kong and the boat trip to the United States?

---

29. See Exhibit B, page 69.

A: My husband wrote Wing Hung Cheong Company and instructed Tom Share Dew in Hong Kong to make the arrangements for us.

Q: Before embarking for the United States, who wrote your husband about the name of the boat and dates of travel?

A: Before embarking for the United States, I wrote a letter to my husband informing him of the boat and dates of travel. (Describe the voyage as it happened.)

Q: Did your husband meet you and your daughter when your boat arrived at the San Francisco wharf?

A: (Answer according to the truth.)

Q: After you and your daughter arrived in the United States and were detained at the Immigration Station for interrogation, did your husband send you any money, letters, food, or clothing? Did you send any letters to him in San Francisco?

A: (Note that if you wrote letters, be sure not to mention any coaching notes.)

Q: How would you describe your husband Yung Hin Sen? His character, appearance, birth marks, gold teeth, et cetera?

A: (Dear Ying, I trust you remember what I look like so I need not write it down for you. Just tell the truth and there will be no mistakes.)

Q: After you were married in China, did any *gam saan haak* [literally, a guest of Gold Mountain, or someone in the United States] visit the two of you whom you knew or talked with?

A: None.

Q: Besides your husband in the United States, is there anyone else in the United States who can testify that you are the wife of Yung Hin Sen?

A: Besides my husband, there are my uncles in the United States who can testify. (In regard to your uncles, answer according to the truth.)

Q: Who else can serve as your witnesses besides your husband Yung Hin Sen and the two named witnesses in the United States?[30]

A: No one else.

Q: When and where did you first meet the named witnesses? And for what reasons?

A: [no written answer]

Q: How many times did you see the named witnesses in China? Where and for what reasons?

---

30. As the blanks that follow indicate, my parents were not sure who the two witnesses were going to be.

A: [no written answer]

Q: How old are the named witnesses? Where were they born? Do they have wives and children?

A: [no written answer]

Q: Besides your husband Yung Hin Sen and the two named witnesses, who else do you know in the United States?

A: [no written answer]

Q: When your uncles and their families who are now in the United States were in China, did they see you and can they act as your witnesses?

A: Before I married and when I was young, I saw my uncles and their families. But when I married my husband, they were not in China to witness the marriage.

(NOTE: If the interrogator asks the new immigrant when your uncles and their families went to the United States from China, and if they ever returned to China, be sure to check on the dates and answer accordingly.)

Q: What villages surround the village where you and your husband were married?

A: [no written answer]

Q: Are there any mountains, rivers, or bridges around the village?

A: [no written answer]

The following is a map of Hin Bin village.[31] The new immigrant and all witnesses must not change anything in their answers in order to avoid discrepancies. If there's anything you do not understand or must change in this coaching book, you must notify me in writing before the new immigrant begins her voyage to the United States by boat.

---

31. As I explained earlier, this is a simplified map of Pai Shan village intended to represent Hin Bin village. Certain changes (noted below) were made to the map in my mother's copy of the coaching book that were not made in my father's copy.

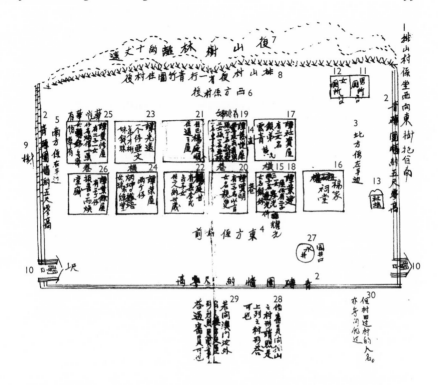

Map of Pai Shan village as it appeared in my mother Jew Law Ying's coaching book.

KEY TO MAP

1. Pai Shan village sits west and faces east. Trees are at the south end.[32]
2. The brick wall is approximately five feet tall.
3. North is to the left.
4. East is in front of the village.
5. South is to the right.
6. West is behind the village.
7. The woods at the rear are about ten yards away.
8. Behind Pai Shan village is a bamboo grove.
9. Trees.
10. Village gate (six feet).
11. Men's outhouse.
12. Women's outhouse.
13. Village shrine.
14. Vertical lane.
15. Horizontal lane.
16. Yung family ancestral hall.[33]

---

32. The following was added to my mother's copy: "Trees are at the south end."
33. Changed from "Kuen Shek ancestral hall" in my mother's copy.

17. Tom Share Dew house. Two daughters named Ngun Dai and Wun Ching. Wong Shee (wife).[34]
18. Tom Yip Ghin house. He has three sons named Choi Kwong, Dat Kwong, You Gong, and one daughter named Ngun Ho.[35]
19. Tom Fat Yuet house. His son died. He has daughter Ngun Dai, one grandson named Ging Kau, and two granddaughters named Ah Gee and Ah Mei.[36]
20. Tom Mai Ming has one son named Yee Yeen and a daughter named Chin Oy.
21. Myself, Yung Hin Sen's house.
22. Yung Hin Gum has a wife Lee Shee and no children. The couple is in their thirties.[37]
23. Tom Kwong Yuan. One son Ah Mon, younger brother Choy Bun, and younger sister Ngun Gee.[38]
24. Tom Wing house. Two sons Bing Sun and Wun Tong. Daughter Kau Dai.[39]
25. Tom Yip Sou house. Has two sons named Wah Yuet and Wah You, and a daughter Jwun Ho.[40]
26. Tom Yip Yee house. Has three sons Jun Hei, Yee Wun, and Tong Sing.
27. Village well.
28. If the interrogator asks about Pai Shan village, answer according to this map.
29. If he asks about your maternal grandmother's house in Macao, answer according to the truth.
30. I didn't ask about the names of the people in Hin Bin village.[41]

---

34. The following was added to my mother's copy: "Wong Shee (wife)."

35. The following was added to my mother's copy: "Son, You Gong."

36. The following was added to my mother's copy: "Daughter, Ngun Dai."

37. The surname Tom was changed to Yung in my mother's copy.

38. The following was added to my mother's copy: "Younger brother, Choy Bun, and younger sister, Ngun Gee."

39. "Chung Pui" was changed to "Wun Tong" and "daughter, Kau Dai" was added to my mother's copy.

40. The two sons' names were changed from Bing Kun and Yut Wing to Wah Yuet and Wah You on my mother's copy.

41. This last sentence was added to my mother's copy.

Jew Law Ying's and Yung Hin Sen's Testimonies, April 2–3, 1941

On March 13, 1941, after a monthlong journey by ship, my mother, Jew Law Ying, and my eldest sister, Bak Heong, arrived in San Francisco and were detained at the temporary immigration station at 801 Silver Avenue.[1] My mother and my father were separately interrogated on April 2 and 3. According to the official transcript that follows, my mother was asked a total of 98 questions, and my father, 102 questions. Although only about a quarter of the questions they were prepared to answer were asked, the line of questioning was similar to that in the coaching book. Both were asked to describe how they met and to give details about their wedding day, their respective family histories, the village where they were married, the house where they lived, and their stay in Hong Kong before my father returned to the United States. Many of the intimate questions asked, such as about the hotel room they shared in Hong Kong and their sleeping and eating arrangements at home, could only have been answered by a truly married couple. They were also asked to identify three photographs and five letters my mother had sent my father as proof of their relationship. (So the coaching book compiler gave my mother the right advice to say she was literate and was therefore capable of writing letters to my father herself.)

---

1. The Angel Island Immigration Station was closed in 1940 after a fire destroyed a number of buildings there.

Neither of my parents had to appear for questioning more than once, which meant there were no major discrepancies between their testimonies. Fortunately, the Sunwui dialect that my father was supposed to speak was very similar to the Heungshan dialect that he actually spoke, as noted by the interpreter in the transcript.[2] *Thus, no suspicion was raised by his speech. As I have noted throughout the transcript, most of my mother's answers were true except for those involving my father's family background as Yung Hin Sen. In those instances, she answered largely according to the coaching book. When she was not sure, as in the question about why my father would marry someone in another district, she said she did not know. Her one big lie regarding her own family background was to say that she had a third brother, Jew Sing Jun. Years later, she admitted to me that my father had instructed her to do so in order to create a slot by which he could help bring another relative over.*

Because my father was a paper son and had testified twice before, upon arrival at Angel Island in 1921 and again in 1936 when he departed for China from Seattle, there was more reason for him to know his paper family history well and to lie in order to cover his tracks. But he obviously had not studied the coaching book as carefully as my mother. For example, he could not remember which direction the head of his village faced or whether my mother's grandparents were living in Macao or Dai Chek Hom village when he was introduced to my mother. He was also more cocky than my mother, as when he chose to focus on the teasing of the bride when describing their wedding day. But each time the interrogator tried to bait him with answers my mother had given, he was always quick with a retort. When he was confronted with a different answer my mother had given about the covering to the kitchen skylight at home, he replied, "If she said that she must be right because I was very seldom in the kitchen and paid very little attention to it." In contrast, my mother answered all the questions with assurance, even volunteering information at times. She felt she had every right to enter the United States. "Why should I be afraid?" she said to me fifty years later. "I wasn't a crook or a robber. If they let me land, fine. If not, too bad. Nothing to be scared about." Both of my parents' ease during the interrogation was noted in the summary, and that, combined with their matching answers, contributed to their passing the test.

---

2. The Chinese dialect of the immigrant was always noted because it was a way to determine whether the immigrant was indeed from the village he or she claimed.

RECORD OF BOARD OF SPECIAL INQUIRY HEARING
U. S. DEPARTMENT OF JUSTICE
Immigration and Naturalization Service
San Francisco, California

Manifest No. 40766/11-13 & 14   Date: April 2, 1941.

IN THE MATTER OF:	At a meeting of a
	BOARD OF SPECIAL INQUIRY
11-13: JEW SHEE (JEW LAW YING),	held at San Francisco, Calif.
Merchant's wife.	
11-14: YUNG BAK HEONG,	PRESENT: Inspector R. F. VAUGHN Chairman
Merchant's daughter.	" H. W. CUNNINGHAM Member
	Clerk W. T. POSEY Member
ex SS PRESIDENT COOLIDGE, 3/13/41	Interpreter J.Q. MOY
(vessel and date of arrival)	

Travel documents presented, if any: For 11-13: American Consular Visa issued in the name of JEW SHEE (JEW LAW YING) as wife of domiciled Chinese Merchant under Sec. 3(6) of Immigration Act of 1924 issued at HONG KONG 2/4/41. The above also covers the accompanying daughter YUNG BAK HEONG, traveling as the daughter of domiciled Chinese Merchant.

Applicant(s) 11-13 *is* sworn and *is* informed of nature of perjury and penalty therefor. If not sworn, state reasons: Applicant 11-14 is not sworn because of age; also too young to testify.

TO APPLICANT(s): If at any time you should fail to understand the interpreter or to understand the meaning of any statement or question in the course of these proceedings, you should so state at once. Do you understand? A. Yes.

Q: What are all the names you have ever used or have ever been known by? A: JEW SHEE nee JEW LAW YING; no others.

Mother (11-13) speaks for daughter (11-14): My daughter's name is YUNG BAK HEONG.

Q: What is your native dialect? A: WONG LUNG DOO Dialect of the HEUNG SHAN District.

Q: Is that the dialect in which you will testify at this hearing? A: Yes.

(IF NOT) Q: In what dialect will you testify, and why will you testify in a dialect other than your native one? A: ____

Q: Your right to enter the United States will be considered by this Board. The burden is upon you to prove that you are not subject to exclusion under any provision of the Immigration Laws, and all evidence in your behalf must be submitted at this hearing. There are present as witnesses *your alleged husband* YUNG HIN SEN. Are there any other persons anywhere in the United States who know of your claimed right to enter the United States? A: Yes.

(IF SO) Q: What are their names and addresses? A: CHUN WING and his wife WONG SHEE, now in San Francisco, address unknown; CHUN WAH, now in New York, address unknown; CHUN FOO, now in San Francisco with his wife LEONG SHEE; CHUN SHEOW, now in San Francisco, address unknown; CHUN MAY NGON, address unknown.

Q: What knowledge have those persons of your claimed right to enter the United States? A: They are my maternal relatives and have seen me in China.

Q: Do you wish to present such persons as witnesses, either here or at any immigration office nearer their residence? A: No.

Q: Have you any letters, documents or photographs which you wish to offer in support of your application for admission? A: No.

Q: At this hearing you may have a relative or an actual acquaintance present, who, if a witness, must have finished testifying. Do you wish to use this right? A: No.

PHYSICAL DESCRIPTION OF APPLICANT: 11-13. (Height in slippers).
    Height 5 ft. 2 1/2 in., complexion *medium*, hair *black*, eyes *brown*, marks or scars: Large flat scar upper left bridge of nose; ears pierced; four vaccination scars on upper left arm and three vaccination scars on upper right arm; flesh mole on right side of neck at collar line; mole underside of right wrist.

APPLICANT QUESTIONED, GIVES FOLLOWING MANIFEST DATA:
Age: 27 years, Chinese reckoning *Sex*: Female *Race*: Chinese
Date and place of birth: CR 4-6-13 (July 24, 1915) at DAI CHEUK HOM
    Village, WONG LUNG DOO Section, HEUNG SHAN District, China.
Marital status: Married. *Calling or occupation*: Housewife.
Ability to speak, read, and write: Chinese only.
Last permanent residence: 73 HAW LON YIN JIN Street, MACAO, China.

Resided there how long: From CR 26 (1937) to CR 29-9 (Oct. 1940)

Name and address of nearest relative in country whence applicant came: My father JEW HIN GWING, DAI CHEUK HOM Village, HEUNG SHAN District, China.

Destined to (Name and address): My husband YUNG HIN SEN, Far East Company, 760 Sacramento Street, San Francisco, Calif.

Purpose for which coming to United States: To join my husband.

Length of intended stay in United States: Indefinite.

Whether ever arrested: No.

Whether ever excluded and deported or arrested and deported: No.

(Other manifest questions and answers where applicable):

Q: When and where were you married? A: CR 26-1-20 (March 20, 1937) at HIN BIN Village, WONG LUNG DOO Section, HEUNG SHAN District, China.

Q: What are all the names you know for your husband? A: YUNG HIN SEN or YUNG NGIP JICK; no others.

Q: On what grounds do you seek admission to the United States? A: As the wife of a merchant.

Q: Of what country do you claim nationality? A: China.

Q: How many children have you ever had? A: One daughter, no sons.

Q: Did you ever have a child that died? A: No.

Q: Did you ever adopt a child? A: No.

Q: Do you have any documentary evidence showing your marriage to YUNG HIN SEN? A: No.[3]

Q: By what custom were you married? A: Old Chinese custom.

Q: When did you first see your husband? A: In CR 25-12-26 or 27 (Feb. 7 or 8, 1937), in NOM SAN Village, WONG LUNG DOO Section, HEUNG SHAN District, China.

Q: Did you see your husband before the actual marriage ceremony? A: Yes. My maternal grandparents CHUN HONG DAI and LEONG SHEE returned to the NOM SAN Village, our ancestral village, from MACAO in the latter part of CR 25 (1936) to spend the New Year holiday there. Shortly after their arrival there from MACAO I also went to that village at my maternal grandfather's request from the DAI CHEUK HOM Village. On

---

3. As a rule, the Chinese did not have birth or marriage certificates.

CR 25-12-26 or 27 (Feb. 7 or 8, 1937), or the day after my arrival in the NOM SAN Village, my husband called at our home there and my maternal grandfather introduced us to each other.

INSPECTOR R. B. JONES REPLACES H. W. CUNNINGHAM AS MEMBER OF THE BOARD.

BY MEMBER R. B. JONES: I have familiarized myself with the evidence thus far adduced in this case.

Q: Where was the marriage ceremony actually held? A: The marriage took place in a house in the HIN BIN Village rented by my husband from YUNG YIP GHIN.[4]

Q: Is YUNG YIP GHIN any relative of yourself or your husband? A: No. He is a resident of the HIN BIN Village.

Q: On the day of the ceremony, how did you arrive at the house of YUNG YIP GHIN? A: By sedan chair.

Q: Did you walk into the house then or were you carried in? A: After I alighted from the sedan chair, my husband and I walked together to the threshold of the house. My husband then entered the house, after which a woman attendant who came with me carried me across the threshold into the house.

Q: Will you describe your marriage ceremony? A: My husband preceded me into our bedroom; then I was carried into that room by a woman attendant. Next my husband left our bedroom to mingle with the guests who had gathered in the house. I remained in the bedroom and occasionally I left the bedroom to appear before guests at their request and served tea to them; occasionally guests would come into our bedroom to look at me. This lasted until a very late hour that night. The following morning at about 11 AM my husband and I went to the ancestral hall in the HIN BIN Village, and there I served tea to some guests who had gathered there. After having done this, we returned to our house, and at about 1 PM I returned to my native village accompanied by two women attendants who had accompanied me from my native village; this return trip to my native village was made in a sedan chair owned by two men. There was a feast held on the day of my marriage but before my arrival in the HIN BIN Village. That was the only feast held in connection with my wedding.

Q: At any time was there any ancestral worship in connection with the ceremony of your marriage? A: No.

---

4. The wedding actually took place in my father's house in Pai Shan village.

Q: Where did your husband stay after you returned to your home village following the ceremony? A: He remained in the HIN BIN Village and I returned to the HIN BIN Village the same day that I returned to my home village.

Q: Did you present your husband with any dowry? A: Yes, bedding, a bureau, a table, two basin stands, two basins, two chairs and two wooden tubs.

Q: Did your husband present you or your family with any gift at the time of your wedding? A: On my first trip to my native village after my marriage, I brought home to my parents some cakes from my husband. That is all.

Q: How long did you remain in the HIN BIN Village after your wedding took place? A: We made our home there for about three and one-half months; we lived in the house rented from YUNG YIP GHIN.

Q: After you left the HIN BIN Village where did you go to then? A: Then my husband and I went to MACAO where I remained with my maternal grandfather.

TO INTERPRETER J. Q. MOY:

Q: In what dialect has the applicant testified? A: WONG LUNG DOO.

AT THE DIRECTION OF THE INSPECTOR IN CHARGE, INTERPRETER EDWAR LEE REPLACES J. Q. MOY.[5] THROUGH INTERPRETER EDWAR LEE:

Q: Have you understood the previous interpreter? A: Yes.

Q: Have you ever visited the native village of your husband, the SIN DUNG Village? A: No.

Q: How does it happen that your husband married you, your home being in the HEUNG SHAN District, rather than someone from or nearer to his native village in the SUN WUEY District? A: I was introduced to my husband by my maternal grandfather. I don't know how they knew each other.[6]

At this point, because of constant interruptions by applicant 11-14 [Bak

---

5. To make sure that the Chinese interpreters remained honest, it was common to change interpreters at least once during the course of an interrogation.

6. Here my mother deviated from the coaching book answer. She should have said that "it was because his parents had passed away and he had no more relatives in Sunwui Sin Dung village."

Heong], board is moved to Matrons' quarters and hearing is recorded in shorthand.

Q: Was the home in MACAO to which you went after leaving the HIN BIN Village in CR 26 (1937) at the same address as that at which you lived just before you came to this country? A: Yes, after living at the HIN BIN Village for three and one-half months I went to my maternal grandfather's house in Macao and lived there until I left for HONG KONG (Changes). After I and my husband left the HIN BIN Village together for MACAO, then on the same day we arrived in MACAO my husband left MACAO by himself for HONG KONG, but he came back five days later and took me to HONG KONG, and we lived in HONG KONG together for a little over three months; then my husband left to return to the United States, and after he left I returned to my maternal grandfather's house in MACAO and I lived there until I left for the United States.[7]

Q: What are the names of your maternal grandparents? A: My maternal grandfather is CHUN HONG DAI or CHUN LUNG, 70 odd years old, now living in MACAO. My maternal grandmother is LEONG SHEE, 70 odd years old, living in MACAO.

Q: What are the names of your paternal grandparents? A: I don't know my paternal grandfather's name. He died when I was very young. My paternal grandmother is LEONG SHEE, 70 odd years old and now living in the DAI CHEUK HOM Village.

Q: Describe your parents. A: My father is JEW HIN GWING or JEW SUN, 48 years old, living at DAI CHEUK HOM Village. My mother is CHUN SHEE or CHUN SUEY KUM, 48 years old, living at DAI CHEUK HOM Village.

Q: How many brothers and sisters have you? A: Three brothers and three sisters.

Q: Describe them. A: My brothers are—

JEW SING HAW, 12 years old;
JEW SING LUT, 10 years old;
JEW SING JUN, 8 years old.[8]

My sisters are—

JEW NGOON JEE, 27 years old; she is my twin;
JEW JIN DAI, 25 years old;
JEW NGAN BUN, 23 years old.

---

7. See page 43, note 13.
8. See page 50, note 25.

All are living in the DAI CHEUK HOM Village except JEW NGOON JEE, my twin sister, who is married to a WONG family man of the SIU CHEUK HOM Village.

Q: Have you ever met any of your husband's relatives? A: None, except the wife of my husband's brother YUNG HING BEW.

Q: Where did you meet her? A: At the HIN BIN Village at the time of my marriage.

Q: Describe the wife of your husband's brother. A: JEW SHEE, about 39 years old; she lives at the SIN DUNG Village, SUN WUEY District.[9]

Q: Is she the only one of your husband's relatives, through marriage or otherwise, who attended your wedding? A: Yes.[10]

Q: Who of your own relatives attended your wedding? A: None of my maternal relatives were present at my marriage. My husband had invited the HIN BIN Villagers to attend the wedding and there were about 30 odd guests at the wedding feast.

Q: Had JEW SHEE, the wife of YUNG HING BEW, made the trip to the HIN BIN Village just to be present at the marriage ceremony? A: According to my husband, she came the day before my marriage to help attend to the details of the wedding and entertain the guests, and she remained at the HIN BIN Village for about ten days and then returned to the SIN DUNG Village.

Q: Do you know if she traveled alone from the SIN DUNG Village to the HIN BIN Village? A: As far as I know she was alone.

Q: Where was her husband at that time? A: He was in the United States.

Q: What are the names of your alleged husband's parents? A: His father was YUNG AH DUNG. He died before my marriage. I don't know when. His mother was WONG SHEE. She also died before my marriage but I don't know when she died.[11]

Q: How many brothers and sisters that you know of does your husband have? A: One brother and no sisters.[12]

Q: Please describe the house of your maternal grandparents in which you were living at MACAO? A: It is a two story residential building, constructed

9. Yung Hin Biew's wife was Jew Shee, but she lived in Pai Shan village.

10. My father's true mother and brother were at the wedding.

11. See page 45, notes 17 and 18.

12. See page 46, note 20.

of brick and faced with cement, and that entire house is occupied by my maternal grandfather's family. The ground floor contains a parlor, three bedrooms, a kitchen, two toilets, a bathroom and also a back yard. The second floor contains three bedrooms, a hallway and a sun deck.

Q: Did your husband pay a visit to your maternal grandparents' home in MACAO before proceeding on to HONG KONG the first time? A: Yes. We arrived at my maternal grandfather's house together in the morning from the HIN BIN Village and my husband stayed there with me until the afternoon of the same day when he left for HONG KONG.

Q: After your husband's first visit to HONG KONG how long did your husband remain in MACAO before you both went to HONG KONG? A: He returned from HONG KONG to my maternal grandfather's house at about 12 Noon and then he explained to my maternal grandfather that he was taking me to HONG KONG to stay for a while, and we left at about 2 PM of that same day for HONG KONG.

Q: What was the reason for this sudden departure for HONG KONG? A: I don't know.[13]

Q: Did you know in advance of the day you departed for HONG KONG that it was anticipated you would go there? A: Yes, he wrote to me while he was in HONG KONG and said he was coming back on the 15th of that month, and that he would then take me to HONG KONG.

Q: Did you know at that time that you were going to live in HONG KONG for an extended period of time? A: That letter did not say how long but he said that he would take me to HONG KONG to live.

Q: Where did you stay while in HONG KONG? A: We stopped at the LOOK HOY HUNG Hotel, which is near the waterfront, and we stayed at that hotel the entire period of about three months.

Q: Do you know the address of that hotel? A: No.

Q: Which floor of that hotel did you live on? A: The second floor.

Q: How tall was that hotel building? A: I don't know for certain but I think it is about four stories high.

Q: Did you occupy one or more rooms in that hotel? A: Only one room.

Q: Did you sleep together in the same bed or in separate beds? A: In one bed.

---

13. According to the coaching book, my mother should have answered, "He had important business in Hong Kong."

Q: Was water obtainable in your room at that hotel? A: Yes.

Q: What was your husband doing in HONG KONG during that three month period? A: He had no occupation.

Q: How did you spend your time then? A: Sometimes we went out walking and sometimes we went to a show.

Q: Did you attend motion picture theaters in HONG KONG? A: Yes, and to a Chinese show once.

Q: Did you make any special trips to a place just outside of HONG KONG for a day's journey? A: Yes. My husband and I rode on the ferry across the Bay to WONG GOCK, and on another occasion we took the train up to the peaks.

Q: Did your husband have any business associations that you know of while in HONG KONG? A: No, not to my knowledge.

Q: Did you return to your maternal grandparents' home in MACAO alone after leaving HONG KONG? A: Yes.

Q: Where did you last see your husband when he left for the United States? A: At the pier in HONG KONG after he had taken me down to the steamer which he took to return to the United States.

Q: About what time of day did your husband board the steamer for the United States? A: I don't remember the exact time but it was in the afternoon. He took me down to the steamer about 12 Noon or 1 PM and I was with him at the steamer for about one or two hours, and then he took me back to the pier and I bade him goodbye there. The steamer was supposed to have sailed at 4 PM but actually it did not sail at that hour because the time was changed and I understand it did not sail until the next morning. In the meantime, I returned to the WING HUNG CHUNG Company, which is my husband's headquarters in HONG KONG. At the time my husband and I left for the steamer we had already taken our baggage out of the LOOK HOY HUNG Hotel to the WING HUNG CHUNG Company. Then on the afternoon of that same day I returned to MACAO by myself.

Q: Did you have any photographs taken while you were in HONG KONG? A: Yes, one; that was when I and my husband were photographed together.

Q: (Showing Exhibit "A") Is this the picture which was made in HONG KONG? A: Yes.

Q: Who are the persons shown in this picture? A: Myself at the left and my husband at the right.

Exhibit A. My parents, Jew Law Ying and Yung Hin Sen [Tom Yip Jing], in 1937.

Q: (Showing photographs marked Exhibits "B" and "C") Who are these people and when was this picture taken? A: Both of them are pictures of myself and my daughter. Exhibit "B" was taken when my daughter was about one hundred days old, and that photo was taken in MACAO. Exhibit "C" was taken just when my daughter was beginning to learn to walk, and that photo was also taken in MACAO.

Q: (Showing letter marked Exhibit "D") Do you recognize this letter?

Exhibit B. My eldest sister, Bak Heong, and mother, Jew Law Ying, in 1938. The Chinese message at the bottom reads: To Bak Heong's daddy, from wife Law Ying and daughter Bak Heong.

A: Yes, that is a letter written by me to my husband acknowledging receipt of the affidavits which he had sent to me and also the money which he sent along with the affidavit which was sent in care of a friend at the WING HUNG CHUNG Company.

Q: (Showing letter marked Exhibit "E") Do you recognize this letter? A: Yes. This is also a letter written by me to my husband acknowledging receipt of the letter which he sent on the 23rd instant through my maternal grandfather. I also informed him that I had arrived in HONG KONG with our daughter and together we went to see the American Consul regarding my papers, and that I would again inform him as to the date of sailing for the United States.

Q: (Showing letter marked Exhibit "F") Do you recognize this letter? A: Yes. This is a letter which I wrote to my husband informing him that our daughter YUNG BAK HEONG had been undergoing treatment for her eyes by a doctor and that everything is all right now and that we would be permitted to sail and that we would board the PRESIDENT COOLIDGE for the United States.

Q: (Showing letter marked Exhibit "G") Do you recognize this letter? A: Yes. This is also a letter written by me to my husband informing him definitely that we were coming aboard the PRESIDENT COOLIDGE on the 22nd day of this month.

Q: (Showing letter marked Exhibit "H") Do you recognize this letter? A: Yes. This is also a letter written by me to my husband, sent by airmail, and in which I acknowledged the letter which he sent to me through my maternal grandfather by airmail and mailed together with $100, and in his letter to me he mentioned something about that if I should run short of money to borrow it from his friend HOM SHARE JOO, the man who looked after my transportation, and in this letter I told him I had spoken of this matter to his friend.

Q: During your stay in MACAO did your husband send regular remittances to support you while you were living with your maternal grandparents after your husband's return to the United States? A: Yes. He sent me some about three or four times a year and in regular sums and amounting to some $200 or $300 a year.

Q: How large a village is the HIN BIN Village where you were married? A: It is a village of about ten houses.

Q: Which way does the village face? A: East, and the head is at the north.

Q: How many rows of buildings are there in the HIN BIN Village? A: The houses are arranged in six rows. The ancestral hall is the first building at the north, and each of the other rows has two dwellings. Including the ancestral hall, there are 11 houses in that village.

Q: Where is the house located which you rented from YUNG YIP GHIN?
A: The second house, fourth row from the north.

Q: Please describe the house in which you lived in the HIN BIN Village?
A: It is a one story adobe house containing two bedrooms, two kitchens,
a parlor and an open court, and the house has a front entrance which
opens into the open court.[14]

Q: Where did you and your husband sleep while you were living in the
HIN BIN Village? A: In the north bedroom.

Q: Did anyone else occupy this house with the two of you? A: No, except for that ten days when my husband's brother's wife stayed with us.
During that period she slept in the south bedroom.[15]

Q: Where were the meals prepared? A: In the north kitchen.

Q: Are there any lofts or balconies in the bedrooms? A: There is a loft
running crosswise in each of the bedrooms but no balconies or sundecks.

Q: Were there outside windows in this house? A: There is a small opening in the outside wall of each bedroom and it has a little wooden door,
but it could hardly be called a window.

Q: Were there skylights in that house? A: One in each of the bedrooms
and one in each of the kitchens. Those in the bedrooms are covered with
glass and so is the skylight in the south kitchen, but the one in the north
kitchen has no covering and is used for smoke to escape.

Q: Is the stove in the north kitchen portable or built-in? A: The north
kitchen is equipped with a permanent stove but not the south kitchen.

APPLICANT VOLUNTEERS: During the period that we lived in this house,
some of my younger brothers visited me in this house.

Q: During your stay in this house were there any special dinners or feasts
or celebrations held during that three and one-half month period? A: No.

Q: When your younger brothers visited you did they remain overnight at
all or did they always return the same day? A: They had to stay overnight.

Q: Did you and your husband make any visits overnight or longer away
from the HIN BIN Village during the time you were staying there? A: No,
but the third day after my marriage I returned to my home at the DAI
CHEUK HOM Village, but I returned on the same day, and one month af-

---

14. This is actually a description of my father's house in Pai Shan village.

15. See page 41, note 10.

ter my marriage I made another trip back to my home village and I was there for about three or four days.

Q: How far is the DAI CHEUK HOM Village from the HIN BIN Village? A: Eight or nine lis[16] to the north of the HIN BIN Village.

Q: Where did you do your marketing while you were at the HIN BIN Village? A: I did not do any marketing during the period I was at this village, but my husband did the marketing at this time and he said he marketed at the DOW MOON Market.

Q: Have you ever been to the DOW MOON Market? A: When I returned to my native village I passed by the DOW MOON Market.

Q: How large is that market? A: It is a very large market but I don't know the number of stores there.

Q: Was your husband with you when you last said goodbye to your relatives in the DAI CHEUK HOM Village before departing for MACAO and HONG KONG? A: About a month before he finally left the HIN BIN Village I made one visit back to my native village and I was there for four days. I went by myself on that trip.

Q: Do you know your husband's occupation in this country? A: He is a merchant and salesman at the YUEN TUNG Company (Far East), 760 Sacramento Street, San Francisco, Calif.[17]

Q: If you are admitted to this country where will you live? A: I will live with my husband. He will provide the place for me but I don't know exactly where.

Q: (Showing photographs of YUNG HIN SEN and JEW LAW YING attached to the affidavit of the alleged husband and father in present file) Who are these people? A: My husband YUNG HIN SEN and myself.

Q: (Showing photographs of applicants on Foreign Service Form No. 257) Who are these persons? A: My daughter YUNG BAK HEONG and myself.

Q: (Showing photograph of YUNG HIN SEN attached to Form 432, dated 10/28/36 in file 12017/51188) Who is this? A: My husband YUNG HIN SEN.

Q: (Showing photograph of YUNG UNG attached to Form 432, dated Nov. 30, 1921 in file 22447/3-20) Who is this person? A: I don't know.

---

16. One *li* is equal to one-third mile.
17. See page 51, note 28.

(NOTE: Throughout the hearing, although unable to testify, YUNG BAK HEONG (11-14) evidenced that she considered applicant 11-13, JEW SHEE (JEW LAW YING) to be her mother by clinging to the mother and resisting any attempt to part them even momentarily.)

TO OTHER BOARD MEMBERS:

Q: Do you wish to question the applicant?

A: BY MEMBER R. B. JONES: No.
   BY MEMBER POSEY: No.

TO APPLICANT:

Q: Have you anything further you wish to state? A: No.

THROUGH INTERPRETER M. J. LEE:

Q: Have you understood the interpreter? A: Yes.

TO INTERPRETER EDWAR LEE:

Q: In what dialect has the applicant testified? A: WONG LUNG DOO.

SIGNATURE OF APPLICANT 11-13 [Jew Law Ying in Chinese characters]
DISMISSED.

I hereby certify that the foregoing is a true and correct transcript of shorthand notes taken on April 2, 1941, notebook 18015.

Stenographer
Interpreter H. K. TANG

HEARING RESUMED APRIL 3, 1941. (Board Room).

ALLEGED HUSBAND AND FATHER SWORN AND ADMONISHED THAT IF AT ANY TIME HE SHOULD FAIL TO UNDERSTAND THE INTERPRETER TO IMMEDIATELY SO STATE; ADVISED AS TO THE NATURE OF AND PENALTY FOR THE CRIME OF PERJURY.

INSPECTOR H. F. DUFF REPLACES R. B. JONES AS MEMBER OF THE BOARD.

BY MEMBER DUFF: I have familiarized myself with the evidence thus far adduced in this case.

Q: What are all your names? A: YUNG HIN SEN or YUNG NGIP JICK. I am also known as Tommy; no others.[18]

Q: What is your natural dialect? A: SUN WUEY Dialect.[19]

Q: Will you use that dialect throughout this examination? A: Yes.

Q: What is your age and place of birth? A: 39 years old, Chinese reckoning, born at SIN DUNG Village, SUN WUEY District, China.[20]

Q: What is your birthdate? A: KS 29-7-15 (Sept. 6, 1903).

Q: How many times have you been out of the United States? A: Just once.

Q: Will you describe that trip to China? A: I departed from Seattle on January 8, 1937 and returned to Seattle Oct. 14, 1937.

Q: What papers have you to show your right to remain in the United States? A: I forgot to bring my Certificate of Identity.[21]

(NOTE: Witness is subject of SF file 12017/51188 which shows his initial arrival and departure through port of Seattle as claimed. He is also subject of Seattle file 7032/3392, which shows his return through that port as claimed. Letter from this office to Seattle dated Jan. 6, 1937, indicates that witness is subject of C.I. No. 35835 but no receipt for such C.I. appears to be in witnesses' file.)

Q: What are your present occupation and address? A: I am a merchant and member of the YUEN TUNG Company, 760 Sacramento St., San Francisco, Calif.,[22] and I live at No. 50-A Beckett Street, San Francisco.

Q: What is your position in that firm? A: Salesman and Stock Clerk.

Q: Since your hearing on Sept. 6, 1940 in which you applied for preexamination of your status in anticipation of the arrival of your alleged wife and daughter, have you daily been occupied in your business at the firm above mentioned? A: Yes.

Q: Why are you appearing here today? A: To testify for my wife JEW LAW YING and my daughter YUNG BAK HEONG, applicants for admission.

---

18. See page 50, note 24.

19. My father actually spoke the Wong Leung Do dialect, which is very close to the Sunwui dialect.

20. My father was actually thirty-seven years old then. He was born in Pai Shan village, Heungshan District, in 1905.

21. Beginning in 1909 the immigration bureau began issuing Certificates of Identity to Chinese immigrants who were admitted or readmitted into the United States as proof of their exempt status. I am indebted to Erika Lee for tracking down this piece of information.

22. See page 51, note 28.

Q: Will you please describe your parents? A: My father was YUNG DUNG or YUNG JING YIN. He died in the Chinese Hospital in San Francisco in CR 18 (1929). My mother was WONG SHEE; she died in my native village in China in CR 25-1-15 (Feb. 7, 1936).[23]

Q: Do you have in your possession the Certificate of Identity which was issued to your father and which he presumably had at the time of his death? A: No. If my father had a Certificate of Identity it might be in my older brother's possession.

Q: Do you have regular contact with your older brother? A: No, not in recent years. I have not seen him for the past five years and I don't know where he is at the present time.

Q: Then you have no means that you know of of ascertaining whether or not he has that Certificate of Identity in his possession? A: No, I have not.

Q: It is necessary for the completion of the records of this Service that there be on file a death certificate and the certificate of identity which belonged to your father. It appears that neither has been submitted to this Service as yet. Will you arrange to have a death certificate prepared and forwarded through your attorney and if possible make an effort to procure the Certificate of Identity belonging to your father and submit it also to your attorney that both documents may become a matter of record at this station? A: Yes, I understand and will do so.

Q: Of what country do you claim nationality? A: China.

Q: Have you registered under the Alien Registration Act?[24] A: Yes.

(NOTE: Witness presents Alien Registration receipt card bearing No. 2549494; same is returned.)

Q: How many brothers or sisters have you ever had? A: One brother, no sisters.[25]

Q: Describe your brother. A: YUNG HING BIEW, 41 years old, now in the United States, but I don't know at what place. He is married.[26]

---

23. See page 45, notes 17 and 18.

24. The Alien Registration Act of 1940 required every alien fourteen years of age or older to register and be fingerprinted within thirty days of arrival in the United States as a national security measure against subversive activities.

25. See page 46, note 20.

26. See page 46, note 21.

Q: What is his wife's name? A: JEW SHEE, now living in my native village in China.

Q: Where did you first meet your wife JEW LAW YING? A: I first met her in her maternal grandfather's home in NOM SAN Village, WONG LUNG DOO Section, HEUNG SHAN District, China, in CR 25, the latter part of the 12th month (January 1937).

Q: Were your wife's maternal grandparents living in the NOM SAN Village before your arrival there? A: No, (Changes) Yes.[27]

Q: Where was your wife living at that time? A: In DAI CHEUK HOM Village, WONG LUNG DOO Section, China.

Q: Where was the marriage ceremony actually held? A: In HIN BIN Village, WONG LUNG DOO Section. I rented the house to get married there and lived there several months.[28]

Q: Who did you rent that house from? A: YUNG YIP GHIN.

Q: Is YUNG YIP GHIN any relative of yours? A: No.

Q: On the day of the ceremony how did your wife arrive at the house in HIN BIN Village owned by YUNG YIP GHIN? A: In a sedan chair.

Q: What took place immediately after your wife alighted from the sedan chair? A: She went into the house and into the bride's chamber—she was carried into the house by a woman. She went into her chamber and sat there in the presence of some women who accompanied her from her home village and also some of my own friends who were invited to come there to see the bride. Those persons in the bride's chamber were teasing the bride by asking her for tea, cakes, lucky money, etc.

Q: Did your wife occasionally leave the bedroom and visit in the other part of the house? A: Yes, she went out to the parlor and to the kitchen and served tea.

Q: What occurred the following morning that was a part of the ceremony? A: The next morning some old people of the village came to the house to tease her again and then she went out to the well to fetch water; when she came back they again teased her. After that she returned to her parents' home and came back to my home that same evening.

Q: Your wife describes an event which took place in the ancestral hall

---

27. According to my mother's testimony, my great-grandparents were living in Macao at the time.

28. See above, note 4.

of the village on that morning. Do you have any recollection of such an event? A: Yes, she did go to the ancestral hall in the company of her women attendants, but she was there for only a short time. I did not go there.

Q: Were there any feasts held in connection with your marriage? A: Yes. There was only one banquet and that took place on the day of the marriage at about 5 PM or 6 PM and the banquet tables were set in the ancestral hall.

Q: At what time of the day did your wife first arrive at the house of YUNG YIP GHIN? A: About 6 PM.

Q: Was there at any time any ancestral worship in connection with your marriage ceremony? A: No.

Q: Did your wife present you with any dowry? A: Yes, one wardrobe, two chairs, one table, one letter trunk, one suitcase, one wash basin stand, one wash basin, some clothes, one gold bracelet and one gold necklace, one spittoon (Changes) two spittoon.[29]

Q: Did you present a gift either to your wife or any members of her family at the time of your marriage? A: No.

Q: How long did you remain in the HIN BIN Village after your wedding took place? A: About three and one-half months.

Q: How large is the HIN BIN Village? A: Ten houses and one ancestral hall.

Q: Which way does the village face? A: East.

Q: Where is the head? A: I don't know.[30]

Q: How many rows of buildings are there in the HIN BIN Village? A: There are five rows of dwelling houses with two houses in each row, occupying the first and second house spaces; the ancestral hall stands in a row by itself at the north end of the village.

Q: Will you please describe the house in which you lived in the HIN BIN Village? A: That house is the second house, third row of dwellings counting from the north. It is a regular five room house, built of dirt, tile floors in all rooms, the open court is paved with stone; it has one outside entrance, located on the east side or front.

---

29. Here my father provided a more detailed answer than my mother, who had replied, "Bedding, a bureau, a table, two basin stands, two basins, two chairs and two wooden tubs."
30. According to the coaching book, my father should have answered, "North."

Q: Which bedroom did you occupy in that house in the HIN BIN Village? A: The bedroom on the north side.

Q: Did anyone else occupy this house with the two of you at any time? A: No, except my brother's wife who stayed there for ten days and sometimes my wife's young relatives came there and stayed with us for a day or two.[31]

Q: Did JEW SHEE, your brother's wife, make the trip to the HIN BIN Village from the SIN DUNG Village just to be present at the marriage ceremony? A: Yes.

Q: Did she make that trip to HIN BIN Village and back again alone? A: Yes, except when she came I went to the boat landing to meet her, and when she returned home I also took her to the boat landing.

Q: Where were the meals prepared in your home in the HIN BIN Village? A: In the kitchen on the north side of the house.

Q: Are there any lofts or balconies in that house? A: Each bedroom has an L-shaped loft and the parlor has an ancestral loft.

Q: Was anything kept in the loft in the parlor during your stay there? A: Yes, there is a piece of red paper with writings representing the YUNG family ancestors, and in front of it is a lamp and an incense burner.

Q: Are any of your ancestors commemorated by that piece of red paper? A: No.

Q: Are there any outside windows in that house? A: Yes, on the outside wall of each bedroom there is a window.

Q: What covers the windows you mentioned? A: It is closed by a wooden door.

Q: Where there any skylights in that house? A: Each bedroom has one skylight and each kitchen has one and they are all covered with glass.

Q: Is the cooking stove in the north kitchen portable or built-in? A: That kitchen has a stationary double stove and two portable stoves, one large and one small.

Q: How does the smoke escape from the permanent stove or built-in stove? A: The smoke rises to the ceiling and through the side openings on the roof.

Q: Are you sure that there is a glass covering over the skylight in the north kitchen? A: Yes.

---

31. See page 41, note 10.

Q: Your wife states that the north kitchen skylight is not equipped with glass and that the smoke from the stove goes out through that skylight. What do you say to that? A: If she said that she must be right because I was very seldom in the kitchen and paid very little attention to it.[32]

Q: How did you occupy your time while you were in the HIN BIN Village for that three months? A: I visited around in the neighboring villages, in DOW MOON Market and on the hills nearby, and at night quite often I went to the ancestral hall and chatted with people there.

Q: Did your wife go with you to DOW MOON Market at any time? A: No.

Q: Who did the marketing while you were in the HIN BIN Village? A: I did.

Q: During your stay in the HIN BIN Village did you and your wife make any visits together to any other village? A: No.

Q: What trips, if any, did your wife make that you know of without you during that three and one-half months period? A: She made four or five trips to her native village. That is all.

Q: How far is the DAI CHEUK HOM Village from the HIN BIN Village? A: About 8 or 9 lis.

Q: What are the names of your wife's maternal grandparents? A: Her maternal grandfather is CHUN HONG DAI and her maternal grandmother is LEONG SHEE. They are now living in MACAO.

Q: Do you know the names of her paternal grandparents? A: No.

Q: What are the names of your wife's parents? A: Her father is JEW HIN GWING, about 49 years old, now living in his home village in China or my wife's native village. Her mother is CHUN SHEE, 49 years old, now living with her parents in MACAO.

Q: How many brothers and sisters does your wife have that you know of? A: She has three brothers and three sisters.

Q: Describe them. A: Her brothers are—

JEW SING HAW, 13 years old;
JEW SING LUT (LEK), 11 years old;
JEW SING JUN, 9 years old.[33]

---

32. Here is an example of baiting by the interrogator and of my father's quick wit.
33. See page 50, note 25.

Her sisters are—

JEW JEE, 27 years old;

JEW DAI, 25 years old;

JEW NGAN, 23 years old.

I know her three brothers are now in MACAO as refugees. JEW JEE, twin sister of my wife, is married to a man in SIU CHEUK HOM Village. I don't know where JEW DAI and JEW NGAN are living at present.

Q: After leaving the HIN BIN Village, where did you and your wife go? A: We went to MACAO and a few hours later I went to HONG KONG, but my wife stayed with her maternal grandparents in MACAO for a few days. Afterwards I returned to MACAO to take her to HONG KONG with me.

Q: When you returned from HONG KONG to get your wife, had she been previously notified that you anticipated taking her back to HONG KONG with you? A: Yes.

Q: How was she notified? A: I sent her a letter.

Q: Where did you stay when you were in HONG KONG with your wife? A: At the LOOK HOY HUNG Hotel.

Q: Do you know the address of that hotel? A: It is on HOY PONG Street, but I don't know the number.

Q: How far is that from the waterfront? A: HOY PONG Street is the waterfront street.

Q: What floor of that hotel did you live on? A: Second floor.

Q: How many rooms did you occupy in that hotel? A: Just one.

Q: Did you have twin beds or one bed in that room? A: Just one bed.

Q: How did you spend your time while you were in HONG KONG? A: I took my wife to visit different places, such as show houses, top of the HONG KONG Mountain, KOWLOON and other places of interest.

Q: How long did you remain in HONG KONG? A: A little over three months.

Q: Did you accompany your wife back to MACAO before you departed for the United States? A: No. My wife returned to MACAO alone.

Q: Where did you last see your wife before leaving HONG KONG? A: At the wharf at KOWLOON when I boarded the steamer for San Francisco.

Q: Did you have any photographs taken while you were in HONG KONG of yourself and your wife? A: Yes.

Q: (Showing Exhibit "A"): Who are the persons shown in this photograph? A: My wife JEW LAW YING and myself.

Q: (Showing Exhibits marked "B" and "C"): Who are these persons? A: Exhibit "B": My daughter YUNG BAK HEONG and my wife JEW SHEE. Exhibit "C": My daughter YUNG BAK HEONG and my wife.

Q: (Showing letter marked Exhibit "D"): Do you recognize this letter? A: Yes. It is a letter written to me by my wife.

Substance of letter by Interpreter H. K. TANG:
"This letter is dated Oct. 9, 1940 and addressed to husband HIN SEN from wife LAW YING acknowledging the receipt of a letter sent her by airmail containing $100 HONG KONG money. She says she was happy to know that affidavits were being prepared for her and her daughter to come to the United States. She was also glad to know that $800 HONG KONG money had been sent to WING HUNG CHUNG Company in HONG KONG asking HOM SHARE DEW to make arrangements for her and her daughter to come to the United States. She said that everything was so high in China and asked that her husband send her $200 HONG KONG money for her expenses."

Q: (Showing letter marked Exhibit "E"): Do you recognize this letter? A: Yes. This letter was also written to me by my wife.

Substance of letter by Interpreter:
"This letter is dated Nov. 3, 1940, written to HIN SEN by his wife LAW YING stating that she had received his letter sent to her through her maternal grandfather. She says she and her daughter BAK HEONG were staying at the WING HUNG CHUNG Co. in HONG KONG; that she had already written to him about the affidavits. She said that she had been to the American Consulate and secured the approval of the American Consul, but the doctor says that BAK HEONG's eyes had to be treated first; so for that reason they had to wait in HONG KONG for a little while longer."

Q: (Showing letter marked Exhibit "F"): Do you recognize this letter? A: Yes. This letter was written to me by my wife.

Substance of letter by Interpreter:
"This letter is dated Feb. 3, 1941, written to HIN SEN by his wife LAW YING acknowledging the receipt of his letter from the United States under date of Jan. 8. She says that her daughter BAK HEONG has had her eyes re-examined, and that the doctor has passed her, but the American

Consul says that the affidavits were not quite ready and asked her to go and see him a week later. Mr. HOM SHARE DEW has tentatively engaged passage for her and her daughter on the SS PRESIDENT COOLIDGE sailing at the end of the month, so when the date of sailing is definitely known she will let him know by letter again."

Q: (Showing letter marked Exhibit "G"): Do you recognize this letter? A: Yes. This letter is dated Feb. 21, 1941 and was written to me by my wife.

Substance of letter by Interpreter:
"This is a letter written by LAW YING to her husband YUNG HIN SEN, dated Feb. 21, 1941. The letter says that her daughter BAK HEONG's eyes have been cured and that the American Consul has given them permission to sail on Feb. 22 for the United States on the SS PRESIDENT COOLIDGE. She says that Mr. HOM SHARE DEW has made all arrangements for them and she asks that when she and her daughter arrive he will meet them on this side."

Q: (Showing letter marked Exhibit "H"): Do you recognize this letter? A: Yes. This letter was written to me by my wife.

Substance of letter by Interpreter:
"This letter is dated Jan. 1, 1941, written by LAW YING to her husband HIN SEN acknowledging the receipt of a letter from him through her maternal grandfather in MACAO and two air mail letters received on Dec. 15, together with $100 HONG KONG money. She says that she and her daughter BAK HEONG were then staying at the WING HUNG CHUNG Co. in HONG KONG and that as soon as arrangements were completed she and her daughter would leave for the United States. She says that she had engaged another doctor to treat the daughter's eyes guaranteeing cure for $100. She has taken treatments for several weeks, but the doctor says that in another week she will be cured. She says that the husband's friend has told her that if necessary he was willing to advance her some money for her expenses. As soon as BAK HEONG has passed her eye examination and as soon as a definite date of their sailing for the United States is known she will let you know by letter again, so don't be anxious about them."

Q: When you were last in China did you visit your home village, SIN DUNG? A: Yes, once.

Q: At what time during your stay in China did you visit your home village? A: I visited that village as soon as I arrived in HONG KONG.

Q: Has your wife ever been to SIN DUNG Village? A: No.

Q: When you returned through Seattle in 1937, you gave the name of your wife, her age and your marriage date and showed her as residing at the time of your re-entry into this country in the SIN DUNG Village, SUN WUEY District. How do you suppose that information got into the record? A: I made a mistake and I cannot explain it.

Q: Would it not seem a little unusual to tie the thought of your marriage which took place in the HIN BIN Village with the name of a village utterly different? A: I am a native of SIN DUNG Village and possibly I was thinking of my own home.[34]

Q: If your wife is admitted to this country where will she live? A: She and our daughter will live with me in San Francisco, but perhaps for a short time we will have to stay in a hotel until we find a place to live.

Q: Do you intend then to continue to support them as your wife and daughter as you have in the past? A: Yes.

Q: (Showing photos of YUNG HIN SEN and JEW LAW YING attached to husband's affidavit, in present file): Who are these persons? A: Myself and my wife JEW LAW YING.

Q: (Showing photo on reverse of Consular Precis of Investigation in the present file): Who are these persons? A: My wife JEW SHEE and my daughter YUNG BAK HEONG.

Q: (Showing photo of YUNG BAK HEONG taken at this station in file 40766/11-14): Who is this? A: That looks like my daughter YUNG BAK HEONG.

Q: (Showing photos of YUNG HIN SEN and YUNG BAK HEONG on affidavit of present witness in file 40766/11-14): Who are these persons? A: Myself and my daughter YUNG BAK HEONG.

TO OTHER BOARD MEMBERS:

Q: Do you wish to question the witness? A: BY MEMBER DUFF: No.
                                   BY MEMBER POSEY: No.

TO WITNESS:

Q: Have you anything further you wish to state? A: No.

THROUGH INTERPRETER LEE PARK LIN:

Q: Have you understood the interpreter? A: Yes.

---

34. Another example of baiting by the immigration inspector and of my father's quick wit.

TO INTERPRETER H. K. TANG:

Q: In what dialect has the witness testified? A: SUN WUEY Dialect, very similar to HEUNG SHAN WONG LUNG DOO Dialect.

SIGNATURE OF ALLEGED FATHER AND HUSBAND [Yung Hin Sen and Yung Ngip Jick in Chinese characters; Yung Hin Sen] DISMISSED

> I hereby certify that the foregoing is a true and correct tran-
> script of testimony taken at the above described hearing.

_____

Clerk

SUMMARY BY CHAIRMAN:

1. JEW SHEE (JEW LAW YING), 11-13 and YUNG BAK HEONG, 11-14, are applying for admission as the wife and minor daughter of a lawfully domiciled Chinese merchant, YUNG HIN SEN. The alleged husband and father was originally admitted to the United States as a son of a Merchant on June 13, 1921. He subsequently departed from this country through Seattle on January 8, 1937 under a Laborer's status and returned through that port on October 14, 1937, thus placing himself in China at a time to make possible his marriage, and paternity to the alleged daughter, as claimed. On September 6, 1940 there was conducted a preinvestigation of YUNG HIN SEN's claimed status as a Merchant and active member of the YING CHUNG COMPANY or the FAR EAST COMPANY. His status then conceded and used as a basis for the issuance of a Sec. 3(6) non-immigrant visa to the alleged wife and daughter does not appear altered since the time of said preinvestigation.

2. Testimony has now been taken from the alleged wife, applicant 11–13 and from YUNG HIN SEN concerning their marriage and subsequent stay together in CHINA. This testimony is [in] very good agreement, both principals testifying freely. No discrepancies worthy of mention were brought out by the testimony. Applicant 11-14 was too young to testify but gave evidence of regarding JEW LAW YING as her mother. Both applicants appear to be about the claimed ages.

(Source: Jew Law Ying, folder 40766/11-13, -14, Chinese Departure Case Files, San Francisco District Office, Immigration and Naturalization Service, Record Group 85, National Archives, San Bruno, California)

MY FATHER TOM YIP JING'S FAMILY

TOM Yuk Wai
1825–1906

KWONG Shee
1847–1897

TOM Fat Ming
1868–19??

TOM Fat Woon
18??–19??

TOM Fat Yuet
18??–19??

TOM Fat Kwong
1882–1920

LEE Yee Oi
1882–1945

TOM Fat Tin
18??–19??

TOM Yeen Kau
1901–1940

TOM Yip Jing
(TOM Share Gow)
1905–1987

JEW Law Ying
1915–1998

TOM Yip Keung
1908–1939

Sharon YUNG
(TOM Bak Heong)
1938–

Sandra YUNG
(TOM See Heong)
1942–

Virginia YUNG
(TOM Bak Kay)
1943–

Patricia YUNG
(TOM Bak Jing)
1943–

Judith YUNG
(TOM Bak Fong)
1946–

Warren Tom YUNG
(TOM Gim Wah)
1948–

MY PAPER FATHER YUNG HIN SEN'S FAMILY

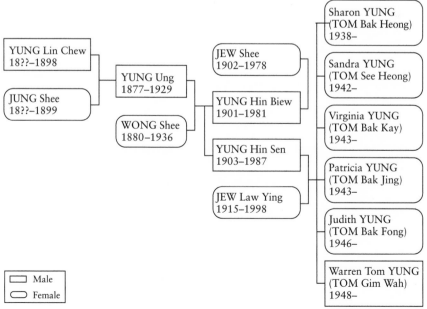

YUNG Lin Chew
18??–1898

JUNG Shee
18??–1899

YUNG Ung
1877–1929

WONG Shee
1880–1936

JEW Shee
1902–1978

YUNG Hin Biew
1901–1981

YUNG Hin Sen
1903–1987

JEW Law Ying
1915–1998

Sharon YUNG
(TOM Bak Heong)
1938–

Sandra YUNG
(TOM See Heong)
1942–

Virginia YUNG
(TOM Bak Kay)
1943–

Patricia YUNG
(TOM Bak Jing)
1943–

Judith YUNG
(TOM Bak Fong)
1946–

Warren Tom YUNG
(TOM Gim Wah)
1948–

Male
Female

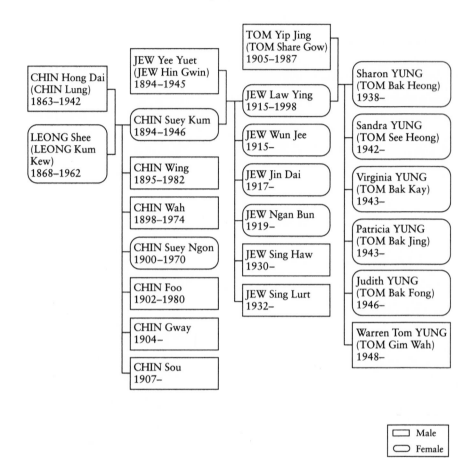

CHIN Hong Dai (CHIN Lung) 1863–1942

LEONG Shee (LEONG Kum Kew) 1868–1962

JEW Yee Yuet (JEW Hin Gwin) 1894–1945

CHIN Suey Kum 1894–1946

CHIN Wing 1895–1982

CHIN Wah 1898–1974

CHIN Suey Ngon 1900–1970

CHIN Foo 1902–1980

CHIN Gway 1904–

CHIN Sou 1907–

TOM Yip Jing (TOM Share Gow) 1905–1987

JEW Law Ying 1915–1998

JEW Wun Jee 1915–

JEW Jin Dai 1917–

JEW Ngan Bun 1919–

JEW Sing Haw 1930–

JEW Sing Lurt 1932–

Sharon YUNG (TOM Bak Heong) 1938–

Sandra YUNG (TOM See Heong) 1942–

Virginia YUNG (TOM Bak Kay) 1943–

Patricia YUNG (TOM Bak Jing) 1943–

Judith YUNG (TOM Bak Fong) 1946–

Warren Tom YUNG (TOM Gim Wah) 1948–

☐ Male
⬭ Female

Oral History Interview
with Jew Law Ying

My parents were always reluctant to talk about their past. I now understand why. Like many other Chinese who came during the exclusion years, they were illegal aliens always fearful of discovery and deportation. It was enough that I knew our real surname was Tom, not Yung, and that my ancestral village was in Chungshan (Zhongshan) District. I was repeatedly told never to divulge this information to any lo fan (white foreigners), otherwise we would all be in trouble.

It was not until I began interviewing old-timers about the Angel Island immigration experience that my parents finally opened up to me. My father, who had been detained at Angel Island for two months in 1921, actually allowed me to interview him for our book. Then after Island was published and I had established my reputation as a historian and writer, my mother allowed me to interview her for my second book, Chinese Women of America. By then she had become a naturalized U.S. citizen and was more willing to talk about her immigration history.

The following interview is a combination of two interviews that I did with my mother, one in 1982 when she was sixty-eight years old and the second in 1987. Both interviews were conducted in Chinese at her home on the outskirts of San Francisco Chinatown. As the historian, I had my agenda; as my mother, she had hers. While I was interested in finding out about her family history and her experiences as a Chinese immigrant woman, she was more interested in impressing me, her fifth daughter, with the hardships and lessons of her life: work hard, suffer for the sake *of your family and children, and above all else, accept Jesus Christ into your life. Although I have taken certain liberties in translating, editing, and reorganizing the interviews for clarity and flow as well as relevancy to the subject matter at hand, I have tried to stay true to her voice and the substance of her interviews.*

Assuming that her version of her life story is closer to the truth than the coaching book or immigration transcript, I have noted discrepancies among the three sources as a way to distinguish the lies from the truth in her immigration history. For example, I believe her story about Ah Kum over my great-grandmother's story to the immigration inspector in 1893; the number of brothers she told me she had over what she reported to immigration officials in 1941; and likewise, her story about my father's family history over what my father wrote in the coaching book. Knowing full well that she has biases and lapses in memory, I tried, whenever possible, to corroborate what she told me with information from interviews I did with other relatives. And to contextualize her story I have included cultural and historical references in the footnotes when necessary.

Aside from helping me to separate the truth from the falsehoods, my mother's interview serves to flesh out and fill in some of the gaps in the immigration documents. Her interview provides a fuller picture of what happened to my great-grandmother in America and in China between and after her appearances before immigration officials. Similarly, it explains what life was like for my mother in China, how and why she chose to marry my father and immigrate to America, and how the Chinese Exclusion Act complicated the process of immigration for women like her. It describes both the hardships she endured in America and her sense of fulfillment in her twilight years. The following is the story of my mother's life as she told it to me.

My mother had seven children. I was the eldest and a twin. The younger twin died at childbirth, so I have two younger brothers and three younger sisters. All the previous generations in my family farmed, so we also farmed. We owned land and planted rice. My mother was born in America. But Grandmother couldn't take the harried life in Gold Mountain. She knew that in China she could have servants and a life of leisure. She took all the children home with her [in 1904]. My mother was eleven years old then. She wasn't very smart, just did what she was told to do. Never had anything to say. She was arranged in marriage to Jew Yee Yuet [a.k.a. Jew Hin Gwing], a Chinese herb doctor. His grandfather left him fifty *mau* (*mou*) of land in Dai Chek Hom [village].[1] When my mother married him, they had land, a big house, and two *mui tsai*. It was a good match. But then his older brother squandered it all on opium, gambling, and women. After they lost all their land, Grandfather [Chin Lung] supported us. Mother would periodically go visit them in Macao and come back with food and new clothes.

When I was seven I went to live with my maternal grandparents in Macao because my grandmother loved me best. (*chuckles*) She treated me like her own daughter. She supported my schooling, so you could say I grew up eating the Chin family's rice and wearing their clothes. They had four *mui tsai* and a head cook, so I didn't have to do any housework. Once a year during vacation time I would return to Dai Chek Hom to visit the family. I usually stayed with an aunt who was a widow in the Girls' House, where we sang, talked stories, joked, and learned about Chinese customs.[2] After I finished elementary school I had to quit [school] because although my grandparents were wealthy, they were very stingy. They said girls became a part of another family when they married, so what was the use of educating them? That's the way it was, so what could I do?

After I stopped going to school, I was sent to collect rent. Grandmother and grandfather had over ten buildings in Macao and about twice a month I went with Fifth Aunt [the wife of Chin Lung's fifth son, Chin Sou] to collect the rent. Whenever I was out collecting rent, Grandmother would tell the *mui tsai* to be sure to save me some food. I especially liked red bean *juk* [rice gruel], and when the weather was hot she would tell the *mui tsai* to cook me some. When I was home, I would sew clothes for myself on Grandmother's old-fashioned foot-pedal machine, the kind that rocked back and forth. On Sundays I would go to church with Grandmother. Both she and Grandfather were baptized at the local Church of Christ. I wasn't baptized until after I came to America and had six children.

[Were you arranged in marriage?] No, Grandfather introduced us when your father came back from America. Your father was very active

---

1. One *mou* is equivalent to .15 acre.

2. Quite common in the Guangdong area of China, a Girls' House was a separate residence for adolescent girls in the village, where they spent the evenings sewing, playing games, telling stories, singing ballads, and preparing for their future domestic roles as wives and homemakers. See Janice E. Stockard, *Daughters of the Canton Delta: Marriage Patterns and Economic Strategies in South China, 1860–1930* (Stanford: Stanford University Press, 1989), chap. 2.

in those days and he often shopped at [Grandfather's] Shanghai Trunk Company [in San Francisco Chinatown]. He also knew Wah Ching [Chin Lung's oldest daughter-in-law], who had a bath house and beauty parlor on Stockton Street. He played *mah jongg* with her. When your father returned to China for a bride at the age of thirty-two, Wah Ching had him bring some head scarves, needles, and slippers to Grandmother and wrote home to recommend your father. At that time I was studying to become a midwife in Canton and was not interested in getting married. Grandmother wrote and told me to accompany her back to Nam Shan village [Chin Lung's native village]. She fooled me into going back to the village to marry your father. Your father's village, Pai Shan, was not far from Nam Shan and she had agreed to give me away in marriage. I agreed to it because I wanted to come to America.

In marriage, a bamboo door should be paired with a bamboo door, a wooden door with a wooden door.[3] Ours was not a good match because your father was poor. He had an uncle lend him $300 to come home for a bride. But he was a Gold Mountain man and that's what mattered. He still had a younger brother who was married with three children in the village to support. His father had died when he was fourteen and he had borrowed money from his uncle to come to America. I knew he was just a laborer who worked on a flower farm.[4] He told me I would have to work hard in America, but I still wanted to come. Your father was older than me by eight years, but that was not unusual for marriages to Gold Mountain men. Despite the age difference, I liked him. He told me that he would go back to America and try to bring me over. He made it clear that he wasn't sure he could do it. I wanted to come to America to open a new road for myself and your two uncles. It was one step at a time.

We were married in 1937 in your father's village. We had a simple but traditional wedding. Just a couple of banquet tables. Your mother rode in a red sedan chair. Your father stayed in China for a few months and then returned to America to take care of the paperwork so I could come. I lived with your paternal grandmother for six months in Pai Shan.[5]

---

3. A Chinese saying meaning that a husband's and wife's class backgrounds should match.

4. Here is evidence that my parents had lied to immigration authorities about my father's family background and occupation in the United States.

5. So my mother did not stay in Macao with her grandparents after my father returned to America, as she had told immigration officials. She returned to live with her mother-in-law in Pai Shan village for three months (not six, as she remarks here) before leaving to give birth in Macao.

She was mean to me and your mother suffered.[6] Everyone called her Kau Ma because she was always arguing with people.[7] She had an evil heart and worshipped money. She insisted that your father buy her all this stuff so she could eat well and dress well. She had pigs and grew sweet potatoes, taro, melons, and green vegetables. I had to work in the fields, carry manure and urine out to fertilize the crops, and help with the harvesting. I never worked so hard. Even after I became pregnant with your oldest sister, I still had to work hard. If I didn't she would complain. When I cooked rice, she was so afraid I would cook too much she rationed the rice out herself. When the rice bin got low, she accused me of stealing. She was even meaner to my sister-in-law, who came from a poor family. After six months of that,[8] I couldn't take it anymore. I wrote your father and said I had to go to Macao to have the baby. He sent me some money and I never went back to live with his mother again. Your sister was born at the Bak Ma Hong Hospital [St. Raphael Hospital] in Macao.

In Macao I rented a room from Grandfather because I was now a married woman. Your father sent money home to support us as well as his mother and brother in the village. He was only making $80 a month as a gardener on a private estate [in Menlo Park, California]. Practically his whole paycheck was sent to support two households in China. After I came to America during the war [World War II], my mother-in-law died and then my own parents. We couldn't get money to them because of the war and they died of sickness and starvation during an epidemic. It was unfortunate that no one helped my mother return to the United States. My uncles said that my mother was like a buddha [sat around all day]. She couldn't work and was too used to having servants. If she came back to America, they would have to find someone to take care of her. Mother was also very frail and nearsighted, unlike my aunt [Mee Ngon], who was smart enough to return to the United States with a brother.

[Why did your grandparents prefer to live in Macao rather than in

---

6. Mistreatment of daughters-in-law by mothers-in-law in China was common. Margery Wolf thinks that Chinese mothers-in-law tyrannize their daughters-in-law as compensation for their own former suffering and in an effort to assert their authority as matriarch and maintain control over their son—the one person who can serve as their "political front" in domestic and public affairs. See Margery Wolf, "Chinese Women: Old Skills in a New Context," in *Women, Culture, and Society*, ed. Michelle Zimbalist Rosaldo and Louise Lamphere (Stanford: Stanford University Press, 1974), pp. 157–72.

7. I later found out from my uncle in Pai Shan village that she was called Kau Ma (literally, Kau's mother) because her daughter's name was Yeen Kau.

8. See above, note 5.

the village?] It was safer and more comfortable. We had a front and back garden and two outhouses. The *mui tsai* would help us flush the toilets by pouring water. There was no tap water, but we had two wells that had water in them all year round. We also had a bathroom: no bathtub, but we used buckets of water to wash ourselves. It was a big house. Two stories tall until Grandfather added a third floor. The Japanese were always bombing the villages, but not Macao. We were safe there.

Everyone said life in America was good, except Grandmother, but I didn't believe her. She warned me that life would be hard there. Before I left for America, she said to me, "Ying, when you go to America, don't be lazy. Work hard and you will become rich. Work and be frugal. Your grandfather grew potatoes [in Stockton] and although I was busy enough at home [in San Francisco], I sewed on a foot-treadle machine, made buttons, and wove loose threads [did finishing work]. I only had one *mui tsai* to help with the children and housework. But I saved enough so that when I returned to Macao, I was able to buy property." Not only did Grandfather have a house built in Macao, but he also built a house in Nam Shan that was two stories tall with concrete walls and balconies. After Grandmother died, all the property went to the sons. Since my mother had married out, we girls weren't entitled to any of the inheritance.

Finally your father arranged for me and your sister [Bak Heong] to immigrate on merchant papers. He was [supposedly] doing business at an import company. I went to Hong Kong and your father sent money to us via the *gam saan jong*[9] run by Uncle Dew [a.k.a. Tom Yip Pooh]. He helped us make the necessary arrangements to come by boat. Your sister was four and I was twenty-seven years old when we came to Gold Mountain on the SS *President Coolidge*. It was 1941.

I heard people say that Gold Mountain was a good place. Like going to heaven. But you really don't know until you've been there. It's been a hard life for your mother all the way.

We were on that boat for over a month. Others got seasick and threw up, but neither I nor your sister [Bak Heong] got seasick. We came by

---

9. Literally, "Golden Mountain firm," an export-import firm doing business between the Americas and China. The firms handled remittances and correspondence of overseas Chinese, provided hostel facilities for emigrants and returning immigrants, helped to process paperwork and book passage for emigrants, and acted as middleman for the sale of immigration "slots."

steerage with lots of people. Slept in separate bunk beds. The food was good except I didn't like any of the meat the way they cooked it. They usually served Western food—lamb chops, beef, chicken. Your sister ate just about everything, but I couldn't.

When we arrived in San Francisco, Angel Island [Immigration Station] had burned down and we were detained at temporary quarters in San Francisco for three weeks.[10] We had to wait our turn to be interrogated. Our name was Yung, so alphabetically we were last.[11] We shared a large room with other women. It was quite comfortable. The air was good and it was spacious. We each had our own bed. Meals were taken downstairs in the dining hall with men on one side and women on the other. We had three meals a day and the food was pretty good. For breakfast we had toast, oatmeal, eggs. The children had milk, and the adults, tea. There was coffee, but we didn't like coffee then. Lunch and dinner consisted of a variety of Chinese dishes with rice, like vermicelli and dried shrimp, steamed fish, chicken, and soup. I ate everything except for some of the meat, which I found too "wild." That's how I got fat coming to America. Your father sent barbecued duck to us at least four times. Once he sent soy sauce chicken. We must have finished three jars of fermented bean cakes while we were there. Bought them at the little store that sold all kinds of snacks. My grandmother had also given us a box of food to take on the trip—cookies, salted plums, oyster sauce, canned fish, fermented black beans. The two of us finished it all before we were landed.

It [the interrogation] was quite simple. They asked me when I married. They asked about my mother and father, where they were born. They asked how many brothers and sisters I had. That was it.[12] It took no more than an hour. I just answered what they asked. Why should I be afraid? I wasn't a crook or a robber. If they let me land, fine. If not, too bad. Nothing to be scared about. Your sister kept crying throughout, she was so shy. As soon as I signed my name, they allowed us to

---

10. She is referring to the temporary detention quarters at 801 Silver Avenue in San Francisco. In later interviews my mother would insist that she had been detained at Angel Island.

11. The order in which immigrants were called for interrogation was based on date of arrival and availability of witnesses, not alphabetical order.

12. Actually, as Jew Law Ying's and Yung Hin Sen's testimonies of April 2–3, 1941 (pages 57–84) show, the interrogation was not that easy. My parents were asked close to one hundred questions about their wedding day, respective family histories, the village and house where they lived, and their stay in Hong Kong before my father returned to America.

land. Yelled out our names and said it's time to go. Everyone was happy
for us. The women who were coming in as paper daughters and had
made mistakes in their interrogations cried when they saw us leave.
They said, "You're lucky Heong Ma" (that's what they called me because your sister's name was Heong) "to be landed so soon. We don't
know when we'll be allowed to leave this place." You remember Feng
Goon's mother? She was stuck there after I left. Her husband was trying to get her in as a paper daughter and she had made mistakes. She
wasn't landed until three months after me. Then there was Ng Feng,
who also came posed as a paper daughter. She cried when she saw me
leave. Burned incense to scare away the evil spirits. She said, "Let's get
rid of the evil spirits so that we can follow Heong Ma." I still remember what she said. There was Mui, Lee, Seeto, many who couldn't land.
Some waited for over a year. Then the war came and they released all
these women.[13]

Your father met us and took us to the Yee Wo Hotel in Chinatown.
We stayed in San Francisco for a few weeks, visiting relatives while waiting for the immigration papers. Then your father took us to live in Menlo
Park, where he had been working with your granduncle as gardeners on
a private estate. They pruned, watered, and mowed the grass. There were
lots of fruit trees—peaches, pears, grapes, and apples—and all kinds of
flowers. The wealthy white boss lived in San Francisco and sent us a check
every month for taking care of her flowers and fruit orchards. Your
granduncle got $100 a month, and your father, $80. That was considered good wages. We were given a shack to live in. No bathroom, no ice
box, just a wood-burning stove and a broken-down bed with a used mat-
tress. I got a job picking suckers [off flowers] for relatives. Started at six
in the morning and returned at six. Twelve hours a day, twenty-five cents
an hour. If the relative had a good year, I would be paid at the end of the
season. If not, he would owe me the money, sometimes for as long as a
few years. Your father drove me there in his old jalopy in the morning
and picked me up at the end of the day. Then I would go get firewood
and cook dinner.

When your second sister was born in the shack, there was only a

---

13. Not all the women were released because of the war. Some were deported. See Mrs.
Chan, interview with Him Mark Lai, Genny Lim, and author, December 14, 1975, San
Francisco, Angel Island Oral History Project, Ethnic Studies Library, University of Cali-
fornia, Berkeley.

kerosene lamp. We didn't have money to go to the hospital.[14] We didn't have a phone, so your father went to the next farmhouse to call this old demon of a midwife to help. She took a long time to come. She was in her eighties and shaking. She felt my womb and said it felt normal, even though my water bag had broken the day before and the baby still refused to come out. Your father lit the kerosene lamp and burned wood in the stove. It was a cold, rainy day in March when I gave birth to your second older sister. Your father helped by boiling water and cutting the umbilical cord. There was a lot of bleeding. I almost died. After a month of rest, I went back to work. Left the two girls at home. Your father and granduncle took turns looking after them. Fed them milk and changed the baby's diapers.

I cried a lot when I first came to Menlo Park. So this was what Gold Mountain was all about! So this was heaven! No bathtub, no ice box, a wood-burning stove, no hot water. I wanted to go back to China, where we had servants to cook and to serve us, where I was happy eating my grandfather's food and wearing my grandfather's clothes. Here I had to do everything myself, including washing the laundry by hand and fetching the firewood. It was a sorrowful three years.

When I became pregnant with your third sister, I said no matter what, I was not going to have the baby in Menlo Park. It was a matter of life and death. I told your father, "Even if you don't want to go to San Francisco, I am leaving." There were two Chinese woman obstetricians in the city and I was determined to have my next child in a hospital. I would find work sewing or doing something. I just didn't want to continue working and living like that in Menlo Park. Besides, we were worried that your father would be drafted.

After we moved to San Francisco, he found a good-paying job working at the shipyard, which exempted him from the draft, and I sewed at home. Your third sister was born at the beginning of 1943, your fourth sister at the end of 1943, you in 1946, and your brother in 1948. Not until you were all in school did I sew in the factory, but I would bring work home at night. I couldn't speak English, so I couldn't work anywhere else but Chinatown. The Chinese always cheated you. You worked all day for low wages. There were no set hours, so you could come and

---

14. My sister Sandy remembers that my father said he was afraid to take my mother to the hospital at night because he might be mistaken for a Japanese American and arrested for breaking the curfew and relocation orders enforced during World War II.

go. When you worked for whites you were paid by the hour so you had to work fast, but the wages were higher. The Chinese paid you by the dozen. If you worked fast, you made more. If you were slow, you made less. I was so-so. I was never let go; I usually quit. All those years, I worked at only three factories. I joined the union sometime in the 1950s. Worked until I was sixty-two. Your father didn't make enough to feed all six of you. And I had to send money home four times a year to my sisters and brothers. Grandfather refused to support them after our mother died.[15]

After sewing all day, I still had to come home to cook and take care of the housework. Your father just worked [outside] and didn't help at home.[16] It was harder than working in China. For eight years, we lived in this two-room apartment on Stockton Street with no private bathroom, kitchen, or hot water. All of you crammed into two bunk beds. Had to cook and boil water by the window on a three-burner stove. That's how I raised you all. Then we moved to a flat in North Beach and things got better.

[What was Chinatown like when you first came?] Things were cheap. You could buy a heavy bag of groceries for twenty-five cents. You could even buy five cents' worth of pork. Now it's at least one dollar. Green onions, ginger, garlic, black beans were free. Innards were given away. Sure, I was only making a dollar or two sewing twelve hours a day, but food and rent were cheap. That two-room apartment [on Stockton Street] was only $18, water included. Rent, telephone, and electricity cost us a little over $20 a month. Now we talk about needing $1,000 a month to cover expenses. And Chinatown wasn't so crowded and unsafe. No one got mugged or robbed. We kept our doors unlocked. People would stay out in the streets until one or two in the morning. Now Chinatown closes down after dark.

[Have your hopes been fulfilled in America?] Yes, considering that I originally hoped for a better future for myself. That has been fulfilled. All five of my daughters have finished school and have good jobs. [My brother—her only son—was in an accident when he was nine years old and has since been institutionalized and confined to a wheelchair.] I feel satisfied with life, especially after I accepted Jesus Christ into my life. Now I'm retired with a good pension and am more active in church af-

---

15. According to Chinese tradition, once a daughter married out, she belonged to her husband's family. My great-grandfather Chin Lung was considered generous for helping his daughter out when her husband fell on hard times. He was not expected to continue supporting her children after her death.

16. In all fairness, my father always helped with the cooking, laundry, and housework.

My mother, Jew Law Ying, with her five daughters in 1946 (from left to right): Sharon, author as baby, Sandra, Virginia, and Patricia.

fairs. I've traveled around a bit and have concluded that America is the best country to live in. Why? First, the mild weather. Second, freedom is good. Third, food is cheap and plentiful. No matter where I go, there's no better place to call home than San Francisco.

(SOURCE: Jew Law Ying, interview with author in Chinese, September 7, 1982, and January 14, 1987, San Francisco)

On July 16, 1998, the day after I turned in the manuscript for this book to my publisher, my mother, Jew Law Ying, passed away suddenly but

Finally, after five daughters, my mother, Jew Law Ying, bears my father, Yung
Hin Sen (Tom Yip Jing), the son he had so long hoped for, Warren Tom Yung.

*peacefully in her sleep while visiting me in Santa Cruz. She was almost
eighty-five years old and was looking forward to the publication of* Unbound Voices. *As my sister Sandy said in her eulogy, "Mom was the matriarch of our family. She was the glue that held the family together. She
worked hard to provide for us and taught us to be woman warriors, to
be a credit to our family, community, and country." I will always remember what she used to say to relatives who would ridicule her for having so many daughters: "Just look at how good my daughters have been
to me. My heart is totally satisfied."*

PART TWO

Bound Feet

Chinese Women in the Nineteenth Century

Few women were among the early settlers who came to California in response to the gold rush. In 1850 there were 12 men to every woman in the state, but among the Chinese population the sex ratio was 39 to 1. By 1900 the numbers of men and women had almost balanced out, except among the Chinese where the sex ratio was 12 to 1. Chinese social mores, as reflected in folk sayings—"Men's ambition is in four directions; women's ambition is in the boudoir," for example, or "A woman's duty is to care for the household, and she should have no desire to go abroad"—dictated that men should leave home to seek their fortunes while women remained behind to care for the family. In addition, the widespread practice of footbinding, which limited physical mobility, ensured that most women would not travel far from home. Of course, not all classes of women followed these social prescriptions. Women from poor families as well as Hakka and Manchu women did not practice footbinding, and silk spinners in the Shunde, Nanhai, and Panyu districts of Guangdong Province joined sisterhoods that openly resisted marriage. But aside from social reasons, women were discouraged from emigrating to Gold Mountain by the great distance, the prohibitive cost of financing their passage, and the anti-Chinese climate in the American West. Given all these considerations, it was cheaper and safer for women to remain in China while their men supported them from across the sea. Later, when Chinese immigrants turned from being sojourners to settlers, they were prevented from sending for their wives and families by the Chinese Exclusion Acts. As a result, the split-household arrangement became a way of life for many Chinese families, separating husbands and wives, fathers and children, for decades.

Although much has been written about the Chinese bachelor society in America, little has been said about the wives who were left behind in China. Supported by periodical remittances from their husbands, they supposedly lived in comfort, attending to the needs of their children and in-laws. Most important, they remained chaste while waiting for the return of their men. Kwong King You's personal story in this section tells us what it meant to be a *sau saang gwa* (literally, a widow with a living husband, or grass widow).[1] In her case, she faithfully waited more than forty years for her husband to return from America, suffering impoverishment during the Sino-Japanese War, the ridicule of jealous relatives, and disturbing rumors that her husband had remarried in America. "A Poem to My Husband Overseas," given to me by a son of a U.S. immigrant, or *gam saan haak,* expresses poignantly the sentiments of a *sau saang gwa* who cries for the return of her husband.

Kwong King You is living proof of the strong influence Confucian teachings have had on the social conduct of Chinese women for centuries. Nowhere is this influence more evident than in the proverbs they all grew up hearing, which I have collected in "Images of Women in Chinese Proverbs." These popular sayings defined women's secondary place in society, reinforcing the common belief that women should be kept uneducated, subordinate to men, and confined to the domestic sphere. At the same time, the proverbs condoned a double standard of moral behavior. While it was permissible for men to engage in extramarital sex, women were expected to remain chaste and faithful to their husbands. These values were all part of the cultural baggage that Chinese emigrants brought with them to the United States in the mid–nineteenth century.

To a large degree, Chinese women's bound lives continued in America. Not only was their social conduct as circumscribed as in China, but alienation and anti-Chinese sentiment in this country compounded the difficulties they faced. Speaking no English, having no independent means of support, and insulated within Chinatown from alternative views of gender roles and relations, most women continued to abide by the Confucian norms of their homeland, maintaining a subordinate role to men

---

1. For a comparable description of life overseas for the husband, or "married bachelor," see Paul Siu, *The Chinese Laundryman: A Study of Social Isolation,* ed. John Kuo Wei Tchen (New York: New York University Press, 1987).

and confining their activities to the private sphere. Regardless of their social status—whether prostitute, *mui tsai,* or merchant wife—they were all considered the property of men and treated as such. Unlike most European immigrant women at the time, Chinese women did not find immigration a liberating experience.

During the early decades of Chinese immigration, the scarcity of Chinese women and antimiscegenation laws created a demand for Chinese prostitution, which was readily filled by the abundant supply of daughters from poor families in China. Whereas prostitutes from other parts of the world came as independent professionals for the easy money, Chinese prostitutes were invariably imported as indentured servants. Protestant missionary women, looking for a way to exert their moral authority, made it their crusade to rescue Chinese prostitutes and domestic slavegirls. Their sensationalistic writings on the enslaved and abusive lives of Chinese women served as a clarion call for social reform and constitute the few records we have of what life might have been like for Chinese prostitutes and slavegirls in America. M. G. C. Edholm's "A Stain on the Flag" is a good example of this genre of writing. Excerpts that include the voices of Chinese girls who were rescued by missionary workers provide a glimpse of the horrible conditions of the Chinese prostitution trade, in which young women were sold for a pittance by poor parents in China and then brought to America and forced into prostitution. As evidence, I have included bills of sale for a Chinese prostitute and a *mui tsai.* In contrast, Suey Hin's story in "Confessions of a Chinese Slave-Dealer" tells us how a Chinese prostitute who was redeemed by a Chinese laundryman later chose to become a madam. Not only was Suey Hin kind to her girls, but she also opted to free them after she supposedly converted to Christianity.

As Chinese prostitution declined, thanks to the efforts of social reformers and the local enforcement of antiprostitution laws, the number of merchant wives increased in response to the Chinese Exclusion Act of 1882, which stipulated that only certain exempt classes—merchants, teachers, students, officials, and visitors—would be allowed into the United States. Following Chinese custom, merchant wives seldom left the house, so there are few first-hand accounts of what their lives were like in nineteenth-century San Francisco. Fortunately, Sui Sin Far, a Eurasian journalist and short story writer, chose to write about Chinese immigrant life, often with great sensitivity and empathy. Her story "The Chinese Woman in America" presents a rosy picture of the merchant wife, apparently content with her lot. In contrast, Louise A. Littleton, writing at about the same time, introduces us to a disgruntled Chinese wife. The wealthy woman she interviewed for her article, "Worse Than Slaves," is a second wife who complains about being confined to the house, treated like a child, and denied the same rights as the first wife. A strong-minded woman, she considers but rejects the possibility of running away to the mission home or seeking help through legal channels. Ultimately, she resigns herself to the limitations of her bound feet and her bound life.

I end Part II with the story of Mary Tape, who, because of a very different upbringing from that of her Chinese peers, was able to speak up for her rights. Her scathing letter of attack against the San Francisco Board of Education, published in the *Alta* newspaper in 1885, probably represents the first time a Chinese woman ever dared to raise her voice publicly against social injustice in America. But it was not the last, as Chinese women began to unbind their feet and their lives with the dawning of a new era.

Images of Women in Chinese Proverbs

"A Woman without Talent Is Virtuous"

Regardless of their educational background, many of the women I interviewed for Unbound Feet *cited Chinese proverbs or folk sayings as maxims they had been raised by and were expected to live up to. For example, the "Three Obediences and Four Virtues" prescribed that a Chinese woman obey her father at home, her husband after marriage, and her eldest son when widowed, and it required of her propriety in behavior, speech, demeanor, and household duties. Similarly, "Marry a chicken, follow the chicken; marry a dog, follow the dog" told women that they had to stick to whomever they married, good or bad. A third popular saying, "A woman without talent is virtuous," warned women not to pursue learning or appear too competent. Women recited these sayings to me as indications of how they had been taught to stay in their proper places—within the domestic sphere and subordinate to men. However, it was obvious that although my interviewees may have tried to live up to some of these idealized norms, in practice they deviated according to the circumstances at hand. When opportunities arose and conditions changed for them in America, Chinese women did not hesitate to leave the home and pursue education, careers, and social activism, in spite of these folk sayings. As other feminist scholars have shown, there is usually a wide gap between ideology and practice, and*

women have always found ways to create space from within prevailing
gender systems to give their lives meaning, solace, and dignity.[1]
    I have collected here some of the more popular proverbs regarding
the status and role of women in traditional Chinese society, as indica-
tions of the bound lives women were expected to lead in the mid–nine-
teenth century when the Chinese began immigrating to America. Intended
as teachings that reinforce Confucian social order and gender ethics, these
selected sayings reflect Chinese society's low regard for women as infe-
rior and subordinate beings relative to men. Other texts that express sim-
ilar sentiments and social ethics include a popular series of instructional
books for women and primers for children.[2] *It should be noted that im-*
perial legal codes worked in tandem with these texts to reinscribe Chi-
nese notions of femininity and women's subordinate status. Men, but not
women, were permitted to commit adultery, divorce, remarry, practice
polygyny, and discipline their spouses as they saw fit. Wives were not al-
lowed to own or control property, and women could not participate in
politics or public activities.[3]
    Compared with the amount of research on sexism in the English lan-
guage,[4] *attention paid to images of women in the Chinese language and*
in popular sayings has been negligible. I found only two articles on the

---

    1. For example, see Dorothy Ko, *Teachers of the Inner Chambers: Women and Cul-*
ture in Seventeenth-Century China (Stanford: Stanford University Press, 1994), and Susan
Mann, *Precious Records: Women in China's Long Eighteenth Century* (Stanford: Stanford University Press, 1997), in which the authors show how elite women were able to
venture into the male domain of literature, public visibility, and responsibility without
threatening or changing the prevailing gender system.
    2. For a discussion of these texts, see Heying Jenny Zhan, "Chinese Femininity and So-
cial Control: Gender-Role Socialization and the State," *Journal of Historical Sociology* 9,
no. 3 (September 1996): 269–89; and Clara Wing-chung Ho, "Gender Role Indoctrination in Traditional China as Seen from Popular Primers Written in Verse," paper presented
at the Women in Confucian Cultures in Premodern China, Korea, and Japan Conference,
June 28–July 1, 1996, La Jolla, California.
    3. See Elizabeth Croll, *Feminism and Socialism in China* (New York: Schocken Books,
1980), chap. 2; and Zhan, "Chinese Femininity and Social Control."
    4. See Joyce Penfield, *Women and Language in Transition* (Albany: State University of
New York Press, 1987); Deborah Cameron, *Feminism and Linguistic Theory* (New York:
St. Martin's Press, 1985); Robin Lakoff, *Language and Woman's Place* (New York: Harper
& Row, 1975); Barrie Thorne and Nancy Henley, eds., *Language and Sex: Difference and
Dominance* (Rowley, Mass.: Newbury House, 1975); and Mary Ritchie Key, *Male/Female
Language* (Metuchen, N.J.: Scarecrow Press, 1975).

subject of Chinese sexist language.⁵ Both authors had combed Chinese dictionaries and etymologies for the meaning of words that incorporated the symbol 女 (woman) as a component. Many of the words they examined have derogatory meanings or represent patriarchal standards of femininity. For example, the Chinese word for "wife," 婦, consists of 女 (woman) holding a 帚 (broom). Contrast that with the word for "man," 男, which is composed of the characters 田 (field) on top and 力 (strength) on the bottom. Not only is a clear separation of men's and women's spheres implied, but obviously the premium placed on the activity of strong men who work in the rice fields is higher than that for women who stay home and do housework. Other examples of words that demean women include 嫵 (to please, cajole, or flatter), which consists of 女 (woman) and 無 (nothing)—meaning that in order to please others, women often have to reduce themselves to nothing; and 嫉 (jealousy or envy), literally a 女 (woman's) 疾 (disease).

Hardly anything has been written about images of women in Chinese proverbs. An article on the subject by Hong Zhang proved my most useful source.⁶ Drawing from two large collections of Chinese proverbs, she examined five hundred proverbs for depictions of women. What she found overwhelmingly were negative stereotypes of women as inferior, subordinate, submissive, and dangerous beings, which strongly reflected the dominant ideologies of a hegemonic Confucian state. As she notes, the oral nature of proverbs allows for a wider distribution of cultural attitudes and social norms, especially among illiterate or semiliterate peasants in rural villages. In this way the state could dictate social conduct and control female virtue among the masses and thereby preserve patriarchal power and stability in the family and the country as a whole more effectively. Since most Chinese immigrants prior to World War II were of peasant background, proverbs become an im-

5. Dali Tan, "Sexism in the Chinese Language," NWSA Journal 2, no. 4 (autumn 1990): 635–39; and Pauline Fong, "The Current Social and Economic Status of Chinese American Women," in The Chinese American Experience: Papers from the Second National Conference on Chinese American Studies, ed. Genny Lim (San Francisco: Chinese Historical Society of America, 1982), pp. 296–99.

6. Hong Zhang, "'Spare Women a Beating for Three Days, They Will Stand on the Roof and Tear the House Apart': Images of Women in Chinese Proverbs," Locating Power: Proceedings of the Second Berkeley Women and Language Conference, ed. Kira Hall, Mary Bucholtz, and Birch Moonwoman (Berkeley: Berkeley Women and Language Group, University of California, 1992), pp. 601–9.

portant source for us to study as a reflection of their social attitudes to-
ward women.

In this section, I have selected from and added to Hong Zhang's list
those proverbs most commonly known among Chinese immigrants in
America. For the convenience of analysis, I have chosen to follow her or-
ganization of the proverbs into four categories: those that (1) highlight
gender differences and the inferiority of women; (2) reflect women's sub-
ordinate role in the family system; (3) express male perceptions of ideal
womanhood; and (4) depict the potential danger in women if uncon-
trolled by men. This list is intended to show some of the sexist cultural
baggage immigrants brought with them from China. Yet as the stories of
women's lives in this book reveal, culture is fluid and the roles assigned
to women in theory and in practice are often quite different. Just as in
China, where women of different classes, ethnicities, and regions devi-
ated from the restrictive norms according to their circumstances, the same
held true for Chinese women in Gold Mountain as they began to create
new lives for themselves in the new land.

WOMEN AS DIFFERENT AND INFERIOR

Confucianism, which by the mid 1800s had governed social conduct in
China for nearly two thousand years, acknowledged men as superior to
women and dictated separate spheres of influence and activities accord-
ingly. Women were considered as different from and inferior to men as
earth is relative to heaven. This was in keeping with cosmological beliefs
that the male was endowed with the positive yang forces (bright, strong,
dominant), while the female held the negative yin forces (dark, weak, and
passive). Originally conceived as equally important and complementary,
through time these elements were rearranged in a hierarchical relation-
ship with yin representing all that was negative and inferior in the uni-
verse. According to Confucius, "Women indeed are human beings, but
they are of a lower state than men and can never attain to full equality
with them."[7] A man's domain was in the public sphere. He was expected
to roam the world and bring glory and prosperity to his family. In con-
trast, a woman's duty was to stay within the inner chambers, manage the
household, and raise the children. Thus, it was more important to edu-
cate sons than daughters. For social order to prevail, everyone needed to
know and maintain their proper places in society and the proper rela-

---

7. Quoted in Croll, *Feminism and Socialism in China*, pp. 12–13.

tionships between people. According to the Yijing, *or* Book of Changes, *"The wife has her correct place in the inner (trigram), and the man has his correct place in the outer."*[8] *It was natural for men to rule, as it was natural for women to submit. The following proverbs speak to this asymmetrical gender system in which women, relative to men, were considered not only different but inferior beings dependent on men.*

The husband is heaven, the wife earth.

夫是天, 妻是地.

Do not regard wives as real human beings, just as you do not regard the spirits of cats as gods.

你把婆娘不要當人, 你把貓鬼神不要當神.

Noodles are not real food; women are not real human beings.

麵條不算飯, 女人不算人.

Men's ambition is in four directions; women's ambition is in the boudoir.

男兒志在四方, 女人志在繡房.

Men travel between counties and provinces, women just run around the kitchen stove.

男子漢走州走縣, 女子只在鍋邊轉.

Men are concerned with plowing the field in the autumn, women with spinning and weaving in the evening.

男子不忘秋耕地, 女人不忘夜紡紗.

A woman does not leave her boudoir; a male scholar does not leave the study.

女子不出閨房, 士子不出書窗.

A woman without a husband is like a house without a roof beam.

婦人無夫房無樑.

Officials depend on their seals, tigers on mountains, and women on men.

官憑印, 虎憑山, 婦人憑的男子漢.

---

8. Quoted in Ho, "Gender Role Indoctrination," p. 3.

A mare is not fit to go into battle. (I.e., a woman cannot take a
  man's place.)
騍馬上不了陣.

A man at thirty is a flower in bloom; a woman at thirty is tea dregs
  to be discarded.
男人三十一枝花, 女人三十爛茶渣.

WOMEN'S SUBORDINATE ROLE IN THE FAMILY

*In the larger scheme of things, Confucian ethics held that women's sub-
ordination to men was essential if social order was to prevail. A good
woman was expected to be obedient and subordinate to men throughout her lifetime. She had few if any opportunities to satisfy her own desires or to garner any real power in the traditional family system, which
was patriarchal, patrilineal, and patrilocal. A son was generally preferred
over a daughter, since it was he who would perform the ancestral rites,
perpetuate the family name, and provide for the parents in their old age.
A daughter, who was destined to marry and leave her natal family, was
considered a drain on the family's resources. Upon marriage, when she
entered her husband's household, she was regarded as an outsider and
expected to obey and serve her husband and mother-in-law. Abuses of
the daughter-in-law were common, and imperial law offered married
women little protection. For example, disobedience to one's in-laws was
a legitimate reason for a husband to divorce his wife, and according to
the Qing code, scolding by a daughter-in-law could mean punishment
by strangulation. The following proverbs reflect a woman's low status
both as a daughter in her natal family and as a wife and daughter-in-law
in her husband's home. Only after a woman had produced a son and become a mother-in-law herself did she gain any respect and power in terms
of running the household and ruling over her daughter-in-law. From this
scenario it is clear that although a woman changed familial roles at different stages of her life, her subordinate position in the Chinese patrilineal system remained constant.*

A girl is born facing out.
女生外向.

Daughters are goods upon which one loses money.
養女賠錢貨.

Raising a daughter is like raising a bandit: you cannot depend on
  either in your old age.

養媛養強盜, 到老勿可靠.

A grown son is an asset, a grown daughter a liability.

兒大一發, 女大一塌.

Ten pretty daughters are not equal to a crippled son.

十個紅花女, 敵不上一個瘸腿兒.

Marry a chicken, follow the chicken; marry a dog, follow the dog.
  (I.e., women have to stick with whomever they marry, good or
  bad.)

嫁雞隨雞, 嫁狗隨狗.

(A new bride) must be the first to work and the last to eat.

作在前頭, 吃在後頭.

(A good daughter-in-law) is never thirsty, never hungry, never
  sleepy, never tired, and never in need of going to the toilet.

不渴, 不餓, 不困, 不累的慌, 不瘟的慌.

Mothers-in-law beating daughters-in-law is justified everywhere.

婆婆打媳天天有.

THE IDEAL WOMAN

From a Chinese patriarchal perspective the ideal woman followed
三從四德 *(the Three Obediences and Four Virtues). She was submissive, industrious, and domestic. Moreover, it was important that she be chaste and forever faithful, even if men were not held to these same standards. Indeed, women who went to great lengths to maintain their chastity and be celibate widows were considered exemplary women, and memorial arches were erected in their honor. On the other hand, women who misbehaved were severely punished. Acts of adultery by women were grounds for wife-beating, divorce, and banishment from one's village. It was also important for a woman to have bound feet, an asset in the marriage market because they signified beauty, wealth, respectability, and sensuality. Proverbs warned, however, that in choosing the ideal wife, men should stay away from women who were too educated or too beautiful, qualities that spelled trouble and possibly disaster. Because the pur-*

*pose of marriage was to beget sons to continue the family line, it was
most important that a wife be able to produce a progeny of healthy sons.
Barrenness was another cause for divorce. As this group of proverbs
indicates, every man hoped for a 賢妻良母 (virtuous wife and exemplary mother), a sure guarantee of a harmonious family and, therefore,
country.*

A man's talent is considered a virtue; a woman without talent is
    virtuous

男子有德便是才, 女子無才便是德.

(A woman's foot) at three inches is a golden lotus, at four inches
    a silver lotus, at five inches a brass lotus, at six inches an iron
    lotus, and at seven inches—shameless.

三寸金蓮, 四寸銀蓮, 五寸銅蓮, 六寸鐵蓮, 七寸不要臉.

Do not talk about physical appearance when taking a wife, but
    look for industry, good health, and filial obedience.

娶妻休論醜與俊, 勤勞體健孝雙親.

A man with a virtuous wife will have few troubles.

老婆賢慧, 老公少災.

One good wife guarantees three generations of good offspring.

娶一輩子的妻, 有三輩子好娃.

Harmonious above, united below; the husband sings, the wife
    joins in.

上和下睦, 夫唱婦隨.

A twice-bleached cloth is no longer good cloth; a twice-married
    woman is no longer a good woman.

再刷無好布, 再嫁無好婦.

A good horse does not feed again on grazed grass; a good woman
    does not get married again to another man.

好馬不吃回頭草, 好女不嫁二丈夫.

WOMEN AS DANGEROUS

*Although relatively powerless, women were said to have the potential to
wield power and disrupt social order, particularly through the harmful*

use of their beauty and speech. The most-cited examples were beautiful women in Chinese history who stole the affections of an emperor, led him astray in excess pleasure, and caused the downfall of an empire: the imperial concubines Meixi, Daji, and Baosi; the consort Yang Guifei; and Empress Cixi. The following proverbs reinforce the popular belief that women by nature were promiscuous, devious, jealous, and distrustful creatures up to no good. Proverbs also warned of the disasters that would result should men choose to listen to the bad advice of women or permit them to overstep prescribed boundaries. To preserve the status quo, it was up to the men to control the women and keep them in their subordinate places, even to the extent of beating them into submission. The legal codes not only stipulated that a wife's jealousy and excessive gossip were conditions for divorce, but they also condoned wife-beating. A husband was never punished for striking his wife unless a serious injury resulted. However, a wife who beat her husband was automatically punished with one hundred strokes. In short, women were regarded as the root of all disasters and therefore in need of male control.

When a woman is in her thirties, her sexual drive makes her a wolf;
  in her forties, like a tiger; in her fifties, like a leopard.
三十如狼, 四十如虎, 五十賽個金錢豹.

The fangs of the bamboo snake and the sting of the wasp are not
  as poisonous as a woman's heart.
青竹蛇兒口, 黃蜂尾上針, 二般不算毒, 最毒婦人心.

Nine women out of ten are jealous.
十個女人九個妒.

Ignorant women make the worst gossips.
無知女人舌頭長.

Real men are not persuaded by pillow talk.
大丈夫弗聽枕邊言.

A man's word is final like a general's command, while a woman's
  word changes by the minute.
男子説話將軍箭, 女子説話時時變.

Let three wives sit together and disaster will fall within three days.
三個老婆一塊坐, 不出三天就有禍.

Let a women work the ox and plow the field and there will be
   a three-year drought.

如娘犁牛, 天旱三年.

A wife married is like a pony bought; I'll ride her and whip her
   as I like.

買來的馬, 娶來的妻, 由我打來, 由我騎.

Better to have a browbeaten wife than a henpecked husband.

著被夫欺, 豈可被妻治.

   (TRANSLATOR: Ellen Yeung)

Kwong King You, *Sau Saang Gwa*

"If I Could Just See Him One More Time"

I met and interviewed Kwong King You, a spry seventy-five-year-old sau saang gwa, *in her home in Nam Shan village, Doumen County, during a research trip to Guangdong Province, China, in 1982.*[1] *Separated from her husband, Ah Fook, for more than forty years, she was still hoping that he would someday return, even though she had heard rumors that he had remarried in the United States. I was introduced to Kwong King You by Chan Gum, a staff member of the Doumen Overseas Chinese Affairs Office, who knew of my interest in overseas Chinese connections to the homeland, particularly the stories of* sau saang gwa.

Throughout my travels in Guangdong Province I visited villages where more than half the population had relatives who had gone overseas. Usually it was the able-bodied men who had left to make a better livelihood in Southeast Asia, the West Indies, or North America. Restrictive immigration laws, financial considerations, and cultural mores had dictated that wives and families be left behind, creating a "split-household" arrangement where husbands working overseas would send remittances home to support the family.[2] *In most cases these emigrant families were*

---

1. I was visiting relatives in Nam Shan village, the birthplace of my maternal great-grandfather Chin Lung. For a report on my trip, see Judy Yung, "Visit to Guangdong Province: Chinese American Roots," *East/West*, May 11, 1983, p. 8.

2. The term "split-household family" is taken from Evelyn Nakano Glenn's "Split Household, Small Producer and Dual Wage Earner: An Analysis of Chinese-American

better off than other villagers, so it was considered desirable for a young woman to become a gam saan poh, *or wife of a Gold Mountain man. If the woman was fortunate, her husband would send letters and remittances home regularly, return for a visit every few years, and eventually come home to stay, a wealthy man. Thus, being a* gam saan poh *meant economic comfort and social prestige. But often, it also meant a long separation. In the worst scenario, the woman might never hear from or see her husband again; yet she was expected to remain chaste and single, suffer the ridicule of people in her village, and somehow find a way to support herself and her family. I heard many sad stories about* sau saang gwa *who had had to sell their children to survive or who had gone insane because of an irresponsible husband.*[3]

One of the saddest stories I heard was told to me by Jew Siu Ping, our tour guide in Sunwui (Xinhui) District, whose own father was a gam saan haak. *Jew said his father left for New York a few months after he returned to marry and never came home again. He worked as a laundryman in New York, sending home about $200 a year with a short letter of "no more than thirty words." To make ends meet, Jew's mother sewed at home by the light of a kerosene lamp. "You see, my mother had bound feet," he told me. "Even if she unbound them, she could not actively work." In tears he said, "It was pitiful seeing my mother waste so many years of her life, struggling as she did, so I wrote and scolded my father, 'How can you face your wife? How can your conscience allow it?'" When word came in 1968 that his father had died, Jew said he felt nothing until he saw his mother cry for the first time. Still crying himself, he said, "As long as he lived, she had hope, not just for the money, but for a letter or the person to return. But now, there was nothing."*[4]

Family Strategies," *Journal of Marriage and Family* 45:1 (February 1983): 35–48, in which she describes the early Chinese American family arrangement as being a "split household," with production (wage-earning) separated from other family functions and carried out by the husband overseas while reproduction, socialization, and family consumption (supported by the husband's remittances) were carried out by the wife or other relatives in the home village.

3. It should be noted, however, that abandoned wives who became destitute could remarry, and there were, of course, stories with happy endings as well. For such stories and an analysis of the predicament of *sau saang gwa* and emigrant families in Taishan County, see Madeline Hsu, "'Living Abroad and Faring Well': Migration and Transnationalism in Taishan County, Guangdong, 1904–1939" (Ph.D. dissertation, Yale University, 1996), chap. 4.

4. Jew Siu Ping, interview with author, Sunwui (Xinhui) District, Guangdong Province, December 9, 1982. The next day Jew shared a poem with me that he remembered from his school days, "A Poem to My Husband Overseas" (see page 123).

Kwong King You had a similar story to tell. In 1927 she felt lucky to be arranged in marriage to a gam saan haak. *During the interview she emphasized how well she got along with her husband, Ah Fook, during the first two years of their marriage. Then he left to work as a seaman for an American shipping line, visiting her in Hong Kong every forty-two days. After the Japanese occupied Hong Kong in 1942, however, communications broke off and Kwong never saw him again. Yet she remained faithful to him, telling me she had no regrets.*

As was the case with many other separated couples, Kwong King You's marriage endured because both partners kept their obligations to each other. Her husband continued sending remittances home, and she remained faithful to him. As Madeline Hsu notes in "'Living Abroad and Faring Well,'" a study of transnational families, even though legal and economic conditions kept Chinese families apart, basic principles and flexible practices of family life enabled wives in China to sustain long-term, long-distance relationships with their men overseas.[5] Believing that a good woman must remain faithful to her husband, Kwong accepted her fate and role as a sau saang gwa, *never questioning the double standards at play.[6] She was also able to withstand the long separation because of the strong support she received from classmates, colleagues, and close relatives, especially her father-in-law and adopted children.[7] Moreover, she was driven to prove her worth by the vindictive remarks and motives of an envious sister-in-law. "I had to stand up for myself," she told me emphatically a number of times. "You can't let people get away with looking down at you."*

Kwong King You appeared small and frail before me, but her penetrating eyes and forceful tone of voice told me otherwise: she was invincible. As I listened to her story of woe, I couldn't help but compare this old woman to the pictures of a youthful Kwong and handsome Ah Fook, dressed in a Western suit and necktie, that hung framed on the wall directly above and

---

5. See Hsu, "Living Abroad and Faring Well," chap. 4; and Paul Siu, *The Chinese Laundryman: A Study of Social Isolation*, ed. John Kuo Wei Tchen (New York: New York University Press, 1987), chap. 9.

6. Although wives in China were ostracized and punished if they did not remain chaste and faithful, their husbands overseas were allowed to frequent brothels and have second wives; see Siu, *Chinese Laundryman*, p. 167.

7. Because of the long separations that made procreation difficult, it was not uncommon for wives to adopt children to carry on the family line, ensure financial stability, and care for them in their old age. See Hsu, "'Living Abroad and Faring Well,'" pp. 172–74; and Siu, *Chinese Laundryman*, pp. 159–63.

Ah Fook and Kwong King You soon after they were married in 1927.

behind her. I had come from across the ocean to hear her story, and she was more than ready to leave her legacy as a good example of a yin chai leung mo (a virtuous wife and exemplary mother), someone who had more than proven her worth to her vindictive sister-in-law, the whole village, and her husband overseas. In the old days the imperial government would have erected a memorial stone arch in her honor. Kwong King You had so much to tell, she required little prodding from me or the government official Chan Gum, who also participated in the interview.[8]

"Lucky to Be Married to a *Gam Saan Haak*"

My *sum* [aunt], who was related to both sides of the family, introduced us. She got a matchmaker to speak to my future father-in-law, saying that I was a good woman, and he agreed to the proposal. Ah Fook came to Siu How Chung [village] hoping to see me, but I was at school so he didn't get to see me.[9] He chose to believe my *sum*, and that was how it

---

8. Chan Gum guided and followed me throughout my visit in Doumen District in 1982. He was a native of the district and a sympathetic listener. I believe his presence at this interview influenced some of Kwong King You's comments about the war years, her retirement benefits, her filial children, and her determination to wait for her husband's return.

9. Kwong King You came from a wealthy family. Her father sent remittances from Cuba, where he had a produce store, to support her education.

happened. I can't remember the date, but I was twenty years old. Yes, [I was considered lucky to be married to a *gam saan haak*].[10]

He was home for twenty-seven months. Then he returned to America. I had one more year of schooling left. He wrote and told me to go to Chow Yung's[11] [midwife] school for the admittance exams. He said that if I had a medical degree I could get into the United States faster. At that time, it was fashionable for married women to go to school, so I followed the girls to school. After I graduated, I went out to practice.

"Every Forty-two Days"

At the beginning, he sent money home for my education. But after he became a seaman on the President Coolidge line he had to have an operation and the doctor told him to rest for three months. He asked someone to write me that he was unemployed and could not send any more money. I almost had to quit school in Canton. But my classmates were good to me. They noticed I wasn't as playful as usual. "Sister Kwong, you look like you have problems. You're not too talkative. Are you all right?" they asked. So I said, "I can't continue with school. I have to leave." I showed the letter to them. They didn't believe I was married until they read the letter. One schoolmate, who was the class president, said, "Don't be discouraged. There's three hundred of us students. If we each give you one dollar, you'll have three hundred dollars." She asked if I had any relatives in Canton. I said, "Yes, there's Dr. Chan." So I went to discuss the matter with sister Chow Yung. She told me, "Don't be afraid. Go ask Fourth Granduncle, because even if he doesn't have the money, his *gam saan jong* does. And if he can't lend you the money, I will." I had already finished one year of school, so I was reluctant to descend from the mountain [to give up my training to become a doctor].

Finally, Fourth Granduncle personally brought me three hundred dollars so that I could continue until I graduated. At the end of the year, Ah Fook wanted to come visit, but I told him not to return because it would disturb my studies. I was close to finishing and I couldn't leave Canton to be with him in the village. At that time, that was how we felt about

---

10. Ah Fook left for the United States with his great-aunt when he was six years old. He returned to Nam Shan village in 1927 for schooling and to get married.

11. According to Chan Gum, Chan Chow Yung had refused an arranged marriage so that she could become a doctor and support all her brothers and sisters through school.

our studies. If you're going to study, then you have to keep at it until you're finished. So although he wanted to return, I told him not to.

He didn't come again until March of the next year. He continued working as a seaman, and over the next five years, while I was in Hong Kong, he would dock there every forty-two days. If the shipment was large, he would stay two nights; if not, one night. Then he would go out to sea another forty-two days before coming back. However, after Hong Kong was bombed by the Japanese [in 1942] he couldn't return because his ship couldn't dock. I was afraid to stay in Hong Kong and took our two adopted children, a son and a daughter, back to Nam Shan on the last refugee boat. He wrote and told me not to worry, and that the next time his ship docked in Hong Kong he would notify me so that I could meet him there. But he quit working on the ships and did not return after that. Then he stopped writing and sending money home because communications were broken off.

"Life Was Hard after That"

After we came back from Hong Kong, life was hard after that. If I didn't have some skill, we three would have died. I worked as a midwife to support my children. Even so, I had to sell our clothes, even my undershirts, to put food on the table. And not even rice, just *jook* [rice gruel]. How I suffered, selling my comforters and blankets to buy eight pigs to raise. Three died and I sold the other five. With the money I was able to buy medicine and set up my practice. People in the village were good to me; otherwise, I would have left for Hong Kong. Every day my table was full of rice and beans [payment from patients]. I was making money then, and I used it all on my children's education. Gee Duk [son] went to Jom Gong for school and Gee Geen [daughter] went to Fat Shan for school. That cost plenty. So whenever I cooked rice, I always threw a handful back. That's how frugal I was until I realized my goals.

Fortunately my children were good to me. They were very respectful. Even when we had no rice, just *jook*, they wanted me to eat first. My father-in-law was good to us. He swore to heaven that as long as he lived, he would support me. He sent us money twice a year, and whatever my sister-in-law got, I got.

I heard people say Ah Fook had died. Others said that after the war started he remarried in America and had children. Even Second Granduncle said so when he came back from America with two hundred dollars and some medicine from Ah Fook. I said to my father-in-law, "I heard people say that Ah Fook's ship was bombed and he died. Is it true?" My *mo* [sister-in-law], who was trying to aggravate me, said, "Second sister-in-law, you don't have anyone anymore. The ship was bombed and he's dead." I knew she wanted me to leave so that she could take our share of the land. I had to struggle on no matter what. (My father-in-law never got along with her. Called her the Empress Dowager.) She shouldn't have said that to me, to wish ill of my family. She was that jealous of me. I stood my ground and smilingly said to her, "First, you are born. Second, you die. That's life. As a doctor I can support my children." I was young then and knew how to stand up for myself. As they say, "Time will reveal a person's true heart."

Ah Fook never told me he remarried in America. You Heung told Ah Go and Ah Go told me, "Second sister-in-law, second brother didn't die. I heard people say he remarried." So I came back and asked my father-in-law if it was true. He said, "That's what kinsmen have been saying, that Ah Fook has remarried. People saw him with children in the streets." Ah Go was trying to comfort me, that he was still alive. I said, "It's better that he's remarried rather than dead." Today, we talk about monogamy. Before, it was "Three wives and four concubines; if your head has enough hair, you can put up with a lot of fleas."[12] There are so few people in this family anyway. It won't bother me if he had eight or ten wives. He has his life and I have mine.

Now that he had remarried, all my colleagues were telling me to remarry. They wanted to introduce me to some doctor. But because of what my *mo* had said to aggravate me, "He's dead," I was willing to sacrifice my entire future and stick it out in Nam Shan. You have to stand up for yourself. You can't let people drive you away by looking down at you. So I wrote Ah Fook. He should have sent for me by then. He was probably afraid I would cause trouble. He used to be afraid of me, always consulted me before he did anything. But because I had written and asked him if he had remarried, he was afraid to write me back. And as long as he didn't write back, I wasn't going to waste money going to Hong Kong to wait for him. I had to make a living at home.

Ah Fook continued to send money through Second Granduncle. Sometimes more, sometimes less, but he always sent something. He was a good person, but maybe because he had remarried and had children he had less money to spend. (People said that he had three sons and that

---

12. These common sayings refer to the practice of polygyny among the wealthy class.

my son, Gee Duk, was older than his son by one year.) It [the money]
was like rain from heaven. No letter, no return address. Maybe he didn't
want his other wife to know. People said it was because he was breaking the law. If he put down his address and I wrote him, people would
know he had another wife and he would be breaking the law. Second
Granduncle told me he couldn't go both ways [be with two wives].

"I Don't Regret Marrying Him"

[Do you blame him anymore? Are you angry with him?] When he first
left, I was very upset and wanted revenge, at least until I reached the age
of forty-five.[13] My colleagues kept telling me not to be stupid. If he remarried, I should remarry. I used to cry tears from my eyes down to my
toes. It's been such a hard life. It was because of my *mo*'s words that I
struggled on. She crossed me for a few *mau* [acres] of land, and that made
me determined to stick it out in the Chan family. I kept saying, "Alive,
I belong to the Chan family. When I die, my ghost will belong to the Chan
family."

[Do you have any regrets about marrying him?] Although ours was
an arranged marriage, we got along well. I don't regret marrying him.
Every personal possession I had—rouge, powder, perfume, even sanitary
napkins, he bought for me. So he was good to me. He bought all the soap
and household items as well. I'm just bitter that I haven't seen him for
so long. For the sake of the children, I didn't remarry. There's always
hope that he might change his mind and come home. That's happened
before to many others who remarried. My hope is that he will someday
return. I will always welcome him back. My mind would be put to rest
if I could just see him one more time.

I know he's still in America. Because some kinsmen scolded him [for
remarrying], he moved away from San Francisco to the countryside. He
still sends money, but he won't write me. Before, he would send it through
one of our relatives. Now he writes to my daughter, Gee Geen. I just received one hundred Hong Kong dollars from him. Gee Duk, my hard-
headed son, said to return the money to him. "It wouldn't cost him anything more to enclose a letter," he said. Gee Geen said, "Let's write him."
He refused, but Gee Geen went ahead.

---

13. Forty-five years of age is significant for a woman as she enters menopause and is
no longer considered marriageable.

"I Just Go Day by Day"

I retired seven years ago, although I'm not the retiring type. I enjoyed working. Everyone at the hospital was good to me. Nobody wanted me to retire but my children. Gee Duk used to scold me and say, "You want to work until you die?" Before, time passed quickly and I didn't even have to cook. There's no fun staying home and doing housework. It's boring at home. I sit until my butt hurts. So Gee Geen knitted this cushion for me. (*pulls seat cushion from under her to show me*)

I know time is running out. I just go day by day. If there's something good to eat, I'll enjoy myself. I'm spending my money as fast as I can. My pension is $44.20 a month. That's enough for an old lady like me. Besides, my children always buy me food whenever they visit. They buy me ginseng twice a month [because] when my appetite isn't good or I'm not sleeping well it helps to take ginseng. Actually, everyone tells me that as long as my voice is strong and loud, I wouldn't die yet. (*laughs*) I only take ginseng to extend my life so I can look after this house my son had built for me two years ago. The old house is up there. (*points in the direction behind her*) My son said it was too inconvenient, so he had this house built. I have my own well. It's considered a good house in this village. My son is a doctor in Macao and my daughter is a doctor at the People's Hospital in Jian On, where my grandson attends school. I usually have two girls stay with me. If I live to be one hundred years old, I know the government will take care of me. I'm not an extravagant person. I live a pretty simple life.

(SOURCE: Kwong King You, interview with author in Chinese, Nam Shan village, Guangdong Province, December 15, 1982)

After an hour of talking nonstop, Kwong King You did not seem a bit tired. I asked if I could take some photographs of her and the framed pictures on the wall behind her. She consented without hesitation. I last saw her standing in front of her doorway, waving good-bye to me. I had promised to try and locate her husband for her. Upon my return to San Francisco, I learned from relatives that he was alive and living in Oakland. He had remarried and had no plans of returning to China. I did not have the heart to write and tell Kwong King You. In 1991, without ever seeing her husband again, she died at the age of eighty-four.

My last image of Kwong King You in 1982.

A POEM TO MY HUSBAND OVERSEAS

Husband and wife, deeply bound, yet forever separated;
The mandarin-duck pillows are soaked with my lonely tears.
When we took our wedding vow: till death do us part—
I did not expect my husband would forsake me.
So far away, the winds did not carry my messages to you;
So difficult, my letters did not convince you to return to me.
Winters come, summers go, so quickly I have become old;
In solitude, we are not together sharing our youthful years.
Ever think of home—is there enough rice and firewood for the day?
Winter clothes on our bodies when it is cold?
Days pass easily; a person ages just as easily.
Springs come, autumns go, old age will soon arrive.
So distant are the mountains and the roads, so endless is my love;
Sitting alone in the bedroom, I no longer care about my appearance.
I had always hoped someday to go away with my husband;
I never expected to be permanently separated, like today.
Pity not the separation of the pith from a ginkgo nut—
But the flow of tears soaking my pillow from night till dawn.

(SOURCE: Jew Siu Ping of Sunwui [Xinhui] District, Guangdong Province, December
10, 1982. TRANSLATOR: Marlon K. Hom.)

一個僑眷寫給海外夫君的回文錦

夫婦恩深久別離，鴛鴦枕上獨淋灘．
當初結髮成偕老，誰知今日受夫棄．
遙去傳書風未便，皆因寫信寄難歸．
寒來暑往催人老，冷落青春兩不齊．
更想家中柴合未，又因身上少寒衣．
日子易過人易老，春去秋來老將至．
山遙路遠情難盡，獨坐閨房懶書眉．
早盼有日隨夫去，誰知今日永分離．
白果有芯還惜別，枕邊流淚到天明．

A Stain on the Flag

M. G. C. EDHOLM

Because of the gold rush, prostitution thrived in predominantly male Cal-
ifornia, and women came from all over the world for the trade. But
whereas most of these women came to San Francisco as independent pro-
fessionals and worked for wages in brothels, Chinese women were al-
most always imported as indentured servants and forced into prostitu-
tion.[1] So great and profitable was the demand for their services that by
1870 Chinese prostitutes outnumbered all other groups of prostitutes in
the city.[2] We know from various studies of the U.S. census that prosti-
tutes also constituted a high percentage of the Chinese female popula-
tion in San Francisco: 85–97 percent in 1860, 63–72 percent in 1870,
and 18–50 percent in 1880.[3] There were reasons for these high percent-

---

1. For a socioeconomic analysis of Chinese prostitution, see Lucie Cheng Hirata, "Free, Indentured, Enslaved: Chinese Prostitutes in Nineteenth-Century America," *Signs: Journal of Women on Culture and Society* 5, no. 1 (autumn 1979): 3–29.

2. According to Benson Tong's calculations from U.S. census data, there were 1,565 Chinese prostitutes (62.6 percent of the Chinese female population) in San Francisco in 1870, compared with 469 non-Chinese prostitutes (.74 percent of the non-Chinese female population). See Benson Tong, *Unsubmissive Women: Chinese Prostitutes in Nineteenth-Century San Francisco* (Norman: University of Oklahoma Press, 1994), p. 98.

3. See Hirata, "Free, Indentured, Enslaved," pp. 23–24; Sucheng Chan, *This Bittersweet Soil: The Chinese in California, 1860–1910* (Berkeley: University of California Press, 1986), pp. 54–55, 62–63; Sucheng Chan, "The Exclusion of Chinese Women, 1870–1943," in *Entry Denied: Exclusion and the Chinese Community in America, 1882–1943*, ed. Sucheng

ages. Not only did Chinese social mores and American immigration policies discourage the immigration of Chinese women, thus skewing the sex ratio, but racial segregation and antimiscegenation laws further ensured that most Chinese immigrants could not have wives and families in the United States. Forced to live a bachelor's existence, many men fell into the habit of frequenting brothels. The ready supply of daughters from impoverished parts of China filled this demand for prostitutes, and enormous profits could be made in the trafficking of Chinese women.

Newspaper accounts, missionary writings, and congressional hearings tell us that most of the women were kidnapped, lured, or purchased from poor parents by procurers in China for as little as $50 and then resold in America for as much as $1,000 and more depending on the market value, which fluctuated from year to year. Because of the harsh physical and mental abuse that Chinese prostitutes suffered, the suspicion is that few ever outlived the contract term of four to six years. Moreover, the bill of sales often stipulated an extension should the woman become ill or pregnant (see prostitute's contract on pages 141–42). According to these sources, the lucky ones escaped sexual enslavement by being redeemed, running away with the help of a lover, committing suicide, or, in the most publicized cases, seeking refuge at one of the two Protestant mission homes in San Francisco.[4]

It should be noted, however, that these sources are highly suspect, given the anti-Chinese climate in the latter part of the nineteenth century and the underlying motives of these publications. San Francisco newspapers sensationalized their coverage of the Chinese prostitution problem in order to sell papers and add fuel to the anti-Chinese campaign. Missionaries played up the plight of Chinese prostitutes and their successful rescue raids in order to win converts and supporters of their cause of moral reform. Congressional committees investigating the Chinese question

---

Chan (Philadelphia: Temple University Press, 1991), p. 107; and Tong, *Unsubmissive Women*, p. 94. Although the accuracy of U.S. census statistics, particularly for a group that is primarily non-English-speaking like the Chinese, is questionable, the manuscript census is one of the few sources available that provides us with any socioeconomic data on Chinese women.

4. See Herbert Ashbury, *The Barbary Coast: An Informal History of the San Francisco Underground* (New York: Alfred A. Knopf, 1933); *Chinese Immigration: The Social, Moral, and Political Effect of Chinese Immigration. Testimony Taken Before a Committee of the Senate of the State of California, Appointed April 3rd, 1876* (Sacramento: State Printing Office, 1876); Otis Gibson, *The Chinese in America* (Cincinnati: Hitchcock & Walden, 1877); and Alexander McLeod, *Pigtails and Gold Dust* (Caldwell, Idaho: Caxton Printers, 1948).

(whether to exclude Chinese immigration or not) heard and published predominantly incriminating reports of Chinese vices such as tong wars, opium dens, and prostitution. Yet in the absence of any unmediated, first-hand accounts from Chinese prostitutes themselves, we have no choice but to utilize these sources.

The following article on Chinese prostitution by Mary Grace Charlton Edholm, which appeared in the Californian Illustrated Magazine *in February 1892, is a good example of this genre of writing. I have selected it for inclusion because it at least provides a variety of personal testimonies by rescued slavegirls that speak to their own experiences and their attempts to escape a life of prostitution. What we need to keep in mind as we read it are the biases of the author, a journalist and social purity reformer who was heavily involved in the temperance movement, women's suffrage, and rescue missions. A member of the First Methodist Church in Oakland, Edholm was a national evangelist for the Florence Crittenton Missions, the purpose of which was to rescue and provide a refuge for white prostitutes. As she wrote in her book,* How to Prevent Traffic in Girls, *Edholm, like many of the missionary women during the Progressive era, wanted to help the "thousands upon thousands of our little sisters writhing under the cruelties and cuts and bruises and oaths and the unutterable atrocities of the brothels."[5] Chinese prostitution, the epitome of female slavery and powerlessness, presented an even more formidable challenge to women like Edholm. Ignoring evidence that some Chinese women entered prostitution knowingly or willingly, mission workers chose to emphasize the enslaved condition of Chinese prostitutes to justify the urgency of their mission.*

In this article, using case examples of successful rescues, Edholm calls attention to the "vile and debasing" enslavement of Chinese women in San Francisco and the "grand" efforts of the Mission Homes to rescue and educate these women. Throughout the article, she describes Chinese prostitutes as helpless victims, Chinese slave dealers and owners as cruel masters who will resort to any means necessary to make their profits, and missionary workers as courageous and noble saviors. By employing inflammatory language and allowing Chinese slavegirls to tell their own melodramatic stories (although there is no way to check the authenticity of Edholm's presentation or the accuracy of her translation), Edholm

---

5. Mary Grace Charlton Edholm, *How to Prevent Traffic in Girls; Personal Experiences in Rescue Work with a Symposium by Prominent People on How to Prevent the Traffic in Girls* (San Francisco: Social Welfare League, 1914), p. 15.

drives home the point that Chinese prostitution is "a blot on the national honor" that clergymen, Congressmen, philanthropists, and all good citizens can help eradicate if they will only insist that the laws against slavery and abuse be upheld.

We should also keep in mind that the short-lived Californian, *which lasted from 1891 to 1894, took a negative stance on Chinese immigration. Edholm's article on Chinese prostitution was part of a special series aimed at showing that "the Chinese are not a desirable addition to our population. In short, continued restriction is needed and demanded."*[6] *Although Edholm does not say anywhere in the article that she is against Chinese immigration, the writings of missionary women such as herself were often used to perpetuate negative images of the Chinese, thus adding fuel to anti-Chinese sentiment and legislation. This effect is ironic, considering that Protestant missionaries were the one group that consistently opposed the Chinese exclusion laws.*

The testimonies of the Chinese women in this article regarding their recruitment, immigration, mistreatment as indentured servants, and eventual rescue are similar to other available published accounts.[7] *Of noteworthy interest in this article, however, are the assertion that* mui tsai *were often groomed for prostitution and the revelation that slave owners might have resorted to crude surgery in order to capitalize on the stereotype that the vaginas of Chinese women ran in a different direction. Because the article is a polemic rather than an informed piece of writing, there are many instances of implausibility, misinterpretation, and overgeneralization caused by the author's biases and lack of knowledge about the Chinese way of life, all of which I have tried to address in the footnotes. For example, Edholm describes the* mui tsai *system as another example of female abuse and enslavement, whereas in fact the Chinese have long regarded it as a form of charity for impoverished girls (see* mui tsai's *contract on pages 142–43). Despite these drawbacks, "A Stain on the Flag" still offers us some rare voices of Chinese prostitutes and the*

---

6. *Californian Illustrated Magazine* 1 (May 1892): 668. The Chinese Exclusion Act of 1882, which suspended the immigration of Chinese laborers to the United States for ten years, was renewed in 1892 for another ten years and extended indefinitely in 1904.

7. Aside from the works cited in note 4, see also Carol Green Wilson, *Chinatown Quest: One Hundred Years of Donaldina Cameron House, 1874–1974* (San Francisco: California Historical Society, 1974); Mildred Crowl Martin, *Chinatown's Angry Angel: The Story of Donaldina Cameron* (Palo Alto: Pacific Books, 1977); and Peggy Pascoe, *Relations of Rescue: The Search for Female Moral Authority in the American West, 1874–1939* (New York: Oxford University Press, 1990).

perspective of missionary women who crusaded to eradicate the prob-
lem. It was mainly thanks to the efforts of Protestant women such as
Margaret Culbertson and Donaldina Cameron that Chinese prostitution
declined by the 1920s.[8]

It was generally supposed that slavery was abolished in the United States
during the administration of Abraham Lincoln; yet, if the facts were
known, as they will be to the reader of the present paper, there exists in
this country, wherever the Chinese have obtained a foothold, a slavery
so vile and debasing that all the horrors of negro American slavery do
not begin to compare with it. In San Francisco, Los Angeles, New York
and other cities where a local Chinatown prevails, women and children
are sold to the highest bidder every month in the year,—not merely sold,
but imported for the purpose, agents being kept in China for this object;
and until the Restriction Act[9] went into operation they were doing a thriv-
ing, land-office business. The negro of ante-bellum days was a prince in
fortune to the luckless Chinese slave: the former was sold to work, while
the latter is selected, bought and handed over for a use compared to which
death would be a happy release. For years this system of human slavery
has been going on. Good men and women, representing the various
churches, have fought it unaided, but it rests to-day a stain upon the
American flag—a blot upon the national honor; and the object of this
paper is to present certain aspects of the crime to the lawmakers of the
country, and to ask how long such things can be in a country that
avowedly offers a refuge to the oppressed of all nations. In the work of
stopping the sale of women and young girls in San Francisco, the hot-
bed of Chinese slavery, especial credit is due the Presbyterians and
Methodists, who have established homes for the rescue and education

---

8. As superintendent of the Presbyterian Mission Home from 1877 to 1897, Margaret
Culbertson devised the technique of rescue work, whereby brothels were raided with the
assistance of the police whenever a Chinese girl or woman sent word for help. Culbertson
was succeeded by Donaldina Cameron, who devoted her entire life to rescue work among
Chinese women. The Presbyterian Mission Home was renamed Donaldina Cameron House
in 1942 in her honor.

9. Edholm is referring to the Chinese Exclusion Act of 1882 here, although there were
other laws that were passed to stop the trafficking of Chinese women, most notably the
Page Law in 1875.

of these girls and women.[10] The annals of these institutions rival Shakespeare for tragedy; and for dark, damning deeds they read more like the records of barbaric ages and heathen countries than those occurring under the full light of Christian civilization.

These homes are sustained by the Board of Missions of these two churches, much of the money being raised by the Women's Missionary societies,—well disproving the old adage that "woman is woman's worst enemy;" for these tender-hearted women labor night and day for the amelioration of their sisters. The records of these two homes show that hundreds of little girls and women have been rescued from this slavery worse than death; and Miss Margaret Culbertson and Miss Houseworth of the Presbyterian Mission and Rev. F. J. and Mrs. Masters, Mrs. Downs and Mrs. Ida Hull of the Methodist Mission, and Rev. M. C. Harris of the Japanese Mission, could a tale unfold that would amaze and horrify the world.

In following the career of these girls after rescue, education and Christianization, the sunny side of Chinese life is shown; and many a pleasing romance of love and courtship, happy marriage and a loving home, echoing with the laughter of little children, represents the payment these workers have received.[11]

First, in regard to child slavery: Fathers, and mothers sometimes, sell or pawn their girl babies; and as they are seldom redeemed they become the absolute slaves of their masters. The Chinese mother has little to say as to the disposal of her children, who belong to her master; and if he sees fit to sell them to others she has no choice.[12] One such Chinese woman, with her little girl six years of age, with a frightened, hunted look, begged the protection of the "Jesus women," as they call the Methodist

---

10. For a history of the Methodist Mission Home, established in 1871, and the Presbyterian Mission Home, established in 1874, see Gibson, *Chinese in America*, and Wilson, *Chinatown Quest*.

11. Once rescued, the young women were brought back to the Mission Home, where they were subjected to strong doses of Christian doctrine and a regimented life of classes and chores. There were some women who, resenting the restrictions and austerity of the Mission Home, chose to return to their former status. Others opted to return to China. Real converts stayed to help with missionary work. A significant number agreed to marry Chinese Christians and start new families in America.

12. Under the *mui tsai* system, it was customary in China for poor parents to sell (not pawn) their young daughters into domestic service, usually with the stipulation in a deed of sale that the daughter be freed through marriage when she turned eighteen. In this way, there would be one less mouth in the poor family to feed and the girl would hopefully

Mission, saying that the man who had bought her six years before, and with whom she had lived, had become tired of the delicate, puny child, and had determined to sell it, as it hindered her from sewing and earning money. She clung to her child with all the tenacity of a mother's love, and resolved that it should be saved to her at all hazards. Then he trumped up a charge that she had won three hundred dollars by gambling, and demanded that she give it to him or he would sell the child.

The poor woman was driven to desperation and knew not what to do. At this juncture she heard of the Mission house, and fled with trembling steps to its shelter.[13]

Her master, Ah Ong, had powerful friends, and resolved that he would not give her up without a struggle. So day by day she was annoyed and alarmed by the frequent calls made by his friends to speak with her trying by every means to persuade her to return. To all their entreaties she gave a firm refusal. . . . Grace Methodist Sunday School assumed the support of little Ah Kum, the child; and thus her mother and herself were saved from a life of slavery and worse. A little over a year ago Ah Kum was married to a Christian Chinaman.[14]

Young Chinese girls are often forcibly kidnaped in China, illegally landed in America, and sold to the keepers of places of ill-repute; and, of the inhuman treatment they receive, Miss Culbertson of the Presbyterian Mission testifies that these cases subjoined could be multiplied a hundred fold. One little slave-girl who was being reared for a revolting life was obliged to sew from seven o'clock in the morning till one o'clock at night; and because she would fall asleep through exhaustion her ears

---

benefit by being fed, clothed, and sheltered in exchange for her domestic labor until it was time for her to be married off. In America, however, because of the small number of merchant families that could afford *mui tsai* and the high value placed on prostitutes, the tendency most probably was to purchase young girls, put them to work as domestic servants in the brothels, and groom them for prostitution rather than marriage. For a success story of a *mui tsai* in America, see the story of Quan Laan Fan in Judy Yung, *Unbound Feet: A Social History of Chinese Women in San Francisco* (Berkeley: University of California Press, 1995), pp. 38–39.

13. This example of agency on the part of a Chinese woman in distress belies the image of Chinese women as helpless victims.

14. A picture of a young woman dressed in Chinese operatic costume was used in the article with the caption "Ah Kum, a Rescued Slave in War Dress." Even if the person is Ah Kum, it is unclear as to why she is dressed in full woman warrior regalia and why the photograph was included.

had been cut, her hands burned, and she had been beaten and tortured frightfully. Another, who had been rescued from a life of shame, had her eyes propped open with pieces of incense wood because they would at times close wearily in sleep after sitting up through long hours. Her eyes were badly lacerated and inflamed by the treatment. . . . [15]

But still worse horrors are in store for the little slave-girl as she nears womanhood; for then she is forced to a life of shame,—*the object of all Chinese slavery;* and if she resists, all the tortures of the Inquisition are resorted to by her cruel masters till she gives herself up body and soul.[16] No need for the Chinese slave to read Dante's "Inferno," or to see the awful horrors of Dore's brush; for her own existence is a living realization of both.

Could there be anything more pathetic than the stories of these few girls, which is the fate suffered by thousands? One girl says: "I was brought here eighteen months ago, and am twenty years old. I was kidnaped in China and brought over here. The man who kidnaped me sold me for four hundred dollars to a San Francisco slave-dealer; and he sold me here for seventeen hundred dollars. I have been a brothel slave ever since. I saw the money paid down, and am telling the truth. I was deceived by the promise I was going to marry a rich and good husband, or I should never have come here."[17]

Another said: "I am seventeen years old. I was born in Canton. When I was ten years old my parents sold me to be a domestic slave. A man brought me here, and he returned to China having sold me for five hundred dollars. I came to this country three years ago. My master wanted to take me to be his slave, but I resisted. I did not want to be his slave.

---

15. Similar horrible stories of child abuse were reported in the San Francisco newspapers, whipping up public sentiment against Chinese slavery and Chinese immigration as well. Stories of Chinese family life and successful outcomes of *mui tsai* were rarely covered in the newspapers.

16. This is a sweeping indictment of the *mui tsai* system that does not take into account the original purposes and positive effects of the system as described in note 12.

17. This and the stories that follow confirm the pattern of recruitment, immigration, and enslavement of young Chinese girls for prostitution as described in other published sources (see notes 4 and 7). Missionary women liked to make the point that the girls were innocent and helpless victims of the prostitution trade in order to appeal to the moral sense of the general public. Edholm made the same point with similar effect in her article "Traffic in White Girls," which appeared in the *Californian Illustrated Magazine* 2 (June–November 1892): 825–38.

He had one wife already."[18] The Rev. F. J. Masters adds in a foot-note, "The girl's master, in presence of Mr. Young of the Episcopal Mission, confessed that his wife bought the girl of a woman for $300." (See the article on Highbinders, by Rev. F. J. Masters, in the January *Californian.*)[19]

Another girl says: "I was sold for $2,970; was a slave in a place of ill-repute; never a wife. I escaped by running to a more friendly Chinaman, who kept me till night, and then, disguised in his American clothes, I was taken to a hotel on Bush Street. My master traced me and sent a spy, who got me into a carriage; but when they tried to take me into a cellar on Pacific Street I screamed so that the police took me from them." When this slave was finally found by the Mission people she was in a cellar under the pavement, watched over by a Chinese master, who was keeping her under the influence of drugs.[20]

In all these sales there is a contract made and given, as there would be in the sale of a horse or cow. As might be supposed, it is extremely difficult to obtain an original copy of one of these documents, but one has been obtained; and a fac-simile of what is probably the only contract in the hands of "American devils," as the Chinese highbinder delights to call us, is shown in the accompanying cut. The black spot upon the left side is the seal of the slave-girl, made by pressing her inked finger

---

18. In this case the Chinese woman did not want to become the second wife, another sore point that offended the moral senses of missionary women and justified rescue. Although illegal and considered immoral in America, polygyny was not so regarded in China, where it symbolized a man's wealth and was often practiced to ensure a progeny of sons. Judging from the household composition in the manuscript censuses as well as published and oral history accounts, we know that polygyny was condoned and practiced within the merchant class in Chinatown until after World War II.

19. Rev. Frederick J. Masters was well versed in Chinese literature and languages. He was a missionary in Canton before he became the head of the Methodist Episcopal Mission in San Francisco in the 1890s. Before he died in 1900 he published two articles in the *Californian Illustrated Magazine*: "Among the Highbinders: An Account of Chinese Secret Societies," January 1892, pp. 62–74; and "Can a Chinaman Become a Christian?" October 1892, pp. 622–32.

20. The sum of $2,970 was a lot of money to pay for a prostitute and perhaps explains the extensive trouble her owner was taking to regain his property. According to one source, the price for Chinese prostitutes rose after the Exclusion Acts were passed and it became more difficult to smuggle the women into the country: "[In] about 1897 girls of twelve to fifteen sometimes sold for as high as $2,500 each" (Ashbury, *Barbary Coast*, p. 181). This case also illustrates the extraordinary efforts made by the young woman to escape and the different parties who attempted to help her, including a "friendly Chinaman," the police, and missionary workers.

Chinese prostitute's contract, dated 1886, stipulating that one Sun Gum, indebted to her mistress for passage from China (costing $1,205), will serve as a prostitute for four and a half years without wages and extend the term by one month for every fifteen days of illness. (Courtesy of Caxton Press)

upon the paper. The contract is given in the original Chinese; the translation would be a *blot upon these pages*. (A careful translation of this slave contract has been made by the Rev. F. J. Masters of the Methodist Chinese Mission of San Francisco; and copies will be provided to clergymen, U.S. Senators, Members of Congress, and those engaged in actual philanthropic work, by addressing *The Californian*.)[21]

---

21. Similar to the contracts signed by white indentured servants recruited to the American colonies in the seventeenth and eighteenth centuries, deeds were customarily drawn

Here is a story a little more in detail, told by a refined Chinese girl, which also shows how they are taught by their masters to perjure themselves so that they may land in defiance of all law. "I am sixteen years old; was born in Canton. My father died when I was two years old, and left my mother and me and a little brother with no one to support us. My mother worked hard as a seamstress, and I helped her when I got older. When I was fifteen years of age arrangements were made for my marriage, and I was betrothed to a man in Hong Kong. I did not see him, as according to Chinese custom we do not see each other. This was on the tenth day of the tenth Chinese month of last year. On the first day of the eleventh month he came up to Canton again with a woman. He sent the woman to see me and to tell me to get ready to go down to Hong Kong with him. I told him that I must wait till my mother came home before deciding. She urged me to go at once, as my husband was waiting. I went reluctantly, but I thought she spoke true. We went down on the steamship *Hankow*. She took me to a house, where we had a room together; but I saw nothing of the man who was to be my husband. After six days the woman left me in charge of a man, who said I had not got to my husband yet, and that I should have to go on a steamer a few days' journey before I saw him. I did not know who the man was. They said I was going to California. We went on board the steamship *Belgic*. When we got to Japan I found we did not get off the steamer, but went on; then I cried to go back to my mother. I cried all the way over.

"There was a man on board who all the time was teaching me what to say. He coaxed me to be quiet, and told me I would have a rich husband and a fine time in California.

"He said I was to say I had been to California before, and had left a year ago. He said I was to tell them my husband was a ladies' bootmaker living on Jackson Street near Dupont, and told me if I made any mistake in my words, and made any fuss, there would be a foreign devil come and

---

up for Chinese women who were sold into prostitution. The deed usually stipulated that the woman had to work as a prostitute for a period of four years without wages in order to pay back debts incurred in her passage from China. Often a clause would be added that should the woman become sick or pregnant, her term of service would be extended. Thus, contracts could easily entrap a woman for the duration of her life. The young women were usually illiterate; thus, thumbprints were used on the contracts in lieu of signatures.

take me away to the devil prison, and I should never see my husband.[22]

"On the third day of the twelfth month I arrived in San Francisco; but it was not before the sixth of that month that I came ashore. On that day a white man came to where I was and called out my name and gave me a white paper, and I went on shore and they measured me.[23] Then I got into a hack with one white man and one Chinaman, and they took me to a house near the court. I was there for several days. I answered all the questions satisfactorily. I swore that my husband lived here, and that I had come to join him. I went again in two or three days till it was all over, and they let me go.

"I went back to a family house; and the next day a slaveholder came to see me, and asked me if I would like to go with her and be willing to go to a house of ill-repute. I indignantly refused, and said I was going to be married in a few days. Then I got suspicious and began to cry; but they told me not to fear, that I was going to a nice place, and would have plenty of food and fine clothes and jewelry, and go to the theater and have a nice time. I cried very much, but it was of no use. The man who brought me over said I must go, and so the money was paid and I was brought. One thousand five hundred and thirty dollars were paid for me. I saw the money paid, and I was taken on the twenty-sixth of last month of last year and placed in her den. They forced me to do their bidding, but I cried and resisted. I did not want to lead this life. They starved me for days, tying me where food was almost in reach of me, which looked so good. Then they beat me time and time [again], and threatened to kill me if I did not behave right. I heard of the Mission, and I waited my opportunity to run, and so I escaped."

Artists have pictured the slave marts of Turkey, where women are being exhibited before the rich possessors of harems, and might find a similar, though more horrible and realistic field, in San Francisco. Among the discoveries made by the missionaries was the fact that there existed a regular slave mart. This is on Dupont Street, and is or was known as the Queen's Room. Here the slaves are brought from the ships as they

---

22. Here, this "refined Chinese girl" is being coaxed to say she is a former resident returning to join her husband in order to bypass restrictions against Chinese immigration. Missionaries often claimed that the girls were coerced into cooperating with their owners by the fearful stories they heard about missionary workers and other "foreign devils."

23. She is probably being measured to see if she fits the physical age of the woman she claims to be.

arrive and are exposed for examination to the various buyers, who rate them according to their various standards of physical beauty.[24] In a number of instances where these sales are consummated the victims are treated in a manner too horrible for publication, but which is supposed to render them more valuable for the purpose for which they have been purchased. A number of such maltreated women were exhibited to a member of the New York Society for the Suppression of Crime within a few weeks in San Francisco Chinatown. This gentleman was visiting the locality with certain officials, *incognito*; and the women were exhibited and the healed wounds pointed out as a curiosity, suggestive of the cunning of the Chinese slavedealer in resorting to a device only employed in the case of the lower animals, to add to their market value. This chamber of horrors is in all probability still open to the possessor of two bits and a "guide" familiar with the worst side of Chinatown.[25]

If any one think these slavedealers give up their prey without a desperate struggle they are mistaken, as these two incidents show. Ah Yung, a woman twenty-two years old, was found by Rev. N. R. Johnston wandering about in Beulah Park, Oakland, and moaning as if in great trouble. She was brought to the Mission, and said: "I was born at Sun Ning; have been in this country two years. Yue Ka Sheng bought me in Hong Kong for $185 for immoral purposes. I had no certificate. I was brought ashore on a writ of *habeas corpus*.[26] The wife of Yue Ka Sheng took me away from here a long distance, where I was sold for six hundred dollars. They beat me and threatened to kill me when I was unwilling to go with them. While I was in the place I was married to Woo Yuen Chee, who paid back the money to my master. My husband went back to China the fifteenth day of the sixth month of this year. After he was gone his brothers wanted to sell me. They beat me and employed highbinders to take me, and gave them six hundred dollars to kill me. I was shot at over

---

24. Similar to the slave auction block, the Queen's Room, also referred to as the barracoon, was a place where Chinese slavegirls were taken upon arrival for inspection and sale to the highest bidder.

25. An ongoing myth that the vaginal opening of a Chinese woman was horizontal rather than vertical has been circulating as folklore since the 1850s. This is, however, the only mention I have seen of the possibility that Chinese slave dealers would resort to surgical illusions in order to reap more profits from their property.

26. A writ of habeas corpus allowed an immigrant who was denied entry into the country and detained for deportation by immigration authorities a prompt decision on the legality of her or his imprisonment. In this way, many Chinese immigrants were able to enter the country despite the stringent enforcement of the Exclusion Acts.

Wong Ting Hing's shop on Commercial Street, but not hurt. They then employed a man to shoot me, but he took pity and sent me to Oakland, and with the money paid him went back to China. I have had two children; the first died and the second was sold by my husband's brothers when it was fifteen months old. I left the child in the room, and when I came back it was gone."[27]

Rev. F. J. Masters relates this story of a little widow: "On the 24th of February, 1890, word was sent to the Methodist Mission that a young Chinese widow, called Chun Kook, was about to be sold into a slavery worse than death. Her husband, to whom she had been married but a few months, died very suddenly, and immediately after his funeral, the widow, who is a very pretty little woman, was taken possession of by her husband's clan. Two big Chinamen, said to be highbinders, were guarding her. The ladies of the Mission and the superintendent undertook to rescue her. We were met by the strongest opposition on the part of the men. They grappled with us, and a hand-to-hand wrestle took place, in which the Chinese became convinced of the superiority of Anglo-Saxon muscle. The woman was rescued and safely housed in the Mission with the household effects which belonged to her. Two more amazed and disgusted looking men could not be found than these Chinamen when balked of their prey."[28]

The famous writ of *habeas corpus* causes endless trouble to these liberators of Chinese slaves; and often justice is defeated and these child-women are in the name of American law handed over to be slaves in the various dens of Chinatown. The well-known case of little Woon T'Sun, in whose behalf Miss Culbertson had to go to court more than a score of times, and for whose return to the dens the slaveowners made such a determined fight, is but one of many.[29] The case attracted the attention of the press not only of California but of the United States. . . .

About five years ago the wife and four of the children of a Chinaman

---

27. This story and the following one speak to another category of Chinese women that missionaries were also interested in helping: widows who suffered abuse at the hands of their husbands' relatives or clan.

28. Note the reference to Anglo-Saxon superiority, in keeping with the white supremacist attitudes of the day. It is hard to imagine two Chinese thugs allowing a group of ladies to wrestle their property from them except that the women may have greatly outnumbered them and the men may have been hesitant to do any harm to a white woman.

29. Because of the high value placed on prostitutes, owners went to great expense to recover their property, hiring highbinders to retrieve the women or paying legal fees to file criminal charges against the women on trumped-up charges of larceny.

died, leaving him a daughter about six years of age. The man had borrowed money from Kum Mah, a Chinese woman, who had long been a
procuress and proprietor of various dens in Bartlett Alley and other parts
of Chinatown. He could not pay his debt, and wanted to go back to
China; and so, to settle accounts and get a little needed money, he sold
his little girl, body and soul, to Kum Mah, and sailed for the Flowery
Kingdom.

Miss Emma Cable was then the house-to-house missionary in Chinatown of the Occidental Board. Like Miss Ida Hull of the Methodist
Mission, she went regularly to houses and dens of vice, where she would
be admitted; for these secluded Mongolian women dearly love these gen-
tle "white sisters,—teaching, bettering, helping and raising Chinese
women and children wherever their kind ministrations will be received."[30] At Kum Mah's place on Bartlett Alley, she found little Woon
T'Sun and for some time taught her with others. Later the little girl suddenly disappeared, and every effort to trace her was fruitless.

Late last fall Miss Culbertson found she was with Kum Mah, her
owner, on Dupont Street, and went on errands every day to one of Kum
Mah's dens upstairs in the "City of Peking," a new brick building on
Waverly Place, where Kum Mah had moved when Bartlett Alley was
closed and the dens "suppressed."[31] Detective Cox was notified, and on
November 16, 1890, he arrested the girl as she was coming out of this
place, and took her to the Presbyterian Home. The girl was a minor in-
habiting houses of ill-repute, and was being raised to become a regular
inmate as soon as her age would permit. Miss Culbertson was soon appointed her guardian, and the bright, little girl at once entered the pure
life and training of the House.

As is always the case, a struggle for the recovery of the valuable piece
of property began, Kum Mah, aided and advised by "Little Pete"[32] and

---

30. From missionary publications we know that missionary women visited Chinese
homes regularly to give lessons on the Bible, domestic and sanitary practices, and English
to the mothers and children. But why would they be welcomed in brothels when it was
well known in the community that missionary women were keen on rescuing Chinese prostitutes and slavegirls?

31. Throughout the nineteenth century, a number of local ordinances were passed
against prostitution in the city, and they were usually more strictly enforced in Chinatown.

32. Also known as Fong Ching, "Little Pete" was a successful shoe manufacturer, member of the Sam Yup Company, and notorious tong-war boss. His criminal career and murder in 1897 are described in detail in Richard Dillon's *The Hatchet Men, 1880–1906* (New
York: Ballantine Books, 1962), pp. 215–48.

some of the most villainous highbinders in Chinatown, secured the professional services of an American attorney, and made application to have May Sing substituted for Miss Culbertson as the girl's guardian. May Sing is a young Chinese woman who was raised by Kum Mah for a life of vice, and who now conducts a house of ill-repute for her.

All little girls bought for illegal purposes in Chinatown are made to work and act as servants until old enough to be inmates of the dens; and this was Woon T'Sun's course of life. As she is now worth fully one thousand dollars in the market, and would be worth double that sum in five years, it is not surprising that a desperate fight is made to recover her by the woman who bought her, by murderous highbinders and others interested.

The case was kept on the docket for many weeks, and attracted the attention of the entire press of the State. The ladies of the Occidental Board appeared in large numbers in court, and one of their members said: "It has been the custom of lawyers who take up these cases to make the affair so unpleasant that no lady would care to appear in court. This plan will not work now; we are determined to see this matter through and find out whether these little girls can be protected by the courts of California. To drive the ladies out of the courtroom, an American lawyer asked Miss Culbertson indecent and insulting questions,—insinuating that they were not fit to have the care of a child, and that they sold children back to slavery for money, and took bribes for letting them go, and other absurd charges. In Victoria [British Columbia] there is a Home like ours, and public sentiment against this slavery is so strong that no lawyer, no matter what his standing, will undertake to recover a girl."

As to the fact of Chinese slavery which the testimony in the case of Woon T'Sun and hundreds of other girls proved, this little paragraph from the decision Judge Reardon in a similar case, where an old hag claimed to be the mother of a rescued girl, adds significant testimony: "In these Chinese cases of maternity claimed, there always lurks a suspicion that the claim is made because, according to Mongolian methods, the child is valuable property. Yet a few years and this infant will, as prices in the slave market rule, be worth from fifteen hundred to two thousand dollars; and it might well be that the grief, real or simulated, of the mother has a money basis. 'Hinc illa lacryma.'"[33]

All lovers of justice will be glad to know that, in spite of all the machi-

---

33. Latin phrase meaning "hence those tears."

nations of the highbinders and their American allies in the guise of lawyers, little Woon T'Sun was given to Miss Culbertson's care, and is to-day one of the happiest girls in the Presbyterian Mission.

To the honor of the San Francisco press be it said, their defense of these helpless girls and their motherly rescuers was most manly. Their *expose* of slavery was fearless. The *Examiner* said editorially, "It is time for people with the instincts of humanity to pay some attention to the proceedings in the courts with reference to the wretched Chinese women bought and sold by their masters, who speculate in their degradation. The Mission Home, presided over by Miss M. Culbertson, has done a noble and arduous work in rescuing these poor women from the hells in which they have been imprisoned. This work has been carried on literally at the point of the revolver against the unremitting opposition of the murderous highbinders, who have been outlawed in their own country and make assassination and every species of crime their profession in this.[34] The odds are fearful, but one would think in such a contest as this the Mission could at least rely on the support of the laws of its own country. . . .

"*The thing must stop.* The laws of California are adequate to protect a band of good women unselfishly working in the cause of humanity and decency; and the public only needs to know what is going on to make its voice heard in a way that will be respected."

All this was foreseen years and years ago by the Chinese merchants, and at the first legislature in the State they sent a petition to the lawmakers to keep out Chinese women of immoral character.[35] At that time there were only a few such in the country, but they were beginning to send to China for ship-loads of slaves for brothels. Then these "heathen" merchants appealed to their "civilized" American brothers begging them to stop the traffic in its incipiency. But the bill was tabled, and the result is, as might have been expected, the traffic has grown to immense proportions. That the traffic exists is well known. Evidences of the horrible

---

34. Although often threatened in writing or with planted explosives, there is no known case of any missionary worker who was actually physically harmed by highbinders. See Wilson, *Chinatown Quest,* and Martin, *Chinatown's Angry Angel.*

35. "A Petition to the State of California to Bar Prostitutes" was signed by the presidents of the Chinese Six Companies and sent to the state legislature on June 1, 1868, spelling out the negative effects of Chinese prostitution on the community and recommending that the Chinese Six Companies be involved in identifying and turning back prostitutes among the new arrivals (California State Archives). I am indebted to Him Mark Lai for this information.

treatment of the victims have been published for years; yet no case has ever been brought into court, no buyer or seller sought to be punished; and the traffic and the slavery go on as steadily, obviously and certainly, as in New Orleans before the war.

Who cares? What are we going to do about it? These noble Methodists and Presbyterians will rescue a few in their Missions. Like Mr. Charles N. Crittenton, the noble philanthropist of New York, who has spent thousands upon thousands of dollars in founding Florence Missions in New York, Newark, Sacramento and San Jose, for the rescue of erring white sisters, these grand Christian people are doing the same for the dark-eyed, dark-skinned sisters of Asiatic birth. But with all their rescue work thousands of these poor girls cannot be reached. Active co-operation and hearty assistance should be given by all who have one drop of Christian blood within their veins. These girls revolt at their horrible lives. But what choice have slaves? Let America blot out yellow slavery as it has blotted out black slavery. Let the Chinese woman as well as the African man point to the stars and stripes and say, No man dares do me injustice under this flag.

(SOURCE: *Californian Illustrated Magazine*, February 1892, pp. 159–70)

AN AGREEMENT PAPER BY THE PERSON MEE YUNG
(Prostitute's Contract)

At this time there is a prostitute woman, Yut Kum, who has borrowed from Mee Yung $470. It is distinctly understood that there shall be no interest charged on the money and no wages paid for services. Yut Kum consents to prostitute her body to receive company to aid Mee Yung for the full time of four years. When the time is fully served, neither service nor money shall be longer required.

If Yut Kum should be sick fifteen days she shall make up one month. If she conceives, she shall serve one year more. If during the time any man wishes to redeem her body, she shall make satisfactory arrangements with the mistress, Mee Yung. If Yut Kum should herself escape and be recovered, then her time shall never expire. Should the mistress become very wealthy and return to China with glory, then Yut Kum shall fulfill her time, serving another person.

This is a distinct agreement made face to face, both parties willingly consenting. But lest the words of the mouth should be without proof, the agreement-paper is executed and placed in her hands for proof. There are four great sicknesses against which Mee Yung is secured for one hundred days, namely, leprosy, epilepsy, conception, and "stone-woman," i.e., inability to have carnal intercourse with men. For any of these four diseases she may be returned within one hundred days.

Truly with her own hands Mee Yung hands over $470.

Tung Chee 12th year [1874], 8th month, 14th day. The agreement is executed by Mee Yung.

(SOURCE: *Congressional Record*, 43rd Congress, 2nd session, March 1875, pt. 3, p. 41)

BILL OF SALE FOR CHUN LAU
(Mui Tsai's Contract)

Bill of sale—I, Lam Tew Kuey of Pak Tsz Sher, situated at the south side of Tuk Chow, make this bill of sale, selling forever our daughter for a slave. Because of being short in food and clothing and generally helpless, my wife and I, after consultation, decided we should sell our own eldest daughter, called Chun Lau, aged 10 years, being born in the tenth month, twentieth day, 3:05 A.M., to be a slave of other people, we receiving therefore 120 taels [$168] toward defraying the cost of bringing her up and other expenses.

The offer was first made to our relatives, but they were not willing to accept. Then the go-between, Mrs. Lam (formerly Miss Chew), brought the matter to the attention of Chew Kuey Lung Tong for him to purchase, which was agreed upon by all parties concerned.

As word of mouth may not be long depended upon, this bill of sale was drawn up the same day the transaction took place, the amount being paid in full in the presence of all concerned directly to me, Lam Tew Kuey, and my wife for our use, not leaving one cent unpaid. This was for our daughter, called Chun Lau, who was the same day handed over to Chew Kuey Lung Tong, to be called thereafter a slave. In after days, when she shall be grown up, Chew Kuey Lung Tong shall have the transferred right of giving her in marriage to whomsoever he may desire. She shall not be redeemed, nor shall any other claim be made for her. If anything unforeseen should happen to her, that must be regarded as from heaven.

This girl is truly the natural born daughter of me, Lam Tew Kuey. No dowry has ever been accepted for her nor earnest money from any one, and there is no debt for which she may be held. The price money is bona fide and this bill is genuine. Should there be anything not entirely cleared up, that shall be a matter for myself and the go-between to settle, and it shall not concern the purchaser.

With faith in each other, it is not necessary to state more, but lest hereafter there should not be evidence, this bill of sale, in which my daughter is forever sold as a slave, is drawn up to be proof.

This shall be evidence of the fact that I have received from Chew Kuey Lung Tong the sum of 120 taels and of the fact that I, Lam Tew Kuey, have sold my own first-born daughter, called Chun Lau, for a slave.

Signed: Go-between, Mrs. Lam, formerly Miss Chew.

Witness to paper: The mother, formerly Miss Jung.

Each signature is made by a thumb mark.

Amanuensis: Lam Lok Kuey.

This bill of sale, selling forever our daughter, Lam Chun Lau, by me, the father, Lam Tew Kuey, for a slave is made this 15th day of the 12th month in the 16th year of Kwong Suey (January 24, 1890).

(SOURCE: *San Francisco Chronicle*, October 27, 1904, p. 9)

Confession of a Chinese Slave-Dealer

How She Bought Her Girls, Smuggled Them into San Francisco, and Why She Has Just Freed Them

HELEN GREY

The following newspaper story about Suey Hin, a Chinese prostitute who became a madam, stands out as an example of how one woman was able to survive the four-year term of her contract, escape enslavement, and move from the rank of oppressed to oppressor by preying on younger women in the prostitution trade. It is also a touching story of how Suey Hin as a young girl was sold into prostitution and later redeemed by a "poor washman" who falls in love with her. Unfortunately, he dies and Suey Hin decides to make a living by opening her own brothel. As the headline and the two inset summaries reveal, the point of the story was to describe the "nefarious" Chinese slave trade, expose the "barbaric" practices of the Chinese, and give testimony to the power of Christianity in influencing one slave owner to free her girls from a life of indentured prostitution. As such, the article is representative of the kind of missionary journalism that was prevalent in the late nineteenth century.

There is, however, a sincere ring to the stories told in this article not found in M. G. C. Edholm's "A Stain on the Flag." While Suey Hin tells the reporter through an interpreter how she was able to buy unwanted baby girls in China for a pittance and smuggle them into the United States as native-born daughters, she also expresses fond memories of her parents and homeland. Rarer still is the image she projects as a benevolent slave owner, someone who empathizes with her girls, especially the one she brings back from her home village in Shantung (Shandong) Province. The descriptions of her interactions with her girls and the stories that they tell the reporter themselves contrast sharply against the mistreatment of slavegirls at the hands of "old hags" described in most other published accounts. For example, during the interview, the girls return from shopping at "a white man's store," indicating that they are free to go out and spend their own money. However, not all the stories are pleasing to the ear, for while one girl's father welcomes his stolen daughter back, another girl's father resells her once he hears that she will be freed. Finally, there is that moving moment at the end of the article when three-year-old Ah San shows her affectionate attachment for Suey Hin, evoking tears on the part of everyone concerned.

Also noteworthy are Suey Hin's dealings with the tongs that control criminal activities in Chinatown and the ingenious ways she tries to prevent missionary women from taking away her girls. Both situations remind us of the race, class, and gender dynamics that affect the livelihood of madams such as Suey Hin and with which they must contend in order to stay in business. Less clear are Suey Hin's real motives and sincerity about becoming a Christian. Is she using Christianity as a way to protect her interests or is she a true convert seeking redemption in the next life? In any case, here we get to see a different side of the prostitution story. One thing is sure: the seven girls soon to be released from prostitution are the true beneficiaries of Suey Hin's "conversion."

SUEY HIN, a Chinese slave-owner, who has been importing Chinese girls into San Francisco for years, has just been converted to Christianity. To show her sincerity she has freed the seven girls in her possession, valued by her at $8,500, and will endeavor to see them safely married. Several of the girls were kidnaped and they will be returned to their parents. In the light of her new faith, Suey Hin uncovers the whole nefarious Chinese girl slave trade in San Francisco, and describes how the girls are sold here among the Chinese for a few hundred dollars. She herself when only five years old was sold into the trade by her own father, and lived out the whole dreadful life to the time when she adopted Christianity.

Suey Hin, importer, seller, keeper of slave girls, has become a Christian. She says her seven girls may go free if they will live a right life. She is the first woman slavekeeper in Chinatown ever known to give up her business for the Christian religion.[1]

She did not intend to become a Christian. She wanted the "white teachers" to be friends because sometimes her girls were sick, sometimes they were kidnaped. Then, shrewd Chinese believe that the white teachers are good friends to have in a contest with highbinders. Suey Hin reasoned that way, and she went about gaining their friendship in the usual shrewd Chinese way.[2]

She went to the lassies of the Salvation Army and asked them to come and pray for her. She returned with them to her little sitting-room, with its great carved and canopied bed, with its shrine and burning punk sticks and prayers on scarlet paper pasted at the side of the altar. "May honorable guests constantly visit this house," and the punctured red paper which makes the money god happy. Only two of the seven slave girls were in the room, and they knelt while the lassies prayed. They could not understand English, so their slaveowner thought the prayers could not hurt them, but it was a way to gain the good will of the lassies. Suey Hin did not understand the prayers herself at first, but the more she did understand them the better she remembered her mother and the old home in Shantung, and how life was before she began to buy and sell young girls.

She owned seven girls. There was Ah Lung, she would sell for $1300, and Ah San, she would bring just as much. Hom Get and Man Yet and Wo Sing, they would each bring $1200. Ah Ho and Ah Ching were both sick, but they were each worth $1000. That made $8200. Little Ah San was only 3 years old, but she was worth at least $300.[3] Eighty-five hundred dollars in all, and Suey Hin would have to give it all up if she be-

---

1. Based on all available published accounts, there were only a handful of Chinese prostitutes like Suey Hin who operated as free agents in America, the best known being Ah Toy. See Lucie Cheng Hirata, "Free, Indentured, Enslaved: Chinese Prostitutes in Nineteenth-Century America," *Signs: Journal of Women on Culture and Society* 5, no. 1 (autumn 1979): 8; and Judy Yung, *Unbound Feet: A Social History of Chinese Women in San Francisco* (Berkeley: University of California Press, 1995), pp. 33–34.

2. Here is an indication that the author suspects Suey Hin's "shrewd" motive in becoming a Christian was to gain the protection and assistance of missionary women, particularly against the threats of highbinders who were hired by tongs to protect their interests in illegal activities such as the prostitution trade.

3. These estimated values are comparable to those given in Herbert Ashbury's *The Barbary Coast: An Informal History of the San Francisco Underground* (New York: Alfred A. Knopf, 1933), p. 181: "During the early eighteen-nineties they ranged from

came a Christian. To be sure she had money put away, but not much. Then she must not leave the highbinders out of her calculations. There was the Hop Sing Tong and their protege tong, the Kwai Hung. They would not forcibly oppose, but they would be very unfriendly.[4]

So Suey Hin took a little room by herself and night and day she considered the problem: "Shall I become a Christian?"

For weeks she lived apart, revolving the whole matter in her mind.

It took Suey Hin five months to "get" so much conversion that she reached the point where she could give up her trade. Then she went back to her home where the seven girls had been under the care of a woman she called her sister.

It was in this home I listened to her story, partly in her own pigeon English and the rest from the lips of an interpreter. And this is the story she told me in her broken pigeon English:

"I am old, very old, too old to be an American. I like Americans, and if I were younger I would be one.[5] Long, long ago I was born in Shantung, where the flowers are more beautiful and the birds sing more sweetly than in any other place. But my people were poor.[6] There was not enough for all our stomachs. Two baby girls had been left exposed—that is, to die, you know. They were born after me and my father said often, 'She is too many.'

---

about $100 for a one-year-old girl to a maximum of $1,200 for a girl of fourteen, which was considered the best age for prostitution. Children of six to ten brought from $200 to $800. About 1897 girls of twelve to fifteen sometimes sold for as high as $2,500 each."

4. The term *tong* refers to any indigenous Chinese fraternal organization founded by Chinese immigrants for mutual aid and protection, including benevolent societies, clan/family groups, trade and craft guilds, and secret societies. Hop Sing Tong and Kwai Hung were secret societies or fighting tongs that were involved with opium smuggling, gambling, and prostitution. Here, Suey Hin is saying that she will have to pay off the tongs before she can free her girls and get out of the prostitution business. According to an article by Frederic J. Masters on highbinders, the tongs that were connected to the prostitution trade included Hip Yee Tong, Kwong Tak Tong, On Leong Tong, and Wa Ting Shan Fong; see "Among the Highbinders: An Account of Chinese Secret Societies," *California Illustrated Magazine* 1 (January 1892): 62–74.

5. Suey Hin is probably speaking about becoming an acculturated American because until 1943 Chinese immigrants could not become naturalized citizens of the United States.

6. As stated in other published accounts, it was poverty that drove parents to give up or sell their baby daughters. Shantung (Shandong) Province, located on the central coast of China, was hard hit by a series of droughts and famines plus overpopulation pressures in the late nineteenth century.

"Once there was an old woman came to our house and she looked at me. I was 5 that year, 6 the next. When she looked at me I was afraid and I hid myself behind my mother. My father told the old woman to go away.

"But that night she came back again and talked to my father and mother. She put a piece of gold money in my hand and told me to give it to my father. I did, for I wanted nothing to do with her. I had enough; yes, I had plenty to eat!

"But that night the old woman carried me away, and I kicked and screamed and said I would not go. I do not remember much more about the beginning. I remember the ship, and I remembered playing with other little girls. We were brought to San Francisco, and there were five or ten of us and we all lived with a woman on Ross alley. Every little while some one would come and see us, and as we grew older the girls were sold.

"One day it was my turn. They said I was 14 years old, but I was really 12. I don't know how much I cost, but I know both my hands were filled three times with all the gold they would hold. The money, you know, is always put in a girl's hand when she is sold.[7]

"Well, then I was a slave for ten years.[8] There was a man who loved me, but he was a poor washman, and he worked eight years and saved all, all the time. I saved all I could get, too, but it took eight years before we had saved $3000. Then we bought me from my owner and we were married.

"Then, ah, it's all of my life I like to think about. It wasn't but two next years, three years. My husband got sick and didn't get any better, and then he died. I didn't have anything but just myself, and I had to live, and I could not live on nothing. No, I had to have things, so I got a little house; you know, one with a little window over the door.[9]

"Then pretty soon I went back to China, but I did not go to my own village. No, my parents would not want to see me.[10] I went to Hongkong and I bought three girls. Two of them are dead, but Ah Moy, that's Ah

---

7. Note the profit that can be made in the prostitution trade. Suey Hin was originally bought in China for one piece of gold, then resold in the United States for three handfuls of gold. She is later redeemed for $3,000.

8. Suey Hin must have been well treated by her owner because most of her peers did not live beyond the four- to six-year terms of their contracts owing to the mental and physical abuse that Chinese prostitutes were known to suffer.

9. In an effort to hide prostitution from public view the city passed an ordinance in 1878 requiring prostitutes to work behind closed doors. Solicitation could only be made through a wicket-covered opening in the door.

10. Most probably because she had become soiled property.

Moy, she was a baby, and I paid her father 50 cents for her. After I had returned here a few months I went back to China again. I wanted to see my village, always I wanted to go back to my home. So I went, but I didn't let anybody know I was there. I went to the place where they put the babies to die. There was a baby there. A little bit of a brown baby, and she didn't look much good anyway. But I wanted some one from my own village, and so I took the baby, and she is Ah Lung. Don't you think she is a pretty girl now? She's not a slave you know. She's a good girl, just the same as white girls. She comes from Shantung, so I say she shall never be like the others. Slave girls most all die soon. It's bad, yes, and only the girls who want to be good and the dear Jesus knows about that. You see she is a girl and her people sold her, so what can she do?

"That trip I brought home four girls besides Ah Lung. You see it was not hard to smuggle the girls into this country then. You can't do it so easy now. Sometimes they come, only sometimes now. You see the Hop Sing tong fix it with the Custom House. They swore to the officers that the children were born here and went to China to visit. Some witnesses come and they say they knew the girl who wants to land was born here, and they tell all about it. Then they say they know she is the same because they saw her when they went back to China. It was not hard to swear them into this country.[11]

"Then I went back once more. That was only a year ago and I brought back six girls. They did not seem to be with me when we got to the landing, but I watched them. I made the girls learn the answers to the questions the highbinders said would be asked by the Custom House. I told the girls if they made any mistakes the white devils would get them. I said white men liked to eat China girls, they like to boil them and then hang them up to dry and then eat them.[12]

"Oh, the girls didn't make any mistakes when the inspector asked them questions and when they were landed they didn't want to run away. I told them that the girls only stayed at the missions till they got very fat and then Miss Cameron and Miss Lake sold them.[13] Oh, I was bad— wasn't I bad? But I love Jesus now.

"One girl I sold to Loo Wing. All the other girls are here now. I will

---

11. One way around the Chinese Exclusion Act was for a new immigrant to claim U.S. birthright and get a Chinese witness to verify that in federal court.

12. See page 135, note 22.

13. Both Donaldina Cameron of the Presbyterian Mission Home and Margarette Lake of the Methodist Episcopal Home Mission Society were known for rescuing Chinese prostitutes.

not make them bad any more. They are all free—they may go or they may stay, but I watch where they go. Hom Get, she is going to China. I bought her in Hongkong. You want to talk to her?"

I said I did, and Hom Get smiled her eyes out of sight and came in with a funny little Chinese swing of her trousered legs. She seated herself as all Orientals do, cross-legged.

"Oh, yes indeed, I'm going home," she said, through the interpreter. "I'm going back to my own home. My father didn't sell me; he would not do it. He just wrote a letter to me. You want to see it? My father he loves me and he doesn't forget. I was stolen. You see my father he quarreled with a man. The man wanted to do him harm. So this wicked man he got another man who knew my father and who lived in Hongkong to write me to visit his family. My father didn't know his enemy was doing anything and he let me go. Then the man took me down town and lost me so my father's enemy could find me.

"Then my father's enemy sold me to Suey Hin and she brought me here.

"My father did not know where I was till the white teachers wrote to him in China. The teachers said I was freed because Suey Hin loved Jesus. Then my father wrote this letter and he sent $70. Isn't that such a lot of money? Don't you think my father loves me? And I'm going home and I will see my sister and I'll see my two brothers, but I, oh, I don't know, you see I'm not like all the other girls at home now. I love Jesus, yes, but then—. You want to see the letter my father wrote?"

While we were talking there was the bustle and chatter of some one coming in. Suey Hin called out and Man Get, Ah Ho and Ah Chung came into the room. We shook hands all around and the girls said they had been to a white man's store to do some shopping. They opened their parcels and showed Suey Hin and me what they had purchased and bragged about how cheap they had bought them. Ah Ching gave a piece of blue ribbon and a pair of long blue silk stockings to Man Get. The girl looked pensive and took the blue things and patted them.

"She has just heard her father is dead. You see I bought her in Victoria [British Columbia]. When I wanted to love Jesus I thought I would ask her father to take her home and get her married. I wrote to him, but you see he is a very bad man. He went right to a man, showed my letter and said: 'You are going to San Francisco. That fool woman gone crazy. You buy Man Get. I sell her cheap.' So he sell her to Loo Wing for $250. He was sure she was very sick, so he sell her very cheap.

"Loo Chee did buy her and then came here to me. He said, 'I will take

Hom Get [Man Get] to her father. He wants her and she can stay at home and be married. He never sell her any more.' You see? He lied.

"I almost let Hom Get [Man Get] go with Loo Chee. He went away, he said, to buy a ticket to take Hom Get [Man Get] to Victoria. But he drop this piece of paper on the floor. Ah San she was playing with Loo Chee and she picked the paper up quick and brought it to me. See, here it is:

BILL OF SALE

Loo Wing to Loo Chee—

April 16—Rice, 6 mats, at $2	$12	
April 18—Shrimps, 50 lbs, at 10c	5	
April 20—Girl, $250	250	
April 21—Salt fish, 60 lbs at 10c	6	
	$263	

Received payment,
LOO CHEE.
Victoria, B.C., May 1, 1898.

"Then I know Loo Wing had sold Hom Get [Man Get] to Loo Chee, but I said no, oh no, not at all! I would not let Hom Get [Man Get] go. Then Loo Chee went to the Kwai Kung [Hung] tong and made a big complaint about me.

"Fong San came and he said I must give Hom Get [Man Get] to Loo Chee or he would make me trouble. After all the money I have paid Fong San. No! Oh, I have given him plenty money to protect me! Well, he knew Hom Get [Man Get] belonged to me because I only said I would send her to her father if he would keep her and get her married. When he sold her that broke the bargain.

"Well, that was two months ago. Last week Fong Sing came to see me. He told us Loo Wing was dead. So now Hom Get [Man Get] has no home and she must stay here and I'll get her married. I won't let her marry any but a Christian man. The blue ribbon she wears? Oh, that's to show she has some one dead. What you call mourning."

While Suey Hin was telling about Hom Get [Man Get] two of the girls brought us tiny cups of tea and confections of dried cocoanut. A little three-year-old girl in a red sam [shirt] and yellow trousers put a doll in my lap. It was dressed in Chinese style most magnificently.

"Lunt gave me," she said, in English.

"You a boy and like dolls?"

"I not boy, I girl; I Ah San." I looked inquiringly at Suey Hin, for the child wore the dress of a boy.

"Oh, yes, she's a girl. I dress her like a boy so the mission people will not steal her. I very cute [smart]! They see I bring her up for a slave girl and then they come and rescue her. Oh, no, no, not at all! I make her look like a boy."[14]

"Where did you get her?"

"Bought her. Bought her when she was ten days old. She's smart. Ah San, come here. Oh, she understands everything! Now, Ah San, sing 'Jesus Loves Me.'"

The little one repeated the sentence and then she said the whole of "The Lord is My Shepherd," and all in very good English.

"What will you do with her?"

Suey's face saddened. You could see she was very fond of the child. "I don't know; maybe give her to the mission. Do you want to go to the mission, Ah San?"

The little face clouded and the tears began to run over the black eyelashes.

Suey gathered the little one up in her arms. Ah San's were not the only wet eyes as she said: "I good, I good girl, Suey."

"What will you do with the other girls?" I asked.

"Oh, I suppose they get married. Only they must marry Christians. I Christian now, and I work always now for Jesus. I used to work hard for the devil, him you call, Satan, but now I work harder for Jesus."

Receptacle for Cast-off Girl-Babies Near Swatow, China[15]

As most people know, the birth of a girl child into a Chinese home is not a welcome event. She is a "go-away child"—that is to say, when married, she leaves her home and goes to her husband's, whereas a son brings home his wife with him. When a Chinese father is reckoning up the number of his household he counts only his sons. The birth of a girl means simply another mouth to fill; and for this sordid consideration baby girls are often not allowed to live. When they are not actually made away with

---

14. This was another tactic employed by Suey Hin to protect her girls from mission workers. Chinese mothers were known to dress their boys as girls to fool the gods who might want to harm their sons.

15. Swatow (Shantou) is a port in Guangdong Province. The following text is the caption to a photo that appeared at the end of the above article.

they are disposed of by some . . . indirect means. . . . Here we see a bas-ket fastened to the wall of the city of Chaochao-foo,[16] some thirty miles up river from the treaty port of Swatow. This basket is for the reception of newly born girls who have not found a welcome in their own homes, a veritable "letter box," where baby girls are "posted." The father may possibly be troubled with some slight scruples about actually killing the infant, so he places it in this strange receptacle, where any one wishing to adopt a female child is at liberty to remove it and do what he likes with it. It is awful practices like this that make the Christian missionar-ies sometimes despair of the Chinese.

(SOURCE: *The Call*, April 2, 1899, p. 25)

---

16. Chaozhou is a prefectural city near Shantou.

The Chinese Woman in America

SUI SEEN [SIN] FAR

Although prostitutes dominated in numbers among Chinese immigrant women in the 1860s and 1870s, married women began to exceed them in the 1880s, owing to the enforcement of antiprostitution measures, the exempt status of merchant wives under the Chinese Exclusion Act, and the marriages of ex-prostitutes to Chinese laborers. By the turn of the century there were reportedly 2,136 Chinese females and 11,818 Chinese males in San Francisco; 62 percent of Chinese women fifteen years and older were married.[1]

Although immigrant wives occupied a higher status than mui tsai *and prostitutes within the patriarchal structure of Chinatown in the latter part of the nineteenth century, all written accounts of their lives indicate that they were still considered the property of men and constrained to lead bound lives. Merchant wives with bound feet were generally sequestered within the home. Those who had* mui tsai *to help them with the household chores spent their time doing needlework and chatting with neighbors. Wives married to laborers generally did not have bound feet, but they were still housebound except when they needed to go out to shop. Aside from cultural reasons, fear of racial assaults and kidnappings kept women close to home. In contrast to the more leisurely lifestyle of merchant wives, laborers' wives were kept busy from day to night at home with wage work, housework, and child care responsibilities.*

---

1. My tally is based on the 1900 manuscript census of population for San Francisco.

Edith Maude Eaton (Sui Sin Far).

Because of the high illiteracy rates among Chinese immigrant women at this time and the lack of opportunities for them to interact with the larger society, few written accounts of their lives exist. As a rule, those articles on the private lives of merchant wives that did sporadically appear in mainstream newspapers and journals were written by outsiders, generally non-Chinese-speaking women with little knowledge of Chinese culture, to satisfy the curiosity of the general public. These articles tended to offer little more than superficial descriptions of a Chinese woman's bound feet, colorful clothing, and cloistered lifestyle, providing little understanding of her thoughts, feelings, and experiences in America. The following article written by Sui Sin Far (literally, "narcis-

sus flower"; pseudonym for Edith Maude Eaton) in 1897 is an exception to this rule.

Born in England in 1865 of a Chinese mother and an English father, Edith Maude Eaton grew up in Montreal, Canada, where she worked as a stenographer, journalist, and short story writer. From 1898 to 1912 she lived and worked in San Francisco, Seattle, and Boston. She died in 1914 at the age of forty-nine, leaving behind a legacy of writings on Chinese immigrant life, including a collection of short stories entitled Mrs. Spring Fragrance *that focused mainly on Chinese women, family life, and children.[2] In recent years Eaton has been acknowledged by scholars in Asian American literature as the first person of Chinese ancestry to write about the Chinese American experience with sensitivity, empathy, and authenticity from an insider's perspective.[3] She has also been credited for defending the Chinese, an unjustly maligned race, and countering popular stereotypes of the Chinese as one-dimensional, unassimilable aliens with her portrayals of Chinese life. Even before her death, she was so acknowledged by a New York Chinese in an article: "The Chinese in America owe an everlasting debt of gratitude to Sui Sin Far for the bold stand she has taken in their defense."[4] And one year after her death, the Chinese communities of Montreal and Boston erected a special headstone for her tomb inscribed with four Chinese characters,* yi bu wang hua *("The righteous or loyal one does not forget China").[5]*

Identifying more with her Chinese mother than her English father, Eaton did indeed set out "to depict as well as I can what I know and see about the Chinese people in America."[6] However, as Annette White-Parks's literary biography of Eaton reveals, she could not speak Chinese and did not live among the Chinese. Her insights were drawn from stories her mother told her about China and visits she made to Chinese

---

2. Sui Sin Far (Edith Eaton), *Mrs. Spring Fragrance* (Chicago: A. C. McClurg & Co., 1912).

3. Frank Chin et al., eds., *Aiiieeeee! An Anthology of Asian American Literature* (Washington, D.C.: Howard University Press, 1974), pp. xii–xiii; S. E. Solberg, "Sui Sin Far/Edith Eaton: First Chinese American Fictionist," *MELUS* 8 (spring 1981): 33; Amy Ling, *Between Worlds: Women Writers of Chinese Ancestry* (New York: Pergamon Press, 1990), p. 40; and Annette White-Parks, *Sui Sin Far/Edith Maude Eaton: A Literary Biography* (Urbana: University of Illinois Press, 1995), p. xxi.

4. Quoted in Sui Sin Far, "Leaves from the Mental Portfolio of an Eurasian," *Independent* 66 (January 21, 1909): 128.

5. Ling, *Between Worlds*, p. 32.

6. Quoted in White-Parks, *Sui Sin Far/Edith Maude Eaton*, p. 44.

homes in Montreal, New York, and San Francisco. According to one of her letters, written while in New York for two weeks, she "saw the Chinese theatres and Joss Houses, visited all the little Chinese women, talked pigeon English to them, examined their babies, dined with a Chinese actress, darted hither and thither through the tenements of Chinatown."[7] *In San Francisco, where she lived from 1898 to 1900, she taught English to Chinese immigrants in the evenings and had Chinese women serve as her guides to Chinatown: "Some little women discover that I have Chinese hair, color of eyes and complexion, also that I love rice and tea. This settles the matter for them—and for their husbands."*[8] *One questions then how much of an insider Eaton really was.*

Judging from one of her earlier essays, "The Chinese Woman in America," Eaton wrote as an outsider but also as a friend who was allowed into the inner sanctums of Chinese homes. She was at the time still living in Montreal but had already visited New York Chinatown, and thus was probably basing the article on her observations of Chinese home life in those two cities. The magazine that published the essay, Land of Sunshine, *was interested in literature that conveyed the "local color" of the American West, and it was for this reason that Charles Lummis, editor of the magazine and Eaton's lifetime correspondent-to-be, solicited her writings on Chinese immigrant life. Eight of her short stories and this essay were published in* Land of Sunshine *between 1898 and 1900, a time in Eaton's life when she was still learning about Chinese culture and becoming familiar with San Francisco Chinatown. Perhaps this is why "The Chinese Woman in America" reads like a generalized, romanticized report by an outsider trying to provide insights into the "odd and interesting" home lives of merchant wives. It offered, as White-Parks points out, "a peephole into a strange and exotic environment."*[9]

Despite these limitations, the article does help readers appreciate the different and not-so-different lifestyles of Chinese immigrant women vis-à-vis the American norm. The trademark of Eaton's writing style was to play with popular stereotypes and turn them on their heads.[10] *Thus, she*

---

7. Letter to the editor of the *Montreal Daily Star*, quoted in White-Parks, *Sui Sin Far/Edith Maude Eaton*, p. 92.

8. Sui Sin Far, "Leaves," p. 131.

9. White-Parks, *Sui Sin Far/Edith Maude Eaton*, p. 94.

10. Annette White-Parks describes this trickster technique in *Sui Sin Far/Edith Maude Eaton*: "Sui Sin Far teases her readers by presenting us with situations and characters that appear to fit stereotypes but in fact disprove them" (p. 135).

describes Chinese merchant wives as quaint, old-fashioned, superstitious, cloistered, illiterate, and demure, but also as outgoing "new women" with feelings, minds, talents, and a deep loyalty to their husbands, families, friends, country, and culture. Their status as women may have been different from that of Western women, but they were equally well loved and cherished as children and accepting of traditional marital customs and their role as wives when they reached adulthood. Indeed, coming to America as a bride in an arranged marriage had its rewards, as Eaton made clear. Most telling are Eaton's detailed descriptions of the women's home environment—a mixture of American and Chinese styles—and the ways that they bonded with their female friends: "there is such a clattering of tongues one would almost think they were [white] American women." Equally important are Eaton's efforts to point out class distinctions among the aristocrats, merchants, and laborers, and where most Chinese wives fit into the picture. Except for a few incidences when she refers to her subjects as children, their country as strange, and critiques their hairstyles and faces, Eaton withholds judgment, choosing instead matter-of-factly to describe what she sees and to keep cultural explanations to a minimum. In her view, Chinese merchant wives were content with their lot and lived the way they did "because that is [the] Chinese way." Considering the lack of first-hand accounts on this subject and the language and cultural barriers at play, "The Chinese Woman in America" was a breakthrough, an important source of information on the private lives of Chinese merchant wives in the late nineteenth century.

With her quaint manners and old-fashioned mode of life, she carries our minds back to times almost as ancient as the earth we live on. She is a bit of olden Oriental coloring amidst our modern Western lights and shades; and though her years be few, she is yet a relic of antiquity. Even the dress she wears is cut in a fashion designed centuries ago, and is the same today as when the first nonfabulous Empress of China begged her husband to buy her a new dress—of a tunic, a pair of trousers and a divided skirt, all of finest silk and embroidered in many colors. A Chinese woman in a remote age invented the divided skirt, so it is not a "New Woman" invention.

The Chinese woman in America differs from all others who come to live their lives here, in that she seeks not our companionship, makes no attempt to know us, adopts not our ways and heeds not our customs. She lives among us, but is as isolated as if she and the few Chinese relations who may happen to live near were the only human beings in the world.

So if you wish to become acquainted with her, if you wish to glean some knowledge of a type of which very little is known, you must seek her out. She will be pleased with your advances and welcome you with demure politeness, but you might wait for all eternity and she would not come to you.

Having broken the ice, you find that her former reserve was due to her training, and that she is not nearly so shy as report makes her. You also find, despite the popular idea that the Chinese are a phlegmatic people, that she is brimful of feelings and impressions and has sensibilities as acute as a child's. That she is content to live narrowly, restricted to the society of one man and perhaps a couple of females, does not prove lack of imagination; but merely that she is ignorant of any other life.

She was born in China, probably in Canton or near that city. When a little girl, she played Shuttlecock, Guessing Pennies and Blind Man's Buff with childish playfellows, boys and girls; and grandfather and uncles kept her awake, when her mother put her to bed, by telling her stories of hobgoblins and ghosts. Amongst her memories of home are little pagodas before which she and her brothers and sisters were taught to burn incense, and an image of a goddess called "Mother," to whom she used to kneel till her little knees ached.

Until about twelve years old, she enjoyed almost as much healthful liberty as an American child; but in China it is not deemed proper for girls beyond that age to have boy playmates.

Then she learned to sew and embroider, to do light cooking and sing simple ballads. She was taught that whilst with them, her first duty was obedience to her father and mother; and after marriage, to her husband and his parents. She never had a sweetheart, but with girl friends would pass the hours in describing the beauties and virtues of future husbands.

In spite of these restraints, her years slipped away happily until time came for her to become an American bride—for the Chinese woman who comes to America generally comes as a bride, having been sent for by some Chinaman who has been some years in the States or in Canada and has prospered in business.

She has never seen her future husband, she has never perhaps ventured outside her native village; yet upon being apprised that for good and valuable consideration—for the expectant bridegroom, like Isaac of old when courting Rebecca, sends presents of silver and presents of gold to the parents or guardians of his chosen—she must leave home and friends and native land, she cheerfully sets about preparing for her journey. She may shed a few tears upon her mother's breast and surreptitiously hug her little sisters; but on the whole, she is pleased.

Her companions and friends usually regard her with envy. None but a well-to-do Chinaman could afford to send for a bride across the sea. The chief reason, however, is that the girl who goes to America does not become subject to her husband's mother, as when a girl marries in China. In that strange land she is obliged to live with her husband's parents and obey them as a daughter; and unless she is of yielding disposition, or the mother-in-law of extraordinary good nature, the result is often unhappiness. If there is a disagreement, it is the duty of the husband and son to take his mother's part, and the wife is made to acknowledge herself in the wrong. The Chinese woman who comes to America is favored also in that she can dress in richer costumes. In China her ordinary attire would consist of cotton, or a combination of silk and cotton, plainly made. The richly embroidered dresses which the Chinese women who come to America are allowed to bring with them are in China worn only by women of rank and position.

The bride comes from a respectable middle-class Chinese family. Aristocratic or wealthy people would not give a daughter to a man living in exile; and Wah Ling, being a big enough man to keep a wife in America, feels himself too big to take a girl from the laboring classes. He wishes his friends to think that he marries well; if he were to choose a girl of mean condition he might be ridiculed. The Chinaman knows little of natural selection; though in his youth he has a sweetheart, when he wants a wife he sends for a stranger.

In China it is deemed altogether wrong for girls "in society" to have men acquaintances; but very poor girls choose their associates as they please without causing remark. Now and then a poverty stricken or outcast maid wins the heart of a Chinaman brave enough to marry her in spite of what his world may say; but such cases are rare. Very few Chinamen are introduced to their wives until after marriage.

The Chinese woman in America lives generally in the upstairs apartments of her husband's dwelling. He looks well after her comfort and provides all her little mind can wish. Her apartments are furnished in American style; but many Chinese ornaments decorate the tables and walls, and on the sides of the room are hung long bamboo panels covered with paper or silk on which are painted Chinese good-luck characters. In a curtained alcove of an inner room can be discerned an incense vase, an ancestral tablet, a kneeling stool, a pair of candlesticks—my lady-from-China's private chapel. She will show you all her pretty ornaments, her jewelry and fine clothing, but never invite you near her private chapel. There she burns incense to her favorite goddess and prays that a son may be born to her, that her husband may be kind, and that she may live to die in China—the country which heaven loves.

She seldom goes out, and does not receive visitors until she has been a wife for at least two years. Even then, if she has no child, she is supposed to hide herself. After a child has been born to her, her wall of reserve is lowered a little, and it is proper for cousins and friends of her husband to drop in occasionally and have a chat with "the family."

Now and then the women visit one another; and when they are met together, there is such a clattering of tongues one would almost think they were American women. They laugh at the most commonplace remark and scream at the smallest trifle; they examine one another's dresses and hair, talk about their husbands, their babies, their food; squabble over little matters and make up again; they dine on bowls of rice, minced chicken, bamboo shoots and a dessert of candied fruits.

The merrymaking over, they bid good-by by clasping their own hands, shaking them up and down and interlacing their fingers—instead of shaking hands with one another.

If it is necessary to pass a room occupied by men, they do so very demurely, holding open fans before that side of the face—not because they are so shy, but because it is the custom of their country.

Although she does not read nor go out to see the sights, the Chinese woman does not allow time to hang heavy on her hands in America. There are many little thoughts in her mind, and she gives expression to them in beautiful fancy-work, representations of insects, flowers and birds most dexterously wrought from silk and beads. This is not useless, from her point of view, for it can be used as presents to distant relations, for the ornamentation of caps for her husband and little son, and also on her own apparel.

She loves flowers, natural or artificial: and if not supplied with the former, makes herself great quantities of the latter and wears them on hair and breast.

She bestows considerable pains on the plaiting of her hair; and after it is done up flat at the back of her head, she adorns it with flowers and large fantastic pins. Her tresses are shining, black and abundant, and if dressed becomingly would be attractive; but the manner in which she plasters them back from her forehead would spoil the prettiest face.

While there are some truly pleasant to behold, with their little soft faces, oval eyes, small round mouths and raven hair, the ordinary Chinese woman does not strike an observer as lovely. She is, however, always odd and interesting.

Needless to say she is vain. Vanity is almost as much part of a woman's nature as of a man's; but the Chinese woman's vanity is not that of an American woman. The ordinary American dresses for the eyes of her friends and enemies—particularly the latter—and derives small pleasure from her prettiest things unless they are seen by others. A Chinese woman paints and powders, dresses and bejewels herself for her own pleasure; puts rings on her fingers and bracelets on her arms—and carefully hides herself from the gaze of strangers. If she has Golden Lily feet (Chinese small feet) she is proudly conscious of it; but should she become aware that a stranger is trying to obtain a glimpse of them, they quickly disappear under her skirt.

She is deeply interested in all matters of dress; and, if an American woman calls on her, will politely examine the visitor's clothing, with many an expression of admiration. She will even acknowledge the American dress prettier than her own, but you could not persuade her to adopt it. She is interested in all you may tell her about America and Americans; she has a certain admiration for the ways of the foreigner; but nothing can change her reverence for the manners and customs of her own country.

"Why do you do that in such a way?" she is asked, and her answer is, "Oh, because that is Chinese way."

"Do it like this," she is told. She shakes her head smilingly: "No, that not Chinese way."

As a mother, she resembles any other young mother—a trifle more childish, perhaps, than young American matrons, but just as devoted. When the baby seems well, she is all smiles and Chinese baby-talk; when he is ill, or she fancies so, she weeps copiously and cannot be comforted. She dresses him in Chinese dress, shaves his head and strings amulets on his neck, wrists and ankles.

She is very superstitious with regard to her child, and should you happen to know the date and hour of his birth, she begs with tears that you will not tell, for should some enemy know, he or she may cast a horoscope which would make the child's life unfortunate.

Do not imagine for an instant that she is dull of comprehension and unable to distinguish friendly visitors from those who merely call to amuse themselves at her expense. I have seen a little Chinese woman deliberately turn her back on persons so ignorant as to whisper about her and exchange knowing smiles in her presence. She is very loyal, however, to those she believes to be her real friends, and is always seeking to please them by some little token of affection.

More constant than sentimental is the Chinese woman. She has a true affection for her husband; no other man shares any of her personal thoughts. She loves him because she has been given to him to be his wife. No question of "woman's rights" perplexes her. She takes no responsibility upon herself and wishes none. She has perfect confidence in her man.

She lives in the hope of returning some day to China. She feels none of the bitterness of exile—she was glad to come to this country—but she would not be a daughter of the Flowery Land were she content to die among strangers.

Not all the Chinese women in America are brides. Some were born here; others are merely secondary wives, the first consorts of their husbands being left in China; and there are a few elderly women who were married long before leaving home. The majority, however, are brides; or as the Chinese call young married females, "New Women."

(SOURCE: *Land of Sunshine* 6, no. 2 [January 1897]: 59–64)

Worse Than Slaves

Servitude of All Chinese Wives

Small-Foot Women Kept as Prisoners

Widows Must Serve No. 1—A White Woman's Hard Lesson in Eastern Ways

LOUISE A. LITTLETON

This article, which appeared in the San Francisco Chronicle *in 1894, stands in marked contrast to Sui Sin Far's "The Chinese Woman in America." It also pretends to provide an insider's look at a Chinese home, but whereas Sui Seen Far presented Chinese merchant wives as content with their lot, Louise Littleton paints a less rosy picture. According to her article, "small-foot" wives are the property of their husbands, "entombed for life," bored to tears, and "weary of being treated as a child." As the second wife, they can at any time be sold "like cows" and, worse, lose their sons, who by Chinese law belong to the first wife.*

What makes Littleton's article plausible and interesting is the access she evidently had to Chinese homes and the logical reasoning behind the voice of the Chinese wife she interviews. Her article begins with a detailed description of the crowded living conditions of the Chinese, down to the exact location of the family shrine in one corner of the room, a gallery of family portraits and "pretty girls" that cover one wall, and the shelves of boxes to be found behind the curtained bed. She writes that when another member—whether it be a second wife or a child—joins the household, a bed space is made by partitioning off a cubbyhole in the room. Only someone who is regarded as a trustworthy friend would be allowed into the inner sanctum of a Chinese home like this. More than likely, Littleton was a missionary who taught English to the Chinese in their homes, since she is addressed as "Seen Sang," or teacher, throughout the interview.

While Sui Sin Far spoke for her subjects, Littleton allows her informant to speak for herself, although one questions the Chinese woman's conversant use of standard and slang English. Was an interpreter employed, or did Littleton make up the conversation? In either case, the wealthy Chinese wife comes across as pampered, forthright, smart, but practical. She complains about being housebound and is so bored that she chooses to pass the time by sewing buttons on overalls. She points out that there is plenty of work for the poor and she is not taking anything away from them. Although generally unhappy about her lack of rights as a second wife according to Chinese law, she reasons that running away to the mission home or appealing to the American court of law would only make matters worse. As she points out, even a Swedish girl, Lizzie, who married a wealthy Chinese man could not do anything when her husband decided to take a second wife. This interviewee has a ready answer to every suggestion Littleton raises. In the end, practicality rules and she resigns herself to saying simply, "He is as good as any Chinese husband would be—what object in leaving him?"

It can be argued that this strong-minded Chinese wife is an exceptional case or that Littleton, judging by the sensational headline to the article and some of her sweeping generalizations and condescending remarks, has projected her ethnocentric biases into the story. Nevertheless, there is a sincere ring to the interview and we benefit from the lively exchange, the candid descriptions of domestic life, and supposedly the private thoughts of one merchant wife.

When a Chinese is poor and owns but one wife, he lives in one small room. His bed, curtained off in one corner, takes up the greater part of it. Within the curtained inclosure a series of shelves is built into the wall to hold the many boxes filled with extra clothing, etc. An American chair or two, an American table, a shelf appropriated to offerings of oranges, tea, rice, sweetmeats, duck, chicken, pork, illuminations of gayly colored candles and punk in honor of the family god and other divinities whose pictures or names are pasted on the wall above. A shrine, underneath this shelf or altar, where the spark of incense never dies nor the tea cup ever empties takes another corner, and now the room is so crowded that husband and wife make their way in and out of the apartment sideways, like a dog.[1] Very little of the

---

1. Here we have an example of Littleton's condescension toward the Chinese.

walls is visible. John[2] believes in the photographer and the *Police Gazette*, and his picture and wife's picture hang side by side in rustic walnut frames, and his friends' pictures and their wives', and all the children, if there are any, and if there are not any it is a wofully unhappy home. The remainder of his picture gallery are "velly pretty girls" in all states of gymnastic poses, dress and undress, cut from flashy "pink" papers.[3]

If children come there is no moving to larger quarters—room for another bed is made by adding a broad shelf away up near the ceiling, which protrudes over the head the whole width or the whole length of the room—a second story as it were—with a very contracted amount of cubic space. Access is gained to this department by means of a common ladder. The goddess of children finds her niche under the head of the parents' bed. Goon Yum, the goddess of mothers desiring children, always has her little illuminated shrine.[4]

There may be one or many wives, a few more chairs and stools, rice bowls and chopsticks, which, with the rich, are of finer ware, but in the main there is very little difference between the homes of rich and poor.[5]

A natural-footed woman has many advantages over the small foot. First, not being an object of special admiration for the opposite sex, her husband may pick a room opening on the street; second, she may come and go as she chooses on the streets, visit places of amusement, native or foreign, do her own meager shopping or marketing, travel in the street or steam cars and see with her own eyes all the wonders of a foreign country.[6] A wealthy man buys a small-foot wife; she comes over the seas to California as a first-class cabin passenger; when she leaves the vessel she is carried in a closely-curtained carriage to her new home, and from the day she enters

---

2. Chinese men were often stereotypically referred to as "John Chinaman" by whites, Chinese women as "China Mary."

3. The *Police Gazette* was published from 1845 to 1932. Originally intended to cover criminal activities, it was bought by Richard Kyle Fox in 1876 and transformed into a popular weekly tabloid that covered sports, the theater, and personal stories. It was known for its pink pages and illustrations of male and female actors and athletes, which explains Littleton's reference to "pink" papers.

4. Goon Yum, also spelled Kuan Yin, is the goddess of mercy, popular among Chinese women.

5. Here we have an example of overgeneralizing on the part of Littleton. Even given the crowded conditions in San Francisco Chinatown, there were major differences between the houses of the rich and the poor.

6. Although it was true that women with natural feet enjoyed more freedom of movement than women with bound feet, in general Chinese women during this time rarely left Chinatown or traveled too far from home out of modesty and fear for their safety.

it is practically entombed alive. Being a small-foot she is, of course, not expected to do anything but look stunning in her big hair done "a la two dragons playing with a pearl," or "a la two phoenixes threading the flowers." She spends much of her time sitting tailor fashion, with both webfeet tucked under, playing poker with her wee servant. Occasionally she toys with a bit of silk and tinsel, actually in one whole year accomplishing the feat of embroidering a pocketbook for her husband.[7] Once a week her mass of hair—the crowning glory of a Chinese woman—is done afresh by the woman hairdresser who has for her clientele the small-feet wives of wealthy men. This important personage is a close observer of society events in aristocratic Chinatown and relates them to her patrons.

The life of a wealthy Chinese woman, rather of a woman belonging to a wealthy man, is most miserable. You will open your eyes in surprise at the great pile of factory overalls on which she is sewing buttons.

"Why do you do this work when you are rich?" I asked one such woman.

"Seen Sang [Teacher]," she said, "would have me go crazy. Can I sit here all day and see the same things I have seen every day for seventeen years, and think the same thoughts I have thought for twenty years? There is plenty of work for the poor people. I do not take it from them, but if I did they are richer than I, for they have big feet and can go everywhere, and every day have something new to fill their minds; while, poor me! In China I was shut up in the house since I was 10 years old, and only left my father's house to be shut up in my husband's house in this great country. For seventeen years I have been in this house without leaving it save on two evenings. Would you take from me my only way of passing the time?"

The Chinese paterfamilias is in his way a very reasonable being. If he has grown wealthy enough to live in good style he buys a small-foot woman to add a distinguished air to his name and establishment.[8] Social laws deprive her from free intercourse with her feminine friends, because she must not travel through the streets, unless on rare occasions after nightfall.[9] She derives no companionship from books because she cannot read. The epitome of politeness in the Chinese woman is absolute ignorance. The only women who can read are the daughters of poor fam-

---

7. Here Littleton is being disrespectful of Chinese women's bound feet, their card games, and their needlework skills.

8. See page 132, note 18.

9. Merchant wives could and did interact with their female neighbors as described in the previous article by Sui Sin Far.

ilies, who are taught the art that they may go out as readers or reciters of fairy tales to the wealthy.[10]

Recognizing his wife's loneliness the Chinese husband breaks the monotony by allowing her an occasional dinner party or by hiring a woman reader to come and entertain her with fairy tales once a week. In this she is treated as a child—only "Arabian Nights" or similar stories are suited to her comprehension, and, as she receives them with the implicit, innocent faith of childhood, they confirm her belief in witchcraft and her conviction in the existence of her Buddhistic pantheon, and make her, if possible, more slavish in her already attentive homage to it.[11] Her lord and master goes still further; he buys her a pot of growing plants, a jews-harp, a harmonica, a canary bird or two, a patent whistle which is supposed to trill like the feathered songster, and above all an expensive European music box which plays from ten to twenty-five tunes, grinding out "The Last Rose of Summer" like a galloping cow, and rendering the farandole from "Olivette" like a funeral dirge. She cannot distinguish one tune from another and cannot adjust the mechanism to either tune or time, but sits back in complacent satisfaction to listen to the noise and watch the prickly cylinder revolve.

The strong-minded woman had all these toys to entertain her, but the charm of novelty had faded; she longed for something new—her husband was about to present her with it in the shape of another wife. The carpenter was already at work partitioning off a cubby hole with a sleeping bunk inside of it for the bride's accommodation.

"Of course you wish my congratulations; you are glad to have constant company and some one to boss."

"No, I'm not; most Chinese women would be, but I'm sorry. And I'm not boss, either, for I'm only No. 2, and have to look down [up] to No. 1. Now, Seen Sang, look; I love my boy—I want him with me all the time, but our custom says: 'No, you are only No. 2; that boy belongs to No. 1; he must never call you mother, but must always owe allegiance to No. 1, who is the true wife, and call her mother.' She wants to see the child—

---

10. In China it was not uncommon for wealthy families to educate their daughters as well as their sons. By this time Chinese parents in San Francisco were beginning to send children of both sexes to the mission-sponsored and public schools.

11. More than likely, the storyteller would narrate Chinese folktales and legends of virtuous women in Chinese history. In regard to "witchcraft," most Chinese immigrants believed and practiced a form of syncretic religion that combined Buddhism, Taoism, local cults, and certain elements of Confucianism. It involved many rites that were performed in the home, including ancestor worship, none of which can be considered witchcraft.

her child she calls him—my child, and so my husband will send him to China in a year or two more and I may never see him again. It makes my heart sorry, but if I had fifty children my feelings would be of no consideration—they would all go the same way. Not one can stay by me and be the support and comfort of my old age."

"But you may go back to him some time?"

"Yes, maybe sometime, if my husband does not get tired of me and sell me to some other man. We are just like cows, excepting No. 1; it is only the first wife he cannot put away so easily; she has all the rights. But if I were to go back I should have to be No. 1's slave, always ready to pamper her every whim and obey her most tyrannical command, and my son could do nothing for me, for he would no longer be my son. You say the Chinese are not an affectionate people. What is there in our domestic life to found affection upon, when our laws maintain that a man may have as many wives as he wishes; that he may put away any or all, excepting the first wife, whenever he wishes; that all the wives must obey No. 1 wife and raise up children to her, and all the children must acknowledge her as their mother? I should like to be a Christian woman, to be governed by Christian laws."

"Be a Christian woman."

"For my husband to sell at once, what should I do?"

"Find a home in a mission house."

"A worse prison than this, with a revolution in my daily habits. I do not desire to be a literal Christian; I do not believe in the Christian religion, but I like the Christian laws. The Chinese in America are governed by the Six Companies, so-called; although there are more companies than that now—common usage makes it six.[12] I could run away from my husband successfully, perhaps, to a mission if I desired. A mission would give me a home for a year; then, at the year's expiration turn me out to marry or to make my own living. Either would mean starvation, death. I am too old for any man to desire in marriage, too helpless in the ways of making money to support myself, too used to the good living my husband provides to be deprived of it; besides, he is as good to me as any Chinese husband would be—what object in leaving him?"

"If he were to die would you grieve for him, for you then would be free to follow your own inclinations?"

12. Also known as the Chinese Consolidated Benevolent Association, the Chinese Six Companies was formed in 1862 to protect the general interests of the Chinese on the Pacific Coast. It originally consisted of six *huiguan* (united clans of people from the same region or district in China), thus its name Chinese Six Companies.

"Oh, Lun [Seen] Sang, how should I ever cease grieving, for I shall then be a worse slave than ever."

"Perhaps if a No. 1 could be found—the real widow acknowledged by our laws—who wished to appeal to our laws she could gain a point."

"Don't believe it," exclaimed the strong-minded woman emphatically. "Look at Lizzie, the Swedish girl who married our wealthiest lottery man in San Francisco. When he took a Chinese girl for his second wife Lizzie was indignant. 'I'll apply for a divorce and one-half the community property. I was married according to Christian laws,' she cried.[13]

"Lok Chee laughed and snapped his jeweled fingers. 'A fig for your Christian marriage and your Christian laws. Behave yourself and I'll always give you an excellent living, and what no Chinese wife gets, plenty of spending money, even if I take a dozen more wives. But don't act the fool and cut your own throat. We Chinese have to do some things with our enterprises in accordance with Californian laws, but we defy all laws and all your lawyers to find how each company or each individual of a company stands financially. I don't dispute that you would gain your divorce, but as to property, not one cent. The Chinese tribunal would not demand it. The Chinese law knows no such thing as community property between husband and wife.

"'To all intents and purposes you are in China and you are governed by the laws of China. The moment you quit my house you cease to have a mite's interest in my estate, and to leave it once is to leave it forever. I have made this concession to your complexion and prejudices—I allow you to be queen over this little house, which, with its plush-covered furniture and velvet carpets, is a miniature palace, and I promise to bring no other wives to share it with you; and on my death you may do with it and all things I leave you as you please; you need obey no other man. But in all other things I do as I choose, and regulate my life upon my own native social customs. So don't act the fool and cut your throat for the sake of 'community property,' which has no existence amongst our people.'"

"Seen Sang, my husband, provides for me bountifully; he is kind and indulgent with me; he is a good husband. But, oh! I am so weary of being treated as a child."

(SOURCE: *San Francisco Chronicle*, October 1, 1893, p. 2)

---

13. Interracial marriages between whites and the Chinese were outlawed in California from 1880 until 1948. But Lizzie could have married Lok Chee in another state such as Washington, where interracial marriage was legal.

Mary Tape, an Outspoken Woman

"Is It a Disgrace to Be Born a Chinese?"

Although Chinese men did not hesitate to speak up and use the courts and diplomatic channels to fight discrimination whenever possible, few women had the resources—English language facility, finances, and adeptness—to do the same on their own behalf. Mary McGladery Tape was one of the few who did. Brought up in an orphanage in Shanghai, she immigrated to the United States with missionaries at the age of eleven and lived for five years at the Ladies' Relief Society (outside Chinatown), where she learned English. In 1875 she married Joseph Tape, a Chinese American expressman, drayman, and interpreter for the Chinese consulate. According to a newspaper reporter who interviewed her in 1892, Mary Tape spoke refined English, was well informed about current events, and was thoroughly Westernized in dress and lifestyle. She was also a self-taught photographer, painter, and telegraph operator, as well as the proud mother of four musically accomplished children.[1] Interestingly enough, nothing was said in the article about the Tapes' lawsuit against the San Francisco school board (Tape v. Hurley) or the publication of Mary Tape's angry letter in the Alta *newspaper on April 16, 1885, in conjunction with the lawsuit.*

It all started when their eight-year-old daughter Mamie was denied entry into their neighborhood public school because the school authorities believed that "the association of Chinese and white children would

---

1. *Morning Call,* November 23, 1892, p. 12.

WHAT A CHINESE GIRL DID.

An Expert Photographer and Telegrapher.

When I was told the other day that somewhere up in the neighborhood of Washington and Stockton streets there lived a young Chinese woman who devoted most of her spare time to photography I was considerably surprised, and felt prone to believe that my informant was telling me a fairy tale.

He insisted, however, that such was the fact, and if I did not believe it I could go and see for myself.

He further told me that her husband was in business on the corner of Dupont and Stockton streets and that his name was Joseph Tape.

I was still incredulous, but went up to see the head of the family and found him in the place designated.

On being asked if the story was true that his wife understood photography, he answered with a laugh and said in as good English as I ever heard in my life: "Yes, sir, and a good many other things, too."

I asked him if I could meet his wife and see some of her work, and he answered:

"Well, I don't know, but you wait here for a moment and I will telegraph and ask her."

The thought struck me as he started up the street that, being in a business that necessitated a good many calls, he probably had a telephone in his house and intended to ask his wife over that if she cared to receive a visitor.

I found this out afterward to be a mistake and that he really did mean to telegraph her, but as this is only one of the many surprises I received during the day, it can better be told later on.

Tape returned in a few minutes and said: "All right; we can go up."

After the shock of hearing a Chinaman say he would telegraph to his wife, I was prepared to see and hear almost anything on reaching the house, but my surprise was

oldest daughter Mamie is quite proficient on the piano."

I expressed a desire to hear the young lady play and imagine my surprise when without any of the backwardness and diffidence of American girls of the same age she took her seat at the piano and began to finger the keys.

The first few pieces I did not know by name, but she soon began to play the "Mocking-bird" and brought out its notes as well as I have ever heard them brought out by an American girl. Her execution was good and her style graceful.

I was more surprised when her mother informed me that she had only been studying four years.

Before hearing Miss Tape play I had the idea that the Chinese as a rule were about as musical as a bassdrum, but then my opinions had been formed through hearing

THE TAPE FAMILY.

their performances in the Chinese theaters or at some public funeral.

She is only sixteen and gives promise of being an excellent physician, as her playing showed that she was in sympathy with her music and did not play merely in a mechanical way.

The second daughter, Emily, is also studying music, but had not advanced far enough to give any public performance.

She had adopted one American custom, though, which showed her patriotism, and that was dancing.

I wanted to ask her to show how far she had advanced in the art, but she felt somewhat constrained before an utter stranger.

Her brother, however, assured me that she was well up in all American dances, and could trip a measure as well as any other girl.

Frank, the only boy, plays the French horn, and is a member of one of the boys' brigades in the city.

He did not have a chance to let me hear him play, but I think he wanted to, for when I left I heard the sweet strains of the horn coming from the back part of the house.

The baby has not as yet begun her musical education, but I have no doubt when she reaches an age suitable to such work she will be as accomplished as her brothers and sisters.

which gave her the highest award for amateur photography.

No one seeing her pictures could doubt that they deserved a reward, as they were fully up to any work done by Americans here in San Francisco, and were far beyond the usual work of amateurs in any country.

The specimens we give with this article are not some of her best efforts, but were picked out because they were family subjects, the figures being those of her children, taken at various times.

Besides being a first-class photographer Mrs. Tape has another accomplishment, which probably no other Chinese woman in the world possesses, and that is the art of telegraphy.

She can send and receive as well as the best operators, and keeps in constant practice by daily use of the instrument, connected with a line running from the house to some point near her husband's place of business.

"You may think it strange," she said, "that I should be able to use the Morse system, and to tell the truth I have never made any practical use of my knowledge. The way my husband and I learned the use of the instrument was through the kindness of a friend, who had a short line in practice on and wished to have somebody at the other end.

"We took it up more to accommodate him than anything else, and both of us soon became proficient in its use.

"Since then we have found it so useful to communicate with each other during business hours when my husband is away from home that we have a private line between here and his office that we use whenever necessary."

The telegraph instrument is on a table in the dining-room and its least click can be heard in any part of the house. Both of the operators handled it in my presence and were as expert as old-time operators.

I thought that Mrs. Tape had about reached the end of her accomplishments, but her husband pointed to a landscape painting on the wall over the piano and informed me that his wife was the artist, and

"Which Hand Do You Choose?"
[Photographed by Mrs. Tape.]

Portrait of Joseph and Mary Tape reconstructed by Tang You Shan from an 1892 wood-cut for *Chinese American Portraits: Personal Histories, 1828–1988* by Ruthanne Lum Mc-Cunn. (Courtesy of Ruthanne Lum McCunn)

be very demoralizing mentally and morally to the latter."[2] *The Tapes promptly took legal action against the board of education. The superior court judge ruled in their favor, basing his decision on the Fourteenth Amendment and California legislation that all children, regardless of race, had the right to a public school education. The school board appealed, but the ruling was upheld in the California Supreme Court. Yet when Mamie Tape, accompanied by two attorneys, reported to the Spring Valley School for class, the principal, Jennie Hurley, refused to admit her on two counts: Mamie did not have a vaccination certificate required by the board of education and the classes were already oversubscribed. Mamie was put on a waiting list while School Superintendent Jackson Moulder hurriedly pushed through an amendment to the school code, establishing a separate school for Chinese children. According to the new bill,*

2. Quoted in Victor Low, *The Unimpressible Race: A Century of Educational Struggle by the Chinese in San Francisco* (San Francisco: East/West Publishing Company, 1982), p. 66.

"When such separate schools are established Chinese or Mongolian children must not be admitted into any other schools."[3]

Seething with anger, Mary Tape drafted the following letter to the board of education, which was read to the board on April 15, 1885, and published in the Alta *the next day. I have followed the newspaper's example of printing the letter as is with all its grammatical and spelling errors intact. This is not to embarrass the writer but to show that despite her imperfect English, Mary Tape had the courage to speak her mind, to chide the school authorities for being racists and hypocrites in no uncertain terms. She obviously believed in the American democratic process and she was determined to see justice done.*

A LETTER FROM MRS. TAPE

The following is a verbatim copy of a letter received from Mrs. Tape, in regard to her children at present attending the Chinese school:

1769 GREEN STREET,

SAN FRANCISCO, April 8, 1885.

To the Board of Education—DEAR SIRS: I see that you are going to make all sorts of excuses to keep my child out off the Public schools. Dear sirs, Will you please to tell me! Is it a disgrace to be Born a Chinese? Didn't God make us all!!! What right have you to bar my children out of the school because she is a chinese Decend. They is no other worldly reason that you could keep her out, except that. I suppose, you all goes to churches on Sundays! Do you call that a Christian act to compel my little children to go so far to a school that is made in purpose for them. My children don't dress like the other Chinese. They look just as phunny amongst them as the Chinese dress in Chinese look amongst you Caucasians. Besides, if I had any wish to send them to a chinese school I could have sent them two years ago without going to all this trouble. You have expended a lot of the Public money foolishly, all because of a one poor little Child. Her playmates is all Caucasians ever since she could toddle around. If she is good enough to play with them! Then is she not good enough to be in the same room and studie with them? You had better come and see for yourselves. See if the Tape's is not same as other Cau-

---

3. Ibid., p. 67.

casians, except in features. It seems no matter how a Chinese may live and dress so long as you know they Chinese. Then they are hated as one. There is not any right or justice for them.

You have seen my husband and child. You told him it wasn't Mamie Tape you object to. If it were not Mamie Tape you object to, then why didn't you let her attend the school nearest her home! Instead of first making one pretense Then another pretense of some kind to keep her out? It seems to me Mr. Moulder has a grudge against this Eight-year-old Mamie Tape. I know they is no other child I mean Chinese child! care to go to your public Chinese school. May you Mr. Moulder, never be persecuted like the way you have persecuted little Mamie Tape. Mamie Tape will never attend any of the Chinese schools of your making! Never!!! I will let the world see sir What justice there is When it is govern by the Race prejudice men! Just because she is of the Chinese decend, not because she don't dress like you because she does. Just because she is decended of Chinese parents I guess she is more of a American then a good many of you that is going to prewent her being Educated. MRS. M. TAPE.

(SOURCE: *Alta*, April 16, 1885, p. 1)

The Chinese Primary School, located on the outskirts of Chinatown, officially opened its doors on April 13, 1885, and Mamie Tape and her brother Frank were among the first to enroll despite what Mary Tape had said in the letter. Only 9 out of 561 Chinese children went to the school during the first year. However, as enrollment increased in subsequent years and students went beyond the eighth grade, Chinese children were finally allowed to attend integrated secondary schools in the 1920s. It was not until 1954 that the U.S. Supreme Court ruled against school segregation in Brown v. Board of Education. In retrospect, had Mary and Joseph Tape not taken legal action, Chinese children would have been denied a public school education for decades more.

It should be pointed out that as an outspoken woman able to stand up for her rights, Mary Tape was a rarity among her peers—the prostitutes, mui tsai, and immigrant wives described earlier. Fortunate to have had an education, a liberal upbringing, financial resources, and a supportive husband, she shines as an early example of an emancipated Chinese American woman and as an antithesis of the Chinese saying "A woman without talent is virtuous."

PART THREE

Unbound Feet

Chinese Immigrant Women, 1902–1929

Although there was a precipitous drop in the immigration of Chinese women to the United States following the passage of the Chinese Exclusion Act of 1882, the situation began to change after 1900 as more and more women, wanting to join their husbands or to pursue educational and employment opportunities, found ways to circumvent the act. Most entered the country as merchant wives, the class most favored by immigration legislation. Before the passage of the Immigration Act of 1924, many also came as wives of U.S. citizens, and after that law barred their entry, there was a significant increase in the category of daughters of U.S. citizens. A small number were also able to come as students, one of the other classes exempted from exclusion. Between 1900 and 1930, the population of Chinese females in San Francisco doubled, from 2,136 to 4,270, while the number of Chinese males held steady at about 12,000.

Compared to their predecessors in the nineteenth century, most Chinese women arriving in Gold Mountain during this period found immigration a liberating experience. Although they still suffered economic hardships and difficult adjustments to life in America, they were encouraged to unbind their feet and their socially restricted lives. Chinese women began working outside the home, getting an education, and participating in community activities. This change in women's fortunes had less to do with the women's suffrage movement in the United States than with the sociocultural upheavals occurring in China and San Francisco Chinatown at the time. In order to throw off the yoke of foreign domination and have China develop into a modern nation-state, reformers and revolutionaries alike were advocating social, economic, and political changes for their country along the lines of the Western model. Elevating the status of women so that they could contribute to the remaking of China was an integral part of the national plan. The campaign included education and equal rights for women and an end to footbinding, female slavery, and polygyny—reforms that Protestant missionaries in China also advocated.

What happened to women in China had a direct impact on Chinese women in the United States. Beginning in the early twentieth century, not only were new immigrants bringing a different set of cultural values with them in regard to gender roles, but Chinese immigrants who had been barred from participation in mainstream American society were also becoming engaged by the political developments in China. Aware that the racial oppression and humiliation they suffered in the United States was due in part to China's weak international status and inability to protect its citizens abroad, Chinese immigrants kept nationalist sentiment alive, focusing their energies on helping China become a modern nation-state even as they worked to change their unfavorable image and treatment in America. As reported in the San Francisco newspapers, Chinese women were becoming "new women" in the homeland, and Chinese women in America were encouraged to do likewise.

From the many editorials, speeches, articles, and poems advocating this point of view in *Chung Sai Yat Po* (*Chinese Daily*), a progressive newspaper founded by Rev. Ng Poon Chew, I have selected three pieces by Chinese women for inclusion in this section. The first is a speech delivered in 1902 by Sieh King King (Xue Jinqin), a student and reformer from China, to a full house at a Chinatown theater. As far as I can tell, Sieh was the first Chinese woman to introduce ideas of women's emancipation as a necessary precursor to national liberation in San Francisco Chinatown. One newspaper reporter noted that her revolutionary ideas and delivery created shock waves in the community and brought about immediate results. That evening women were allowed for the first time to sit in the main dining hall at a banquet held in Sieh's honor and enjoy the same food as the men.

The second selection is a speech by Mai Zhouyi on the importance of education for Chinese women, given at the Presbyterian Church in Chinatown in 1903. Mai, an educator, journalist, and missionary worker, was trying to join her husband in New York, but because of immigration complications she was detained at the Pacific Mail Steamship Company's shed at the San Francisco wharf for over a month. Incensed by this humiliating experience, she seized the opportunity to protest the mistreatment as well as to speak up for women's education and the human rights of all Chinese immigrants.

Echoing the nationalist and feminist sentiments of Sieh King King and Mai Zhouyi is the third selection, "No More Footbinding," an anonymous song of twenty-four stanzas that was published in the literary section of *Chung Sai Yat Po* in 1909, at the height of the anti-footbinding movement in China. It was but one of many diatribes aimed at "barbaric" Chinese customs that filled the newspaper until legislation passed by the new Chinese republic began to put a stop to all such practices. Like the first two selections, "No More Footbinding" reflects the reformist views that were beginning to take hold in China and San Francisco Chinatown after the turn of the century.

Arriving in the early twentieth century, Chinese women such as Wong Ah So, Law Shee Low, and Jane Kwong Lee, whose life stories follow, found unprecedented opportunities to become "new women." Born around the turn of the century in the same area of Guangdong Province, all three women immigrated to America in 1922. Wong Ah So and Law Shee Low came as obedient wives from sheltered and impoverished families, while Jane Kwong Lee immigrated as a student after graduating from a missionary school in Canton. Wong Ah So's start in this country was not altogether unusual: she was sold into prostitution but, with the help of Donaldina Cameron, was able to start life anew married to a Chinese merchant in Boise, Idaho. Law Shee Low found life in America unexpectedly full of struggles and hardships, but she managed, with the help of her husband, to raise eight children and takes great pride in that accomplishment. With the help of relatives and a scholarship from Mills College, Jane Kwong Lee earned a master's degree in sociology. Instead of returning to China to teach as she had planned, however, she ended up marrying, raising two children, and finding great satisfaction in her job as a community worker in Chinatown. All three immigrant women were able to improve their economic situation and find fulfillment in their lives in America, owing to their own hard work and strength of character to be sure, but also to the changing socioeconomic landscape that conditioned their lives.

The beginning of the twentieth century was marked by the Progressive Era, a time when women were entering the public arena to effect social and moral reform. Protestant missionary women played a major role in Chinatown by providing a safe refuge for abused women, educating girls and women, and encouraging their participation in organized activities outside the home. It was thanks to their initiative that the Chinese YWCA was founded in 1916. The earliest social service organization to be established by and for Chinese women in San Francisco, the YWCA provided women with English classes and translation services, helped with immigration, employment, and domestic problems, and was a springboard to social and political activism. Jane Kwong Lee directed its programs from 1933 to 1944, doing much to influence the changing status and role of Chinese women. Her autobiography, excerpted in this section, provides a telling look at the new opportunities for women in Chinatown during these years.

Chinese women also took the initiative to start their own organization. In 1913 a group of Chinese women from San Francisco and Oakland got together to form the Chinese Women's Jeleab [Self-Reliance] Association for social intercourse, education, and mutual assistance. The organization was unique in that it was not affiliated with a church or nationalist cause. Although short-lived, its membership was at one point two hundred-strong and consisted of both immigrant and American-born women. As indicated by the organization's statement of purpose, which concludes this section, the Jeleab Association, following the example of progressive women in America, expanded on Sieh King King's point of view, advocating self-reliance and collective effort as a way to attain women's equality. As such, the organization represented a giant step forward in the overall process of social change for Chinese women in America.

Sieh King King, China's Joan of Arc

"Men and Women Are Equal and Should Enjoy the Privileges of Equals"

On November 3, 1902, Sieh King King (Xue Jinqin), an eighteen-year-old student from China and an ardent supporter of the Baohuanghui,[1] made Chinese women's history when she stood before a Chinatown theater full of men and women and "boldly condemned the slave girl system, raged at the horrors of foot-binding and, with all the vehemence of aroused youth, declared that men and women were equal and should enjoy the privileges of equals."[2] Her talk and her views on women's rights were inextricably linked with Chinese nationalism and the 1898 Reform Movement, which advocated that China emulate the West and modernize in order to throw off the yoke of foreign domination. Modernization included elevating the status of women to the extent that they could become "new women"—educated mothers and productive citizens capable of contributing to the building of a stronger China.

Sieh King King's speech, covered in both the English- and Chinese-language newspapers, caused a sensation because it was the first time that such feminist ideas, already prevalent in China, had been introduced in San Francisco Chinatown and by a Chinese woman. As noted by the

---

1. The Baohuanghui (Protect the Emperor Society) was a reform party that advocated restoring the deposed Ming emperor and establishing a constitutional monarchy in China.

2. "Leads Her Sisters Out of Bondage: Chinese Woman Begins a Crusade against Social Conditions in Her Country," *San Francisco Chronicle*, November 3, 1902, p. 7.

LEADS HER SISTERS OUT OF BONDAGE

Sieh King King, China's First Woman Reformer.

Chinese Woman Begins a Crusade Against Social Conditions in Her Country.

Sieh King King's landmark speech as reported in the *San Francisco Chronicle*, November 3, 1902.

San Francisco Chronicle *reporter, both men and women "listened like zealots . . . with every sign of approval."*[3] *Although young, petite, and female, Sieh King King was taken seriously because she had already developed a reputation as China's Joan of Arc before coming to the United States, where she hoped to further her education.* According to Chung Sai Yat Po, *her fame as a patriot and orator was established in 1901 when she delivered a stirring speech before five hundred people in Shanghai, protesting the Chinese government's intention to grant Russia special rights in Manchuria after the Boxer Rebellion failed.*[4]

Newspaper reporters attributed her progressive views to her family and educational background. A daughter of a liberal-minded merchant from Heungshan (Xiangshan) District in Guangdong Province, Sieh King King attended missionary schools in Shanghai and Tientsin (Tianjin), where she was heavily influenced by Western ideas. Upon arrival in San Francisco she immediately caused a stir when she went out "for a spin in the park" in the company of Chinese gentlemen without a female chaperone.[5] *The same newspaper article also reported that Sieh insisted that Chinese women be invited to a banquet to be held in her honor and that they be allowed to sit in the main dining hall with the men. Her plans were to return to China after six years of advanced schooling in America and advocate for women's education.*

Unfortunately, Sieh King King's rousing speech that afternoon was never fully recorded. We do, however, have two abbreviated versions of her speech, published in Chung Sai Yat Po *and the* San Francisco Examiner, *respectively. Both versions emphasized the ongoing reformist line of thinking that linked Chinese nationalism with women's emancipation. China could not be saved, it was believed, as long as half its population was subjected to the crippling practice of footbinding and kept ignorant and unproductive. Both articles are included here in their entirety for purposes of comparison. While* Chung Sai Yat Po *was faithful in describing the form and substance of Sieh King King's speech, including her polite style of speaking, the* Examiner *was more straightforward, noting only the composition of the audience. Neither reporter*

---

3. Ibid.

4. *Chung Sai Yat Po*, August 31, 1901, October 23, 1902, and January 21, 1903. The Boxer Rebellion (1900) was an antiforeign, anti-Christian uprising led by a secret society whose members believed that they were immune to bullets.

5. "Chinese Joan Urges Reform: Sieh King King of Shanghai to Lecture on Broader Life for Countrywomen," *San Francisco Examiner*, November 2, 1902, p. 41.

was as embellishing as the Chronicle *writer quoted above. In that Sieh King King's speech was delivered in Chinese, the first article printed below, from* Chung Sai Yat Po, *was probably more accurate than the second one, from the* Examiner.

SPEECH BY MS. SIEH KING KING

At the invitation of the membership of the Baohuanghui of San Francisco, Ms. Sieh King King was scheduled to speak at noon on November 3 at the Dangui (Red Cassia) Theater. An audience of several thousand men and women gathered there early to hear her speak. When Ms. Sieh had not arrived by 12:15 P.M., Mr. Xie Kuangshi of the Baohuanghui stood up and addressed the audience, regaling them with accounts of the accomplishments and virtues of women from the past. Finally, at 12:45 P.M., Ms. Sieh appeared on stage, accompanied by Ms. Liu Yonglian of San Francisco, and was greeted with warm applause from the audience. After she had sat down and sipped some tea, Ms. Sieh got up, bowed to the audience, and began to speak.

"The purpose of my trip to America is to study, not to make speeches. Since members of the Baohuanghui have been kind enough to overlook my ignorance and ask me to speak about current affairs, I find it difficult to refuse them, so I will try my best to satisfy their request. But the problem is that being of the weaker sex and young in years, I lack knowledge and experience. I know very little about the state of the world or the situation between the East and the West. I have nothing worthwhile to say and hardly know where to begin. However, since I am Chinese, they have asked me to speak about China.

"Today's China is extremely debilitated. If one traces its cause, one finds it in the crushing oppression suffered by women there. Women, on their part, have also given up and neglected their responsibilities. This is why the country is in such a weakened state. Of all that women have to endure, none is worse than having their feet bound. Not only does it make walking and working difficult for them, but it also breaks their spirits. As such, the body serves no purpose. And since women have absolutely no learning, how can one expect them to help the country prosper and the family thrive?

"If we want women to fulfill their duties, we must educate them. It is imperative that schools for women be established all over the country so that all twenty million women in China can acquire reasoning and practice professions, thus allowing them to move forward on a complementary footing with men. If we can accomplish that, then it would be impossible for our families not to thrive and our country not to be strong.

"I am presently in America to observe and study women's education in the West in order to gain some insights, so that when I return to China I can do my part in advancing the education of women. I hope that every one of you will also do your part and contribute your wisdom and efforts to help revitalize China. Wouldn't that be a most happy venture?

"I beg your indulgence for my foolish ramblings and welcome your suggestions and criticisms."

At the conclusion of her speech, Ms. Sieh walked to the front of the stage, bowed, and then returned to her seat. Because the crowd was large and noisy, it was difficult to hear her, so I could only record her main ideas. After the speech, Messrs. Wang Jianzu, Cheng Xingnan, Tan Bokui, and Xie Xingchou also took turns addressing the audience until 1:45 P.M.

(SOURCE: *Chung Sai Yat Po*, November 3, 1902. TRANSLATOR: Ellen Yeung.)

SIEH KING KING TALKS ON THE POLITICAL CONDITION OF HER COUNTRY

Sieh King King, the Chinese new woman, appeared at the old Washington-street Theatre yesterday morning, under the auspices of the Chinese reform movement, and gave a short discourse on the principles advocated by that society. The gallery of the theatre was reserved for those of her sex, while the lower floor was crowded with Chinese and some Caucasians, all eager to hear and see this far-famed Oriental.

Sieh King King chose as the subject of her discourse, "The Political Conditions of China," and said in part:

"The political condition of China is dangerous in extreme. There is oppression from within and from without, for the government and from foreign nations in all directions. It is high time that the men, and also the women, for the women are a part of the nation, exercised themselves and saved their country. To accomplish this end education is the prime factor. To do this systematically and procure the quickest results we must begin with the youth and educate the boy and girl equally. In China the girls are generally ignorant, but it is not their fault. Their parents do not teach them, but when they are yet in tender years their feet are bound and they undergo a life of seclusion. Both these exigencies weaken their health, they become timid, and also have no opportunity for personal observation or education. These are bad customs and should be reformed. To effectually carry out this crusade against injustice to our sex and to save our country we must lay aside all these traditional customs and become modernized. I urge all my countrymen and women to act as one of our great statesmen said, 'to try our best and do out utmost until our energies are exhausted.'"

In an interview Sieh King King said: "I did not come to your country to talk on this subject, but am here to further my education. I shall reside with my uncle in Berkeley and attend the university there. I attended the convent of Shanghai one term and also the Jesus College there one term before coming to this country."

(SOURCE: *San Francisco Examiner*, November 3, 1902, p. 7)

After this speech, Sieh King King was mentioned in the San Francisco newspapers two more times. Charles K. Moser did a full-page story about her in the Chronicle *on March 1, 1903, reiterating her background history and political goals and describing the difficulties she was facing as a student at the University of California, Berkeley. Because of her limited English she had secured the services of an interpreter and had moved in with a white American family. Her plans, she told Moser, was to study American life thoroughly and return to China to teach her people "the true, natural philosophy of living instead of sleeping—of progress instead of stagnation." She added, "China doesn't need missionaries, but she needs teachers of commerce, of industry and liberal thought."*[6] *Later that year Sieh King King gave another "eloquent and inspiring speech," this time to an exclusively female audience of two hundred, at the Dangui Theater in Chinatown, in which she again "expounded her views on the role of Chinese women and the need to abolish outdated Chinese customs and emulate the West."*[7] *After that she was not mentioned again in*

---

6. Charles K. Moser, "China's Joan of Arc," *San Francisco Chronicle*, March 1, 1903, p. 2.

7. *Chung Sai Yat Po*, October 12, 1903.

the local English- or Chinese-language newspapers.[8] *But what she advocated on behalf of Chinese women—unbound feet, education, equal rights, and public participation—would remain at the heart of social change for Chinese women for the next three decades.*

---

8. According to Louise Leung Larson's autobiography, *Sweet Bamboo: Saga of a Chinese American Family* (Los Angeles: Chinese Historical Society of Southern California, 1989), pp. 51–52, Sieh King King left San Francisco and went to Los Angeles in 1905 to stay with the family of Tom Leung, an active Baohuanghui member. She was allegedly involved in a plot to assassinate the Empress Dowager and restore Emperor Guangxu to the throne. She spent three years there helping to take care of the children while attending Los Angeles High School. In 1908 both the Empress Dowager and Emperor Guangxu died before the assassination plans could be realized. According to Larson, Sieh King King went on to graduate from the University of Chicago, marry a fellow student, and return to China, where her husband started a chain of banks.

Madame Mai's Speech

"How Can It Be That They Look upon Us as Animals"

Mai Zhouyi, a merchant's wife and a teacher from Canton, shared a similar background and point of view with Sieh King King and Mary Tape. All three women were educated by missionary teachers, influenced by Western thinking, financially secure, and known for speaking their minds. In addition, Mai shared Sieh's skills as an orator and was equally committed to promoting women's education as a way of strengthening China. Prior to immigrating to the United States, she was a teacher at Peidao Girls' High School, editor of the Lingnan Women's Journal, *and a missionary worker.*[1]

In April 1903 Mai Zhouyi immigrated to the United States to join her husband Loo Lin (a.k.a. Lu Zhinang), a New York restaurateur and partner in two other business firms. After a stormy journey across the Pacific she arrived in San Francisco to find that she could not be landed as a merchant's wife because her husband, owning a restaurant, was considered a laborer according to the McCreary Amendment of 1893.[2] *Along*

---

1. *Chung Sai Yat Po*, May 22, 1903.
2. Congress passed the McCreary Amendment in 1893 hoping to curb the fraudulent use of the merchant exemption. The amendment defined a merchant as "a person engaged in buying and selling merchandise, at a fixed place of business, which business is conducted in his name" (28 Stat. 7, sec. 2). The New York immigration official who ruled on Loo Lin's case chose to stick to this definition and declared him a laborer for owning a restaurant even though he was engaged in other business ventures and the main floor

with other Chinese arrivals at this time, she was detained in the ware-house of the Pacific Mail Steamship Company, a two-story shed at the San Francisco wharf, to await clearance for admittance into the country. According to Chung Sai Yat Po, *Mai was held for over forty days while her attorneys took her case to the federal courts in Washington, D.C. During that time she started a school for other women detainees and complained about the filthy, depressing, and humanly uninhabitable conditions of the wooden shed to newspaper reporters. At one point she became so sick that she had to be seen by a woman physician. "I feel like a criminal who will never be called to trial or sentenced," she told a* Chung Sai Yat Po *reporter.[3] Because of her illness, she was finally released on bond and instructed to go to Canada to await a teacher's visa from China that would admit her into the United States. Prior to leaving for Canada, she agreed to speak at the Presbyterian Church in Chinatown on the topics of missionary prospects in Canton and the education of Chinese women.[4]*

The following speech, which Mai delivered to a mixed audience of some 1,500 Chinese and whites, men and women, on June 8, 1903, and which was published in Chung Sai Yat Po *two days later, focused on two subjects—women's education and the ordeal of detainment. In arguing on behalf of women's education and rights, Mai Zhouyi followed reformer Sieh King King's line of reasoning: educated women make better mothers; better mothers make better citizens; better citizens make a stronger China.[5] Whereas Sieh did not see Christianity as part of the solution, Mai did. "Reverence for Jehovah is the root of wisdom," she said. Like Sieh and other feminist thinkers, Mai advocated that China should learn from the example of Western countries but not to the extent of putting individual needs above the collective good. It was a matter not of working against men to improve women's lot but of working with them to improve China's standing. "We must remain patriotic," she told her sisters in the audience.*

---

of his building was devoted to selling Chinese goods, with his restaurant occupying a secondary position on the floor above (*San Francisco Call*, May 24, 1903, p. 29).

3. *Chung Sai Yat Po*, May 22, 1903.

4. *Chung Sai Yat Po*, May 22, 25, 29 and June 2, 8, 1903.

5. These sentiments appeared repeatedly in *Chung Sai Yat Po* between 1900 and 1912. See Judy Yung, "The Social Awakening of Chinese American Women as Reported in *Chung Sai Yat Po*, 1900–1911," in *Unequal Sisters: A Multicultural Reader in U.S. Women's History*, ed. Ellen Carol DuBois and Vicki L. Ruiz (New York: Routledge, 1990), pp. 195–207.

Mai Zhouyi's speech offers us one of the few public indictments we have of discriminatory treatment against Chinese immigrants who were detained in the Pacific Mail Steamship shed prior to the opening of the Angel Island Immigration Station in 1910. Although it was known that the accommodations stank from the odors of sewage at the wharf, was dark, overcrowded, unsanitary, and a firetrap, this was not what Mai chose to complain about.[6] What irked her most was the low regard given to Chinese arrivals compared to Europeans, Japanese, Koreans, and Blacks. In her eyes, even the animals and cargo were treated better, leading her to exclaim, "Are we Chinese not made of flesh and blood? Do we not have souls?"

Like Mary Tape, Mai Zhouyi had a mind of her own and was not one to keep her opinions and feelings quiet. When she overheard two inmates protesting their mistreatment, she did not hesitate to chime in with her point of view on the matter. In an earlier article published in Chung Sai Yat Po *on May 23, 1903, she expressed her determination to pursue all legal channels to adjudicate her right to enter this country. "The outcome of this case doesn't affect just me," she pointed out, "but all Chinese men and women coming to the United States in the future." The* San Francisco Call *concurred: "Unless the findings of the New York customs office in the case of Mrs. Loo Lin [are] reversed by the Treasury Department, the legal status of practically every Chinese merchant in America will be affected."[7] As the reporter noted about her speech, Mai's presentation was clear, passionate, and inspiring. According to another source, "the story of her sufferings caused tears to spring to the eyes of the usually stolid sons of Han, and . . . [white Americans] expressed themselves shocked that such conditions could exist in a civilized country."[8] Mai Zhouyi is an example of an emancipated woman who was*

---

6. After repeated complaints from Chinese community leaders and missionary workers about the unsafe and unsanitary conditions of the detention shed, Immigration Commissioner General F. P. Sargent inspected the facility himself on November 18, 1902, and was forced to agree. Upon his recommendation, funds were appropriated to build a new immigration station at Angel Island to accommodate Chinese and other aliens coming from Asian countries. See Mary Roberts Coolidge, *Chinese Immigration* (New York: Henry Holt, 1909), pp. 299–300; H. M. Lai, "Island of Immortals: Chinese Immigrants and the Angel Island Immigration Station," *California History* (spring 1978): 90; and Lucy E. Salyer, *Laws Harsh as Tigers: Chinese Immigrants and the Shaping of Modern Immigration Law* (Chapel Hill: University of North Carolina Press, 1995), p. 63.

7. "Affects Status of Rich Chinese," *San Francisco Call*, May 24, 1903, p. 29.

8. Jean White, "The Woman's Hour in China," *Forum* 57 (April 1917): 426–27.

able to speak up not only for her own rights but for the rights of her countrymen and women.

"Sisters, don't say that educating women serves no purpose for home and country. Look for the cause of prosperity in all the Western countries and you will find it in their pool of talented people. Talented people come from learning; learning comes from teaching; and teaching begins at childhood. What we see and hear when we are young remains imprinted in our memory and is not easily forgotten. Therefore, in order to properly educate our young, we must look to our mothers, for they are the ones whom the children cluster around the whole day, while the fathers spend most of their time away from home. If the mothers are uneducated and just allow their children to indulge themselves in idle play, the children's formative years will be wasted and their future will be adversely affected. However, if the women of today will make the effort to learn and understand their duty to the country, then when the time comes they will be able to educate their children, from whose ranks talented people will surely come. Why worry, then, that our country will not be prosperous and strong someday? Right here and now I dare say this: The key to a country's prosperity lies in its women's propensity for learning.

"It may be difficult to find a good school for girls, but if female students are steadfast in their pursuit of knowledge, they will excel and surpass even their teachers. My sisters, we must keep love of country in our hearts. Don't let the weakness of China and the strength of another country turn away your patriotism and discourage you from learning. As they say, good or bad, it is still our country. Since we know our country is weak, we should seek the cause of its weakness. If another country is strong, we should search out the reason for its strength. There are four hundred million of us men and women in China. If we all do our best for our country, though weak at present, China will someday become strong.

"Since landing here, I have spent forty-odd days in the wooden house. All day long I faced the walls and did nothing except eat and sleep like a caged animal. I saw five Chinese ships arrive one after another. Others—Europeans, Japanese, Koreans—were allowed to disembark almost immediately. Even the lowly Black people were greeted by relatives and allowed to go ashore.[9] Only we Chinese were not allowed to see or talk

---

9. It is ironic that Mai Zhouyi can, on the one hand, argue eloquently on behalf of human rights and, on the other hand, denigrate Blacks.

to our loved ones. In low spirits, we waited for the customs officials to collect our papers and interrogate us. After a few days, we were herded into a cart and escorted by armed guards to the wooden house. From then on, we could no longer set our eyes on our friends and relatives. Frustrated, we could only sigh and groan. Even the cargo was picked up from the docks and delivered to its destination after customs duties were paid. Only we Chinese were denied that right. How can it be that they look upon us as animals? As less than cargo? Do they think we Chinese are not made of flesh and blood? That we don't have souls? Human beings are supposed to be the superior among all creatures. Should we allow ourselves to be treated like cargo and dumb animals? If someone as ignorant as I refuse to be regarded as such, one can imagine how you, my brothers and sisters sitting in this audience, would feel.

"They said that the passport I used to come to the United States was not in order. Who knows how many people have been subjected to this kind of capricious harassment? Why then do we Chinese come to this country? All because our country is weak. While in the wooden shed, I heard someone who was angry say that should China become strong someday, he would kill all white people to get even. Then I heard someone who was more moderate say that if China should become strong and prosperous, he would make the Americans pay for this day by treating them as harshly as they had treated us. I, of course, also expressed my feelings. What I would do is quite different. If China should become strong one day, I would have a big stone tablet erected at each trading port to commemorate how America kept us in captivity. But I would have 'Please enter' carved on it to show the world that in spite of the unkind treatment accorded us by the Americans, we Chinese would treat others more generously. Such a response would be far superior to killing or retaliating in kind.

"There is a saying, 'Wisdom is the root cause of a country's prosperity.' If we want China to prosper, we must first seek wisdom. The Bible says, 'Fear Jehovah, for that is the root of all wisdom.' My brothers and sisters, fear and respect God and we will attain wisdom. If we want others not to ridicule us, we must not give them cause to laugh at us. Men should not be too self-aggrandizing and women should not be too self-depreciating. We are all wise in our own ways and if we all discharged our responsibilities, China will naturally become strong.

"At present, women in China are beginning to become educated and more aware of their obligations to their country. Some of the prominent women like Zhang Zhujun and Du Qingchi are teaching their students about patriotism.[10] Those who study under them are growing in numbers. This is evidence that Chinese women are catching up with the modern world. My dear sisters, we must take heart. We are human beings, not to be compared to animals or goods. We must work together so that we can stand in equality and liberty. This, then, is my fondest hope."

All the men and women in the audience applauded these noble sentiments. Madame Mai's speech, which lasted over an hour, was clear, passionate, and inspiring. The audience would have loved to hear more from her but Madame Mai was scheduled to go to Victoria by boat that afternoon.[11] Due to the trip she could not stay longer and took her leave.

(SOURCE: *Chung Sai Yat Po*, June 10, 1903, pp. 1–2. TRANSLATOR: Ellen Yeung.)

---

10. Zhang Zhujun and Du Qingchi were both strong advocates of Chinese women's emancipation through education. Although neither of them ever made a trip to the United States, their writings and speeches on women's rights were published in *Chung Sai Yat Po* (October 25, 1902; June 8, 9, 10, 11, 1904; and July 27, 1904).

11. From Victoria, Mai Zhouyi was scheduled to go on to Vancouver and then by train to Montreal (*Chung Sai Yat Po*, June 10, 1903). According to the *New York Times*, September 22, 1903, p. 1, she was finally admitted into the United States as a schoolteacher.

No More Footbinding

ANONYMOUS

Inspired by palace dancers in the tenth century, footbinding was widely practiced in China for close to one thousand years until it was denounced by reformers and missionaries and outlawed after the 1911 Revolution. The practice involved tightly wrapping the feet of young girls with bandages until the four toes were permanently bent under in the direction of the sole and the whole foot compressed to a few inches in length. Despite the excruciating pain that it caused, mothers continued to subject their daughters to this crippling custom because bound feet were considered an asset in the marriage market, a sign of gentility and beauty. Indeed, women took pride in their small feet. From the male perspective, bound feet were sexually appealing: the smaller the foot, the more alluring the woman. The practice also served to keep "proper" women immobile and dependent, cloistered and chaste. However, it did not always ensure a life of leisure. There were known cases of women with bound feet who did heavy labor within the home or out in the fields.

Throughout the centuries male liberal thinkers were the chief opponents of the practice, beginning with Che Ruoshui in the Song dynasty (960–1276), who asked, "What is the use of binding and restraining [the feet in this way]?"[1] In the eighteenth century Yuan Mei, Yu Zhengxie, and Li Ruzhen, all of whom supported greater freedom for women, openly de-

---

1. Quoted in Howard S. Levy, *Chinese Footbinding: The History of a Curious Erotic Custom* (New York: Walton Rawls, 1966), p. 65.

nounced sexist practices such as footbinding and the double standards of chastity. The Manchus, who ruled China during the Qing dynasty (1644–1911), did not believe in footbinding and issued numerous prohibitions banning it, but to no avail. The Taiping rebels, who sought to free China of Manchu rule, also tried unsuccessfully to abolish footbinding in an effort to treat women as equals and encourage them to join them in battle. But it was not until foreign missionaries gained a foothold in China after the Opium War that bound feet came to symbolize the oppressed state of Chinese women and the decadence of old China. Reformer Kang Youwei shared the missionaries' point of view. "Foreigners laugh at us . . . and criticize us for being barbarians," he wrote to the Qing emperor in 1898 in "A Memorial Requesting a Ban on the Binding of Women's Feet." "There is nothing which makes us objects of ridicule so much as footbinding."[2]

Given its reformist and Christian perspectives, it is not surprising that Chung Sai Yat Po *took the lead in condemning footbinding in America, where a small number of women still followed the practice.[3] Echoing arguments circulating in China at this time, front-page editorials urged an end to footbinding for the following reasons: it was a barbaric custom, detrimental to a woman's health, unnatural, caused unnecessary pain and suffering, and prevented women from contributing to the Chinese nationalist cause. One editorial specifically urged Chinese women in America to discontinue the practice, asking, "How can men treat their wives with such contempt? How can women treat their bodies with such contempt?" Three reasons were given as to why women overseas would choose to have bound feet: the parents were obstinate and at fault; husbands prized and encouraged its practice; and women in general were still uneducated and unenlightened. Its eradication, the editorial concluded, depended on family upbringing and formal schooling for girls.[4] Articles also compared the practice of footbinding to the wearing of corsets, reminding readers that sexist fashions were not confined to the East. In one such article, a physician was quoted as saying that both practices were barbaric: they hindered a woman's freedom of movement and were equally harmful to her health. In an editorial note at the end of the article, the reporter commented,*

---

2. Ibid., p. 72.

3. Only merchant wives who immigrated before the 1911 Revolution had bound feet. For a discussion of *Chung Sai Yat Po*'s stance on footbinding, see Judy Yung, "The Social Awakening of Chinese American Women as Reported in *Chung Sai Yat Po*, 1900–1911," in *Unequal Sisters: A Multicultural Reader in U.S. Women's History*, ed. Ellen Carol DuBois and Vicki L. Ruiz (New York: Routledge, 1990), pp. 195–207.

4. *Chung Sai Yat Po*, December 9, 1907.

"Once the Natural Feet Society succeeds in releasing our women from suffering, I suspect the practice of wearing corsets will also decline."[5]

In 1907 a literature section consisting of poetry, essays, historical biographies, and short stories was added to Chung Sai Yat Po. *The following anonymous song, "No More Footbinding," appeared in that section in 1908. I suspect by some of the references to "ourselves" and its refined literary form that it was written by a highly literate woman. The original Chinese version was written in the* bailan *(literally, "plain olive") style of Cantonese opera with the cadence and rhyme scheme of 3-3-5. Like modern rap, the song was intended to be chanted against the background beating of a block of wood in the shape of an olive with no other musical accompaniment, thus the term* bailan. *Because of its popular form and the reformist arguments against footbinding that it employs, the song was probably written by someone involved in the anti-footbinding movement.*[6] *One thing for sure is that it was written soon after the death of Emperor Guangxu and the Empress Dowager in 1908, because the new emperor, Xuantong, was credited in the song for issuing and enforcing a decree against footbinding. However, this celebratory note was premature, for it was not until after the Republic of China was established in 1911 that the formal abolishment of footbinding began to take effect. Following the example of women in China, Chinese women in America also began to unbind their feet (a process that was just as painful as having them bound) and to stop binding their daughters' feet. By the 1920s, the only trace of footbinding that remained in America was the unnaturally small feet of older women encased in specially made leather shoes.*

A girl's feet, yes, a daughter's feet—
A natural part of the body.
Be he a son, be she a daughter—
All born from the same mother.

---

5. *Chung Sai Yat Po,* August 13, 1909. The Natural Feet Society was established in Shanghai in 1895 by a group of European missionary women. Branches of the society sprang up throughout China, reaching thousands of people through its mass meetings and publication of songs and tracts. Members vowed not to bind the feet of their daughters or to allow their sons to marry women with bound feet.

6. For other examples of poems that denounced footbinding, see Levy, *Chinese Footbinding,* pp. 82–85; and Ono Kazuko, *Chinese Women in a Century of Revolution, 1850–1950* (Stanford: Stanford University Press, 1989), pp. 30–32.

The ten toes are like brothers,
Siblings living in harmony.
They wish for wholesome prosperity,
Sharing what heaven has endowed.

For what reason, ladies, may I ask:
When did this evil custom begin?
Why, be she young or old, rich or poor,
Shrink the feet to three inches?

A life in the inner chamber, a living hell,
In solitary confinement,
Beneath her hemline, bound into a tight bundle—
Layers upon layers of restriction.

Walking slowly, moving gingerly,
Ever fearful of toppling over.
Clogged circulation, congested respiration,
The pinching pain of pecking birds.

Such suffering for one born a daughter:
No wonder she enjoys not longevity.
What crime has she committed in her girlhood?
Why subject her to such cruelty?

Narrow and pointed shoes are not for walking;
Why must we do such a thing to ourselves?
Why, may I ask the mothers—
Why are you treating your daughters in such a fashion?

People say, a girl without bound feet—
No man would desire for a wife.
Such reasoning, such incivility—
All leads to sickness and disease.

This is biologically unsound;
A contradiction to a superior human race.
It is indeed good news: "Reform is here!"
The government has issued such a decree.

Manchurians and Hans may now intermarry;
The imperial house is showing its benevolence
The officails and gentry are earnest advocates,
Womenfolk should bear this decree in mind.

From Minister Xi, Minister Shen,
And the governors of Yunnan and Sichuan,
All written in plain words, circulated in newspapers.
People are amused by the decree.

Emperor Xuantong and his Prince Provost
Strictly enforce the new policy.
The governor of Sichuan and Grand Marshall Zhao
Make public speeches in every city.

Patrolling policeman would say:
The intention to reform this practice is not evil;
Another police officer would comment:
Minister Gao has sent orders to every department.

First reach the provincial capitals, then the entire province,
Make sure that the decree will be uniformly enforced.
Then send out officers and advocates,
Make people aware and responsive to the cause.

Superior people set the trends;
They'll take the first step to loosen the bindings.
Now she can walk, attend school;
How can she not be happy?

Schools for boys, schools for girls—
An idea as bright as candlelight.
An imperial edict, an order from the government;
There will be no going back to suffering.

Don't worry that people will laugh at her—
A woman with feet as big as a boat.
Don't believe what they say—
Skirts and dainty shoes are a perfect match.

Never a civilized country
Allows people to bend and twist their feet;
Never a civilized person
Speaks maliciously of another's deeds.

No one should allude
That a woman with natural feet will have no proposal from any man.
No one should believe
That a woman with natural feet will not find a good husband.

From now on, let's hurry the reform;
Everyone supports it in all sincerity.
Nevertheless, it will be enforced;
No one escapes the fines and penalties.

Factories for women workers; schools for young girls—
All require financial support.
Dear ladies, learn from this song:
Once, twice, thrice, until you remember it well.

Be brave, be gracious;
No need to be modest and reserved.
Don't follow the barbaric customs;
Don't sever ligaments and break bones.

This is a call for compassion for our lives;
Kindness for humanity.
Without it, dear ladies—
Our life may be shortened and in jeopardy.

Impeded mobility leads to illness—
You were digging your own graves at an early age.
Don't treat this matter as trivial talk;
Don't take this policy ever too lightly.

(SOURCE: *Chung Sai Yat Po*, September 15, 16, 1908, p. 5.
TRANSLATOR: Marlon K. Hom.)

勸不纏足歌

女兒足，女兒足，本是天生肉．是男兒，是女兒，同是母生育．
千趾頭，如弟兄，同胞本和睦．望發達，望完全，享受天然樂．
卻為何，婦女們，染此怪風俗．無老幼，無貧富，三寸金蓮縮．
深閨門，嚴禁錮，儼如活地獄．裙邊下，纏角黍，層層加束縛．
緩緩走，慢慢移，生怕身顛仆．血氣滯，不流通，疼痛如雀啄．
因此故，女兒家，少受長命福．閨閤中，犯何罪，受茲刑慘酷．
尖尖履，行路難，此孽由自作．問何為，母親們，待女不賢淑．
他說道，不纏足，不如夫家欲．這都由，不開通，釀成病虛弱．
生理學，全不講，焉知強種族．幸得好，許開放，論旨出內閣．
滿與漢，許開親，皇家待不薄．官與紳，多提倡，女眷膺誥軸．
錫制臺，岑制臺，總督官滇蜀．編白話，刻報章，眾人曾玩索．
宣統朝，攝政王，新政人都服．川總督，趙大帥，隨處多演說．
這習慣，責巡警，改良意不惡．巡警道，高大人，告示徧各屬．
先省城，後全省，禁止是一律．又派員，多勸導，喚醒人知覺．
上等人，開風氣，放足先一著．行道路，進學堂，那些不快活．
男學堂，女學堂，此理明如燭．皇家旨，官家示，此事無反覆．
莫說是，大如船，怕受人戲謔．莫說是，小弓鞋，方配裙一幅．
斷無有，文明國，足下拳而曲．斷無有，文明人，背後生謗讟．
斷無有，天然足，誇口無媒妁．斷無有，天然足，東床無坦腹．
從今後，速改良，大家須踴躍．若不然，行強迫，罰錢躲不脫．
女工廠，女學堂，款項正需索．婦女們，把這歌，一一當三復．
放大膽，學大方，無待詳斟酌．切莫效，野蠻風，纏斷筋和骨．
這都是，愛百姓，一片慈心伏．惟恐你，婦女們，有妨生命促．
少運動，病奄奄，未老填溝堅．莫說是，非政體，此言太瑣屑．

Wong Ah So,
Filial Daughter and Prostitute

"The Greatest Virtue in Life Is Reverence to Parents"

In 1922 Wong Ah So, the eldest of five children, was betrothed by her poverty-stricken mother to Huey Yow, a Gold Mountain man, in exchange for a bride-price of 450 Mexican dollars. Happy to be leaving China for a better life in America, Wong arrived in San Francisco only to discover that she had been sold into prostitution. For the next year she was forced to work as a prostitute in various small towns and to borrow $1,000 to pay off Huey Yow, who was threatening her life. She was resold to another madam in Fresno, California, for $2,500. Then one evening at a tong banquet a friend of her father's saw and recognized her; ten days later she was rescued by Donaldina Cameron.

Fortunately for Wong Ah So, prostitution was on the decline by the time she arrived in America, thanks to the efforts of Chinese reformers, Protestant missionaries, and those who supported the social purity movement.[1] As her story demonstrates, Chinese women brought to the United States as prostitutes at this time continued to suffer undue hardships but benefited from the sociohistorical forces then working to eliminate prostitution in the city. Moreover, testimonies such as Wong Ah So's

---

1. In 1870, the peak year of prostitution, the manuscript census listed 1,426 or 71 percent of Chinese women in San Francisco as prostitutes. By 1900 the number had dropped to 339, or 16 percent, and by 1910 to 92, or 7 percent. No prostitutes were listed in the 1920 census, although newspaper accounts and the records of the mission homes indicate that the trafficking of Chinese women was still going on.

reveal the inner workings of the Chinese prostitution trade, some of the coping mechanisms women employed to deal with their enslavement, and the escape and rehabilitation process that was possible through the help of missionary workers like Donaldina Cameron.

There are two versions of Wong Ah So's story. One was told to a sociologist investigating race relations among Asians on the West Coast and published in a collection of life histories.[2] The other was told by Donaldina Cameron and published in a Presbyterian magazine that promoted missionary work at home and abroad.[3] Both are rare first-hand accounts that describe in detail the life history and thoughts of a Chinese prostitute. I have chosen to reprint both versions for the different information and insights they shed on Wong's life. On the one hand, we have a sociological account that provides a complex and moving picture of the predicament Wong found herself in. We see her as a happy bride leaving China and sense her shock when she discovers she has been tricked into prostitution. We are moved by her sense of self-sacrifice, forgiveness, and filial duty, and by her efforts to support her family in China and keep them from "losing face." Finally, we feel her relief when she is finally rescued by Donaldina Cameron. The missionary version, in contrast, recounts matter-of-factly how Wong was sold into prostitution and the unscrupulous practices of her "husband" Huey Yow. It reads more like a court transcript than an escape narrative, given its emphasis on Wong's innocence and the terms of her enslavement, with no mention of "prostitution" and little said about the rescue itself.

Both versions included a touching letter at the end, supposedly written by Wong Ah So to her mother prior to her rescue and apparently translated by a missionary worker. This letter, along with others in Wong's file

---

2. Under the direction of Robert E. Park of the University of Chicago, the Survey of Race Relations was launched in 1923 to study the assimilation process and race issues among Asians on the West Coast. The two-year project involved a group of sociologists who utilized the method of life histories to interview more than three hundred Chinese and Japanese Americans about their lives and encounters with racism. Wong Ah So's story was among the interviews selected from the survey for inclusion in *Orientals and Their Cultural Adjustment*, Social Science Source Document, no. 4 (Nashville: Social Science Institute, Fisk University, 1946).

3. Donaldina Cameron, "The Story of Wong So," *Women and Missions* 11, no. 5 (August 1925): 169–72. *Women and Missions* was published by the Women's Committees of the Boards of Missions of the Presbyterian Church in the U.S.A. from 1924 to 1945. Its target audience was Presbyterian women. The magazine reported on missionary work abroad at orphanages, schools, and hospitals as well as in the United States among immigrant populations.

at the Presbyterian missionary archives, attests to the fact that some pros-
titutes were able to stay in touch with their families in China and to
send them remittances periodically. It further confirms Wong's strength
of character, love of family, and belief in Buddhism, fate, and filial piety—
driving forces that kept her alive and above the degradation of forced
prostitution. Subtly, Wong hints in the letter that she has contracted a
venereal disease and that she has more than proven her worth as a daugh-
ter. She asks her mother not to underestimate the value of any of her chil-
dren. "A son is a human being, and so is a daughter," she wrote. As in
her story about Wong Ah So, Donaldina Cameron deleted all references
in the letter to the act of prostitution and to Wong's illness, at one point
substituting the word "slavery" for "prostitution." Because the socio-
logical version of the letter is probably more accurate, I have chosen to
reprint it over Donaldina Cameron's version.

STORY OF WONG AH SO—
EXPERIENCES AS A PROSTITUTE

I was born in Canton [Guangdong] Province, my father was sometimes a sailor and sometimes he worked on the docks, for we were very poor.

I was 19 when this man came to my mother and said that in America there was a great deal of gold. Even if I just peeled potatoes there, he told my mother I would earn seven or eight dollars a day, and if I was willing to do any work at all I would earn lots of money. He was a laundryman, but said he earned plenty of money. He was very nice to me, and my mother liked him, so my mother was glad to have me go with him as his wife.

I thought that I was his wife, and was very grateful that he was tak-ing me to such a grand, free country, where everyone was rich and happy.

When we first landed in San Francisco we lived in a hotel in China-town, a nice place, but one day, after I had been there for about two weeks, a woman came to see me. She was young, very pretty, and all dressed in silk. She told me that I was not really Huey Yow's wife, but that she had asked him to buy her a slave, that I belonged to her, and must go with her, but she would treat me well, and I could buy back my freedom, if I was willing to please, and be agreeable, and she would let me off in two years, instead of four if I did not make a fuss. She said that so I would be quieter about it. I did not believe her, I thought that she was lying to me. So when Huey Yow came I asked of him why that woman had come and what she meant by all that lying. But he said that it was true; that he was not my husband, he did not care about me, and that this was something that happened all the time. Everybody did this, he said, and why be so shocked that I was to be a prostitute instead of a married woman. I asked him, "What is a prostitute? Am I not your wife?" And he said, "Couldn't I just say that you were my wife? That does not make it so. Everybody does this sort of thing. The woman gave me money just to bring you over."

I was in that life for seven months, and then I was released. I don't know just how it came about, but I know it was through a friend of my father's that I met at a banquet.

It was a party given by the Tong men, where slave girls are invited, who sit and eat and drink with the men. Suddenly I saw a friend of my father's come in, a man who had seen me less than a year ago. Although I was all dressed up so grand he recognized me, and the first chance he had, he came and asked me, "Are you not so and so's daughter?"

Of course, under the circumstances, I refused to admit that I knew my own parents, for fear that I would disgrace them, but he insisted, and finally he took me aside and forced me to admit it, and asked, "How is it that you have come to this?" He explained that if I would tell him all he would find some way to get me out of that. So I told him all.

The reason why I did not tell him at first was because I wanted to shield my mother. I felt that my father was absolutely innocent, because one day I heard him tell my mother that if any evil should befall me in America he would hold her responsible, and I felt that now the evil was done and there was no need for her to suffer for it.

About ten days after the party and the interview with this man I was rescued and taken to the mission. I don't know just how it happened because it was all very sudden. I just knew that it happened. I am learning English and to weave, and I am going to send money to my mother when I can, I can't help but cry, but it is going to be better. I will do what Miss Cameron says.

LETTER FROM WONG AH SO TO HER MOTHER FOUND IN SUITCASE AFTER ARREST IN FRESNO, FEBRUARY 7, 1924

To My Honorable Mother, Greetings:

I have left you for several months. I hope you are well and so my heart will be at peace. I received your letter and heard about the children. I am very glad to receive this news.

Your daughter has come to America. I have been ill for several months and have not yet recovered . . . [ellipsis in original]. The man, Huey Yow, who brought me to California, compelled me to pay him one thousand dollars. I have already done so.

Mother, you must be sure to take good care of yourself and not worry. This illness of your daughter is not very serious. In a few days probably there will be two or three hundred dollars sent you for New Year's.

Your daughter's condition is very tragic, even when she is sick, she must practice prostitution (literally, do business with her own flesh and skin).[4] Daughter is not angry with you. It seems to be just my fate. In ancient times, the Chinese legends say, there was a man, Man Jung, who wept under a bamboo tree out of filial reverence for his parents. Another man, Wong Cheong, was going to Peking to see the Emperor to ask redress for wrongs done his parents, and it was so cold he must sleep on ice. These two great heroes left their honorable names behind them as examples of filial piety.[5]

After I have earned money by living this life of prostitution, I will return to China and become a Buddhist nun . . . [ellipsis in original]. If, having earned money for my mother, I am able to expiate my sin also by becoming a nun, I shall be grateful to my mother. By accomplishing these two things I shall have attained all the requirements of complete filial piety.

If people treat me kindly, I shall be kind to them. Since I have not done evil to others, why should others do evil to me? At home, a daughter should be obedient to her parents; after marriage to her husband; after the death of her husband, to her son. These are the three great obediences.

Be sure not to have any trouble with Ah Gin and Meung Ping. As in the building of a house there are twelve beams and you do not know which is the strongest, so in a family you cannot judge which will be the

---

4. In another letter addressed to her mother, Wong Ah So wrote, "Every day I have to be treated by the doctor. My private parts pain me so that I cannot have intercourse with men. It is very hard. . . . Next year I certainly will be able to pay off all the debts. Your daughter is even more anxious than her mother to do this. As long as your daughter's life lasts she will pay up all the debts. Your daughter will do her part so that the world will not look down upon us" (Wong Ah So, letter to her mother, file 260, Donaldina Cameron House, San Francisco). I am grateful to Peggy Pascoe for sharing her notes from the Presbyterian missionary archives with me. See her discussion of Wong Ah So's life story in *Relations of Rescue: The Search for Female Moral Authority in the American West, 1874–1939* (New York: Oxford University Press, 1990), pp. 163–65.

5. These stories come from the Chinese classic *Twenty-four Acts of Filial Piety*.

most dependable one. A son is a human being, and so is a daughter. At home, everybody looks down upon a daughter. How is it now? When I was at home, Mother, you looked down upon me as a daughter. Since daughter came to California, by right she should forsake you. But, in thinking it over, the greatest virtue in life is reverence to parents, so I am keeping a filial heart. My present misfortune is due to the sins of a previous incarnation. Now I may be somebody's daughter, but some day I may be somebody's mother.

(SOURCE: *Orientals and Their Cultural Adjustment*, Social Science Source Documents, no. 4 [Nashville: Social Science Institute, Fisk University, 1946], pp. 31–35)

THE STORY OF WONG SO
DONALDINA CAMERON

"Sing Yow, a Chinese woman of immoral character living in San Francisco, paid Huey Yow, a Chinese man, member of the Hop Sing Tong (Chinese 'highbinder' tong) $500 with which to go to China and there secure for Sing Yow a Chinese slave girl. Huey Yow went to China in 1922, and through Wong Sing Kuey at Hongkong negotiated with my mother for my purchase. Huey Yow paid the sum of $450 Mexican money to my parents.

"I was told by my mother that I was to come to the United States to earn money with which to support my parents and my family in Hongkong. Huey Yow secured a Chinese paper, purporting to be a certificate of marriage. No legal ceremony of any kind was performed. Huey Yow taught me to claim him as my husband, so that I could be landed on my arrival in the United States. In accordance with my mother's demands I became a party to this arrangement. On my arrival at the port of San Francisco, I claimed to be the wife of Huey Yow, but in truth had not at any time lived with him as his wife.

"Immediately upon my landing I was turned over to Sing Yow who placed me in a life of slavery. Sing Yow told me that she had paid Huey Yow $500 to go to China and bring me to the United States.

"After placing me in a life of slavery, Sing Yow took me to various small towns, making me earn for her. Later Sing Yow brought me back to San Francisco, and in San Francisco Huey Yow began to make demands upon me for extra money over and above what I was earning for Sing Yow. I told him that I did not have any money to give him. He then attempted to take certain of jewelry which I was wearing. When I remonstrated with him, he drew a pistol and threatened my life. I pleaded with Huey Yow to spare my life for the sake of my parents and family in China.

"Just at this time Sing Yow returned, and found me weeping. I told her it was impossible for me to meet the constant demands for money that Huey Yow was making upon me, and that I would rather in some way raise a sufficient amount to pay him off finally. Sing Yow then inquired how much Huey Yow would demand for final settlement. He said $650 if paid within a week; if not, he would ask more. It was impossible to raise this sum within a week's time, so he then demanded $1,000. Knowing that Huey Yow was guilty of three murders, I was in such fear for my own life that I agreed to go to Stockton and borrow from different parties this amount of money.

"I then went to Stockton, secured the thousand dollars, and returned to San Francisco. On the Chinese eleventh month, the eighth day, at the Hop Sing Tong ('highbinder' tong) headquarters, I paid Huey Yow $1,000 in the presence of Sing Yow, Wong Wai Sum, president of the Hop Sing Tong, Jeah Jai Yen and several other members of the Tong. At that time Huey Yow gave me a written receipt for the money paid and a guarantee signed by himself and Wong Wai Sun to the effect that he would cease to molest me or demand money from me.

"'*Receipt:* I, Huey Yow, write this receipt to Bo Lin (Wong So). Bo Lin is my good friend and now Bo Lin wants her freedom. She is willing to give $1,000 to Huey Yow. After the money is received, Bo Lin is released from Huey Yow and Huey Yow cannot go after her to demand more money or trouble her. Even though Bo Lin should gain $100,000, Huey Yow cannot demand more from her. Fearing that verbal evidence is not strong enough, this receipt is given as evidence. Witness: Wong Wai Sun, 12th year of the Republic of China, 8th day of the 11th month. Signed by Huey Yow's own hand.'

"Following this transaction in San Francisco, Sing Yow took me back to Stockton and arranged with Chun Huen, the Chinese woman who conducts the San Joaquin Lodging House in Fresno Chinatown, to become her partner. Chun Huen paid $2,500 to Sing Yow and I was taken to Fresno to live with this new owner.

"When I came to America I did not know that I was going to live a life of slavery, but understood from women with whom I talked in Hongkong that I was to serve at Chinese banquets and serve as an entertainer for the guests. I was very miserable and unhappy. My owners knew this and kept very close watch over me, fearing that I might try to escape. My family are very poor in China and kept writing constantly to me asking for money.

"When representatives from the Chinese Mission found me in Fresno, and I was taken to the Home and offered liberty, I gladly accepted it."

(SOURCE: *Women and Missions* 11, no. 5 [August 1925]: 169–72)

A year later, after learning how to read Chinese and English and after becoming a Christian, Wong Ah So agreed to marry Louie Kwong, a merchant in Boise, Idaho. Her connections to Cameron and the Presbyterian Mission Home did not end there, though. A few years later, Wong wrote to complain about her husband and to ask Cameron for advice. Louie Kwong had joined the Hop Sing Tong, refused to educate his three daughters (by a previous marriage), had struck her and refused to pay her old boarding fees in the Mission Home, and worst of all, threatened to send for a concubine from China because she had not borne him a son. As Peggy Pascoe notes in Relations of Rescue, *compared with Wong Ah So's earlier letter in which she totally accepted her place in the traditional Chinese gender system, this letter, where she dares to challenge her husband's decisions and conduct, shows how her ideals had changed since her rescue.[6] In support, Cameron promptly sent a Chinese missionary worker to investigate the matter.[7] This act must have helped because five years later, in the following letter to Cameron, Wong Ah So wrote about being happily married and "busy, very busy" raising her husband's three daughters, their own two sons and a daughter, plus an adopted daughter and a brother-in-law's ten-year-old son. She also talked about returning to China only to find that her mother had died and entrusted her with the lives of her two younger brothers and two younger sisters. Louie Kwong had evidently turned a new leaf, perhaps because Wong had finally borne him sons. His three daughters were receiving an education and he was willing to support all of Wong's siblings. Throughout the letter she expressed appreciation for what Cameron and the Mission Home had done for her and reiterated her sincere commitment to Christianity. In Cameron's words, "God spoke definitely to Ah So through His own Word and a broken life was given over to be re-*

---

6. Pascoe, *Relations of Rescue*, pp. 163–65.

7. Letter from Wong Ah So "to Lo Mo and all the Teachers," dated October 24, 1928, file 258, Cameron House, San Francisco.

built."[8] *The sociologist who interviewed Wong Ah So for the Survey of Race Relations would, following the reasoning given in the introduction to the publication* Orientals and Their Social Adjustment, *probably say that here was an example of cultural change as a result of contact with Western civilization.*[9]

December 28, 1933

My Dear Lo Mo [Mother]:

It has been a long while since I have written you, but there has not been a moment in which I have not thought of you and friends at the Mission Home. I hope this Christmas has been a joyous one.

Lo Mo, I am so happy that you have found such a wonderful place for the fifty dollars. Your suggestions are always for the best and where it will receive the most good. I am happy to have you carry out your plans.

We came back to America last year in May. We felt that a living was much easier to make in this country than China. With these small children, it will take a long while before they are able to care for themselves. We stayed with friends while our home was being built. I have been busy, very busy since then. Mary and Eva are in Hong-kong going to school. We felt it was an opportunity for them to receive a Chinese education, something that they could not attain here. They are cared for by their Ki Neang and Ki Yea [god-grandparents], who are both Christians.

My sister is also staying with them. They are always thoughtful of you too. They are all living in our home. My sister has become a Christian. She and my adopted girl were baptized this Christmas. I adopted this girl from my father-in-law who wished to take her as his second wife. Upon hearing this, I immediately took her to my home. She is now going to school with my two girls and sister. She is happy and I have named her Wai Goy. This is interpreted as God's love, and I love her.

My mother died before our return to China. Before her death she said she could not entrust the two smaller brothers and two sisters to anyone excepting myself. On my return I tried my best to fulfill her wish and

---

8. Donaldina Cameron, "New Lives for Old in Chinatown," *Missionary Review of the World* 57 (July–August 1934): 329.

9. *Orientals and Their Social Adjustment*, p. i.

care for them. One of the sisters is married and the other one staying with the three girls.

The two smaller brothers are in a Christian home for children. These two boys have not yet been baptized but want to become Christians after they grow older. My married sister is baptized and a Christian woman. I am very grateful and thankful to God that my husband is willing to care for these smaller brothers and sister and help them.

On November 3d this year we had another baby girl. Her name is Ruth. William is well and goes out with his father on the truck every day. He enjoys working with his father. Paul is growing to be a big boy. He has a cold now and does not feel so well. He is running around and is learning to talk.

I am taking care of my brother-in-law's son. He is a little boy about ten years old. He minds very well and wishes to become a Christian and live a Christian life.

Mae (our daughter) will graduate from the University of Washington this coming June. She wishes to return to China to do work. She studies bacteriology at the university.

Lo Mo, when I look at my three children, I always think of you and your workers at the Mission Home. If it were not for your help, I would not have what I do. I am again very thankful to you. When these children grow up, I hope they will do God's work and be His disciples. There is a lot of His work to be done in this world especially in China where so many are suffering both mentally and physically. Mary and Eva will return to this country next year and finish their work and then return to China.

The girls and I are getting along fine. You need not be worried of that. I am again grateful and thankful to God for His help.

I hope you will take good care of yourself and please give my love to teachers.

Lovingly yours,

Ah So

(SOURCE: Donaldina Cameron, "New Lives for Old in Chinatown," *Missionary Review of the World* 57 [July–August 1934]: 329)

Law Shee Low, Model Wife and Mother

"We Were All Good Women—Stayed Home and Sewed"

In 1922, the same year that Wong Ah So was sold into prostitution and brought to America, Law Shee Low was arranged in marriage to a gam saan haak *and immigrated as the wife of a U.S. citizen. Like Wong, she was glad to be leaving poverty conditions behind and she remained true to her filial and marital duties as an obedient daughter and virtuous wife. But unlike Wong's mock marriage to Huey Yow, Law's marriage turned out well. While her husband worked as a cook in a restaurant, she stayed at home and sewed for a living, did all the housework, and took care of their eight children. During the Great Depression, when her husband was unemployed, she took over the role of chief breadwinner, and after she became a widow in 1956 she managed to support the family with the help of the older children.*

After interviewing Law Shee Low for the Chinese Women of America Research Project in 1982, my sister Sandy Lee remarked, "There must be many, many Mrs. Lows in San Francisco whose entire lives are devoted to their children and center on Chinatown. When their children are all grown and married, they seem so vulnerable and lost." Sandy was the perfect person to interview Law Shee Low: she is fluent in Cantonese Chinese and knows how to relate to the old-timers. From her two-hour interview with Law we learn of the change in family fortune that caused her to marry a gam saan haak, *the ordeal of detainment at the Angel Island Immigration Station, her hardworking life in America through the depression and war years, and her constant devotion to her family.*

In 1988, while doing research for Unbound Feet, *I interviewed Law Shee Low twice at her home, each time for two hours. I chose to focus our interview on gender issues. I wanted to know how she was raised and treated as a girl in China, her experiences as a wife, mother, and working-class woman in America, and how she was able to cope with the many limitations placed on her as a Chinese woman. I found Law a willing and forthright interviewee. She did not mind my personal questions about such matters as birth control and she was candid and consistent in all her responses. You can tell how pragmatic and religious she has always been by her favorite refrains: "That's how it was" and "Thank heaven." Law Shee Low believes in making the best of every situation and puts her faith in fate and in* tin wong *(literally, the king in heaven). She lives a simple life and follows all the rules. She is a survivor, a kindhearted soul, and a remarkable woman in her own right.*

The following life story of Law Shee Low is a combination of her words from the three interviews. From her perspective, we come to understand what it means to be a model wife and mother in America—the personal sacrifices that role demands as well as the personal satisfaction gained. We also see that women like Law did not consider their lives oppressive. She may have been housebound and stuck in low-wage work, but she was not subordinate or totally dependent on her husband. From her vantage point, it was a matter of the family working together as a team for economic and cultural survival. Because she also contributed to the family income, ran the household, and provided cultural sustenance, her and her husband's relationship was interdependent. Nor did she regard her housework and child care duties as a form of exploitation. Immigrant wives like Law Shee Low viewed the home as their domain and ruled it proudly and efficiently. Although family life exacted a heavy toll on women's personal lives, it also served to sustain them. Working hard had meaning for Law because it enabled her to fulfill her filial and marital obligations as well as provide a better future for her children.

Finally, as isolated, apolitical, and traditional as her life as a Chinese immigrant woman may appear to be, coming to America proved to be a liberating experience for Law Shee Low in a number of important ways. For one, America allowed her to escape from hunger and poverty. "At least here in America, my children all have a good future," she said. "If I had remained in China, we might have all starved to death by now." For another, she found new resources and opportunities in America which gave Chinese women like her more leverage in dealing with racial, gender, and class oppression. She relied on other women and clansmen to

*help her got through the immigration process at Angel Island, find work
in the community, give birth to her children, resolve differences between
her and her husband, and adapt to life in America. Although she did not
read the Chinese newspapers or participate actively in community affairs,
Law Shee Low was made aware of the changing attitudes toward Chinese women through her husband and neighbors. As she noted in one of
the interviews, after the 1911 Revolution it was no longer "fashionable"
to practice footbinding or have concubines and mui tsai in China or Chinatown. And housebound though she was, Law knew about the Christian organizations that rescued prostitutes, helped abused women, and
provided education for children and immigrant wives such as herself. She
was as patriotic as anyone else in the community during the war years
but was prevented from participating in the war effort because of her
limited time and money.*

*Although life in America presented Law Shee Low with opportuni-
ties to depart from traditional gender roles and relationships, she found
certain traditions worth keeping. For example, she was very aware of the
changing fashions for women, but she still preferred to wear Chinese
dresses. "More and more of the Chinese ladies changed to Western-style
clothing after World War II," she noted, "but the American dress just
does not feel comfortable to me." To this day she wears Chinese dresses
that she made herself. Her beliefs in the proper role of women, family
collectivity, and folk religion have also continued to serve her well. Ultimately, these beliefs helped Law Shee Low to overcome the many hardships she has faced as a Chinese woman in America.*

"The Bandits Came and Took Everything"

Before the bandits came, the living conditions were not too bad.[1] If you
had money, you could stay home and take it easy. If you were poor, you
could still farm or hire yourself out as a farmer. Life was very simple.
We had a bit of money because my grandfather owned land. We had three
generations living under the same roof and we all got along fine, including
my sisters-in-law. Then when I was twelve years old, the bandits came
and took everything. They destroyed our farmland and property and we

---

1. Political and social upheavals continued unabated after the 1911 Revolution as Sun
Yat-sen's government fell apart and warlords fought for control of China. Banditry was
rampant in many parts of the country, particularly in the emigrant villages of Guangdong
Province.

became poor. There was no calling for doctors, so my father went to the city to be a teacher. But he had a hard time collecting tuition; the students were so poor. Sometimes they would pay him with clothes, sometimes ten *gan* [catties] of sweet potatoes or ten *gan* of preserved olives.[2] Every other day my sister and I would carry our baskets over to help him lug it all back. After two years of almost no pay, he returned to the village and became a doctor again.

We had many *mui tsai* before, at one time at least three. We had slowly married them off one by one. When we became poor we couldn't afford to buy new ones. There was no more money for my sister and me to continue with school, so we stayed home and learned to cook and take care of the house. We were very capable and we learned fast. We did all the water carrying and washing. Every morning we had to draw water from the well for cooking, for tea, and for washing. My grandmother, mother, and an aunt all had bound feet, and it was difficult for them to get around. When they got up in the morning I had to go fetch the water for them to wash up and carry the night soil buckets out. Every day I swept the floor, washed the dishes, chopped wood, and tended the garden. We also had to wash the floor whenever it rained because the brick floors would get so dirty. I would help grandmother with the cooking, and until I became older I was the one who went to the village marketplace every day to shop.[3] My brothers never helped us. They continued going to school. It was work for girls to do.

"My Husband Was a Christian in America"

My parents decided to marry me off to a *gam saan haak* from the next village. We were poor and there was no other way. If we had money, I'm sure my mother would have kept me home instead. We had no food to go with rice, not even soy sauce or black bean paste. Some of our neighbors even had to go begging or sell their daughters, times were so bad. So my parents thought I would have a better future in Gold Mountain. My husband was thirty-four years old to my eighteen years. His father died when he was seven. He had an uncle who sponsored him to America as his paper son when he was sixteen. There, he sewed in order to pay back the debt. He said he was a salesman in a clothing store. My

---

2. One *gan* is equivalent to one and one-third pounds.

3. It was all right for Law to go to the marketplace and shop as a girl, but once she became a woman Chinese custom dictated that she not mix with men in public places.

grandmother didn't like him, but the matchmaker was able to convince my grandfather. It was a blind marriage. I didn't even have the nerve to look at him when he came over to our house for a visit. Oh, we were so stupid then!

My husband was a Christian in America, so we had a Christian ceremony. He got an American minister to perform the ceremony. I wore the traditional Chinese tunic and skirt set but had an American-style veil and carried a bouquet of flowers. My parents didn't object, since China was starting to become more modern. After the wedding we lived in this big house in Shekki that was rented from another Low person for eight dollars a month.[4] There was his sister—the one who had a nervous breakdown because her husband in America had left her childless and never bothered to send money home—her mother-in-law, and some *mui tsai*. They gave us part of the house to live in until we left for America nine months after we got married [in 1922].

"It [Angel Island] Was Like Being in Prison"

I came as the wife of a U.S. citizen. My husband didn't have to stay at Angel Island [but I did]. Unfortunately, he forgot to give me some papers and so they wouldn't let me off the ship. All the other Chinese passengers got off, then the Japanese women. There was this young kid, a son of a friend of mine, who didn't have his papers either. The two of us had to wait almost half a day, standing throughout because there were no chairs. Fortunately, we arrived during the daytime and it was nice weather. But we were beginning to worry that they would not take us to Angel Island. The kid was only nine years old and skinny. He began to cry. I was young then and able to endure it.

[Upon arrival] we didn't have to take a full physical examination, just give a stool sample. They gave us each a basin, and fortunately I was able to eliminate and passed. Those found with hookworm had to go to the hospital. Liver fluke was considered incurable.[5] There was a young bride who had it and was deported. After that, we were told to leave our luggage in the storage shed by the pier and just take what we needed. We would be allowed to retrieve things later. I put some clothes in a bag and took some bedding—a comforter, blanket, and two pillows—that

---

4. Shekki (Shiqi) is the county seat of Chungshan (Zhongshan) District in Guangdong Province.

5. See page 15, note 11.

my husband had given me. The kid was to stay in our [women's] barracks, but his father hadn't given him anything to take except a big towel for washing.[6] So he helped me lug the bag and bedding up the stairs into this big room. There were about six or seven women [in the women's barracks] and four double-decked bunk beds, all with springs but no bedding.[7] I took the top bunk and gave one of the pillows and the blanket to the kid. Later when I left, he returned my things to me. I often wonder what happened to him.

It [Angel Island] was like being in prison. Every morning we would all get up at 6 A.M. and they would let us out for meals and then lock us up again when we came back. The food was terrible! We always ate after the men were done. The bean sprouts were cooked so badly you wanted to throw up when you saw it. There was rice but it was cold. I just took a few spoonfuls and left. Same food all the time, either bean sprouts or cabbage. We began craving salted fish and chicken. We wanted preserved bean paste. The food was steamed to death; it smelled bad and tasted bad. The vegetables were old and the fatty beef was of poor quality. They must have thought we were pigs. Whenever my husband sent me food—*dim sum* [Chinese dumplings and pastries], cantaloupes, Chinese sausages—I would share it with everyone. The old white lady we called Ma delivered it.[8] They would call out my name and search it for any hidden coaching notes.[9] The kid's father never sent him anything good to eat. That was sad because he didn't like the food. He stuck with me, since he was alone and he knew me.

There was nothing much to do. Ma was a good person, brought us knitting things, but we didn't know how [to knit]. She was willing to teach us, but we weren't in the mood. Once a week she would take us for a walk up the hill. I never went. Mostly, we just sat there and waited out the days, staring out the windows. We hardly even chatted. No ar-

6. Men and women were segregated at Angel Island. Boys under the age of twelve generally stayed with their mothers in the women's barracks.

7. Most other women I interviewed for the book *Island* recalled that there were between thirty and fifty women in the barracks at any one time.

8. Deaconess Katharine Maurer was appointed by the Women's Home Missionary Society of the Methodist Episcopal church to tend to the needs of Chinese women at Angel Island.

9. Relatives were known to sneak in coaching notes through the Chinese kitchen staff or in the mail to help a detainee pass the interrogation. In Law Shee Low's case, her husband did not even prepare a coaching book for her to study, believing that since she was a legal immigrant, she should have no trouble passing the examination.

guments, no jokes. Everyone was just worried about not being able to land. There were two women who had been there for over three months. They didn't cry, didn't seem to care. They even sang sometimes and joked with the cleaning man. Whenever Ma offered to take us out for walks, just the two would go. They were friends and appeared very happy and carefree. The younger woman was very nice and helped us dress our hair. They had little going for them, but they managed to struggle on. Later, when they told us that people had hung themselves in the bathroom, we were afraid to go to the bathroom alone.[10] Even when we went to bathe, we made sure we had company.

One woman who was in her fifties was questioned all day and then later deported, which scared all of us. She told us they asked her about [life in China:] the chickens and the neighbors, and the direction the house faced. How would I know all that? I was scared. Later [on her tenth day at Angel Island], when I went for the interrogation, they told me to drink a few mouthfuls of cold water to stop the fear, so that's what I did. There was an inspector, a Chinese interpreter who was very nice, and a white girl taking notes. The white inspector asked when did I marry, what is my surname, my age, and that was about it.[11] When the interpreter asked me whether I had visited my husband's ancestral home during the wedding I said no because I was afraid he was going to ask me which direction the house faced like the woman told me and I wouldn't know. Evidently, my husband had said yes. So when they asked me again [this time in the presence of her husband] and I said no again, my husband said, "*Choi* [For fortune's sake]! You went; why don't you say so?" The immigration officer hit the table with his hand [in objection] and scared me to death. So I quickly said, "Oh, I forgot. I did pass by [in the wedding sedan chair] but I didn't go in." So they let me land. But when they led me back to the barracks I thought I would be deported, so I cried. Later, they called me to get ready to leave on the four o'clock boat for San Francisco. So I quickly changed my clothes and the others happily helped me

---

10. Although there were few documented cases of suicide by Chinese immigrants at Angel Island, rumors circulated that women, after hearing they were to be deported, committed suicide by hanging themselves in the bathroom.

11. According to Law Shee Low's interrogation transcript, which is in the possession of her son Victor Low, she was asked a total of fifty-one questions about her family, her husband's family, their marriage and living quarters in Shekki, and their trip from China to America. Because of a discrepancy in her and her husband's testimonies, she was recalled for a second interview, in which she was asked four specific questions about their wedding.

pack. Only the kid was sad to see me go. I just hope the other ladies took care of him.

"We Worked Like Crazy"

When we got here, lots of people had no work. We were so poor we just had pickled vegetables for dinner. We rented a room on Stockton Street for eleven dollars a month. We did everything in that one room: sleep, eat, and sit. We had a small three-ring burner for cooking. There was no ice box, and my husband had to shop for every meal. We did not use canned goods and things like that. We ate only Chinese food. There was no hot water, and we would all hand wash our clothes. We used to dry them on the roof or in the hallways. That's what happens when you are poor. It was the same for all my neighbors. We were all poor together.

My husband worked as a cook in a restaurant twelve hours a day for $60 a month. It was a restaurant run by a Low in Chinatown that catered to Blacks. There were fights all the time, frightening and brutal. Sometimes they couldn't pay for their meals. It only cost ten or fifteen cents a meal, they told me, but people were poor. His [her husband's] earnings barely covered the rent and food. I had to learn how to sew, so my husband bought me an old-fashioned sewing machine and when he got off work from the restaurant he would teach me how to sew.

The building we lived in was filled with Lung Do people, about six or seven households.[12] Many people in our building sewed, men included. At first someone from the Low clan brought me things to sew a dozen at a time, then every day by the dozen. Someone else showed me how to do the seams and how to gather. This one teacher I had—a Mr. Wong from a neighboring village—specialized in baby clothes with beautiful decorations, embroidered pockets and all. He taught me well and I made over two dozen pieces a day. The pay was over a dollar a dozen. I did that for ten years or so. It wasn't a lot, but it helped to cover some of the food and rent. I just gave it all to my husband, since he did the shopping.

Usually he bought enough for one meal—pork, vegetables, fish, and that was all. Whatever he brought home, I cooked. Later, I would ask him to buy a chicken to make soup. Sometimes we would pay to have men deliver the groceries to us. You just called and they delivered. That

---

12. Law Shee Low is from the Lung Do region of Chungshan District. Immigrants from that district dominated the sewing trade in San Francisco.

Law Shee Low and her eldest daughter, Ruby, in 1924. (Courtesy of Law Shee Low)

way with children at home you didn't have to go out and waste time shopping. They would deliver pork and vegetables, and then you could cook a simple meal like pork hash and vegetables. In those days, we had only two meals a day. My husband might help make the rice, but I always did the cooking.

I had a total of eleven children—seven daughters and one son survived. They were all born at home. Who had money for the hospital? Sometimes one of the neighbors would help me. If not, I managed myself. That's the way it was. Many [of my neighbors] had ten or more children. [Was it because women then didn't know about birth control?] We didn't know. We would be pregnant every year without realizing it. Even if we didn't want it, we didn't have money to go see the doctor. The midwife wanted us to have more babies. She was having a hard time because no one could afford to pay her. She charged $25 a baby. I lost two sons [in childbirth]. Another died when he was three. We didn't have any money and he had a bad cough [pneumonia]. Their father sent him to the public hospital and he got worse. The doctors were no good. He kept losing weight, so we brought him back to Chinese Hospital. He died soon after. He was a good boy. I cried for years; it was so tragic.

Fortunately, he [her husband] liked kids. Other men would beat their children and kick them out of the house. He wasn't like that. He never changed their diapers or carried them, but he bought food for the kids. There was a woman who had eleven kids. On the sly she bought a barbecued duck and fed it to the kids, afraid that if the husband found out he would beat her to death. She told us. Other men would scold their wives for having girls. One woman who had four children told me her husband would drag her out of bed and beat her because she didn't want to have any more children. We heard all kinds of sad stories like that, but my husband never picked on me like that.

[Was he a good husband?] He wasn't a bad person and he did care about me. Sometimes he would help me hang out the wash. When he was afraid I wasn't eating, he would tell me to eat more. He was just a bit stubborn. When he was first unemployed [during the depression] he went and played Chinese dominoes one night. When he came back in the early morning I said to him, when he presented me with a chicken, "I don't want to eat your chicken; I don't like you to gamble." So he stopped gambling and spent more time sewing. But he continued going out every day, right after he ate. We didn't talk much. We didn't argue. Good or bad, we just struggled on as long as we had work to do.

[You didn't find staying home like being in prison?] There was no time to feel imprisoned, there was so much to do. We worked like crazy. We had to cook, wash the clothes and diapers by hand, [clean] the floors, and sew whenever we had a chance to sit still. Who had time to go out? I sent all the kids to the Baptist church on Sunday, but with so much to do I had no energy to go myself. There was a nice missionary lady who tried to teach me English when I first came to San Francisco. But after I became busy with my baby, I told her not to come anymore. There was no time to attend [the family association] banquets, get involved with any women's group, or even help with the war effort. I wanted to help, but we were barely able to keep ourselves alive. And with one baby after another, there was no time for things like that.

When I first went out to sew I put my daughter, who was a few months old, in a basket. But after a few weeks of that I came back to sewing at home. It was much easier. At home I could work and take care of the children. There were jobs for women in the cannery and fruit orchards, but I couldn't do that because of the kids. Besides, it wasn't proper. Nice Chinese ladies always stayed home and took care of the housework, children, and husband. It was a pity, but that's the way life was for us ladies then. It was the same for all my neighbors. We were all good, obedient, and diligent wives. All sewed; all had six or seven children. We did not go out and waste our husbands' money. Besides, we were so dead poor, who had the money to go shopping for new clothes? Every now and then, he [her husband] would buy me some material and I would make clothes for myself and the kids. As for shoes, since I didn't go out, one pair of shoes would last me ten years. I just tried to send money home whenever there was money to spare.

I heard there was a building known as the Empress Building in Chinatown, where the wives beat the husbands if they were unemployed or did something wrong. But it wasn't so in our building. We were all good women—stayed home and sewed, had the delivery man bring the groceries so we never had to go out. Once in a while a widow in our building would take us out to visit friends in the evening when there was no sewing to do. Three or four times a year she would take us shopping. On New Year's eve she would take us out to buy flowers. Later, when the children were older, I would take them to go see Chinese movies every Saturday.

"So We Struggled On"

[Do you remember the depression in the 1930s?] Those were very poor and tough years for us. When my uncle who became penniless died and we were all asked to help with the funeral expenses, we could only afford to give a few dimes. We were so poor, we wanted to die. My husband had taken our savings and opened a restaurant in Oakland with a friend. He took my sewing money and lost it all. Then he went to Suisun to pick fruit. When there was no more work, he had to go to Vallejo. [He] just made $40 a month at this restaurant; he gave me $20 and kept $20 for himself. I sewed at home and made another $30 or $40. So we struggled on. Then business got slow at the restaurant and he quit and came back. We got two machines and we both sewed at home. He would help with the easier pieces and I would do the harder ones. Then things got worse and we had to use up our savings. When we had no money for rent, they tried to evict us. We convinced them to give us some time.

Joe Shoong was giving out rice, so my husband went and carried back a fifty-pound sack.[13] Food was cheap then. A dime or two would buy you some *sung* [vegetable or meat dishes to go with the rice]. Things got better when Roosevelt became president. Their father [her husband] got in line for milk and relief funds that the government passed out [to the unemployed]. He also enrolled two of the kids in the nursery school at the Chinese YWCA. Two white women took care of them for a few hours every day, gave them breakfast and naps.

"Thank Heaven for Getting Us Through"

I sewed at home until my youngest daughter was five. By that time they didn't allow us to sew at home anymore. So I sewed in the factories for another twenty, thirty years, until I was sixty-five and able to retire. Sewing was better than picking shrimp; it was cleaner. There were many different patterns, but once you learned the pattern, it was easy. I would stop work to go shop at twelve. Then after I prepared the food, I would go back and sew. I always came home at five to cook dinner. At six we had dinner. Then I usually brought home some odds and ends to finish. At one point I also baby-sat one of my granddaughters for a few hours. I would take her to the factory while I worked. Then I would take her shopping at twelve. Then when I went home to prepare the food she had her milk and napped. After my daughter came to pick her up I would go back to the factory and sew.[14] Between the children and sewing, I never had a free moment. Thank heaven I had good health and was able to go on like that for years.

---

13. The wealthiest Chinese American at the time, Joe Shoong owned the National Dollar Stores sewing factory and chain of retail stores. He was Law Shee Low's clansman and landlord. See Sue Ko Lee interview (pp. 387–407) for the story of the 1938 National Dollar Stores strike.

14. Conditions at Chinatown garment shops did not improve through the years. Most women worked an irregular schedule that revolved around family responsibilities. It was standard practice for Chinese seamstresses like Law Shee Low to work long hours under unsanitary conditions for low piece-rate wages.

Fortunately, all the children came out well. They never gave me any trouble. I never had to scold them. They went to school, came home and ate, then went to bed. They even took care of their own weddings. We didn't have any money to help them. But they understood my situation and have always been good to me. My oldest daughter was sick for a long time, and my husband had a heart condition for quite a few years before he died. My sewing money barely covered the rent. Fortunately, they [her children] all helped pay for the food. I thank heaven for getting us through those hard years. Now they always remember my birthday. They chip in for my rent, the electricity, insurance, everything; and they give me spending money. For the last ten years I've been able to send money home to China. They asked me who I wanted to live with, but I decided living here by myself was more convenient. They are worth all the struggles.

(SOURCE: Law Shee Low, interview with Sandy Lee in Chinese, May 2, 1982, San Francisco, Chinese Women of America Research Project, Chinese Culture Foundation of San Francisco; interview with author in Chinese, October 20 and 30, 1988, San Francisco)

Jane Kwong Lee, Community Worker

"Devoting My Best to What Needed to Be Done"

I first became aware of Jane Kwong Lee in 1982 while working on Chinese Women of America: A Pictorial History. *As coordinator of the Chinese YWCA, she had written an article, "Chinese Women in San Francisco," that appeared in the June 1938 issue of the* Chinese Digest, *which served as the voice of second-generation Chinese Americans. The article highlighted the history and changing roles of Chinese women since the gold rush era, as well as publicizing the services of the Chinese YWCA. In my research for* Unbound Feet *I found other articles she had written in* Chung Sai Yat Po *about the Chinese YWCA and the need for women to get involved in the war effort. Then, while teaching at Cornell University, I met an old friend of hers, Ruth Young, who showed me an unpublished autobiography written by Lee in 1977, titled "A Chinese American." I remember being excited at this new find, because her thick manuscript of over four hundred pages was full of rich details about her childhood, education, and family life in China and her experiences as a student, worker, mother, and community activist in San Francisco Chinatown in the 1930s and 1940s. She had written the autobiography for her children, so there were also many Chinese legends and moral lessons embedded in the text. My assumption had been that Chinese women did not leave any written trails; yet here was evidence to the contrary. And luckily, she was still alive and willing to be interviewed.*

Jane Kwong Lee was someone who not only had lived an extraordinarily active life as a Chinese woman in San Francisco but was also a participant-observer of Chinese American women's history. Her experiences as an immigrant woman, training as a sociologist, involvement with the Chinese YWCA, and perspectives as a community organizer and feminist made her an important informant for my study. Twice in the fall of 1988 I interviewed Jane Kwong Lee at her home in El Cerrito, California. I feel fortunate to have met and interviewed her then because she died a year after our meeting, leaving a copy of her autobiography in my keeping.

She was eighty-seven years old at the time of our interview. Although petite and frail—she needed the aid of a cane to get around—Lee still had a good memory and a commanding voice. The door would be left unlocked for me and she would greet me from the kitchen table as I entered. I would join her at the table and for the next two hours she would tirelessly answer all of my questions about the family, working, and social-political lives of Chinese women in San Francisco. Much of what she told me reinforced my own conclusions derived from other sources, in particular that social change for Chinese American women came about as a result of the women's emancipation movement in China and economic conditions in America. Her responses possessed a quality of personal detachment, probably because I was asking for her opinions about and observations of Chinese women rather than her own experiences as one, which I knew had already been recorded in her autobiography. I have thus chosen to excerpt portions of her autobiography rather than use her interviews to tell her life history here.

Jane Kwong Lee was born in Toishan (Taishan) District, Guangdong Province, in 1902. Her father was a businessman in Australia, and his remittances allowed her to attend a missionary school for girls in Canton. There she studied both English and Chinese and became exposed to Western ideas of democracy and feminism. Upon graduation Lee convinced her mother to sell some of the family's land to pay her passage to the United States. In 1922 she obtained a student visa and left China, planning to earn a college degree and return home to a prestigious academic post.

Although Jane Kwong Lee could speak English and was not burdened by family responsibilities, she still faced problems adjusting to life in America. Of foremost concern were her financial needs. Mills College in Oakland offered her a scholarship, but she had to find work to cover her living expenses. Despite her educational background and bilingual abilities, Lee could only find work sewing flannel nightgowns, peeling shrimp, sorting fruit, and cleaning house. Unaccustomed to such hard work, she did not stay long in any of these jobs. Then again, she knew full well that these were but temporary jobs for her, whereas the other immigrant women workers would never have any other option.

Upon graduation Jane Kwong Lee had another rude awakening. All along she had believed that education would be the key to her economic independence, and so she had striven to go as far as she could, finishing high school in China, then a bachelor's degree in sociology at Mills, and, after her marriage and the birth of her two children, returning to Mills to earn a master's degree in sociology and economics. Her educational achievements, however, did not translate into economic rewards. She had not anticipated discrimination in the labor market, nor had she reckoned on the responsibilities associated with marriage and children, which prevented her from returning to China to assume that prestigious teaching post. Like other Chinese American women with college degrees, Lee learned that she could not find work in her profession outside Chinatown because of racial prejudice. She felt fortunate, then, to finally land two part-time jobs teaching in a Chinese language school and working at the Chinese YWCA.

Jane Kwong Lee's autobiography provides us with a rare portrait of a Chinese immigrant woman who worked tirelessly for the well-being of her community, thereby gaining the respect of that community. As the coordinator of the Chinese YWCA from 1935 to 1944 she provided assistance to foreign-born women regarding immigration, health and birth control, housing, domestic problems, and financial aid. For second-generation women she organized clubs, classes, and programs that met their specific social needs. Because of her bilingual skills, Lee was able to do outreach for both groups; she also utilized the local press to publicize and promote the YWCA's services, while at the same time echoing Sieh King King and Mai Zhouyi's feminist sentiments about women's equality. As an example of her journalistic writings and outreach efforts, I have included her article "Why Chinese Americans Should Support the Young Women's Christian Association."

In conjunction with her work at the Chinese YWCA, Jane Kwong Lee also assumed a leadership role in helping Chinese families weather the depression and organizing women to contribute to the war effort in both China and the United States during World War II (see pages 347–55 and 432–51). Once her bilingual speaking abilities and organizational skills became known, Lee was courted by Chinatown churches and organizations as well as women's groups outside the community to speak on behalf of the Chinese YWCA, the Chinatown community, and various nationalist and women's causes. As her autobiography indicates, Jane Kwong Lee served as a crucial link not only between two generations of Chinese women, but also between those women and the Chinatown community, between the Chinese community and the larger American society, and between her newly adopted country, America, and her birthplace, China. And thanks to her supportive husband, James Lee, she did it all without neglecting the needs of her family.

"Two Girls in a Row Were One Too Many"

My ancestors were farmers. A farmer's life was rigorous, demanding, and regimented by the vagaries of nature. The average household had a pig, a dog, some chickens, and ducks or geese. There were a couple of water buffaloes in the village corral; these were used to pull the plows tilling the furrows in the rice fields. Two youths worked as cowboys taking the buffaloes to the nearby hills to pasture. Men worked outside and the women attended to family chores.

I was born in one of these houses. My grandfather was a successful farmer, but my father did not till the soil. He went to join his fourth uncle in Australia when he was seventeen. After a few years in the "New Gold Mountain," as Australia was known, he returned to the old village to be married. My mother was the daughter of an "Old Gold Mountain" man, one among thousands of Chinese laborers who built the transcontinental railroad in the United States. After my sister was born, my father went overseas again. I was born after his second return home.

I was the second daughter, and two girls in a row were one too many, according to my grandparents. Girls were not equal to boys, they maintained. Girls, after they married, belonged to other families; they could not inherit the family name; they could not help the family financially no matter how good they were at housework. In this atmosphere of emotional depression I was an unwanted child; and to add to the family sadness, the weather seemed to be against me too. There was a drought, the worst drought in many years, and all the wells dried up except one. Water had to be rationed. My long (youngest) uncle went out to get the family's share daily. The day after I was born, the man at the well gave him the usual allotment, but my uncle insisted on obtaining one more scoop. The man asked why, and the answer was, "We have one more mouth." Then, and only then, did the villagers become aware that there had been a baby born in their midst. My grandparents were ashamed of having two granddaughters consecutively and were reluctant to have their neighbors know they had one more person in their family. They wanted grandsons and hoped for grandsons in the future. That is why they named me "Lin Hi," meaning "Link Young Brother." They believed in good omens and I did not disappoint them. My brother was born a year and a half later.

"I Wanted to Be Economically Independent"

Revolution was imminent. Progress was coming. Education for girls was widely advocated. Liberal parents began sending their daughters to school. My long aunt, sixth aunt-in-law, godsister Jade and cousin Silver went to attend the True Light Seminary in Canton.[1] Women's liberation had begun. It was the year 1911—the year the Qing Dynasty was overthrown and the Republic of China was born.

[Even] before the declaration of independence from the monarchy, the under-current of free thought had permeated the land. Old traditions began to crumble. Blind obedience was resented. Human dignity was gradually recognized. Women with small feet were advised to unbind them. Slavery was denounced. Men with long queues were urged to cut their hair. Equality of the sexes was secretly discussed. Feudalism was soon to be replaced by democracy.

Just at this juncture of social change, I started to attend school [at True Light Seminary]. I was nine years old—ten years according to the Chinese calendar. The curriculum was built around the Christian doctrine. The Bible was the prime textbook. I, as a beginner, was given a "three word" text printed in three-word sentences to be read and recited to the teacher every day. Discipline in the classroom was rigid. Students stood up and bowed to the teacher when she came in. No noise was tolerated; any conversation was silenced by the reproving voice of the teacher. A class period lasted fifty minutes. At the end of the period, the school bell rang for recess and students rushed out to relax in the corridors. At the end of ten minutes, the bell rang again and the routine of classwork resumed.

To me the last year in grammar school was a turning point; our class was given instruction in the English language. It was an innovation and we were proud of it. In no other girls' school in Canton was English be-

---

1. The True Light Seminary, now a middle school, was a private missionary boarding school for girls and women supported by the Presbyterian Missionary Board in the United States.

ing taught. English was highly respected at the time. There was a saying to the effect that the Western wind was slowly penetrating the East and old customs were changing. It was expected that a person with a knowledge of English would have better occupational opportunities in the future.

We were enthusiastic, and I, especially, was looking forward to many more years of schooling. Quite a number of my classmates, however, did not have the same ideas toward education as I had. Some could not afford the tuition any longer and had to drop out. Some thought a liberal education was not a guarantee toward a livelihood. Hence, a few of my classmates left True Light Seminary to enter technical institutions; others stayed home and eventually got married. I thought otherwise. I enjoyed studying; I took pleasure in reading and exploring different ways of making a living. As long as my family could pay my tuition, I hung on, no matter how frugal [I had to be]. I wanted to be economically independent. In that sense, it was clear in my mind that I had to have as much formal education as possible.

[In 1917] the new school was built in [White] Crane Cave, a stretch of country land bordering a tributary of the Pearl River. The school was an extension of True Light Seminary. Our teachers were the product of highly respected American educational institutions. Miss Law got her Master's degree from Mount Holyoke, one of the most prestigious women's colleges in the United States. She taught me English grammar, without which I could never have gotten into college. Besides Miss Law, there was Miss Fletcher, who had a year's sabbatical from a California school district to teach us English and history during my second year there. She was an exceptionally dedicated instructor who made me do my homework and enjoy its result.

Another teacher I remembered vividly was Miss Margaret Mar, who taught us piano lessons. Miss Mar was an accomplished pianist, but did not know a word of Chinese. She could not pronounce our Chinese names correctly, but she had a solution to this difficulty; she gave us English names. She would give each of us several girls' names and let us choose the one we liked best. That was the beginning of our Jane, Nancy, Helen, Doris, Dorothy, etc.; these aliases stuck with us all our lives.

The importance of English was emphasized, but we did not neglect our Chinese. A Chinese scholar commuted from the city three times a week to our school to teach us old Chinese literature. We listened to the detailed explanations of every complicated word and lengthy discourse on the historical background of the incidents mentioned in the lessons.

Every week we were asked to hand in Chinese compositions to be graded by their quality of thought as well as literary expression and style. Student activities increased as time went on. To stimulate cultural achievements, a school journal was published, a piano recital was presented, not to mention the different kinds of sports we played—volleyball, baseball, and horseback riding. To further arouse our curiosity for knowledge, we periodically invited renowned personalities to speak to us about current events. One speaker was Miss Sz[e]to, who had received her Master's degree from an American women's college and was currently the Dean of Girls at Canton Christian College. She spoke on the status of women in China. The main point of her thesis was that women should get up and fight against the stigma of inferiority and for equality with men. "We should not be playthings of men anymore," she said. "We should get rid of the double standards." We applauded her. We were still hesitant in accepting far-advanced ideas of women's independence, albeit mentally we wished we were independent.

Above all, the most urgent, enthusiastic, and absorbing extracurricular activities were those growing out of the May Fourth student movement in 1919. The Twenty-One Demands from Japan stirred up strong resentment from the students as well as the whole Chinese population.[2] We boycotted Japanese goods and bought only native-manufactured fabrics. We participated in demonstration parades in the streets of Canton. Student delegates were elected to attend discussion meetings in Canton; once I was appointed as one of two delegates from our school. Our twofold duty was to take part in the discussions and decisions and then to convince our schoolmates to take active parts in whatever action was decided. It was a year of turmoil for all the students and of exhaustion for me. . . .

To be a medical doctor had been my dream ever since I was first subjected to a vaccination by my Fourth Granduncle's daughter-in-law, who was one of the pioneer women physicians in Canton. It would give me not only financial independence but also social prestige. Alas, hope without financial support was futile. My mother would not listen to my pleas.

---

2. In 1915, while the European nations were preoccupied with World War I, Japan pressed on the Chinese government a list of Twenty-one Demands for special concessions and privileges. The Chinese bourgeoisie and students protested by boycotting Japanese goods. Then at the conclusion of the war, the Versailles Treaty allowed Japan to take over German concessions in Shandong Province, sparking a nationwide protest and cultural revolution known as the May Fourth Movement.

Jane Kwong Lee (right) with her best friend in Canton in 1920. (Courtesy of Priscilla Lee Holmes)

It was not that she did not want her daughter to succeed; it was simply that my father did not send enough money home to support the family and at the same time continue to send my brother and me to boarding schools.

Just at this time a cousin returned to China from the United States on a business trip. He explained to my mother, while visiting us in Canton, that he could take me to the United States on a student visa. He was taking his married niece to join her husband in Detroit and I could be company for his niece. My mother was interested in the prospect of my trip with her and the bright future that I might bring to the family. At the same time, I was also delighted, although a little dubious. I privately thought that if, with a big IF, I were allowed to go to America I would study to get my B.A., M.A., and Ph.D. and then return to China to obtain an academic position in a middle school or a college. It was a beautiful picture. Instructors with B.A.'s from American universities received much higher salaries than graduates from local colleges. After much consideration my mother said she would be able to finance my trip. She would sell the property in Dongshan. If there was not enough money, she would borrow the rest from the husband of our second slave girl, Ah Hung.[3] [At their last meal together] we sat down cheerfully to a nice dinner with steamed chicken as the main course. According to our dialect, the word "chicken" symbolized good luck, which my mother, above anyone else, would wish me to have in my stay in the Golden Mountain.

"The Dreary Life of a Working Overseas Student"

The steamship *China* had docked at one of the waterfront piers in San Francisco. There was a hubbub of hustle and bustle aboard the ship; passengers preparing to disembark, stewards helping guests on their departure, and immigration officers ready to question aliens, some of whom had to be transferred to Angel Island for detention and further interrogation.

I was more fortunate because I came as a student who occupied a first-class cabin on the steamship. I was not detained except to answer a few pertinent questions. As I was leaning against the upper deck rail watching the traffic alongside the pier, a fellow passenger called me and said that I was wanted downstairs. I went directly to the cabin where the immigration officers were conducting their business. There I was asked to sit down in one of the two chairs there and was shown the papers bearing my name. I was asked my age, date of birth, and other information as appeared on my passport. It seemed that I satisfied the examining officer and was told that was all. . . .

Until now [about a month later] I neglected to write my mother, in-

---

3. Ah Hung had been married off to a rich, old merchant in Hong Kong as a concubine. As Jane Kwong Lee wrote in her autobiography, "She was thought to be fortunate because his wife was living in the country and she was living in Hong Kong with her husband, who showered her with whatever material comforts she needed."

forming her of my safe arrival. She wrote me inquiring about my voyage to America. I did not know why I delayed in writing to her; perhaps it was due, in part, to my resentment of my own precarious financial condition. . . . I wrote to my mother at last, apologetically, telling her of my arrival in San Francisco and of staying in cousin B. S. Fong's house.[4] At heart I was sorry for myself; I wished I were a boy. If I were a boy, I could have gone out into the community, finding a job somewhere as many newcomers from China had done. Once, before I left home, my mother had said to me that she reared me as if I were a son; I wished I were a son.

After a short time of idleness, I set out to look for work. Someone took me to the Joe Shoong sewing factory on Washington Street in which women, mostly of the first generation, were busily sewing dresses.[5] The fashion at the time was to have coarse embroidery done on ladies' apparel. I was asked to do some of the embroidery, which was easy for me. I did not hate the work, but after a few hours, I was bored; and by the end of the week, I was ready to quit.

I went to see my aunt, who introduced me to Miss May Yee, a devout Christian of the Oakland Presbyterian Church. She took me to see a Caucasian lady who wanted someone to help her with the housework. The house was very nice, and the old lady made a bed out of the couch in the corner of a spare room for me to stay. There was not much work to do as there were only two adults in the house, the lady and her husband, who worked all day and came home for dinner after work. I was permitted to sit at the table to eat dinner with them. It seemed that they, out of Christian compassion, were willing to hire a needy Oriental girl whom they did not look down on as if she were servant. They were extraordinarily nice to me. On Saturday, the lady cleaned the kitchen, including washing the walls and ceiling, and I had to help. It was hard work! I could not take it! After a week, I told the lady that I wanted to leave. She was exceedingly kindhearted and asked May to come take me home. She paid me $5.00 for the work I had done for her. I appreciated her generosity, but at heart I felt that I was not equipped to be a domestic. . . .

Teaching school became a routine for me and I had time to spare for

4. B. S. Fong and his wife Emily were affluent relatives who lived in a three-bedroom unit over a Chinatown storefront. They provided Jane with her own room, financial support, and important contacts, enabling her to strike out on her own sooner rather than later.

5. See page 222, note 13.

other activities.[6] I looked around to see if I could get another part-time job to brighten my financial picture. I learned of people shelling shrimps and was anxious to know whether I could do it. One Saturday afternoon I followed a friend to visit a family in a tenement house. The corridors were dim and the small window in the back room of the apartment was the only outlet for air and light. The mother and daughter were sitting at the kitchen table shelling shrimps; their fingers flew in putting shrimp meat in one bamboo tray and shrimp shells in another. They were experts! They shelled so fast that I could hardly see what they were doing with the boiled shrimps they picked up from the big, round container in the center of the table. I tried to imitate them. Alas! As soon as I held the shrimp between my thumbs and forefingers of both hands, the shrimp broke while the shell was still clinging to the meat. I realized then that I could not make my living by shelling shrimps even if I might be able to endure the foul, fishy smell permeating the whole atmosphere. . . .

[As a student at Mills College,] I lounged in a day student room near the front of the campus. Between classes I usually went to the library; I would sit there facing the front lawn for hours to think about nothing in particular. I felt very lonesome and would write letters to old friends and old classmates, lamenting about the dreary life of a working overseas student. Once in awhile I would wander around the running creek, reciting in my mind old sayings in Chinese literature to amuse myself. In fact, I was disappointed in coming to America. My conditions were not what I had expected. I reflected that were I still in China, I would have had a teaching position in a school just like some of my old schoolmates did.

All this time I had the ambition of preparing for a medical career. That was why one day I wrote a school friend asking for advice as to what courses I should take in order to switch to medicine in case I would be able to do so in the future. My friend told me that the best courses to take would be in the natural sciences. The natural science course I took during the first year was Physics I. It was, to me, very simple because most of the basic theories I had already taken in my subfreshman class in China. The most difficult class was French, which was really foreign to me. I could write the spellings but could not maneuver my tongue to utter the correct pronunciations.

To me, at the time, an obvious difference between American and Chi-

---

6. Jane had found a part-time job teaching in the Chinese language school of the Chinese Episcopal Church in San Francisco.

nese students was that an American would be quick to raise her hand in response to the professor's questions whereas a Chinese would keep quiet unless she was asked particularly by name. I usually sat back quietly; the professor might think I was dumb, but I did not care. I was used to the old Chinese way of thinking—receive what you are taught and do not oppose what the teacher tells you—in short, keep quiet. . . .

During the summer, I went out to earn some money. There was a cannery in Oakland owned by Mr. Lew Hing, a very rich man by Chinese standards. It employed many factory workers in the summer, and I followed some Chinese women to work there. I got up early and wore my blue overall smock to go to work as a fruit-cutter. My job, as was the job of all the women sitting on the benches facing the boxes, was to cull the good fruit and put them in boxes on one side and throw the bad ones in the boxes on the other side. The first fruit I picked were cherries; big, dark, red and juicy Bing cherries. As I sat in front of those tempting cherries, I could not resist the desire to put some into my mouth. Later on, the supervisor stopped workers from eating the fruit, but by the time the order came the cherry season was virtually over. Then we culled apricots, using the same procedure—putting the good ones in one box and the bad ones in another. We did not eat the apricots; I did not like apricots, anyway. After that we started to cut peaches. We had to buy a little knife and spoon to cut and take the pit out. I could not cut fast enough. I had made a little money, but not as much as the ladies who came from the villages. These women, used to heavy work, had strong hands and arms which helped them to make ten times as much money as I did. My wages averaged only about a dollar a day while the others made about ten dollars. Still, I was proud that I could class myself as a working college student.

"I Was Not a Run-of-the-Mill Housewife"

After graduation, there were two questions in my mind. Should I go back to China or should I stay in this country? To return to my native land at this time was not exactly what my mother expected, I was afraid, because she would like me to either marry or be economically independent. As I did not as yet have any prospect of a steady position, I tried to stop thinking of going back unless I had earned enough money to pay my ocean liner fare and to sustain myself in my mother's house while waiting for a job. On the other hand, if I stayed in this country, what kind of an opening could I get, if at all, in the face of severe racial discrimination in every walk of life? Since I had already begun taking some graduate courses, why not continue to study as I wished? As I looked around for a way out of my dilemma, I got married and started out as any ordinary housewife. . . .

My daughter was born in the old Fabiola Hospital [in Oakland]. The fee was $100, which was considered high. I stayed with my baby in the hospital for four weeks before going home to the attic bedroom at my aunt's store. In a few days my baby's skin began to break out in boils. The doctor asked me to move into a more sanitary place right away because the heat in the attic where we lived was too hot and unfit for the newborn baby. Immediately my husband and I with our baby moved to a third-floor flat on Webster Street just two blocks away.

I nursed my baby but had a hard time pacifying her at night when her skin bothered her. Mentally I was in anguish but could not help her. Later in life my daughter had this skin trouble off and on, and I blamed my own imprudence of living in an unhealthy attic. It also shows how poor mothers and their offspring might suffer all their lives no matter how blandly social workers explain family difficulties. . . .

On a cold night in January, 1931, my son was born. Remembering my daughter's skin trouble, my husband and I decided to leave him in the hospital for awhile so as to be sure that he would get the right care. He stayed in the hospital for four months. When he was brought home, he was healthy and strong. Our family was complete and we had a girl and a boy to continue the family name after us. I felt that I had done my duty as a wife. Many Chinese might think that a wife should bear as many sons as possible, but I did not approve of such thinking.

While taking care of my children and doing routine housework, I found a little time to rethink my life. Was I in a rut? Why did I get a higher education? Had I utilized my formal training? Should I stay at home merely to be wife and mother? My thoughts were confused at first, but gradually my ambition to reach out beyond the four walls of a home seemed to attract my imagination. I said to myself: Why not try to accomplish what I had started to do at the time I left China [pursue graduate studies]? In addition, I had more reason to improve myself now than before; I had a husband and two children. Marriage, to me, was a two-way proposition: the husband had the duty to maintain a family, and so had the wife who should contribute her share of responsibilities. Furthermore, society still discriminated against married women. A married friend once said to me, "When you are single, people admire you and are ready to assist you; but once you are married, you are finished." She must have experienced this sad situation herself before she could utter such a bitter opinion. Anyhow, it aroused my suspicion about social disrespect for a married woman. I was furious with myself when I heard criticisms against housewives. Some people would say, "Look at so and so; she has a college degree but what does she do? Just stay home and wash diapers!" I could not stay put! I had to show them that I was not a run-of-the-mill housewife who looked up to her husband's good will alone.

"It [the YWCA] Was My JOB, in Capital Letters"

In the two years of graduate study, I had a vague idea of possibly returning to China to teach. When I was not immersed in the process of getting my assignments done, I would picture to myself the image of a middle school teacher in Canton where teachers were highly respected, dedicated educators. Were I in such a place, I would be able to put my knowledge gained in America into practical use. I would fit the principles I learned from the West into pragmatic lessons to equip Chinese students for their daily lives. [But] my family was here and I surely should stay in this country permanently. [So] in spite of my ambition to teach in China, I did not go back after all. I had been thinking of seeing my mother again before it was too late. By the time I graduated from Mills College the second time [in 1933], it was really too late. My mother had passed away. . . .

To stay home and take care of my children was, of course, my primary concern; but in the midst of the depression period, it was necessary for me to seek employment. Since I had earned a higher academic degree, I felt that it was imperative for me to keep on pushing for an opening in a more rewarding profession. Where could I go? I could not expect to get any answer from a Caucasian establishment which was prejudicial to Orientals. Once, I took up a suggestion from a friend to see about an opening in a public office. I entered the lobby where a secretary said the boss was out to lunch and would be back soon, and would I like to sit down and wait? I said I would and sat down for almost an hour. At last the secretary said that Mrs. So and So was not coming back that afternoon and she was sorry. At that, I was dismissed! On my way out, I peered into the inner office and saw a lady there. Was that the Mrs. So and So? I did not know, and I had no choice but to leave!

Fortunately, I was sought to work for the Chinese YWCA in San Francisco. At that time the San Francisco YWCA had built a Residence Club on Powell Street. The Board of Directors also included in their plan a new Chinese YWCA building near the Residence Club, facing Clay Street. After the dedication of the new building, the Chinese Committee of Management looked for someone who could speak Chinese to contact its Chinese-speaking members.[7] In their search for a suitable person, they sent me a letter asking if I was available. I was interested, but with reservations. This offer was only a part-time situation and I had to have baby sitters; it was not economical for me to commute to San Francisco every day for a few hours just for a part-time pay.[8] I laid the letter aside and continued thinking in two divergent directions; to get a job and to care for my children. I hesitated.

Fortunately again, I was told by someone that the Hip Wo [Chinese] Language School in San Francisco was looking for a teacher in the fall. Reverend Tse Kai Yuen [Kei Yuan], then the minister of the Chinese Presbyterian Church, knew that I was available for employment and recommended me for the position. He was bold enough to say that I could fulfill the responsibilities of a teacher of the junior class, which was the highest in the whole school. I was overjoyed. I was thinking that I could combine two part-time jobs into one full-time position, and I could then have someone look after my children. It was a God-sent opportunity, I thought, and came home with an optimistic anticipation of a working mother who not only could use her ability to improve her economic condition, but also to meet the challenge that her academic learning had provided for her.

Chinatown was a compact community. Every important move in any of the organizations was announced in the local papers. As I was appointed the community worker of the Chinese YWCA, the news was known all over town. Some of my friends congratulated me for being lucky enough to be employed by such a prestigious organization. However, I did not delude myself. I knew I had to work hard in order to get any recognition from the community which, to my amazement, was already accepting me as one of its leaders. A short time after I started work at the YWCA, Mr. B. Y. Leong asked me to speak to the Union of Churches meeting at which members of the Protestant churches would

7. Although founded in 1916 by white missionary workers, the Chinese YWCA was run by and for Chinese American women. In 1932, at the height of the Great Depression, the Chinese community donated $25,000 toward a new building. Architect Julia Morgan volunteered her services and designed both the Residence Club on Powell Street and the Chinese YWCA building on Clay Street. The latter building was recently sold to the Chinese Historical Society of America.

8. At the time, Jane Kwong Lee was still living in Oakland, where her husband operated a meat market.

attend. I had spoken at public gatherings in Oakland and attracted attention from the crowd. With pleasure, I accepted the invitation to speak.
Whether or not I made any impression from the first speech I made, I
did not know; but I knew that I was asked to speak to church groups
again and again in the future. It was a good omen for me to take part in
the Chinese community life of San Francisco.

In the next two years of my life, I actually divided my attention in
three different directions—my family, the YWCA, and the Chinese language school. Aside from providing the necessary care for my children,
I did not have any other worries for my family as they were healthy; my
husband left for work in the East Bay every morning without asking me
to prepare breakfast and came home after work to look after the children. I considered myself lucky to have his cooperation in raising two
normal children and maintaining a normal family life. At the YWCA I
really contributed a great part of my energy. Even though my official
hours were about four hours in the afternoon, I actually planned and
worried about the procedure and methods of carrying out the day's work.
In fact, it was my main concern as a college-trained person to handle social problems as they arose. In a way, it was my JOB, in capital letters.

The schools, in my view, were equally important. They provided the
needed corrective force for Chinatown's smooth pattern of living. On
top of [assisting] children of Chinese descent to [prepare for] their future careers, the Chinese schools actually helped in checking the behavior of unruly children. We did not have so-called "delinquent youth."
One of the reasons, I assumed, was that the Chinese schools kept them
in school all day, every day, and half a day on Saturday and Sunday. No
matter how naughty a child might be, he could not have time to [get into
trouble]. As most parents sent their children to these schools, there was
hardly any [unoccupied] child [who could] perform any illegal act by himself or by grouping together with his peers for violence. I was happy to
be included on the staff of a Chinese language school.

In turning my attention to the position of Community Worker, I had
a varied spectrum—a link between persons, between individuals and
groups, between groups and groups, and between country to country,
even. For instance, when I interpreted for a Mrs. So and So, this was a
connection between her and her physician; when I asked a girl to be a
member of a club, I acted as a link between this girl and the YWCA;
when I went out on a financial campaign for a school house, I acted as
a link between the school house and the community in which the school
house was to be erected; and when I volunteered to get help from Amer-

ica for flood victims in China, I acted as a link between China and America. Thus, I considered my job as a very important and beneficial one, and I was doing it with deep dedication and zeal. Later on, I might be accused of being too career-minded, but I could not help my professional attitude of devoting my best to what needed to be done. I might have to apologize to my children that I should have given them more of my time and care, but I have to admit that my love for them has never diminished an iota, no matter how deeply involved I was in community affairs.

(SOURCE: Jane Kwong Lee, "A Chinese American," unpublished manuscript in my possession)

WHY CHINESE AMERICANS
SHOULD SUPPORT THE YWCA

In May of this year, the national YWCA held its general meeting at Colorado Springs. Attendees included delegates from Africa, Asia, Europe, and the United States, representing the four races. Topics discussed included academic, agricultural, industrial, and commercial issues, plus problems of mutual concern and their solutions. The goal was to foster understanding among people and to promote peace. This is a good example of the global and universal nature of the YWCA. Moreover, the mission of the YWCA is consistent with the goals and direction of every country in the world, China included. That is why the YWCA chapters in the schools, cities, and rural areas of China have been flourishing. A few years ago, the operation of these groups was made possible by donations from American philanthropists and Western-trained directors. Now, because of the economic depression, the West can no longer be concerned with the Far East. But since capable women have surfaced in China, the local branches can function under Chinese management. This is actually the best possible development and calls for rejoicing among overseas Chinese. As for the YWCA in Chinatown, it deserves no less attention, for it is an integral part of the larger movement.

Not only that, but the degree of the YWCA's success reflects the extent of our society's development. Why do I say this? It is because women constitute half of the human race. And if women, who make up half of the human race, do not unite and improve themselves in the areas of character, intellectual, physical, and social development, then no matter how high-minded and knowledgeable the men—the other half of the human race—are, the entire society will not advance. In old China, men were held to be better than women. Men had more ambitions and were educated so they could roam the world and bring glory to their family. Women, on the other hand, were considered virtuous if they remained uneducated.[9] They were passed over and confined to their bedchambers, ignorant of the world and its affairs. That is why the Chinese people have become weak and it is so difficult to help them. Yet those with foresight have long realized that liberating women so that they may develop and improve themselves is something that should not be delayed.

Then too, we should give our support to the organizations that are worthwhile and withdraw our support from those that are not. Let's look for a moment at the worthwhile work of the YWCA. To women, the YWCA provides training and assistance, such as classes that teach them skills, lectures that improve their knowledge, arts and craft workshops that help them to pass their leisure time. To other community agencies, it offers cooperation. And to anyone who seeks aid, be it a single person, a family, or a group, it gives assistance in the spirit of charity. For example, it offers job referrals to those who need jobs, financial assistance to those who need money, and translation services to those who do not know English. To the country, it offers patriotic women willing to do their best under any circumstance. In summary, the function of the YWCA is to help women develop their abilities as well as to help society advance. Isn't the YWCA a beneficial organization worth supporting?

Editor's note: The YWCA in San Francisco Chinatown is a newcomer among the various other charitable organizations, but because it provides needed services in the spirit of giving, this latecomer is gaining in reputation and popularity. For example, it sponsors Mandarin language classes with volunteer instructors; organizes fund-raisers to aid refugees in China and visits to comfort soldiers wounded in battle against the Japanese; sponsors social functions for women; and overall helps to improve the Chinese American community. All these public services have benefited the Chinese here and brought glory to China.

The YWCA's splendid new site has been made possible through the support of Chinatown's residents and community leaders. Surely they will want to finish what they have started by continuing to give generously to the organization.

(SOURCE: *Chung Sai Yat Po*, August 15, 1936, p. 1. TRANSLATOR: Ellen Yeung.)

---

9. For a discussion of other such sexist sayings, see "Images of Women in Chinese Proverbs," pp. 103–12.

The Purpose of the Chinese Women's Jeleab Association

LIU YILAN

Even before the Chinese YWCA was established in 1916, Chinese women in the San Francisco Bay Area had taken the initiative to organize the Chinese Women's Jeleab [Self-Reliance] Association in 1913. Following the example of other American clubs, they had even filed incorporation papers at the state capitol, stating as the group's purpose "social inter-course, benevolent work, educational advantages, and mutual assistance and benefit." According to an interview with one of the founders, Mrs. C. G. Lee [Clara Lee],[1] that appeared in the San Francisco Chronicle*—complete with a photograph of thirty-eight of the group's members flanked by the American flag and the club's Chinese banner—the Jeleab Association was inspired by the 1911 Chinese revolution and by the membership policies of the Chinese Native Sons of the Golden State, which excluded women.[2]* The club was unique in that it was unaffiliated with a church or nationalist cause and its membership consisted of immigrant

---

1. The daughter of liberal parents Rev. Chan Hon Fun and Ow Muck Gay, Clara Lee was born in Portland, Oregon, in 1886. The family moved to Oakland before the 1906 earthquake, and Clara remained there after her marriage to Dr. Charles Goodall Lee, the first Chinese licensed dentist in California.

2. Elizabeth Young, "The Most Unique Club in America: A Club of Chinese Women," *San Francisco Chronicle*, February 8, 1914, p. 5. The Chinese Native Sons of the Golden State changed its name to the Chinese American Citizens Alliance in 1928, after the Native Sons of the Golden West refused to give them affiliated status. Its bylaws were not changed to admit women members until 1973.

The top half of a full-page story in the *San Francisco Examiner* on February 8, 1914, featuring the Chinese Women's Jeleab Association. Founding president Mrs. C. G. Lee [Clara Lee] appears in the top left corner.

mothers and American-born daughters, all of whom lived in Oakland and San Francisco.

A more elaborate statement of purpose appeared earlier in Sai Gai Yat Po/Chinese World *as follows. Prepared by Liu Yilan, most likely a member of the new organization, the article pressed the point that Chinese women's subordination was due to their lack of self-reliance, which in turn was due to their lack of education. While the writer followed the reformist point of view in linking education to women's equality, she took it a step further by encouraging women to take advantage of opportunities in America to elevate their status and that of their sisters in China. The key to women's self-improvement and the purpose of the Jeleab Association, she concluded, was for women to band together and learn from each other. In this sense, the self-initiated association represented a new awakening in the social consciousness of Chinese American women, a recognition of a higher status of womanhood to which they and their counterparts in China could aspire. Moreover, juxtaposed against the comments of Clara Lee in the* Chronicle *interview, Liu Yilan's views in this article indicate that the membership was indeed bi-*

cultural and intergenerational, and that a strong blend of Chinese na-
tionalist and American progressive thought had gone into the founding
of the organization.

For several thousand years a black curtain has shrouded the women of
China, blocking their view of the sky. How can men—living under the
same sky and on the same earth as women, members of the same human
race in the same universe—presume to be superior to women, trampling
them underfoot, humiliating them, and making them serve men's every
whim? As for women, they have suffered these indignities and humilia-
tions without questioning; living or dying at men's every command. This
is such a tragedy! All this is because women are not self-reliant. And yet,
before one can be self-reliant, one must have education.

In our ancestral country education in the home is missing, education
in society is poor, and education at school is also lacking. No wonder
women cannot stand on their own feet. But if they were living in this republic, where education flourishes and women's rights are allowed to
develop, then the situation would be entirely different. Women who are
born and raised here have the chance to enter school when young and
to receive the same education as men. Even the older women who come
from China feel inspired, after being continuously exposed to talk of freedom and equality and after seeing for themselves the elevated status enjoyed by women here as opposed to the inferior position of women back
home. They begin to think and question: Why is it that there are those
who can lord it over others while I am a slave? Why is it that some can
be in heaven while I am in hell? Questioning leads to realization, and
with realization comes resolve. One could hardly be considered human
if one did not take urgent steps to become self-reliant.

Although to be able to stand on one's own feet requires learning and
knowledge, yet learning can be improved through interactions with others and knowledge can be increased through the exchange of information. It is important that we broaden our contacts by making new friends
and not keep to ourselves and become limited to our own little world.
If we women are to become independent, we must form a large group
so that we can cull and share ideas and benefit from each other. Therefore, those of us who are of like minds have decided to form this group
and call it the Lü-Mei Zhongguo Nüjie Zilihui [Chinese Women's Self-
Reliance Association]. Our goal is to cultivate self-reliance in each of us
and, furthermore, to promote and propagate this concept in China, so

as to strip away the black curtain that has blocked women's view of the sky for thousands of years. This, then, is the purpose of our group.

(SOURCE: *Sai Gai Yat Po/Chinese World*, September 22, 1913, p. 12. TRANSLA-TOR: Ellen Yeung.)

In 1914 the Chinese Women's Jeleab Association boasted a membership of two hundred women, some of whom met regularly in the parlor of the Chinese Native Sons of the Golden State in Oakland. An evening class was started to teach the illiterate how to read and write Chinese, under the direction of Mrs. T. L. Lee, a Baptist minister's wife, with plans to tackle English next. Another class met every other Monday for instruction in using American sewing patterns. Seventy-five years later, Clara Lee noted in an interview with me that the Jeleab Association, despite its auspicious beginnings, disbanded a few years later. "It didn't last very long," she said. "Some lived [too far away] in San Francisco, and some moved away later."[3] But the seeds of self-reliance had been successfully planted in women like Clara Lee, who, aside from being among the first Chinese women to register to vote, went on to join the YWCA, the International Institute, and Fidelis Coterie, and devoted much of her life to volunteer work on behalf of immigrant women and the Chinese community in Oakland.

---

3. Clara Lee, interview with author, July 31, 1989, Alameda, California. I first interviewed Clara in 1986 when she was 100 years old. She passed away in 1993 at the age of 107.

PART FOUR

First Steps

The Second Generation, 1920s

Coming of age in the 1920s, second-generation women, unlike their mothers, were not fettered by bound feet; nor were they as restricted by Chinese tradition. As Rose Chew notes in her essay on the second generation, they spoke English, went to public schools, and were influenced by their teachers, peers, and popular culture to be modern in appearance, outlook, and lifestyle. While the first generation had been concerned with economic survival, this generation wanted to become a part of mainstream America. However, they were prevented from doing so by intergenerational and cultural conflict at home and by racism, sexism, and economic segmentation in the larger society. As expressed by an anonymous second-generation woman in an essay titled "The Oriental Girl in the Occident," many young Chinese women found themselves in limbo, having broken their links with the East but as yet unconnected to the West. Placing their faith in Christianity was one solution, according to Janie Chii and other Chinese American Christians. Another solution, advocated by social worker Rose Chew, was for the second generation to take "the best of the East and the West" and shape a new cultural identity for themselves.

As the life stories and writings of the seven women in this section demonstrate, it was not easy being a second-generation Chinese American in the 1920s. The need to negotiate between cultures, as well as between the American ideals of democracy and the realities of racial exclusion, elicited a variety of responses based on the interplay of historical forces, cultural values, family circumstances, and individual personalities. Some, like Alice Sue Fun, Esther Wong, and Gladys Ng Gin, acquiesced to parental expectations and the limitations placed on them by the larger society. Others, like Tye Leung Schulze, Rose Yuen Ow, and Flora Belle Jan, chose to challenge social restrictions and define their own positions in American society. Those with progressive parents had an easier time of it. Florence Chinn Kwan's parents were Christians and Chinese nationalists, and they encouraged her to pursue higher education and go serve China in its hour of need. Rose's parents likewise supported her education and then her career as a cabaret dancer. Often, once they became economically independent, Chinese American daughters were able to break away from the confines of home and the control of their parents. With her earnings, Alice was able to dress in the latest fashions and travel; Rose was able to take dancing lessons and convince her father to let her perform in vaudeville; and Flora Belle was able to pursue the lifestyle of a flapper and leave home for college.

Most Chinese American women tried to become a part of mainstream America while retaining certain elements of their cultural heritage. Indeed, taking pride in their ethnic culture was one way for them to deal with the marginalization they experienced in the broader society. They proudly spoke both Chinese and English, ate Chinese and Western food, and celebrated Chinese and American holidays. Like other American adolescents influenced by the lure of U.S. consumerism in the 1920s, those who could afford to do so dressed fashionably, went to movies, dances, and picnics, and participated in sports, though usually in a segregated setting because of racial exclusion. Similarly, they accommodated discrimination in the labor market by finding sales, clerical, and professional jobs in Chinatown or going to China, where their scientific, business, and professional skills could be put to good use.

Compared to their mothers, second-generation women were, in general, better educated, more economically mobile, and more socially active. Because of their birthright as U.S. citizens, they were also more politically involved, participating in American politics and contributing to Chinese nationalist causes. As soon as women's suffrage was won in California, Tye Leung Schulze became the first Chinese woman to vote. Others, as Rose Chew indicates in her essay, followed suit and went so far as to campaign for political candidates.

Another difference between the two generations was in marriage. Western notions of romantic love influenced many to break with the Chinese tradition of arranged marriage. Against her parents' wishes, Alice

Sue Fun fell in love with her Chinese school teacher and left home to marry him. Tye Leung Schulze ran away to the Presbyterian Mission Home to avoid an arranged marriage and later suffered social ostracism for marrying outside her race. Not only did all of the women featured in this section choose their own spouses, but they were more often than not equal partners in their marriages. Their husbands were more willing to share in the housework and child care, discuss decisions affecting the family, and confide in them.

Finally, second-generation women were more literate, articulate, and interactive with the larger society than was the first generation. Fortunately for me and the public record, they left a trail of stories, writings, and oral histories behind. I found the oral histories of Esther Wong and Flora Belle Jan in the Survey of Race Relations collection at Stanford University. Conducted in the 1920s as part of a sociological investigation into race relations on the West Coast, these interviews ring with an immediacy and truth not obtainable in retrospective interviews today. Nevertheless, it should be noted that the investigators had an agenda of sorts: they were seeking to prove that, contrary to popular nativist and racist opinions, "Orientals" such as Esther and Flora Belle were assimilable and could become good Americans.

The two essays by Tye Leung Schulze and Florence Chinn Kwan about the importance of Christianity in their lives were given to me by their children, who fortunately saw the value of preserving their mothers' writings. The life story of Rose Yuen Ow, the cabaret dancer, came from an interview that Him Mark Lai and Philip P. Choy of the Chinese Historical Society of America had the foresight to do in 1970. Although I tried to locate Rose and her family for a follow-up interview, I was unsuccessful. Alice Sue Fun was someone I had known for years from my work at the Asian Branch Library in Oakland, California, and Gladys Ng Gin, the only illiterate member of this group, was a good friend of my sister Sharon. Both have passed away since I interviewed them. Although of the same generation, these women all tell different stories about how they took the first steps, crossing race, gender, class, and cultural boundaries, toward claiming their rightful place in American society.

The Oriental Girl in the Occident

ONE OF THE "SECOND GENERATION"

In 1926 the following article on the cultural dilemma of second-genera-tion Chinese American women appeared in Women and Missions, *the same Presbyterian women's journal that published Donaldina Cameron's "The Story of Wong So" a year earlier (see pp. 201–10). It may seem odd that such an article would be published in a journal that purportedly fo-cused on mission activities among foreigners throughout the world and at home. But given that all Chinese in America, regardless of birthright, were considered foreigners at this time, it is not odd at all. The title, "Ori-ental Girl in the Occident," by objectifying Chinese women as the ex-otic "other" from the reference point of Western superiority, reinforces this perspective.[1] Similarly, the author's use of "American" in this arti-cle to mean white American relegates all Chinese Americans, even those born in the United States, to foreign status.*

---

1. The term "Orient," meaning East, was coined by British imperialists in the sixteenth century to locate Asia far to the east of London, then the center of world power. From this position of Occidental or Western superiority, "Oriental" was commonly used in refer-ence to Chinese, Japanese, or Korean people until the 1960s, when Chinese and Japanese American activists called attention to its derogatory connotations of exoticism and inferi-ority. Since then "Asian American" has become the preferred name, in recognition of the group's common history of oppression, geographical origins, panethnic identity, and po-litical destiny.

According to this anonymous writer, the second-generation Chinese American woman lives in limbo, "neither East nor West and yet is the product of both." Influenced by popular culture and what she learns from her white peers, she yearns for a life far different from that of her mother's generation—a life of "excitement and thrills" away from the social restraints and crowded living conditions of Chinatown. But as she ventures out in pursuit of the good life, how is she to preserve her "finer character"? What is to become of her?

Although the writer acknowledges the structural barriers that prevented second-generation women from acculturating into mainstream American life—overcrowded housing and low-wage jobs—she does not bother to probe the underlying sources of these problems. Alien land laws, housing covenants, and rental practices that discriminated against the Chinese kept them living in substandard tenement buildings within the bounds of Chinatown until after World War II. Even the most qualified and westernized Chinese Americans were told "We don't hire Orientals" when they applied for jobs outside Chinatown, except in cases where their "picturesque" appearances might draw customers. Considering the religious tenets of the publication, it is not surprising that Janie Chii, responding to "One of the 'Second Generation's'" query at the end of her short article, would tell the writer to rely on Christianity to overcome all obstacles and problems.

Despite its lack of analysis and any concrete solution, "The Oriental Girl in the Occident" still conveys a strong sense of the frustrations Chinese American women felt as they tried to define their position in American society in the face of cultural conflicts at home and discrimination on the outside. The stories of second-generation women that follow in this section not only expand on this dilemma but also show the diverse ways that individual women resolved the conflict for themselves.

The problem of the second generation is familiar to all who are interested in newcomers to American shores, but most people think of it in relation to the European immigrant. That the problem is even more serious among the Orientals in America the following article makes plain. The writer, a university graduate, the daughter of Christian parents, is a young Chinese woman of the second generation in America who is doing Christian work among girls of her own race in a big western city. She speaks out of a full heart. The question with which she closes her query is answered by Mrs. Janie Chii, another second generation young Chinese woman, who frankly confesses the darkness of the situation, but is confident that Christ can bring it light.

An interesting development of the East in the West is the second generation Chinese in America. Particularly interesting is the second generation Chinese girl. She is a thing apart from her sister of the older generation who was bound by the traditions of many centuries. Freed from old restraints, yet hampered by many new problems which she meets in her daily living, she is still an uncertain quantity. Consciously and unconsciously she reflects the conflict within her caused by her Chinese heritage and American environment. She has broken her link with the East. She has not as yet found one with the West.

The second generation Chinese girl in America easily assimilates the West as it is seen outwardly. She can quickly become American in speech and in dress. With her limited resources, she keeps pace in fashion with the American girl of today. She wants the same things; she enjoys the same things. To her people she seems extreme when compared with the old concept of the Chinese woman. She is extreme, because she is always ready to try the new. Not being guided by any criterion, her values for the time being become mixed. The rules of conduct which serve her parents do not hold for her—she is of another world than they. She needs new rules, but she is yet to find them.

The Chinese community in the West is usually crowded into a small area and in an unattractive locality. Particularly is this true of San Francisco, where a population of over 8,000 Chinese live in an area of about fifteen blocks. In such crowded quarters, the average Chinese home is naturally limited in space. Tenement buildings shared by many families take the place of separate dwellings. The average home may consist of three rooms, two of which are bedrooms and one living and dining room combined, which also serves as a sleeping apartment at night—and this for an average family of say seven in number. Common stairs, common halls, common sanitary facilities, community kitchens are features of the typical tenement home. There is no privacy. Neighbors and relatives come and go at will.

Family ties are very essential to the average Chinese. They are still essential to the second generation Chinese girl. But she is generally dissatisfied with her crowded home conditions and the resulting lack of privacy. She has no time when she can be alone. She has no place where she may receive her friends, where she is free from the curious eyes of neighbors living in too close proximity.

Her parents submit to present living conditions. They know of no other, perhaps, or they bow to the inevitable. But the second generation Chinese girl belongs to another world. She knows, to some extent, better living conditions and she strives for them. Expressed or unexpressed, she thinks, "I do not want to live as my parents do. I *cannot* live as they live." In some instances she may succeed in changing to a slight degree her home conditions. More often, to escape from them she spends her leisure hours outside her home. With this comes the greater freedom from restraint. Occasionally she is forced to live apart from her family, and this also results in greater freedom.

Economic pressure at home forces the second generation Chinese girl early into the world of industry. Here also she has problems. Employment for her is limited. Professional work to some extent is open to her, and there are in her group a few doctors, teachers, social workers, nurses; but opportunities in this field are open only as the Chinese community grows. With the restriction on immigration of the Chinese since the Exclusion Act, the number in the community has decreased and is steadily decreasing. Higher education is dearly loved by the Chinese, but what urge is there for the average girl to go on in school if economic conditions at home force her to employment and she feels that her prospects are not any better after years spent in higher education?

Hence the second generation Chinese girl may be employed as a stock-girl in American stores, elevator operator, errand girl for specialty or millinery shops, waitress, stenographer, bookkeeper, bank clerk, operator in hairdressing shops, clerk in Chinese shops dealing with oriental goods, maid in American homes, or in some capacity where her picturesque appearance is an asset—in such capacity as the girl who passes bread or cigarettes in restaurants with occidental patronage. Her wages are low, usually the minimum.

In positions where picturesque appearance and conduct are required, how can the second generation Chinese girl put right values first? How can she preserve her finer character and expression when the occidental community, especially for business purposes, demands otherwise? Her parents cannot help her—their rules of conduct do not hold in this new field.

In her social life the Chinese girl meets with new problems. Her social contact with Americans of the right sort is limited. She gets her knowledge of social America from the "movies," from the street, from what she hears from the girls in service in homes. She wants to be American and she has always a struggle in her mind as to what is right and what is not right in respect to occidental thinking. She teems with the life that urges on this new generation of Americans. She wants excitement and thrills. She wants to live.

Average home conditions make it impossible for her to receive her friends at home so what is more natural than that she should spend her leisure hours away from home? Therefore she meets her friends outside, in the streets, in restaurants, or in some public place. Her means of social expression are found in theater, in restaurant parties, in dances, in automobile rides.

In her social life, in business, in home, the Chinese girl of America ventures with her greater freedom into new fields. Yet greater freedom does not bring with it greater wisdom. Governed by neither the West nor the East, yet influenced by both, she plunges heedlessly into new experiences in her quest.

What will be the outcome in the development of the second generation Chinese girl of America? How will she find herself, she who is neither East nor West and yet is the product of both? It is an interesting conjecture.

The Answer to the Problem

What the outcome will be? We shall never know. The social and economic problems of the second generation Chinese girl of America will never be solved; and the life of a non-Christian girl is surely a tragedy!

Yet all is not as hopeless as it seems to the Christian Chinese girl. *Christianity* enables her to overcome all obstacles, all problems. She does not grope in darkness as her sister who is without Christ, and she does find herself after she has found Christ. *Jesus* is her answer, and she can say as David said in the Psalms, "He only can."

                                                             Janie Chii

(SOURCE: *Women and Missions*, 3, no. 5 [August 1926]: 174–75)

Manifestations of Modern Influences on Second Generation Chinese

MISS ROSE CHEW

As if building on the preceding article concerning the cultural dilemma of second-generation women, this article discusses similar issues but in more depth and from a sociological perspective. The author, a daughter of Rev. Ng Poon Chew and a second-generation Chinese American herself,[1] was a social worker at the International Institute when she wrote this essay for the "Survey of Social Work Needs of the Chinese Population of San Francisco." The survey, conducted under the auspices of the Community Chest of San Francisco and published in 1930, at the beginning of the Great Depression, was aimed at defining the welfare needs of the Chinese community, particularly in the areas of child care, housing, health, recreation, education, and employment.[2] A second survey was completed in 1935 under the auspices of the California State Emergency Relief Administration.[3]

The point of this article was to describe the "modern" influences of

---

1. Rev. Ng Poon Chew (1866–1931) was editor and publisher of the progressive Chinese newspaper *Chung Sai Yat Po* and an eloquent advocate on behalf of Chinese Americans.

2. Similar to today's United Way, the Community Chest was the fund-raising arm for various community organizations in the city.

3. Both surveys are cited in earlier studies of San Francisco Chinatown. The 1935 survey is available from the Bancroft Library at the University of California, Berkeley, and the San Jose Public Library. The 1930 survey I accidentally found in an upstairs closet of the International Institute of San Francisco, where Rose Chew was previously employed.

American life on members of the second generation as compared to the "traditional" ways of their immigrant parents. In so doing, Rose Chew was careful to avoid any denigration of Chinese culture and to acknowledge the range of responses of the younger generation to the acculturation process. Unlike the previous writer, she openly discusses the racial discrimination that prevented Chinese Americans from finding better-paying jobs and living outside of Chinatown. In drawing comparisons between the two generations, the article provides a wealth of information on just how different second-generation men and women were in appearance, thinking, and lifestyle. For example, they generally spoke English more fluently than Chinese, enjoyed American jazz and movies over Chinese opera, embraced American democratic ideas, and followed Western wedding customs. Second-generation women now tended to work outside the home—as waitresses, stockgirls, teachers, bank tellers, and operators of beauty parlors. But their aspirations to acquire "the best in American living and culture" were thwarted by racial discrimination. What was to become of them? Here, Rose Chew offers a more realistic and practical solution than Janie Chii did in the preceding selection. The second generation, she says, should strive to adopt the best of both cultures, thus asserting their identity as a rich mixture: not as Chinese, not as Americans, but as Chinese Americans.

An attempt to show manifestations of modern influences in the life of the second generation Chinese is necessarily based on observations made through personal knowledge of the Chinese community. No adequate statistics are possible in the treatment of this subject which is so general and takes into account so many factors. The second generation group as a whole shall be considered, not taking into account either extremes—those who are American in every way and those who have not been influenced greatly by modern trends due to extremely Chinese background in family life.

The Chinese Community is rather closely confined within a certain number of blocks, a restriction due to the impossibility of expansion on three sides (business district, commission market district and North Beach district) and to prejudice which makes expansion rather difficult on the remaining side. In spite of being more or less limited to a certain area, the second generation Chinese (or rather first generation Americans of Chinese parentage) have been greatly affected by modern influences, that is, influences other than Chinese. These influences are very evident when one compares similar phases in the life of the older group and younger group, with respect to the economic, social, civic and cultural factors.

Employment is a question of paramount importance to the second generation Chinese because of the vast problem it presents in the lack of opportunities of employment open to them. The problem is not so acute with the first generation, as the majority of them are absorbed in the various businesses in the community itself. The following lists of some of the occupations of both groups give in a measure the differences in employment interests between the two groups:

Some Occupations of First Generation	*Some Occupations of Second Generation*
Bazaar Owners and Clerks	Bank Clerks
Bath House Owners	Bond Brokers
Barbers	Beauty Parlor Operators
Chinese Drug Stores (Herbs, etc.)	Chemists
Chinese Grocery and Vegetable Store Owners and Clerks	Clerks in Bazaars
Cleaners and Dyers	Clerical Workers (General Office)
Cooks	Dentists
Coffee Shop Owners and Waiters	Doctors (Western trained)
Chair Repairers	Drug Stores (American)
Domestic Help	Draymen
Herbalists (Chinese herb doctors)	Elevator Operators
Hotel, Rooming House, Apartment House Owners	Engineer (Civil, Electrical, etc.)
Jewelry Shop (Chinese)	Garage—Auto repair shop
Laundries	Interpreters—Court, etc.
Ministers	Insurance Brokers
Newspapers (All printed in Chinese)	Librarians
Pawnbrokers	Nurses
Restaurant Owners & Managers	Newspapers (Two of the six papers in the community managed by second generation but printed in Chinese—necessitating a Chinese Education)
Shrimp Industries	
Shoe Repairing	
Sewing Factories	
Street Fruit Stands	Pharmacists
Salmon Canneries	Salesmen of various sorts
Tailors	Social Workers
Teachers in Chinese Language	Stenographers
Vegetable Peddlers	Stock Girls
	Teachers in American Schools
	Waitresses in American Tea Rooms, etc.
	Waiters

Mr. Ching Wah Lee of the Chinese Y.M.C.A. has made a very interesting study of the occupations of the Chinese University of California
graduates from 1921 to 1928 and the number in these occupations, taking into consideration only the second generation. He has also studied
the number of students in occupations for which they had training and
the number in occupations for which they had not the training in college, which they have entered because there was opportunity for employment. There is apparently much waste in the matter of training when
considered from the standpoint of the employment which the students
are able to secure after college.

The older generation Chinese have built up businesses of their own
which are in the main non-competitive with the American businesses and
dependent to a great extent on the support of the Chinese Community
itself. Practically all the first generation are absorbed in these businesses
with the exception probably of the laborers and domestic helpers. Very
few of the second generation are employed in the work of the older group
because there are no openings for them and also because the younger
group is not trained to do such work. Not many of the younger group
outside the professions have developed businesses of their own. The second generation tends to enter professional work (and only a certain number can be absorbed in the community) or work for which their western
training qualifies them. A quite recent development is the stock exchange
branch in the Chinese Community managed by second generation men—
which is absolutely the outgrowth of American influences.

A striking contrast can be shown in employed women. About fifteen
or twenty years ago, it was the exception for Chinese women to be gain-
fully employed outside the home. It is quite the general thing for women
to be employed outside the home now. For the second generation girl, her
employment frequently takes her outside the community in work where
her costume is a requirement, such as waitresses in tearooms and restaurants, stock girls, elevator operators, etc. Herein is also a problem which
must be met—the effect of such employment on character—employment
dependent primarily upon attractive costumes rather than upon qualifications and ability to do the work.

It is interesting to note that in the Chinese Community itself, among
the second generation women, there are two teachers in the public school,
two doctors, a dentist, a manager of a branch bank where practically all
the workers are Chinese women, a number of nurses, four beauty parlors owned and operated by Chinese women. This is without doubt the
result of modern influences.

Because of their western training, the second generation Chinese young people must look for employment outside the Chinese community. The limited opportunities in employment constitute a very great problem in the life of the second generation Chinese. Professor Eliot Grinnell Mears in his recent book "Resident Orientals on the American Pacific Coast" considers this problem very fully.[4] He shows clearly from statements of employers, etc., the occupational handicaps of the Oriental, due to union labor opposition and group and individual preferences. He says "the vocational problem for the American-born of Oriental parentage is serious because of an assumption on the part of many employers, even when they are free from race prejudice themselves, that their employment of oriental workers would be criticized by others." Recently a worker of a local social agency interviewed the employer of one of the large department stores in San Francisco and was told that "the store had a definite policy not to employ Orientals; that as far as the management was concerned, they would not make this ruling, but there was trouble in the departments where the white help object to working with Orientals." Where prejudice is added to competition, the employment situation becomes acute and is so for the increasing group of second generation Chinese who because of their western training is a part of the American community, but who has great difficulty, in spite of training and ability, in finding a place in the economic life of that community.

In their social life, American influences are as strongly manifested. Take, for instance, their club life. The first generation Chinese are practically all members of family associations, district associations, and the Chinese Six Companies. Membership in these organizations is dependent upon the family to which one belongs or the district from which one came or whether one is a Chinese or not. Very few of the second generation are active in these groups. They have clubs of a different sort— social clubs (membership in which is dependent not upon family or district or nationality, but upon one's group of friends), a University Alumni Club, a fraternity of University men, the Native Sons group, Young Women's Christian Association and Young Men's Christian Association clubs, Boy Scouts, High School Clubs, an Athletic Council, etc. American influences are distinctly seen here in the type of clubs formed and in the activities they carry on.

---

4. A key player in the Survey of Race Relations in the 1920s, Eliot Grinnell Mears went on to publish some of the findings in *Resident Orientals on the American Pacific Coast: Their Legal and Economic Status* (Chicago: University of Chicago Press, 1928).

Athletics play a strong part in their recreation life—track meets, basket ball leagues, tennis tournaments, etc., which are not confined to boys alone. In the social activities of the clubs and also of individuals of the second generation, there are the usual rounds of card parties, dinner dances, dances, week-end parties, all activities which are markedly different from the social life of the first generation. At a recent dance of one of the larger clubs, an American from the East exclaimed "Why, these are Americans!" He had been told of the western influences on the Chinese young people, but only realized it fully when he attended the dance and saw this actually with his own eyes. His one criticism was that the program preceding the dance was too much American Jazz! Where the older group attend the Chinese Theaters for amusement, only about 10% or less of the younger group attend these theaters. The latter more frequently go to the American movies or theaters.

There is this noticeable fact in the social life of the second generation in general, the lack of opportunities for a natural intermingling socially with American groups. Having been thrown back upon themselves through opposition from without in the way of prejudice, the group has developed a social life within themselves and invisible barriers have been built consciously or unconsciously around them for protection, barriers which are visibly manifested by the limits of the community. Group self-consciousness has developed to a marked degree. There have been attempts made by outside groups and groups on the inside to penetrate this difficulty, but barriers which have been the growth of such a long period are not easily broken down.

In the political life of the second generation Chinese, American influences doubtless hold sway. First in the matter of citizenship, except for a few exceptions of very early days, the entire group who can vote in the community is restricted to those born in this country. A large group of Chinese young people do vote. In matters which are of great interest to the country, this interest is reflected in the community itself. At the last presidential election, a Smith club was established in the Chinese community with Chinese members who were very active in behalf of Smith. The names of at least two women appeared in the preliminary letters sent out. In the same way, there was an active group in the community in favor of Hoover. It is interesting to note that a Chinese was put up for election at a city election, sponsored by a group at North Beach. Whether he was elected or not is not important. The fact remains that the second generation Chinese is gradually ready to enter the civic life of the city. As to their adherence to the old country, there is very little indication. To many the country of their parents is a foreign country. Their interest in the happenings of the old country is stimulated by the interest of the older group. To the majority, this is their country and here they expect to remain.

Manifestations of American influences on their cultural life are equally apparent. Education is essentially American, in spite of the Chinese Language Schools in the community, while the education of the first generation is generally Chinese. Practically every second generation child has elementary education. A large number continue their study in high school and a considerable number—increasingly so—attend the universities. This alone is indicative of American influences.

Language is an important factor pointing to these influences. English is used as often, if not more so, than Chinese, particularly in club meetings, in play [and] in social activities. A large number of the second generation would find it difficult to give a talk in Chinese. Some even are unable to speak Chinese or speak it with difficulty. Publications issued by the second generation clubs are practically always in English. American books and periodicals are read rather than Chinese books and periodicals.

Chinese customs followed by the older group, such as feast days, New Year's customs, etc., do not mean so much to the second generation except as they help to increase their holiday spirit. Many have been discarded. Marriages are hardly ever arranged according to old customs. It is a matter of personal choice, nor does it matter so much, as formerly, whether a girl marries or not. Marriage ceremonies are western rather than Chinese. At the same time, divorces are more frequent, not only with the second generation, but also with the first generation.

In the matter of dress, practically all the men wear western clothes. This is entirely true of the second generation Chinese men. With the second generation women, this is the general thing—costumes being worn usually where their employment demands them. And so on, down a list, such as music, parental authority, standards of living, manner of living, medical care, etc., one can find every indication of American influences.

This is but a hasty review of some of the outward indications of changes in the Chinese community due to American influences. The best example is the second generation Chinese himself. The outward indications point in a measure to inward changes, manifestations of which are not so tangible. But it is without doubt that western influences have changed the thinking of the group.

With the changes, problems arise. As we have previously stated, there is the problem of employment adjustment for the second generation group. There is a need of a greater choice of where to live which would ultimately mean a more natural intermingling with other groups and a lessening of the group's self-consciousness as a segregated community. With more diverse places of residence, the intermingling would begin at an earlier age where the children, not segregated in one school, could at an early age begin to know others, have the customary give and take with children of their own age but with different heritage, and lose in a measure the self-consciousness of their nationality and race which has been so fostered in a segregated community. There would be an opportunity of acquiring and knowing the best in American living and culture. The customary gulf between the first and second generations in America is greater in the case of the Chinese, primarily because of the vast differences between the customs of the East and West. In this gulf lies a great problem for the Chinese group. It is not so much a problem of not enough American influences (for they are very evidently present), but a problem of helping the younger group, while acquiring western ideals and culture, not to throw away their Chinese heritage, but to appreciate the culture of their parents and to cultivate this appreciation in order to make their lives as American citizens richer by this heritage. A slow, sure growth with the retaining of the best of the old and adding to this foundation the best of the new is more healthy than an indiscriminatory throwing away of old things and the taking on of new things.

(SOURCE: Community Chest of San Francisco, "Survey of Social Work Needs of the Chinese Population of San Francisco," 1930)

Alice Sue Fun, World Traveler

"A Rebel at Heart"

I will never forget Alice Sue Fun. She was so full of life and had such a cheerful disposition that whenever she entered the Asian Branch Library in Oakland, where I worked from 1975 to 1981, her mere presence would light up my day. At eighty years old, she kept busy traveling, knitting, sewing, and coming regularly to borrow Chinese novels to read. I remember showing her our collection of historical pictures of old Chinatown. When we came across one of Arnold Genthe's photographs, captioned "Waiting for the car," showing a Chinese family in holiday attire standing at a street corner in Chinatown, she said excitedly, "That's me and that's my sister, brother, mother, and uncle. We're all dressed up because my uncle was taking us to our aunt's house to baai nin [pay respects at Chinese New Year]. Look at me in those Chinese shoes," she laughed. The picture was taken right before the 1906 earthquake and Alice was about five or six years old, wearing a beaded headdress, embroidered tunic, trousers, and platform slippers, and holding a handkerchief in her right hand.[1]

In 1982, after I had left the library and was working on the Chinese Women of America exhibit and book project, I contacted Alice Fun and

---

1. See Arnold Genthe, *Old Chinatown* (New York: Mitchell Kennerley, 1913), p. 17. The photo was reprinted in Judy Yung, *Unbound Feet: A Social History of Chinese Women in San Francisco* (Berkeley: University of California Press, 1995), p. 110.

arranged to interview her at her home in Oakland. She was at that time the only Chinese resident of the plush St. Paul's Tower senior home that faced Lake Merritt. Her sunny studio apartment was full of plants, books, and her fine needlework. In two sessions and for a total of five hours, she cheerfully and patiently answered all my questions about her childhood days in San Francisco Chinatown, the 1906 earthquake and fire, the 1915 World's Fair, the jobs she held, her two marriages, and her travels around the world. Fortunately for me and for posterity, Alice loved being photographed, and she also enjoyed playing photographer. She shared with me a priceless photo album of black-and-white snapshots dating to the early 1900s that was filled with pictures of outings with family and friends to Golden Gate Park, Muir Woods, and the beach; visits with relatives in Fresno, Stockton, and Oakland; close-up portraits of family and friends; her married life in New York; and her trips around the United States and abroad. The photos bore playful captions inscribed in Alice's neat handwriting; one read: "Look carefully [and] you will see Goldie [her sister] falling from a swing on the roof with Ma and everybody watching. Look again if you do not see. 1913." Many of the photos showed Alice in a wide range of fashions. I have selected a number of these to complement her interview.

Alice Sue Fun's life spanned ninety years, from 1899 to 1989. She grew up in a sheltered environment, in an age when Chinese girls were expected to give unquestioning obedience to their parents, stay close to home, and help their mothers with income-generating work, shopping, and housework. Nurtured in Chinese culture, she spoke Chinese at home, ate Chinese food, celebrated Chinese holidays, learned to appreciate Chinese opera, and attended Chinese school after public school. Working-class parents like Alice's could not afford to support their children beyond grade school and usually expected their daughters to contribute income to the family until they were old enough to be arranged in marriage. In Alice's case, her mother pulled her out of public school after the sixth grade so that she could help out at home.

At fifteen, Alice was finally able to strike out on her own. She found a job as a stockgirl at a department store downtown and then as a salesgirl at a Chinatown curio shop, both jobs considered good for a young Chinese American woman at that time. Making more money than her mother, who sewed at home, and being able to keep half her earnings to spend as she liked no doubt gave Alice a sense of independence and explains her ability to dress in the latest fashions and to socialize as much

Alice Sue Fun in 1915: "At that time everybody wore Chinese clothes in Daai Fau [San Francisco]. You were considered a *faan gwai lo* [foreign devil] if you wore Western clothes."

"My brother Thomas loved to take pictures. He got me to dress in his clothes [and pose for him]."

Alice Sue Fun (fifth row, second from the left) attending the True Sunshine Chinese Language School in San Francisco.

Alice Sue Fun with her first husband in New York City: "Everyone in New York wears Western-style clothes, not like in San Francisco. . . . I knew how to make my own clothes, so I could always dress nice."

Alice Sue Fun (left) and friend at the Panama-Pacific International Exposition in 1915.

Bathing at Asbury Park, New Jersey, in 1919: "At that time it was considered daring to bare your arms. . . . I never swim, just get my feet wet."

Visiting friends on a farm in Connecticut.

as she did. It also freed her of traditional gender-role constraints. Against
her parents' wishes, she married her Chinese teacher and moved to New
York. When the marriage failed, she got a job working as a maid and
companion to actress Lola Fisher, which exposed her to Western culture
and allowed her to travel to different parts of the United States and Eu-
rope. That experience changed her life and, as she remarked in the in-
terview, "made a different person out of me."

"I Remember the Earthquake Very Distinctly"

I was born in San Francisco on Washington Street, 809 Washington Street.
My father ran a *daap sik gwoon*, a boardinghouse where the bachelors
came just to eat. Just two meals a day. Nine o'clock in the morning, four
o'clock in the evening. They paid so much by the week, so much by the
month. My father owned a place like that on Pacific Street when the earthquake came. My mother didn't know how to read or write but she was
an intelligent woman. She remembered every story that was told her and
she told us these old Chinese legends and ghost stories when we were
children. She took in sewing. At the time, no women went out to work.
She had five children already, how could she work? I had an older brother,
two younger sisters, and a younger brother at the time of the earthquake.
[Tell me what you remember about the 1906 earthquake.] I remember the earthquake very distinctly. That morning everything fell off the
shelves. We had one of those stoves made out of brick. My father cooked
and the stove had crumbled. So my father was very worried about the
stove and [how] he was going to put it back together again. But very
soon we had to evacuate the place. All my father took was some bedding and a set of ivory chopsticks. We went to Washington Square, over
in North Beach, and slept on the lawn. They had bread lines there and
all that. I had my younger brother by the hand and my mother was pregnant. Oh, it was hard then. After three days we came over to Oakland.
I remember we lived in a tent by Lake Merritt. And then my father dug
clams and got sick eating them. Contaminated water, you know. He died
soon after of typhoid fever. My sister was born four days after my father died. There was nothing my mother could do. She had six children.
At that time, you know, no welfare, nothing. So she remarried a year
later. My stepfather, he was a cook on one of those revenue cutters that
go out when boats come in, that brings the custom official out there. He
baked bread and everything right there on board ship. He brought home
pies once in a while, pumpkin pies I remember. He brought us up, really.

"Mother Watched Us Like a Hawk"

In 1908 we moved back to San Francisco and I began Oriental Public School, from 9:00 to 2:30.[2] Right after American school, we went across the street to True Sunshine Chinese School, from 2:30 until 4:30 or 5:00. Came home and did a lot of housework for my mother—washed dishes, scrubbed the children's clothes by hand, helped her sew. At that time, a lot of the men's pants had to be hand-finished. Many women did that kind of work at home. We had to hem the trouser legs, add the waistband, make the buttonholes, all by hand. That's how I learned to sew. I even sewed clothes for my younger brothers and sisters, using those old foot-treadle machines. Everything was used. I would take an old shirt apart and repiece it together for Little Brother's trousers. Eight or nine years old, I was cooking rice. If I burnt the rice, I would get a *ling gok* [a knuckle-rap on the head]. A lot of strength went into it, too. [Was your mother strict with you?] Pretty strict. Whenever we misbehaved, she would use a switch on us, whip us until flower patterns [black and blue marks] broke out, hit our legs until it was one long welt. So we never dared misbehave again. It wasn't easy. Mother watched us like a hawk. We couldn't move without telling her. We were never allowed to go out unless accompanied by an older brother, sister, or somebody else.

[What do you remember about San Francisco Chinatown?] Well, my mother use to send us kids to do the shopping. Remember Sang Wo? I always went there to shop—pork, tofu, bean sprouts, whatever my mother told me to go buy. In those days, for five cents you could buy four cakes of tofu and get some green onions free. (*laughs*) Imagine, you could request some bean sauce to go with the tofu and they would give it to you free. If anyone had a cold, my mother would have us go to Oi Wa Tong to pick up some herbs for fifteen cents, no more than twenty cents, and they would throw in some sweet dates to sweeten the bitter taste. We would bring it home, Mother would boil it, we would drink it

---

2. Originally established by the San Francisco School Board as the Chinese Primary School in response to *Tape v. Hurley* (see pp. 171–75), the school became Oriental Public School in 1906 to accommodate Japanese and Korean students. Under pressure from the Chinese American Citizens Alliance, which found "Oriental" offensive, the board changed the name to Commodore Stockton Elementary School in 1924. More recently, in October 1998 the school board decided to rename the school Gordon J. Lau Elementary School in honor of the first Chinese American elected to the San Francisco Board of Supervisors, in 1977.

and get well. It was very common, like going to a drugstore and getting aspirin.

"The Highlight of My Life"

[Did your mother ever go out?] Only once or twice a year with the whole family. Once every few years we would board the streetcar and go out to Golden Gate Park. We would stroll around the gardens and that was considered a big deal. (*laughs*) The only other time she went out was to go see the Chinese opera. She took us along because she didn't want to leave us alone at home. And anyway, it was not acceptable for her to go out alone. There were two operas a day. It cost a little over a dollar for the grand admission ticket, but after nine o'clock the admission would be lowered to twenty-five cents. Free for children if accompanied by an adult. The place was noisy. Everyone ate and talked during the opera. It was like a picnic. People would bring a big shopping bag with, imagine, a roast squab and things like that! But that's how I learned to love the opera.

[Do you remember the World's Fair in 1915?] Oh yes! It was once in a lifetime and we saved to go see the fair. For about twenty cents a day you could spend the whole day there. My mother also went many times. You don't just see it once because there were so many things to see. I saw lots of pavilions from different countries, but I liked the Chinese pavilion best. You know why? Because they had Chinese art, ceramics, furniture, carvings, ivory, and fine embroidery. And I've always loved embroidery—I used to look forward to attending embroidery class at the Congregational church on Saturdays. I was quite a young lady then and I enjoyed the entertainment—the aquacade and the creation of the earth. I remember it was very interesting, you know, how Adam and Eve were created, how they produced clouds, all the beautiful things on the stage that rotated around. It closed at the end of 1915 and it was the highlight of my life.

"She Thought a Girl Shouldn't Learn So Much"

I went up to the sixth grade and then my mom said, "You've learned enough now." So she made me quit school. I never finished elementary school because she thought a girl shouldn't learn so much. I was about fifteen, I think. At that time I liked school and my teacher liked me. My teacher cried and I cried. Someone asked if I would like to go to work and my mother let me. So I was a stockgirl in the millinery department at I. Magnin. When people got through with the hats you just put them back where they belonged, in the stockroom or in the drawers. And in the morning, you brushed the hats, dusted them a bit, that's all I did. I think I got something like twenty-five dollars a month. They paid us in gold pieces. I gave half of that money to my mother and kept half myself. One summer, it got quiet and they laid me off. Somebody asked if I wanted to work in an art goods shop. So in 1917 I started working at the Canton Bazaar. I was a salesgirl. That's all they ever hired, a girl to sell things and wait on customers. I worked six days a week and got Sundays off. They had lots of good furniture—ebony furniture—pictures, toys, Japanese dishes and kimonos, cloisonné and ivory from China. They were very nice and kind to me. And I got dinner there too. They had a kitchen upstairs and we would close the store at around four and go upstairs for dinner. I think I stayed there for about two years and then I got married.

[How did you meet your husband?] He was a schoolteacher at the Yeung Wo District Association, where my two brothers and I went. That's how I met him. Fell in love with him. He left to go to Vancouver to teach, and I went to Seattle to marry him. My mother was very opposed to my choice because he was poorer than a church mouse. We moved to New York, and because he didn't know English I had to wait on tables in a Chinatown restaurant to support him. That's how the marriage terminated. It was hard work but what else was there to do? Discrimination was very strong in those days. We were together six years.

"Made a Different Person Out of Me"

Then I got a job working with an actress [Lola Fisher] as a companion-maid. Those years with her I traveled a lot—Washington, Philadelphia, Chicago, Atlanta, St. Louis, Cincinnati. And she took me to Europe. We went to Switzerland and France. Everything was first class. I took care of all her luggage and her clothes. Whenever we moved to a different theater, right away I found my way by cab or by public transportation to the theater, got all her clothes hung up and pressed. The hard ones were the one-night stands. Then we had to pack everything in a trunk after the performance before the men came to pick up the trunks. But then I knew just how to do it and I could pack good with tissue paper and everything so things didn't get too wrinkled. I enjoyed it [the job] because it was easier than working in a restaurant. She paid me thirty-five a week, while at the restaurant I made about fifteen or twenty a week. But it kind of tied you down because you had to be with her all day, all night, especially when she traveled. And of course, there wasn't much time for yourself. She didn't get up early (*laughs*), so that was good for me. I always got up early in the morning and browsed all around town. I shopped all over Paris. She said, "Don't go out by yourself because French men love little Chinese girls." Tried to scare me, but I wasn't scared because I always liked to go out by myself, even now.

Those few years with her broadened my mind, made a different person out of me. Sometimes, not having much schooling, I made a lot of mistakes in my English, but she corrected me, nicely, you know. I learned to read because she encouraged me. When I was in Switzerland, I had a lot of time because she was waiting to recuperate and didn't need me. There was a library in the hotel where we lived, and she said, "Go down to the library and get some books to read." So I sat in the garden and read. She was very good to me, but I knew I had to quit after four years because I knew I shouldn't stay with her anymore. She had tuberculosis and that's very contagious. So I moved back to Daai Fau [San Francisco] and stayed with my parents. I made up my mind I wasn't going back to New York and I told my husband so.

(SOURCE: Alice Sue Fun, interview with author, February 28, 1982, Oakland, California)

In 1933 Alice Sue Fun remarried and with her husband Joe Fun operated a corner grocery in Oakland while raising three children. When he died in the 1950s she sold some of their property and took a trip around the world. Having invested wisely in stocks and real estate, she was able to retire in comfort. When asked what made her so independent and forward-looking, she replied, "I guess I was born different. Both my stepfather and mother were very strict and that [made me into] a revolutionist and a rebel at heart. If I died today, I would say that I had a happy life. I don't moan about the past. What's the use? The good old days will never be back again. I know you can never buy four cakes of tofu for a nickel anymore and at the same time ask for some free sweet cucumbers and red ginger!"

Alice Sue Fun died peacefully in her sleep at the age of ninety.

Rose Yuen Ow, Cabaret Dancer

"I've Lived a Full Life"

A contemporary of Alice Sue Fun, Rose Yuen Ow was born in Grass Valley, California, in 1895, the eldest of five children. Her father, who had immigrated from Chungshan [Zhongshan] District in Guangdong Province when he was seventeen, was a cook in a mining town when he was introduced to a young woman who had come from Hong Kong with the Chinese consul. When they married, she was only fifteen, and a few years later she gave birth to Rose. The family moved to San Francisco Chinatown when Rose was six years old. There her father found a job as a "bar boy" at Long's Bar on Jackson Street. In 1905, the year before the earthquake and fire, her mother died at the young age of twenty-eight.

In this interview with Him Mark Lai and Philip P. Choy of the Chinese Historical Society of America in 1970, Rose recalled her life growing up in San Francisco Chinatown and how she became a cabaret dancer, going on to perform in the Ziegfeld Follies. Like Alice, she resented the many social restrictions imposed upon her by an insular and "old-fashioned" Chinese community, but she also appreciated the rich cultural environment in which she was raised. Similarly, she found vaudeville a mixed bag. She was well received as a performing artist, but that was partly because she was a novelty act.[1] Rose was very aware of racial discrimina-

---

1. Without taking away from their talented abilities, I should point out that "Oriental" performers during this period, including the Chung Wah Quartet, Honorable Wu's Chinese Showboat Revue, and later, the Forbidden City nightclub entertainers, were popular

tion. In the interview she described how whites taunted the Chinese, and how Chinese audience members, including the Chinese consul, were not allowed to sit downstairs in some of the theaters where she performed. Compared to most of the other women in this section, Rose was quite daring for her time, partly because her parents were "open minded" and supportive of her education and independent ideas. Not afraid to talk back to the elders in the community who tried to interfere with her life, she took the initiative to take dancing lessons in order to make a career in show business and then found ways to convince her father to support her aspirations despite the Chinese community's condemnations. Given the limited opportunities open to Chinese American women in the early 1900s, Rose made the most of the situation, thus paving the way for other young women to work outside the home and outside Chinatown. She was someone who was able to cross race, gender, class, and cultural boundaries and deserved, at the age of seventy-five, to proclaim, "When I die, I can say I've lived a full life."

"It Was Really Hard Being a Chinese Girl in Those Days"

The Chinese didn't want the girls to go to school in the old times. I was twelve years old before I started school. Very old-fashioned in those days. Even when my mother and father let me go to school, the cousins criticized. I went to Oriental Public School until I finished the eighth grade. They criticized me for being out in the streets, even for eating cherries in the streets. They would tell my parents on me and say it wasn't lady-like to eat in the streets.

All the mothers wanted their daughters to go to work but they were afraid of gossip. I think I was the first or second one to start working in Chinatown at a [moving-]picture place. I sat there and sold tickets. The cousins immediately told my father to get me home. Later when I was older and went downtown to work in the nightclub for Westerners, everyone talked about me. Said I worked and roamed around the streets.

In those days, Tait's Cafe was the biggest cabaret in San Francisco. They

---

largely because of their exotic appeal to an "Occidental" audience. For more information about these performers, see Thomas W. Chinn, *Bridging the Pacific: San Francisco Chinatown and Its People* (San Francisco: Chinese Historical Society of America, 1989), pp. 211–15; and Lorraine Dong, "The Forbidden City Legacy and Its Chinese American Women," *Chinese America: History and Perspectives, 1992* (San Francisco: Chinese Historical Society of America, 1992), pp. 125–48.

purposely hired two Chinese girls to pass out hot biscuits when dinner started. Then after dinner, we came around again to pass out peppermint candy. Chinese men would follow me all the way downtown to see where I was going. They talked and everyone in Chinatown talked about you. Not nowadays. You can do anything and nobody in Chinatown would care. It was really harsh in the old days. They didn't want Chinese girls doing that [kind of work]. Always butting into your business. So one time I got so mad, I said, "Come on in and look." They had followed me to the door. They were all closed minded, the Chinese in the old days. Now it's a little too open. Before, you couldn't even move. I didn't dare walk the streets with a Westerner alone. I would always drag a friend along.

My mother and father were both open-minded. My mother was very open-minded. When I was young, my mother made me Western clothes to wear. I was so happy when I got to wear Western clothes in grammar school because very few people did. Only two families were up to date— Joe Shoong's wife's family—the Soo Hoo's. They always wore Western style and we envied them. Then there was Sammy Tong's family—the actor. When I asked my mother to bind my feet, she scolded me. Now I thank my mother. But then it was fashionable to have bound feet.[2] I thought they looked so genteel and tiny. So I said to my mother, let me bind my feet too. She said no! She died when she was twenty-eight. I was only nine. In the old days, they married too young—at fourteen or fifteen.

In 1913 I ran for Chinatown queen and won.[3] It wasn't a matter of intelligence or beauty, just popularity. I was working at Tait's and very popular there. This Fong girl got jealous I won the title. Said I wasn't fair. People from Elk's Club and Olympic's Club use to come to Tait's to eat. They wanted to surprise me, refused to buy tickets from me. Then last minute, they sent a $500 check up to the headquarters. So they said it wasn't right. So everyone fought about it. My father was willing to call out the tong to help, but I told him not to, that it wasn't that important to me. I would rather give the title away so I gave it to Lew Hing's daughter—Francis Moon's wife [Rose Lew]. They came up to me at the

2. Footbinding was widely practiced in China and among the Chinese merchant class in America until it was banned after the 1911 Revolution. See discussion on pages 194–96.

3. The beauty contest was actually first held in 1915. Initiated by the Chinese Six Companies, the competition for the title of Chinatown queen emulated the American cultural practice of crowning festival queens. The winner—whoever sold the greatest number of raffle tickets—was to preside over Chinatown celebrations in connection with the Panama-Pacific Exposition. The coronation ball was held at the classy Fairmont Hotel.

Fairmont and said I was the real queen. Chinatown was really bad in those days. They even sent out white notices saying nasty things about me.[4]

In those days, no white would go out with a Chinese. They looked down at the Chinese. The Chinese were treated as bad as the Blacks. It was pitiful the way the whites taunted us. Before, Chinese were not allowed to sit downstairs at the Pantages Theater [downtown]. It was really hard being a Chinese girl in those days.

"The Traditional Holidays Were Festive"

When we turned twelve, we were not suppose to go out anymore. We were stuck at home and not permitted to say anything. Only in groups did we go out. Once a year, we would go downtown to shops like the Emporium—we called it Sap Baat Gwok [literally, eighteen countries]. After the new year, we got to prepare for Baai Chat Je [Festival of the Seven Maidens].[5] It was like a girls' club. Eight or nine of us would get together to work. It was a lot of work making flowers, the bridges, and the seven sisters all standing there. We used sesame seeds and rice to decorate the cups and plates. It took months. If you were young, you would display only four tables. Six or seven tables were considered a big deal. So you put on these pretty displays on the tables and people from the streets would come up and look. People would praise the best displays. The point was to see which family had the most talented girls. On that day [of the festival] we would get together and go out, a whole bunch of us. We would walk together in pairs. That's how we girls did it in those days.

[Chinese New Year] was festive. There were firecrackers, and *lai si* [lucky money given in red envelopes] was a must. It was quite rigid: when-

---

4. Only bad news and death threats were printed on white paper.

5. Also known as the Festival of the Cowherd and Weaving Maiden, this holiday is celebrated on the seventh day of the seventh month according to the lunar calendar. Legend has it that the Weaving Maiden in heaven fell in love with a mortal Cowherd. After their marriage her loom, which once wove garments for the gods, fell silent. Angered by her dereliction of duty, the gods ordered her back to work. The Queen Mother separated the couple with the Silver Stream or Milky Way and allowed them to meet only once a year on the seventh night of the seventh month, when the Silver Stream is spanned by a bridge of magpies. On this day, maidens display toys, figurines, artificial fruits and flowers, embroidery, and other examples of their handiwork so that others, especially prospective husbands, can judge their skills. See Carol Stepanchuk and Charles Wong, *Mooncakes and Hungry Ghosts: Festivals of China* (San Francisco: China Books and Periodicals, 1991), pp. 80–84.

ever you saw kids, you had to give. It was usually ten cents. A quarter
was considered a lot. All the kids had banks for the *lai si* and pretty
clothes. Girls would comb their hair up and wear flowers. It was very
pretty and colorful. They wore high wooden shoes. [It lasted] seven days.
No [lion dancing], just firecrackers to bring good luck to the house. People
would *baai nin.* Women went to all the homes of friends. Took fruit and
went everywhere.

[During Baat Yuet Sap Ng (literally, eighth month and fifteenth day,
or Mid-Autumn Festival)][6] people prayed to the gods and placed food
on the altar. We had fresh lichee, dragon's eye, pomelos. [Da Jiu (Feast
of the Hungry Ghosts)][7] I remember because people were afraid of the
ghosts, they made effigies and lit lanterns and marched at night. They
were big effigies and frightful. They would parade around at twelve midnight.

"They All Knew Us as Rosie and Joe"

I was working in the cafe passing out candy. I was stationary watching
the people dance and Mr. Tait jokingly said, "How would you like to do
something like that, Rosie?" I said, "Fine." I had a [Chinese] boyfriend
[Joe Hall] who was studying pharmacy. So I told him the boss said I
should learn dancing and he would hire me to dance. He said, "All right,
let's take a few lessons." I was quite bold because the boss hadn't said
he would hire me, just how would I like to do that? In those days, there
was the waltz, the fox-trot, the cakewalk. So that was three dances. Then
we improvised a Chinese dance. So after a few months of lessons, I
thought I was all ready. I was that brave. So I said to the boss, "Mr. Tait,
I'm ready for you." He had forgotten all about it. So he said, "You're
ready for what?" Scared me. "I'm ready to dance for you," I said. There
were two floors then, a beautiful ballroom upstairs and a dining room

---

6. The Mid-Autumn Festival falls on the fifteenth day of the eighth lunar month. This
is the time set aside by farmers to enjoy their successful harvest and for women to make
offerings of melons, moon cakes, and pomegranates in honor of the full moon.

7. This festival occurs on the fifteenth day of the seventh lunar month and is intended
to pacify the ghosts of strangers and the uncared-for dead, those who had died without
descendants and before their time, such as murder victims or suicides. Denied entry into
heaven, these ghosts are temporarily released for a month to seek other souls to take their
places in hell. The living use lanterns in the water to guide them away and place food outside homes to buy them off. See Stepanchuk and Wong, *Mooncakes and Hungry Ghosts,*
pp. 71–79.

downstairs. Just then this French woman said she refused to dance in the dining room. She would only dance in the ballroom—more high class. So Mr. Tait was having a little trouble. So he said, "Tomorrow, you go upstairs and dance for me." So we bravely danced for him. And Mr. Tait said, "Fine, very good." So he decided to put "Rosie and Joe" on next week. So I became scared. How was I going to tell my father that I was going to dance?

My boss took a great big picture of both of us posing how to dance. After my picture appeared in the morning paper and it had gotten all over Chinatown, I ran up to see Mr. Tait and said, "Mr. Tait, you can't put my picture in the paper." I was crying. "What's the matter with you," he said. "People give thousands and thousands of dollars for publicity." I said, "I don't care for publicity." I was just afraid my father would see it. Everyone in Chinatown saw it, it was such a big picture. So I told him [my father] I'm not going to dance but I just put my picture in the paper to fool the public that I was the dancer so that they would come. My wages were raised to $200 a week and I brought home the money.[8] I gave it to him and he said, "What, all that big money?" And I said, "Yeah, I have a raise and I have to work night time." So I lied to my daddy again. He didn't say anything. My daddy is a very easy-going Chinese man anyway. I told him if I didn't work, who would support him? His relatives? He said he didn't want people talking about me. I retorted, "Are they going to feed you?" So I started dancing for over a year. My father didn't know anything about it, that I was really dancing.

So come about 1915, Raymond Hitchcock came to San Francisco. He was a big star, you know. And he said, "How would you like to go to New York?" I jumped. I go to New York? They were asking me to go to New York? To be a show, in the big theater. So I didn't know what to do. So I made up my mind and went home to tell my daddy again. "I'm going to New York." And he said, "What for?" And I said, "To go dance." "You don't know how to dance." And I said, "No I don't but I go there and they will teach me how." We were only eighteen or nineteen years old then. "So nobody go with you?" "Oh, I will find a girl to go with me." So I took my partner's sister with me to New York to keep me company.

So we get to New York and we were very lucky. We got to know some

---

8. Rose had previously made $60 a week passing out candy.

big brokers and got a chance to play the big theaters like Palace Theater in New York and the Ziegfeld Follies. So Raymond Hitchcock took me there and he wanted to buy me some new shoes. "And how much money do you want for your new shoes, children?" I said, "Three dollars." You see, you can't buy any shoes in New York for three dollars. So he gave us twenty or forty dollars. In those days, we all wore three dollar shoes, nothing higher than that. And no silk stockings.

I'll tell you about another experience we had. He [Hitchcock] gave us spending money and the hotel was paid for. Three of us, we spent our last nickel and no money, go without dinner. We didn't know how to go downstairs and sign. So we had some Chinese friends call on us that night. "You had dinner yet?" And we said yes although we just had sardines and crackers. So we went up to look for Mr. Hitchcock. "What do you want, children?" And I said, "We want some money. We have no money to eat on." So he said, "What's the matter with you? Why don't you go downstairs and just sign your check and we will cover it?" That's my experience in show business. We had money but we didn't know how to get it. We thought they would come around every week and give us some money, but he [Hitchcock] went out of the city for a couple of days, so we had sardines and crackers for two days. (*laughs*)

[Did a lot of Chinese come to see you perform?] Lots. Because Chinese were performing, so they came to support us. In Vancouver, even the Chinese consul came. I got mad when they won't sell me a ticket for them to sit downstairs. So I screamed at them. She said it's the people in town who would object. Of course, the Chinese were a bit sloppy. They would wear their Chinese slippers. Vancouver and Victoria Chinese were very old-fashioned. Typical Chinese with queues and open shirts. Only in Vancouver and the Pantages in San Francisco did Chinese have to sit upstairs. The Orpheum on O'Farrell Street, one of the most high-class theaters, didn't discriminate. Every year we played the vaudeville show there. Also the Golden Gate [in downtown San Francisco].

So we were pretty lucky after we went to New York. We worked with Jack Benny, Marx Brothers, Will Rogers, and that's how I started my show business. Altogether fourteen years of show business [1915 to 1929]. Then the movies, the talkies came in. He [Joe] didn't want to give up but I wanted to give up because the shows were all closing. And we weren't used to booking week to week. We were so used to booking season to season. We traveled around all the big cities. They called it the key circuit. Same town over and over again back east. Our stage name was Chung and Rosie Moy.[9] They, the Westerners, all knew us as Rosie and Joe.

(SOURCE: Rose Yuen Ow, interview with Him Mark Lai and Philip P. Choy, September 9, 1970, San Francisco; transcript of talk by Clara Lee and Rose Ow before the Chinese Historical Society of America, April 9, 1974, San Francisco, Him Mark Lai private collection)

Rose and Joe quit the stage in 1929 and returned to San Francisco Chinatown, where Rose worked as a cashier in a restaurant for the next forty years. The two adopted a daughter named Barbara. "All my life it's people," she said in the interview. "I miss it [show business] but my husband missed it more. He loved it. If he were here, he'll get up and dance for you." Joe passed away in 1960 and Rose remarried. Unfortunately, I was not able to find out what happened to Rose after this interview.

---

9. "Moy" was her Chinese given name.

Tiny

TYE LEUNG SCHULZE

I first heard of Tye Leung Schulze in 1977 while interviewing Thomas Wu, Henry Tom, and Fred Schulze about their memories of the Angel Island Immigration Station. Fred mentioned that his mother was the first Chinese woman to be hired by the civil service to work at Angel Island and that she was also the first Chinese woman to vote in an election. As I found out later in subsequent interviews with Fred and his sister Louise Schulze Lee, their mother was a remarkable second-generation Chinese American woman in many ways.

Tye Leung Schulze was born in San Francisco in 1887 and died in 1972 at the age of eighty-four. She was a tiny woman—only four feet tall—but she had a big heart and a strong will. At twelve she escaped an arranged marriage by seeking refuge at the Presbyterian Mission Home. She stayed on to help rescue and interpret for Chinese prostitutes, and she took charge of planning the meals for the Home. In 1910, while working at the Angel Island Immigration Service as assistant to the matrons, Tye met and fell in love with Charles Frederick Schulze, an immigration inspector of German and Scottish descent. Against their parents' wishes and California's antimiscegenation law, the two got married in the state of Washington, where interracial marriage was allowed. Both lost their civil service jobs at Angel Island as a result. In 1912 Tye Leung Schulze made newspaper headlines for being "the first Chinese woman in the history of the world to exercise the electoral fran-

Tye Leung Schulze as a young woman. This photo appeared in the local newspapers in 1910 after it was announced that "Miss Tye Leung, interpreter of
the Presbyterian Mission Home, San Francisco" had been appointed to a government position at Angel Island. (Courtesy of Frederick L. Schulze, Louise
Schulze Lee, and Donaldina S. Lee)

chise."[1] While her husband Charles worked at the Southern Pacific Railway Company as a mechanic, Tye went to school to learn bookkeeping

---

1. "Modern Chinese Adopt the Auto: President of Oriental Republic and Local 'Suf-
fragette' Are Motor Fans," *San Francisco Call*, May 19, 1912, p. 63. Accompanying this

This photograph of Tye Leung Schulze as a progressive woman behind the wheel of a Stude-baker-Flanders car appeared in the local newspapers in 1912 after she became "the first Chinese woman in the world to vote." However, according to her son, Fred Schulze, she never owned or drove an automobile in her life. (Courtesy of Frederick L. Schulze, Louise Schulze Lee, and Donaldina S. Lee)

and later landed a job as a night-shift operator at the Chinatown Tele-phone Exchange.[2] They had four children and chose to live close to Chi-natown. Committed to serving her community, Tye spent many years providing interpreting and social services to the Chinese people in San Francisco.

Both Fred and Louise Schulze remember their mother as a warm, gen-tle, and loving person who was well respected in Chinatown despite the fact that she had married outside of her race. At the time of our inter-view, Louise generously shared with me the following autobiographical essay that she had found among her mother's possessions. The title,

---

article on Tye Leung Schulze being the first Chinese woman to vote in an election was a photograph of her behind the wheel of a Studebaker-Flanders car that Dr. Sun Yat-sen sup-posedly also drove. According to the article, "Miss Tie [Tye] believes in the automobile and regards it in its various functions as a mark of progress—her own watchword." In-terestingly enough, according to her son Fred Schulze, Tye never owned or drove an au-tomobile in her life.

2. Until dial telephones became available, the Chinatown Telephone Exchange operated a switchboard at 743 Washington Street that received all calls for Chinatown. Twenty-two women worked as operators, working three shifts around the clock. They were expected to know English and five Chinese dialects, had to memorize over 2,100 phone numbers, and handled an average of 17,000 calls per day. Given the limited job opportunities for Chi-nese American women before World War II, this was considered a good job for that time.

Tye Leung Schulze with her two sons, Theodore (left) and Frederick (right).
(Courtesy of Frederick L. Schulze, Louise Schulze Lee, and Donaldina S. Lee)

*"Tiny," refers to the nickname Donaldina Cameron gave Tye because of
her size. Written in Tye's neat handwriting on lined paper, the essay is
undated but most likely was written late in her life, judging by the end-
ing. Nor is there a clear indication as to whom it was written for; possibly for her children, possibly as a tribute to Donaldina Cameron, whom
Tye remained close to until Cameron's death in 1968.*

*On six sheets of paper we learn Tye's entire life story, from birth and
early childhood in a large and poor family to her retirement from the
Chinatown Telephone Exchange and many hours of volunteer work in
the Chinese community. The one theme that stands out in this essay is
the important role that Christianity and Donaldina Cameron played in*

*her life. The church provided Tye with an education, helped her return
to her family after her mother sold her into domestic servitude, rescued
her from an arranged marriage she rejected, provided her family with
shelter after the 1906 earthquake and fire, and recommended her for the
civil service job at Angel Island. In conclusion, Tye acknowledges
Cameron for helping her become who she was: "I owed a lot to Miss
Cameron who was so tender and good teaching [me] the ten years I spent
with her, to know what's right and wrong." Similar to the sentiments expressed by Chinese American Christians in this section, "Tiny" is a testimony to the important influence of Christianity in the lives of second-
generation women.*

*Aside from being a rare document of a Chinese American woman's
reflections on her own life, "Tiny" also provides us with insights on family life in San Francisco Chinatown, the limited jobs that were available
to Chinese women in the early twentieth century, their early challenges
to prescribed gender roles, and the outcome of an interracial marriage.
Except for only the occasional correction of a spelling error in brackets
for clarity, I am including the story here as it was originally written, in
the loving voice of Tye Leung Schulze herself.*

Born Aug 24, 1887 at 14 1/2 Ross Alley San Francisco, Calif. Father &
Mother came from China at the age of eight. They were married between
16 and 20 yrs of age. To my knowlege there were 8 children (6 girls and
2 boys).[3] They have no chance for education. My father's income was
$20.00 a month working in a shoe shop, have to support his Uncle and
Aunt who raise him, and brought him to this country. My Mother help
my marternal Grandmother who has a broading [boarding] house for
girls on Jackson St. near Grant Ave. My oldest sister also help her at the
age of 14, as an errand girl and help cooks.

As far as I can remembered we all occupied two rooms. During the
blue ban plea [bubonic plague] Chinatown was quarantine, but our family was kept well.[4] I used to go to two glambling [gambling] houses to

---

3. According to Fred Schulze, "My mother being the youngest in the family was the
most *baak yim* [mischievous]. By *baak yim* I don't mean bad but daring to do things that
others don't" (interview with author, January 26, 1989, San Francisco).

4. In 1900, in an attempt to snuff out Chinatown's economic life, San Francisco's board
of health alarmed the public by announcing the existence of the bubonic plague in Chinatown. A quarantine was imposed to prevent any Chinese from leaving the area. After

get the left over from their meals to feed our family. When Grandmother return to China, my mother ran a broading house at Ross Alley. My oldest sister and I help clean up, errands and cooking.

There was a mission school on Stockton St. I was allowed to attend to learn English. The teacher who was a missionary in China spoke flun [fluent] Chinese, started that school under the presbyrian [Presbyterian] church, now at 925 Stockton St. The teacher who was Miss Wesley, later Mrs. Cook, was very fond of me. She got a liken [liking] of me and got me clothes, bath me, took me to different church meetings and showed me off, for she taught me to sing. At that time I don't know what was what. At the age of nine, my mother sent me to one of her friend's house to live as an errand girl. This family was nice to me. My father's uncle took me, to go to the school teachers, he told me my mother sold me to her friend that I will not be able to come home. I took his advice, and was home after. Was able to attend school and Sunday school at times. Because, no girls were allow to go out much. They must stay home learn to sew, and housewife's duties. At the age of 13, my oldest sister was to be married a man at Butt[e], Montana. But she left home with her suitor instead. My folks wanted me to take her place, but I was still too young, but at the same time I refused. Then the mission home heard about the case, Miss Donaldina Cameron and my school teacher Miss Crather rescue me and took me to Miss Cameron's home at 920 Sacramento St. in 1901. I stayed there and learned Christianity and became a Christian woman. During my stay at the home, I had good exprinces by helping intrepreting for the girls staying at home for shelter. Most of the girls are slave girls from China. I used to be so happy to know that I know and have my parents although they were not Christian. They were nice and loved me dearly. During the fire and earthquake of 1906, Miss Cameron with forty in the family, also took my parents to give them shelter in San Ra[fa]el, Calif. Until they came back to San Francisco, after about four months. After the New Home was built at 920 Sacramento, most of the girls wanted to go out to school to get a better education, but in gratutude I want to stay with Miss Cameron to help in the home, intrepreting and ordering food for the meals. In 1910, the Commissioner of Immigration needed a Chinese woman to help the matron, for the Chinese

---

the Chinese filed suit against the board of health, Judge William Morrow declared the quarantine arbitrary and racist and ordered it lifted. See Charles J. McClain, *In Search of Equality: The Chinese Struggle against Discrimination in Nineteenth-Century America* (Berkeley: University of California Press, 1994), chap. 10.

woman who comes from China, who had to be detain at Angel Island until their cases are OK and landed.[5] By recommendation of Miss Cameron, I served as an intrepreter for the government from 1910 till 1913. Then I met my husband. He is not my own race, naturully. We had to go to Vancouver, Wash. to be married. His mother and my folks disapprove very much, but when two people are in love, they don't think of the future or what happen. My husband's mother lost her husband since she was eighteen years old and live till she was seventy-four years of age. My husband resigned from his job as an inspector, because of the racial prejudice. It was hard for him to get a steady job, till later he work for the S. P. Co. as machinuc [mechanic] on Dictaphone and typwriter.[6] We have four children, two boys and two girls. I went to work at the fair ground of 1915 the Chinese Tea Garden, for one year, when my second boy was three months old.[7] My mother died in 1912. Cared and buryed her. In 1914 two weeks after my second was borned my father died. Buried him. In 1917 I worked in a draying concern, for ten years, to take telephone calls. Later find out I have to take care the books. I took up bookkeep at Mu[n]son private school at night three times aweek for 10 months. Was taken sick. The two boys were care for by the Chung Mee [Mei] home for one year.[8] I work at the Chinese Hospital as an admitance clerk and bookkepper, also as a social worker in the clinic. The telephone co., China Exchange, needed a night operator. I was pregant

---

5. Actually, according to a letter to the secretary of commerce and labor from the commissioner-general of immigration dated February 7, 1910, a Chinese woman was sought chiefly to look out for prostitutes among the recent arrivals: "It should be borne in mind that the prevention of importations of Chinese women for immoral purposes cannot be frustrated without something of this character being done, a person of their own sex and race being the only channel through which definite evidence of the intentions of these women could be secured." I am grateful to Erika Lee for sharing this letter that she found in the National Archives. There is, however, no evidence that Tye Leung Schulze accommodated the needs of the immigration officials. According to her son, she probably tried to do what she could during the interrogation "to lead them [the arrivals] on to the correct answer" (Fred Schulze interview).

6. Charles Schulze worked for many years servicing dictaphones and typewriters for the Southern Pacific Railway Company.

7. The Chinese Tea Garden was part of the Panama-Pacific International Exposition that was held in San Francisco in 1915.

8. Established by the American Baptist Home Mission and the San Francisco Bay Cities Baptist Union, the Chung Mei Home for Chinese Boys operated from 1923 to 1955, first in Berkeley, moving in 1933 to El Cerrito. It mainly sheltered and cared for Chinese boys who were orphans, wards of the court, or from broken homes.

so I thought was a good chance, worked for twenty years. And had two girls borned to me. Cared for my children day and work at night. My husband stayed and cared for his mother till 1930. He died 1935. I was still working with the phone co. till 1946. When the Veteran's family was able to come to the United States,[9] I was called to help the Immigration Office to do the Inpretering. Was employed for one year. During my life I do interpreting for Chinese people who needed my help, to doctors, attorneys or court. My schooling only to the six grade beside the ten months of night school at Mu[n]son school, but I learned a lot by expriences.

I owed a lot to Miss Cameron who was so tender and good teaching why the ten years I spent with her, to know what's right and wrong. Still we are all human.

(SOURCE: Fred Schulze, interview with author, July 23, 1979, and January 26, 1989, San Francisco; Louise Schulze Lee, interview with author, November 7, 1988, San Mateo, California; Tye Leung Schulze, "Tiny," Frederick L. Schulze and Louise Schulze Lee private collection)

---

9. She is referring to the War Brides Act of 1945, which was amended in 1947 to admit Chinese wives and children of U.S. citizens on a nonquota basis.

Some Rambling Thoughts on Why I Am a Christian

FLORENCE CHINN KWAN

Unlike the other Chinese American women in this section, Florence Chinn Kwan was born to and raised by progressive-minded Christian parents who encouraged her to pursue higher education and allowed her to choose her own husband. This in large part explains how she later earned the distinction of being the first Chinese woman to graduate from Mills College, with a B.A. degree in English (1919), and the University of Chicago, with a master's degree in religious education and sociology (1920). Most Chinese American women at this time still received a limited education, being groomed instead for marriage and motherhood. Considering Chinese sexism, combined with limited financial resources and the dim job prospects for any Chinese American college graduate, higher education was for the most part not a viable option for second-generation women, at least not until after World War II.[1]

Although her mother tried to arrange a marriage for Florence when she finished high school, her father told her, "No, go to college and get

---

1. Florence Chinn's master's thesis, "Religious Education in the Chinese Community of San Francisco" (University of Chicago, 1920), which covers the early history of religious education in San Francisco Chinatown and advocates that churches begin addressing socioeconomic problems in the community, made the point that only girls from Christian families were encouraged to pursue an education. According to Beulah Ong Kwoh's study "Occupational Status of the American-Born Chinese College Graduates" (Master's thesis, University of Chicago, 1947), until the 1930s very few Chinese women graduated from college (p. 130).

your Ph.D. and then go back to China to teach English."[2] *Florence decided to quit after her master's degree and return to San Francisco to work as the associate secretary of the Chinese YWCA. In 1923 she married physician Sung Tao Kwan, whom she had met in Chicago, and went to live in China with him for the next twenty-six years. While her husband worked as a neurosurgeon at the Peking Union Medical College Hospital, Florence volunteered at a dozen service organizations, including the YWCA, and raised three children. In 1949, after the Communist takeover, she and the family returned to the United States.*

I had long known of Florence Chinn Kwan through my research on the Chinese Women of America Research Project. I finally had the opportunity to meet her in person and to interview her in 1988. She was at that time ninety-one years old. She had slowed down considerably but was still attending church on Sundays and, occasionally, the Chinese Senior Center in Berkeley. And as I discovered from the three times I interviewed her at her home in Berkeley, her memory was intact. She credited her good physical and mental health to her daily routine of calisthenics and acupressure. She also spent a good part of each morning working on her memoirs, which she hoped to leave to her children and grandchildren. Those days she tired easily, and I was careful to stop the interview at the first sign of weariness. Even so, each of our sessions lasted over two hours. I found her to be a soft-spoken and gracious interviewee, able and willing to recount her past in detail and to reflect on the changing role of Chinese American women.

Florence Chinn Kwan passed away in 1993, leaving in my care the manuscript of a speech she had given to a youth group at the Chinese Congregational Church in San Francisco in 1966. I include this speech here because I believe it represents Florence's perspective on life and her testimony, similar to Tye Leung Schulze's, of the important role that Christianity has played in the lives of second-generation women. In contrast to many of her peers, Florence faced relatively few restrictions growing up in San Francisco Chinatown. Her Christian parents dressed her in Western attire, rarely disciplined her, and her father often took her with him on outings to the park or downtown. As Florence points out in the speech, the warmth of her parents' Christian love, their commitment to do good deeds, and their ability to educate themselves and make themselves over in a new land were not lost on her. Learning from their ex-

---

2. Florence Chinn Kwan, interview with author, October 7, 1988, Berkeley, California.

Florence Chinn Kwan (front row, second from the left) attended the Oriental Public School from 1909 to 1912. (Courtesy of Florence Chinn Kwan)

amples, she devoted her life to working hard for a better world through "positive acts." From her patient and giving husband, Florence learned to appreciate nature and Chinese culture. Thus, like Rose Chew, Florence advised young Chinese Americans to "select the best in both cultures."

First of all, let me say that I am very grateful to you for inviting me to come and talk to you of the Christian influences and experiences in my personal life. It is not because I think I can be of help to you, but rather to thank you for giving me the opportunity of searching within myself of how God has helped and guided me all these years.

I understand that you are making a study of Christian Commitment. What is commitment? In Webster's Dictionary, it says that commitment is a state of being bound or pledged.

To me, the word commitment means an obligation pressured from outside so that one is bound to act accordingly. To me then, Christian commitment means that a Christian is bound and pressured into doing Christian deeds. I do not want to think that this is so, but rather to think that being a Christian is a great privilege that God has bestowed on every individual. When one is a true Christian, he is *free*, not bound or obligated as in commitment. He is *privileged* to know the difference between the right and the wrong and will *voluntarily* and *naturally* choose the right. Christianity then, gives us the privilege of using our intellect which is God-given. Of course, my interpretation of the word "commitment" may be different from the accepted meaning you understand it to be.

When I was young, my parents gave us children certain rules to live by—"do this" and "don't do that"—all in a negative approach. But in their daily lives, my parents exemplified their actions as true Christians. This was the positive approach which influenced me most. We were shown the way; we were impressed and we remembered.

Thinking back, as far back as the fourth or fifth years of my childhood, I was surrounded by the warmth of my parents' Christian love. Naturally there were tiffs and spats between them—few and far, but they always ended on their knees asking for God's forgiveness. This impressed me much even as a child.

Our father's influence was felt by us through his gentleness, honesty, humility and great Christian love for all. He was a missionary teacher of this church—teaching English and preaching to Chinese immigrants in the evenings.[3] Why evenings? Because at that time, there were very few Chinese families. The Chinese here were mainly male immigrants who had come to earn gold dollars to send back to their families in the villages to better their living and also to educate their sons. These men worked mostly as cooks, pantry boys, and in laundries, etc. After their work in the evenings, they would come to our mission and learn the English language. Although his salary was very small, my father did not seek to enlarge his income. I still remember that once he was asked to take a day time job that would not interfere with his evening work. He replied that he was not interested and that doing God's work was enough.

In every way, my father was always improving himself physically, men-

---

3. Chin Quong was fourteen years old when he left China for San Francisco in 1872. During the day he worked in his uncle's laundry; at night he studied English and the Bible at Rev. William Pond's Congregational church on Brenham Place (now Walter U. Lum Place). Before returning to China in 1879 to marry Yee Fung Soo, he worked as a pantry boy for a white family in the well-to-do neighborhood of Pacific Heights. His wife stayed in China until Chin Quong was able to send for her in 1897. By then he had made four trips to China, siring two sons. Florence was born soon after her mother's arrival in the United States. Two more sons were born after her. Chin Quong lived with his family on the top floor of the Congregational church, where he preached on Sundays, ran a Chinese language school for children in the basement in the afternoons, and taught Chinese immigrants English during the weekday evenings. He died in 1944 at the age of eighty-six.

tally and spiritually. He was interested in Nature and all of God's world. He walked miles every day and took us to the park daily. He read profusely. I remember that he would hold me on his lap while reading in his study. He was quite artistic and used to draw pictures for me when I was a child. He would practice for hours on writing Chinese characters. His writing was considered very good, especially the small block type. He was a self-educated man—a self-made man.

My mother was a fine Christian woman, patient, honest, intelligent, alert and humble with a great capacity for learning. Her father was a fine village teacher and to our surprise she did not receive any education from her father. She was the only daughter with four brothers. She related to us of how her father loved her the most and when in the classroom, would have her on his knee. In those days, girls were not supposed to receive any education. If she did, I am sure she would be a great social worker. As far back as I can remember, she was always helping the sick and the needy by going to their homes, cooking for them and caring for them all without compensation.[4]

Mother was self taught in the art of reading the Chinese characters. She never learned to write. In our childhood, when our father was teaching my younger brothers and myself the Chinese characters, she would sit beside us sewing with her eyes and ears wide open. In this way, she learned much faster than we did. We had our English lessons to do and they were easier. Not much time was spent on our Chinese lessons. Mother studied the Bible and was able to read it from cover to cover. When we came from China in 1936, mother was 78 years old. Every evening we would find her reading the daily Chinese newspapers far into the night. She was very active mentally up until the time of my father's death at the age of 88. She was 86.

After my return to San Francisco in 1949, from Peking, I was told by all who knew them, and there are many, both old and young, how wonderful a couple they were, a true Christian couple, shining with real genuine Christian love. How fortunate I was to have had such wonderful

---

4. Yee Fung Soo was born in Canton, China, in 1858. She joined her husband, Chin Quong, in San Francisco in 1897 when pregnant with their third child, Florence. She was a forward-looking woman, choosing to unbind her feet after the 1911 Revolution. Although housebound according to Chinese custom, Yee Fung Soo took in sewing and peeled shrimps at home to supplement her husband's meager salary as a missionary teacher. She helped to organize the Women's Missionary Society, which paid for a woman to preach in the villages of Guangdong Province. She died in 1954 at the age of ninety-six.

Florence Chinn Kwan (back row, far left) at the YWCA Conference in 1915. (Courtesy of Florence Chinn Kwan)

Christian parents! I prayed to God to give me the strength to follow in their footsteps.

During my junior high school years and up through my senior high days, I taught English to Chinese immigrants at our home for a big salary of $5.00 per month teaching five days a week. When I received my first pay, of course I gave it to my mother. My parents were very happy and the whole family rejoiced with me. Father suggested that I contribute the sum to the Women's Missionary Society of our church, which I gladly did even though we knew we needed it ourselves.

Even after college, when I was a Y.W.C.A. secretary up to the time of my marriage,[5] all my salary went to the general coffers of our family. My brothers did the same. When we needed money, mother would give it to us. This was our family life, a life of closeness to each other, a belonging to each other, helping and sharing—a very happy family.

---

5. As associate secretary of the Chinese YWCA, Florence organized social activities for the girls, taught immigrant women English, took them shopping downtown, and helped them with domestic problems. She also helped form the Girls of the Chinese Congregational Church, forerunner of the Square and Circle Club, a women's service organization that is still active today.

Although we had very few possessions, we were happy—much happier than some of our friends who had everything. God was with us helping and guiding us. My father, my brothers, and myself were accused for many acts that people said we did, but we were not alarmed nor worried. Mother told us that when we were among people of this world working with them, there is bound to be jealousy and contention—that if we think what we did was right in the eyes of God, we need not heed their accusations.[6] God would right the wrong done us, we need not worry. Up to this day, I have tried to adhere to these words of my mother's and pass them on to my children and to all who would listen. With God in us, we need not worry. In these troubled times, the only wise thing to do is to work hard for a better world, not by talking only, not by hurting others, not by protesting, etc. . . . , but by positive acts. First, we must find ourselves and let God in. When He is in us, then with Him as guide, we are bound to reach the goal in our Christian lives.

For my undergraduate work, I attended Mills College. For my graduate work in sociology, I was accepted by the University of Pennsylvania in Philadelphia. My credentials and baggage were sent ahead as I wanted to do some sightseeing in Chicago. There I was told by some friends of my father's that the University of Chicago was best known for sociology since the great sociologist, Jane Addams, was there at Hull House. Somehow this friend of my father's maneuvered a scholarship for me from the Theological Seminary of the University of Chicago. Here it was that I met my husband where he was doing his pre-medical studies. If I had gone on to Philadelphia, I would never have met him. I believe that God directed me to Chicago. People may say it was fate. But what is fate? I believe that fate is what God has planned for each of us—and God planned that we two must meet. God has been with us throughout our 43 years of married life, giving us three wonderful children and eight darling grandchildren.

My husband has been and still is a great source of influence to me. I admire his patience, untiredness, tolerance, humility and unselfishness. He is a person of integrity, honesty, and trustworthiness. He has a good sense of humor—a person of creativity, resourcefulness and of great intellect. While at college, he was awarded a gold medal for being the most

---

6. In another essay titled "Me and My Church," written in 1969 (in the possession of her daughter Jeanne Fong), Florence remarked on how some "misguided" youths in the church had accused her father of mismanagement. He evidently weathered the storm because he stayed with the church until his retirement in 1928.

well-rounded student, intellectually, physically and spiritually. I thank God for giving me such a wonderful partner!

A great lover of the out-doors, he has unfolded to me the wonders of God's world—the animals, the fish and plant life.

He has directed my attention to the great Chinese culture, both past and present. It is a rich culture, one of which every Chinese should be proud of. I hope that you, your children and children's children will foster and nurture this culture. Even the foreigners know how precious the Chinese culture is. They are learning our language, our art, our philosophy etc. . . . , imitating our fashions and our way of life. There are good and the bad in both the American and Chinese cultures. You are fortunate to be able to select the best in both cultures.

Several years ago, my husband and I rededicated ourselves at a Billy Graham rally here in San Francisco. We thank God for bringing us here at a time when there was great turmoil in China. We came here for one year's trip not knowing that we were to settle here for the rest of our lives. God has given us Grace and His plan for us is unfolding day by day. He has given us much—we are rich in His love.

I would like to end my talk with a few words of advice that I came across. I hope you will integrate these thoughts with your own in your daily lives.

> The best thing one can give is forgiveness to your enemy
> > Tolerance to your opponent
> Your heart to a friend
> > A good example to your child
> Good will and love to a father
> > To your mother, a conduct that will make her proud of you
> To yourself, respect
> > To all men—LOVE

(SOURCE: Florence Chinn Kwan, interview with author, October 7, 12, and 14, 1988, Berkeley, California; Florence Chinn Kwan, "Some Rambling Thoughts on Why I Am a Christian," Jeanne Fong private collection)

Story of a Chinese College Girl

(The Conflict between the Old and the Young)

ESTHER WONG

Caught between two generations and two cultures, Esther Wong initially chose to conform to the gender-role expectations of her parents.[1] *Born in China in 1903, she came to America with her mother and sister to join her father when she was five years old. As a child she helped out in her father's garment factory, working long hours after school six days a week. At the age of twelve she was put in charge of supervising twenty-five male workers in the factory. "I simply never had a chance to play in my life," she said in the following interview. "I have never been to a dance, never had a caller that I received, although some have come, never had what is called 'fun' in my life." Then when her mother became ill, Esther was the one who had to nurse her and take over all the household chores. All this she did willingly, despite her father's indifference toward her and the preferential treatment given her brother.*

Esther was especially careful about her public image, always fearful that she might be criticized for behaving improperly. "I had the right Chinese manner, very cold and proper, which the Chinese look for in women." She made sure that she kept an appropriate distance from men

---

1. Although the original document in the Survey of Race Relations collection does not identify the college girl in this interview, I came to the conclusion that it was Esther Wong based on another Survey interview that did identify her. Esther Wong also appears as Jade Swallow in her half-sister Jade Snow Wong's autobiography, *Fifth Chinese Daughter* (New York: Harper & Bros., 1950).

and became annoyed when they did not do likewise. Even when she helped her father out with political fund-raisers, she purposely avoided attending any of the banquets so that she would not be criticized for mingling with men.[2] But when her parents began to arrange her marriage, she finally rebelled and stood her ground by threatening to leave home. Slowly she gained her freedom by breaking away from the social restrictions of her home life. She found a job at the Chinese YWCA and supported herself through Mills College. Upon graduation she went to China to teach, remaining there until 1937, when war broke out between China and Japan.

When interviewed for the Survey of Race Relations in 1924, Esther apparently had much to say about what was wrong with Chinese families, the public schools, and the Chinatown community. Speaking from her own personal experiences, she criticized Chinese parents for not understanding their children, for working them so hard, and for their harsh treatment of daughters compared to sons. Her recounting of the anti-Asian attitudes of one teacher in itself is a strong indictment of racism in the public schools. Acknowledging social problems in the community, she criticized employers for labor exploitation, the churches for not working together, and organizations like the YWCA for not getting to the root of problems. What comes across in Esther Wong's interview is the frustration a second-generation Chinese American woman feels when the old ways no longer work in an ever-changing society. At the same time, her words speak to the concerns and willingness of the second generation to work "nobly and tirelessly" for the betterment of their community.

My grandfather was a merchant, a very successful one, and after business hours he was a student of the classics, so that my father was brought up in that atmosphere. He [her father] married in China and then, when the oldest child, that was I, was three years old he came to America, and we came on, my mother and sister and myself, two years later. My father had at first a very hard time; he was young, and trying to manage a business and none in the business gave him credit for knowing anything, so they all cheated him. So, after awhile, his health broke down, and he went to San Diego to live, and left us here to get along the best we could.

---

2. Conservative Chinese decorum dictated that women should not mingle freely with men in public.

Mother took in sewing, and we used to help her, too. I was then eight years old, and my sister was about six. That was a kind of sweatshop work, but it was not very hard, as we rented rooms in the family of a missionary. We had pleasant rooms, and sunshine, and even after the missionary left, another Christian family took their place so we have had that sort of influence, even from the first. When I was nine, father came back and he had learned a good deal about taking care of his health, so he made very good rules for himself and for us, and since then he has never been sick and is very, very strong, always active and doing something.

He cannot understand how anybody can get tired, and ever since we were small he has expected us to do really more than we could. We always heard that we were lazy, but this is what we did. I myself was a child worker in a factory, my father's clothing factory it was, and that is why I know what child labor is, and *just* what it is, I simply never had a chance to play in my life. I began grammar school when I was eleven, but before that father had taught us in Chinese. We used to have a little class with him at six o'clock in the morning. At eleven years of age I began school, and after school hours, from three to nine I worked in the factory every day but Sunday; Saturdays I worked all day. I earned all my way through grammar school, every cent that was spent for my schooling, and I completed the eight grades in four years. Then I worked my way through high school, also in the factory, but earning more. I sometimes could speed up to ninety cents an hour, but my average was about seventy-five cents.[3] At sixteen I had for the first time control over my own money, before eleven I did not know how a nickel looked, or what it was for. My mother was very sick for a year while I was in my fourth year at high school, and part of the time I stayed at home, and acted as nurse, as mother refused to go to a hospital. I also did most of the cooking and cleaning for the family, my sister helping at times, when she could. I sometimes wonder how I did all that, but I did. The strange thing about my early factory work was not so much the long hours, but the responsibility. When I was twelve my father gave me the oversight of twenty-five men; I was to give out material, see that their work was right, see that the factory was kept clean, etc.

My father, at that time, had no boys and he started in to train me as

---

3. Her speed and earnings are quite good when compared to immigrant women like Law Shee Low, who was making about two dollars a day sewing at home (see p. 218).

if I was a boy; he always tried to make us think things out, gave us problems in arithmetic, told us stories, discussed what was right and what was wrong with us, in fact he could be a wonderful companion, and I could have loved my father very much, only he would not try to understand us.

When I was thirteen my brother was born and then he lost interest in us girls, did not care to bother teaching girls, and seemed to forget what we were like. When we were small he used to work at a machine next to ours, and when we were all busy he would tell us stories as we worked; but later he became very stern and cold and did not try to understand us at all.

My brother has a great deal of spending money and a bank account of his own and can do just about as he likes. We girls were expected to do everything and to pay for our room and board, which we thought was hard, as that is not the Chinese way, usually that is given to children. One reason for this conflict which has grown up between the old and the young in our family was the question of marriage, which came up when my mother was very ill. I was doing the housework, studying very hard at high school, getting ready to graduate, and nursing my mother, when two suitors appeared.

It is the custom, when one parent is about to die, for the daughters of marriageable age to marry, thus going at once into another family and give the departing parent assurance that the daughters are to be safe and well cared for. One suitor was a distant cousin that I did not know very well, and had never suspected of any such feeling. My mother was in favor of him. My father was against him, but in favor of another man about twenty-seven years old, who had been divorced from his wife, but my mother hated the thought of that. Divorce nearly always means something queer in China. I was seventeen years old, and I hated them both, and I stood out against them all. I finally said that I would pack my suitcase and go, if they did not stop this torture. It was bad enough, having parents do the matchmaking, but when they did not even agree on the man, and began quarreling about it, as they often did, it was terrible. Then my sister, who was only fifteen, had a suitor, too, and she used to tell him to his face, "I don't like you! I won't have you!" But still he hung around, and my two used to come around often, so that I was nearly crazy with all this on my mind.

About this time, too, I had one teacher who was awfully hard to get on with. All my teachers had been good to me, kind and helpful, but this one was an Englishwoman, and she did not like Orientals, and none of them could stand her, they always got out of her class, all but one Japanese girl and me, and I stood her the longest, for fifteen months, then I had to get out of her class, although I lost credits by doing so. She was the only teacher of French in the whole school. This teacher always tried to stir up this Japanese girl and me against each other. She would praise one and slam the other, which ever one she felt like hurting, and would say "Why do you let the representative of that nation beat you—you ought to be ashamed!" When I would stay out to nurse my mother and bring notes explaining she would make jokes about it, and once she said, "Why, I thought your mother died long ago!" Towards the last I had to do some sight-reading for her, and I was very much frightened. She was a very stern teacher, with very strict rules about everything. You had to stand just so far from your desk, hold your back just so, and everything. Well, I read for her, and there were no mistakes. She just looked me over, from head to foot, for a minute, and I did not know what was coming, but was frightened. Then she said very slowly, "Well, you read all right, but I don't like you. You belong to a dirty race that spit at missionaries."

I felt almost frozen with horror, then I began to get crimson, I was the only Chinese in the room. The other students were shocked, too, but they soon forgot it; I never could. She gave me new slanders each day, so I felt that I could not finish the last six months with her, and dropped the class. She sent for me, and asked, "By what authority have you dropped my class? Don't you know that you can't possibly graduate without it?" I said I thought I could, that I had talked with other teachers. "No, you can't!" she said, "I will see about that!" So she went to all the other teachers but they all felt sympathy with me, and knew the case, so she could do nothing. I already had eighteen points and I only needed fifteen, but she thought that I needed her class to get the bare fifteen. After I left she seemed to get better, sent messages to me once or twice and asked after my mother, but then it was too late.

Miss M. helped me a great deal, with encouragement, and she gave me a chance in the "Y" to work my way through college.[4] At first I thought I would like to make this my life work, but now that I have been in the work for a few years it seems to me that it is largely palliative; although the work is constructive and necessary; as far as training for leadership is concerned, I feel that I would now like to get at the roots of wrongs, and I want to see happier homes.

---

4. Myrtle Mills was director of the Chinese YWCA from 1916 to 1926.

I have been very active in church work for a number of years, and once I spoke before a missionary society where there were really more men than women. I was talking about what we can do right at home, because only a few of us have money to go to China to work, and asked what can we do right here? Afterwards a large number of the young men came up and hung around to tell me how interested they were. I said to the superintendent, "You have a very fine lot of young men right here, to begin on!" and she said, "Yes, but we need workers!" I said "Would you like to have me come here to help?" and she said, "Why, would you come?" I said, "Yes, I will come, I should like to do something like that!" So she said, "Well, what would you like to do best, down here?" And I said, "I would like to have a class of young men, if that is possible, since they are the founders of homes, and more depends on them than on anything else."

So I began with that class of men who were there that day, and some others. There are twelve men in the class, although that is of course very strange, for a Chinese girl to be instructing men in anything of this kind. We are studying the modern version of the Bible, and they are intensely interested, all come regularly and we have a great many discussions. There is one man in the class who is about forty-five years old, and he always disagrees with everything I say, and contradicts me, but I never have to defend myself unless I want to, because some young men will speak up quickly and say, "That is not so!" But after class they always go out without speaking to me because it would not be good Chinese manners for them to stop and speak to me, or say they liked it, or anything like that. Now I have another class, also, of Chinese women and girls. This is harder, because they are all of such different ages, and cannot all understand either Chinese or English alike. In this class we discuss American ways.

As you asked me, I never had much trouble with pupils falling in love with me, that I knew of, except one time. That was awful. I was teaching a class in English, to young men from China, at a night school, and one young man that I never suspected sent a message to me that he would like to marry me. When I would have nothing to do with him he tried to burn down my father's factory. We don't know, but we think he must have been the person, for we had no other enemy, and that is the Chinese way. He thinks if he can make a girl poor, and have no friends, then he can step in and rescue her, and make her happy. He did the same thing to a man friend of mine who tried to tell him to have more sense and leave me alone. He threw a blazing ball of cotton, soaked in chemicals, into the factory, the first time through the letter-slot, and another time through the transom. But my father happened to be there both times and put them out. The second time it fell within a few inches of a great pile of a hundred dozen garments all ready to be shipped, and just missed a whole box of papers, but my father got it out in time. Afterwards this man went away, but he wrote us some queer letters. Another pupil sent me a gold ring, but mostly they behaved very well, and did not bother me. It is very annoying, when they act that other way.

My sister, two years younger, also earned her way through high school by working in the factory, and has even bought her own piano, as she wants to be a musician. We expect a sort of crisis when I get through college. You see, by Chinese tradition and custom, if my father wanted to retire now, he could do it, and I, as the oldest, would have to support him.

Two girls that I know had a father about sixty years old, but he did not look more than fifty. He sold out all of his business to get money to go to China and live. After about three or four years he came back to America and the two girls had to support him, working in a tearoom to do so. Finally, after three or four years, he got tired of that, produced some more money from somewhere or other, and went back to China. If a girl marries, under such circumstances, however, she is free, except that she may have to support a new family. It is very hard for Chinese girls because marrying always means off with her own family and taking on a new one.

I was brought up in the very strictest Chinese way. I have never been to a dance, never had a caller that I received, although some have come, never had what is called "fun" in my life. Father did not believe in it. He was one of the prominent leaders of the Chinese National League of America,[5] and acted as Treasurer, handling large sums of money. I used to be all alone in the office, receiving large sums, but was perfectly safe, none ever spoke to me except when necessary, because I had the right Chinese

5. The Guomindang or Chinese Nationalist Party was founded by Dr. Sun Yat-sen following the successful overthrow of the Qing dynasty and the establishment of the Republic of China in 1911. Under Chiang Kai-shek's rule beginning in 1925, the Guomindang stood in opposition to the Chinese Communist Party, which was founded in 1921. In 1949 the Communist Party took control of China, driving Chiang and the Guomindang to the island of Taiwan. Until the United States normalized diplomatic relations with the People's Republic of China in 1979, the Guomindang exerted great influence in the Chinese American community.

manner, very cold and proper, which the Chinese look for in women, and so I was not even spoken to, except in a business way. These League Teams always end in a feast, but though I was on many different teams at different times I never went to a feast, and so I could not be criticized.

Perhaps you could not find a family that would better illustrate the conflict between the old and the new. We were brought up more strictly than most girls, even according to Chinese ideas, and my sister and I have kept these habits, never going to dances, or having company, always working. At the same time I now live quite independent of my family, I have cut myself off, made myself free. My father hardly knows what I am doing, he does not know at all what is in my mind. My father is a very clever man. He did not learn to read English, only to speak in the most ordinary way, but somehow he learned all about electricity and how to repair the electric sewing machines in our factory; and though he never studied carpentering, and things are done differently in China, he built an addition to our factory himself, with his own hands, and he is always studying and reading in Chinese in medicine, philosophy, history and biographies of great men, whenever he has time. If he could have learned to read English, perhaps he would have understood us better.

When my mother died, my father had a right to keep me home from school, and to use all my time, but he did not, and after one year he married, so then we girls were free from the housework. My stepmother is only a year older than I am, now she is twenty-five, and she has two little children. They each have bank accounts, and she has [one], as well as my brother. Something is put in each week. If my father should die, everything would go to my brother, except perhaps a little to my stepmother and the children. If they had nothing, it would be the duty of my sister and myself to support them, as we are older than my brother, although he would have all the property.

My brother is eleven years old. Oh, yes, I like him very much, although he may be a little spoiled. The way that I stopped living with my family was this. We used to have breakfast at eight, dinner at twelve, and supper at four-thirty. That was all right, I could do my work and eat at those hours with the family. But all of a sudden my father changed all of those hours, breakfast at 9, etc., so that I could no longer do my work and eat at home. He did not give any reason, and I simply stopped eating at home; but I sleep there, with my sister.

One thing that is very discouraging for us, when we hope to see an improvement in the second generation, are the traps that are set for our boys, to exploit them, and make fools of them, even criminals. Once we lived next door to a factory where they made flannel shirts for men; they paid good wages there, and the boys made lots of money. But there was only a thin board partition between the factory and our home, and we could hear all that went on there. The boys used to work until nine o'clock, and then the proprietor introduced a gambling game. At first he used to lend the boys money to play in it, and make a kind of joke of it. Afterwards the boys got perfectly crazy about it, and they would play every night, after work, until one or two o'clock, and lose every cent that they made. So, in time, the proprietor got back all of the money that he spent for help, and there was no way to stop him. The police tried to reach [the boys], and some detective used to listen in at our house, but they never could get the boys to testify against him. The mothers of those boys were in despair. But one thing the Chinese do not seem to see, this is, "that as you sow, so shall ye reap." They don't seem to have any sense about that.

One mother that I know kept her boy all day long at a machine. He never, never had a chance to play, and when he would run away, as he did when he was let out to school, she would beat him. Finally she had him chained, actually *chained* to his machine, but one day he succeeded in filing himself loose, and went away, never to return, he thought. He went to Portland and joined a Tong, becoming one of their soldiers, living on a salary from them.[6] But after awhile he heard that his father was very sick, and he felt sorry, and came home to see him before he died.

The father died before he got there, but his mother was glad to see him, and she gave him $700.00 to buy his freedom from the Tong, so that he could go to work. But he could not work any more. He had been loafing around as a Tong man for too long. Now he has joined two Tongs, instead of one, and does nothing at all, just loafs around, living on his two salaries from them, and ready to do what they want, if they need him. His mother cannot see that she helped to bring that about. They never seem to see what they do has consequences.

About the Churches, and the Missions helping? Yes, they do, but they would help more if they were united. It was the fault of the Americans in starting so many Missions up here, and it seems so strange that the Christian Churches, that preach love and peace, should not agree with each other. There are eleven churches in this small district, and each one wants more authority. So the Chinese boys say, "You ask us not to fight, why should we get into your fights?" If the churches were united in one

---

6. She is referring to the secret societies that were engaged in criminal activities.

big church, not each one poor and struggling, each one trying to raise money from the Chinese, it would be a lot better. They are all too poor to do much, are always trying to raise money, and never have much. Then, I am sorry to say, when they get a really good man they do not always appreciate him. They are jealous of his influences, some prominent men do not dislike what he preaches, but they feel he has too much power, which goes with popularity. We had really one very fine man here in the Y.M.C.A. He was full of splendid plans, he started outdoor sports for the boys, he got them all working and was loved by everyone. You could not help but like him. But he went a little too fast, and got some jealous workers down on him. You have to go very slowly in Chinatown. So finally he had to leave, and he went to some other place, and that was the only really good man we have had. Mostly they don't do much, they avoid having enemies, but that is about all.

It is very discouraging for anyone who is trying to do anything, but the only way is to go very, very slowly. It is apparently the slow, patient workers who have the right vision who help and construct. That is the only way that I have been able to do anything at all. Education does not always help. It is knowing the people, and then, by following the highest ideals, to work nobly and tirelessly. That is the only way that good can be brought about, to replace the evil. Please do not think for a minute that I wish to minimize the work of the Y.W.C.A. It is only a personal ambition of mine to want to get at the roots of things. The Y.W. has done more good in the community in the last five years than all the churches combined. The Y.M. is in need of a proper leader, otherwise it would be ready to do its very best for the young boys, which it has done in the past, to combat evil influences which young people are bound to come across in their lives.

The problem of poverty in Chinatown is largely bound up with the large size of their families, but if you say to a Chinaman, "Why have you so many children, so that you cannot support them all?" he will say to you, with a pitying smile, "Don't you know that a farmer lays up stores for the winter? We lay up children for our old age, so that we may be taken care of." If you say, "Well, then, why have stunted or sickly children?" They will not understand you, they do not think that far, they do not think that sickness or health is the consequences of the way you live, but just fate, a consequence of bad luck or something outside of your control.

(SOURCE: Box 24, Folder 54, Survey of Race Relations Collection, Hoover Institution on War, Revolution, and Peace, Stanford University)

Flora Belle Jan, Flapper and Writer

"I Long for Unconventionality and Freedom"

In direct contrast to Esther Wong, who tried to comply with her parents' expectations, Flora Belle Jan responded differently by rebelling against prescribed gender roles. She was what was known as a "flapper" in the jazz age of the 1920s, someone who defied social control and conventions, who was modern, independent, sophisticated, and frank in speech, dress, morals, and lifestyle. Caught in the webs of two cultures and marginalized by white American society as well as the Chinese American community, she found a way to define her own identity and express her social dissatisfactions through writing.[1]

The third child in a family of eight children, Flora Belle Jan was born in 1906 in Fresno, California. Like Esther Wong's parents, Flora Belle's parents were Cantonese-speaking immigrants from China. Although relatively well off—they owned and operated the Yet Far Low Restaurant in Fresno Chinatown—they did not encourage any of their sons or daughters to pursue higher education. They were also quite strict with Flora Belle, wanting to maintain control over her comings and goings and mold her into a "proper" Chinese woman, though they evidently failed.

Influenced more by her teachers, peers, books, and popular culture than by her conservative parents, Flora Belle showed signs of rebel-

---

1. A longer article, "'It Is Hard to Be Born a Woman But Hopeless to Be Born a Chinese': The Life and Times of Flora Belle Jan," appeared in *Frontiers: A Journal of Women's Studies* 18, no. 3 (1997): 66–91.

Flora Belle Jan in 1925. (Courtesy of Flora Belle Jan's family)

liousness at an early age. In the following interview from the Survey of Race Relations *collection, she described how she began questioning "the old Chinese ways and ideas" as a little girl. She also pointed out that she was just as critical of social conventions in the larger American society. To expose the hypocrisy that she saw among her peers, Flora Belle wrote scathing articles, poems, short stories, and skits, some of which were published in the* Fresno Republican, San Francisco Examiner, *and periodicals of local and national Chinese student clubs.[2] In one article, "Chi-*

2. Chinese student clubs were organized in colleges and universities throughout the country after the turn of the century when the numbers of students from China began to increase. In 1911 the Chinese Students' Alliance in the United States of America was officially constituted; it was responsible for organizing a national conference every four

natown Sheiks Are Modest Lot; Eschew Slang, Love-Moaning Blues,"
reprinted below, she used the latest slang to poke fun at her Chinese male
friends, while in two other sketches, "Old Mother Grundy and Her Brood
of Unbaptized Nuns" and "Miss Flapper Vampire," she chose to ridicule
certain characteristics of the modern flapper.[3]

Although I could not interview Flora Belle Jan (she died in 1950), I
was able to interview her sister Bessie and Flora Belle's two daughters
(whose names I am withholding on request).[4] Her daughters generously
shared some of the letters that Flora Belle wrote to her childhood friend
and lifetime confidante Ludmelia Holstein from 1918 to 1949. From these
interviews and letters I was able to reconstruct Flora Belle's life story and
her struggles as a second-generation Chinese American woman with aspirations to become a famous writer. Like other American girls who came
of age in the 1920s — a decade marked by postwar prosperity, consumerism, and a revolution in manners and morals on the part of
youth — Flora Belle was interested in the latest fashions, romance, and
having a good time out dating and attending parties, none of which her
parents approved. According to her sister Bessie, Flora Belle was an avid
reader and had a vivid imagination and flair for writing. She was also serious about pursuing college and a writing career, ambitions that her parents likewise did not support. Their opposition, however, did not stop
her and she was able to find part-time jobs as a housekeeper, factory
worker, salesgirl, and waitress that allowed her to fulfill those goals.

After graduating from Fresno Junior College in 1925, Flora Belle
moved to San Francisco to attend the University of California, Berkeley.
Living on her own in the city gave her free rein to indulge her youthful
whims, although she faithfully wrote letters home to her father in Chinese. She joined the Chinese Students' Club, signed up to write for the
college newspaper, went to fraternity parties, and competed for the title
of Chinatown queen. But she was unable to integrate into the larger social circles on the college campus. Because of racial exclusion, she could
not join any of the white sororities or date any of the white fraternity
boys. Even so, according to her last letter to Ludmelia from San Fran-

---

years and publishing the Chinese Students' Monthly, which reported on student activities
and included articles on Chinese cultural and political topics. Local clubs also had their
own publications.

3. Unfortunately, I was not able to locate copies of either skit.

4. Bessie Hung, interview with author, June 30, 1989, San Francisco; Flora Belle Jan's
two daughters, interview with author, August 6, 1989.

cisco, within six months excessive partying, romantic relationships with the wrong men, and "scandalous" newspaper columns had earned her a bad reputation in the close-knit, conservative Chinese community. She decided to accept an offer from sociologist Robert E. Park and transfer to the University of Chicago to study journalism.[5] There she was able to complete her B.A. degree and launch her career as a writer, serving as literary editor of the Chinese Students' Monthly, *a feature writer for the* Chicago Daily News, *and belonging to the Poetry Circle, American Literary Association, and Order of Book Fellows. But then she met and fell in love with a graduate student from China. They married in 1926, had a son a year later, and left for China in 1932, where they made their home for the next sixteen years. Those years would be difficult for Flora Belle as she tried to adapt to life in China, raise a family of three children, and find work as a journalist during a time when China was at war with Japan. Her health declined and her nerves shattered, never to recover. In 1950, a year after she was able to return to the United States with her two daughters, she died of high blood pressure and kidney failure at the age of forty-three. Her children had these words inscribed on her gravestone: "A journalist and feminist before her time. A talent and beauty extinguished in her prime. Our beloved mother."*

Although Flora Belle Jan did not fulfill her dream of literary fame before she died, she did leave behind a legacy of writings about her time. From among her newspaper articles, short stories, poems, and book reviews, I have selected her satire on Chinatown sheiks, a short story about a Chinese American flapper, and a poem addressed "To a Chinese Mother" as examples of her writing talent. Arranged in the date order in which they were published, they show her development as a person and a writer. "Chinatown Sheiks Are Modest Lot" represented her debut as a Chinese flapper and writer in a major metropolitan newspaper; in it she showed off her command of English slang and her unusual views on Chinese American life. Contrary to the prevailing stereotypes of the emasculated Chinese coolie or the diabolical Fu Manchu, the Chinese American men she described knew how to "shimmy 'Chicago,' and tango . . . buy candy for the Shebas, take them to the theater, sing them all kinds of 'I've got the blues' songs, and do everything else that American sheiks indulge in." Al-

---

5. Robert E. Park headed the Survey of Race Relations project and was known to recruit "Oriental" students to work with him at the University of Chicago. See Henry Yu, "Thinking about Orientals: A History of Race, Migration, and Modernity in Twentieth-Century America" (Ph.D. diss., Princeton University, 1995).

though initially amused by her writing, the San Francisco Examiner *soon let her go for being "too inexperienced for a metropolitan daily."*[6]

Her short story *"Afraid of the Dark,"* published in the Interpreter, *an insert of the* Chinese Students' Monthly, *appeared while Flora Belle was a student at the University of Chicago. It shows Flora Belle to be a romantic dreamer with a vivid imagination. The story's heroine, Ming Toy, closely resembles Flora Belle in a number of revealing ways. A daughter of a "chop suey palace proprietor," Ming Toy insists she's an American flapper, refuses to honor her ancestors, and leaves home for college. There she is found one evening cowering before the ghosts of her grandfather's past, proving that she is not as brazen as she is made out to be. Her poem "To a Chinese Mother" was also published in the* Chinese Students' Monthly. *By then, Flora Belle had completed her college education, was married, and had just given birth to a baby boy. The voice we now hear is that of a mature and subdued woman in search of ways to deal with the burdens of marriage and motherhood. She had yet to experience the worst years of her life, in war-torn China, which would temper her "flapperism" and reinforce her faith in America.*

INTERVIEW WITH FLORA BELLE JAN,
DAUGHTER OF PROPRIETOR OF THE
"YET FAR LOW," CHOP SUEY RESTAURANT,
TULARE ST. AND CHINA ALLEY,
FRESNO, CALIFORNIA[7]

Miss Jan is a graduate of the Fresno High School and has taken two years in the Fresno State College. She is a leader among the native born Chinese, very much interested in writing, dramatics and social life.

---

6. Letter from Flora Belle Jan to Ludmelia Holstein, July 16, 1924.

7. According to a letter addressed to Robert E. Park dated June 1, 1924 (Box 12, Survey of Race Relations Collection, Hoover Institution on War, Revolution, and Peace, Stanford University), investigator Merle Davis interviewed Flora Belle Jan. He was evidently fascinated by her keen intellect, outgoing personality, and unconventional outlook, for he wrote in the letter to Park that "Flora Belle is the only Oriental in town apparently who has the charm, wit and nerve to enter good White society. . . . She is both a horror and source of pride to her staid Chinese friends, and is quite the talk of American town." In other words, she confirmed Park's theory that all ethnic groups, including "Orientals," were assimilable. See Robert E. Park, *Race and Culture* (Glencoe, Ill.: Free Press, 1950); and Yu, "Thinking about Orientals," pp. 41–54.

Flora Belle Jan as the only female officer of the Chinese Students' Club of Fresno in 1924. (Box 3, Survey of Race Relations Collection, Hoover Institution on War, Revolution, and Peace, Stanford University)

She entertained me [investigator Merle Davis] in her father's upstairs restaurant for about an hour. My first approach was through Miss Purcell,[8] but was unsuccessful and I finally saw her by presenting my card directly.

She said, "Would you like to hear something about my life? I will tell you if you are interested. I was born here in Fresno Chinatown and attended the city schools and graduated from the High School and have had two years in the State College. When I was a little girl, I grew to dis-

---

8. Amy Purcell was the superintendent of the Baptist Chinese Mission and Flora Belle Jan's Sunday schoolteacher. This is how she described Flora Belle in an interview with Merle Davis: "She is an unique girl. Very keen, unconventional, bright student, good writer. . . . She would like to go on with her education at the University of California, but her parents objected. She needs the advice and help of a good friend. She runs around with the native young Chinese boys, who are as American as she. Last night I saw her go tearing along in a big car with a boy's arm around her neck. At the same time I think Flora Belle is amply able to take care of herself and will not get into serious trouble." See "Flora Belle Jan, Interview with Miss Amy Purcell, Superintendent of Baptist Chinese Mission," 1925, Box 9, Folder 9, Survey of Race Relations Collection, Hoover Institution on War, Revolution, and Peace, Stanford University.

like the conventionality and rules of Chinese life. The superstitions and customs seemed ridiculous to me. My parents have wanted me to grow up a good Chinese girl, but I am an American and I can't accept all the old Chinese ways and ideas. A few years ago when my Mother took me to worship at the shrine of my ancestor and offer a plate of food, I decided it was time to stop this foolish custom. So I got up and slammed down the rice in front of the idol and said, 'So long Old Top, I don't believe in you anyway.' My mother didn't like it a little bit.

"As I grew older I came to see that American life is also full of conventionality and foolish customs and it has become a fad of mine to study these things and to write about them. I long for unconventionality and freedom from all these customs and ideals that make people do such ridiculous and insincere things.

"I have written a good deal in local papers about Chinese life. Much of this had displeased the Chinese people of Fresno. My article on 'The Sheiks of Chinatown' (a description of the young sports of China Alley) was a takeoff on certain well known native-born Chinese. It made a terrible fuss in Chinatown. I have had three blackmailing letters sent me for writing so openly about Chinese life. One of the Chinese students from North China became very angry at my article on the Sheiks and wrote me a very long, fat letter attacking me and picking to pieces everything that I had said. He thought that I was trying to disgrace China, which I distinctly was not, but only trying to have a little fun with my Chinese friends. All Chinatown got very excited and two of the boys, one from North China and the other from South China, fought a kind of a duel over it. North boy said that I had disgraced China. South boy said No, that we should be too proud to let a little dust like this hurt us. A delegation of Chinese students met me at college and I challenged them to show what I had said that disgraced anybody or anything. They put on their spectacles and after ten minutes could not find anything. I said, 'Ta ta, Kiddos, when you find any disgrace you just put me wise. I can't wait all day.'

"It is very funny to watch the snobbishness of the girls at the state college. I listen to the Sorority girls talk over possible candidates to membership in their sorority. It runs something like this, 'Girls, what do you suppose, Jane Smith whom we've been rushing is impossible. We've just found out that her father once drove a delivery wagon. They live in such a nice house and she wears such pretty clothes, who would have dreamed it. My, she's such a nice girl, it is really too bad.' I happen to know that some of these very girls have families where the men are working at shop work and day labor and where the mothers do their own work. They judge people entirely by the clothes they wear and the amount of money they spend, and they get awfully stung in this way sometimes. Of course being a Chinese girl, I'm not eligible to membership in a sorority, but some of the girls are awfully good to me.

"I have written a sketch of American girls, called 'Old Mother Grundy and her brood of unbaptized nuns,' which takes off some of the characteristics of the modern flapper in American society.

"At the Community House last week our Chinese Club gave a play called, 'Miss Flapper Vampire,' that I wrote. I was the leading character and about five young men played in it with me. There was a large audience of Americans. Afterward we danced and the American girls danced with the Chinese boys and I danced with American young men."[9]

(SOURCE: June 5, 1924, Box 28, Folder 225, Survey of Race Relations Collection, Hoover Institution on War, Revolution, and Peace, Stanford University)

CHINATOWN SHEIKS ARE MODEST LOT
Eschew Slang, Love-Moaning Blues

Introducing to the San Francisco public Miss Flora Belle Jan, Chinese flapper, who will discuss for your edification and entertainment the Chinatown sheik! Miss Jan has roped and tied the English language in a manner that would have made Noah Webster marvel and whether you are interested in the Mendelian law of the variation of characteristics or such anatomical curiosities as the "bee's knees" and the "flea's whiskers," you will find it requires a nimble mind to go a-sheiking with a Chinese flapper. Miss Jan contributes the following monologue on "Sheiks of Chinatown":

The Mendelian law of the variation of characteristics is surprisingly true. Though individuals may appear similar in every way, they are never exactly alike.

For instance, in my wanderings through San Francisco's Chinatown, I heard rumors of Chinese sheiks, and further rumors of more sheiks. Immediately I thought of bandolin hair, sideburns, jazz, slang and the

---

9. According to Davis's letter to Park, the interracial dancing caused "quite a furor" in town.

thousand other things that comprise the make-up of the beloved creatures from Sahara.

I thought, too, how it would interest the public to know the Chinatown Sheik, the Worshipped of the Celestial Queens. I deluded myself
into believing it an easy task to persuade one of the idols to admit he
was topnotch, the cat's eyebrows in sheikdom, and to let his photograph
appear among a galaxy of fawning maidens.

Say! Did Napoleon anticipate Waterloo? Have newlyweds ever painted
rolling pins on their wedding cakes? If they had had the foresight—oh,
well, at least they make glorious illustrations of the human version of
sapwood, deadwood, and asphaltic concrete—and I, another example.

Here's where Mendel's law comes in, showing the difference between
Chinese sheiks and those of some other nation. The dreamy-eyed Valenti-
nos hate publicity. If permitted by the roof garden proprietors, they would
shimmy "Chicago," and tango (and take it from me, they know how!).
They buy candy for the Shebas, take them to the theater, sing them all
kinds of "I've got the blues" songs, and do everything else that American sheiks indulge in: but they'll be dawgoned if they want the world to
know about them! If Diogenes were looking for a modest man, wouldn't
he have a paralytic stroke to learn that he needn't use a lamp?

Of course the Great American "Slanguage" is an indispensable tool
of sheikhood, but the Oriental sheiks do not pollute their vocabulary
with expressions like "bees' knees," "fleas' whiskers," and "come on,
babe, let's cheese it to the Saturday night hop."

Far be it from me to even suggest that they are effeminate Tagalongs,
so delicate that they say, "Oh, dear," when they mean "Suffering cats!"
Neither are they smooth, sinister Landrus nor silver-tongued Spaniards.
They are just Chinese Sheiks who say anything they please any time, but
they are not very guilty of hammer-murdering the English tongue.

It would be extreme to say that the Chinese sheiks know every item
in the etiquette book, but they certainly have digested many rules. At a
party held at a Chinese roof garden last evening, the sheiks knew so much
about etiquette that they discussed the subject of manners with genuine
ease. They ate with their knives on purpose to show how ungraceful and
uncharming they could be. Truly, it was on purpose!

Contrary to the popular imagination, the literature read by the Chinese sheiks does not consist wholly in True Confessions, Love Stories and
Whizz Bangs. Those sheiks laugh at sentimental girls who spend a portion of their weekly allowances piling up dime novels for the rag man to
take away. It is difficult to interpret their literary taste. Some, I must ad-

mit, are lenient toward Elinor Glyn, but others would love to see her books at the bottom of the sea. Writers like Gertrude Atherton and Ruby Ayres have a better following.

As for religion, Chinese sheiks have as much religious fervor as some Americans; that is to say, sometimes they have no religion at all. But that is not vitally important. They are sheiks, whether they believe in Buddha or Sikh.

They don't pretend to be highbrow. They wouldn't muse over "Humoresque" and other classical numbers when they can secure a moaning saxophone and play, "You know you belong to somebody else, so why don't you leave me alone?" But say, if anyone insinuates that they are a million miles from the highbrow, I'll take off my French heels and knock him for a set of mah jongg!

(SOURCE: *San Francisco Examiner*, March 27, 1924, p. 9)

AFRAID OF THE DARK

Do you believe that ghosts, like bootleg liquor and human stowaways can be smuggled across the United States border? Of course, I don't either. But on the other hand, there is the case of Ming Toy.

Ming Toy, daughter of a chop suey palace proprietor at 1007 1/2 Chinatown Alley, is a beautiful and a brazen child. Her shoulders are, so the California artists say, incomparable, and her sulky pomegranate mouth has been deemed worthy of attention and of praise, not only by the susceptible Pacific coast poets, but by more ordinary men as well. The sons of Japanese samurai, the nephews of Korean intellectuals, tennis-playing American university instructors, and the whole tribe of native sons from Chinatown's suavest sheik to its earnest be-tortoise-shelled medical students, cluster about Ming Toy's doorstep as iron filings cluster about a magnet.

Ming Toy is very beautiful, and she is very brazen. She has refused to honor her ancestors, she has ridden through Chinatown Alley on horseback, she has traveled alone in a sleeper, she has walked upstairs at three o'clock in the morning and called out, "Hello, folks," while her little Chinese-American girl friends were paddling upstairs in stocking feet so as not to be heard. She has written stories about Chinatown society that almost precipitated a tong war. In fact, Ming Toy has so thoroughly shocked the older generation of Chinatown by her attempts to behave like an American magazine flapper that various men offered to pay for the eastern university education that they knew Ming Toy had set her heart on. "Any strings to the offer?" said Ming Toy in her hard-boiled way, and did not accept.

Ming Toy Leaves Chinatown Behind Her

When the disapproval of Chinatown's older generation became too hot for Ming Toy, she left for the East to get a university education for herself. Ming Toy has never seen China, and has no desire to see China. Ming Toy was born in Chinatown, but she has no desire to live in Chinatown. Ming Toy is an American.

One night an American student found Ming Toy cowering on the steps of a university building, looking much less brazen than usual. "Waiting for someone?" he inquired. "No," said Ming Toy, "I'm afraid to walk home in the dark." The young man took her home. "And why are you afraid?" he inquired. Ming Toy did not want to say. She confessed that she had always been afraid of the dark, because there were so many ghosts about. What sort of ghosts? They were ghosts,—Chinese ghosts,—who had haunted Ming Toy's grandfather. And why had they haunted him? Ming Toy didn't know; there was some mystery about it, and her parents had never told her.

"Ming Toy isn't the hard-boiled child she thinks she is," said the American to a fellow student from Boston's Chinatown. "Do you know that she is afraid of the dark and that she believes that ghosts who haunted her grandfather in China, follow her around the streets of Boston?"

"Ah," said the Chinese-American gravely. "I understand. You see her grandfather was the village executioner. He went insane before he died because he was haunted."

"By the same ghosts that haunt Ming Toy?"

"The very same."

"Does Ming Toy know that her grandfather was an executioner?"

"No indeed. If Ming Toy knew that she would feel disgraced. And we Chinese do not wish Ming Toy to feel disgraced. I can assure you that not even Ming Toy's worst enemies in Chinatown will ever tell her that the ghosts she is afraid of are the ghosts of the men whom her grandfather executed."[10]

(SOURCE: *The Interpreter* 6, no. 7 [September 1927]: 17–19)

---

10. Malicious ghosts who died before their time either as murder victims or suicides were known to haunt those from whom they sought revenge.

TO A CHINESE MOTHER

Small in stature, glossy-haired,
    Young in face, though wan.
Forgotten have you how you fared
    In your bridal caravan?

Skin of velvet, luscious eyes,
    Wide in childlike gaze—
How are you able to disguise
    The sorrow of those tortured days?

Was love a duty, or duty, love,
    When brides were tagged a price
And sent to market in a drove
    Fat purses to entice?

Ten years have gone, and you are free,
    Your sons your only care.
How could those years of slavery
    Still leave you young and fair?

You smile at questions, shake your head,
    And work the silken floss
Of the multi-colored petal threads.
    Mute, on the years you've lost.

Can it be you think it folly
    To mourn over what must be.
That our lives are mapped out wholly
    By the Gods of Destiny?

If from your face, serene and calm,
    I can gain your philosophy,
I would fear no torrents of grief or pain,
    From all desires would I be free!

(SOURCE: *Chinese Students' Monthly* 25, no. 4 [March 1930]: 160)

Gladys Ng Gin, Cocktail Waitress

"That's What Happens When You're Illiterate"

I met Gladys Ng Gin through my oldest sister, Sharon. They were mah jongg buddies and Sharon thought Gladys, who was eighty-five years old at the time, might have some interesting things to say about her life in San Francisco. Gladys agreed to let me interview her in her Chinatown apartment one Friday afternoon. Her husband was home and sat through half of the interview before getting up to go out. He said very little and his presence did not seem to affect Gladys' spontaneous responses to my questions. Gladys appeared much younger than her age and was fashionably dressed in a colorful silk blouse and a pair of black slacks. I found her easy to talk to. She had a good memory and provided detailed answers to my questions, probably because she was illiterate and has always had to rely on her memory. Indeed, her knowledge of life was based both on practical experience and on hearsay. "You just have to learn by listening and remembering no matter what," she said at one point in the interview.

Although a second-generation Chinese American of the same age, Gladys had very different experiences from those of the other women in this section. As a young girl, she was taken to live with her grandmother in a poor village in China, where she grew up deprived of an education. By the time she returned to the United States at the age of fifteen, she was too old for school and her mother needed her to go to work. Despite her lack of education and inability to speak English initially, Gladys was able to find decent-paying jobs. She said it was because she was lucky, but from the interview it is obvious that it was also because of her willingness to work hard, her ability to compensate for her illiteracy, and her agreeable personality, which won the help of many people. Her philosophy was always, "If you're good to others, others will be good to you." In addition, her mother was more open-minded than her girlfriends' mothers were. She allowed Gladys to attend church socials and did not object to her bobbing her hair or, later, working in a nightclub.

From everything I have read and heard through my interviews with second-generation women, I know that racial and gender discrimination often made it difficult for this generation to fulfill their potential and adapt to mainstream American life. Yet when I asked Gladys if she had ever experienced discrimination as a Chinese person or a woman, she said definitely not, noting that everyone had always been friendly and helpful to her. Although that may be the case, a number of incidents that Gladys recalled indicated that she had experienced discrimination. She cited the Chinese proverb that "a woman without talent is virtuous" and recalled how she and her sisters were left in China, but not her brother, and how girls were not given as much education as boys. Although she was aware that her first jobs required her to wear Chinese clothes to contribute atmosphere, she did not consider this bad in any way. On the contrary, she was convinced that if she had the same education and qualifications as a white person, she would be treated equally. Given Gladys's life story that follows, it is understandable how and why she could have reached this conclusion. I have intentionally rendered Gladys's story in the ungrammatical way in which she spoke.

"They Don't Teach Us, So How Can We Learn?"

I was born in San Jose in 1903. We moved to San Francisco after the [earthquake and] fire of 1906. When I was four or five years old, I was taken to China. Didn't come back until I was fifteen. That was because we had a big family, three girls and one boy, and my father was the only one working. He was a chef in a big hotel in San Francisco working for Westerners. Only thirty dollars a month, but considered a good salary. My mother took us all back to China to the village. She came back with my brother and left all the girls with my grandmother to care for so that she could come back and work.

We lived with my grandmother and aunt in Sunning [Taishan District]. It was very poor there. Everyone farmed. I had to help with the farming, cut firewood. I cried day and night to come back at that time. And then, we didn't know how to read. My mother sent money back for us to go to Chinese school. The man we called *ah gung* [grandfather], who had the same surname, was the only one in the village who could read and write in Chinese. He received the letters and money [from my mother] and spent it on opium. We don't know nothing about it. Then when we came back and mother told us to write *ah mo* [grandmother] that we had arrived, we couldn't. She said, "You've been back there for over ten years and had schooling and can't write a letter?" But we had not attended school for even one day. That was really sad, but that's what happens when you're illiterate.

Soon after my mother returned, my father left for New York. He always sent money home, but he never came back. Passed away in Boston and they sent his bones back to the village. So my mother had to work hard to raise us. She knew English, so she could take jobs outside. That was because she came over [from China] with missionaries when she was nine and went to American school. Surprise [people that] she could write, play the piano, and sing because she lived with the American people. I don't know too much [more] about her background. I don't even know my mother's name until a couple of years ago when she passed away. She never talked about her background. I don't know why. Even when she chatted with others, she didn't want us to hear. Funny thing. That's why [you can't say that] people before were dumb. They don't teach us, so how can we learn?

After she [her mother] came back with my brother, she sewed in the factory, and later she worked at the steamship company in engine service until the company closed down. Then she worked at the Oriental Bank (that's the Canton Bank) until the bank closed. She was unlucky. Later [she worked at] the telephone company for many years until she retired. Before she retired, whenever there was an investigation, about Chinese women or the tongs, she was the only one who knew English to make long-distance calls. In the old days, when there were tong wars in Chinatown, in the middle of the night when there was news about who killed who, even if my mother was asleep, they called her and told her to hurry and get to work to talk to the investigators. She had to call long distance to tell others in the small towns about the recent killings. It was very rough and people were always fighting.[1] When she saved some money

---

1. Tong wars—internecine feuds between rival secret societies—were rampant in Chinatown from the 1880s to the 1920s.

she sent me and my older sister back [to America]. By that time, we could work.

"We Just Worked and Stayed Home"

We were very poor but [there was] nothing much [we could] do since we had no education. After the World's Fair in 1917, Chinese girls came out to work. Not the high-class jobs of course. Pick shrimps for six cents a pound, ten cents to hem one pair of pants, cannery work, waitress, and things like that. Most of my friends only went up to the third grade because they [the parents] were afraid [we] would fool around with boys. Very old-fashioned.

Three days after we came back, I went to work at the California Theater at Market and Third, right at the corner. It was a big theater and it just opened. George Ong's father was a recruiter and looking for twelve young women to be ushers. What did I know? Can't even read one, two, three. We two sisters signed up. He said we were the right age and we were just needed to usher, to read the numbers and find seats for people. They wanted us to dress in Chinese clothes, which we always did anyway. So we learned right away. Blossom Yim's mother in our building— she went to college—taught us the first ten numbers in the middle of night. (We had to start work the next day.) "One," she said to remember *faan* "*woon*" [rice bowl]; "two," remember "*to*" *hau sui* [spit]; "three"—we couldn't turn the tongue right [to imitate the sound]. It took us ten minutes to get it right, it was so hard. So after we learned the first ten numbers, we could do the rest.

Seventy-five dollars a month made me so happy. It was very good. We worked from opening to closing time. Even if there was nothing to do, you had to stand there. The recruiter took us to work and back. We had to walk because it cost five cents for carfare. We came back [home] after 11 P.M. together. We gave the whole paycheck to Mother and she gave us one dollar a week for spending money. It cost ten cents for lunch— bean sprouts and rice at an upstairs restaurant near the theater. No meat. We had to provide our own Chinese clothing made of cotton that we had brought from China. It was white cotton that we had to starch and iron—hard work. We worked for six months. Gradually they laid off the Chinese women, one by one. When they first opened, they just wanted to use Chinese kids as novelties.

[What did you do after that first job?] Worked in the cannery, the California Cannery Company at Fisherman's Wharf. They hired all Chinese women. My brother-in-law was the foreman. (He was an American-born. Came from a small town and met my sister at the cannery.) It was a big cannery. We cut fruit, canned fruit, watched the machines. My job was to cut fruit. It was easy. Like peaches, you cut it and take the pit out, put the peach by size in different pans. The hardest was pears. You had to peel it, split it, and take out the pit—three motions. It was long-term work but cheap wages. Five cents per crate of fruit to open. One dollar to cut up 100 pounds of stringbeans to can it. When you poured 100 pounds on the table, it was like a mountain. One dollar for all that would scare anyone. You had to pick off the ends and break them into even lengths. We made a little over one dollar a day, which was considered good. We worked until one in the morning and walked back from Fisherman's Wharf, a whole bunch of us Chinese women since we all had to work late. Worked seven whole days. The check for six days we would give it all to Ma. There was a separate check for Sunday that we kept. In the old days, over twenty dollars a week was considered a lot. We got double pay on Sunday. We kept it and Ma never knew. We cheated on her because otherwise we would not have any money. We had no allowances. Not like now, you get allowances without doing anything.

We just worked and stayed home. Lucky we had church for a couple of hours each week. There were two services, eleven to one [during the day], seven to nine at night. The only enjoyment we had were at church socials and picnics. Not like now, dancing and partying; no such things. The first time I bobbed my hair, I was so afraid my mother would be upset, but she just looked and walked away. Another friend on purpose cut her hair on payday so that when she saw her mother, she called attention to the paycheck and her mother shut up. Some of my friends' mothers were very mean. They were afraid to ask if they could go out. But not my mother. I would always ask and she always said yes. She never spanked or scolded us, but if the floor was dirty when she looked at it, you know you better get the broom fast and sweep the floor. In the old days, kids were more mature. We had no choice but be obedient. There was no time to be naughty. After work, we came home, ate, and went to bed. Same thing day in and day out.

"Smart at Learning Things"

After I knew a little English, I went downtown to work and ran an elevator at Willard's Department Store on Geary, between Grant and Stockton. Some Chinese girls who were stockgirls introduced me. [I worked]

Gladys Ng Gin as a cocktail waitress in 1936. (Courtesy of Bill Gin)

from nine to six, six days a week. Off on Sunday. We had to wear Chinese style top and pants. You were considered lucky to find such a *si man* [genteel] job. Seventy-five dollars a month was very good. That's sixty-three years ago when I was in my twenties. [Did you experience any discrimination?] I tell you something funny. When I use to run the elevator, they would never ask about the hat department, but the millinery and I would say no, we didn't have that. The boss was in the elevator and laughed. So how lucky. Then underwear, they would say lingerie. How am I suppose to know what lingerie was? So you just had to learn it by listening and remembering no matter what. Everyone was friendly. When you didn't know how, they always taught you.

I stayed in that job until I was in my thirties. After that, the first bar [nightclub] in Chinatown, Chinese Village, wanted a cocktail waitress.

I didn't know anything about it, so Emma Chan, who used to work at Temple Bar Tearoom as a cocktail waitress, told me to take the job. I said I didn't know the difference between gin to rum, scotch or bourbon. But she wanted me to go because it was good money—ten dollars a week, but great tips. So she took me to see Charlie Low, the owner. She told him, "This is my friend, Gladys. She's never done this before and you'll have to excuse her if she makes mistakes. It's not because she's my friend but she's smart at learning things." So she pushed me into it. I told her, "Emma, don't go. I'm scared. Keep me company for at least an hour." So she stayed and helped me take orders when it was more than two customers. So she was very nice to show me how.

I never went to school, so I can't read English or Chinese, but I had to speak English at work. Like in the elevator, they would ask where the coats or dresses were and I had to say which floor. It was hardest working at the bar. I had to memorize more than a hundred kinds of alcohol because I couldn't write. You ordered, and I told the bartender. Then the bartender made the drink and I served it. But you have to remember what each customer is drinking. It took too long to write it down. Sometimes you go for another order and then come back for the first drink. It use to be very festive at the bar, like a parade. The night of the Rice Bowl,[2] I was dizzy with work; worked until 5 A.M. After two years at the Village, Charlie Low opened Forbidden City and asked me to work there. I worked a total of eleven years. During the Second World War it was good money—fifty, sixty dollars a night in tips alone—wow! Right after the war, no more business and soldiers to spend money, so I retired in 1946.

[Was your mother against your working at a nightclub?] She didn't care. Many people were against it, said anyone who worked at a bar was no good, letting people caress you. But you don't have to let people do that if you know how to take care of yourself. Americans hug for no reason at all, as long as you're friends. Putting their arms around your shoulders, that's nothing. And dance, that's nothing. [Were the customers mostly white?] Yes, it [the Village] was the only one in Chinatown. Charlie [Low], Dr. [Margaret] Chung, Dr. Collin Dong were the big bosses, and they knew all the Caucasians. So very few Chinese would go for drinking at a bar. They did it in the Chinese restaurants.

---

2. Rice Bowl parties, featuring festive parades and cultural entertainment, were held in San Francisco Chinatown in 1938, 1940, and 1941 to raise money for the war effort in China.

"You're Good to Others and Others Will Be Good to You"

I was twenty-one when I got married. Someone at CACA [Chinese American Citizens Alliance] introduced us.[3] He's American-born [as were most of her friends]. Worked at a bar. We stayed in Chinatown and had a boy and a girl. [Did women in those days know about birth control?] No, even after you got pregnant you were afraid to talk about it, and you didn't go see the doctor until you showed. Not like now—your period is late by a few weeks and you go see the doctor. No such thing. Everybody did the same thing and you learn it. I had both of mine in the hospital, but a lot of my friends didn't because they were afraid or didn't know how to speak [up]. But my friends were very good to me. As I say, you're good to others and others will be good to you. A friend who was very frank said, "Gladys, you have to go to the hospital," and introduced a woman doctor to me. My boy was born at St. Luke's, and my girl was at Children's [Hospital]. For my boy, they kept me for twelve days. For my girl, I wanted to return by New Year's Eve, so after six days the ambulance drove me home. No such thing as health insurance then, but it was cheap—thirty to thirty-five dollars.

[Has your marital relationship been pretty equal?] My husband and I get along fine. You can see that. If he wants to go out, he goes out. He's going to play mah jongg now (*as her husband gets up to leave without saying anything*). I don't bother him. A retired man, what can he do? [After they were married] he mostly worked in the countryside. My mother and sister helped me. At least the kids could go somewhere after school. My mother worked the night shift [at the phone company]. My husband came home every so often. We spent our own [earnings], but he sent money home every month. Things were pretty good by then. Wages were good. We were very satisfied. I've been pretty lucky.

[What was life like during the depression?] I was okay, but my sister had a hard time. She had seven children and her husband had heart trouble. Died when her youngest was three. She had public assistance. Instead of money, she was given fifty or a hundred pounds of potatoes, a sack of flour, butter, and things like that. Every six months she would go buy shoes from Bally's shoestore. A woman would go around and check out your living arrangements. My sister had seven children and was liv-

---

3. By then Glady's mother was allowing her to attend dances. She remembers, "Gradually, when CACA opened, my mother let us wear American dresses, low neck and lace. She embroidered some flowers on it and let us wear it to the dance at the grand opening."

ing in a two-room place. They made her move because that wasn't sanitary. So they helped her find a cheaper place in our building that had three bedrooms. It was cheaper because it was in the basement. My sister worked at home. She would make bean paste and take it to the vegetable market to sell; crochet purses for $4 that I would bring to Forbidden City to sell for $20. Sold like hotcakes. So that's how she raised the seven kids.

My mother was working at the telephone company. It was sad that when the telephone company checked on the ladies, they didn't have much education and thought they would be laid off because of their age, so they all reported they were five years younger. So when they applied for social security, they also reported younger ages by five. Same with the retirement funds. That's why my mother had to work an extra five years. And she only survived [her retirement] by twelve days. Unlucky. She could have enjoyed five more years of her retirement fund and social security.

[Did you ever experience discrimination because you were a woman?] No, everyone was friendly. Chinese always looked at females differently; for example, the old saying *Nui ji mo choi bin si dak* [means that it is a virtue] to be illiterate and stay at home. It wasn't until later that women went out to work. Like now, if young people didn't have a good education, they could not get good jobs. Now my grandchildren all make good money, $50,000 a year in computer work. As long as you're well educated, the Westerners won't look down at you. You can do what they can do. People always say it's discrimination, but it isn't. If you have a good education, they will give you a good job. That's my understanding. If they gave me a good desk job, I couldn't do it.

(SOURCE: Gladys Ng Gin, interview with author, November 4, 1988, San Francisco)

My sister Sharon said up to the end, Gladys was always worried about dying a painful death. But she died peacefully in her sleep in 1989. She was eighty-six years old.

PART FIVE

Long Strides

The Great Depression, 1930s

Americans nationwide were hard hit by the Great Depression. The Chinese community in San Francisco, however, was not only spared some of the worst hardships, but in some ways Chinese women came out ahead. Even during the worst years of the depression, before President Franklin Delano Roosevelt's New Deal went into effect, there were no breadlines or traces of Hoovervilles in Chinatown; nor were Chinese violently scapegoated by white workers as they had been in the depression years of the 1870s. Ironically, the segregated economy and community resources of Chinatown—developed as an outcome of Chinese exclusion and exploitation in America—protected residents from the worst effects of the economic downturn. And for the first time in their history, Chinese Americans, who had always been marginalized, became beneficiaries of federal relief programs and were welcomed into the rank and file of the ascendant labor movement. Although hundreds of Chinese men lost their jobs as cooks, seasonal laborers, and laundrymen, most Chinese women continued to find employment in the female-dominated areas of sewing, domestic service, and sales and clerical work. Less affected by unemployment than their men, assisted by federal relief programs, and encouraged by political radicalism during the depression era, many Chinese American women were able to improve their circumstances as well as assume a larger share of responsibilities for their families and community. Thus, the Great Depression both required and allowed them to make long strides during a time of setbacks for most other Americans.

Certainly, Chinese women and families did suffer during the depression, as Law Shee Low and Gladys Ng Gin attest in their stories on pages
221–22 and 326–27. "We were so poor, we wanted to die," recalled Mrs.
Low when her husband was laid off and work for her as a seamstress
became scarce. With four young children to feed, they dipped into their
small savings, sought help from clansmen, and accepted federal aid.
Gladys said in her interview that although she and her mother remained
employed, her sister Kathy, who had seven children and a husband with
heart trouble, had to apply for public assistance. Thanks to the New Deal,
Kathy received groceries, clothing, and shoes and was moved to better
living quarters. Being resourceful, while she stayed home to care for the
children, she made bean paste and crocheted purses to sell at the farmer's
market. Adding to these stories is my grandaunt Wong See Chan's account below of the Great Depression: "The 1930s were the hardest years
for us. I just went from day to day." After the family fortune was lost,
she had to pawn her jewelry, borrow money to buy food to feed their
six children, undergo an abortion, and finally go on welfare until her husband found work as a seaman and she was able to open a beauty shop
in Chinatown. According to the writings of Ethel Lum and Jane Kwong
Lee included in this section, living conditions in Chinatown improved
during the depression, and although going on relief may have been seen
as an "inalienable right" to American-born Chinese, it was still a hard
pill for the Chinese community to swallow. For many, it was a matter of
"losing face," and therefore a last resort.

Even more so than their mothers, second-generation Chinese American women had more to gain than lose from the depression. For the most
part, the race- and gender-segregated labor force protected them from
unemployment. Jobs such as housekeeping, cannery work, sewing, wait-
ressing, running elevators, and professional, sales, and clerical work in
Chinatown remained open to them. In addition, the New Deal, a bud-
ding tourist industry, and the favorable political climate offered them new
opportunities to make strides in terms of their work, family, and political roles. Ethel Lum, for example, owed her job as a social worker to the
New Deal, and Gladys Ng Gin got her start as a cocktail waitress because of the entrepreneurial foresight of second-generation Chinese
Americans who saw tourism as Chinatown's way out of the depression.
Eva Lowe, inspired by Chinese nationalism and radical politics in the
1930s, became active in progressive organizations, making "soapbox"
speeches in Chinatown to condemn Japanese aggression in China and
demand action from the Chinese Six Companies on behalf of the unem-

ployed. Influenced by her family upbringing, Christianity, and the rise in second-generation leadership, Alice Fong Yu became a community organizer after she moved to San Francisco from Vallejo, California. She was instrumental in founding a number of service organizations and devoted much of her life to community service and Chinese nationalist causes. In addition, we have an interview with Sue Ko Lee, who participated in the 1938 National Dollar Stores strike—Chinese women's earliest stand against poor working conditions in the garment industry. As she told me, they would not have gone on strike and won without the support of labor unions that had been strengthened by prolabor federal legislation.

Aside from oral histories, many of the following selections come from the *Chinese Digest*, a news magazine published between 1935 and 1940 serving the interests of American-born Chinese. Women's issues, in particular, were well represented in this weekly and, later, monthly publication. Clara Chan, for example, had a regular column on women's fashion; Ethel Lum wrote on sociological topics, including women's issues; and Alice Fong Yu's "Jade Box" featured women's fashions, recipes, and social as well as political news. Indeed, according to the pages of the *Chinese Digest*, the second generation, less affected by unemployment, continued their quest for the good life even as they concerned themselves with the social needs of their community, civil rights, and the war in China. As examples of their writings and viewpoints, I have included some of Alice Fong Yu's columns, as well as Ethel Lum's and Jane Kwong Lee's articles on community welfare. Finally, thanks to Sue Ko Lee's foresight, we have first-hand news clippings and bulletins of the 1938 National Dollar Stores strike drawn from her scrapbook. The combined voices and writings in this section provide us with an inside look at how Chinese women in San Francisco were able to make long strides during the Great Depression.

Ethel Lum, Social Worker

"Careful Social Planning Needed"

During the depression, with the launching of New Deal programs, Chinese Americans were encouraged to enter the field of social work. Ethel Lum was one of eleven Chinese social workers hired by the civil service during those years to administer to the welfare needs of Chinatown. Her job was to make home visits, dispense financial aid, and help clients adjust to the economic situation. The depression marked the first time the U.S. government provided assistance to the Chinese American community, and Ethel, along with her second-generation peers, were determined to seize the opportunity to improve living conditions in Chinatown.

In 1935, when Thomas W. Chinn and Chingwah Lee started the Chinese Digest, *a news magazine geared to the interests of the second generation, they recruited Ethel Lum to write a column titled "Community Welfare."*[1] *For the next year she provided news and commentary on the social needs of Chinatown, covering the effect the depression was having and describing educational and social services available in the community. She paid particular attention to women's issues. Her articles on the depression, reprinted here, support the argument that the Chinese in*

---

1. Published from 1935 to 1940, the *Chinese Digest* advocated tourism as a viable economic base for Chinatown and the ballot as the political means by which second-generation Chinese Americans could fight racial discrimination and improve living conditions in Chinatown. The periodical also supported the war effort in China and made it a point to feature news and stories of interest to women.

333

San Francisco not only weathered the hardships better because of their segregated economy and access to essential services but also gained quite a bit by the New Deal. Chinatown did receive a good share of public assistance in cash benefits, Works Progress Administration (WPA) jobs, and social service programs, which in turn helped to improve living conditions. Women and families, in particular, benefited from better housing, nutrition programs, and a new nursery school and a public health clinic, thanks in part to the advocacy efforts of second-generation Chinese Americans like Ethel Lum.

In a sense, Ethel was the moral voice for the community. Certainly, the long-term negative effect of relief was uppermost in the minds of many Chinese Americans. As she observed in "Chinese during Depression," although the Chinese had come around to recognizing public assistance as their "inalienable right," they did not become dependent upon it. In the second article on the WPA, Ethel proudly pointed out that more than half of the Chinese on the relief rolls had switched over to the work program, even though it meant less income for them. As hardworking people, Ethel wrote, the Chinese would rather work than accept charity. Indeed, the Chinese in San Francisco were probably the earliest group in the country to get off welfare, thanks in large part to young businessmen who had the foresight to promote China trade and tourism in Chinatown as soon as prohibition laws were repealed in 1933.

Ethel Lum's article "Chinese Nursery School," which describes how the collective efforts of individuals and agencies helped to establish a much-needed nursery school in Chinatown, reveals her concern for the community's working mothers and young children. Months of planning and fund-raising, initiated by a group of social workers and volunteers, had already gone into the project before the federal government suddenly stepped in and "practically forced" a nursery school on the community. Within a year, Ethel happily reported, the benefits of outdoor activities, nutritious meals, quiet naptimes, and group learning had produced a new breed of eager, bright-eyed, independent children. Here was yet another concrete example of the positive effects of the New Deal on Chinatown.

Aside from recording the different kinds of public assistance given the Chinese American community during the depression, Ethel Lum's articles also provide an inside look at the problems involved with dispensing aid. She was quick to criticize American government agencies for inefficiency and lack of social planning, as shown, for example, in the ways they set up the WPA guidelines and the nursery school in Chinatown. Ethel also blamed first-generation Chinese for not taking more ini-

tiative to effect social change in their community. In her view, they were too set in their ways and ignorant of the benefits of Western health care and child-rearing practices. At the same time, however, she failed to acknowledge that racial discrimination played a large part in causing not only unhealthy living conditions in Chinatown but also the relegation of Chinese to the lower strata of the labor market. When race relations improved and opportunities opened up for Chinese Americans during and after World War II, they did not hesitate to move out of Chinatown and move up in the labor market. Despite its blind spots, Ethel Lum's column in the Chinese Digest *provides important documentation on how Chinese men and women in San Francisco weathered the depression and of the important role the second generation played in helping their community deal with the pressing issues of unemployment, housing, health, and child care.*

CHINESE DURING DEPRESSION

Since March of 1931, when the first Chinese family applied for unemployment relief, the number of Chinese in San Francisco receiving assistance from the State Relief Administration has grown to approximately 2300, almost one-sixth of the entire Chinese population of San Francisco. This relief load consists of approximately 350 families, 25 unmarried women, and 500 unmarried men.

The relief originally took the form of groceries sent from a local Chinese food store to the families, a basket once a week for the large families, once in two weeks for the smaller families. The amount and type of food was carefully arranged and selected to offer the most nutritional values. In addition, milk was delivered daily. To permit a free selection of food, a system of weekly orders or vouchers was attempted in October, 1933. The food orders were called for and taken to the various stores to be filled as wished.

Cash Relief Now

Cash relief, introduced in San Francisco in February, 1934, is now the sole form of assistance. A weekly check is sent to each family or single individual, the amount of which provides for expenditures for food, rent, utilities, and clothing, budgeted on the number of persons in the household. In addition, surplus food commodities and surplus clothing are periodically distributed. Provision for medical care is centralized in a Central Medical Bureau, to which agency all requests for medical assistance are referred, and where minor ailments are treated. More serious or specialized cases are referred to other private or public clinics in the city.

The Chinese social service staff numbers eleven workers, seven women and four men. The case aides (visitors) have at least one contact a month with each case, generally a visit in the home. Not only do the workers assist in the dispensing of financial assistance, but they also attempt to aid their clients to adjust to their environment, physically, mentally, and emotionally. Because of language difficulties and differences in habits and customs, the Chinese on relief have always received special consideration, and have been treated fairly and justly. They receive identically the same allowance for food as do the white families; whereas in several counties in California, Chinese and other racial groups, Filipino, Mexican, etc., are accorded a lower food budget, a difference of from 10 to 20 per cent, on the belief that these racial groups have less expensive diets.[2]

Relief Classified

A recent study of the occupational history of the heads of families revealed that the greater part of these family men were formerly employed as cooks and business men. Among the single men, a more unstable group of workers, a majority of them were previously engaged as seasonal workers, laundrymen, and cooks. The following list will give a comparative study of the occupations of both types of men and occupations:

Farm or seasonal workers, single men, 25.5 per cent; family men, 8.8 per cent. Laundry workers, single, 21.3 per cent; family, 3.4 per cent. Cooks, family and hotel, [single,] 15.2 per cent; family, 20.4 per cent. Kitchen helpers and waiters, single, 14.1 per cent; family, 8.3 per cent. Semi-skilled workers: garment makers, printers, broommakers, tinsmiths, single, 9.4 per cent; family, 16.8 per cent. Housemen, janitors, gardeners, single, 5.7 per cent; family, 9 per cent. Clerks, office aides, salesmen, single, 5.7 per cent; family, 17.1 per cent. Business operators, single, 2.1 per cent; family, 12.3 per cent. Professionals: teachers, laboratory technicians, single, 1 per cent; family, 3.9 per cent.

---

2. This equal treatment in San Francisco may have been due to accusations that had circulated in the community a year before charging the authorities with providing Chinese families less relief because of their lower standard of living. In response, the federal government had assigned a bilingual social worker to investigate and correct the situation.

Improper Housing

Aside from unemployment, the most serious problem confronted in this relief population is that of improper housing, with its injurious implications with regard to health. The situation is complicated by the high rentals in Chinatown and by the lack of buildings in the vicinity of the community into which the families can move.[3] A recent investigation of housing conditions among 119 relief families showed that these families, with 622 individuals, live in only 268 rooms, or an average of 2.2 persons to a room. This figure of 2.2 does not begin to describe the inadequacy of the situation, since many of the rooms reported were merely cubicles or partitions not sufficiently large to comply with U. S. housing standards. The fact that out of 119 families only 40 have private kitchens, and only 25 have private bathing facilities gives a better picture of the congested conditions. Considerable work has been done by the Chinese social service workers in encouraging and promoting better living conditions, and when one compares present conditions with those of ten years ago, one is struck by the noticeable difference.

Health Standards Raised

In general health habits, there has been a definite raise in standards. More contacts and greater acquaintance with the clinics have lessened the distrust and disdain of Western methods of medicine.[4] The sick and bedridden are more willing to enter the public hospitals, no longer with fear of "not leaving them alive."[5] The amount of milk now consumed by families on relief far surpasses the quantity previously consumed. One of the most gratifying responses to clinic care is the confidence shown by the Chinese mothers in the prenatal clinics. Over 90 per cent of all child births and maternity cases within relief families are taken care of by the prenatal clinics of the San Francisco Hospital in conjunction with the Chi-

---

3. Actually, it was not the lack of available housing but housing discrimination in the city that prevented Chinese from moving into better housing after World War II.

4. This was in large part due to the bilingual skills and efforts of Mickey Fong, the first Chinese American to be hired as a public health nurse, in 1931.

5. It should be noted that far from being distrustful of Western medical practices, the Chinese community established its own Western hospital (Chinese Hospital) in 1925 because the county hospital discriminated against Chinese patients and failed to meet their language and cultural needs.

nese branch of the board of health. Many of the mothers are even willing to have their babies delivered in the hospital, there to remain the customary period of ten days.

Moral Effect of Relief

The question of whether public relief has had any moral effect upon the Chinese people may be answered in many different ways. There is discernible, however, a definite change of mental attitude toward dependence upon public support. The Chinese as a race have always prided themselves for their independence and self-respect. They "dig their own wells, plow their own fields, and earn their own food and drink." The government does not owe them a living; it merely offers protection for them to labor in peace. As a result of the continued acceptance of relief, there has developed in the Chinese a changed attitude toward the entire situation. The first few families who found it necessary to accept relief were looked down upon as accepting "charity." Gradually, as the economic depression become more widespread and more people were compelled to seek public assistance, there came the recognition that it is the duty of the "public government," the great "wong gar" [literally, "imperial family"], to provide for every one's needs. This recognition of a new "inalienable right," the right of an individual to indefinite support at public expense, is something foreign to the Chinese mind.

(SOURCE: *Chinese Digest*, November 22, 1935, p. 10)

THE W.P.A. AND CHINATOWN

Interested observers of the relief situation in Chinatown will wish to know what changes the new Works Progress Administration program has wrought in the community. As early as October, 1935, Chinese cases have been transferred from the relief rolls to the work program. Today the situation may briefly be stated as follows: Out of the approximate 500 "single" men formerly dependent on direct relief from the State Relief Administration, 331 are now working on W.P.A. projects; of the approximate 350 families, 164 have one member employed on W.P.A. work. All of these people, with but a few exceptions, are working at the lowest occupational level, unskilled labor, at $60 a month for 120 hours of work.

Comparative Figures

Only one member out of each family household, no matter how large, can be certified for full time W.P.A. work. Furthermore, W.P.A. workers are ineligible for supplementary relief from the State Relief Administration, whether it be cash, medical service, surplus clothing or food commodities. The amount of income from W.P.A. work as compared with the amount of relief previously granted may be seen from the following figures:

Total number of families on W.P.A., 164. Total earnings on W.P.A., $9,840 (@ $60 per month). Total W.P.A. earnings plus average outside income, $10,878.12 (average outside income $6.33 per month). Total income while on direct relief $11,444.81 ($69.79 per family). Difference $566.69 per month.

Total number single men on W.P.A. 331. Total earnings on W.P.A., $19,860. Total income while on direct relief, $5,438.33 (average $16.43 per person). Excess $14,421.67 per month

From these figures it is apparent that the families are earning from W.P.A. employment, $566.69 a month less than what they received while still on direct relief. On the other hand, the single men are now earning almost four times what they were previously granted.

Although these comparisons may seem astonishing, yet one is not fully aware of the great discrepancies until one examines the situation of the larger families. Of the 164 families mentioned, 74 of them with from 2 to 4 members, are better off on W.P.A. work, a total excess of $1,137.01 per month, or an average of $15.36 per family per month. The 90 remaining families, with from 6 to 11 members, earn a total of $1,703.70 a month less than their income while on direct relief. This deficiency ranges from $6.62 per month for the 6-member family to $48.40 for the 11-member family. (The present incomes have been calculated to include average outside earnings of $6.33 per family per month in addition to W.P.A. wages.)

The Individual and the Family

The W.P.A. has therefore succeeded in redistributing Uncle Sam's wealth among the Chinese relief population irrespective of size of family or budgetary needs. The lone individuals and the smaller families earn more than they need, while the larger families earn below their subsistence level. The aims of the W.P.A., to give employment to the relief public on the

basis of ability to earn as governed by professional classification, have
not been realized in Chinatown. On account of the differences of occupations of the Chinese from those of the general population, the W.P.A.
cannot offer the variety of occupations adaptable to the Chinese. Again,
because of the lack of higher-paid projects where Chinese can be conveniently placed, they have almost all been assigned to unskilled labor.[6] The
redistribution of public money, at least for the Chinese, has consequently
been inversely proportional to the needs of each family instead of directly
proportional to the earning power.

Among the 331 single men now working on labor projects, we find
that their median age is 52 years, and that 28 per cent of them are 60
years or more. This latter group of men, though physically able, are practically unemployable, even in economically normal times. Their employment records show that they have had no steady employment for
the last five years, that at the most, they can earn barely enough through
seasonal or casual work, to keep themselves from starvation. Thus, in a
program to provide work for the needy, a large portion of the income is
allotted to a group of individuals who otherwise may be considered to
have retired from the field of employment.

Surprising to say, although the larger families, by leaving the relief rolls
to accept W.P.A. work, will earn considerably less than their relief budgets, yet they have not been known to refuse such work on these grounds.
The larger number of cases still remaining on the relief rolls has been a
result more of the failure of the W.P.A. set-up to mobilize rapidly enough
to accommodate the large number than of any hesitancy on the clients'
part to accept such work. Or, in some cases, social, mental, or medical
problems may prevent the employable member temporarily from taking
the job. The desire of any normal, self-respecting Chinese to work for a
living is greater than any temptation to live at ease upon free "charity."
Besides, to these people of steady working habits, any type of labor is
welcome to break the monotony of idleness.

Social Consequences

What social consequences will result from such a work program? To the
single men, it means increased income and a greater purchasing power,

---

6. Here the author fails to acknowledge the racially stratified labor market that kept
Chinese out of the better-paying jobs.

even over and above the average income for this group in normal times. That any appreciable portion of this income will go towards improving housing conditions is a matter of grave doubt. The influence of deeply-rooted habits and customs will preclude any thought of change in environment.[7] The expectation that such a work program will not be permanent will not be inducive towards altering their mode of living. The amount of money to be spent for rent, utilities, and food will therefore remain about the same, and any increase will be negligible. Since these bare necessities will consume about one half of the $60, where will the remainder go? It is estimated that this "excess" will be spent in three ways: the payment of old debts, the increased support of dependents in China, and greater indulgence in leisure-time pleasures. The few theatres in the vicinity of Chinatown, the pool rooms, the "lucky" parlors may hope for more thriving business in the immediate future.[8]

For the smaller families the increase in income is not great, since these families generally have more than one employable member. They were able, even while on relief, to supplement their budgets by irregular income through casual employment. These 70 and some odd families will undoubtedly continue to live on the same standard as when receiving direct relief.

Readjustments Necessary

The plight of the larger families is easily imagined. The reduced income means a strenuous struggle to "make ends meet." It means a more exhaustive search for all available sources of additional income. At this point, the majority will contend that since many of these families never earned more than $60, even before the depression, there should be no difficulty for them to return to former standards. While this assertion may be true, it must be remembered that when these families received larger incomes when they came on relief, their living standards have been greatly raised, as evidenced by better living quarters, more varied diets, and more educational opportunities. A relapse to former living conditions is not so simple as it sounds, for it is physically and psychologically

---

7. Here the author blames the victim rather than the structural barriers that kept Chinese poor and confined to a ghetto.

8. Part of this money probably also went to the war effort in China. Despite the depression, the Chinese in San Francisco managed to send over $5 million to China between 1931 and 1945.

much easier to raise one's living standard than to lower them. The problem here of adjustment is not one to be treated lightly.

The most immediate changes to take place among these larger families placed on W.P.A. work will be the surrendering of many things which formerly were necessities, but now have become luxuries. There will be a move towards reducing rentals by returning to smaller and poorer quarters. The consumption of milk will be drastically cut. There will be less money for recreation, for leisure-time enjoyment. Many of the children will not be able to continue attending the Chinese evening schools. Unless the W.P.A. can provide medical care these families will be unable to afford medical attention except for emergencies.

Social Planning Urgent

The continued efforts of the social workers to keep mothers of large families home to care for their children will prove of no avail now that the mothers are virtually forced to seek gainful employment to supplement W.P.A. wages. They will be found in garment factories and shrimp companies, leaving their babies at home alone or in the care of older children.

Chinese social workers are of the opinion that these problems of social rehabilitation, while associated with the W.P.A. programs, are not actually caused by the W.P.A. They are problems which could be foreseen at the height of the present relief program, and which grew out of the long siege of unemployment upon Chinatown followed by the many experimental attempts of the public government to relieve the economic distress. At no time is careful social planning and individual case work more needed in this "depression weary" community.

(SOURCE: *Chinese Digest*, January 10, 1936, pp. 10, 15)

CHINESE NURSERY SCHOOL

A nursery school in Chinatown has been a long felt need. In no other district in the city are there so many working mothers, such crowded living conditions, and such lack of play space. The habit of taking children to factories is not only unlawful but detrimental to their health. It is indeed a miracle that through the years there have been no serious accidents to children playing around dangerous machinery and in poorly ventilated factories. On the other hand, leaving infants and pre-school children at home alone, often behind locked doors, is equally alarming. Especially is this true of those homes where gas plates, matches, or running water are within reach of the children, who are usually confined with few, if any, toys. The ill effect of both these conditions on the children, psychologically as well as physically, cannot be overestimated.

There have been various attempts by different groups in the community to establish a nursery school for these children. The lack of economic means and the failure of the community as a whole to recognize the need have been the greatest obstacles. The most recent attempt gave birth to the present Chinese Nursery School, now in its second year of existence. Its background history, though brief, is interesting.

Working Nucleus

At a social workers' meeting in September, 1933, comprised of workers from all social, religious, and health agencies in the community, the founding of a nursery school was suggested as the most practical project the group can undertake to improve Chinatown's social conditions. The first step in this direction was the organization of a committee to study the requirements, equipment, and the cost of running such a school. The Dept. of Public Health supplied the requirements and the Golden Gate Kindergarten Association submitted budgets. The possibility of Community Chest aid was questioned, but it was ascertained that a project must run successfully a full year before the Chest would even consider rendering assistance. The interest of the Chest was, however, assured, and the committee went ahead with its plans.

The location of an available space in this congested area constituted the next problem. After exhaustive search, the largest and most conveniently situated yard for play was found to be the yard of the Chinese Presbyterian Home, open on Joyce Street. Miss Donaldina Cameron also offered the use of the entire first floor of the Home, with the exception of an office, as quarters for indoor care and play, eating and sleeping.[9] The Golden Gate Kindergarten Ass'n offered to supervise the school and to provide the salary of a full time teacher for one year. A private gift of $500.00 for necessary alterations was promised. On top of these ten-

---

9. By this time prostitution had declined considerably and the Presbyterian Mission Home was turning its attention to the growing numbers of neglected children.

dered resources, subscriptions and pledges from interested friends were solicited.

Unexpected Developments

While these plans were being considered, the Federal Emergency Relief Administration [FERA] suddenly issued a summary notice that it would start a nursery school in Chinatown only if on the following day, arrangements could be made to enroll the children and open school. The social workers acted rapidly, and overnight twenty children, from relief families, were gathered together. Thus a nursery school was practically forced upon Chinatown, with no time to hold a committee meeting or, officially, to accept the project. April 28, 1934 marked the opening of the school, with offices and dressing room facilities in the basement rooms of the Chinese Y.W.C.A. and utilizing as playground the Presbyterian Home yard across the street.

The yard, sheltered by a high fence, is ideal for the children's use, remarkably comfortable even on foggy days. The first summer, the children, in sunsuits whenever the weather permitted, actually "lived" in the yard. They immediately showed the good effects of sun baths, milk, and tomato juice.

After July, 1934, with dishes and food supplied by the FERA, a daily nutritious lunch was served. At first the strange food was merely sampled, but soon all were eating diligently and were asking for second helpings. The effect of the lunch soon showed, in improved muscle tone and general well-being, if not always in increase in weight.

Cots, provided in December, 1934, were placed in the spacious gymnasium of the Y.W.C.A., and real rest in one's own bed, with no distractions, was enjoyed by the youngsters. It took some time before they became accustomed to sleeping soundly for two hours. At this time, the school period was lengthened to 3:00 P.M. Rest has done as much as, if not more than, the food, and it is difficult to recognize the eager, bright-eyed, independent children as those who entered some months ago.

Present Conditions and Staff

When the FERA was dissolved in August and September of 1935, the school was threatened with disruption. For four months, no public funds were received, but the teachers gladly volunteered their services. What money on hand from contributions was used to provide for daily lunches and sundry expenses. From the beginning of this year to the present time, funds from the Works Progress Administration [W.P.A.] have made possible the continuance of this good work.

A head teacher, a nurse, two assistant teachers, a cook, and a handyman make up the present staff, of which one is a Chinese nutritionist. Thirty-three children are now enrolled, with an average attendance of 25. These children, 2 to 4.5 years, come from families on relief, families employed by the W.P.A., or families of inadequate income. The outside employment of the mother or the presence of health problems in the home is a general prerequisite for admission. The school charges no fees.

Beneficial Care

The benefits which a nursery school offers to any group of children are doubly productive of results among the Chinese. The social environment, where the child is placed among equals, is difficult for the average Chinese home to duplicate. Learning how to play and to acquire good group habits are privileges not easily obtainable for these children. The majority of them receive little individual care at home. The busy parents cannot take time to watch a child go through the routines which form part of his training, even such a trivial thing as the putting on of a shoe or stocking. The nursery school, moving at the child's tempo, allows time for the gradual mastery of these tasks.

The equipment of the school, toys of all kinds, chairs and tables, have in great part been donated by American friends. Here, as in most cases, the community waits to be served and is slow to respond with contributions. The Chinese habit of taking things as they are explains, to a great extent, why almost all social reforms or social experiments usually originate from outside the community.

Future of the Nursery

The future of the school is rather doubtful. The original small committee turned over its work, in January, 1935, to a larger committee composed of influential women representing various social and educational agencies throughout the city. While the FERA was carrying on, the committee decided to remain in the background. Should W.P.A. funds be exhausted in the near future, it is hoped that the committee will take action to cope with the situation. The permanent housing of the school is still the most important problem since, on account of other plans, the offer of the Presbyterian Home has been withdrawn. May the committee find ways and means of establishing a permanent nursery school in Chinatown, the need for which has been amply proven.[10]

(SOURCE: *Chinese Digest*, February 28, 1936, pp. 10, 14)

---

10. A full-time day nursery for children was established at the Chinese YWCA in 1939, thanks to the efforts of the Community Chest and the generosity of Joe Shoong, owner of the National Dollar Stores.

Jane Kwong Lee, Community Worker

"A Richer Life for All"

In 1933 Jane Kwong Lee graduated from Mills College with a master's de-gree in sociology, but like many other Chinese American college graduates at this time, she was unable to find work in white establishments because of discrimination.[1] She settled for the part-time position of community worker at the Chinese YWCA, where she provided assistance to immigrant women on health and birth control, housing, domestic problems, and ap-plications for government relief. In this capacity, she wrote the following article, "A Resume of Social Service," which was published under Ethel Lum's "Community Welfare" banner in the Chinese Digest. *Being an im-migrant herself, as well as bilingual and bicultural, Jane had a better un-derstanding of the immigrant generation than Ethel and other American-born Chinese. She was thus able to provide concrete examples of the effects and limits of public assistance on the lives of Chinese immigrant women.*

As she explains in the article, Chinese on relief might appear happy, but inside they felt defeated and humiliated. Practically speaking, they did not look upon welfare as their "inalienable right" but as "a matter-of-fact," a temporary arrangement to help them through the depression. Although the relief money was enough to keep them from starvation, it was not enough to provide them with decent living quarters. Speaking for the Chinese YWCA, she delves into the question of moral dangers raised earlier by Ethel Lum. What should be done about the spiritual or

---

1. For the beginning of Jane Kwong's Lee story and earlier writings, see pages 224–41.

Jane Kwong Lee with husband, James, daughter, Priscilla, and son, James Jr.,
upon receiving her master's degree in sociology and economics at Mills
College in 1933. (Courtesy of Priscilla Lee Holmes)

social needs of young people during this economic slump? Here, Jane
demonstrates her public relations and organizing skills by describing the
range of services at the YWCA, which were designed to meet everyone's
needs, and expressing her willingness to cooperate with other agencies
for the common good of the entire community.
  In the following excerpt from her unpublished autobiography, "A Chi-

Jane Kwong Lee

nese American," Jane elaborates on her observations and job as community worker. In particular, she focuses on the "wretched situation" that large families had to face during the depression. Here she brings up the sensitive issue of birth control, describing how one Chinese woman took the initiative to have an abortion rather than bring one more hungry mouth into an already impoverished family. While she could not openly recommend abortion as a way out of their misery, Jane did what she could to help women obtain birth control information, taking them to the clinic and acting as their interpreter. Indeed, it can be said that access to birth control, which started during the depression, helped to make life more bearable for Chinese women—on whom the responsibility for taking action usually fell—and resulted in a considerable decrease in the size of Chinese families.

Writing decades later with the benefit of historical hindsight, Jane was able to lend meaning to the changes occurring in the community at the time. She saw a mother-in-law dispute for which she was called to interpret in family court as a sign of family disharmony caused by modernization. When she was later asked by the San Francisco civil service to interview Chinese-speaking candidates for the position of social worker, Jane saw this as a significant move towards providing bilingual services in the community. And in the conclusion to the excerpt from her autobiography, she blames racial discrimination for keeping the Chinese down, something that Ethel Lum failed to see at the time.

A RESUME OF SOCIAL SERVICE

We imagine Chinese have established the reputation of being humble, industrious, and peace loving. We mind our own business and dislike being drawn into trouble with any Westerner. If others try aggressively to drive us out of our jobs, we quietly leave and try to dig out something elsewhere. This is both our virtue and our weakness. In this physical world, where aggressiveness and self-defense are badly needed, we lose our battle for livelihood.

Mere Existence

In this depression, it is a sad destiny for the 2,000 Chinese dependent upon the public relief agencies. We are thankful to the government for giving them the necessities of life.

However, would the public like to know how we feel? Let me draw an illustration: There is a family with a father, mother, and five small children. The father was unemployed for several years before he obtained work relief. The family is expressively grateful, for they are no longer afraid of starvation. Outwardly, the mother appears happy. Yet, when I talk with her further, I can sense the struggle within her. She cannot bear the thought of being on the relief roll. The people in China think she is enjoying life here in the "Golden Mountain." She dares not inform them about the family's sufferings and hardships. If she does, she would "lose face." Although the relief money is enough to feed and clothe the family, it is not sufficient to allow for better living quarters than the two rooms they now occupy, without a private kitchen or a private bath. She can afford no heat in the rooms even when the children are ill in bed. This family is on the bare existence line. As in many other cases, at first she felt humiliated about her surroundings. Later on, she got used to it. Now she regards relief as a matter-of-fact.

Dangers of Present Conditions

This presents a dangerous condition. We must help our own people. The government can provide us with the bare necessities of life, but cannot give us the real thing which enables us to grow spiritually healthy and happy. What is this intangible "something"? We cannot see it with the crude material eye. It is the real core of life, without which, life is next to nothing. Furthermore, without it, we will create self-destruction.

The third generation will not grow up satisfied with present conditions. Without real and true appreciation of life and its appurtenances, these young people will follow either of these roads: first, they will become pessimistic, careless, and hateful of life—the road of race-suicide; second, they will become resentful, radical, rebellious, and will resort to unlawful actions—the road to crime.

Are we going to let the young people in relief families follow either of these two roads? Or are we going to help them avoid these dangers? If we think that these people should be trained to love and to struggle for a richer life, we should try to care for them in addition to giving them food, clothing, and shelter.

Social Agencies at Work

Where can we find a suitable place to train them? I dare say it is the Chinese Y.W.C.A. and other social agencies. The churches can help those religiously inclined. The Y.M.C.A. can work with boys and men. The relief visitors can comfort individuals with kind words. The Y.W.C.A. can help all groups. To be more exact, I would like to outline the program of work in the Y.W.C.A.:

I. Individual service:
We are always ready to help those who come to ask us for personal help. Our employment department is every day receiving calls, and we are constantly recommending persons to fill these positions. We offer our help as interpreters for those who visit clinics and who are unable to speak English.

II. Group work:
There are clubs and classes in which members receive instruction and recreation. The Girl Reserve Clubs are for the high school students; the bridge, sewing, cooking, Chinese, and English classes for young people; the "965 Club" for girls and young women in industry and business. The children's group enjoys a good time in play, handicraft, songs, and storytelling. In the near future we hope to work with other groups in satisfying their recreational needs—whether it be the "need" of the high school girl to learn tap dancing, or that of the college graduate who is interested in the world's most difficult problems.

All these groups plan their own programs within the bounds of the Y.W.C.A. purpose. They identify themselves with the Association by their willing participation in the efforts to realize the purpose of a richer life for all people.

III. Community programs:
Even though the Y.W.C.A. is primarily for young people, we realize that the Chinese Community needs a center to which all groups of people can go. Therefore, there are programs arranged for this purpose. The building is available for the use of any group provided general interests of the whole community are regarded.

IV. Recreation center:
The building is open to all girls and women from 10:00 A.M. to 10:00 P.M. They can enjoy basketball, badminton, and other sports here. The health education department instructs members in the rules of good health. All who come in should feel at home in the Y.W.C.A., which is maintained for physical and spiritual health.

All for a Richer Life

Within the framework of this program, the secretaries of the Y.W.C.A., with the approval of the committee of management and the board of directors, try to meet the needs of the community. However, without the cooperation of the workers at large, we can do nothing.

Every agency has its particular function, and we hope to merge our efforts with others in helping individuals find that "something" which enables them to grow spiritually and intellectually for a better future.

(Source: *Chinese Digest*, December 20, 1935, pp. 10, 14)

COMMUNITY WORKER AND SCHOOL TEACHER

As I was employed during the depression years, I personally felt the trauma of my poor neighbors and friends, not to mention myself. Those who had big families suffered the most. Money, money, money! Where was there money for expenses and food? There were no government subsidies in the beginning. Later on, there was government surplus food given to the poor, but the canned goods were alien to the Chinese appetite. Red carrots were not to their liking; yet they had to endure the unpleasantness. Still later, they were issued allotment cards to buy food from a Chinese grocery store which could supply them with essentials. Life was not at all satisfactory.

A poor family with six small children could subsist, but if a seventh child came along, could the mother cope with the family's wretched situation? I doubted it, and I have an example to illustrate my point. Mrs. T. had six small children, ranging in age from one year six months to nine years. Her husband had been a store clerk, but recently was unemployed because of not enough business. She was getting groceries through the allotment card. Whenever a child had a cold, she just concocted some Chinese tea and forced the child to drink it; there was no money to pay for an herbalist. One day she came to me and talked about being pregnant. She complained that she did not know what to do if she had another child. We sat and talked for a long time, but no solution arose; all I could offer was sympathy and advice for her to do the best she could to keep the family's health. In a week she came back to see me as if she had a solution to her dilemma of whether she should have another child or not. She did not tell me her decision, but asked me for $5.00, which I gave her as a token of goodwill; I never expected her to pay me back.

I thought to myself, "Poor Mrs. T., I wish I could help her more." Surprisingly, I was astonished a few weeks later that she returned to me the borrowed money. Without my coaxing, she confided to me that she had an abortion. She explained that after seeing me the last time she went to see a Mrs. So and So who knew how to direct pregnant mothers to have their wombs washed.[2] It was very safe and easy, she said. She just stayed in the doctor's office for a few hours and then went home without any ill-effects. I listened with interest but could not utter any dissident opinion. She seemed happy to have solved her family problem and said, "It is better this way. I cannot afford to have another baby." What could I say? Should I show moral or religious indignation, or should I show her that I sympathized with her for her right action? I could do neither because I was a worker with a prestigious organization which also had the duty to help the unfortunate. Abortion was illegal then and is still a moot question.

Aside from a position of helping or not helping a pregnant woman, I actively cooperated with the Planned Parenthood Association to help women before they got pregnant. Sometimes a public nurse would call me up saying that a Mrs. So and So seemed to need birth control information and would I be able to take her to the clinic for help, since she herself, being a public nurse, was not permitted to act in this capacity. I answered that I would gladly do whatever was helpful to the woman. It was always my duty to be in a position to help anyone in the community as I could.

The procedure in directing the woman to the birth control clinic was similar to the steps in taking a sick woman to a hospital clinic. At the birth control office, the doctor, after examining the woman, would ask her to step down from the examining table and crouch on the floor with a rubber cup in her hand to fit into her vagina. As I stood beside to interpret the directions of the doctor, she slowly learned how to smear some jelly on the cup and press the cup in her. After that, the doctor examined her again to see if she got it in right. If it was correct, she then was given some jelly and a rubber cup to be used at home. Usually no fee was charged since all these women were poor. It seemed that it worked for most of them as I had several calls from these women who wanted their

---

2. In an interview with me years later, Jane Kwong Lee mentioned a community grapevine that helped pregnant women get to doctors who performed abortions. "The cost was very reasonable and it was safe," she said (interview with author, October 22, 1988, El Cerrito, California).

jelly supply replenished. Once a doctor suggested that a man could help the control of the number of children in a family if the father would undergo a vasectomy. I mentioned it once to a head of a big family, but he did not seem to be interested. The time had not arrived for males to take the responsibilities of birth control as they do now.

In interpreting for women, I was only asked once to go to the family court with an older lady who complained that her daughter-in-law was not treating her right. I went early in the morning with her to face the family court judge, who was solemn and courteously asked her what was wrong. She said, and I interpreted for her, that her daughter-in-law threatened her and she was afraid. The judge then asked her son, who was also in court, for his side of the argument. The son held up a hammer in his hand, saying that his mother had threatened his wife with that instrument. After a long pause, the judge dismissed the case. At that time the mother-in-law and her son and daughter-in-law were not living together. This showed that the two generations were having difficulties even at the time when Chinese were still thought to be peace-loving people who could tolerate mothers-in-law living with their "modern" children.

Gradually, public agencies realized that Chinese-speaking workers could help their clients much better. Accordingly, the San Francisco Civil Service Commission held a Chinese language examination for social workers. For the first time two Chinese-speaking examiners were included on the examining team. At that time it seemed that the Reverend T. T. Taam and I were known to be able to translate Chinese into English and vice versa and had the time to volunteer for the service. Both of us sat in to ask some questions in Cantonese after the applicants had written their answers put out to them on the blackboard. There were just a few applicants and those who passed the written and oral examinations were people who had lived in Chinatown or had been studying in the Chinese language schools. Slowly, but inexorably, the community was changing from the Cantonese-speaking to the English-speaking language.

The two years of experience in community work and school teaching[3] had given me a keen insight into the relationship between the Chinese and the so-called American societies and its consequences. There was an absolute discrimination in housing and a segregation in primary

---

3. Jane Kwong Lee was holding two part-time jobs at this time: community worker at the Chinese YWCA and Chinese school teacher at the Hip Wo Chinese Language School.

education. Whenever there was supposed to be equality among the races, it was only a token appearance. It would take the Second World War to abolish racial prejudices.

(SOURCE: Jane Kwong Lee, "A Chinese American," unpublished manuscript in my possession)

Wong See Chan, Hardworking Wife and Mother

"The 1930s Were the Hardest"

In 1982, while researching Chinese American women's history, I asked my grandaunt Wong See Chan for an interview. She was married to Chin Wing, the eldest son of my maternal great-grandfather Chin Lung, the Potato King. She was also the one who had befriended my father in San Francisco and recommended that he marry my mother in China. Now both in their eighties and retired, my grandaunt and -uncle lived on Jasper Place in the Telegraph Hill district of San Francisco. As I puffed up the steep incline one sunny afternoon, I wondered how either of them could make the climb. They were home waiting for me and happy to see me. With his failing eyesight, balding head, and weak constitution, I could see that Granduncle, who was eighty-eight, had really aged since I'd last seen him. However, Grandaunt, who was one year younger, was as energetic as ever. She had a clear memory and spoke in a loud voice. Although they knew I had come to hear her story as an immigrant woman, Granduncle stayed to listen, occasionally interjecting his opinions. At times, Grandaunt would openly criticize him about something he had done in the past. That's when I realized they had this love-hate relationship. Although Granduncle could be a tyrant, it was Grandaunt who wore the pants in the house.

Wong See Chan was from Mong Shan village in Chungshan [Zhongshan] District, the same area from which my parents emigrated. She married my granduncle when she was seventeen and came to America with him and their three-year-old son in 1920. Because Chin Wing was born

Wong See Chan in the 1930s. (Courtesy of Chan Wing Family)

in the United States, she was admitted as a wife of a U.S. citizen. Although she married into a wealthy family, she did not have an easy life. "We were not fated to get along," she said of her mother-in-law (my great-grandmother Leong Shee), who gave her a really hard time in China. Grandaunt and Granduncle had seven children—three sons and four daughters. One daughter died in infancy. During the Great Depression, Chin Lung lost most of his fortune and had to leave America debt-ridden as a "laborer" instead of a "merchant."[1] Chin Wing tried to hold on to some of the assets his father left him, but to no avail. He was not a good businessman

---

1. For Chin Lung's story, see pp. 17–19.

and had to foreclose on the Shanghai Trunk Company and their apart-
ment building on Powell Street. When Granduncle became unemployed
it was Grandaunt who ended up finding a way to support the family.

Fifty years later, Wong See Chan was apparently still bitter about the
outcome of her marriage. During the interview, although she was pleas-
ant enough, she took every opportunity to vent her woes—her sick child-
hood, wretched life under a tyrannical mother-in-law, and hardworking
years in America married to a gam saan siu ye (spoiled son of a rich Gold
Mountain man). Because of the Great Depression and an irresponsible
husband, she had had to sell her jewelry, undergo an abortion, go on wel-
fare, work long hours at her beauty shop, and raise their six children prac-
tically single-handed. Wong See Chan's story attests to the ability of Chi-
nese immigrant women—unlike many other Americans, whose marriages
and families fell apart during the depression—to cope with the financial
and emotional stress of the period while keeping their lives intact. In the
case of my grandaunt, she found solace and strength in her Christian faith
and in the words of her father, who taught her: "The most important
thing is your character."

"I Was Like a Sick Cat"

I was born in Mong Shan village. I had two younger sisters and one younger
brother. My parents farmed and had a small store that sold sundry items.
Our place was small and there were many children. So as the oldest, I lived
in the Girls' House up the alley.[2] We chatted and learned to sing and embroider. Then I got sick in my teens. I had chills until I was seventeen. Off
and on I would get the chills and then run a high temperature until my
eyesight became blurred. So I was always in bed. I was like a sick cat.

My father and your great-grandfather [Chin Lung] were friends. Father gave him a welcoming party when he returned from America [in
1904]. Your great-grandfather took a liking to me and wanted me for a
daughter-in-law. Said we [she and Chin Lung's eldest son, Chin Wing]
played well together. So I was betrothed when I was ten years old. That
was the custom in China. It was arranged between the fathers.

[How old were you when you married?] At seventeen I rode the big
red sedan chair.[3] I got married in July. It was so hot that I got sores from

---

2. See page 89, note 2.
3. See page 38, note 4.

sitting in the sedan chair. It was very sad. But it was considered a fancy affair. (*laughs*) I was just seventeen and a sick weakling at that.

"Mother-in-Law Worked Me to Death"

A month after we married he [her husband] returned to America. I stayed in the [Nam Shan] village with his mother and worked like a slave. She forced me to pound and grind the rice every day. His mother was very cruel to me. She wanted to work me to death. I had to get up at three in the morning to wash the rice. The slavegirls would report to my mother-in-law at around 9 P.M. and ask if there was anything else she wanted them to do. She would ask, "What is *that* one doing?" "She's still pounding the rice," they replied. "Oh, you can go to bed then." So I was worse off than the slavegirls.[4] But I knew that if you lead a righteous life, God will see it.[5]

Sometimes the slavegirls asked me to go get water from the well. She would scold and forbid me to go again. Said that she didn't want others outside to say she was using me to fetch water from the well. But at home she could work me to death. One time when her [porcelain] pillow fell off the dresser and broke, she said it was my pillow. Every morning I would greet her and comb her hair. She would begin to scold me right there and then. I just learned to ignore her.

[She didn't beat you, did she?] No, but she forced him [her husband] to beat me. Once when my mother was going to marry off one of the slavegirls, the one who had been like a sister to me, my mother asked me to go to the wedding. As soon as he [her husband] came back, she told him I had been asking to go to my mother's home. "Who knows what lover she has?" So she told him to beat me until black and blue welts broke out. He did this a number of times. [Why didn't she beat you herself?] She didn't have the strength, but her troublemaking was bad enough. When my younger brother who was visiting one time saw my husband beat me, he left, saying he had *mo min* [literally, no face, meaning he was too humiliated] to stay. She was very wicked. In a way I can't

---

4. Many other Chinese immigrant women I have interviewed, including my own mother, have told me similar sad stories about abusive mothers-in-law. For an explanation, see page 91, note 6.

5. My grandaunt did not become a Christian until the family moved to Macao in 1916 to escape bandits in the villages. After she immigrated to the United States, she attended the Chinese Presbyterian Church in San Francisco regularly.

blame him [her husband] because a son must obey his parents. But while there's filial piety to one's parents, there's also love for one's spouse. So how can you do whatever your mother says? That was the first thing that was wrong with our marriage. But God was supporting me, so it didn't hurt me.

"A Hard Life in America"

If it wasn't for the war [World War I], he [her husband] wouldn't have returned to China [in 1915]. He was afraid of being drafted. [Turns to her husband to ask why he returned. He replies that his younger brother had been a gambler and the tongs were after him, so his father decided to bring them back to China.] In 1920 we left for America. I came as the wife of a U.S. citizen. Our three-year-old son came with us. We went first class on a Japanese ship. Shared a cabin with bunk beds. I was a little seasick but managed to leave the cabin for meals.

[Did you have to go to Angel Island?] (*nods*) I got mad when they tried to take my son away, so they let my son stay with me. I was there for half a month [waiting to be interrogated]. Stayed with other women in a big room. We got along and chatted, but my son kept fussing and crying for his father. If his father had remembered to bring our photographs, we would have been landed immediately, but he forgot, so we had to stay at the island. [The interrogation] was hard, but I answered truthfully, since I wasn't assuming a false identity. I answered all the questions right.[6]

[Was life hard in America?] Very hard. We lived a few months in Oregon because your great-grandfather [Chin Lung] owned a farm there. He [her husband] didn't like farming and I became pregnant, so we returned to San Francisco. The minister's wife at the Methodist church knew Cantonese and came to teach me English, but then before long the baby was born. One after another, seven in all, so I didn't have the time or heart to study. I lost out. I tell others who say it's too hard to learn

---

6. According to my grandaunt's immigration file in the National Archives, my granduncle had neglected to submit two photographs of their son to the Immigration Service as required. Nevertheless, the interrogation went smoothly, with only one minor discrepancy about where their wedding feast had taken place (Wong See Chan, folder 18891/2-12, Chinese Departure Case Files, San Francisco District Office, Immigration and Naturalization Service, Record Group 85, National Archives, San Bruno, California).

English in America that they must, no matter how hard it is. I was stupid because I didn't get the chance.

We lived in a crowded storefront. There were three families—mother-in-law, younger sister-in-law, and us. Each family had a room. We had a kitchen and a bathroom. No hot water. I had to wash diapers by hand in cold water for three of my babies—see how crooked my fingers are? (*holds out her hands*)

I sewed in Chinatown across the street from our house on Sacramento Street. Sewed flannel nightgowns until 12 midnight. We got paid in gold coins. It wasn't a hard job, but all that lint ruined my nostrils. When there was no more work, we peeled shrimps. Then we moved to Powell Street and ate our meals at the store [Shanghai Trunk Company] on Stockton Street [where her husband worked as an accountant].[7] I was still breast-feeding my son when I decided to go to beauty school [downtown]. There was a Mrs. Quock who said she would translate for me, so I followed her to school.[8] I would go half a day and then go home to breast-feed my son. After I weaned him, I was able to spend more time at school. Just when I was making some headway I became pregnant again. So I was forced to abort it; otherwise I would not have been able to finish school. So it was too bad for that child.

[Was it hard getting the license for the beauty shop?] It was very hard, but I was determined to do it. Others took half a year, but it took me over a year. I went every day with my suitcase. At night I practiced on friends. The point behind my opening a beauty shop was to keep my family together. If you work outside, your children will scatter like sand. With a beauty shop, I could watch the kids and we could live behind it. After dinner, I could oversee their homework. Sometimes after homework, we would play poker or "donkey" [card games] and they would jump with joy.[9]

[How was business?] So-so. The shop was on Stockton near Jackson

---

7. Her daughter Penny Chan Huie later told me that Grandaunt did all the cooking at the Shanghai Trunk Company: "She cooked for twenty, thirty people. Worked four woks over a wood-burning stove in the basement of the store" (interview with author, November 21, 1988, San Francisco). Keep in mind that my grandaunt was about five feet, two inches tall and probably weighed no more than one hundred pounds.

8. My grandaunt was allowed to use an interpreter in class and at the time of the licensing examination.

9. By then my granduncle was a merchant seaman and rarely at home.

Street. Permanents weren't popular yet. Most came for the marcel look. A few prostitutes came to have their hair done. [How could you tell they were prostitutes?] You couldn't tell by their appearance. They talked about it. They were not ashamed. It was just another line of work. It was busiest at New Year's. I worked from morning until 3 A.M. the next day. Slept for two hours and then had my next customer come at 5 A.M. There was the bathhouse to manage too.[10] Your father helped me out occasionally while this one (*nodding at her husband in the room*) was still sleeping. I operated the beauty shop for eighteen years [from 1930 to 1948], until they wanted the building back and we moved here to Jasper Place. Still, customers continued coming back to me.[11]

"You Marry a Chicken, You Follow the Chicken"

The 1930s were the hardest. You had to live day by day. I can tell you this in front of him. (*nodding toward her husband*) He gave me a quarter to buy food for dinner. I bought two sand dabs for five cents. Ten cents for three bunches of vegetables—two bunches for stir-fry and one bunch for soup. Ten cents for pork. What else can you eat for a quarter? Some fish, meat, and vegetables—that would be enough for a good meal. But he didn't like steamed sand dabs, so he flipped the fish dish over and even the children didn't have any to eat. He was that mean, like his mother! (*raises voice indignantly*) He didn't care about the children. I'm not lying.[12]

There was nothing I could do. "You marry a chicken, you follow the

---

10. Penny told me her mother worked from seven in the morning until midnight, seven days a week. The children helped with the bathhouse: "People who lived in Chinatown then had no private baths. So for 35 cents, they got one tub of water. If they ran a second tub, they had to pay 15 cents. Every time someone finished a bath, we had to clean up the bathroom. Remove all the dirty towels, put out a new bar of soap, dust the dresser, sweep the floor, and scrub the tub with Lysol" (Penny Chan Huie interview).

11. Penny said that afterward, her mother became bored and went to work as an inspector in a jeans factory close to home. She didn't retire until she was eighty-two. "She didn't need the money; she needed to get away from my father," Penny explained. "You know there was love between them, but they couldn't stand being around each other" (ibid.).

12. Although my grandaunt did not mention this, Penny later told me that my granduncle lost all the properties Chin Lung left him after he returned to China in 1933. He even had to pawn all of my grandaunt's jewelry to make ends meet. "But we never felt deprived," she said. "My mother made it doing the hairdressing. She made sure we had three meals, treats, and all that. And we had our birthday parties—fried chicken, cake, and ice cream" (ibid.).

chicken. You marry a dog, you follow the dog."[13] Even if he beat me, I
had to follow him. My father was very strict. He told me that no matter what, I cannot make the Wong family lose face. "Don't divorce like
others," he said. "No matter how hard it is, you have to endure it. You
cannot disgrace the Wong name. The most important thing is your character." He loved me, so I did whatever he told me to do. Even now, no
matter how hard it is, I have to endure it.[14]

"I've Settled Down"

[I enjoyed] Chinese opera and movies, mah jongg. But later when crime
went up I quit everything—mah jongg, movies, cigarettes. [Women
smoked then?] Lots of women smoked. I started smoking when I was a
teenager. My father bought me a water pipe when I was thirteen. Everyone in the family smoked. I smoked until after I got married and his
mother scolded me for smoking. When I came to America, I started smoking cigarettes. All my grandchildren told me to quit, so I did.

[Are you glad you came to America?] No matter how hard life was,
it was better than staying in China. All my children are doing well now.
We didn't let them speak English at home. That's why they can speak
Chinese, but none of my grandchildren can. All six of my children had
to stop speaking English as soon as they came through the door. I said
because I didn't know English, if you spoke English you must be scolding your mother. They all complained the rules were too strict, like in
sports, but my second son, who is a doctor now, is glad he can speak
Cantonese. I had them bring their friends home. I didn't want them fool-
ing around outside. That's why I had the beauty shop.[15]

[When did you become a citizen?] In 1950. I got to vote for Eisen-
hower. My daughter was my witness. They didn't ask much, just how

---

13. An old Chinese proverb. See "Images of Women in Chinese Proverbs" on pages
103–112, for other sexist sayings.

14. Penny recalled that her parents were constantly arguing. When the situation became unbearable, her mother would go to the Chinese Presbyterian Church for help. "She
went there a couple of times, and each time it got ironed out and she came home" (Penny
Chan Huie interview).

15. According to Penny (ibid.), my grandaunt brought them up biculturally. She knew
how to cook American food like hamburger pie, turnovers, macaroni, and pot roast as
well as traditional Chinese dishes. The children were raised celebrating Chinese New Year
and the Mid-Autumn Festival as well as Thanksgiving and Easter. And they all went to
church on Sundays.

long I had been in the United States. They asked me what I thought symbolized America. I said, "The flag." They asked how many stars and stripes? I answered in Chinese. (They allowed interpreters then.) I've voted in every election since.

[Is there anything you don't like about America?] Not much. It's been 62 years and I've settled down. When I first came, I cried day and night, wondering when I would be able to go home. (*laughs*) I kept worrying about my mother and cried every day. Now that I don't have a mother or father to worry about, I've stopped wanting to go back to China. [Do you have any regrets?] I don't think about the past anymore. If I did, I would have died a number of times.

(SOURCE: Wong See Chan, interview with author in Chinese, March 5, 1982, San Francisco)

My grandaunt Wong See Chan passed away in 1987, outliving her husband, Chin Wing, by five years.

Eva Lowe, Fighter for the Underdog

"You Have to Stand Up for Your Rights:
Nobody Will Give You Anything for Nothing"

The depressed times gave rise to radical politics throughout the country. As conditions in Chinatown deteriorated and its established leaders refused to seek outside assistance, the unemployed found a new political advocate in the Huaren Shiyehui (Chinese Unemployed Alliance), a group formed by the Chinese Marxist left to organize the working class and aid the unemployed. In 1931 the alliance led a march on the Chinese Six Companies to demand immediate relief. Among them was twenty-two-year-old Chen Junqi, the only female member of the organization. At a mass meeting following the march, in a loud and clear voice she presented their demands for (1) shelter and food for the unemployed, (2) free hospital services for the unemployed, (3) free education for unemployed women, and (4) an employment office, to be administered by a board selected by the Shiyehui.[1] Who was this woman and how did she become a political activist during the depression? I suspected but could not confirm that Chen Junqi was Eva Lowe until I interviewed her in 1989.

I first met Eva Lowe in 1982 while working at the Chinese Culture Center in San Francisco on the Chinese Women of America research project. She was at that time in her seventies, a petite but energetic woman who volunteered in the center's gift shop. The project staff (Genny Lim, Vincente Tang, and myself) all knew Eva as the proud mother of Dr. Rol-

---

1. *Chung Sai Yat Po*, March 24, 1931, p. 3; March 29, 1931, p. 2.

land Lowe, chief of surgery at Chinese Hospital, board president of the Chinese Culture Foundation, and a respected community leader. I had heard that she had been quite a political "rabble-rouser" in the 1920s and 1930s. Considering how housebound and politically inactive most Chinese women were in those days, I found this hard to believe. When we finally got around to interviewing Eva, we found her to be quite a storyteller and "a fighter for the underdog," as she repeatedly described herself. This is her story, based on Genny Lim's interview with her in 1982 and my later interview with her in 1989.

Born in Fort Bragg, California, in 1909, Eva Lowe was the fourth girl of five children. Her father was a cook at a lumber mill. Her mother died when she was four years old and Eva was raised by her aunt and uncle in Fort Bragg until she moved in with her eldest sister's family in San Francisco, accompanying them to China in 1922. Upon her return in 1926, she attended high school and became involved in the Chinese Students Association, a leftist organization.[2] After graduating from high school she found a job ironing in a Chinatown garment factory and later worked as a waitress in a Chinese American restaurant downtown. During the depression years she became involved with the Huaren Shiyehui, making soapbox speeches and supporting demonstrations on behalf of the unemployed. In 1937 Eva went to live in Hong Kong with her husband, Lawrence Choy Lowe, and son, Rolland. China was at war with Japan, and Eva did her part by volunteering at the China Defense League, where she worked with Madame Sun Yat-sen. Returning to California in 1941, they settled in Oakland, where the couple ran a grocery store until Lawrence died in an automobile accident in 1962 and Eva moved back to San Francisco.

In the following interview, Eva Lowe vividly recalls a number of racist and sexist incidents in her life that made her initially ashamed of being Chinese. She also reflects upon a number of influential factors that turned her life around, encouraging her to be politically active in fighting dis-

---

2. The Chinese Students Association was founded in San Francisco in 1927, ostensibly for social and educational purposes, but it was more of a political organization that supported the Guomindang left-wing faction and opposed foreign imperialism in China. The group claimed a membership of three thousand before it was raided by the San Francisco Chinatown Police Squad and closed down for alleged Communist activities in 1929. See Him Mark Lai, "To Bring Forth a New China, to Build a Better America: The Chinese Marxist Left in America to the 1960s," in *Chinese America: History and Perspectives, 1992* (San Francisco: Chinese Historical Society of America, 1992), pp. 12–14.

Eva Lowe (center) with friend Connie Ulz (left) and unidentified friend (right) having fun at "Chutes at the Beach" in 1930. (Courtesy of Eva Lowe)

crimination and injustices: the free rein she had living with her sister, the rise of Chinese nationalism and leftist politics in Chinatown in the 1920s and 1930s, her reeducation in China, and a Chinese feminist and scholar who befriended her on a boat trip back to the United States. While passionate on the topics of discrimination and civil rights, Eva was evasive about her involvement in Chinatown politics. Only when presented with articles from the Chung Sai Yat Po *newspaper that named her as a speaker at a Huaren Shiyehui rally in 1931 did she begin to discuss this chapter in her political life.*[3] *Considering the red-baiting that led to the demise of the left movement in Chinatown in the 1950s, her willingness to talk at all about Chinatown politics speaks to her candor and commitment to social change. "I was always a tomboy, always questioning how come boys can do that but a girl can't," she said at one point in the interview. As her story reveals, being a girl never stopped Eva from acting on her political convictions.*

"I Didn't Feel Proud to Be a Chinese"

[After] my mother came to America, she gave birth to four girls. My [paternal] grandmother was mad at her and wanted to go back to China to help my father get a concubine [who hopefully would bear sons]. Before she left for China, my mother, who was a very smart woman, told my sister to hide the jewelry. So by golly, my grandmother said, "I'm going to China now. Where's the jewelry? I want to give it to the concubine." So my mother said, "You look for it." She went to her room and couldn't find it. She said, "Where's the jewelry? Where's all the jewelry?" My mother held out her hands and said, "It's all here. You want it, you take it." My grandmother scratched the back of my mother's hands—all bleeding—but she couldn't get anything off. So she screamed very loud, "*Sam po da ga poh* [daughter-in-law is hitting the mother-in-law]!" She made my mother kneel down and *jam cha* [serve tea] to ask for forgiveness. My mother did that, but she [grandmother] didn't get any jewelry. You know why? My mother wanted the jewelry to give her daughters when they got married, not because she wanted the jewelry for herself.

Later on, my mother had a son. So my father sent a cable to my grandmother in China. My grandmother wanted to come back to take care of my mother, but she had arthritis in her foot and couldn't walk. That's why she never came back. Then my mother died. They called it consumption [tuberculosis]. I guess it was because we lived down in the basement on Sacramento Street [where her father operated the Lincoln Shrimp Company]. And after she died, my younger sister died and my baby brother died. So we [father, second sister, and she] moved back to Fort Bragg to live with my aunt and uncle.

In Fort Bragg, my uncle knew lots of English, so we had American

---

3. I showed her the articles from *Chung Sai Yat Po*, March 24 and 29, 1931, when I interviewed her in 1989.

newspapers. I would always look at the cartoons. The Chinese were always drawn as very inferior, with a long pigtail. I had this feeling that I was not proud to be a Chinese because gee, the Chinese looked so bad in those cartoons. When I was in the first grade and we walked to school, the boys in my class called me "Ching Chong Chinaman." I had a straw hat with a brim around it and they threw horse manure all over it. One time my aunt was bathing me in one of those galvanized tubs (we didn't have a bathtub) and noticed my back was all bruised. She asked me, "What happened?" I said, "*Faan gwai jai*"—we always said *fan gwai jai* for foreign devil boys—"threw rocks at me." My uncle got mad and he took me to school the next day. The teacher asked me which kids did it and I pointed at them. Those boys had to stay behind. So we all knew something was going to happen. We stood behind the door. The teacher slapped their palms with a ruler. Afterward, they were very good to me.

When I stayed with my auntie, I learned a lot from her even though she was strict. And oh, she used to beat us up, my sister and me. I knew my aunt liked my second sister more than me. My second sister never said anything—the Chinese say *ho pei hei*, a very good temperament. Me? I'm more of a tomboy. If somebody accused me of something that wasn't right, I would say something right away. Being a girl, that's one strike against you. They always said girls shouldn't do this, girls shouldn't do that. So I had it in my mind when I was twelve years old, how come boys can do it and girls can't do it? I didn't say it because when we were small, we're not supposed to talk back. You talk back and you get a slap in the face.

"I Began to Be Proud"

I returned to San Francisco to live with my oldest sister and help her take care of the kids. Gradually I wanted to learn Chinese. I was in Chinese school and I began to be proud [of being Chinese.] My sister was living on Jackson Street near Kearny. Near the Kearny corner there used to be a shooting gallery run by the Japanese. And I had to go past there to take the garments she [her sister] finished [sewing at home] back to the garment shop. From there I would get a new batch to take home. I always passed there. In response to Japan's Twenty-one Demands of 1915, I used to yell, "Hell, hell, hell, Japanese go to hell."[4] So one time she [the pro-

---

4. See page 230, note 2.

prietor] had a broom ready for me. And that was the end of it. I never told my sister. Otherwise I would get a licking. When they were burning the Japanese merchandise, I was just a little kid, about nine or ten years old, but I started to hate the Japanese.[5] That's why when my sister and brother-in-law took their family to China, I fought to go. My uncle and aunt told me not to go. "Don't go to China. You cannot come back. They're going to marry you in China." But I said I wanted to go because I wanted to learn Chinese. Afterward when I went to China, I went to Chinese school and I learned Chinese history; so many thousand years ago, the Tang dynasty and all kinds of dynasties until the end of the Qing dynasty and how the imperialist countries came over. Like Dr. Sun Yat-sen said, *gwa fun* [literally, a cut-up melon]—China was cut up like a watermelon and each imperialist European country had a part of it. I remember when I was in that class, I cried. You know, China used to be so strong and now it's [come to] this.

On the way back to America, I met this lady on the ship. She was a well-read woman and had brought lots of books from Shanghai to read. She explained to me what is socialism and opened my mind about inequality for women in China. She gave me lots of books to read, especially about women's rights and how Chinese women were oppressed. And then by golly, I thought about how my stepmother married my father with a rooster. You see, my father was in America. My mother [had] died. And right away my grandmother wanted a daughter-in-law to take care of her. She [her stepmother] never knew my father. It was a blind marriage and when she married, the rooster represented my father [in the ceremony]. And then my father came home [to China]. He was a sick man and died a few months later. So she's a widow. She has a boyfriend. I don't know how friendly they were but he's [in the] Chan family too. So after dinner in China in the summer we [would] sit outside in the courtyard and fan ourselves until sundown. This young man would always come and sit right there too. Nothing happened until my adopted brother saw this boy go into my stepmother's bedroom one day. So he hollered and the whole village kicked her out and forbade her to come back to the village. It's true. I read lots of books about how if a Chinese

---

5. A series of boycotts and public burning of Japanese-made goods was instigated in Chinatown in the fall of 1919 to protest the Japanese takeover of German concessions in Shandong Province at the conclusion of World War I according to the terms of the Versailles Treaty.

woman—even a widow—fell in love with another man, they would put her in a *jue lung* [a pig's cage] and throw her in the river.

"I Always Like to Do Things for the Underdog"

When I was in high school, I was in that Chinese Students Club. At that time we had lots of memorial days. "5-30," May 30th, that's the day the British killed our students and workers in Shanghai.[6] *Jai naam chaam on*, the Jinan [massacre].[7] On "6-23," *gwok chi* or "Humiliation Day,"[8] our student club would make speeches on the corner of Waverly [Place]. *Da do dai gwok jue yi*, down with imperialism! A lot of people gathered on the street and we would remind people about what the imperialists did on that day to the people of China. Several times I was the only girl [among the students]. Once I spoke over in Oakland, another time inside the Chinese Catholic Center on Stockton Street. My sister was there. She said, "You talk too loud." You see, my voice was strong even though I was konked out [overtired]. (In school I was always second instead of first in class because I was a loudmouth.) I still remember coining the slogan "If you have money, give money. If you have muscles, give muscles. I have neither money or muscles, but I can lend my voice to the cause."

At that time, the Guomindang had lots of power in Chinatown.[9] They were against the Chinese Students Club. I asked several girlfriends to join. They came to the meetings and that was it. What did we talk about? We

---

6. The May 30th Incident commemorates the day in 1925 when Chinese demonstrators protesting mistreatment of workers in British and Japanese-owned factories were fired upon by British soldiers in Shanghai. Twelve were killed, dozens injured, and some fifty students were arrested. Public outrage at this incident led to strikes, boycotts, and protests throughout China.

7. The Jinan massacre occurred on May 30, 1928, when Chinese and Japanese troops clashed in Shandong Province during Chiang Kai-shek's Northern Expedition, resulting in the loss of five thousand Chinese lives.

8. On June 23, 1925, a huge rally of Guangzhou protesters consisting of college students, soldiers, industrial workers, and farmers was fired on by British and French troops in the foreign concession area of Shamian Island. The demonstrators were responding to the May 30th Incident in Shanghai and calling for a major strike against the British. This time fifty-two Chinese were killed and over one hundred were wounded. The strike and massive boycott of British goods that followed in Hong Kong lasted sixteen months.

9. See page 303, note 5.

talked about what the foreign countries did to the Chinese. Nothing else. But they were labeling us Communists and all that. So my girlfriends got scared and quit. And I asked her, "Did we talk about communism? Did we talk about socialism?" "No." "What we talked about?" "Well, we talked about anti-imperialism." "Are you in favor of it?" "Yeah, I'm in favor of it." "But why are you scared?" (See, I'm a fighter.) "Well, my father said so and my father is a Guomindang [supporter]." So all my girlfriends quit except me. I believed in what they [the Chinese Students Club] did.

You know the longshoremen's strike in San Francisco? Harry Bridges organized it. People who worked as longshoremen had to wake early in the morning and stand in line at the hiring hall. Rain or shine, you had to wait. Then if the people should like you, you get a job. Otherwise, you don't get a job. So they organized a union and the union hall called people to work, not wait outside in the rain and beg for a job. They had a strike and the police killed several people. So they had a parade right on Market Street.[10] Another time there was a hunger march in San Francisco. During the depression years a lot of people had no work and they had a big march. There was a whole mass of people marching on Market Street, [shouting] we want work, we want work! I was the only Chinese woman watching these things. The Chinese would say I am a good fighter because I always like to do things for the underdog.

"You Have to Stand Up for Your Rights"

That depression year I saw an ad that said they wanted to hire a seamstress on Third Street. I remember I went over there and asked for the job. I had that ad from the newspaper and she said, "We don't hire Orientals." Not Chinese, but Orientals.[11] I said, "You have the ad there." She told me, "Well, I don't mind, but I don't think the workers would be willing to work with you." Now you cannot say that. You'll be sued, right?

I was a waitress, but not in Chinatown. In Chinatown there were more men than women, so those women who waited on tables had to be very

---

10. On May 9, 1934, San Francisco longshoremen struck for a shorter workweek, higher pay, union recognition, and union-run hiring halls. Police and scabs were called in by employers in an effort to break the strike, which resulted in a bloody battle. A general strike was called, bringing the city to a standstill for three days. The settlement in October won the longshoremen union recognition, union-controlled hiring halls, a thirty-hour workweek, and a pay increase.

11. See page 251, note 1.

tough. This is what I heard, so I never worked in Chinatown. I would rather starve than work in Chinatown. I worked in a white place because the people treat you better. If anyone tried to get fresh with me, I just go tell my boss (I'm a tough lady), "You better wait on him." "What's the matter?" I said, "He caressed my hand." "That's nothing." I said, "If you want me to wait on him, I'll tell him to get out." This guy was a steady customer. He came every week to eat, so I never wait on him. When he comes in, I tell my boss, "Chan *suk* [uncle], he's yours." So one day Chan *suk* came out and said, "This man wants to talk to you." He apologized, "I'm sorry, will you wait on me from now on?" Which I did. You have to stand up for your rights. Nobody will give you anything for nothing.

You know, I was living with my Caucasian girlfriend. She didn't like living in Chinatown, so I compromised with her. She wanted to live in Nob Hill, so we went to rent an apartment there. She saw it first. She said, "I'll bring my girlfriend to see it." Sunday, we ring the manager's doorbell. She opened the door and said, "This is your girlfriend?" My Caucasian girlfriend said, "Yes." She said, "We don't rent to Orientals." Finally we found one up in Russian Hill on Broadway [Street]. The landlord said to me, "If anybody asks about you, say 'I'm the maid.'" (*laughs*) But at that time, it hurt. Now when I tell people from Hong Kong about it, they can't believe it.

That's why I tell the newcomers from Hong Kong, "You lucky you come now. We Chinese fix the kingdom for you to sit in." Who started it? I want them to remember the Black people started it. I've been to New Orleans and I know how it was. The streetcar, the front is white and the back is Black. They have signs and they don't call them Blacks. They call them Negroes. And even the drinking fountain is divided. I saw how the Black people live. I don't have to tell you how they fought for civil rights. When they won their civil rights, indirectly we Chinese people got it too. Of course if you're not conscious of that, it will go backwards again. That's why I support the C.A.A. [Chinese for Affirmative Action].[12]

When my birthday comes, I'll be seventy-three. I read about [veteran Cantonese opera star] Hung Sin Nui in the Chinese newspapers.[13] They

---

12. The Chinese for Affirmative Action is a civil rights organization in San Francisco established in 1969 to advocate for equal opportunities in education and employment on behalf of Chinese Americans.

13. At the time of this interview, Hung Sin Nui (Hong Xian Nü) was touring the United States.

interviewed her in New York. They asked her, "How come you're so youthful?" She said, "Physically, I'm old, but my thinking is young." I think that's most important. Don't think of how old you are. Think young. That's more important.

(SOURCE: Eva Lowe, interview with Genny Lim, July 15, 1982, Chinese Women of America Research Project, Chinese Culture Foundation of San Francisco; and interview with author, November 13, 1989, San Francisco)

In her twilight years, Eva Lowe continues to fight for the underdog by doing her civic duty. At the time of the second interview she was volunteering at the Chinese Culture Center, the Chinese Hospital, and University of California's Moffitt Hospital (UCSF Medical Center). And every election day, she works at the polls. "Not that I want that $35," she said. "I believe in bilingual elections and I'm just proud to be a Chinese American."

Alice Fong Yu, Schoolteacher and Community Organizer

"I Wanted to Help People, Not Run Their Lives"

Looking at the social, fashion, and sports pages of the Chinese Digest, *one would not think there was a depression going on in the 1930s. In direct contrast to Ethel Lum's and Jane Kwong Lee's descriptions of hard times in Chinatown, other columnists in the same publication chose to write about Chinese Americans competing in sports, learning the latest dance steps, going to the beauty parlor, and worrying about what to wear to the next formal dance. The different concerns between generations and classes as reflected in the* Chinese Digest *indicate that the depression was not a bread-and-butter issue for everyone in the community.*

"Lady P'ing Yu's" column for women, "The Jade Box," offers us one entry into the minds and hearts of second-generation Chinese American women during this period. Written by schoolteacher Alice Fong, "The Jade Box" featured short essays on fashion, recipes, and Chinese culture as well as women, community, and political issues. As Alice later explained to me in an interview, she chose to write under a pseudonym because she did not want to be in the limelight. "I wanted to help people, not run their lives," she said. "So they called me Lady P'ing Yu."[1]

Born in the mining town of Washington, California, in 1905, Alice

---

1. The pseudonym is also a play on Alice Fong's Chinese name, Fong Yu P'ing. She added the surname Yu (a different Chinese character from that of her given name) to her name after she married Jon Yu in 1940. Alice Fong Yu, interview with author, June 29, 1987, Piedmont, California.

Fong Yu was the second of eleven children. Her father, Fong Chow, ran a general merchandise store and operated the Omega gold mine. Her mother, Lonnie Tom, was from Marysville, California. In 1916 Fong Chow lost the mine and decided to move the family to Vallejo, California, where he opened a grocery store. Alice attended school in a one-room schoolhouse and remembers white classmates making fun of the Fong children. "When we would play games, they wouldn't hold our hands, as if they would be contaminated, and so they wouldn't accept us," *she said.[2] Her parents advised them to ignore the "barbarians," get a college education, and go work in China. However, upon graduation from San Francisco Teacher's College in 1926, instead of going to work in China, Alice became the first Chinese schoolteacher to be hired by the San Francisco school district.[3] In 1940 Alice married Jon Yu, a journalist for the* Young China *newspaper. They had two sons, Alon and Joal. Despite being overworked and underrewarded, Alice stayed with the school district for forty-four years, retiring in 1970.*

In 1937, when Alice began writing her column for the Chinese Digest, *she had already developed a reputation as a community organizer.* "Being so useful in the community, they put me in everything," *she recalled.* "I was always the superintendent wherever I went."[4] *A founding member and first president of the Square and Circle Club, the earliest and most enduring service organization of American-born Chinese women, Alice helped raise funds for Chinese orphans, the elderly, needy families, and war relief in China; register Chinese Americans to vote; campaign for political candidates; and lobby for improved housing and recreational facilities in Chinatown.[5] In her capacity as a teacher at Commodore Stockton Elementary School (previously, Oriental Public School), she helped found the Chinese chapter of the Needlework Guild, which sewed clothes and provided shoes to needy children and assisted families to apply for relief during the depression. Alice also helped to organize the first Lake Tahoe Chinese Young People's Christian Conference, in which Chinese Americans from all over California came together to discuss com-*

---

2. Ibid.

3. With similar support from their parents, Alice's sisters did equally well as the earliest Chinese American women to enter certain professional fields: Mickey Fong became a public health nurse; Marian Fong, a dental hygienist; and Martha Fong, a nursery school teacher.

4. Alice Fong Yu, interview with author, June 29, 1987.

5. Founded in 1924, the Square and Circle Club is still active in San Francisco today. Its name comes from the Chinese round copper coin with the square hole in the middle and the motto, "In deeds be square, in knowledge be all-around."

Alice Fong Yu, founding president of the Square and Circle Club in 1924.
(Courtesy of Alice Fong Yu)

mon problems and concerns. On top of all that, she was a forum leader,
fund-raiser, and den mother for the Chinese YWCA. "Whatever the com-
munity needed, we got involved in," she said.[6]

Much of this volunteer spirit and concern for the well-being of the
community is reflected in her writings, a selection of which appears here
and in the next section on the war years. Politically astute and a feminist
as well, Alice wanted to address the interests of her intended female au-

---

6. Alice Fong Yu, interview with author, June 29, 1987.

dience with her articles on fashion, men, marriage, and recipes even as
she advocated on their behalf. At one level, her column shows how far
removed second-generation women were from the desperate economic
times being experienced in the rest of the country.[7] At another level, "The
Jade Box" demonstrates the desires of Chinese American women to hold
on to their Chinese heritage while they tried to acculturate into main-
stream American life. Equally important, Alice's writings reveal an all-
around Chinese American woman who is principled, witty, bicultural,
and equally confident and effective in the domestic and the public sphere.

COLOR-CHAFING TO CLUBWOMEN

Just when the world, the intelligent world, was getting nauseated with
the patriotic purity purgings and the shameful spread of race hatred
among the less democratic nations, and when we were vociferously praising the more enlightened ways of life and government in this country
where we can still doff our hats to whomever we like, this had to happen to take the joy out of life. The "color line" once more became a point
of issue and definitely caused a battle in the ranks of local American clubwomen when the constitution of the City and County Federation of
Women's Clubs was amended to bar non-Caucasian clubs from membership.[8] Some of the much heated clubwomen, doing considerable chest-
heaving, said that though they would be willing to work for "colored
women," they wished—oh, so ardently—to reserve the right to choose
their own club friends, and so on, ad nauseam.

It's just this high and mighty "holier than thou" attitude of "working for" and not "working with" people that makes this world so divided in spirit. I am sorry for the Federation. It had a wonderful chance,
in this cosmopolitan San Francisco, to make world history for the cause
of international peace and good will, but that's gone with the wind.

I don't like living alone, so I think I shall join the Commonwealth Club.
Its members are talking of an Asia House where they can expand their
inter-racial contacts—with no constitutional amendment to restrict them!

---

7. Whereas Chinatown had recovered from the Great Depression by this time (1937),
recovery for the rest of the country was delayed by a recession in 1937–38 and not fully
achieved until the United States entered World War II in 1941.

8. The Square and Circle Club had applied for membership into the Federation of
Women's Clubs and had been refused on racial grounds.

I doff my bonnet to Mrs. Richard Simons, Mrs. W. F. C. Zimmerman, Mrs. Letitia Farber and Mrs. S. S. Abrams, leaders in the losing battle. Thank goodness, I can still do that.

(SOURCE: *Chinese Digest*, March 1937, p. 10)

FASHION TID-BITS
Prevue of the Easter Parade

Spring is here. And how do we know? In the midst of February sunshine and showers, haven't we seen a sprig of daphne pinned to a smart lapel (or if you'll digest the latest Paris note, you'll be doubly smart by pinning on two boutonnieres, one for each of your own smart lapels) and aren't hyacinths and tulips, true forerunners of spring, blooming gaily in florist show windows?

But we aren't too enchanted by the season's loveliness to note that brilliant, flower-splashed prints are appearing all over the landscape from smart Grant Avenue stores to equally smart Market Street shops. And for you blessed souls who are determined to have your Easter outfit in all its glory and perfection it isn't a bit too early to plan it now.

To begin with, choose the basic note of your costume, and mind that costumes are THE essential this year. The standard trio is navy, beige, and grey, with perhaps the first two running a shade ahead in milady's favor . . . anyhow you can't go wrong with any of them. For those fair ones (and we mean "fair" *both* literally and figuratively) an experiment with the new thistle shade might prove helpful. This definitely established color is a cross between a dulled orchid and ashes-of-roses. And it combines beautifully with navy.

Now you can let your imagination run rampant on your splashy prints or solid color dresses. Boleros and redingotes can't be beaten in point of popularity. Necklines are either very high or very low. They may be trimmed with lingerie touches or unadorned . . . that's up to you. Skirt lengths vary from 13 to 14 inches from the ground. For you 'n me, 12 or 13 inches are dandy. Don't be afraid of shortening your last year's skirts . . . a few inches may be the difference between your looking "Oh, pret—ty good" and really chic.

Suits are going bigger than ever in the fashion limelight BUT get yours with excellent fabric and tailoring because it is something you'll derive joy from each time it returns from a trip to the cleaner's . . . it'll have that "just bought today" look. The charming feature about suits is that you can vary them with a change of accessories . . . that's a real economy. AND, speaking of accessories, those are all-important little things that can make or mar an outfit. Hats, thank heavens, are styled with the idea of being becoming as well as attractively feminine to all of us rather than to just a few. We've previewed the new collection and, take our word for it, it's de-lovely.

Luise Rainer as O-lan in the "Good Earth" does not have to worry about her clothes from one season to another, but, fortunately, or unfortunately, you 'n I have to.[9] We've previewed the coming trend in feminine fashions, and your Easter will be all the more happier if you choose the proper costume to wear.

(SOURCE: *Chinese Digest*, March 1937, pp. 10–11)

ON THE STATUS OF WOMEN—POINT OF VIEW

The inhibited Chinese female in the days of pre-Republic China accepted marriage as a matter of course, much as she did the natural facts of life—birth, reproduction, and death.[10] It was something that had to be, something over which she had no control. As it would have been unnatural for her not to do so, in due time she was married. An intelligent modern Chinese woman today either chooses to marry or to remain single. Broadly speaking, she marries because she knows that marriage is a natural state. Luckily the clamor for independence and freedom has not served to still the inner heart-beat for the instinct of motherhood. In spite of careers to occupy her intellectual life, she is able to accord to marriage and motherhood its proper place in her life.

But many ultra-moderns who pride themselves as being non-conformists, fail to see any longer the necessity for marriage. They claim economic independence, the single standard, the access to a better and unfettered life. Liberty, equality, and fraternity are theirs. Of what need is there for men? No pleasures are denied them. They have unlimited choice of companionship with both men and women. And as long as there is poverty and sickness in society, they will have the privilege of mothering and caring for

---

9. The film *The Good Earth*, based on Pearl Buck's novel of the same title, had just been released to critical acclaim in the community, even though Luise Rainer was given the lead role of O-lan instead of Anna May Wong.

10. In 1911 Dr. Sun Yat-sen's Revolutionary Party successfully overthrew the Qing dynasty and established the Republic of China, ushering China into the modern era.

children. Why then join the already numerous rank of the disillusioned and neurotic wives? Moreover, a wedding ring is no sure symbol of a safe and easy haven nor does love conquer all. How well they know that the present divorce rate indicates an unfortunate state of unsuccessful alliances!

According to the Chinese, the two components of life representing the female and male principles are Yin and Yang. Without them, life is without its heaven and earth, its light and darkness, its good and evil, its positive and negative forces of nature. They represent the qualities of passiveness and activity, of tenderness and hardness, rest and motion. As Yin embodies both peace and love—the ideal of Chinese life, it has therefore been considered the superior and the more essential.[11]

Fundamentally, then, woman is equal and complementary to man and the sexes should be so in life. In truth, however, woman is the fountainhead of life as she holds the power of giving and enriching life. To me, true womanliness then is femininity without parasitism, strength without hardness. Hence, there is definitely a career in marriage for the modern woman. It may not be essential to overcome loneliness or to satisfy the desire for children but it is a vital means to a full and complete life. And it is within the power of every intelligent and creative woman to provide for that which man eternally seeks—the totality of life.[12]

(SOURCE: *Chinese Digest*, June 1937, p. 8)

CHINATOWN MEN

It has not been within the province of the Jade Box to editorialize on our second generation manhood but the Chinatown Crier's comments on Chinatown Women last month provoked me to vow in defense of my sex to write something on what our men should know and do about themselves.[13] But now on second thought, tit for tat writing doesn't seem to me to be

---

11. Here, Alice is reinterpreting Chinese cosmology from a feminist perspective. Yang, representing the male, is commonly understood to be superior to Yin, the female (see discussion on pages 106–7).

12. Alice Fong Yu herself married late in life—at the age of thirty-five, three years after she wrote this column.

13. In response to Jane Kwong Lee's article "Chinese Women in San Francisco," first published in the *Pan-Pacific* magazine and reprinted in the *Chinese Digest* in June 1938 (pp. 8–9), the "Chinatown Crier" (editor William Hoy) had questioned the bright picture painted of Chinese American women as emancipated, enlightened, and a perfect blending of the East and the West (*Chinese Digest*, May 1938, pp. 2–3).

either elevating or constructive. Furthermore, I don't think men can take criticism or defeat as gracefully as the fairer sex. And too, we know instinctively that women have a great deal to do with men being what they are so we simply cannot point a finger at their faults without feeling a little guilty ourselves.

If men prefer women to be streamlined homemakers (cooking and sewing considered) as well as being the last word in multiple performance outside our homes, this to me should be cause for female jubilation. For isn't this a healthy sign that men at last are no longer jealous of our brains and are willing to live and work on a par with us? On the other hand, if Chinatown men are guilty of lukewarm interest in our homes, aren't we as mothers and wives to blame for not making our homes a place where they can find relaxation and comradeship in reading and listening to good music for instance, and where they can take pride in building lovely surroundings and cultivating flower gardens for us?

Turning from our own homes, let us look at the community and social projects which work for the elimination of filth, disease, and social and juvenile delinquency. National and world thinking have been directed in various ways to achieve for all men more abundant living and greater happiness in better housing, superior recreational facilities and more healthful conditions of work. All these efforts, in the last analysis, exalt the home and youth, both of which should be very close to the hearts of all women. And if Chinatown men are disinterested or indifferent to these community, social, national and world problems, I am afraid it is because Chinatown women have not found it their duty to direct their thoughts to these things. Therefore, although we can tell the Chinatown Crier that we, too, can say a thing or two about our Chinatown men, we prefer at this time not to judge, but to give a little thought to what has been said about man's ability to rise no higher than the level of woman.

(SOURCE: *Chinese Digest*, June 1938, p. 10)

GOOD RICE AND HOW TO COOK IT

Beggar, commoner, lord, or king, one can hardly resist a bowl of steaming hot rice. So it was with Wang Lung in "The Good Earth."[14] Perhaps

---

14. This same issue of the *Chinese Digest* included a number of favorable reviews, interviews, and ads about the newly released film *The Good Earth*.

you wondered how he could relish so many bowls of rice—why, you even thought: It's just like eating plain boiled potatoes with neither salt, cream, nor butter.

Ah! But Wang Lung is eating rice prepared the way it has been prepared for as many thousands of years in China as you can count on your ten little fingers—the way the finest culinary wizards prepared it for the emperors—the way the peasant woman cooks it for her family—the way we cook it in San Francisco's Chinatown.

We think of it as a simple everyday operation. But many of us have often asked, "How do YOU Chinese cook rice?"

To which we endeavor to explain:

First, use an ordinary covered pot, NOT a double boiler. Next, the grains must be cleaned and rinsed until the water runs clear. (China rice is a finer, smaller and shorter grain, and not as glutinous as Texas or California rice.)

Since the art of Chinese cooking is handed down from generation to generation, the question of how much water should be used is answered by "experience"—depending on the grade and type of rice used—and, ladies, therein lies the secret of cooking rice that is rice and not mush. It is, however, safe to say that the amount of water should not rise more than one to one and a half inches above the grains.

The pot is put on a medium fire. Allow it to simmer rapidly until all the water has evaporated. Refrain from lifting cover to peek at it, but as soon as you hear it crackling, turn the fire very low.

Your worries are now over. You may tune in on Ben Bernie or even finish a few squares of that quilt you started—was it last Spring?

Come back in 20 minutes. Lift up the cover, and you have a pot of rice fit for the KING—of your household and your heart!

(SOURCE: *Chinese Digest*, March 1937, p. 11)

MY FAVORITE RECIPE
Gai Jook (Chicken Gruel)

For cold weather, warm food. Why, of course, that goes without saying! And the best part about serving Gai Jook or, for that matter, any kind of Jook on a chilly, foggy San Francisco evening is: you can prepare it hours ahead of time, and be the perfect hostess that you no doubt are. When you decide on Jook for refreshments—or shall I say re-warm-ment?—you can rest assured that you will have your chance to win the bridge prize of the evening, too—(although it would not be exactly good etiquette to win one's own prize)!

The usual consistency in serving a party of 12 is one and one-half bowls of rice to six quarts of water. This varies considerably depending on the individual taste. After your first experience, you should be able to judge accordingly.

During a spare moment in the day, the rice may be cleaned. Season with half a teaspoon of salt and a few drops of cooked peanut oil, which any good cook of Chinese food should have handy. Let the rice stand until you are ready to start the Jook cooking, or, at least for half an hour. My dear ladies, these few drops of oil and half teaspoon of salt mean the making or unmaking of your Jook.

Clean a two and one-half pound chicken. Put in kettle of four quarts of boiled, salted water. Simmer for 15 minutes. Remove from kettle. Be sure to save stock. When chicken cools, bone and dice.

Four hours before serving time, add two quarts of cold water to seasoned rice, bring rapidly to a boil. Add chicken bones and the four quarts of stock, and let simmer on very low fire, but high enough to keep Jook bubbling.

If desired, pork soup bones may be added. However, they should first be parboiled, then seasoned with salt and allowed to stand for 10 minutes before adding to the stock and rice water.

In the meantime there will be a lot of chopping and mincing to do. Well, why should I scare you by making you think it's going to be such a tedious process? For diligent young ladies, and also men (if you read my column), all this preparation should not take more than half an hour. Mince one pound of pork, chop up two pieces of chone choy [Chinese green onions] very fine. The following is optional: mince two pieces of red ginger and four pieces of sweetened Chinese cucumbers.

Half an hour before serving time, add the pork and chone choy. Just before serving, add chicken meat. Bring to boil (but never turn gas high after it has once come to a boil, else the rice will be scorched), then add one tablespoon each of ginger and cucumbers. The balance may be served on a relish dish, and left to the individual taste.

I don't believe I should pamper you by letting you enjoy your game of bridge so wholeheartedly, because this Jook does require a little looking into every now and then. Aside from that, all you need do is—shall we say, "dish it out" when you sense that first yawn coming on.

And once again, we cannot get away from our indispensably famous soy sauce. Serve this in a small fancy dish, and let your appetite take its course.

(SOURCE: *Chinese Digest*, January 1938, pp. 9, 18)

MY FAVORITE RECIPE
Har Yuk Won Ton (Shrimp Meat Ravioli)

Just a cloudful of the tastiest morsels you can think of—that's har yuk won ton—"won ton" meaning "swallowed by clouds." Isn't that romantic? But then anything pertaining to ancient historic China is romantic.

Service for eight, with exquisite rice bowls, white inside, with a border of pink and green blossoms; clear jade green outside, with an allover pattern of a head of bokchoy. Complementing the bowl, pick out a spoon fresh as a day in May, with its matching pattern of bokchoy. Along with this lovely setting one uses a pair of ivory chopsticks. They come in sets of ten pairs, although they are also sold separately—some with square heads, some with round heads, and even some which are screwed together in the middle. Wouldn't it be fun to have a fork like that—then just as we think we've picked up that mouthful of peas with such elegant grace, it could somersault on us!

As I was saying—service for eight:

Take two pounds of lean pork and a pound of jumbo shrimps shelled. Grind together. Season with salt, soy sauce, and just a dash of pepper. Add 2 tablespoons of flour so that the meat will stick together.

You will need 2 pounds of "won ton" paste squares. I wish I could relate to you the interesting process by which this particular paste is made—pounded out thin and transparent by a huge bamboo rod about a foot in diameter.

Using a small stick or a bamboo chopstick, take a dab of the minced meat, place in one corner of the paste squares, and roll very loosely half way across. This leaves 3 corners of the square paste free. Take the 2 corners at the base of the triangle (the ones closest to you). Draw and pinch together with a dab of beaten egg. This finishes one ravioli. But don't despair, after the first dozen or so, you'll find that it is more fun than work. Place finished ravioli on the platter. Avoid crowding, as it will make them less fluffy.

Make a good soup stock with: pork bones and Chinese mushrooms. Keep boiling rapidly for 20 minutes.

Add ravioli one by one. Stir with chopsticks to prevent sticking.

When soup comes to a boil, continue bubbling for 2 minutes. The ravioli are now cooked.

For this service for eight, I would suggest cooking only half the ravioli first, then remove from stock and cook the other half.

This is truly a magnificent dish, for just by merit of its decorations, you can boast of different varieties of won ton.

Top it with thin strips of Chinese roast pork and you have "cha siu won ton."

Top it with one piece of roast duck, one piece of cold chicken, 2 generous slices of roast pork and 1/2 a hard boiled egg, and you have "chop suey [literally, a mixture] won ton."

Top it with a nice juicy, fat leg of roast duck and you have "op duey won ton."

Garnish with curry, ketchup, and roast pork strips and you have "sam jup [literally, three flavors] won ton."

This is getting too strenuous for my appetite now, so may I bid you "Joy Geen" until we meet again!

(SOURCE: *Chinese Digest*, June 1938, p. 10)

Sue Ko Lee and the 1938 National Dollar Stores Strike

"It Changed Our Lives"

In 1938, at the tail end of the Great Depression, 108 Chinese garment workers organized against unfair labor practices at Joe Shoong's National Dollar Stores sewing factory, forming the Chinese Ladies' Garment Workers' Union (LGWU) and going on strike for fifteen weeks. It was at that time the longest strike in the history of San Francisco Chinatown. Their hard-won victory was due as much to their determination to win as to the economic and political circumstances of the depression that nurtured their union activism. The Wagner Act of 1935, which granted organized labor the right to collective bargaining, had resulted in the greatest organizing drive in the history of the labor movement. Large numbers of racial minority and women workers were recruited into unions for the first time. Thus, with the support of white labor unions and the rise of leftist organizations in Chinatown, Chinese women were encouraged to stand up for themselves and work across generational, racial, gender, and political lines to improve working conditions in Chinatown.

When I began researching Chinese American women's history in the early 1980s, there was only one in-depth article about the strike, written by Patricia M. Fong in Asian American Review, *a publication of the Asian American Studies program at the University of California, Berkeley.[1] Although it was well researched and provided many details on the garment*

---

1. Patricia M. Fong, "The 1938 National Dollar Strike," *Asian American Review* 2, no. 1 (1975): 183–200.

industry in California, the causes behind the strike, developments during the fifteen-week strike, and the aftermath of the strike, the author relied exclusively on English-language materials from newspapers and the union archives. There were no Chinese voices. And the conclusion—that the garment factory and union gained more from the strike than the workers—troubled me.[2] I was determined to interview the strikers and get the inside story. In particular, I wanted to know from their perspective: What led up to the strike? What sustained the strike for so long? What role did the International Ladies' Garment Workers' Union (ILGWU) play? More important, what role did Chinese women play in the strike and how did it change their lives?

It was difficult finding anyone involved in the strike to interview. Finally I located Sue Ko Lee, who was a buttonhole machine operator at National Dollar Stores at the time of the strike and who afterward became a labor organizer for the ILGWU. Over tea and gingersnaps in her kitchen one sunny afternoon, I interviewed Sue about the events. She was seventy-nine years old and retired, living alone in a comfortable house in El Cerrito, California. I found her to be a quiet, soft-spoken person, though occasionally my line of questioning would provoke an angry or spirited response or two. This happened when I asked her about Joe Shoong (owner of National Dollar Stores), Jennie Matyas (ILGWU labor organizer), the debate over the strike settlement, the significance of the strike in her opinion, and the reason she left labor organizing. While transcribing the interview, I noticed that I had repeatedly tried to put words into her mouth—to have her tell me that the garment workers had not been used by the union, that the women had played an active role in this strike, and that, as a result, their lives had changed dramatically. But Sue Ko Lee had a mind of her own. At times, she would nod in agreement and not elaborate further. Other times, she would contradict me with justifiable reasons. As an example:

JY: Why were all the officers of Local 341 [Chinese Ladies' Garment Workers' Union] Chinese men when the women members outnumbered the men?

SL: The men were not as afraid as the women at that time. (I didn't say

---

2. Specifically, this is what Fong said in the conclusion: "Who received the most satisfaction from the outcome? Probably the ILGWU, the National Dollar Stores Ltd., and the Golden Gate Manufacturing Company. The workers were (sold out by the union?) dissatisfied with the terms of the contract, and they all lost their jobs within two years, and the union could not really help them much afterwards" (ibid., p. 196).

all the men were not as afraid.) They were [the] decision mak ers.
[Women] didn't want to assume the responsibility. (I won't want to
assume the responsibility at that time either.) They had families and
they just [went] out and work to earn a little extra money.

JY: Even though the men were the officers and leaders, did the women
participate just as actively in the strike as the men?

SL: (*nods*)

JY: Did they have a say in the decision making?

SL: Oh, sure.

JY: Did the women speak up during the meetings?

SL: Not too much, but they understood the issues. They [just] weren't
use to speaking up and taking the leadership role.

*I appreciated her honesty and I was grateful to have found someone
willing to talk to me about the strike. So you can imagine my delight
when, without my prompting, Sue Ko Lee produced her scrapbook of
the news clippings, newsletters, bulletins, and photographs she had kept
in connection with the strike and her work with the ILGWU. With her
permission, I have included a selection of these news articles and bulletins following her interview.[3]*

*Sue Ko Lee was born in Honolulu, Hawaii, on March 9, 1910, and grew
up in Watsonville, California, the eldest of ten children. At eighteen, she
married Lee Jew Hing, who had immigrated to the United States in 1921
and was working as a bookkeeper at National Dollar Stores. They made
their home in San Francisco Chinatown, where they had two sons. Soon
after their marriage Sue Ko Lee found a job at the National Dollar Stores,
and before long she was embroiled in a strike that would irrevocably
change her life.*

"We Weren't Bad Off"

Did you know almost everyone had to work for Joe Shoong's Dollar
Stores? Because you couldn't get out of Chinatown and work anywhere

---

3. In 1995, with Sue Ko Lee's permission, I deposited the scrapbook in the Labor
Archives and Research Center, San Francisco State University, for safekeeping and the use
of other researchers.

Sue Ko Lee with her husband, Lee Jew Hing, and son, Stanley, in 1930. (Courtesy of Sue Ko Lee)

else. You either worked in a laundry, restaurant, or your own barbershop. Women got into [it] because there were no other opportunities for them [except] pick shrimp at home. There weren't too many employers. All my family worked for Joe Shoong . . . all my brothers, my sister Mary, even my brother-in-law. It was [also] a matter of family connections. My husband got his job because his uncle was working for Joe Shoong.[4]

4. Joe Shoong emigrated from Chungshan (Zhongshan) District, whose people controlled the garment industry in San Francisco Chinatown. The tendency was for employers

In those days, as long as there was a machine empty, anyone could get a job since they didn't pay union wages and it was piece rate. There were no controls until Roosevelt came in.[5] We come in and go as we liked. There was no set time. They opened until nine at night. I didn't see any sweatshop conditions there. The National Dollar Stores was clean and a good-size factory because they made all the things that were sold in their [retail] stores, simple things like flannel nightgowns, cotton housedresses, aprons, satin bloomers, all women's clothing. The factory was well lit. It was not in the basement but above ground with windows that opened on one side. Only the cutting room and rest rooms were downstairs.[6]

I started learning on the most difficult machine—the over-lock with three needles. It worked over the seams that were trimmed off on the inside of the garment. I learned all the special machines. My husband had a steady job and was making $125 a month [as a bookkeeper]. I was averaging 25 cents an hour or something like that. I wasn't a very fast worker or a slow worker, just an average worker. And I couldn't work full time because my children came in 1927 and 1929. At $125 a month and with rent at $35 a month, we weren't bad off. We never had to live in places with community kitchens and all. [Did you make enough money to take care of expenses?] Yes, and enough for him [her husband] to send money home to his family [in China]. They never forget that, no matter how hard things got.

"Wages Was the Main Thing"

I wasn't in the beginning of it [the strike]. I was working there, but I wasn't involved until later. You see, they [the union] came to organize us. The white shops were already organized, and the white shops were clamoring that the contractors were sending work out to the Chinese workers and that was a thorn [in their side]. So they had to organize the

to hire people from their own districts; thus, workers like Law Shee Low (see pages 211–23) and Sue Ko Lee who were from Chungshan easily found jobs at the National Dollar Stores factory. However, the kin relationship made it difficult for workers to protest any labor exploitation or mistreatment.

5. She is referring here to the National Recovery Administration codes, which provided workers with set minimum wages, hours, safety standards, and collective bargaining rights.

6. The National Dollar Stores factory specialized in women's light apparel for exclusive distribution to its thirty-seven retail outlets on the West Coast. The factory was known for being the largest, cleanest, and most modern garment factory in all of Chinatown. Joe Shoong was a millionaire and generous philanthropist.

Chinese to counteract that [underbidding of Chinatown shops]. They tried and tried but they couldn't break the [racial] barrier until Jennie Matyas came.[7] She was talking to people there, and that's the time I became aware of it. They had to get enough signatures from the workers for the local before they could present it to the employer to have a union.

[Did you sign up?] I must have, although I can't remember now. You see, in each shop, they get the cutters first because if they don't cut, you don't have any work. We had a group meeting to talk about it.

[Was there a dispute over wages?] Yes, wages was the main thing. The depression was over and the hour wage laws were in effect and we weren't getting the thirty-three-and-a-third cents an hour. They were cheating on us. The hours were not kept legally. What they did was say what you earned was [based on] how many hours you worked to make the thirty-three-and-a-third cents.[8] And there was already a home work rule, but they were [still] sending a lot of home work out. (My husband knew because he kept the records of that.) I think that was the incentive for the workers to join the union of their own will. The employer[s] definitely said they didn't want a union.

After the majority of the workers voted for a union shop, establishing the Chinese LGWU under the ILGWU, National Dollar Stores sold the Chinatown factory to Golden Gate Manufacturing, a new company formed by two former managers of the National Dollar Stores. Seeing this move as a subterfuge to freeze them out and break up the union, the Chinese LGWU voted to call a strike and began picketing the National Dollar Stores factory and its three retail stores in San Francisco. Their demands were recognition of a union shop, $20 wages for a thirty-five-hour workweek, and a guarantee that National Dollar Stores would buy all its manufactured goods from Golden Gate and that Golden Gate would provide work for a minimum of eleven months of the year to its workers.

---

7. Jennie Matyas was a dedicated socialist and labor organizer for the ILGWU. For her life history and her memories of the 1938 strike, see "Jennie Matyas and the ILGWU," oral history conducted in 1955 by Connie Gilb, Regional Culture History Project, Bancroft Library, University of California, Berkeley, 1957.

8. No one else mentioned the "doctoring" of time sheets. Sue Ko Lee may be confusing this illegal practice from later years with what was going on at the National Dollar Stores factory at the time.

"We Were Determined to Close Them Down"

[How were you able to keep the strike going for fifteen weeks?] We organized our shifts, and the ones on the picket line were all together. We never mentioned anything about why we are doing this. What is there? Maybe they won't reopen the shop for us? There was no other recourse. There was nothing else. We were determined to close them down if necessary.

We all did it with the Chinese leadership and advice from the top because we didn't know anything. They had to tell us what to do. The men were not as afraid as the women at that time. (I didn't say all the men were not as afraid.) They were [the] decision makers. My husband was the vice-president and wrote all the bulletins that went out in Chinese. [Women] had families and they just [went] out to work to earn a little extra money. They didn't want to assume the responsibility. (I won't want to assume the responsibility at that time either.) They [women] weren't used to speaking up and taking the leadership role but they understood the issues. When you see a woman like this (*points to a picture showing an older Chinese immigrant woman picket*) on the picket line, isn't that something? They stuck in there too.

[Who was running the strike?] We all worked on the [picketing] schedules and all, but the legal stuff, they [ILGWU] had to do it for us. Everything had to be okayed by the officers of the [international] union because they might be liable and they were footing the bill. [With] the support of the white people, the union people, we closed the downtown [retail] store.[9] I don't know what we felt then. Certainly, Jennie Matyas made a difference.

[Can you tell me why Jennie Matyas was so effective with the Chinese?] She's not Chinese, but she's a woman. She's very dedicated and very honest and sincere. (Now you read about the corruption in the unions. I don't think you could corrupt her.) She really wanted to help us. I think it was also the large company [National Dollar Stores] that people did not like. I remember we were on the picket line and here came

---

9. The ILGWU not only took care of legal matters, but it also conducted the negotiations, provided relief monies, sponsored English classes for the workers, and sought the sanction of the San Francisco Labor Council and cooperation of the Retail Department Store Employees' Union. Only when the white retail clerks refused to cross the picket line at the three local National Dollar Stores, thus closing down the retail outlets for two weeks, did Joe Shoong feel compelled to deal with the strikers.

Mrs. Shoong and she said, *"Ni di sui tong yan* [these awful Chinese]!"
So she's not Chinese, right?!

[Did you get any support from the Chinese Six Companies?] Of course
not! They were against us. We had the whole Chinese community
against us. They didn't do anything, but they didn't show us any support because we were all called troublemakers. It was unheard of! [But]
we knew the union was behind us. The union would come by with donuts
and coffee in the morning. Then we went back to the union hall for meetings. [What were some of the difficulties during the strike?] Survival. We
got the strike benefit—five dollars a week, but that won't pay your rent.
Thirteen weeks, that's three and a half months.[10] If we got any help, it
was borrowing from our relatives. I don't know how we managed. But
when you're young, you don't think about these things.

[At any time was there any disagreement between the union and the
workers?] Not until the time of the contract agreement. Jennie was trying to get them to accept it, and some of the militant workers were against
it. It just wasn't good enough for them. And I said, at least that's something to begin with. And that's when she [Jennie Matyas] noticed me. It
may not be what you wanted, but you take the best there is. At least you
got something for one year. And maybe something better would come
out of it. If you take longer, people are not going to stand around here.
They can't afford to.

*The contract called for a closed union shop; a 5 percent raise (to $14 per
week except for apprentices); a forty-hour workweek, with time and a
half for overtime; a paid holiday for Labor Day; enforcement of health,
fire, and sanitary conditions; guaranteed half-day of work whenever
workers were called in; a shop steward authorized to collect dues and
deal with grievances; the right to a hearing before an arbitration committee in the case of a dispute over the contract or a questionable discharge; a price committee to step in whenever piece rates did not yield
the minimum wages for 75 percent of the factory workers; and an agreement that National Dollar Stores continue contracting work to the
Golden Gate Company. The vote was close: thirty-one for the agreement,
twenty-seven against. Workers went back to work a few days later. But*

---

10. The strike actually lasted 105 days, or 15 weeks, from February 28 to June 8, 1938.

when the contract expired one year later, the Golden Gate Manufactur-
ing Company conveniently went out of business.

"The Best Thing That Ever Happened"

They closed the factory while we were picketing. Then because we picketed the downtown stores, they sold it [the factory] to Golden Gate and
disengaged themselves from the main store. The contract said they had
to stay open a year, so they stayed open a year and then closed it.

[What happened to everyone after the factory closed?] A lot of them
went to work for white shops because the union found them jobs. You
don't know how hard Jennie Matyas worked to get us into the white shops
downtown. I heard this later: Edna was a presser. She didn't have any parents and she and her sister lived alone. So Jennie tried to place her, to get
her into a white shop. The employer was willing, but the workers rebelled.
They didn't want any Chinese because of the reputation that the Chinese
will work for nothing and cut the wages down. Finally she got Edna in
and she proved her worth. And after that, the door opened and employers began asking for Chinese workers. That's how the Chinese workers
got out of Chinatown to work elsewhere. And that's the turning point for
workers in Chinatown. Because of the garment workers' strike in Chinatown, everything changed. Later, the restaurant workers had shorter
hours, days off. In my opinion, the strike was the best thing that ever happened. It changed our lives. We overcame bigotry, didn't we? The war
came and that helped because there was a labor shortage. But even if it
hadn't come, we would have still broken the barrier. Otherwise, we would
have still been stuck in Chinatown working among our own race.

I know it was a turning point in my life. My husband went to work
in a downtown shop [as a cutter] in clothes and suits. I worked the machines for a while in the little shops, and then Koret took over and that's
how I got into quality control. I had a tape measure around my neck to
make sure the button holes were spaced out [correctly]. (Koret had very
good standards for their workmanship.)

[What was the main difference between working in Chinatown and in
a white shop downtown?] You made more money and had set hours. You
didn't jump in and out of the shop. You worked eight to five and there
was holiday and vacation pay. It was still piecework, but the price had to
come up so that you made your minimum. It's controlled that way. So

Sue Ko Lee (second from the right) with co-workers in the 1940s. (Courtesy of Sue Ko Lee)

the faster ones can make more, but at least the slowest ones made the minimum. During the trial period they paid to make up the difference in order for you to make the minimum, but after the trial period, if you can't keep up, they have a right to let you go. But in Chinatown, they just cut your hours on the records. I remember there was a fire in one of the little shops I was working for, and because they had insurance I was paid for staying home. If it was a Chinese shop, you would get nothing. Then through the union bargaining, we got health insurance and death benefits.

[Did they mistreat you in any way?] No, I won't let them. We had no problems getting along with the people in the shops. There was no discrimination. Where I worked I was respected. I'll just cite you a few instances. I was working on the floor at Koret during the Second World War.[11] A co-worker told me another woman working the floor got a raise. "You go ask for a raise," he said. On another occasion, I was on the floor trying something on the machine, tucking. I didn't like that job, but I was willing to try any machine. Most people won't because if they went

---

11. A floor person took care of the workers, including the distribution of work to them.

slow, it would lower their average. So this lady came to me and said, "Why didn't you tell me you can work on that machine?" I said (*smiling smugly*), "You never asked me."

Later in the 1950s, I stopped working at Koret and went to work for the union [Local 101 of the ILGWU]. It started with the strike. I was working in the shop and was drawn into it.[12] They needed someone with language skills, so I was appointed the business agent. That's when I became a delegate to the convention.[13] [Was there any racial discrimination in ILGWU?] No. I was secretary of a *white* union. There were Blacks in there too, and we all got along. After the war [ILGWU was successful in getting other shops in Chinatown to unionize] because they worked through the manufacturers. If you send your work out and you're a union shop, you have to send it to a union [factory]. That's how they organized them. Otherwise, they would never be able to organize them and they won't strike. At least they [Chinatown workers] gained something. They never had death benefits and health insurance before. Now they have.

In a way the Chinatown shops are good for the people who cannot get out of Chinatown transportation-wise or know their way around. But the contractors are so greedy. You know the manufacturers pay them the price and overhead on top of the piece rate but they don't pass that on to the workers. Just like in real estate, they hurt their own people. And here these employees feel sorry for their employers. They give them the sad story, "You run through this at this price or we don't get any work." I know for a fact that the manufacturers pay them the same rate as they pay downtown and pay them for the overhead. But they're not happy with the overhead; they have to cheat the workers.[14] That's what gets me disgusted! That's why I got out of it. I could have just gone along with it and take my pay. I would have been rich by now. But I can't take that out of the dues of the people. I'm not that kind of person.

---

12. According to Sue Ko Lee, after the Golden Gate factory closed and the ILGWU was able to place workers in white shops, the Chinese LGWU disbanded and Chinese garment workers began joining Local 101.

13. Under Jennie Matyas's mentorship, Sue Ko Lee became secretary of both Local 101 and the San Francisco Joint Board. She was a delegate to the 26th National ILGWU Convention in Cleveland, Ohio, in 1947.

14. Then and now, Chinatown garment shops have had to underbid downtown shops to get work. Unfortunately, owners make up for it by downsizing their employees' wages. More recently, there have been efforts to hold manufacturers accountable for working conditions in contract shops and to form alliances among manufacturers, contractors, and organized labor in order to compete globally without undermining decent working conditions.

I thought maybe I could help Chinatown, but I couldn't do it. (sighs) It's frustrating. They [Chinese workers] don't want to do anything for themselves. They want you to hand them the benefits, and still they won't fight for them. It's not like the Black people, [who are] more aggressive. Your mother is at the age where she can't understand it, but those younger ones, they should know better.[15] I tried to explain to them, but they just don't want to change. So I said what's the use of me hanging around? I can't do anything. So that's why I quit the union in the 1960s and went to work for the state in the employment service.

(SOURCE: Sue Ko Lee, interview with author, October 26, 1989, El Cerrito, California)

Sue Ko Lee died of cancer on May 15, 1996. The last time I saw her was on October 28, 1995, at the book party for Unbound Feet. *Proudly sitting on stage at the Chinese Culture Center in San Francisco Chinatown, she was one of seven outstanding women being honored that day.*

FROM SUE KO LEE'S SCRAPBOOK

In a light-brown-covered scrapbook Sue Ko Lee had carefully arranged and preserved an array of English- and Chinese-language newspaper clippings, mimeographed pages from union publications, handwritten Chinese bulletins, and photographs—all documenting the 1938 strike and her ILGWU activities. From them we get a detailed account of an intraethnic class struggle and the tactics employed by both sides—the Chinese garment workers and their employer, millionaire Joe Shoong. At stake were the reputation of Joe Shoong, on the one hand, and the rights of Chinatown workers to unionize and demand better working conditions, on the other. Both sides vied for the support and approval of the Chinese community, appealing to its sense of righteousness and to Chinese nationalist solidarity.

---

15. During the interview I told Sue Ko Lee about my mother's experience working in union shops in Chinatown from the 1950s to the 1970s. She felt so beholden to her employers that she was willing to "doctor" her time sheets and be paid piece rate and below the minimum hourly rate. Many other women did likewise because they felt obligated to their employers or were afraid of losing their jobs. Also, because of their cultural background, Chinese women, even today, are more apt to cope by accommodating rather than confronting; on the latter point, see Chalsa Loo, "Slaying Demons with a Sewing Needle: Gender Differences and Women's Status," in *Chinatown: Most Time, Hard Time* (New York: Praeger, 1991), pp. 188–211.

As the following excerpts from bulletins, news clippings, and newsletters show, Joe Shoong went to great lengths to fight the union, demanding an election of the workers, changing the ownership and name of the National Dollar Stores factory, getting a court injunction against the pickets, suing the union, and finally closing down the factory when the contract expired. In the National Dollar Stores' "Statement to the Public" of March 2, 1938, Joe Shoong tried to come across as the benevolent employer, upstanding citizen, loyal Chinese nationalist, and victim of union tactics. In response, the Chinese local provided a reasoned point-by-point rebuttal that was published simultaneously in the Young China *newspaper, arguing that the workers were victims of Joe Shoong's mistreatment and unscrupulous tactics. Over and over again, the Chinese LGWU issued bulletins that explained the union's position to the Chinatown community. These were often couched in leftist political rhetoric— labeling Joe Shoong a capitalist, arguing that the worker's welfare is the nation's welfare, and calling on workers to fight to the end to raise their living standards. The union even went so far as to join forces with leftist organizations such as the Chinese Workers Mutual Aid Association.[16]*

The excerpts from union publications show that throughout the strike the Chinese garment workers were determined to win. In the spirit of union solidarity, they kept fellow union members apprised of the situation, continued to bolster the membership's morale, and constantly expressed appreciation for all that the ILGWU was doing for them. They apparently really felt that "the ILGWU is behind us; we shall not be moved." Even after the strike was over and victory won, they remained stalwart members of the labor movement and avid supporters of Chinese nationalist causes. In the September 21, 1938, bulletin printed below, they expressly made the connection between U.S.-China foreign relations and interethnic workers' solidarity, urging all of Chinatown not to cross the picket lines at department stores downtown "for the sake of national reputation and of promoting friendship between Chinese and American workers." Later, the Chinese local also contributed to the strike fund of other unions, campaigned against antilabor legislation, participated in the protest against U.S. shipment of war materials to Japan, and supported the boycott of non-union-made lisle stockings, which women wore in order to boycott Japanese silk products. Unfortunately, Chinese

---

16. The Chinese Workers Mutual Aid Association was established in 1937, following a successful strike against the Alaskan Packers Association, to unite Chinese workers for the purposes of improving working conditions and raising their status in labor unions.

women's involvement in the labor movement proved short-lived as the movement dissipated with the coming of war, the end of the depression, and the repression of the left following World War II.

A LETTER TO THE PUBLIC REGARDING THE STRIKE

Dear Fellow Countrymen:

Why are we striking and picketing? We are striking for better wages from the factory owner so that we can support our livelihood. This is not something that we want. However, since last October, because of inflation, we have had difficulty making ends meet. That is why we mobilized our fellow workers to fight for equality and decent wages. It has been three months since we formed our union. During these three months, we have tried repeatedly through peaceful methods to negotiate with the owner, but he has consistently used the oppressive tactics of the capitalist to stall for time. He forced us to have an election in the presence of his representatives to rectify the formation of the union. Supervised by the National Labor Relations Board and with a full quorum of workers, the election was carried out and our union received due recognition. Subsequently, his legal representatives signed an agreement with our union lawyer, but he continued to use all kinds of stalling tactics to defuse our unity. Then on top of that, he tried to turn the situation around by changing the name of the factory. His goal is to break our ricebowl. Therefore, we have no choice but to set up a picket line to fight for fair treatment.

February 26, 1938
All the workers of the National Dollar Stores factory

(SOURCE: Handwritten Chinese bulletin. TRANSLATOR: Ellen Yeung.)

A STATEMENT TO THE PUBLIC REGARDING THE DAMAGES DONE TO BUSINESS BY THE CHINESE LGWU STRIKE AGAINST NATIONAL DOLLAR STORES

Beginning February 26, the Chinese Ladies' Garment Workers' Union has been sending its members to picket our stores on Market Street, Mason Street, and Fillmore Street as well as our warehouse. The damage this is doing to our business, however, is not as significant as the impact it has on the whole overseas Chinese community. Our company had on February 8 sold the factory located at Washington and Kearny to the Golden Gate Manufacturing Company. That company had received State government approval to establish itself as a business and had also published a notice in the newspaper to raise capital by soliciting shareholders. Not only is their name different from ours, but their organization is different. They have absolutely no relationship with us. As for the negotiations going on between labor and capital, when the factory changed hands the Golden Gate Manufacturing Company agreed to continue the negotiations with the union. And instead of pursuing the matter with them, the union turned around and picketed our company. The union is in error for not being able to tell the difference. Moreover it is a great pity that they are hurting a Chinese business. Our company has always extended cooperation and excellent treatment to the workers. We have always adhered to government regulations regarding work hours and wages and have never oppressed anyone or reduced anyone's wages. Therefore these workers of the Golden Gate Manufacturing Company are totally out of line in picketing us and distributing flyers in the name of the workers of a non-existing National Dollar Stores factory in order to confuse the public. In this time of national disaster, when unity among ourselves is crucial, it is really sad to think that such an unfortunate incident has happened. Because we are concerned that our countrymen may not know the truth, we are providing a brief explanation so that you may understand that we are the innocent victim in this dispute.

National Dollar Stores
March 2, 1938

(SOURCE: *Young China* newspaper, March 5, 1938, p. 4. TRANSLATOR: Ellen Yeung.)

ANOTHER LETTER TO THE PUBLIC FROM LOCAL 341, THE CHINESE LADIES' GARMENT WORKERS' UNION

Yesterday we read the ridiculous statement from the National Dollar Stores. It is not even worth a response from intelligent people, but because we are concerned that our countrymen may not know the truth, we are providing a brief explanation of the oppression suffered by members of this union.

According to National Dollar Stores, "Beginning February 26, the Chinese Ladies Garment Workers Union (LGWU) has been sending its members to picket . . . " Our sending members to picket National Dollar Stores was not really something that we wanted to do, but because of the low wages, the inflation, and the downward spiral of living standards, we had no choice but to raise the issue of a wage increase with the owner of National Dollar Stores. Instead of responding, the owner evicted four union members from the factory. After the attorney and the officers of the union took up the matter, the owner reinstated the four workers to their original jobs and recognized the Chinese LGWU.

At first he agreed to open negotiations with the union regarding wages and working hours. Then he reneged on his words and refused to recognize us, demanding instead that the workers vote in an election supervised by the National Labor Relations Board. The majority voted for a union, so finally the representative and the legal counsel for National Dollar Stores signed a document recognizing the union and agreeing to start negotiations over wages, working hours, and other issues. In the latter part of January, National Dollar Stores scheduled a meeting with our union representative at the Palace Hotel, at which time our union representative presented their company representative with a copy of the contract. Representatives and legal counsels from both sides also met on January 28 at the union attorney's office to sign a document stating that the National Dollar Stores factory was now a union shop, meaning that it cannot hire non-union workers. In the midst of negotiations, National Dollar Stores resorted to trickery, suddenly changing the name of the factory. They refused any further negotiations with the union but continued the talks about wages and working hours under the name of the Golden Gate Manufacturing Company. Meanwhile, Golden Gate Manufacturing Company refused to provide any satisfactory responses and instead stalled for time. Work at the factory became unsteady. That was why union members were forced to strike.

National Dollar Stores said that they have "always extended cooperation and excellent treatment to the workers . . . have never oppressed anyone or reduced anyone's wages . . . " When workers ask for a wage increase from the employer and the latter evicts them, is that not oppression? Where in this case is the excellent treatment? When the National Recovery Administration (NRA) codes were in effect, weekly wages were at least $18, $19. After the NRA codes expired, wages were slashed to $13.30, a reduction of $5.60. How can the employer claim not to have reduced wages? All this constitutes oppressive treatment of workers by the employer.

National Dollar Stores also said, "In this time of national disaster . . ." If the owner of National Dollar Stores is really interested in China's welfare, he should negotiate with the workers in good faith and allow workers to make a decent living so that they can afford to buy Chinese war bonds. We can barely survive on $13.30 a week, let alone contribute to the war effort. If the owner of National Dollar Stores is someone who is understanding, then he should negotiate with the union and raise the wages of the workers. Then not only will the workers benefit, but China will as well. We trust that wise people in the community will be able to judge for themselves as to who is right and who is wrong in this present dispute.

March 5, 1938

(SOURCE: *Young China* newspaper, March 5, 1938, p. 4. TRANSLATOR: Ellen Yeung.)

TO THE MEMBERSHIP OF OUR ILGWU

The Chinese article on the opposite page is a letter written by our Chinese strikers to our membership. The underneath is a translation of it by Alice Dong, a striker.

April 30, 1938

Dear brothers and sisters,

We, the members of the Chinese Ladies' Garment Workers' Union, Local 341, send our greetings to you all, and wish to bring to your attention the existence of our strike, now more than nine weeks old.

Ever since the end of last year, after we were granted our charter, we tried our utmost in every way to get an agreement from our employer, the National $ Stores Ltd., to assure us higher wages and better working conditions. In reply to our demands, our employers asked for time to consider the terms. Meanwhile, pending negotiations, the name of the factory in which we were working was changed from the National $ Stores Ltd., to the Golden Gate Mfg. Co., and our employer claimed the factory was sold.

When we heard of the sale of the factory we believed at the time, and still do believe now, that such a sale is only a means used by our employers to break our unionization and to avoid further responsibilities toward us. The strike was called February 26, and we started immediately to picket the factory and the three National $ Stores in San Francisco.

We continued to picket peacefully for three weeks until the firm obtained a temporary restraining order against us. This prevented us from picketing the stores. The hearing on the temporary injunction was held on April 12, '38. We did not as yet get our decision, but we sincerely hope that when it comes it will be in our favor so that we shall again be able to picket the stores, as we now picket the factory.

We appreciate deeply the help and the assistance that all the officers of the San Francisco locals, and Miss Jennie Matyas, our organizer, are giving us in our strike. We take this opportunity to thank them all and individually.

We also thank our headquarters, the ILGWU, in New York City, for all the support extended to us: moral support, economic support, legal support, and financial support. Every week a relief sum is handed to each of us to take care of arising needs. Legal advice is given readily whenever troubles or complications happen. With such supports behind us, we know we cannot fail. We will fight our fight to the end, and hope to raise the living conditions not only for ourselves but for the other workers in Chinatown as well.

Words cannot express our gratitude. All we say and sing forever is:

> "THE ILGWU is behind us
> We shall not be moved."

We thank you all for the nice Easter party given to us and to our children, also.

Strikers of Chinese Ladies' Garment Workers' Union
Local No. 341

(SOURCE: *Union Bulletin*, May 1938)

ILGWU LOCAL #341, CHINESE LADIES' GARMENT WORKERS' UNION BULLETIN

Dear Fellow Workers and Union Members:

Our request to the owner for a wage increase, reduction in work hours, and improved treatment not only failed to get the owner's sympathy and consent, but instead caused him to reveal his vileness and treachery. First he pretended to recognize the union and negotiate a contract in good faith. Then he changed the name of the factory in an effort to avoid further negotiations with the union. Then under the new name he tried to draw up a contract with the clause stipulating that "National Dollar Stores and the new company are not responsible." He would open the factory only one or two days a week, thus using economic pressure to intimidate the workers. Fortunately, our workers stood together and maintained a united front.

On February 26, the head of our local chapter mobilized all workers to begin picketing the National Dollar Stores factory and its three retail stores in San Francisco. That was two months ago. Then in the middle of March, while we were picketing, the owner obtained a temporary injunction from the court which stopped our picketing at the retail stores, but not at the factory. We are now waiting for the judge's final decision. We hope that the judge, who should be like a father to us, will base his judgment on law and justice, allowing us to resume picketing in front of the three retail stores so that we can continue our long-term struggle for justice from National Dollar Stores.

During our struggle, we have been lucky to have the backing of our New York headquarters, including material and moral support as well as financial, promotional and legal assistance. Dear workers, we must struggle on. No matter what happens, we must fight to the end, so that the support from our New York headquarters will not be in vain. We also hope that you members in all the other local chapters will help to publicize our situation in your areas and continue to give us your moral support.

Happy May First [International Workers Day].
Chinese Ladies' Garment Workers' Union, Local #341
May 1, 1938

NOTICE REGARDING THE STRIKE
BY EMPLOYEES AT THE EMPORIUM

The Japanese invasion of China has brought about a national unity of such magnitude as has never been seen before. While the common people in China are sacrificing for their country, we overseas Chinese, besides giving financial assistance, should try actively to lobby through diplomatic channels for support for China. Our intense efforts have gained us the sympathy of all kinds of American workers and have generated a lot of moral and material support. However, we have not attained our goal of stopping the loading and unloading of Japanese goods and the shipment of weapons and ammunitions to Japan. In order to succeed, we need to work harder from now on to strengthen the bond between Chinese and American workers.

Recently, because of economic strife, workers at the Emporium, Woolworth, and a dozen other stores went on strike and began picketing the stores. Since we are not directly involved, we do not have a stake in which side is right or wrong. However, as long as the dispute is going on, we Chinese should not cross the picket line and enter any of the stores to shop so as not to give American workers a bad impression of us. Our Chinese community does not lack wise people who understand the implication of all this. However, there is always that small minority, who, for the sake of saving pennies, would cross a picket line to patronize a store. For the sake of national reputation and of promoting friendship between Chinese and American workers, we publish this notice hoping to call everyone's attention to the present situation.

Chinese Workers Mutual Aid Association
Chinese LGWU
September 21, 1938

THE CHINESE LOCAL EXTENDS GREETINGS

The following is a translation of the Chinese Greeting on the opposite page, which besides being in our Bulletin, was distributed among a thousand Chinese workers in Chinatown. The Chinese, as well as the English translation, was written by the Chinese members, themselves.

"We greet the New Year with new hopes. A year has passed since our local was organized. In the last year we won our first strike for union recognition, and better wages. Our strike lasted 105 days. We owed our success to the solidarity and determination of our members to fight 'to the end' to raise our living standard.

"We are grateful to our International for the fullest moral and financial support which it gave us so generously. We are grateful to the S.F. Joint Board and their officers for their generous help, also.

"We are also grateful to Local 1100 for the full support they gave us in our strike.[17] We shall never forget it.

"We enjoyed the privilege of a union shop for over half a year, and we wish the rest of the Chinese garment workers were with us. With the beginning of the new year, we hope that they will realize, as we have realized, that a union will help them win better living conditions in all Chinatown.

"We greet everyone of our friends in the ILGWU, and wish you all a happy and prosperous new year."

Chinese Ladies' Garment Workers' Union
Local No. 341, ILGWU

(SOURCE: *Union Bulletin*, January 1939)

---

17. Local 1100 was the Retail Department Store Employees' Union, whose members refused to cross the picket lines at the three National Dollar Stores retail outlets, thus closing down the stores for two weeks.

PART SIX

In Step

The War Years, 1931–1945

World War II was a watershed event for all Americans. It brought the Great Depression to an end and marked the beginning of significant socioeconomic and political change for women and racial minorities. It also encouraged Americans from all walks of life to put aside their differences and pull together in a national effort to win the fight against fascism. Chinese Americans were very much a part of this effort. Indeed, because of the War of Resistance against Japanese military aggression which had been waged in China since 1931, they had even more at stake in this struggle than most other Americans. In stark contrast, Japanese Americans were seen as enemy aliens, stripped of their civil rights, and 120,000 of them were herded into concentration camps for the duration of the war.

Moved by Chinese nationalism, American patriotism, and feminism, Chinese American women responded to World War II with an outpouring of highly organized activities in the areas of fund-raising, propaganda, civil defense, and Red Cross work on the home front. While some enlisted in the armed services, many others went to work in the defense industries and private sectors outside Chinatown for the first time. The war years thus provided Chinese American women with unprecedented opportunities to improve their socioeconomic status, broaden their gender role in the public arena, and fall in step with fellow Americans during a time of national crisis.

Soon after Japan attacked Mukden and Shanghai on September 18, 1931, and January 28, 1932, respectively, overseas Chinese reacted with anger and dismay. Putting aside their political differences over the Communist-Nationalist fight in China, they beseeched Generalissimo Chiang Kai-shek to do the same and concentrate instead on resisting the Japanese. War relief and national salvation organizations formed in Chinese communities across the country and thousands of dollars were immediately raised and sent to support General Ma Zhanshan's troops in the north and General Tsai Ting-kai's troops in Shanghai, both of which armies had valiantly fought back the Japanese despite Chiang's orders to retreat.

From Chinese newspaper accounts of this period we know that immigrant women, believing that "everyone, man and woman, has a responsibility in the rise and fall of a nation," lent their voices and energies to the war effort from the very beginning. In rallying others to join them, patriotic women such as Zuo Xueli, in a speech reprinted in this section, argued that defeating the Japanese would improve China's international status and lead to better treatment of the overseas Chinese. Others like Man Yun and Jane Kwong Lee tried to arouse the patriotic spirit of overseas Chinese women by citing the heroic deeds of revolutionary women in history. In their articles in this section, they wrote that by contributing to the war effort women would be able to prove themselves worthy of gender equality; by helping to liberate China, they would be advancing the women's movement.

By the time war was formally declared between Japan and China in 1937 there were seven women's organizations in San Francisco busy with war-related work. Among the earliest was the Chinese Women's Patriotic Club, which, in the *Chung Sai Yat Po* article included in this section, called on overseas Chinese women to emulate their heroic sisters in China and help the country recover its national honor. In another article taken from *Chung Sai Yat Po*, members of the Women's War Zone Refugee Relief Committee pleaded with overseas Chinese to purchase more "mercy dollars" so that they could buy the necessary materials to make winter clothing for refugees in China. The story of Lai Yee Guey, a seamstress and mother of six children, illustrates the patriotism of Chinese immigrant women who became involved in the war effort. Despite her busy life as a self-employed dressmaker and homemaker, Lai always found time to march in the patriotic parades or dig deeper into her pocket to buy another war bond.

Speaking on behalf of second-generation women, Alice Fong Yu, in articles reprinted from the *Chinese Digest*, called on women to boycott silk stockings and give generously to war relief. She herself set a good example by leading members of the Square and Circle Club to put on fashion show benefits, volunteer for Red Cross work, and lobby Congress to declare an embargo against Japan. May Lew Gee, who was a shipyard worker during the war, recounted in an interview how everyone, including herself, walked the picket lines at the waterfront. "My mother went, my grandmother went, and we all went whenever we had time after school," she said. "It was just such a strong feeling against the Japanese because we knew that all that scrap metal that went over to Japan was used for ammunition to fight China."

Without doubt, the most visibly active commandos on the home front were Jane Kwong Lee and Dr. Margaret Chung. Both were instrumental in mobilizing support for the war efforts in both China and the United States. As the coordinator of the Chinese YWCA and a respected member of the Chinese community, Jane concentrated on drumming up support from within Chinatown, while Dr. Chung, a well-known physician and patron of the arts, focused on outreach in the larger society. Jane's article from *Chung Sai Yat Po* and excerpts from her unpublished autobiography, "A Chinese American," provide us with detailed evidence of her dual allegiance, leadership abilities, and tireless efforts in propaganda, fund-raising, and Red Cross work. As for Dr. Chung, news clippings and an autobiographical essay she wrote for television tell us that she was equally active and effective in making speeches, organizing fund-raising benefits, and volunteering for the Red Cross. Her essay also explains how she came to "adopt" 1,500 American aviators and how she helped lobby Congress to pass the bill that established the Women's Navy Auxiliary, or WAVES (Women Accepted for Volunteer Emergency Service).

The selected writings in this section also speak to the opportunities that opened up to Chinese American women after the United States entered the war. As sociologist Rose Hum Lee notes in her article "Chinese in the United States Today," because China was an ally of the United States, American attitudes toward Chinese Americans improved and they were now welcomed in the armed forces and in jobs previously reserved for whites only. To Rose Hum Lee, this was a good sign of social acceptance and assimilation for Chinese Americans. For San Franciscans like Jade Snow Wong and May Lew Gee, the booming war economy meant well-paying jobs in the shipyards. In an article titled "Marinship Chinese Workers," Jade Snow Wong, who worked as a private secretary in Marinship (located in Sausalito), wrote about the range of jobs taken by Chinese workers at the shipyard and the patriotism that inspired all of them to do their best in building ships to free their homeland. In my oral history interview with May Lee Gee, she reflected on the good pay, assembly line work, and positive experience she acquired from working as a tacker on the graveyard shift at one of the Kaiser shipyards in Richmond.

We know that close to twenty thousand Chinese Americans served in the armed forces, but no one knows for sure how many of these GIs were women. Having interviewed seven of these women myself, I know Chinese American women served as aviators, nurses, therapists, and office workers in the army, air force, and navy. Among them was Corporal Ruth Chan Jang, who in her interview describes how military service turned her life around. The experience gave her self-confidence, a wider perspective, new friends, and the opportunity to travel, learn new skills, and avail herself of GI benefits after the war. So rewarding was her experience in the service that she proudly said, "I would love to be buried at Arlington National Cemetery."

Together, the voices and stories in this section speak to the important role that women from all walks of life played in helping China and the United States defeat their common enemy and win the war. As a result, in the wake of victory on August 14, 1945, Chinese American women, who had given generously of their time, money, and energies through a protracted war of fourteen long years, found themselves in step not only with the rest of their community but with the larger society as well.

Women's Role in the War of Resistance

"Everyone, Man and Woman, Has a Responsibility
in the Rise and Fall of a Nation"

*As Sieh King King pointed out in her speech on women's rights in 1902,
the future of China depended on the contributions of all its citizens. China
would never become a strong nation as long as half its population remained shackled, uneducated, and unproductive in the public arena. This
link between nationalism and feminism was raised each time China faced
a national crisis in its fight against feudalism and imperialism—during
the 1911 Revolution, the 1919 May Fourth Movement, and then the War
of Resistance against Japan. With each crisis, Chinese women on both
sides of the Pacific were called to contribute to the nationalist cause and
prove themselves worthy of equal rights. They always came through with
flying colors, but rarely were they duly rewarded.*

*Even more so than with past nationalist causes, immigrant and Amer-
ican-born women were visibly active in the War of Resistance. They were
concerned about the grave developments in China and especially out-
raged by reports of Japanese atrocities against women and children.
News from China constantly reminded them that their motherland was
under brutal attack and that the national crisis demanded the contribution of every son and daughter. The slogan "Everyone, man and
woman, has a responsibility in the rise and fall of a nation" became the
rallying cry for women's participation in the war effort in China as well
as overseas.*

The following articles, gleaned from Chung Sai Yat Po *and the Chi-*

nese Times,[1] *reflect the sentiments of immigrant women from Guang-dong Province, who understandably felt closer to China than the sec-ond generation. From the first article, "Kang-Ri Holds Rally," I have excerpted the speech delivered by Miss Zuo Xueli at a meeting in San Francisco sponsored by the Zhonghua Minguo Guomin Kang-Ri Jiu-guohui (Republic of China Association for National Salvation and Re-sistance to Japanese Aggression).[2] Like Sieh King King, Zuo Xueli was a foreign student and a political activist. Prior to coming to San Fran-cisco she had attended a student convention in Chicago, where the Chi-nese Students Association of North America was founded for the pur-pose of calling on the Chinese government to stop the civil war and on all Chinese to unite in resisting Japanese aggression. To further this goal, the student organization successfully organized an anti-Japanese rally in Chicago, in which more than one thousand Chinese Americans marched in the dead of winter under the banner "Japan Is Public En-emy No. 1."[3] Now, in trying to arouse the nationalistic spirit of over-seas Chinese in San Francisco, Zuo Xueli made the point of connecting their mistreatment in America to the low international regard for China. If we can defeat Japanese imperialism, she argued, then the world will look at us with respect. Acknowledging the valiant contributions of over-*

1. *Chung Sai Yat Po*, started by Rev. Ng Poon Chew in 1900, favored reform in China and advocated equal rights for all Chinese Americans, including women. The *Chinese Times* was founded by members of the Chinese American Citizens Alliance in 1924 to cover is-sues of civil rights, community welfare, Chinese nationalism, and economic opportunities. Both newspapers were Chinese-language dailies. *Chung Sai Yat Po* enjoyed a wide circu-lation among Chinese Americans until its decline in the 1930s. The *Chinese Times* con-tinues to be read by old-time immigrants, but the majority of recent immigrants today fa-vor the daily newspapers based in Hong Kong and Taiwan.

2. The Kang-Ri Association was organized by General Fang Zhenwu during his visit to San Francisco in 1936 for the purpose of resisting Japanese imperialism. General Fang supported the anti–Chiang Kai-shek left faction of the Guomindang. The association co-existed with the Chinese Six Companies' Meiguo Huaqiao Ju-Ri Jiuguo Houyuanhui (As-sociation of Chinese in America Backing Resistance to Japan and National Salvation) un-til the two merged in 1937 to become Lü-Mei Huaqiao Tongyi Yijuan Jiuguo Zonghui (Chinese War Relief Association of America). See Him Mark Lai, "Roles Played by Chi-nese in America during China's Resistance to Japanese Aggression and during World War II," in *Chinese America: History and Perspectives, 1997* (San Francisco: Chinese Histori-cal Society of America, 1997), pp. 75–125.

3. Zuo Xueli, "Yijian xiaoxiao de dashi: Xie zai Zhicheng kang-Ri shiwei dayouxing zhihou" (A small matter of great importance: the anti-Japanese protest march in Chicago), *Chinese Students Monthly* 1, no. 5 (April 1935): 30–33.

seas Chinese in the building of the American West as well as in the 1911
Revolution in China, Zuo Xueli encouraged every man and woman in
the audience to continue to work hard and support China in its present
crisis.

In the second article, *"Let the Overseas Chinese Women's Movement*
Unfold," Man Yun, taking advantage of the occasion of International
Women's Day, linked the Chinese women's movement with the War of
Resistance. As she notes, only by liberating China could women liberate
themselves. Thus, the course of the women's movement must be redirected
to mobilizing all women to participate in the war effort. Then, remind-
ing her audience of their traditional fighting spirit as Guangdong women,
she called on them to shore up their combative strength and support the
efforts of their revolutionary sisters in China.

Soon after Japan's attacks in Manchuria and Shanghai, women's or-
ganizations formed across the country in support of the war effort. In
San Francisco alone seven women's groups were organized, on the basis
of nativity, class, age, and political orientation, to do fund-raising, Red
Cross work, picketing, and publicity. The earliest and most radical group
was the Funü Ju-Ri Jiuguohui (Chinese Women's Patriotic Club), con-
sisting of well-educated immigrant women who were critical of Chiang
Kai-shek and the right wing of the Guomindang. As early as 1932 they
fired a letter off to their much-admired leader Song Qingling (Madame
Sun Yat-sen), complaining about Chiang's stance of nonresistance and
vowing to do what they could to help China recover its lost territory
and reclaim its honor. "In the face of the destruction of our country and
home, calamity and danger, how can we not give voice to our grief and
anger?" they wrote in the letter, which was reprinted in Chung Sai Yat
Po *(March 16, 1932, p. 3). The club members firmly believed that the*
rise and fall of a nation were the responsibility of women as much as of
men. To this end, they tried to mobilize other Chinese women to join their
group and support their cause. Their recruitment notice, reprinted be-
low, spoke of the club's purpose and the urgent need for women to rise
to the occasion.

In contrast, the Funü Zhanqu Nanmin Chouzhenhui (Women's War
Zone Refugee Relief Committee) was a more conservative group of work-
ing-class immigrant women organized by the Chinese War Relief Asso-
ciation in 1937 to collect clothing and supplies for refugees in China and
to participate in various parades and demonstrations. As the last article
below indicates, members may have been less critical of Chiang Kai-shek,
but they were just as committed to the cause of national salvation. By

selling "lucky coins" and "mercy dollars" to purchase sewing material and by contributing their labor, they were able to send numerous crates of winter clothing and supplies to China during the war years. Such were the kinds of contributions that Chinese immigrant women made to the war effort, which in turn allowed them to move into the public arena and fall in step with the men in their community.

KANG-RI ASSOCIATION HOLDS RALLY
SPEECH BY MISS ZUO XUELI

It is the sacred duty of the Chinese in America to resist Japanese aggression and save China. Everyone, man and woman, has a responsibility in the rise and fall of a nation. What I would like to discuss with you are some ways to advance the interests of the overseas Chinese. (1) Enhance the international status of the Republic of China; (2) abolish all unequal treaties and develop the industries and businesses of overseas Chinese; and (3) publicize the valiant contributions made by our forefathers to gold mining and railroad construction in order to help dispel discrimination against the Chinese in America.

During this trip I have passed through the towns where our forefathers worked, and I have met many patriotic Chinese who told me about the many bitter experiences that overseas Chinese have had to suffer. It pains me even to speak of them. All of these problems cannot be solved unless all the Chinese in America join together to resist Japan and save China.

With China facing a national crisis, if we don't take immediate steps to defend and protect our country, then I fear the future standing of the Chinese in America will be even lower than that of the Blacks. If we can unite and resist Japan, recover our lost territory, and defeat Japanese imperialism, then our allies will look at us with respect. The Chinese in America played a historic and honorable role in the establishment of the Chinese Republic.[4] I hope that you can summon forth those same energies and continue the struggle to complete this historic mission.

(SOURCE: *Chung Sai Yat Po*, August 19, 1936, p. 3. TRANSLATOR: Ellen Yeung.)

---

4. With the generous support of overseas Chinese, Dr. Sun Yat-sen's revolutionary forces were able to overthrow the Qing dynasty and establish the Republic of China in 1911.

LET THE OVERSEAS CHINESE WOMEN'S MOVEMENT UNFOLD (IN COMMEMORATION OF MARCH 8)

MAN YUN

At this time when blood and fire cover the land, and the sound of cannons fills the air, March 8 Women's Day is once again upon us. The giant wheel of time has arrived at a turning point in history. Gunfire and cannonfire have sewn a new outer garment for this year's Women's Day. The struggle against invasion has become top priority in the current agenda of the women's movement. Today we should commemorate March 8 not just in our hearts, but in our actions as well.

Thirty-three years ago in March, American women held a huge demonstration and parade in their struggle for women's rights. The next year (1910) delegates at the International Conference of Socialist Women in Copenhagen approved [Clara] Zetkin's proposal to celebrate International Women's Day annually on March 8. Thus began the international women's movement.

In the spirit of March 8, Chinese daughters shook off the manacles and shackles from their bodies and left their secluded chambers for the outside world to fight for freedom and equality. They freed themselves from their bonds to follow the road of human rights and independence. For several decades, the women's movement has continued in this spirit, surging forward.

However, since the formation of a united front against Japanese aggression on the part of the democratic nations, the women's emancipation movement has entered an epochal new stage. In order to adapt to changing realities, the women's movement has had to change its agenda. For if the anti-aggression democratic alliance fails, then so will the women's emancipation movement. Thus, in order for our women's movement to unfold, our course needs to be direct participation in the struggle against Japanese aggression.

Most overseas Chinese women here came from Guangdong. The vigorous, enterprising and combating spirit of the Guangdong people can be seen in these women, and the history of the Guangdong women's movement is something in which we can take pride. Progressive Guangdong women gave of themselves to further the 1911 Revolution, plotting the battle of Huanghuagang.[5] During the Northern Expedition there

---

5. The battle of Huanghuagang (Yellow Flower Ridge) outside Canton was a heroic but abortive attempt by the Tongmenghui (revolutionary party) to overthrow the Qing

was a commando unit made up of women warriors.[6] People like Song Qingling and He Xiangning were among the prominent vanguards of the women's movement in those days.[7] During the May Fourth Movement, first the United Guangdong Women's Society, then the Alliance of Guangdong Girl Schools came into being, calling for women's participation in politics, freedom in marriage, and equality in education.[8] Then during May 30 the Guangdong women's movement joined the grassroots liberation movement, which called for the protection of mothers, women workers, and equal pay for equal work.[9] At the time of the massive strikes in Guangdong and Hong Kong, more than ten thousand women participated. The Guangdong Women's Liberation Society at that time accomplished much work of historical significance.[10]

From the "9-18" incident to the "7-7" incident, Guangdong women saw a new direction for their work as they gained in national consciousness.[11] During the past few years of war, the women's movement has merged with the national liberation movement, and the Guangdong

---

dynasty. It was a heartbreaking and costly defeat in terms of casualties to Dr. Sun Yat-sen's army. Seventy-two martyrs were later buried at Huanghuagang.

6. The Northern Expedition was a military campaign led by Chiang Kai-shek in 1926 against the regional warlords in central and northern China in an effort to unify China. Its progress was delayed by the split between the Chinese Communist Party and the Guomindang, and the expedition was not completed until 1928.

7. Song Qingling (1883–1981) was the wife of Dr. Sun Yat-sen and his constant companion, aide, and confidante from their marriage in 1914 until his death in 1925. She identified with the left Guomindang and was pro-Communist in her political outlook. Song Qingling was active in war relief work during the Sino-Japanese War and was made honorary chair of the Women's Federation of China in 1957 and honorary president of the People's Republic of China in 1981. He Xiangning (1877–1972) was the first woman to join the Tongmenghui and to be elected to the Guomindang's Central Executive Committee along with Song Qingling. She too contributed to war relief work among refugees and troops during the Sino-Japanese War and was made honorary chair of the Women's Federation of China. Both Song and He played active roles in the women's movement in China.

8. See page 230, note 2.

9. See page 371, note 6.

10. The Guangdong Women's Liberation Society was founded in 1925 in Guangzhou to fight for the legal, educational, and worker rights of women. It actively supported the demonstrations against the British in Guangzhou and Hong Kong that year as well as the Northern Expedition in 1926. The society also published a newsletter, *Guangmin* (Brightness).

11. The "9-18" incident refers to September 18, 1931, the day the Japanese army used the pretext of a mysterious explosion on the South Manchurian Railway line to attack Shenyang (Mukden) and in short time occupied all three provinces in Northeastern China. The "7-7" incident refers to July 7, 1937, when the Japanese army attacked at Marco Polo Bridge outside Beijing, launching the Sino-Japanese War.

women's movement has flourished as a result. Countless women have thrown themselves into the mighty torrent of war. The women's movement has spread from the urban areas to the impoverished villages of the remote countryside. Even peasant women have risen up. In the past the Guangdong women's movement has had many exemplary individuals, such as Song Qingling and He Xiangning, who have been pragmatic throughout their lives. Women such as the two Deng sisters [Huifang and Yingchao] and Liu Qunxian are all outstanding cadres in the women's movement.[12]

Now let us turn to the overseas Chinese women's movement here. In recent years a number of women have also awakened and freed themselves from the confinement of the kitchen and child care to work for war relief, displaying their talents in many ways. In the past few years, as the women's movement began to spread, the feudal atmosphere lifted and there has been a decrease in superstitious practices. Young and old alike seem to be more aware of themselves and of their motherland. This is a development worth rejoicing, and also reflects the dawning of a new era.

Yet, viewed from the current crisis, in order to arouse all overseas Chinese women to actively participate in the war effort, as well as to build up our own combat strength for survival, the overseas Chinese women's movement must intensify its efforts. It needs to mobilize and organize all overseas Chinese women to join directly and indirectly the struggle against Japanese aggression, to save China from destruction, and thereby work for our own liberation and create a brighter future.

In these past years, many educated women have come here from our motherland. At the same time we have an already existing pool of dedicated comrades. If they can team up together, get organized, form a strong core of leadership to assume the heavy burden of the women's movement, and, with concrete plans, speedily and earnestly labor on, there will come a day when the overseas Chinese women's movement will take hold and grow.

---

12. Deng Yingchao (1903–92) was the wife of Zhou Enlai and one of thirty women in the Long March. She was active in women's organizational work and land reform, and held important posts in the Women's Federation of China and Chinese Communist Party. Deng Huifang (1891–1976) joined the Tongmenghui in 1908 and took part in both the 1911 Revolution to overthrow the Qing dynasty and the subsequent Northern Expedition against the warlords. During the Japanese invasion she organized a local guerrilla group to battle the Japanese. Liu Qunxian (1907–41) joined the Communist Party in 1926; she was active in the labor movement and a commanding officer of the women's contingent in the Long March.

Today, in celebrating March 8, we must dedicate ourselves to working for the success of the overseas Chinese women's movement. Rise up, all you overseas Chinese women revolutionaries!

(SOURCE: *Chinese Times*, March 8, 1942, p. 3. TRANSLATOR: Ellen Yeung.)

MEMBERSHIP DRIVE BY THE
CHINESE WOMEN'S PATRIOTIC CLUB

The Chinese Women's Patriotic Club[13] was established three years ago. Its mailing address is 1026 Powell Street. It is now organizing a drive to recruit members. The following is their recruitment notice:

The Club was established in the winter of 1932, when the Short Bandits [Japanese] invaded the province of Heilongjiang and General Ma Zhanshan emerged to resist the powerful invaders with just a brigade. The sight of his flag fluttering aloft was greeted with thunderous cheers, and overseas Chinese opened their hearts and their pockets to donate to the troops. Believing that everyone has a responsibility in the rise and fall of a nation, we gathered over ten women friends and formed the Chinese Women's Patriotic Club. We also proposed that the members should give according to their means and, in addition, should solicit donations from friends and relatives in order to provide aid [to China]. At the conclusion [of our solicitation] we were able to remit a total of $600 to General Zhu Qinglan to send on to the Volunteer Army of Manchuria because by that time General Ma had already withdrawn his troops owing to lack of support.[14]

Since all this has already been reported by the various Chinese newspapers, there is no need to repeat everything here. However, the crisis threatening China is growing worse every day and the ambition of the Japanese keeps on increasing. Yet all that the authorities in charge do is keep making concessions and retreating. Even so, that has not satisfied the appetite of the Japanese. Sometime in the future, China will have to take a stand and fight—an inevitable outcome.

In anticipation of the impending disaster and out of fear for the future of China, we are planning ahead. We need to enlarge our member-

---

13. The Chinese name of the Club was Funü Ju-Ri Jiuguohui (Chinese Women's Society to Resist Japan and Save China).

14. At that time, $600 in Chinese currency was approximately equivalent to $150 U.S.

ship so as to recruit able women the likes of Hua Mulan and Qiu Jin to come up with *wo xin chang dan* strategies to resist Japan and save China.[15] We must treat this with a sense of urgency and learn about ourselves as well as our enemies.[16]

Liang Hongyu beat the drums and enemy soldiers were slaughtered.[17] Hong Xuanjiao took the bracelets off her own wrist to give to the troops.[18] These women can serve as our models. All that we are saying is the result of long and deep reflection. Won't you sisters who share a love for China rise up and join us?

(SOURCE: *Chung Sai Yat Po*, March 6, 1935, p. 2. TRANSLATOR: Ellen Yeung.)

---

15. A legendary woman warrior, Hua Mulan lived in what is today Hunan Province sometime during the Tang dynasty (618–905). She disguised herself as a man in order to take her aging father's place in the Chinese army. Well versed in the martial arts and in military strategy, she won many battles against the Tartars and was promoted to the rank of commanding general. After twelve years of war, she returned home a hero. Declining the emperor's offer of a high post for her outstanding service to the country, she chose to reunite with her family and resume the domestic role of a Chinese woman.

Qiu Jin (1875–1907) was a poet, fighter for women's rights, and revolutionary martyr. When her arranged marriage failed, she left China to go study in Japan. There she became involved in Dr. Sun Yat-sen's Tongmenghui. Upon her return to China she taught at a girls' school, founded a women's magazine, and engaged in subversive activities against the Qing rulers. While still plotting the revolution in Zhejiang, she was arrested and executed.

Wo xin chang dan (literally, "to sleep on firewood and taste gall") strategies refer to the story of Goujian, king of the state of Yue. He was ignominiously defeated by King Fucha's armies from the state of Wu in 494 B.C. Two decades later, Yue recovered and returned to defeat Wu. It was said that while plotting his vengeance King Goujian slept on firewood and tasted gall to remind himself of the bitterness and humiliation of his defeat.

16. The implication here is that by knowing both sides well, victory can be assured.

17. Liang Hongyu (1127–79), a favorite subject of popular lore and drama, was the daughter of a border garrison officer in the Southern Song dynasty. Her father taught her martial arts and military strategies. After his death she was left destitute, so she became a courtesan and later married Han Shizhong, a junior army officer who, with her assistance, rose to the rank of general. Liang Hongyu was given the title of Lady Defender after she exposed the plot of a coup d'état by a group of treacherous military officers. She is best known for her role in the victory of a decisive battle against the advancing Tartars when she beat the war drums to arouse the morale of her husband's badly outnumbered troops.

18. Hong Xuanjiao lived during the time of the Taiping Rebellion (1850–64). She was the sister of Hong Xiuquan, leader of the rebellion, and the wife of Xiao Chaogui, her brother's trusted lieutenant. An able sharpshooter and military commander, she led female troops into battle, defeating Qing forces at Zhenjiang City. After her husband was killed in the battle of Changsha, Hong Xuanjiao escaped to Nanjing with her son and was not heard of again.

WOMEN'S REFUGEE RELIEF COMMITTEE PLEA
TO OVERSEAS CHINESE: PURCHASE MORE
"MERCY DOLLARS" TO HELP WAR VICTIMS

Because of the repeated attacks on Shanghai by the brutal Japanese, the government is determined to mobilize the entire country to engage in "scorched earth" warfare to defend our sovereignty. Our countrymen's sufferings are too great to describe. My fellow compatriots should exhort one another to keep the faith and remain devoted to the cause, to combine our minds and strength, to join hands and stride down the wide avenue of national defense and war relief work, and struggle to save our suffering compatriots and restore our nation. In order to do this, we, driven by our conscience and motivated by sincerity, have assembled patriotic women from all walks of life to form this group, and, exhausting our meager strength, are working together to sell "mercy dollars" in the hope of amassing a large sum of money to buy cloth, cotton and woolen fabrics, to make winter clothes to be sent quickly to the war zone to aid the refugees.

At this time when the country is in danger of being overrun by invaders, war refugees are everywhere, and the wails and moans of the hungry and the cold fill the air. Those who can hear are sad, and those who can see shed tears. We are duty-bound to help relieve such suffering. One more "mercy dollar" sold means one more victim's life saved. Our group feels strongly that as long as the war continues, the war relief effort must go on without even a day's interruption. There is a saying, "To save a single life is better than building a seven-story pagoda." We entreat all our compatriots not to shy away from doing good, but wholeheartedly embrace this just cause. Fathers should order their children and older brothers should exhort their younger brothers to be generous, dip into their pockets, and support this act of mercy.

(SOURCE: *Chung Sai Yat Po*, September 27, 1937, p. 2. TRANSLATOR: Ellen Yeung.)

Lady P'ing Yu on War

"Women, Show Your Stuff"

Second-generation women, not to be outdone by their mothers, also did their part for the war effort in China. The Square and Circle Club, whose members were predominantly business and professional women, raised money for cotton uniforms, surgical supplies, and airplanes, volunteered for the Red Cross and Aircraft Warning Services, participated in parades and protests, and pressed Congress to break its neutral stance and declare an embargo against Japan. Under the capable leadership of Alice Fong Yu, the club became particularly well known for two female-gendered activities: fashion show benefits and the boycott against silk stockings.

The Chinese fashion shows were major productions that featured scores of Chinese American women modeling elaborate clothing from the Tang dynasty to modern times, to the accompaniment of instrumental music. "They were very popular in those days," recalled Alice. "After each show, we had to let the audience out the back door. As soon as we let one group out, new people were pushing in already—just one show after another."[1] The fashion show, which also went on the road in chartered buses to small towns outside San Francisco, did much to generate support for the war effort as well as promote appreciation for Chinese culture.

---

1. Quoted in Diane Mei Lin Mark and Ginger Chih, *A Place Called Chinese America* (Dubuque, Iowa: Kendall/Hunt, 1982), p. 84.

*The boycott against silk stockings, started at the suggestion of U.S.
Senator George Norris of Nebraska, was part of a national movement
to boycott Japanese goods. Since 90 percent of the silk in women's hosiery
came from Japan, wearing cotton instead of silk stockings was one direct way women could express their opposition to Japanese aggression
in China. In New York, the Friends of China Committee organized a large
demonstration on December 11, 1937, in which more than five hundred
Chinese women marched down Fifth Avenue carrying banners that read,
"We'd rather wear cotton stockings than silk ones." In San Francisco,
the Square and Circle Club led the boycott. Wearing lisle stockings, club
members appeared in publicity photos with the caption, "Be in style, wear
lisle," in* Life *magazine as well as local publications.*

*Writing under the pen name Lady P'ing Yu, Alice Fong Yu used the
"Jade Box" column in the* Chinese Digest *to promote her point of view
on the Sino-Japanese War. First of all, she agreed with other women
pacifists that war was neither right nor reasonable. "Women know better," she wrote in the first article reprinted below. "Relatively speaking,
women actually die piecemeal as they watch their sons taken from them
to be slaughtered." They know the futility of war. Thus, women must do
their share to save China and ensure world peace, whether it be in Red
Cross work or in boycotting silk products. "But are our prestige-seeking and face-saving men ready to help them?" she asked.*

*Alice strongly supported the "Non-Silk Movement" and took every
opportunity to remind women not to buy or wear silk stockings. In response to a letter from a "Mere Male" criticizing Chinatown women for
not honoring the boycott, she openly chided those women who would
express horror at the rape of Chinese women by Japanese soldiers and
yet continue to wear silk stockings out of vanity. "It is the money which
Japan gets from our trade that goes to pay for the countless people massacred throughout China," she wrote in an article titled "Each Individual Must Show His Stuff." Strategically set in the middle of the "Jade
Box" page was a description of how women in China had given up cosmetics and fashion for first-aid and military training. The implication was
that Chinese American women should follow the example of their patriotic sisters in China and voluntarily forgo individual pleasures and luxuries for the nobler cause of the common good.*

*In the third article printed below, "Spirit, You Can't Explain It," Al-
ice chose to describe the spirit behind the picket lines at the San Francisco docks as a way of raising women's political consciousness. For five*

*consecutive days in December 1938 more than five thousand people, the
bulk of them Chinese, had come out in the winter cold and rain to protest
the shipping of scrap iron to Japan. Holding picket signs that read, "Prevent murder of Chinese women and children!" they sang and marched
to the stirring tune of "March of the Volunteers" (later to become the
national anthem of the People's Republic of China). As far as Alice was
concerned, this was the kind of nationalist spirit that should move women
to boycott silk stockings and give generously to the war effort and, ultimately, help China win the war.*

FOR PRESTIGE AND FACE

For prestige, face, or honor, men have been sentimentally whipped into
making and tolerating war. Whether in single combat or in groups, they
have gone forth to war to die a glorious death, so they thought, but death
nevertheless. And, paradoxically, man actually can be made to believe
that to die is more beautiful than to live.

But women know better. For to them empty glory can neither fill empty
hearts nor replace hollow hopes. The world torn and bleeding from the
barbarity of war is but the pulling on the heartstrings of women everywhere. Relatively speaking, women actually die piecemeal as they watch
their sons taken from them to be slaughtered. Mothers suffer from the
mutilations and bleeding of their sons' bodies, which are but parcels of
their own flesh and precious blood. This insufferable agony and horrible dying bit by bit has always been women's lot to face—a form of death
which men will never be capable of experiencing.

For this reason, men never knew that women have always longed for
peace. But now men are coming to see the futility of war because it is
bad economics. War is wasteful and destructive. It doesn't pay, as it were,
so men are ready to organize for the preservation of peace. Even the idea
that war is neither right nor reasonable is rapidly gaining favor with them.
In spite of war bombs and planes raining death everywhere, tremendous
forces are at work to influence public opinion to make effective healthy
conditions of peace. Accordingly, men in high places and men of wisdom
are being very helpful in that they are actually keeping calm and cool in
the face of much emotional recklessness and mass hysteria. This situation presages world sanity, and I dare say it can go a long way in con-
trolling war as unwarranted sentiment can make war. In this regard the

world appears hopeful to me. You may call this wishful thinking, but I am betting on sane thinking to win peace. The reason is simple, for there is really no reason for war.

Our women of Chinatown are doing their share in helping China and the world to win peace. In the face of much madness and unbridled sentiment they are showing their restraint and much of it is reflected in our own people. Unlike the last time when war raged in China there has been no attack or animosity of any kind against the Japanese people here. There has been no thought of revenge or retaliation. Our one thought has been the relief of the victims of the terrorist acts of the Japanese madmen. The women of our community are to be complimented. Many hours have been spent by them in the making of flowers and lapel coins for money,[2] in making bandages and in mending of old clothes to send across the sea to alleviate suffering.

Foremost of these women to be commended is Dr. Margaret Chung who has through her winning personality won much sympathy and generous contributions for the purchase of medical supplies to send to the war zone.[3] Others deserving praise are the leaders of the Chinese Y.W.C.A. and the members of the Square and Circle Club. The former group is asking other women of the community to work unitedly and tangibly with women of the world to banish war from the face of the earth,[4] and the latter has initiated a campaign urging the women of Chinatown to minimize the use of silk in the hope of crippling Japan's economic ability and staying the hands of her militarists.

I think this is a praiseworthy example of women everywhere who are wholeheartedly for the cause of sane thinking and intelligent restraint for the winning and preservation of peace. But are our prestige-seeking and face-saving men ready to help them?

(SOURCE: *Chinese Digest*, October 1937, pp. 12, 19)

---

2. As fund-raising activities, women and children made crepe paper flowers and "lucky coins" (Chinese coins tied with a red-white-and-blue ribbon to be worn on lapels) to sell.

3. Dr. Margaret Chung, the first Chinese woman physician in California, lectured and fund-raised widely for the war effort in China. For her story and contributions at the home front, see pages 452–64.

4. Jane Kwong Lee, who was coordinator of the Chinese YWCA at the time, was a strong advocate for peace and women's involvement in war relief work. Her story follows on pages 432–51.

EACH INDIVIDUAL MUST SHOW HIS STUFF

Dear "Mere Male,"

I read the letter which you wrote to a certain young lady and found it most interesting.[5] I certainly agree with you that there is an appalling lack of conscience among many Chinatown girls who continue to buy the "latest shades" in silk stockings to help extend Japan's ability to get more munitions with which to shoot down our helpless brethren across the seas.

Ever since the beginning of this unholy Japanese invasion of China, small groups of individuals in Chinatown took up the stand of E. Stanley Jones, noted American missionary, and others that the only course open to us was to pronounce a moral judgment of condemnation on Japan's aggression in the Far East and to implement this moral condemnation by an economic withdrawal, for "we cannot economically support what we morally condemn." In other words, Japan must pay for this war through her trade abroad and if we continue to buy from her, we help to provide her with the cost of this war. It is the money which Japan gets from our trade that goes to pay for the countless people massacred throughout China.

As you know, Chinatown merchants as a group have submitted to the coercion of group conscience and have openly stopped their trade with the Japanese. And you must know also that notwithstanding severe penalties, many individual businessmen have not seen fit to express their moral condemnation in this practical and vital way of withdrawing from Japan all economic support.

You will realize, "Mere Male," that this is what burns people such as you and I up so. You find people vociferous in their condemnation of the horrors of war and pitifully verbose in their sympathy for the poor refugees, and yet they do not refuse to buy Japanese goods or to spend lavishly on private parties and buy the best wine or champagne in the market.

As a matter of fact, you're absolutely right about many of us being hypocrites. I actually know women who weep openly and sicken over the ghastly reports on the rape of Chinese women by Japanese soldiers,

---

5. I was not able to find this letter anywhere in the *Chinese Digest*.

and yet feel no shame to have their money go to support these soldiers on Chinese soil by continuing to buy Japan[ese] silk.

The fact is, as you say, the vanity of many women is stronger than their feeling for their sisters across the Pacific and whatever moral judgment they may have toward this war.

I expect you know that the China War Relief Association, the most influential and representative organization existing in Chinatown, made the unfortunate mistake of trusting women to their own conscience to register their disapproval of Japan's acts and has not concerned itself with the lisle hosiery and cotton movement. Silk is the lifeline which connects Japan with credit and resources abroad and Chinese women in America can exert considerable strength toward severing this strong and important link.

But you see, people still lack individual discipline to overcome selfish desires, and individual willingness to forego immediate pleasures and luxuries to gain nobler group objectives is obviously not sufficiently apparent among many. And because of the lack of group pressure in Chinatown, the individual woman feels uncompelled to register her moral protest by withdrawing her economic support of Japan's atrocities and to get others to do so. Is it any wonder then, that force is still most frequently resorted to in order to gain immediate results?

Frankly speaking, we as individuals generally contribute to our own undoing. When we are unwilling to recognize the heritage of determination, endurance, and courage which is ours and devote this heritage to worthy uses, unbearable external forces will compel us to exercise it. Then it will be too late to regret our course.

We know full well that words alone cannot help stem the tide of Japanese aggression. It requires something more than that. Witness the films which picture the unspeakable horrors to which the Chinese people have been subjected in the sack of Nanking[6] and the indescribable suffering of China's population today. Although laboring against great odds, their patriotism and fortitude are doing justice to their glorious heritage. What they are accomplishing over there, caught in a veritable inferno, are never-to-be-forgotten monuments to Chinese humanity and heroism.

I know you will agree with me that every Chinese man or woman who

---

6. On December 12, 1937, the Japanese army entered the capital city of Nanking and within weeks not only looted and burned the defenseless city but systematically raped, tortured, and murdered three hundred thousand Chinese civilians. See Iris Chang, *The Rape of Nanking: The Forgotten Holocaust of World War II* (New York: Basic Books, 1997).

lives in the United States, a paradise if ever there was one, must not wait until he or she is forced to show of what stuff he is made.

War Sets New Styles in Chinese Women's Fashion

A year of war has found Chinese girls spending less time in dressing and beautifying themselves. Today from city streets to country roads in the interior, one finds robust and sun-tanned Chinese women whose chief interests are first-aid and military training rather than fashions and amusements.

In pre-war years, Chinese women spent millions of dollars on imported cosmetics and clothing. Now they are wearing serviceable native-made dresses. Their faces are clean of powder and rouge, their hair unwaved but neatly combed, thus saving money for caring of their destitute friends, relatives and fellow-countrymen. Long streamlined gowns are being out-moded by sleeveless, up-to-the-knee dresses which afford more ease, comfort, and economy in making. Japanese cotton-goods and Western-styled silk stockings find little popularity in China's inland where cheap and durable substitutes can be purchased everywhere.

Black satin dresses, hitherto considered out of vogue by modern Chinese misses, have made a wholesale re-appearance on the streets this summer. In many places the wearing of [a] white dress, which easily draws the attention of Japanese bombers, is banned. Also, uniforms of different styles and hues are worn by many Chinese girls who are members of different wartime organizations.

(SOURCE: *Chinese Digest*, November 1938, p. 6)

SPIRIT, YOU CAN'T EXPLAIN IT

From one of our own Chinatown leaders I learned that one can't describe spirit. It was at the time of the loss of Canton and the Wuhan area, China's darkest moment of her crisis, I thought.[7] But the occasion did not alter a bit the faith of our leaders who are still confident of China's ultimate victory. I was wonder-stricken at their spirit.

---

7. In October 1938, the Japanese took Canton after successfully occupying Peking, Tietsin, Shanghai, Hankow, and Nanking. The Chinese armies tried to stand their ground in

Two determined pickets at the San Francisco docks in December of 1938.
(*Chinese Digest*, January 1939; Courtesy of San Francisco History Center,
San Francisco Public Library)

"I can't explain it," this leader said. "We only reflect the spirit which
is in our people. Listen to their songs." Then he sang the Song of the Volunteers—"Cheelai: Arise, ye who would not be slaves! With our flesh
and blood we will build our new Great Wall. People of China, answer
your country's call!"—Some of us listeners caught the same spirit. He
didn't have to explain further.

I was asked about the picket lines at the demonstration last month
against the loading of scrap iron for Japan. There were men and women
bowed with age, women who had bound feet dragging their children
along for support, college rah-rah boys, fur-coated and lisle-hosiery-ed
society matrons, and pretty young coeds, all in orderly procession and
unashamed to carry the banners of protest. They were out there from 7
A.M. to 5 P.M. for four days. They sang songs and improvised lyrics to
old familiar tunes. Neither rain nor early rising in the dead of winter fret
those people. Others hearing about the demonstration were wonder-
stricken at their spirit. Could I explain it to them? No, but I told them
about the songs which came from the hearts of those people. I think some

Wuhan, where the government had taken refuge, and successfully beat the Japanese at
Taierzhuang in northern Yangzi, but the recovery was short-lived. Wuhan was abandoned
in the same month.

of them understood the spirit of the Chinese people for the first time. The spirit that will win the war for China.

Have you that spirit? If you can't explain a certain feeling which makes you want to wear lisle hosiery, give generously to war relief, and sing Cheelai, you've got it.

(SOURCE: *Chinese Digest*, February 1939, p. 6)

Jane Kwong Lee, Community Worker

"To Save Our Motherland and Promote
Our Status as Women"

At the time of World War II, Jane Kwong Lee was director of the Chinese YWCA.[1] Owing to her bilingual skills, strong political and feminist consciousness, and reputation in the community, she was the ideal person to mobilize a community divided by age, gender, nativity, class, religious, and political differences. And to this end, she worked diligently and tirelessly from the time Japan invaded China in 1931, to the Pearl Harbor attack in 1941, to her resignation from the YWCA in 1944. As the fearless commando on the home front, she did everything from writing plays to making speeches at street corners, from teaching courses on first aid to stripping cars for scrap metal. Under her capable leadership, the YWCA became the focal point for women's contributions to both China's and America's war efforts. Wherever there was a need—whether in door-to-door solicitation, Rice Bowl parades, picket lines, Red Cross work, or entertaining soldiers on leave—the Chinese YWCA was always involved.

Jane Kwong Lee's writings in the Chinese newspapers and her unpublished autobiography, "A Chinese American," offer us some of the best details about the impact of war on Chinese women and the range of war-related activities in which they engaged on the home front. They also reveal her diverse talents, leadership skills, political acumen, and unwavering dedication to the causes of Chinese nationalism, American democracy, and Chinese American feminism. After attending a national

---

1. For the first parts of Jane Kwong Lee's story and her earlier writings, see pages 224–41 and 347–55.

YWCA conference in Atlantic City, New Jersey, in April of 1940, Jane reported on what was discussed about the war in China. In two front-page articles in Chung Sai Yat Po, she carefully laid out her observations and arguments for action. She wrote that although Americans were more interested in the war in Europe than in China, given their democratic tendencies they could easily be persuaded to help a weak ally under attack. She strongly suggested that Chinese American youths, well versed in English and international politics, should be the ones to solicit widespread political and financial support, although everyone should work together to rouse the humanitarian spirit of the American public. In a special effort to mobilize Chinese women to action, Jane also pointed out that the war effort provided women an opportunity to prove themselves worthy of respect and equality: "If we Chinese women can work with the men at the war front as well as behind the lines, then who can look down on us? Who will dare say women are not equal to men?"

Representing the YWCA at Chinese War Relief Association meetings and as a member of the relief association's propaganda committee, Jane Kwong Lee took her responsibilities seriously and worked hard to do her part hosting receptions for Chinese dignitaries, sponsoring speakers at the YWCA, speaking out at rallies herself, and networking with other community organizations. She even gave playwriting a try. Although she would be the first to admit that the Chinese-language plays she wrote, directed, and sometimes acted in were "crude" if not "amateurish," they did serve to promote the war effort.[2] Tickets were sold in advance to audiences who came as much for the cause as for the entertainment. In keeping with Jane's own nationalist and feminist convictions, the plays were generally about heroic actions by Chinese women involved in war work, based on newspaper reports. "The intent was to show the audience the voracity of the war," she wrote in her autobiography. "Thus, their emotions were aroused to give whatever they could afford to alleviate the human sufferings of war."

OBSERVATIONS FROM ATTENDING
THE NATIONAL YWCA CONFERENCE

From April 10 to 16, over 2000 women, some from the Far East, some from Europe, representing YWCA groups in every country, convened at

---

2. Jane Kwong Lee's plays are collected in "Lianzhen chu ji" (Collection of plays by Lianzhen), unpublished manuscript in my possession.

Atlantic City and reaffirmed the YWCA's position for more than eighty years—that of service toward humanity in the spirit of universal love. What was discussed can be summed up under the following three topics: (1) the trend of modern religion; (2) the implementation of a democratic government; and (3) the building of a world community. This writer participated in the conference as a delegate and came away deeply impressed. I would like to report on the more important discussions by both male and female compatriots, all of whom were interested in social and national issues.

1. American women can indeed boast of equality with their men.

The March newspapers from the motherland gave extensive coverage of the events and essays celebrating March 8 [International Women's Day]. While women leaders in the motherland were all raising their voices to clamor for "women's liberation," we, on the other hand, could not find any mention of March 8 in the American newspapers. It was as if American women no longer cared to fight for a higher status and for issues regarding their rights. But in reality, they have already risen to a higher status and attained their due rights. That is to say, the women issue is no longer a unilateral problem, but a national problem for all its citizens, and thus a problem for all of the world's people as well. If the problems of the world were solved, then the women's question would no longer be a problem. This is proof enough that the status enjoyed by American women is equal to that of men, that they are on the same footing as men. And that was made very clear at this week-long conference.

2. American women are very concerned about the world situation.

The conference lasted only six days but during that time, all items, big and small, were resolved on schedule. It was only when questions relating to war or peace were raised that people became agitated. For example, questions such as "Should the United States offer financial assistance to the countries at war? Are England and France fighting for democracy? How to prevent the United States from being sucked into the whirlpool of the European War and thus avoid repeating the disaster of 1917?" took up a lot of discussion time. This showed that American women are extremely attentive to the European war situation. Young students, in particular, did not want to see the slightest excuse for war result in sending American youths off to Europe to be needlessly sacrificed. Therefore they wanted a well thought-out position which would, on one hand, preserve peace for the United States, but, on the other hand, also be compassionate toward people and weak nations suffering oppression.

3. The average American is gradually forgetting the war in the Far East.

Since war broke out in Europe, the focus of attention for all Americans has shifted from the Pacific to the Atlantic. One reason is that news of war in the Far East is like yesterday's news, and does not generate the kind of attention comparable to that created by headlines about the European war. Another reason is that people in the Far East are ethnically removed from Americans. On the surface, the Far East problem is a problem of the yellow race. Therefore it is not as close to the heart of Americans as the problem in Europe, which is seen as a problem of the white race. Moreover, Americans are hardly suffering any losses in the Far East, but the world war in Europe has caused a lot of damage to men and women in the United States. That is why all discussions about international issues during the conference were set in the context of the European War. In particular, women students and young people in industry and business have little time to devote to the war on the other side of the Pacific.

4. Americans are extremely sympathetic to China's cause.

Although the European War has captured the attention of Americans, yet the United States is still a free, democratic country. The American people, steeped in the traditions of democracy, are constant champions of weak nations that have been invaded. China has been at war for close to three years, and in reality has already won the approbation and recognition of the American public. Therefore, at the conference, whether in small groups or as a whole body, as soon as the subject of China and Japan was broached, the participants were all in favor of the arms embargo against Japan, of financial assistance to the Chinese government to resist the invaders and of raising funds for the relief of Chinese war refugees.

I would like to share a few thoughts about my observations of the above.

1. Chinese women need to rouse themselves and seek to attain a higher status for themselves.

The status that American women enjoy today did not develop by chance. They had to prove their abilities through difficult stages before they earned public recognition of their rightful status and rights. If we Chinese women can work with the men at the war front as well as behind the lines, to build up our nation and protect our citizens, then who can look down on us? Who will dare say women are not equal to men? As an overseas Chinese woman with over two years of experience in the resistance effort, I dare say that overseas Chinese women do possess abilities worthy of respect from men. Sisters, I urge you to intensify your efforts. However, short-term enthusiasm without requisite training is useless to the cause. Take American women, for instance. If not from higher education, where else could they have gained the knowledge to discuss world problems? Therefore, given the wonderful opportunity that overseas Chinese women have to pursue knowledge, we should forge ahead in promoting our status until we are equal to American women in every respect.

2. Overseas Chinese youths must take up the duty of public relations.

Although the American public has expressed sympathy towards our war effort, yet the world situation is changing too rapidly for the average person to focus his attention on Europe and Asia at the same time. Americans may be willing to help our resistance movement financially and materially, but they have a strong aversion to war. They want to avoid American involvement in the European War, and in order to keep America out of that war, they have urged their government to implement an isolationist diplomatic policy. Although it has not harmed China directly, that policy has made it difficult for China to obtain American aid. That is why overseas Chinese youths, with their facility in the language, their understanding of the world situation and their knowledge of the law, must at all times call the American public's attention to the situation in the Far East and to the State Department policies regarding the Far East, so that Americans will not forget our war for democracy and freedom.

3. Overseas Chinese must at all times rouse the spirit of humanitarianism in the American public.

During the past two years, the Rice Bowl Movement in all the cities across the United States has gained the sympathy and support of the American people, a sign of proof that there are many benevolent and compassionate individuals in the United States.[3] However, since war broke out in Europe, refugees have been on the rise in that continent. After the war between Russia and Finland, former president [Herbert] Hoover immediately spearheaded a big campaign to raise funds for the refugees in Finland. When Norway was invaded, Americans again showed their sympathy. During the past year, because of the persecution of Jews by Germans, Jewish refugees arriving in the United States have also received aid from many charitable organizations. Because of this desire to help European refugees, American efforts to help Chinese refugees have inevitably become diluted. However, if overseas Chinese everywhere could work continuously to generate publicity and devise meaningful ways to raise funds to aid the refugees, they could rouse the spirit of humanitarianism among charitable individuals in the United States, so that even if the Americans wanted to forget us, they would not have the heart to forget our refugees in China, who have been living in hell. Only then would we have discharged our duty as overseas Chinese to save our motherland and help our own people.

4. China-born and American-born Chinese must work closely together.

In recent years, young men and women all over the world have grown very active. While American youths, in particular, have gained a lot of attention, there is no lack of overseas Chinese youths who can carry out important social responsibilities. And since they are steeped in the tradition of democratic rule, they are perfectly willing to discharge whatever duty is required of them when it comes to the war in the motherland for freedom and independence. However, due to special circumstances, most of them have not had the chance to become familiar with the language and culture of the motherland. Because of that, those overseas Chinese born in the motherland should try to treat them with understanding, offer them guidance and show them trust. Everyone should work together, shoulder to shoulder, so that Chinese youths here can continue in the patriotic tradition of their progressive forebears and engage in the long struggle to save the motherland.

It is with sincerity that I offer the above observations. I am willing to join overseas Chinese men and women across the United States, in mu-

---

3. The Rice Bowl Movement, an advocacy effort for war relief in China, sponsored patriotic parades and cultural festivals in Chinese communities throughout the United States to raise money and spread the word.

tual support and encouragement, and race down the path of national defense and construction towards the finishing line of victory and success.

(SOURCE: *Chung Sai Yat Po*, May 2, 1940, p. 1; May 3, 1940, p. 1. TRANSLATOR: Ellen Yeung.)

CHINESE WAR RELIEF

China was invaded long before the beginning of the Pacific War.[4] Chinese all over the world started to work for war relief. We in San Francisco organized a "Save the Country Association" [Chinese War Relief Association], combining all sectors of the community and having its headquarters in the Six Companies building on Stockton Street. America was still at peace. Scrap iron was being shipped from the wharf to the Orient to supply Japan's war needs. One morning, a large group of Chinese men and women, carrying large placards, marched down to the pier to picket the ships. The demonstration lasted more than a week. We did not know whether or not it had any effect on trade between Japan and the United States; all we knew was that we did not want America to help our enemy kill our people in China.[5]

At the same time we went out to campaign for money for refugee relief. Teams went from door to door collecting contributions. Everyone was very enthusiastic. The whole city was in a tense mood. Newspapers were publishing all the war news and reporting all the cruel actions of the Japanese soldiers. We were especially touched by the news that soldiers not only killed, but also raped women and girls. Virginity was precious to every Chinese girl, and purity to one man was of paramount importance to a Chinese woman. Upon hearing such sad news about women and girls suffering such indignities from the enemy, we women here in a foreign land were exceedingly angry. We tried to think of some

---

4. As far as the Chinese were concerned, World War II started on September 18, 1931, when the Japanese army attacked Mukden and occupied Manchuria.

5. Jane Kwong Lee is referring to the Chinese picketing at the San Francisco docks that took place December 16–20, 1938. In the short run, the large protest won the support of longshoremen, who refused to cross the picket line to load the SS *Spyros,* as well as called attention to the war in China against Japanese aggression. In the long run, it launched a national embargo movement that resulted in President Franklin Delano Roosevelt signing an act halting the sale of arms to Japan in 1941.

indirect action that might help. I put out a skit to show that women wanted to do what they could.

Here, Jane included an English translation of her one-act play "Boycott Silk Stockings," in which five Chinese American women resolve not to buy or wear silk stockings for the duration of the war.

The one-act play I put out reflected the opinion of all Chinese women in Chinatown. We did not buy and did not wear silk stockings during the war. We wore lisle stockings. Later, much later, nylons were created; they were called glass stockings and the price was quite high.

Before the fall of Hong Kong, refugees from the North flocked South, and we were told that they needed clothing. Therefore, we went on a clothing collection campaign. I was instrumental in obtaining an empty store on Waverly Place as the receiving station. Old clothing was dumped there every day. Some were dirty, although wearable. I had to arrange them in a closed room for fumigation by formaldehyde. After they were supposedly "clean," I and some volunteer ladies packed them into cartons which were carried by volunteer trucks to the pier to be shipped to Hong Kong for distribution to needy refugees. Those were very busy days for me! Only after Hong Kong fell [in 1942] were we told to stop collecting used clothing.

At the same time, propaganda was going on strong. I, as a member of the Propaganda Committee, wrote quite a few stage plays to arouse sympathy from residents in Chinatown.

Here, Jane included an English translation of her five-act play "Blood Stains Rivers and Mountains," in which two female college students become aviators and go to China "to sacrifice for our country." Although they both fall in love, they nobly put their country's interest ahead of marriage. "We are people who have high ambitions! We should do something great. We should do something for society, for the country, and for the world before we marry." Both die martyrs while serving in the Guangdong Air Force.

The war in China was becoming rampant. The Japanese army was sweeping in from the North. The Nanking government had to flee to Chungking. Overseas Chinese were increasing their efforts for relief. Mr. B. S. Fong was chairman of the Save the Country Association, and all representatives from all the family associations were diligently doing their best to help. Propaganda was intensified. The Chinese-speaking population felt that if China were lost to the Japanese, they would have no country to go back to. They would be virtually people without a country because Chinese were not allowed to be naturalized to become American citizens.[6]

At the same time there were a number of delegates from China to propagandize for the war. There was one Miss Young Wai Mun [Yang Hueimei], who was said to be so brave as to carry the Chinese national flag to the fighters defending Shanghai. She was adored by all the inhabitants of Chinatown; and when she made an appearance at the Chinese YWCA auditorium, the hall was jammed. She made a very appealing speech.[7] Of course, she spoke in Mandarin, which had to be interpreted by someone from the community who understood her language. She stayed in the Chinese YWCA residence and I had to be considerate of her needs. . . .

During war time, there were quite a number of young people's clubs which were active in propaganda too. Some clubs specialized in Chinese music and others liked to put out athletic programs or dramatic presentations in order to attract attention to the importance of helping to win the war. One of the more active dramatic clubs was called the Low Fung Club, whose members asked me to be one of their advisors. For awhile I was very much interested in their activities. The members were intelligent young men and women who recently came from China. Low Fung was the name of the bridge in Northern China where the Japanese first started the Sino-Japanese war.[8] These young people were enthusiastic in doing whatever they could to augment the war effort. They even put out a little booklet to commemorate their activities. When the United States

---

6. This changed in 1943, when Congress repealed the exclusion laws and granted Chinese aliens the right to become naturalized U.S. citizens.

7. Yang Hueimei, famous for carrying the Chinese flag and supplies across enemy lines during a decisive battle in Shanghai, was given a hero's welcome when she came to San Francisco in 1938, after attending the Second International Youth and Peace Conference in New York. In her speech she called on overseas Chinese to "unite and fight to the end, for the final victory will be ours" (*Chung Sai Yat Po*, November 9, 1938, p. 2).

8. The Low Fung Drama Club or Lufeng Huajushe (Lufeng Vernacular Dramatic Society) was founded in 1940 to produce plays in support of the war effort in China. Its name derived from "Lugouqiao," or the Marco Polo Bridge, where the Japanese army attacked China on July 7, 1937, launching the Sino-Japanese War.

entered the war, most of them were drafted into the Armed Forces and some of them were incapacitated. They were really war heroes, both in terms of the Sino-Japanese War and in terms of World War II.

As a member of the propaganda committee of the Save the Country Association, I continued to put out stage plays, no matter how crude or amateurish, to attract attention to the war in China even before World War II extended to the United States. The following is another example of my propaganda effort—a five-act play, put out in June, 1938, before the Fall of Canton [in October 1938].

Here, Jane included an English translation of "To the Front," a play that depicted the plight of refugees and the dangerous work of female commandos at the war front.

The above play was presented in June, 1938, for the relief of Chinese war refugees. All the scenes were based on newspaper reports. It was to show the audience the voracity of the war. As overseas Chinese did not experience the trauma of the actual fighting, they were shown what it was like for their own country to suffer in China. Thus, their emotions were aroused to give whatever they could afford to alleviate the human sufferings of war. I wrote the play and many other plays like this for propaganda purposes. I also did the directing and coaching and all other work pertaining to the staging in the play. Incidentally, I acted the part of the crazy old woman in this play and received long applause from the audience. We have to remember that it was war time and public response was geared to war time emotions.

(SOURCE: Jane Kwong Lee, "A Chinese American," unpublished manuscript in my possession.)

WARTIME ACTIVITIES

It was an unforgettable December morning. As I was descending the stairs with my children to attend church, I was startled by the surprised voice of my cousin on the first floor saying that Pearl Harbor was being bombed by Japanese airplanes. In a hurry to prepare myself and my children for church, I had not had time to listen to the radio as usual. After the sad news was heard, all of us were stunned. I did not tarry to find out what was to come next. It seemed inevitable that the United States would go to war with Japan. We were saddened and felt helpless.

We in the Chinese community had been busily doing war relief work; it was for a war far away in the Orient. It concerned us only in the way of raising money for refugees with whom we had a genuine sympathy. This time, however, it would be different. It would not only cause us a lot of anguish, but would also cause us personal sacrifice or death. We just had to wait and see.

In my employed position I began to assume more responsibilities. Due to personnel changes, I was named "Administrator" instead of "Coordinator." The change in title meant that in addition to coordinating the YWCA-wide program, I had more freedom to expand or limit the work of the Chinese YWCA. Before I was given full range of my exercise of power, though, I was instructed to take a refresher course at the National YWCA headquarters in New York.

Since it was wartime, my traveling East was looked upon as more than a mere occupational trip. To all Chinese it was thought of as a representation from the San Francisco Save the Country Association to arouse patriotism from other associations.

From this viewpoint, I was welcomed in New York and Washington, D.C. by friends and family association members. As soon as I arrived in New York, a delegate from the Louie, Fong, Kwong Family Association met me at the train station and took me to Chinatown for supper. The next day the same lady took me to visit the Fong Family Benevolent Association and to have lunch in Chinatown again. There were other dinners in my honor. When I left New York, a couple of gentlemen from the Fong Association took me to the station to see me off. In Washington, D.C. I was honored by several old friends and acquaintances. All these gestures were not based on my personal merit, but on my reputation as a person with a mission from San Francisco because I was one of the members of the Propaganda Committee of the Save the Country Association. I accepted the honor and worked hard at my assigned post for the war. . . .

As soon as I returned from the East, I immersed myself again into war relief work, except that this time the involvement was deeper and more complicated. The Chinese YWCA had always received requests for a "mother's helper." We would recommend school girls to American homes after school to help out in preparing food for dinner and in cleaning up afterwards. Some girls were asked to live in the homes, but most preferred to return to their own homes after work because in this way, the girls said, they were not at the beck and call of their mistresses. A "mother's helper" would receive about $5.00 a week or $20.00 a month. In those days wages were low, and school girls who could earn a few extra dollars for their own expenses were usually very bright and ambitious.

After the United States' declaration of war, the entire employment picture for these girls brightened. They did not have to work for a pittance. As manpower became scarce, some mothers were desperate. Our office telephone was flooded with frantic calls, but our desk clerk simply took the messages and politely answered that we would do our best. After awhile everybody realized that requesting for help in homes was futile; no one would take a housework job when there were high-paying positions begging to be taken. Even school girls could fill in where vacancies were left open by adults who went to work in shipyards or defense industries.

The fear of enemy bombing was real. Citizens were warned not to strike matches at night so as not to attract attention from the air. Households were informed to put up black curtains. Because the YWCA, as a social organization, could not stop its group functions in the evenings when lights were necessary, we had to put up black curtains. The auditorium-gymnasium windows were high and the hanging of the curtains required a lot of planning and labor on the part of the staff. After the curtains were up, we opened them in the day time and closed them at night. The whole city was dark. Fortunately there were no muggings or any kind of unlawful violence. Aside from the fear of bombing, there was an absolute absence of robbery or bodily attack. Those were the good old days! I could walk on the street at night without fear of having my purse snatched or my person molested. I cannot do that now!

Once in awhile sirens sounded. Whenever we heard the sirens, we hurried to the nearest shelter. Once I walked from the YWCA building on Clay Street to the shelter at Grace Cathedral on Taylor Street. It was a clear evening and stars were twinkling overhead. I was fascinated by the quiet beauty around me and unconsciously stopped in the middle of the street to gaze at the sky. All of a sudden I heard someone say, "Mrs. Lee, hurry! You will be killed!" I turned and saw Mr. Lee Poon Lum [Lim P. Lee, who later became postmaster of San Francisco]. Fortunately it was a false alarm. . . .

There was a lot of confusion in the first days of the war. Japanese people had to sell or give away their businesses. Chinese merchants again started taking over the stores on Grant Avenue. There was a spirit of revenge everywhere; the Chinese hated the Japanese and the Caucasians would have nothing to do with them. The Japanese secretary of the Japanese YWCA at one staff meeting reported that many Japanese ladies joined the YWCA with the idea that the YWCA could help them in some way; but, alas, the YWCA could do nothing for them.

At this time of history, the similarity of appearance between Chinese and Japanese was a problem. Chinese might be mistaken as Japanese by Caucasians who could not tell the difference. Furthermore, we might be mistaken by our own countrymen because there is really a very minute difference or no difference at all in the features of the two races. Very often I was mistaken for a Japanese woman. Japanese are usually short, but there were many Chinese who were short also. Japanese eyes are more slanted, some said, but there were many Chinese who had slanted eyes. Some also might say that Japanese have bowed legs which make them walk awkwardly, but there were many Chinese who had bowed legs. On the other hand, there were many Japanese who did not have bowed legs and could walk much better than other people. There was a strong argument at one of our war relief association meetings. In the end, a resolution was passed that all Chinese would carry identification cards with their photos on them so that, when encountered by either Caucasians or other Chinese, they could pull out their cards and not be harmed. After that, everyone in San Francisco Chinatown could have a personal card with a photo pasted on it and signed by the Chinese Consul General.[9] I had my card properly made out and carried it in my purse wherever I went. No one ever asked to see it.

As World War II progressed, Chinese women devised more ways to help the war effort. A group of ladies gathered in the lobby of the Chinese YWCA daily to make paper flowers for sale. The project was similar to the veterans' selling of paper poppies. When the crepe paper flowers were ready for sale, they were arranged nicely in bamboo baskets. One girl would carry a basket and another carried a tin can. The girls would stand on a street corner peddling the flowers at ten cents each and ask the customers to put the money in the can. When all the flowers were sold, they would return to check with the person in charge. At the end of the day the money was delivered to the Six Companies, where the Save the Country Association treasurer included it in its War Relief Fund. We did not raise money for the people [refugees] in the United

---

9. Chinese Americans, wishing not to be mistaken for Japanese, also displayed signs in their windows announcing, "This is a Chinese shop," or wore buttons that read, "I am Chinese."

Jane Kwong Lee's identification card during World War II. (Courtesy of Priscilla Lee Holmes)

States because the United States was not locally invaded as China was by the enemy.[10]

After the conclusion of the paper flowers project, the women thought of something else. Someone suggested a jewelry raffle. It was a big and welcomed idea. As a rule every woman had some gold or jade trinkets which could easily be taken out of storage. It happened at the time that a principal from a girls' school in Hong Kong was in this country to raise funds for a new school building. Because of the war, she was stranded here. Her name was Mrs. Chan Ng Mun Chee [Wu Minchi], a refined educator.[11] She was exceedingly enthusiastic and donated a diamond bracelet as the first prize. A lady from a neighboring town donated a beautifully embroidered white satin bedspread as the second prize. Other women donated their heirlooms with gracious dispatch. A former lady principal of a school in Singapore took off a red jade ring from her finger and said she hoped it would help a little. As I received it from her, I re-

---

10. However, the Chinese community did give generously to the U.S. war effort via war bonds and fund-raising benefits. The Chinese chapter of the American Women's Volunteer Services had a war bond booth in Chinatown that drew an average of $1,000 a day.

11. Wu Minchi was also an organizer for Madame Chiang Kai-shek's New Life Movement, which advocated a mixture of Confucian ethics and Christian values intended to guide women's behavior and encourage their participation in war relief work.

alized red jade was rare and felt that the person who won it should know the value of it. The whole chest of these valuables were put before a group of women who classified the pieces according to their estimated worth. Then tickets were printed to be sold at $1.00 each. Teams were organized to sell them, not only in San Francisco, but also in the surrounding cities and towns. At the end of the drive, the chest of jewelry was brought into the Six Companies hall where the winning tickets were picked. I headed the committee of women announcing the winners. At first there was quite a group of men in front of the hall talking loudly, but after I made a couple of remarks, the voices quieted down; I was surprised by my own clear and emphatic speech.[12] The winning numbers were printed in the newspapers and all winners came to the Chinese YWCA to claim their prizes. The money [$6,723] had already been given to the war relief. It was considered a success.

At the beginning of the war, the whole population was aroused and enthusiastic. People would donate money for the war effort without much urging. However, as time dragged on, some people seemed exhausted and began to feel unconcerned. They needed to be reminded that the war was still on. The propaganda committee met every week to assign work for the coming week to be done. The most important item was the public appearance of a member at street corners to arouse the interest of the listening passersby. Whenever my turn came, I accepted it with stoicism.

The usual procedure was for me to ride in a sound truck provided voluntarily by the Golden Star Company.[13] The truck, with a martial song blaring, would go around all the busy streets of Chinatown and then stop at Grant Avenue and Clay Street. I would talk by microphone to an invisible audience. My voice could reach all the people on the streets and in the stores. It was similar to a Salvation Army street corner meeting except that my talk was about our country at war, and the Salvation Army was talking about God. It was a unique experience for me.

Not only materials were needed to win the war; Christians thought

---

12. Because of her loud voice, bilingualism, and oratorical skills, Jane Kwong Lee was a popular speaker at churches and community organizations. As she told me in our interview on October 22, 1988, "I have a loud voice. I can speak without a microphone and people can still hear me. So people tell me, you will live to a hundred years old because you have a long voice—*cheung hei* [long-winded]." Jane Kwong Lee passed away at the age of eighty-eight.

13. The Golden Star Chinese Hour, founded in 1939 by businessman Thomas Tong, broadcast music, news, and commentaries nightly in Cantonese over the radio until its demise in 1978.

of asking for Divine guidance. They asked for God's mercy for the suffering Chinese. They would pray individually and they expressed their feelings in their churches. Gradually they felt that individual prayers in private were not enough; they wanted concerted voices to be heard in heaven. Thus a prayer meeting was held every Sunday afternoon in one of the churches. At first the meetings were crowded and the prayers were long and earnest. Slowly the crowd became smaller and smaller; during the last days of the war the church was almost empty. The war was still not won. Where were those faithful Christians who cried out in the beginning for God's pity for the Chinese and for God's wrath upon the Japanese? I participated in those meetings and I did not ask whether or not the praying individuals were sincere. Emotions can play tricks!

Money was still the vital item. The Chinese government issued war bonds and urged all of us to buy them. They had dividend coupons. I bought quite a few and immediately after the war cut a couple of coupons for dividends. Unfortunately, the Chiang [Kai-shek] government went bankrupt later and the bonds became only waste paper!

The most effective and emotional arouser for patriotism was the parade. We had parades for all excusable pretexts. The most laudable was the "Double Ten," the date of the proclamation of the Chinese Republic [October 10, 1911]. All elements of the Chinese community participated in the long line of paraders led by the Cathay Band.[14] During the war, one feature added to the parade was a big Chinese flag held horizontally to the road by ladies, young and old, to receive donations for war relief. As the flag passed by, onlookers on the sidewalk and on the store balconies would toss coins and currency onto the flag. When the flag became too heavy from the pennies, nickels, dimes, and dollars, someone from the Association treasury committee would scoop the cash into a bank canvas bag to be counted for refugee relief.[15] Gathering money this way was much easier than approaching donors individually.

The most memorable parade was the "Rice Bowl Parade." It was one

---

14. The Cathay Club Boys Band, which played American music, was organized by the Chinese Six Companies in 1911. At its peak, the band had more than a hundred members and played all over the United States, winning numerous prizes and trophies. It disbanded in 1962. See Thomas W. Chinn, *Bridging the Pacific: San Francisco Chinatown and Its People* (San Francisco: Chinese Historical Society of America, 1989), pp. 55–59.

15. Measuring seventy-five feet long and forty-five feet wide, the Chinese flag weighed over three hundred pounds and required one hundred women to hold it aloft. During the "Double Seven" parade in 1942, to cite but one example, a total of $3,417.97 was collected from the flag.

feature of the Rice Bowl Festival. Buttons were made to sell for fifty cents each. On the evening of the parade, the streets were jammed. All visitors were asked to buy buttons, and the response was tremendous.[16] I sat inside the Six Companies giving out buttons and receiving money and did not have a chance to watch the parade.

The war across the Pacific intensified. As the United States was one of the Allies, the United States would not help the Japanese in any way and scrap iron was needed for America. One day an elderly lady came to the Chinese YWCA and asked to see me. When I met her, she explained that a group of patriotic women were going to a used car lot to remove the trimmings from the abandoned old automobiles for whatever scrap [iron] could be salvaged. I agreed to cooperate. I accompanied her to a junkyard and started to strip an abandoned car. In the process, I thought this was a wasted effort. I continued to take off the draperies, carpets, and whatever was removable by hand. The bare auto body was left for the yard manager to turn over to the factory to make ammunition. I thought the ladies were overzealous, and after the first day of volunteering with them, I quit.

The United Service Organizations (U.S.O.) movement was spreading all over the country. The YWCA, being a social and service organization, participated in whatever was appropriate for servicemen on leave. We at the Chinese Center sponsored a social program every Thursday.[17] There was dancing and conversation with volunteer hostesses. Refreshment was served by the ladies who knew how to cook delicious Chinese food. These ladies were members of different prestigious clubs in the Bay Area who would not otherwise bother to perform kitchen duties outside their own homes. Wartime was different. The response to serve was spontaneous.

In war time food supplies were not plentiful. Food stamps were distributed. In the beginning, volunteers in Chinatown gathered in a borrowed hall for duty in issuing stamps. Meat, especially, was in short sup-

---

16. During the Rice Bowl Festival, held in San Francisco Chinatown in 1938, 1940, and 1941, everyone entering Chinatown had to wear a "Humanity button" or suffer the consequences of being tried before a "kangaroo court" of volunteer judges and fined up to hundreds of dollars. Two hundred thousand people packed the confetti-filled streets of Chinatown during the first Rice Bowl Festival and contributed $55,000 to war relief in China. In 1940 and 1941, $87,000 and $93,000 were raised respectively.

17. Popularly referred to as the "Chinatown Canteen," the weekly event at the Chinese YWCA was orchestrated by Chinese women and paid for by contributions from local residents and businesses.

ply and butcher shops were careful to inspect the value of the stamps. Inevitably there were rumors of black markets and under-the-counter sales.

As the Red Cross was sponsoring first-aid classes for everyone who cared to attend, I quickly enrolled. Later, when I finished the class, I joined an instructor's course. The reason was that I needed to translate the knowledge into Chinese so that other Chinese in the community could know what was needed. After I received an instructor's badge, I started first-aid classes in the YWCA gymnasium for women and girls. In turn, the graduates of those classes received their Red Cross buttons.

I was also invited to give instructions to some Chinese men in a club-house. Meanwhile, I was asked to teach a class at Chung Wah [Chinese Language] School. These students were exceptionally bright and answered correctly all the questions I put to them. All the classes were conducted in Cantonese Chinese.

China was America's partner in the war and the name of Madame Chiang was popular among all Americans. She came to address Congress and in passing through San Francisco, all the Chinese in China-town gave her a tumultuous welcome.[18] The dinner held in her honor was $10 a plate; it was considered expensive in those days. She appeared at the Palace Hotel and many Chinese saw her. One of the girls who saw her came back with high praise for her beauty. She exclaimed, "Wow, you should see how straight she stood! She's really queenly!" Madame Chiang was the originator of the New Life Movement, and when she was here she invited all the leaders of the club in town to see her in her hotel suite.[19] I did not go because I was not a member.

During war time, as well as at any other time, the question of nutrition was important. The problem of malnutrition began to arouse thoughtful attention, and the value of vitamins also began to be emphasized. There was a nutrition course offered at the U.C. Extension campus in San Francisco and I enrolled in the course. I was exceedingly diligent in taking notes

18. In 1943 Madame Chiang Kai-shek toured the United States on a goodwill mission to drum up support for the war effort in China. Educated at Wellesley College and an accomplished orator who spoke impeccable English, she received a standing ovation when she spoke before Congress. It was partly due to her efforts that the Chinese exclusion laws were repealed that same year.

19. The Funü Xinyunhui or New Life Association was a prestigious women's organization dedicated to the principles of Madame Chiang Kai-shek's New Life Movement (see above, note 11). The San Francisco chapter actively sponsored speakers to talk about the war in China, conducted classes in Mandarin Chinese, and held fund-raisers for war relief.

and reading up on references. What I had in mind was that I could teach a class in nutrition in Chinatown. Accordingly, after the conclusion of the class, I advertised in the local language papers of the establishment of such a class and invited anyone interested to attend free. I thought the knowledge would be valuable to everyone and was quite disappointed when only one Chinese school teacher attended. Then and there I realized that adult education was not popular. I had to think of some other way to impart my knowledge to the community.

The best way, I thought at the time, was to inform the public of the importance of nutrition by entertainment, the kind of entertainment I had been presenting periodically for the past several years. Therefore, undaunted, I concocted a variety show and invited the whole community to come and enjoy it. I wrote a three-act play to be performed by my Chinese class students. The W.P.A. provided artists who painted scenes for the play; and above all, the Dairy Council dispatched a speaker to talk about the different kinds of food we consume. Her talk was illustrated by dishes of Chinese food showing the different nutrients in the different vegetables and meats. Before the talk, I distributed printed sheets containing information about nutritional values to the audience. On the evening of this program, the auditorium was filled to capacity and the latecomers had to stand leaning against the side walls. They came to see the show, but to me, they came to be informed of something vital to their health. I was satisfied, but was so physically and mentally tired that I could not sleep that night; I had overexerted myself.

I prepared programs such as this partly to entertain for the sake of fellowship and partly to draw the attention of the public to various timely subjects of common interest. I was enthusiastic about my job, but the job was absorbing too much of me. At last I began to reexamine my ambition as a group social worker. Why not change jobs, I asked myself. The job at the YWCA demanded my time mostly in the evenings when my children needed me most. If I were to get a job working in the daytime, I would be with my family more. After careful consideration, I resigned.

(SOURCE: Jane Kwong Lee, "A Chinese American," unpublished manuscript in my possession)

After resigning from the YWCA, Jane Kwong Lee moved to the East Bay to live. She returned to San Francisco to work at the Chinese YWCA for a few years after the war and then got a job as a translator for Chinese

World, *a bilingual newspaper that was critical of both the Guomindang and Communist Party. When the newspaper folded in 1969, she helped her husband operate his grocery store in Oakland until a series of robberies and burglaries forced them to sell the business and retire to El Cerrito. Her husband died in 1984, Jane Kwong Lee in 1989.*

Dr. Margaret Chung
and the Fair-Haired Bastards Club

"Necessity Is the Mother of Invention"

While Jane Kwong Lee proved to be an important link between differ-
ent factions in the Chinatown community during the war years, Dr. Mar-
garet Chung was invaluable for her medical expertise and connections
to the larger society. After the Japanese attack on Shanghai, she volun-
teered for medical service at the front lines but was dissuaded by both
the Chinese and American governments. "They felt I could do more good
raising funds for medical supplies here in this country," she told radio
audiences.[1] A charismatic figure and a patron of the arts, she took it upon
herself to lecture all over the country on behalf of the war effort in China
and to use her social connections in show business to sponsor benefit
performances in local theaters outside Chinatown. After the Japanese at-
tack on Pearl Harbor, Dr. Chung redoubled her efforts in propaganda
and Red Cross work, making speeches on radio and through the lecture
circuit. She also put in many volunteer hours at the local Red Cross sta-
tion she helped to establish and taught classes in first aid and home nurs-
ing to Chinese American women. Dr. Chung is probably best known for
starting the Fair-Haired Bastards Club, the Phi Beta Kappa of aviation,
and least known for her contribution to the establishment of the Women's
Navy Auxiliary, or WAVES, both of which she discussed with pride in
the following autobiographical essay written for a television show that
was never produced.

---

1. "To Aid War Benefit," *San Francisco Chronicle*, September 18, 1937, p. 11.

After a successful benefit show to raise funds for medical supplies, Dr. Margaret Chung personally prepares the shipments to be sent to China. (*Chinese Digest;* Courtesy of San Francisco History Center, San Francisco Public Library)

Margaret Chung was born in Santa Barbara, California, in 1889, the eldest of eleven children. Her parents emmigrated separately from China in the 1870s and were both devout Christians. Her father was a farmer, fruit peddler, dairyman, and ranch foreman at various times, but "never made more than $45 a month in his life." Her mother was rescued from a brothel and educated at the Presbyterian Mission Home. They were married in 1888. Unfortunately, both her parents became invalids when Margaret was quite young, her mother with tuberculosis and her father with rheumatism. The responsibility of supporting the impoverished family thus *fell on her shoulders, and as Margaret put it, she quickly learned what was meant by the phrase "Necessity is the mother of invention." Amazingly, she nevertheless managed to put herself through college and medical school by winning scholarships, selling medical supplies, and lecturing on China. In 1916 she graduated from the University of Southern California's College of Physicians and Surgeons, becoming the first Chinese woman physician in California. After a brief stint as resident physician at Kankakee State Hospital in Illinois, she returned to California and worked at the Santa Fe Railroad Hospital in Los Angeles before making the move to San Francisco in 1922. Although she had intended to serve the Chinese community there, she found her poor ability to speak Chinese a barrier and ended up building a white male clientele that apparently preferred a female doctor's gentler ways.[2] Nevertheless, the Chinese community always took pride in her accomplishments, especially during the war years when she came through with flying colors on the home front.*

I was born on the soil, drank the water, and breathed the air that is America. I was educated on the taxes of free men whose foresight it was that everyone in this country should be literate and enlightened. I am particularly grateful to be a citizen of the United States with all of its privileges because my parents and my forefathers were Chinese, and had I been born in China I probably would have been thrown down the Yangtze River for I was the oldest of eleven children and most of us were girls. My father was poor, and I do not remember that he ever made more than $45 a month in his life. My mother, who was tubercular for twenty-six years before she died, had married when she was very young.

Fortunately for me, both my parents were Christian and, therefore, believed in giving their daughters an equal opportunity to go to school. My early childhood was very sad. I remember when I was about five, watching with horror as my mother leaned over an ash can, hemorrhaging from the lungs as a result of tuberculosis. About every month I would stand at the foot of her bed all night long giving her teaspoonfuls of salt which is what the doctors at that time ordered in an effort to stop the hemorrhage. For twenty-six long years, each month there would be sev-

---

2. Judy Wu's study of Dr. Margaret Chung's life adds that her status as a transplant from Southern California and questionable sexual orientation contributed to her marginalization in the Chinese American community; see Wu, "Mom Chung of the Fair-Haired Bastards: A Thematic Biography of Doctor Margaret Chung (1885–1959)" (Ph.D. diss., Stanford University, 1988).

eral nights that I would stand, agonized with terror, watching her die a little at a time. It was logical then and inevitable that being the oldest of eleven children, most of them a year apart, that I had to wash the diapers for all of them, feed them—usually there were at least two on diapers and two on milk bottles, that I would have to do the cooking and the cleaning and take care of my mother as best as a little child of that age could. Frequently, I fainted from exhaustion and malnutrition.

My father, who was a good, honest, decent, God-fearing Christian, tried very hard to make a living for his large family and was at different times a Chinese art dealer, a farmer, fruit peddler, foreman of a ranch, truck driver, dairyman. When he was bedridden with rheumatism and I was about ten, I had to go out and try to make a living for all of us, so I would harness the two horses to a low drainage truck. I was too small to reach the horses' necks with the harness, so I would pull them alongside of a large packing case. They were gentle, and I had no difficulty in hitching them up, and I would haul freight. My first job was moving fifty chairs to the Congregational Chinese Mission for which I received a dollar and a half. I was in the fourth grade at the time and could make out Bills of Lading, so for many weeks I took freight to and from the Santa Fe Freight Depot. . . .

Several years later, my mother and the children and I would go up to Mower Park and pit apricots. We got nine cents for pitting a fifty pound lug box full of apricots. I was a homely little child, and there were always some pretty teenage girls around whom the boys liked. The boys would give them the large ripe apricots which they could simply run a knife through and slip the pit out, whereas they would give me the small green ones. I would have to cut clear around the apricot and then pull the two sides open. Needless to say, I did not make very much money pitting apricots, but it was sort of fun because we always took along a tent and camped out, and I still like to go out camping once in awhile and cook over an open fire.

While in the seventh and eighth grades in grammar school, I went to work in a chop suey restaurant in order to help out with the family finances. After school I would go to this restaurant and clean the tables, fill the salt and peppers, mop the floor, wait on tables, and sometimes would do a little cooking in the kitchen. For all of this work from 3:30 in the afternoon until 3:00 in the morning seven days a week, I received the sum of six dollars a week.

Later on, the *Los Angeles Times* put on scholarship contests every summer, and for two years I received scholarships to the University of

Southern California. My third year and fourth years I won scholarships
by entering the oratorical contests. When I went to medical college, I
earned my way by selling surgical instruments, rubber gloves, surgical
aprons, and supplies. In my junior and senior years in medical college,
we had to go out to the County Hospital for much of our clinical work,
and when I was too broke to pay the carfare to and from the County
Hospital and the medical school I would borrow a penny or two from
some of the boys, shoot craps with them until I won about thirty-five or
forty cents which would be enough to buy a half a pie, a sandwich, and
assure me of carfare for the next day.

During my first year in medical college, I slept in a tent in somebody's
back yard with my mother who was very, very ill, and she died a couple
of weeks after the first year of medical school was over. My sister, Anna,
put in long hours helping to take care of Mother, and actually she has
been a mother to the rest of the brothers and sisters after Mother died.
Those very grim days we scarcely had enough to eat. All the time that I
was in medical college I do not remember having three square meals a
day. The manager of a restaurant would sometimes give us trimmings
from ham and bacon rind. My sister, Anna, and I would use these to flavor
whatever vegetables we could get hold of which might be cabbage,
cauliflower, or spinach, and sometimes, on rare occasions, string beans.
Try it sometime. It really makes a tasty dish, and as necessity is the mother
of invention so my sister and I became very good cooks because we had
learned in the years of poverty to make very common ordinary things
tasty. . . .

[Upon returning from her first medical position at the Kankakee State
Hospital] I was on salary at the Santa Fe for taking care of people who
were members of the Santa Fe Hospital Association, but when I took
care of their families I could charge a fee. I had my offices, telephones,
and secretaries free and was working up a very fine practice among some
of the new people of the musical world like Charles Wakefield Cadman
and Carrie Jacobs Bond, who frequently came to my house and played
some of their newest compositions.

I performed a couple of operations on a man and his wife, and he happened to be the Los Angeles Manager for United Artists when it was composed of Mary Pickford, Douglas Fairbanks, D. W. Griffith, and Charlie Chaplin. This man and his wife were so pleased with the results of
the operation that they decided to go to San Francisco for a little trip
while they were convalescing and invited me to go along. I accepted with
alacrity and fell in love with San Francisco at once. At that time, there

were no Chinese doctors practicing American medicine and surgery in Chinatown, and I thought I saw a great future here. . . .

My first few years in San Francisco were rather disheartening. I knew very few people socially, I lived alone in a hotel. I was afraid to go out and visit many Chinese people because of my limited Chinese. They thought me "high-hat" because I didn't accept their invitations where, as a matter of fact, I was embarrassed because I couldn't understand their flowery Chinese. Working for a living, getting a medical education, and caring for an invalid mother and a large family, had given me no opportunity to learn the Chinese language, much to my regret.

Then I began taking care of some of the policemen on the force and their families, and gradually I began to get a very fine clientele among the white people. Living as I did at a hotel, I was called upon to take care of patients who needed a physician in the hotel, and gradually several other hotels in the area began calling upon me for my services when they needed a physician. Now most of my clientele is composed of white patients, and a large percentage of them are men. I have always been used to taking care of men, of course when I was in the Santa Fe Railroad the majority of the patients were men, and when I came to San Francisco within a couple of years I'd found that sometimes men prefer to go to a woman to have their surgery done because they think perhaps she might be gentler. . . .

Then came 1937 when Japan first began invading Manchuria and Mongolia, and I could see that war had not only gone into China but was threatening the United States. I began making speeches to organizations like Pro America, speaking in different colleges and wherever clubs would have me speak. I would go and speak of the dangers of war which threatened them, urging them to write to their congressmen and their public officials to put an embargo against selling scrap iron to the Japanese.

I sat on the verandah of my little apartment on Telegraph Hill overlooking the waterfront, and each week I would see the big Japanese ships come in, unload, and in about a week's time they would be loaded again and on their way to Japan. I told people that this same scrap iron would be used as bullets and ammunition against their own sons, but very few people paid heed to me at that time. However, many times after 1941 people who had heard me speak in these meetings would come up to me on the street and say, "How right you were, if we had only listened to you." However, the American Red Cross was alert as always and began making preparations as far back as 1939 for the day when we would be attacked, and there were stations in San Francisco where people were taught First Aid and where women worked feverishly to make bandages and dressings. I volunteered my services to the American Red Cross at that time and helped to establish the Emergency [Room] in the basement of Grace Cathedral on Nob Hill. Some people do not realize how efficiently and foresightedly the American Red Cross works, but when the Japanese struck on December 7, 1941, we worked feverishly and by 10:00 that night huge packing cases were loaded upon the decks of the U.S.S. MARIPOSA and were sent away out to Pearl Harbor. For this work I was fortunate enough to receive a citation from the American Red Cross which reads:

> In recognition of meritorious personal service performed on behalf of the nation, her Armed Services, and suffering humanity in the Second World War.
>
> Signed: President Truman

The Origin of the Fair-Haired Bastards

In 1931, when Japan began her ruthless, savage invasion of China, a very handsome young man strode into my office one never-to-be forgotten day, and offered his services to fly for China. He announced that he wanted to bomb Tokyo out into the middle of the Pacific, which I still think was a whale of a good idea, but the United States government frowned upon it at the time. . . . Ensign Stevens G. Bancroft brought in his credentials when he first came. He was a graduate of Pensacola Flying School, had had a year's active duty at sea, and a thousand flying hours to his credit. He had been an all-American tackle at the University of California, a hearty hero, hale fellow well-met, a "wolf" among women but a natural leader of men. He lived with his buddies in a small bungalow in Berkeley, and to put it mildly, it was a constant "rat race" and a "dog fight." There never was a dull moment, and mischief was always brewing. . . .

The first seven [of his buddies] came over to San Francisco one night when I invited them for dinner. They were two hours late, because they couldn't find anyone who would lend them the fare to get over on the trans-bay ferry. Finally they found a girl who loaned them $5.00, and they showed up at nine o'clock for dinner, and those seven boys ate enough for twenty-five people! They ate everything except the eggs, which I passed around several times. Finally, Bert Schwarz, #6, blushed to the roots of his blonde hair and said, "If you don't mind, Dr. Chung, we'll skip the eggs this time. The egg man is the only guy who has given us any credit in the last six weeks, and we've had nothing but eggs for breakfast, lunch and dinner, and we are about ready to cackle and lay a couple of eggs ourselves!"

Needless to say, they were very welcome for dinner almost every night for many happy months, and lest there be some misunderstanding, please let me clarify the atmosphere by stating that feeding them was *not* an act of charity. It was the most selfish thing I've ever done because it was more fun than I had ever known in all my life.

They were and still are the most glorious specimens of real American manhood, and having them around was more fun and happiness than I had known existed! It opened up a brand new world for me, taught me to laugh (don't forget that up to this time I had been too busy in a struggle for a mere existence to laugh or to have fun). Here were seven All-American football heroes, with a hilarious sense of living, and from this sprang the famous Bastard's Club, which is now recognized by the United States government as the finest organization of active aviators in America. Known the world over as the Phi Beta Kappa of Aviation! . . .

One evening after dinner, we were all sitting in my office. Red spoke up and said, "Gee, you are as understanding as a mother, and we are going to adopt you; but, hell, you are an old maid, and you haven't got a father for us!" Feeling facetious that night, I cracked back at them, "Well, that makes you a lot of fair-haired bastards, doesn't it?" And, quick as a flash, they pounced on that idea and said, "Swell! We'll call ourselves your fair-haired bastards from now on, and we'll spread your fame into every corner of the world!"

That sounded like idle chatter then, but eleven years later they had made good their boast. In every corner of this planet, wherever men were flying and fighting for Democracy, I had valiant sons fighting the Axis aggressors. From the frozen wastes of Kodiak, Alaska, to the burning deserts of Arabia and Africa I had glorious sons who were winging their way to make this world a decent place to live in. From Suva, New Caledonia, Midway, and the high seas, I have had letters written on Mother's Day—to send me greetings! In Burma and Australia, England and Portugal, I have precious sons who are proud to be called my "Fair-haired Bastards"—and they meet and recognize each other all over the world by silver rings and little green jade Buddhas I gave them for luck and to keep them safe. . . .

Known to all of them as "Mom," Dr. Margaret Chung ended up "adopting" 1,500 aviators. She took a personal interest in all of them, giving each one a jade Buddha as a talisman, writing them letters, sending them gifts on holidays, and welcoming them into her home whenever they were in town. She also organized the Golden Dolphins, consisting of crew-men of U.S. submarines, and the Kiwis, a women's auxiliary that included such notables as Amelia Earhart and Alice Roosevelt Longworth. Because of these connections, Dr. Chung was asked by the Chinese government to recruit the first 200 American aviators for the renowned Flying Tigers, and for her services in the war effort she became the first woman in the United States to receive China's prestigious People's Medal in 1945.

Origin of the WAVES

In 1942, when there was such a desperate need for men to fight on the front lines, I wanted to do something actively to help in the war effort. I had a pair of trained hands, a medical degree, and I felt that there were a great many other women in the United States who wanted to do their part in the war effort, so I went to Washington, D.C., told some of my sons in the Congress that I wanted to offer my services to the United States to free someone else to go out and fight at the front, and they realized that there was a need and a place for women in the war effort, but there were no laws which permitted women to be taken into the Armed Forces. So I thought of a bill which was introduced into the House of Representatives by my son, Congressman Melvin Maas, and introduced into the Senate by another of my sons, Senator Raymond Willis of Indiana, and aided and abetted by another son, Senator Happy Chandler, who was then head of the Military Affairs Committee.[3] . . .

On March 8 Ruth Chatterton and I flew to Washington, D.C., where we were met at the airport by Ruth Judge, Mrs. #68; Lt. Harry Sartoris and his wife; also George and Mrs. Brainard, #370. We went to the home of Frank Morse, then to the home of Lt. Col. and Mrs. Campbell Judge, #368, whose son, Billy, is one of my dear grandchildren.

---

3. According to Captain Joy Bright Hancock, U.S. Navy, the Bureau of Aeronautics was having difficulty proposing legislation for the establishment of a Women's Navy Auxiliary when Dr. Chung, wanting to join the Navy herself, offered her help. She was successful in getting her "sons," Representative Melvin Maas and Senator Raymond Willis, to introduce identical bills in the two houses of Congress. See Joy Bright Hancock, *Lady in the Navy: A Personal Reminiscence* (Annapolis, Md.: Naval Institute Press, 1972), p. 54. I am indebted to Judy Wu for this citation.

That evening Lt. Commander Frank Weld, my beloved #502, brought Ailene Loveland, Kiwi #120, who was the secretary for Senator Raymond E. Willis, #124. Besides being very beautiful and lovely, she was brilliant, and was considered by a great many people in Washington "the smartest senator on the Hill." She knew all the ins and outs of Washington, all the intrigue and the technicalities. She was invaluable as a walking encyclopedia of the nation's capitol. She was an indefatigable worker on my Women's Navy Auxiliary bill; she never relaxed her vigilance nor her interest, and she reported from time to time the progress of the bill. . . .

I called up Congressman Maas, who was just leaving on the next plane for New York, where he was on the investigation committee of the Normandie. I said, "Can you wait twenty minutes for me? I must see you immediately." He yelled, "Come right on over." Ruth and I tore up to his office where he greeted us with open arms and a great big smile. I introduced him to Ruth, who was delighted to see that he wore his green jade Buddha on his watch chain in full view for the whole world to see. I told Congressman Maas what I wanted, and he said, "I am amazed, Mom, that no one has ever thought of such a bill before. There is a similar one for the Army, which has been introduced by [Congresswoman] Edith Nourse Rogers of Massachusetts, which is in discussion now; but I do not see why someone did not think of a similar bill for the Navy. I have just recently returned from a trip to England where I saw women doing every sort of work that men are able to do, and doing a very good job at it."

The next day I went to lunch again in the Senatorial sanctum sanctorum, the Senate lunch room, with Ailene Loveland, Senator Raymond Willis, and his niece. I knew there was no time to let grass grow under my feet, so during the luncheon I asked Senator Willis if he would lend his support to the Women's Navy Auxiliary bill. Up to that time, Senator Willis had felt that a woman's place was in the home, and was not particularly enthusiastic about having a women's auxiliary in the Navy. His young niece spoke up and said, "I think you will have trouble getting this bill passed, Dr. Chung, because the people of the South will object to having colored people in the Navy, and it is certain that as soon as the colored people hear about this, they will volunteer and want to join." I answered, "Well, the people from the South are going to have to make up their minds very soon as to whether they prefer to have colored people fighting for them or have the Japs and Germans in our hair." Senator Willis overheard our discussion and apparently my retort to his niece sold him on the idea of women in the Navy Reserve. He pledged that he would lend his support to the bill when it came before the Senate. He more than kept his word, for not only did he support the bill when it came before that august body, but it was he who introduced that bill into the Senate. . . .

We ran into a little difficulty from one of the Senators who fought against the measure. Just about at that time a newspaper had been writing a series of very salacious articles about this gentleman and apparently they had dates, times, and names to back up their claims. It began to be so bad that the Senate had formed an Investigating Committee, and about the time that he bucked my bill, another one of my sons, #98, Senator Happy Chandler of Kentucky, who was head of the Military Affairs Committee at that time, called me up on the phone and told me that they were having trouble getting the bill passed in the Senate. Impatiently, I said to him, "Well, aren't you going to do anything about it, son? I don't want to filibuster on the thing for six months, and I don't want it on somebody's desk for two years. The need is urgent, and we must have action immediately, and the bill must be enacted as soon as possible." He promised me faithfully that he would do all in his power, so he went to the Senator who was under fire at that particular time and said, "Senator, I have been an orphan for many, many years. The only Mom I have ever known was Mom Chung, and this Naval Auxiliary bill is her brainchild and her bill. Senator, if you will let my Mom's bill pass exactly as she wrote it, I will do all in my power to call off the Senate Investigating Committee." So, a compromise was made, and, in the vernacular, we horse-traded.

When I was still in Washington, I remember vaguely that there was a thing called lobbying. I did not know what it meant, but I thought it meant standing out in the lobby of the House and Senate and buttonholing every Representative and every Senator, but I didn't know who they were or what they looked like, and I didn't have time to contact each one of them. I went to one of my daughters. She calls herself my old forty-niner, Alice Roosevelt Longworth, daughter of President Theodore Roosevelt and widow of Nicholas Longworth, the Speaker of the House. I told her that I needed her help and asked her if she would contact the members of the Old Guard for me and ask them to help enact the bill. Then, because it was during a New Deal regime, I went to another one of my daughters, Kiwi #130, Mary Early Holmes (her brother was Steve Early, Executive Secretary to Franklin Roosevelt at the time). I asked Mary if she would help me get the bill passed, and she said, "I would be happy to help you, Mom, because I think it is a good idea. What would you like? A large cocktail party or a small dinner party?" I said, "A small dinner party." So, on the following Wednesday, I went to Massachusetts Avenue, and we sat down to dinner. Mary Holmes had one end of the table, I was at the other end, and seated around us were the Democratic Whip of the House, Speaker Sam Rayburn, a couple of Judge Advocates, some Senators from different states who could really swing the New Deal vote. As we finished the soup course, "Mom, tell these gentlemen about your Bastards Club." Well, that settled them into listening, and I started to tell them the origin of the Bastards Club. Then Mary said, "Mom, tell these gentlemen what you are here in Washington for right now." Briefly, I told them that I was hoping to have a bill introduced and passed with their help which would enable women to join the Armed Forces and serve their country. Mary said, "Don't you think that's a good idea?" They agreed that it was. Mary said, "When Mom's bill comes up before you in the House and the Senate, would you all vote for it?" They said they would, so . . . with the good help of loyal citizens like Alice Roosevelt Longworth working on the Old Guard and Mary Early Holmes working on the New Deal side, we finally got a bill passed in Congress which was called at first the Women's Navy Auxiliary Bill. Later, it was known as the Waves Bill. So successful has that department become that they are no longer known as WAVES but are part of the regular Navy.[4]

(SOURCE: Margaret Chung Collection, Ethnic Studies Library, University of California, Berkeley)

After the WAVES was established, Margaret Chung's popularity as a national figure peaked. Century Fox proposed to do a movie about her life, and newspapers mentioned that "Mom Chung" would surely be included in any history of World War II. In preparation, Dr. Chung began writing her memoirs after the war, while continuing to direct war relief projects for China and to give speeches at military affairs. Although no film on her life ever materialized, the love and respect of her military sons

4. According to Hancock (ibid., p. 56), Congress finally passed the WAVES bill (Public Law 689) owing to the intervening support of Eleanor Roosevelt and President Franklin Delano Roosevelt, who signed the bill into law on July 30, 1942. However, the Women's Armed Services Integration Act, which granted servicewomen regular military status, was not passed until June 12, 1948.

and entertainment friends remained steadfast. Many of them were at her bedside when she became ill with cancer. And when she died in 1959 at the age of sixty-nine, she had a funeral befitting a public figure. Among her pallbearers were Admiral Chester W. Nimitz, Mayor George Christopher, and famed conductor Andre Kostelanetz.

Chinese in the United States Today

The War Has Changed Their Lives

ROSE HUM LEE

Rose Hum Lee was a graduate student in sociology at the University of Chicago when she wrote this article, proclaiming that the "crisis of December 7 has emancipated the Chinese in the United States" and presented them with "another stepping stone toward complete assimilation." As her article notes, China's allied relations with the United States had changed the lives and outlook of Chinese Americans throughout the nation, allowing them to find well-paying jobs in the war industries and private sector, enlist in the armed forces, and participate in the political arena on the home front. More important, they could look forward to the repeal of anti-Chinese laws that had denied them basic civil rights, such as the right to become naturalized citizens and to own property. "Surely, racial discrimination should not be directed against those who are America's Allies in the Far East and are helping here in every way to win the war," she wrote.

Rose Hum Lee wrote this article from the vantage point of three authoritative positions: as a second-generation Chinese American, as someone who had recently returned from witnessing war conditions in China, and as a scholar who was about to embark on a major study on Chinese Americans under sociologist Robert E. Park at the University of Chicago. Born in Butte, Montana, in 1904, Rose was the second oldest of seven children. Her father, Hum Wah Lung, had come from Guangdong Province in 1878 and worked his way from California to Montana as a water carrier in a mining camp, a laundryman, and a restaurateur before

opening a Chinese merchandise store in Butte Chinatown. After her fa-
ther died, her mother, Hum Lin Fong, took over the business and con-
tinued to encourage all the children to pursue business and professional
careers in China. Upon graduation from high school Rose married Ku
Young Lee, a China-born engineering student, and went to live with him
in China, where she worked as a secretary for various government bu-
reaus and business firms.[1] When war broke out with Japan she helped
to organize emergency social services for refugees and war orphans in
Canton, adopting one of the orphans and bringing her back to the United
States in 1939.

Back in the States, Rose continued to help in the war effort, lecturing
across the country and participating actively in the American Women's
Volunteer Services. With the support of her mother, she went on to earn
her B.S. in social work from the Carnegie Institute of Technology in 1942
and entered the graduate program in sociology at the University of
Chicago. She would finish her Ph.D. in 1947, writing her dissertation on
the Chinese in Butte, to complete two other major works on Chinese
Americans and urban planning, and earn the distinction of becoming the
first woman and first Chinese American to head a sociology department
at an American university.[2] As a student of the University of Chicago's
prestigious School of Sociology, she adopted Robert E. Park's theory of
race relations—that all minority groups, following his posited assimila-
tion cycle of contact, conflict, accommodation, and assimilation would
inevitably integrate into mainstream America.[3] She was apparently opti-

---

1. The marriage ended in divorce. In 1951 Rose married Glenn Ginn, an American-born Chinese lawyer from Phoenix, Arizona.

2. Rose Hum Lee's Ph.D. dissertation was "The Growth and Decline of Chinese Communities in the Rocky Mountain Region," University of Chicago, 1947. Her two major publications were *The City: Urbanism and Urbanization in Major World Regions* (Philadelphia: J. B. Lippincott, 1955) and *The Chinese in the United States of America* (Hong Kong: Hong Kong University Press, 1960). Rose joined the sociology department at Roosevelt University in Chicago in 1945 and became the chair of the department in 1956. For Rose Hum Lee's family history and biography, see her dissertation, pp. 352–55; and Barbara Sickerman, ed., *Notable American Women: The Modern Period* (Cambridge, Mass.: Harvard University Press, 1980), pp. 414–15.

3. According to Henry Yu's analysis, Rose Hum Lee took Robert E. Park's assimilation theory one step further by positing that racial prejudice and the clannish ways of Chinese Americans could be eliminated by eradicating all physical and cultural distinctions through intermarriage. See Yu, "Thinking about Orientals: A History of Race, Migration, and Modernity in Twentieth-Century America" (Ph.D. diss., Princeton University, 1995), pp. 216–31.

mistic that World War II would finally allow this to happen for Chinese Americans. Rose Hum Lee passed away in 1964, soon after she received the B'nai B'rith Woman of Achievement Award for her contributions to ecumenical cooperation.

One hundred and thirty million Americans were very little aware on December 7 of the eighty thousand Chinese in the United States. But by noon of December 8, the country's declaration of war on Japan and similar action by the Republic of China had made the two nations allies. Since then the outlook of the Chinese living in this country has been considerably changed by Pearl Harbor.

One half of our Chinese population lives on the West Coast. San Francisco and the Bay Region have approximately 30,000, Los Angeles 4,500, Seattle 3,500, Portland 2,000. Most of the others are located in large cities in the East and the Midwest; New York, Chicago, Cincinnati, Detroit, and Cleveland have sizeable Chinatowns. In out-of-the-way towns are lonely laundrymen silently washing and ironing. Wherever the Chinese are, it has been possible to count the variations in ways they can earn their living on the fingers of the hand—chop suey and chow mein restaurants, Chinese art and gift shops, native grocery stores that sell foodstuffs imported from China to the local Chinese community.

In San Francisco's Chinatown, merely from force of habit, signs saying, "This is a Chinese Shop" are still displayed.[4] But they no longer are needed; the section today is completely Chinese. The fifty Japanese shops fringing upon or in Chinatown have had to liquidate and Chinese have rented the stores.[5] One of the most attractive shops is being run by a second generation Chinese-American young woman.

Throughout the Chinatowns in the United States there is a labor shortage. For the first time since Chinese labor exclusion began, absorption of the Chinese into American industry has been significant. Whether in New York, Los Angeles, San Francisco, Chicago, or in Butte, Mont., the service in Chinese restaurants is slow. Four restaurants in New York's Chinatown have closed their doors in the past few months. The propri-

---

4. Such signs were put up at the start of the war by Chinese businessmen afraid of being mistaken for Japanese.

5. Given no more than a week to dispose of their possessions before their relocation to concentration camps for the duration of the war, many Japanese Americans on the West Coast were forced to sell their properties at a great loss.

etor of Li Po, an up-to-date cocktail-chop-suey place located in "Chinatown on Broadway" in Los Angeles, said sadly: "I was just ready for another venture. But I can't now. No men to run it."

They have gone in the army and navy, into shipbuilding and aircraft plants. Even the girls are getting jobs. A personal column of the *Chinese Press* notes:[6] "The newest on the defense payrolls are Jane Sai, stenographer; Rose Hom, timekeeper; Jimmy Hom, welder; J. Eric Hom, carpenter." And another item says; "In Fresno, Chinese boys and girls are training at the NYA resident project for employment with Consolidated Aircraft."[7]

The same issue carried the announcement that the associate editor, William Hoy, is donning a uniform. This brilliant young inductee is one of the best informed persons on the history of the Chinese in California.[8]

In War Industries

In Portland, Ore., the Chinese Consul, Silwing P. C. Au, and his wife have done much to promote interracial understanding. For three years they have worked to get Chinese assistants and cooks into the hospitals at Vancouver Barracks. The Chinese make good workers: they are taciturn, orderly, and perform their duties well. Meetings with the union leaders have smoothed out some labor difficulties and paved the way for absorption of many Chinese-Americans into war industries. Recently the restaurant unions invited the Chinese restaurant employees to join their ranks. Although very few Chinese have joined so far, the invitation is significant. Mrs. Au is active in the League of Women Voters, the American Association of University Women (she was recently invited to be the program chairman for the coming season), in the National Federation of Women's Clubs, as well as in the Chinese-American Women's League, and in all organizations aiding in relief for China.

Only a handful of stores dot the so-called Chinatown in Minneapolis.

---

6. After the demise of the *Chinese Digest* in 1940, the *California Chinese Press* was started by Charles L. Leong and William Hoy to continue serving the reading needs of second-generation Chinese Americans. The newspaper went out of business in 1952.

7. The National Youth Administration was established by President Franklin Delano Roosevelt during the Great Depression to provide education and work experience for out-of-school young people between the ages of eighteen and twenty-five.

8. As associate editor and later editor of the *Chinese Digest*, William Hoy did some of the earliest research on Chinese American history.

In June, when the city turned out to welcome fifteen war heroes from the East Coast, tiny Chinese-Americans wearing their gay costumes waved welcome to the visiting celebrities. The flag of the Republic of China elicited thundering applause. The proprietor of the city's only Oriental gift shop liquidated his business last winter at the height of a busy Christmas season and entered a war industry. His wife, likewise a Chinese-American, works in the same plant. An American-born University-of-Minnesota-trained master in architecture found work in a war industry—the first technical job he has held since his graduation fifteen years ago. Previously he had to be satisfied with managing his father's restaurant, but now, his American-born, business-trained wife is doing that.

In the Pittsburgh and Philadelphia communities, shortage of help has been acute for so long that not even labor imported from other cities can ease the situation. In New York, students who used to earn money as "extra waiters" during the weekends have found employment in industries working on lease-lend material for China.[9] The China Institute in America has placed many trained young men in American industry as technicians, chemists, and engineers.[10]

An officer of the China Institute, Dr. B. A. Liu, has been making a tour of the large universities to get in touch with Chinese students, many of them stranded in this country as a result of the war. The Department of State announced in April that such students would be given opportunities to gain practical experience or be assisted financially to complete their technical training. The response of American industry has been heartening. Industrial, transportation, and scientific organizations have absorbed many scientific and technical students. Other students hope for employment in educational institutions, libraries, foundations, hospitals, publishing houses; and as translators. Meanwhile, those who need to complete their training are being assisted by the Division of Cultural Relations of the State Department. More than a hundred have been awarded temporary grants to continue with their courses or to take up practical training in line with their studies. (More recently the Chinese government has delegated the responsibility of supervising the education and

9. The Land-Lease Act of 1941 allowed the United States to give aid to its allies during World War II. The country spent millions of dollars in funding, material and equipment, and personnel to meet the emergency needs of China.

10. The China Institute of America was founded in 1926 to help students and scholars from China adjust to life in the United States. Today, it continues to offer classes, lectures, and a newsletter featuring book reviews and upcoming events.

training of Chinese students in this country to a committee headed by
Dr. T. V. Soong, Chinese foreign minister, now in Washington.)[11]

In the Armed Services

Portland's Chinese community sent a contingent of thirty-three trained
pilots to Generalissimo Chiang Kai-shek before December 7.[12] With
America in the war as an ally, those now in training will be pilots in the
United States Air Force. The Generalissimo has urged Chinese men here
to enlist in the armed forces of the United States as a demonstration of
China's complete cooperation with the United Nations. The removal of
restrictions in the United States Navy and Naval Reserve has started a
drive for 500 Chinese as apprentice seamen. Heretofore, Chinese were
restricted to enlistment as messmen and stewards. The recent requirements for enlistment are American citizenship; ability to pass the navy's
physical examination; age seventeen to thirty-one for the navy and seventeen to fifty for the naval reserve.

New York's Chinatown cheered itself hoarse when the first draft numbers drawn were for Chinese-Americans. Some below-age boys tried to
pass on their "Chinese age," which is often a year or two older than the
American count. Since their birth certificates told a different tale, they
had to be patient and wait.

There are only eleven Chinese-Americans of draft age in Butte, Mont.,
and all have enlisted or are serving Uncle Sam in some other way. One
in the army was promoted to be sergeant, and has gone overseas. A fam-

---

11. T. V. Soong (1894–1971), a financier and official of the Chinese Nationalist government from 1927 to 1949, became foreign minister in 1942. He is the brother of the famous Soong sisters (Ai-ling, Mei-ling, and Ching-ling) and brother-in-law of Dr. Sun Yat-
sen and Generalissimo Chiang Kai-shek.

12. Encouraged by the Guomindang's slogan "National salvation through aviation,"
Chinese Americans started aviation clubs in New York, Los Angeles, San Francisco, and
Portland in the 1920s. Thirty-two graduates from the Portland school joined the air force
in China in 1933. Among them were two women, Hazel Ying Lee and Virginia Wong. Unfortunately, at that time women were not allowed in the Chinese air force. Lee returned to
the United States and was killed in an accident while serving in the Women's Airforce Service Pilots (WASP) Program. Wong chose to remain in China, contracted malaria, and died
a year after her arrival. See Him Mark Lai, "Sprouting Wings on the Dragon: Some Chinese Americans Who Contributed to the Development of Aviation in China," in *The Annals of the Chinese Historical Society of the Pacific Northwest* (Bellingham, Wash.: Chinese Historical Society of the Pacific Northwest, 1984), pp. 179–83.

ily with three sons has one in the medical corps, another in the army air corps, the third in the navy. In another family with three sons one, an engineer, is in the East in a lease-lend organization, and the other two, both engineering students, are reserves in the air corps until they graduate.

K. S. Jue, president of the Shiu [Sue] Hing Benevolent Society,[13] speaking of home front activities, said: "San Francisco has gone over the top in its recent Red Cross drive. We raised $18,000 for the campaign. In the Defense Bond Drive, we bought over $30,000." This is in addition to all the war relief the Chinese here have been sending to China and in response to the demands of relatives across the Pacific.[14]

Civil Rights for Our Chinese Allies

This year, at the recent convention of the California League of Women Voters in San Francisco, the following resolution was passed:

> Recognizing the racial discrimination shown in several Asiatic Exclusion Acts passed by our government over a period of sixty years, the California League of Women Voters accepts its responsibility for education as to the history and effects of the Exclusion Acts leading toward effective opposition to racial discrimination in immigration laws, and asks that the National League send material to all State Leagues.

It is significant that this step towards righting an old wrong should come from California, where the Chinese exclusion movement first saw birth as a state issue, gradually to become national policy. While the exclusion sections of the Immigration Act of 1924 were aimed primarily at rapidly increasing immigration of Japanese picture-brides in the early years of the twentieth century, they worked even more hardship among the Chinese immigrants.[15] The solution to the problem of Oriental immigration promises to be not exclusion by law, but intelligent restriction and selection of those who desire admittance into the country. It seems to the Chinese that those of us not born here should be eligible to become citizens through a process of naturalization as do those who come from other lands; and that the right to own property as citizens should

---

13. The Sue Hing Association, consisting mainly of Chinese from the Kaiping District of Guangdong Province, was formed in 1878. It became the seventh association to join the Chinese Six Companies in the mid-1880s.

14. By then, the Chinese in San Francisco had already contributed over $3 million for war relief in China.

15. See page 11, note 4.

be acknowledged. Surely racial discrimination should not be directed against those who are America's Allies in the Far East and are helping here in every way to win the war.

It has long been recognized that "cheap labor" was not eliminated by the series of exclusion laws. Immediately after the passing of those laws, "cheap labor" was supplied by incoming Mexicans and Filipinos.

Every thinking Chinese in this country and in China hopes that the American people will advance the social, political, and economic status of the Chinese in the United States. To be fighting for freedom and democracy in the Far East, at the cost of seven million lives in five years of hard, long, bitter warfare, and to be denied equal opportunity in the greatest of democracies, seems the height of irony. With the absorption of the Chinese in industry and the proof that they are good workers, loyal citizens, and faithful to the United Nations' cause, racial barriers and prejudices should break down now and for all time.

In California, today, there are fourth generation Americans—Chinese-Americans who speak no Chinese. They live on close terms with their American neighbors, enjoy the same recreation and health facilities offered to their fellow citizens. For them the present crisis is another stepping stone toward complete assimilation. No longer do Americans think of the Chinese as mysterious Orientals from a little known land. Most of these Chinese living among them are fellow citizens. The rest of them, as well as their cousins in the old country, are Allies. The crisis of December 7 has emancipated the Chinese in the United States. It is up to the American people to effect the emancipation by law.[16]

(SOURCE: *Survey Graphic: Magazine of Social Interpretation* 31, no. 10 [October 1942]: 419, 444)

---

16. On December 17, 1943, in response to Japanese propaganda and as a goodwill gesture to China, an American ally in World War II, Congress finally repealed the Chinese Exclusion Acts, establishing an annual quota of 105 Chinese immigrants and granting naturalization rights to Chinese persons in the United States.

Marinship Chinese Workers
Are Building Ships
to Free Their Home Land

CONSTANCE WONG [JADE SNOW WONG]

*War production revitalized the San Francisco Bay Area, which developed
into the largest shipbuilding center in the world during World War II.
After the Japanese attacked Pearl Harbor, thirty-nine shipyards sprang
up in the Bay Area, ready and eager to build the Liberty cargo carriers
and large tankers needed for America to win the war. Because of the labor shortage as well as federal guidelines against discrimination in hiring, all of the major shipyards were willing to hire racial minorities and
women.[1] Chinese Americans, who had long been excluded from industrial employment but who were now seen in a more favorable light by
white America, were among those recruited. By 1943, approximately five
thousand Chinese Americans, five hundred to six hundred of whom were
women, were employed in defense-related industries in the Bay Area. Of
the total Chinese population in San Francisco, one-fourth were so employed, and Chinese workers made up 5 percent of the shipyard labor
force.[2] In contrast, some fifteen thousand Blacks (approximately 40 per-*

---

1. The six largest shipyards in the Bay Area at the time were the Kaiser yards in Rich-
mond, Mare Island Navy Yard in Vallejo, Naval Drydocks in San Francisco, Marinship in
Sausalito, Moore Dry Dock Company in Oakland, and Bethlehem Steel in Alameda and
South San Francisco.

2. Xiaojian Zhao, "Chinese American Women Defense Workers in World War II," *California History* 75, no. 2 (summer 1996): 141. For a larger study on the subject, see her
Ph.D. dissertation, "Women and Defense Industries in World War II," University of California, Berkeley, 1973.

cent of their population) made up 20 percent of the shipyard labor force in the Bay Area.

Marinship in Sausalito boasted of 360 Chinese workers among a work force of 16,000 and took pride in being the first to launch a Liberty Ship in honor of a Chinese statesman—the SS Sun Yat-sen. In a special issue of its publication Marin-er *on "The New China," Marinship had nothing but praise for its Chinese American workers: "They are practical, teachable, and wonderfully gifted with common sense; they are excellent artisans, reliable workmen, and of a good faith that every one acknowledges and admires in their commercial dealings."[3] In the same issue, Kenneth Bechtel, president of Marinship, said as much in a letter sent to Generalissimo Chiang Kai-shek, praising the Chinese workers' patriotic drive and crucial contributions to war production: "We have learned that these Chinese-Americans are among the finest workmen. They are skillful, reliable—and inspired by a double allegiance. They know that every blow they strike in building these ships is a blow of freedom for the land of their fathers as well as for the land of their homes."[4]*

Constance Wong, a private secretary at Marinship, echoed these same sentiments in a separate article. A second-generation Chinese American born and raised in San Francisco Chinatown, she understood the history, hopes, and unfulfilled dreams of her community. With clarity and empathy she wrote about the mixture of immigrant and native-born Chinese Americans from all walks of life who had been able to find jobs at the shipyard, ranging from floor sweepers, cooks, and clerical workers to burners, draftsmen, and boilermakers. Though diverse in background and skills, they were singular in purpose. "They are giving their all to the job because they know from their Chinese countrymen what Japanese warfare is all about," she wrote. "Chinese at Marinship are each in his or her own way working out their answer to Japanese aggression: by producing ships which will mean their home land's liberation."

Soon after the war Constance Wong would write her memoirs, Fifth Chinese Daughter, *under her Chinese name, Jade Snow Wong, in an attempt to provide Westerners with a better understanding of Chinese*

---

3. "We Like Our Chinese," *Marin-er*, June 26, 1943, p. 2.
4. Editorial page, ibid., p. 4.

American life and culture.[5] *The autobiography covered her childhood years as she negotiated between two conflicting cultures, and her young adult years when she struck out on her own, earning a college degree in economics and sociology from Mills College in Oakland in 1942. Then she was told by a job counselor that because of racial discrimination she had no hope of finding a job outside Chinatown. Thanks to a turn of historic events, she was able to prove the counselor wrong. Following in her sister's footsteps, Jade Snow Wong landed a job at Marinship as a clerk-typist, working forty-eight hours a week for $160 a month.*[6] *Aside from drawing good pay, she was able to contribute to the war effort and gain experience in the larger work world. On her own initiative, Jade Snow Wong entered an essay competition sponsored by the* San Francisco Chronicle *on the problem of absenteeism among defense workers, in which she suggested that a vitamin supplement would help prevent colds and that labor and management should get together to solve the basic problem of low morale. Her award-winning essay earned her the honor of launching the next Liberty Ship at the Kaiser Richmond yard, which she did amid great accolades from the press, her family, and the Chinese American community. It was following this major accomplishment that she wrote the following article for the* Marin-er.

Across the waters of the stormy Pacific, China, the mother country from which American Chinese derive their ancestry, is fighting desperately to expel the enemy from her land. Here, the Chinese of this bay area, who hold their heritage dear because they are Chinese as well as American citizens, have found an important way to help China—by building ships.

As they lay lines on steel, straighten plates, weld in the double bottom, they are fighting for China. For even if the ships they are helping to build may not be carrying supplies directly to China, they are helping the United Nations and speeding the day when China will receive the full aid she needs so desperately.

---

5. Jade Snow Wong, *Fifth Chinese Daughter* (New York: Harper & Bros., 1950). As the first major publication by a Chinese American woman, the autobiography received critical acclaim, and it has been translated into seven foreign languages and made into a film by PBS television.

6. Her sister Mary or Jade Precious Stone worked as a draftswoman at Marinship.

Jade Snow Wong (left), assisted by her sister Jade Precious Stone (right), prepares to christen the Liberty Ship SS *William A. Jones* in 1943. (Courtesy of
Jade Snow Wong)

Striking Contrast

I cannot help but think of the contrast between the present life of these
Marinship Chinese, and life as it must have been in pre-war China, twenty
years ago. One was a bookkeeper in a village rice store, another a respected
teacher of Chinese classics, the third a housewife dutifully caring for home,
babies, and chickens. Whatever the occupation, it was characterized by
leisure and stability for these were the characteristics of their culture.[7] But

_____

7. Life in China was far from leisurely and stable at the time of massive migration to California in the mid–nineteenth century. Peasants in Guangdong Province were particularly

rumors of golden fortunes in America reached the Cantonese, and they came over in search of comfortable savings with which they could return to China. The immigrants settled together in a location now world-famous as colorful San Francisco's Chinatown, for their protection, pleasure, and convenience—not for the tourist glamour which has suddenly been Chinatown's to commercialize consciously in the last five years. Chinatown meant home to the Chinese. It was where they could have their controversies settled, their grievances aired by Chinese tradition through their own governmental organizations. It was where they could have their imported delicacies, their bamboo shoots and bird nests. In Chinatown they could attend their operas, sit around evenings to philosophize. Barred from United States citizenship, they held fast to things Chinese and memories Chinese.

Some of them, true to plans, made their fortunes and returned to China, but some of them liked it here, liked the idea of bringing up their children in America and sending them to college, liked their comfortable businesses in Chinatown.

The second generation from its infancy learned about their heritage—Chinese ideas, ethics and ideals of their elders. Their American heritage they learned from their teachers. According to their adjustments, many of them retained basic Chinese characteristics, while others became extremely Americanized. Some chose to follow their fathers' well-established businesses. Others went into the professions—doctors and lawyers, serving the 18,000 Chinese who populate San Francisco.[8]

Best Workers

With this war, Chinese workers have entered war industries in enormous numbers, applying to their jobs the same loyalty, patience, care, while preserving that individual dignity which they are proud to claim as a Chinese characteristic. Marinship foremen and supervisors will tell you that some of their best workers are Chinese. They are giving their all to the

---

hard hit by poverty conditions and political instability caused by imperialist incursions, peasant rebellions, interethnic feuds, and natural calamities. Even after the 1911 Revolution and the establishment of the Republic of China, life for most Chinese remained precarious as first the warlords, then the Communists and Nationalists, and finally the Japanese fought for control of China.

8. It should be noted that until World War II most Chinese Americans had no choice but to work in Chinatown because of racial discrimination in the larger labor market.

job because they know from their Chinese countrymen what Japanese warfare is all about.

At Marinship, a mixture of older and second generations comes from all walks of life. Some are university graduates, some are older Chinese who were perhaps printers or cooks, some are women who were sheltered housewives. I know two mothers who for years had sewn coveralls for my father with their children under their eye while they worked, and kept house also. Now they are at Marinship picking up litter paper—and they don't understand a word of English! It is a revolutionary turn to Chinese family life.

The paper picker-uppers who keep the yard neat, the cook who prepares wholesome food, the burner who cuts with precision and patience, the draftsman who draws with care and accuracy, the timekeeper who records working hours, the boilermaker helper who fills the buckets with essential shifters' hardware, the girl who makes travel reservations—these Chinese at Marinship are each in his or her own way working out their answer to Japanese aggression: by producing ships which will mean their home land's liberation.

(SOURCE: *Marin-er*, June 26, 1943, p. 3)

Following the publication of this article, Jade Snow Wong developed a back problem and had to undergo surgery. Also realizing that she had little hope of advancement because of gender discrimination, she left her job at Marinship and embarked on a career as a writer and ceramist. In 1950, the same year Fifth Chinese Daughter *was published, she married Woodrow Ong, an American-born Chinese businessman. They had four children—Mark, Tyi, Ellora, and Lance. In 1975 she wrote* No Chinese Stranger, *in which she described her new roles as wife and mother, and her first trip to China, an experience that helped her reconnect to her cultural roots and reappraise her ethnic identity.[9] Despite her busy schedule as a homemaker, artist, and world traveler, Jade Snow Wong has always found time to volunteer with organizations such as the Mills College Alumnae Association, Chinese Culture Foundation of San Francisco, California Council for the Humanities, and San Francisco Public Library. Today, at the age of seventy-seven, she still operates her gift shop and travel agency, Jade Snow Wong, in San Francisco.*

---

9. Jade Snow Wong, *No Chinese Stranger* (New York: Harper & Row, 1975).

May Lew Gee, Shipyard Worker

"I Was a Tacker on the Graveyard Shift"

The largest shipyard in the San Francisco Bay Area, the Henry J. Kaiser shipyard in Richmond, boasted that it employed twenty thousand women out of a total work force of ninety thousand, as well as five all-Chinese male work crews in pre-fab that were always ahead of schedule. Chinese women workers, however, were integrated into the various units as office clerks, draftswomen, welders, burners, and in other semiskilled positions. Although there were older, married women such as Ah Yoke Gee, mother of six and a welder in Richmond yard Number Two, and Minnie Lee, who worked in the electric shop in yard Number Three along with her two daughters and one daughter-in-law, the majority were single, second-generation women with at least a high school education, like May Lew Gee, who worked as a tacker in yard Number Three from 1942 to 1943.[1]

May Lew Gee was born in Chico, California, in 1924, the eldest of five children. Her parents were devout Presbyterians. When she was eight years old her father died, and her family moved to San Francisco Chinatown. She said she was always more liberal than her Chinese peers in San Francisco. "Most of the girls I went to school with had really old-

---

1. Kaiser had four shipyards: Richmond Number One, Number Two, Number Three A, and Number Three. A tacker roughly fastened pieces of plates together for the welder to weld over to desired standards. For a study of Chinese women shipyard workers, including profiles of these women, see Xiaojian Zhao, "Chinese American Women Defense Workers in World War II," *California History* 75, no. 2 (summer 1996): 139–53.

*fashioned parents and they had to go by very strict Chinese customs,"
she told me in an interview. "My mother was born in China, but she
spent her first years in a small town [Chico] where there were only three
or four Chinese families. She adopted a lot of new customs and did not
question any of the things I did because other people did them too."
This liberal upbringing helps to explain May's political activism today
and her attitude toward discrimination: "I have been very lucky all my
life. I have never really experienced discrimination. If there was, it didn't
bother me because I figured it wasn't my problem. It's other people's
problem if they don't accept me. I've never let it deter me from doing
anything."*

*As I listened to May Lee Gee's life story one Saturday morning in her
ice cream parlor in Pacifica, California, I came to understand what she
meant by that last statement. Among her many accomplishments, she has
been a shipyard worker, WAC (member of the Women's Army Corps),
restaurateur, and realtor. She was the first Chinese to buy a house in
Pacifica, has served seventeen years on the Pacifica Water Board and twelve
years on the Planning Commission, was the only woman member of the
Cathay Post No. 384 (a Chinese American veterans' group), incoming
president of the Kiwanis Club, and had just been reelected to the Central
Democratic Committee of San Mateo County at the time of our interview. Of course, it also helps that May has always been an energetic person, requiring only four or five hours of sleep, an attribute that sustained
her through the shipyard days when she worked the graveyard shift.*

*Although May has much to share about her long and active life, I asked
her to focus on her memories of World War II, particularly working in
the shipyard. She started with what she remembered about the Sino-
Japanese war effort in the community, and I could sense her patriotism
rising as she described events surrounding the attack on Pearl Harbor.
"There was this giant headline that said, 'WAR!' It struck me and I was
just shocked." As shipyards began recruiting heavily in Chinatown, the
word got around to May, who was ready for a job but, even more, a patriotic job.*

"They're Sending Scrap Metal to Japan to Kill Our People!"

[Do you remember any of the activities in support of the war effort in
China?] Oh yeah, we used to picket down at Pier 45 when they were

shipping scrap iron to Japan.[2] We used to have fund-raisers in Chinatown to send money back to Chiang Kai-shek to fight the Japanese. And
my mother used to fold bandages with the Red Cross. Then all the women
used to march down Grant Avenue during the parades. They would carry
this huge Chinese flag, about the width of the street, down the street.
People used to throw money into the flag and then they would take that
money as a contribution to the war effort.[3]

[Who did you go with to picket?] My mother went, my grandmother
went, and we all went whenever we had time after school. That was part
of living in Chinatown. It was pretty close knit. When we picketed at
the waterfront, everybody was invited down, anybody who could spare
the time. They used to go in shifts. There were hundreds of people, [in-
cluding] young children, ladies. Some women came with their babies. We
just kept picketing. It was like a demonstration today, except it was a
peaceful march. Some people carried signs. We walked around in a circle and I would be reading my homework while doing it. (*laughs*) That's
the first time we ever did that. It was just such a strong feeling against
the Japanese because we knew that all that scrap metal that went over
to Japan was used for ammunition to fight China. And we couldn't just
sit back and let them do it. Every time they loaded a ship, we would have
a demonstration to alert the people: "This is what they're doing. They're
sending scrap metal to Japan to kill our people!"

Immigrant women like my mother were expected to help because that
generation had ties with the mainland. We were more removed and we
didn't feel the same ties. During my three years at Francisco Junior High
School, we had one Japanese student, a girl. And she and I were very
good friends. Yet after the Japanese invaded China, I didn't hold it against
her because it wasn't her fault but her government's, her ancestors'. Even
when I went down to picket at Pier 45 against the scrap iron shipment,
she and I were still friends. I guess it was because we didn't connect ourselves with China, so we didn't connect her with Japan.

"Everybody Was Just Stunned"

[Can you describe your reaction to the Pearl Harbor attack?] I remember it was on a Sunday. I was in church, the Chinese Presbyterian Church

---

2. See page 438, note 5.
3. See page 447, note 15.

on Stockton Street. The service was at noon. Someone came up to the pulpit in the middle of the service with a little note. And the minister looked at the congregation and said, "We've been attacked at Pearl Harbor. Let us pray." So we all prayed. I was seventeen then, and it just didn't register with me. War was something that happened elsewhere.

At that time, I was working part-time in a little cafe on Polk Street. Right after church service, I took the bus up Sacramento Street, all the way to Polk Street. I got off the trolley and there was this giant headline that said, "WAR!" It struck me and I was just shocked. By the time I got to the cafe, all the radio stations were giving an account of the attack. All of us huddled in front of the radio. Most of the women were crying because we were scared. We were at war. The streets were quiet and we didn't have any customers all day. Everybody was just stunned.

"It Was the Patriotic Thing to Do"

The war had just started in December 1941. Within six months Kaiser had built three shipyards over in Richmond, and shipyards were springing up in Sausalito, Hunter's Point, Benicia.[4] There were jobs all over the place. Everyone was going over to Richmond. It was part of the war effort. It was the patriotic thing to do, to work in some kind of war industry. That was also the natural thing to do in those days. By the time you were in the junior year of high school, you were preparing yourself for employment. I think 75 percent of the women went to work in some office. Not very many [families] could afford to send their children—especially girls—to college. It was very difficult to even get a civil service job in those days. [Was it because there was discrimination?] I think so. We never questioned it. We just said, "Well, I don't think they're hiring anybody for this, that, or the other." So we never even bothered to try.

[How did you end up working at Kaiser?] I think someone told me they were hiring, because the grapevine was terrific. I just went over to Richmond. They had hiring halls over there and they just about took everyone. We joined the Boilermakers' Union and they placed you.[5] They

---

4. See page 473, note 1.

5. The American Federation of Labor negotiated a "closed shop" agreement with shipyard employers in April 1941 that granted union control over employment, upgrading, and seniority. The Boilermakers' Union controlled 65 percent of job classifications in the shipbuilding industry. See Xiaojian Zhao, "Women and Defense Industries in World War II" (Ph.D. diss., University of California, Berkeley, 1973), p. 110.

had to train us because nobody had experience building ships. I think I had one or two weeks' worth of on-the-job training. It was very brief.[6]

I started out as what they called a tacker. They tacked together pieces of metal where you put up the bulkhead—the upright partition that separated parts of the ship. Then the welder came by and welded the pieces together. The welders had to be journeymen, experts, so they wouldn't burn holes into the metal. Because I was so small [five feet tall], I kept working the double bottoms [the space between the inside and outside of the hull]. The double bottoms are about four feet tall. And at that time, we were making $1.26 an hour. That was good wages. Everybody else was making 25 cents an hour working elsewhere. And when you became a journeymen, you made $1.38 an hour. That was great money.

[Were there a lot of Chinese working there?] Quite a few because the pay was so good. Some were older men who were not eligible for the draft. Lots of women too. Most of the Chinese people worked the day shift. I worked the graveyard shift because we got a night differential. We got [15 percent] more pay. We started at 12:30 and ended at 8 o'-clock in the morning. I used to go down to the ferry building and take the ferry boat at night. It docked right near the shipyard and took about twenty minutes. In those days, it was very safe. Chinatown had restaurants open twenty-four hours. There was no violence, no fear, and no difference between day and night.

Then there was overtime on weekends—Saturday and Sunday. At the beginning, they didn't have it. Then after that, the shipyards were going seven days a week, twenty-four hours a day continuously. Sometimes on weekends, they had to put on more people when there was a rush job or they were behind schedule. I would go in both days if it was offered. At that time I was just a kid, just out of high school. I had a lot of energy. The graveyard shift and overtime gave me a little more money, and then it gave me more free time during the day for my other activities. (*laughs*) I usually got off at 7:30 or 8 o'clock and I slept about four or five hours. Then I had my afternoons or evenings free for activities—dances and church activities.

[Did you have to wear special clothing?] Yes. When we got to work,

---

6. In order to speed up production, shipyards operated on an assembly line and prefabrication basis, training large numbers of semiskilled workers in a few weeks to perform specific tasks. Also, because women were perceived as temporary workers, it was not considered necessary for them to acquire a comprehensive knowledge of the trade. See Zhao, "Women and Defense Industries," pp. 87–93.

we would change into our work clothes. We wore black hoods that you pulled down to protect your eyes. We had the really heavy, heavy leather jackets, overalls, and boots. (They issued them to you and took it out of your paycheck.) And we had to learn to use machines and carry our lines down from the machines to where we were working. It was just like an assembly line. You did the same thing over and over again. They figured that's the best way to get the most work out of you because you were familiar with what you were doing. [Did you find the work monotonous or dangerous?] No, we never even thought about it. We heard about accidents, but I never saw any.[7] We heard about people drowning, [who] fell off the ship because they were careless. Maybe they fell asleep and fell overboard. But we never paid much attention. We just kept working. Every couple of days there was a new ship and you started all over again. It went on twenty-four hours. You might be working on a ship for a couple of days. Before you know it, you come back the next day, you had another ship, another hull to start up. They were building them faster than you could even count. It took a few days to build a ship, and they always launched it during the day shift [so she never got to see it.][8]

[Were the Chinese segregated into their own units?] No, I think it was such a big yard that the Chinese got spread out. [Were the Chinese mainly at the lower-level jobs?] There were quite a few Chinese people who were more educated and they probably got advancements, but I think most Chinese were inexperienced and had to start at the beginning level. [Did you see any evidence of discrimination?] Not while I was there. There were a lot of Blacks from the South who were working there. There was a terrific mixture and everyone was there to do a certain job, to build ships so they could go and fight the war.[9]

[How did working in the shipyard affect you?] To me, it was a job. It

---

7. Actually, accidents were common occurrences in the shipyards, where tools often flew in the air without warning and safety regulations were not always enforced. See ibid., pp. 210–11; and Sheila Tropp Lichtman, "Women at Work, 1941–1945: Wartime Employment in the San Francisco Bay Area" (Ph.D. diss., University of California, Davis, 1981), chap. 4.

8. Much profit and patriotism rode on the speedy construction of the warships. The average construction time for Liberty Ships in 1942 was 105 days, and in 1943, 50 days. Richmond Shipyard Number Two set an unprecedented record at the end of 1942 by completing the SS *Robert E. Peary* in four days. See Zhao, "Women and Defense Industries," pp. 231–33.

9. Compared to Black shipyard workers, who were discriminated against in hiring, training, and promotion, Chinese workers received better treatment, most likely because they

was something everybody wanted to do to contribute to the war effort. I thought it paid well, it was a living. I learned a skill I never used. But every time I see an electrode, a Holbart machine, a Lincoln machine, or people welding, it always brings back memories, good memories because I had contributed something.

(SOURCE: May Lew Gee, phone interview with author, June 25, 1994, and in-person interview with author, July 16, 1994, Pacifica, California)

In 1943 May Lew Gee left her shipyard job to accompany a pregnant friend home to Detroit, Michigan. Then because she had difficulty finding transportation back to San Francisco, she decided to enlist in the Women's Army Corps. Like Ruth Chan Jang, whose story appears on pages 486–95, May did her basic training in Des Moines, Iowa. Afterward, she was assigned to Camp Roberts, California, where she worked in intelligence. Upon leaving the service in 1945, May took advantage of the GI bill to attend secretarial training school in San Francisco. But instead of becoming a court reporter as planned, she married Wing Gee, had four children, and moved to Pacifica, where she has lived for the past forty years. She just recently closed her Pacifica Ice Creamery, supposedly to retire, but in her last letter to me she wrote, "I am now associated with the Pacifica Chamber of Commerce (some retirement!!)."

---

were fewer in number and regarded as model workers. However, few opportunities existed for Chinese Americans to advance to supervisory positions. According to the women in Xiaojian Zhao's study, the better jobs usually went to white workers, but unlike their male counterparts, very few Chinese women experienced any direct conflicts with other workers or their supervisors; see Zhao, "Chinese American Women Defense Workers," p. 150.

Ruth Chan Jang,
U.S. Air Corps Corporal

"I Would Love to Be Buried at Arlington"

Approximately 11 million Americans were inducted into the U.S. armed forces between 1941 and 1945. Among them were some 20,000 Chinese soldiers and 350,000 women volunteers. I found out that 6,527 Black women joined the Women's Army Corps, but so few Chinese American women volunteered that I could not find the exact number. Yet I was able to interview seven such women in the course of my research. There was Helen Pon Onyett, who served in the Army Nurse Corps, tending the wounded aboard transports off North Africa. She remained in the services and was promoted to the rank of full colonel in 1971. Marietta Chong Eng joined the WAVES and was assigned to Mare Island as an occupational therapist. Maggie Gee was one of two Chinese American women to volunteer with WASP (Women's Airforce Service Pilots Program), transporting military aircraft around the country. Jessie Lee Yip and Charlotte Sexton were teletypists, and May Lew Gee did intelligence work while in the WAC during World War II.[1]

The seventh woman I interviewed was Ruth Chan Jang. I didn't have to meet her in person to get to know her; I warmed up to her almost immediately as I interviewed her over the phone one evening about her ex-

---

1. For their stories, see Judy Yung, *Chinese Women of America: A Pictorial History* (Seattle: University of Washington Press, 1986), pp. 66–77; and Yung, *Unbound Feet: A Social History of Chinese Women in San Francisco* (Berkeley: University of California Press, 1995), pp. 252–60.

perience in the Women's Air Corps. She had been referred to me by David Lee, past president of the Chinatown Post of the Veterans of Foreign Wars in San Francisco. I was trying to complete Unbound Feet *and wanting to include more stories of Chinese women who had served in the military. Part of the problem was that despite the special efforts of Madame Chiang Kai-shek and WAC recruiters to lower height and weight requirements and entice women to form an all-Chinese women's air unit, Chinatown parents just did not want their daughters to volunteer for military service.[2]*

Because Ruth lived near Sacramento, a good four-hour drive from me in Santa Cruz, she agreed to let me interview her by phone. It turned out to be an enjoyable and informative conversation. She did not hesitate to share with me her innermost thoughts about how she was treated in the WAC and the impact of military service on her outlook in life. In a very sincere voice she told me the following story.

"I Really Believe It Would Shorten the War"

I was born in Walnut Grove [California] but then I only lived there ten years. Then we moved to Locke.[3] From there I graduated from high school and came up to Sacramento to go to community college. In those days, they didn't believe in putting girls through college, so I had to do it on my own and I had to work as a live-in maid. I got room and board and twenty dollars a month and that was *big*. (*laughs*)

It was Sunday afternoon. After I got through with my morning duties

---

2. Jessie Lee Yip, who joined the reserves after the war and became a recruiter in San Francisco Chinatown, said most Chinese parents then were conservative and against their daughters enlisting (interview with author, November 2, 1989, San Francisco). Many parents also believed what they read in the Chinese newspapers, that women were being used as prostitutes in the armed services. This may have been part of the slander campaign against the WAC that Bettie J. Morden discusses in her study *The Women's Army Corps, 1945–1978* (Washington, D.C.: Center of Military History, United States Army, 1990), pp. 10–11.

3. Located twenty-five miles south of Sacramento, the town of Locke was built on land leased from the George Locke family in 1915 by a group of immigrants from Chungshan (Zhongshan) District after a fire destroyed their homes in nearby Walnut Grove. Chinese farm laborers and their families exclusively inhabited the town until the 1970s, when white Americans began to move in. For a history of Locke, see Jeff Gillenkirk and James Motlow, *Bitter Melon: Stories from the Last Rural Chinese Town in America* (Seattle: University of Washington Press, 1987).

working for this lady, I went downtown. While I was shopping on K Street, I heard someone talking about the news: Pearl Harbor had been bombed. What was my reaction? Well, do you remember the general from China, Tsai Ting-kai?[4] He came to the United States to raise money and we were all very patriotic at that time. We grew up with this notion [of patriotism] because my parents were [patriotic]. And we donated to his cause and all that. So I was very unhappy that they [the Japanese] did such a thing. But I had no intention of joining the service because the service didn't have a good reputation in those days. My parents told me, "Don't go in because the service women go in there to serve the men." That's what was implied in the Chinese papers.

By that time I had quit my job. Because they sent the Japanese to camp,[5] there were jobs available for us. So I went to work for the state [as a stenographer]. Then when my [white] girlfriend said, "Let's go in," I said, "That's a good idea." I was tired of office work. She said to go into nursing. I said, "No, I don't want nursing." So that's the reason: to change the type of work.

They were supposed to give us what we wanted, but after you get in, you don't get it. (*laughs*) I promised my family I would not be out of California. I asked to be stationed here in California and that I wanted to go to air controller school. That's the kind of thing I wanted to do. I thought it was so glamorous. So I went into the Air Force [Women's Air Corps] and she went into the WAVES and we split up.

Everybody was very patriotic in those days. Not like now. It may sound kind of corny, but the reason I volunteered was I really thought I would shorten the war if I put in my time. I had a good job with the state, and I got paid well. And I had girlfriends to run around with. I've never told anyone, but I really believed it would shorten the war and then the fellows would come home. And my brother would come home.[6]

I found out later they had to investigate me by calling my postmistress.

---

4. Hailing from Guangdong Province, the same place from which most Chinese immigrated to the United States, General Tsai Ting-kai became a hero in 1932 when he led the Nineteenth Route Army in a valiant fight against the superior forces of the Japanese army in Shanghai for thirty-four days before retreating.

5. She is referring to the mass internment of Japanese Americans during World War II.

6. Her brother Edward W. Chan, the oldest in the family, was then stationed in Chungking as part of the all-Chinese American 407th Air Service Squadron of the Fourteenth Air Force (Flying Tigers).

They thought we [Chinese Americans] might be subversive. (*laughs*) Her name was Pauline Stambaugh. She was the only white person who worked in Locke at the time. Her [post] office was right in our house. They always asked her about people who lived in Locke. I guess she knew all about us. I didn't even know they checked with her. She told me when I came back on furlough.

My mom and dad thought I would never pass the physical. They gave us a complete physical. They listened to your heart. They looked at your hair to see if you had lice, how you walked, and your teeth. I passed it. [My parents didn't think I would pass] because I always had menstrual pain. I didn't tell the service about that. What I did was get my doctor to give me a prescription before I went in and then when I had pain I would take those pills. When they ran out, I would have them refilled.

They [the military] treated me *very* well—much, much better than the white people down the river [treated her]. We were segregated in Locke and Walnut Grove. All the Chinese and Japanese went to Oriental School and white people went to white school. When you got to high school, then you mixed. That's why we had an accent. We didn't learn to speak [good English] until we were ten years old because we didn't have [role] models. At school, we all spoke Chinese or maybe Japanese, and the teacher was the only one who spoke English. When we came home, our parents spoke Chinese. Coming from Locke, I wasn't a city girl and I had never traveled that far. So I was *very* nervous. (*laughs*)

"The Only Chinese in My Unit"

My parents discouraged me from signing up, but after I went in, they were very happy. Because I told them what kind of work I did. We did have a job in the service and we had basic training, [which] was very hard. We had never trained like that before. You get up at the crack of dawn. Sergeant comes in, blows the whistle, and you all get up and do calisthenics in front of your bed. And you have to do that at least forty-five minutes. Then you have to make your bed. You know how the military is, you have to make it to certain specifications. It has to be real tight. Your shoes have to be lined up and your closet clothes have to be lined up. Everything has to be real neat. And they come around and inspect everything with the white gloves on. Then after that, you go to breakfast. After breakfast, you march and march and march out in the field. We also saw a lot of training films about the care and usage of gas

Ruth Chan Jang in winter uniform during basic training in Des Moines, Iowa.
(Courtesy of Ruth Chan Jang)

masks and so forth. I was stationed at Des Moines, Iowa, and we did
that for six weeks.

There were thousands of people there in Des Moines, but I was the
only [Chinese]. No Blacks. One Mexican girl. Everyone else was Caucasian. Like I said, they treated me *very* nicely. Maybe it was because I
was the only Chinese. One night, they gave me a surprise birthday party.
I never had a birthday party in my life. You know the Chinese don't cel-

ebrate until you're sixty years old.[7] I was like the pet because I was one of the youngest ones there. I had just turned twenty-one before I went in.

We lived in barracks just like the men, in double-decker bunk beds with wood frames. It was very embarrassing for me to take a bath in the open shower. I wasn't used to it. Even in high school, we had little booths. But then, I got used to it. And I didn't get the job I wanted. Worked in a hanger doing clerical work. Didn't even get to do dictation. It was just a very menial type of job, very unimportant. It was because my clerical test score was high. My spelling, grammar, letter-writing were good so they put me in clerical work. It was really unfair because we had only been trained for that in [public] school. When they gave me those spatial relations tests, I didn't know what it was. If they were to test me now, I would score high because I know what they're going for. But at the time, coming from the country, I didn't know. They had asked me what I wanted to do, but I didn't get it. (*laughs*) And I was too dumb to protest because I didn't know how. If you come from the country, there's a lot of things you don't know. You just do what they tell you to. (*laughs*)

"No Chinese in Georgia!"

I thought I would go back to California, but they shipped us to Moody Field, Georgia, instead. That's forty-five miles from Jacksonville, Florida. And no Chinese in Georgia! [I was there for] one year. Then I complained to my captain. I told her the sad story, "There's no Chinese here. I'm lonely. I don't get to go home because I'm too far away."

But I was active. I played basketball twice a week, and then on Fridays they flew us to different bases to play basketball against other girls' teams. Not in the private airplanes, but those army air force planes that had no insulation and no chairs. You just sat on crates. It was very primitive when you come to think of it. I don't know why I did it. Now you couldn't pay me to go.

In those days you couldn't fly, but a lot of times the test pilots I worked for would say, "Here, go get a parachute and come with us." And stupid me, I would go with them. They would fly real high up, cut the motor off, and dive. Then they'd pull up again. That's the kind of thing they did and I used to go up with them even though it was against the rules.

---

7. Following Chinese tradition, birthdays are only celebrated at birth and after a person reaches sixty and each subsequent decade.

But they didn't let us near the instruments. We didn't get to do fun things like that. (*laughs*)

[Did you experience any discrimination in the armed forces?] I was the only Chinese on the basketball team, and all the other teams we played were white. I think because I was the only Chinese, they liked me very much. If there was a whole bunch of us, like we had in Locke, mostly all Chinese, and you tried to mix with the whites, then you'd get discrimination. But if you're the only one, you're a specialty I think. (*laughs*) I experienced more discrimination at home way afterwards. I remember in the late sixties, I had gone back to work as a steno, a secretary they call it. She [a white girlfriend] would be late all the time and I was always on time. The boss never said anything to her. I was late once and he called me down. Little things like that. You still get it here, but not in the service.

I was very active and I loved being able to play basketball. But still I missed Chinese company. I didn't have any Chinese boys to go out with. Then when I did go out to what they called the noncommissioned officers' club, where they had dancing and you drank beer or whatever, I still missed Chinese people. I couldn't even go out to a restaurant and have Chinese food. So my captain was kind enough to have me shipped to New York the second year.

"Big Thrills in New York"

I worked in the hospital as a secretary to the nurses at Mitchell Field. That's in Long Island. And I met a lot of nice Chinese people in Long Island. They invited me to their restaurant to celebrate Chinese New Year. In those days, rich people in New York lived in Long Island. They had beautiful homes there and they liked to entertain WACs away from home. Quite often I was invited to their homes. They were real nice to me, much better than the Caucasian people who came from down the river [in Locke and Walnut Grove].

When I first got in the service, they didn't know anything about Chinese people. So the captain asked me to give an orientation class. I myself didn't know anything about the Chinese except from my parents, who were peasants from a small village in Guangdong. I didn't have a very high esteem of Chinese culture because I didn't know anything about it. That's when I got interested and went to the base library. Looked up China and studied it for a long time. I found out that not all Chinese ate rice, and little things like that. Then I gave my talk and they all liked it.

I told them about the different dialects that I spoke, homey things like that. They got interested and they started looking into Chinese things. I think they were interested in China because China was on our side in those days. A lot of them were sent to China later on. And a lot of our boys came back wounded and were sent to the station hospital in Mitchell Field.

As secretary to the nurses, I was treated real nice. I didn't have to go in during the middle of the night. In fact, they even let me live in the nurses' quarters. I didn't have to live in the open barracks like the other girls. I had my own room. And I got to eat in the hospital instead of in the mess hall. Sort of special treatment. Like, you're supposed to pull KP duty once every other month or so. All the two years I was in, I only had it once. Well, the nurses liked me. I would do things without them telling me. I didn't have to be told all the time. Towards the end, it was hard to get promotions, but my nurses got me one. I was promoted to corporal. That was a big deal in those days. I didn't have to take any tests or anything. They just recommended me.

The pay then—about fifty dollars a month—was considered good because we had room and board. All the food you wanted to eat. Clothing was supplied to you too, even underwear. (Ugly underwear. Khaki-colored ones.) Remember in the old days, you had to wear these sort of rayon stockings? They supplied that too. All your shoes. Everything. The only thing you had to buy was shampoo or soap if you didn't like theirs. We even got cigarettes free. (I didn't smoke that much but it was the *in* thing to be smoking. That meant you were grown up.) So I saved enough money to buy bonds every three months to send home.

Sometimes on Saturdays, I would go to the non-officers' club to dance. I loved to dance. Learned how to lindy-hop from the white soldiers. The men never gave me a hard time. They would dance with me. Not the officers, but the enlisted men. I also had these passes to take wounded soldiers to plays and light operas. They were free tickets. I just had to accompany them like their nurse. So I got to see all these plays.

Every chance I had, I went to the Metropolitan Art Museum. Because it was so big, you couldn't cover it in one day. I went to Central Park and looked at the gardens. And there were the cathedrals and the Cloister, where the monks lived. My big thrill was going to this garment district and buying a black lace dress. I didn't know my way around, but I had three girlfriends [in the service] who were from New York. One sang light opera. I got friendly with her because I loved listening to her sing. I went to Brooklyn and stayed overnight at her house. She taught me

Italian ways, how they made wine and pizza from scratch. Then I met another girl who took me home to New Jersey. She was a Polish girl. Then another Jewish girl who lived in the Bronx. She would take me around New York.

The war ended and I was discharged. So I served two years. I didn't want to stay in any longer because I was still doing secretarial work. So when I came back, I used the GI bill to go to community college. But I dropped out to get married [to Harry Jang, a Chinese American architect] and raise a family [of three children]. When I finally finished school and got my credential in adult education, I was fifty-six years old.

"I Came to Feel Much Better about Myself"

[What was most memorable about being in the WAC?] You mean the nicest feeling? Oh, friends I've made there. They treated me very nice. I was one of them, whereas here [outside the service], I wasn't. [Here] you hung around the Chinese people or the Japanese people. Over there, I was accepted. They never made me feel like you had to hang back and be subservient. I was more like a leader. I was the captain of the basketball team. So I felt very good.

And my bosses were good. They recommended me for promotion. I didn't have to ask for it. They just surprised me and gave it to me. And when I first got in there, I loved the food. We never ate like that before. You got chocolate cake, dessert at every meal. We didn't have dessert at home. When I worked for the Caucasian family, I was the maid. And I ate after they ate, and in the kitchen. I know all the people complain about the food, but I loved it because we didn't have it at the time. Lots of meat, real butter, real milk. It was all very good.

It [the WAC] got me to see that there are good people out there. And I came to feel much better about myself. I learned never to be ashamed about Locke or about my Chinese background. Lots of people who come from Locke won't talk about Locke because they think it's lowly. They don't even want to speak my dialect because it sounds real peasantlike. Well, I'm proud I can speak it. And I'm proud that my parents came from such poor beginnings, and look where we are now. When I was growing up, though, I was ashamed of it because we were segregated down there and made to feel like you're not a real citizen and you don't belong here. So I had that feeling until I grew up and began to see things differently.

Everywhere I went [I was the only Chinese]. I heard of another Chinese from here, but she died some time ago. Her name was Winnie Jang and she was from Courtland. In fact, Judy, I would love to be buried at Arlington, but I don't know how I can get there because you have to be a hero. The only thing I can think of so far is because there are so few Chinese women [in the military]. I would like to be buried there with my husband [who also served in the air force]. All I need is a little niche to put my ashes there at Arlington. I think it would be nice because we've visited Arlington twice and looked at the gravestones. I guess without realizing it, we must be very patriotic.

(SOURCE: Ruth Chan Jang, phone interview with author, July 8, 1994)

In December 1997 Ruth's husband, First Lieutenant Harry Jang, suffered a stroke and passed away. A recipient of the distinguished Flying Cross for his service in World War II, he was cremated and buried with full military honors at Arlington National Cemetery. A spot has been reserved for Ruth to be buried beside him.

Lai Yee Guey and Lorena How, Mother and Daughter

"Making Marks for Heaven"

I first heard of Lai Yee Guey through my sister, Sandy Lee, who was help-ing me find Chinese immigrant women to interview about the war years. Although I had found many articles and photographs in the newspapers and archives showing both immigrant and American-born women active in fund-raising, Red Cross work, political rallies, and defense jobs, I was having trouble locating women who were willing to talk about their role in the war effort. Finally, Sandy thought of an old friend of hers, Lorena How, who agreed to share her vivid memories of her mother's patriotic efforts during the war years. Although a second-hand account (her mother, Lai Yee Guey, died in 1949), the interview turned out to be a rich recounting of one immigrant woman's struggles to support her family of six children through the depression and still find the resources to express her patriotism toward China and the United States during World War II. It also proved to be a powerful story of a loving mother who knew how to care for a disabled daughter and teach her how to stand up for herself.

Lorena How was born in San Francisco in 1932 with a congenital heart defect. The fifth child in a family of three daughters and three sons, she had a difficult childhood. Often sick and in the hospital, she struggled to get through high school and, later, college, though in the end she succeeded. Because of her interrupted education and poor health, Lorena found it hard to make friends at school. Her physical appearance did not help mat-

ters. She was only four feet nine inches tall and weighed less than eighty-five pounds. She appeared pale, with one eye bigger than the other, and was required to wear thick eyeglasses. It also did not help that her father was considered "crazy" in the community. (He claimed to know how people could determine the sex of their unborn children, was into numerology, and espoused anticommunist rhetoric on every public occasion.) Consequently, Lorena spent a lot of time at home with her mother and came to know her well—so well that her siblings would come to her, the "lieutenant," if they wanted anything from their mother, the "general."

The following interview, condensed from a four-hour conversation between Sandy and Lorena, is as much a portrait of a patriotic feminist as of a smart businesswoman and devoted mother. A born storyteller with a sense of humor, Lorena recreates in graphic detail the circumstances of her mother's life in China (not only is Lai Yee Guey given an education, but she gets along with her in-laws), her ability to establish a business at home sewing Chinese dresses while raising six children, her struggles with an incompetent husband and a disabled daughter, and through it all, her unwavering support for feminist and patriotic causes. We come to know an industrious woman who works from 8 A.M. to 3 A.M. seven days a week, stopping only to cook for the family and celebrate Chinese New Year. Yet she makes sure that her children learn to appreciate their bicultural heritage, that they assume responsibilities both at home and as individuals. And whenever called upon to give to her community or her country, Lai Yee Guey always found a way. (Lorena has photographs of her mother and children making "lucky coins" for the war effort, of her mother and brother Art picketing at the San Francisco docks to protest the shipping of scrap iron to Japan, and of her mother marching proudly with an American flag in the Victory Day parade.)[1] Underneath her hard exterior, Lorena tells us, was a compassionate woman with progressive views. Of the many lessons in life that Lorena learned from her mother, the one that has had special power for her all these years is the advice she gave Lorena on her first day back to school: "Other kids might see you and laugh at you, but don't let it bother you. Because you were sick; you're not stupid."

---

1. See Judy Yung, *Unbound Feet: A Social History of Chinese Women in San Francisco* (Berkeley: University of California Press, 1995), pp. 234 and 243; Yung, *Chinese Women of America: A Pictorial History* (Seattle: University of Washington Press, 1986), p. 77; and below, p. 508.

"She Was More Fortunate Than Others"

In 1914 or so, my father [Joe Chan How] went back [to China] and married my mother.[2] It was all prearranged, a blind marriage. At that time my mother was about sixteen or so. But she was more fortunate than others because during her time, when she was nine, ten years old, they usually had their children's feet bound. My grandfather was quite progressive. During the 1911 Revolution he had his queue cut and he would not let his daughters have their feet bound. He also insisted that they go to school.

My mother told me that when they were first going to school, walking through the village, men would stand by the side heckling them. "What do you want to go to school for? Do you want to get smart enough so that you can sell your husband? You don't need to go to school. You'll end up washing diapers anyway." She was fortunate she had three years of Chinese school.

When my mother married my father, my grandfather [Lai's father-in-law] was a scholar who taught school in the little schoolhouse next to our house in the village. Instead of saying that the daughter-in-law had to serve the mother-in-law and all that, my grandfather was quite modern and progressive in his thoughts. He said, "Since we have *mooi nui* [slavegirls], you don't have to take care of the house. Why don't you attend school with the young men?" So my mother sat in the back of the classroom and had another half a year of school with her father-in-law, which was very unusual in the old days. Then she was pregnant with my oldest sister [Mamie] and she naturally could not attend school any further because you do not show yourself when you're pregnant.

When she arrived in 1923 I think everything was novel to her. But she was not afraid for the simple reason that she had so much support when she was in China from her father-in-law, mother-in-law, and aunts. And because she also had attended school, she was more confident coming to a new country. So it wasn't too much of a struggle at the beginning.

"The First Chinese Woman to Have Her Own Business"

My father didn't have a steady job, so [my mother] started to pick shrimp. From there she went on to sewing, since she had learned sewing from

---

2. Joe Chan How immigrated to the United States in 1910 when he was nineteen years old. He lived with his granduncle, a gambler, and attended grammar school in Berkeley. According to Lorena, "He was the best tailor west of the Mississippi, specializing in men's clothes—suits, pants, vests, and overcoats."

the Girls' House.[3] There was a sewing factory on Commercial Street, the cleanest, biggest shop in Chinatown. Run by a Mr. Lee. Had about four rows of machines. Linoleum on the floor and bathrooms that were clean. It had a little cooking area for the ladies if they wanted to cook, but most of them went home for lunch because everybody just lived about four blocks away at the furthest. So my mother started sewing there until she was showing with Betty [her second child]. She went home and continued picking shrimp, which was delivered up to the house, at five cents a pound.

Then before my brother [Jon] was born two years later, my mother decided since she's better at sewing and she can't go to the sewing shop because of the two babies, she would open her own business. So my mother was the first Chinese woman to have her own business in Chinatown. Instead of sewing for the manufacturer, what she did was go into dressmaking, specializing in Chinese kimonos, also known as *cheong saam*. I asked her one time, "When you started to sew, weren't you scared?" She said, "Well, I made up my mind to be a dressmaker. So my customer came in with three and a half yards of material. First I asked her, 'How much is it and where did you buy it?'" I said, "Why did you ask her that?" She said, "Oh, in case I made a mistake, I can run down to Emporium, get three and a half yards and do it over again." So she was quite brave. Then she found out it really was enough to support the family.

"She Kept Her Sense of Acceptance and Hope"

The beginning [of the depression] was easy for my mother, but as time wore on, 1927, 1928, the pressures were mounting because she was pregnant with my second brother [Pat] and my father wasn't working. She was making Chinese dresses for a living. The next thing you know, she realized that the whole family depended on her and her alone. And this was just before the depression in 1929. About 1930, after my brother [Pat] was born, she had a miscarriage or abortion. I guess the pressure and the unhappiness got to her. I was born in 1931, right in the depression. And I was born with a congenital heart defect. So with five children and a husband that was irresponsible (my father was an artist and a poet and quite a man about town), it was quite a struggle for my mother. But she kept her sense of acceptance and, at the same time, hope. I re-

---

3. See page 89, note 2.

member her telling me when I was six going to kindergarten again (I started at five but because I was sick with pneumonia, appendicitis, had all my teeth pulled out, and in the convalescent hospital, I took a year off), when I started school again that morning, she combed my hair and said, "You're going back to kindergarten again. Other kids might see you and laugh at you, but don't let it bother you. Because you were sick; you're not stupid." That's something I have kept in my mind all these years. Even with all her problems, she always encouraged me to look ahead, to do my best.

You would think that I would be the last straw. You come over with all this hope and you don't know what you're going into but it must be better. Then there's no job, your husband's sort of irresponsible, all these children, and then she winds up with me. I remember one time when I was about three, the doctor said I was too weak and my mother had too much on her hands and the best thing was to put me in a sanitarium. I went there and it cost twenty-five dollars a month. In those days that was a lot of money because men in Chinatown were making thirty to fifty dollars a month. If you're lucky, you work for the whites for sixty-five or seventy-five dollars a month. She accepted all this and not once did I hear her complain, saying, "You're so much trouble" or "I wish I didn't have you." She only told me, "Well, it's not what you wanted, so whatever you can do, you just go ahead and do it."

She was a very religious person. Not so much [in the sense of] going to church, but she had this philosophy that if God made you, God will provide for you somehow. She always accepted whatever the gods offered her. She even saw to it that our religion was taken care of. (Betty, Pat, and I were Catholics, my father was Methodist, Mamie was a Baptist, and Arthur didn't believe in anything.) She said, "You guys can believe in Jesus. That's fine because Jesus wants you guys to be good. My *tin san* [god in heaven] wants you to be good too." And on Fridays she would always have one dish for the Catholics. Either fried eggs, raw tomatoes with sugar and oil, or fish. So she was very democratic in that. She didn't believe that your Jesus is the God, but because you believed he is, that was good enough for her. So long as you have a god that you're afraid of.

"She Was Very Understanding"

We thought she was very strict and we were really afraid of her. She was under a lot of pressure and we didn't understand. All we knew was that

our mother was very snappy all the time. As a matter of fact, my brothers and sisters always called her the general because she just gave the orders and we had to carry it out. No one had to pick up after us. She just
laid down the law. Saturday, you did this and that. You had to do this,
do that, before you could go to the school picnic. My mother just said
sai dei [wash the floors] and everyone *sai dei*; *sai yi* [do the laundry] and
everyone *sai yi*. And I was the lieutenant because I always got along with
my mother. Because I was sick all the time, I stayed home and talked
with her all the time. So anything they wanted to ask for, they always
told me to ask my mother and they usually got it.

I was very fortunate that I could talk to her, although I was afraid of
her too. I remember one time at school, we had a record dance. And this
fellow said he'll take me to the dance. Well, I said I had to go home and
ask my mother. Went home and took one look at her, I didn't even ask
her. Ran down and told the guy, "No, I don't think my mother will let
me go." Of course now we understand why she seemed so *ok* [mean],
but she really wasn't. Because as I talked with her, she was very understanding. I remember one time I couldn't eat. I just sat there crying. I
had this lump in my throat from four o'clock to nine o'clock. That's five
hours. Then after dinner my mother finally asked me, "What's the problem?" You know what the problem was? I was playing with scissors and
I snipped one pair of satin pants she was working on. And I knew she
was going to kill me. So I was really crying before she even found out.
So I told her. I said, "I was playing with the scissors and I cut your pants."
And she looked at it. And I guess she saw how scared and petrified I was
all night. She just said, "That's okay. It's not the end of the world. You
tell me." So she said, "We can fix it. I'll just cut some more material and
do it again." She didn't have to tell me not to play with scissors again
because I ain't going to play with no scissors again. So she was quite understanding and real progressive in her thoughts.

"Quite a Seamstress and Businesswoman"

We were living in a three-room place and it was quite crowded, so we moved
into this big, gigantic house [675 Commercial Street, where Lorena was
still living at the time of the interview]—fourteen feet wide and sixty feet
long, three stories. We paid $50 for the whole building. My mother, being
a pretty good businesswoman, decided to rent out the store [downstairs]
for twenty-five dollars—that paid half of the rent—and take in borders at
five or ten dollars, then the rent would be only fifteen. Then we used to

have a great big room downstairs, and she rented it out to the gamblers. The understanding was that they used the room from eight to twelve.

Then in 1937 they put up a sign saying the house was for sale. So my mother was saying, "My goodness, I just moved over here and now I have to move again?" So she asked the real estate man, "Can I buy it?" At that time the real estate man didn't know it and she didn't know it either, that unless you're an American citizen, you can't buy it.[4] But the man told my mother, "Sure, you got money, you buy it." So she said, "How muchee?" And the man said, "Two thousand nine hundred fifty dollars, lady." So she told the man, "Okay, I buy it." Then the question came up as to, "Are you a citizen?" "No." "Your husband a citizen?" "No." "Well, who's a citizen?" The only one is Betty, but she was only twelve years old at that time. So legally she can't buy it because she's under age. We were very fortunate to have a very good friend, who is a Dr. Lee, a Chinese herbalist doctor. He was a citizen and my father's best friend. One day my mother and father went up to talk to him. And he said, "Very simple. Do you trust me?" My mother said, "If we didn't trust you, we won't be telling you all these problems." And he said, "I'm a citizen and I'll buy it in my name for you. When your daughter is of age, I will write it back in her name." So that's how we got the building.

She was a good businesswoman and she worked in the morning, eight o'clock until three o'clock at night, sewing at home. She made these Chinese dresses from scratch. The customer comes in; they have a fitting. She'll cut it, and it'll take three days to finish one Chinese dress. At that time she was charging about three dollars a dress. So it's a dollar a day, thirty dollars a month. That was pretty good. But she did not have enough money saved [for the house] for the simple reason that she also had to feed six children. [Her youngest child, Arthur, was born in 1933.] Then she had a sick one that had to go to the hospital every now and then for twenty-five dollars a month. And she refused to go on welfare. She said, "As long as I can work, we will not go on welfare." So she didn't have the down payment, which was two hundred dollars. But by that time my sister Mamie was a dressmaker and shared the store on Clay Street with my father.[5] She saved enough money to give my mother the down pay-

---

4. The Alien Land Law of 1913 barred all "aliens ineligible to citizenship" from owning land in California, and only Asian immigrants were not allowed to become naturalized U.S. citizens at that time. The law was not repealed by California voters until 1956.

5. According to Lorena, "Mamie sewed strictly Western clothes—dresses, skirts, suits, and coats. My father specialized in men's clothes—suits, pants, vests, and overcoats. And

ment for the house. And the monthly payment was thirty seven and a half dollars. So she was able to lower her own rent by buying the house. As soon as Betty was eighteen, Dr. Lee turned it back to my sister.

[How did your mother come to sew for Gump's?] One day the Gump's designer walked by Mamie's store and asked her if she could find a lady who sewed Chinese gowns. So it just fell in place. I took over when my sister got married. I was about twelve. I use to deliver, take the measurements back and read them to her. She'll cut it and I'll bring it back for fitting. And after the fitting, I'll bring it back and she'll finish the garment. I'll take it back down there and make a bill.

She was an outstanding seamstress. I know she made a dress for Madame Chiang Kai-shek, although Madame Chiang Kai-shek didn't know that she made it for her. But she [Madame Chiang] did ask who was the dressmaker. She said, "I have never worn a Chinese garment so comfortable in the collar. Even my own tailors can't sew like that." She wanted to know who it was so that she could have more dresses made. But my mother said, "Forget her, I have enough customers."

My mother went into her own dressmaking business because she had so many young children. She didn't want to leave them at home while she went to sew in the sweatshop. So she figured [this way] she could be with her children and make money at the same time. She started sewing at eight in the morning. By the time we started school, we managed our own breakfast, just chocolate and toast. But afternoon at twelve o'clock, it was rice. She'll cook that and we'll come home for lunch. Then when we came home from school at three-thirty in the afternoon, she'll take a coffee break. At eight o'clock at night, we had our main dinner of rice and Chinese dishes. About ten o'clock, she would have a cup of coffee and sew until three. So she only slept between three and eight. That's five hours of sleep a day.

"We Had Everything"

From eight to fourteen years old, those years were very happy for me. I was making the grades in school and I didn't have to go to hospitals anymore. My mother and father weren't screaming so much, and we were in this new house with a lot of space to run around. I could take any

---

my mother specialized in Chinese gowns. So we had it all covered." But as she pointed out, whereas mother and daughter could make a living from sewing, her father could not. "Because he was such an artist and perfectionist, he never got any clothes done."

schoolmates home because my mother preferred we come home and play instead of out in the streets or at other people's houses. I felt we were very fortunate. We had a whole flat, whereas a lot of people had just two rooms. We had our own bathtub, the first washing machine in the neighborhood, the first radio. We had the first cars because my father went out and bought twelve (one at a time and all used ones). We had all the modern conveniences and we had a lot of room.

We had everything. Twice a year my mother would cook an American dinner—Thanksgiving and either Christmas or Easter. Besides all the Chinese holidays, we celebrated all the American holidays. At the end of the year, she [Lai Yee Guey] always went to the temple to give thanks to the gods for giving her a good year. At the beginning of the year, she would go to the temple again to ask the gods to give her another good year. At home she also baai san [worshipped], not to any picture or idol. She just set it [the altar] by the window because she believed in her god in heaven. She always bought gai [chicken] and foh yuk [roast pork] and a little bit of fruit. (Not too much because she didn't like to eat it and it was expensive and the kids wouldn't eat it.) Then at baat yuet sap ng [Mid-Autumn Festival] she thanked the Moon Goddess for the harvest.[6] She also made jung [glutinous rice dumplings] for ng yuet jit [literally, festival of the fifth month, or Dragon Boat Festival].[7] Every year she took a week off at Chinese New Year—New Year's Eve through the seventh, when she hoi nin [started the new year off with a special family meal]. Then she'd go back to work from morning to night, seven days a week. My mother also believed in the Christmas tree. I still have some ornaments that she bought when she first came [to America].

"Mister Nine of Chinatown"

[So life was getting better by the late 1930s?] Financially, my mother was a little bit better, but emotionally, my mother was not doing very well because by that time, my father was into partying and writing poetry. And he had this theory teaching people how to have boys or girls. In the

---

6. See page 276, note 5.

7. The Dragon Boat Festival, which occurs on the fifth day of the fifth lunar month, is rooted in fertility rites to ensure abundant rainfall in southern China. It is celebrated with river parades, dragon boat races, and offerings of jung (zhongzi) to China's well-known patriot Qu Yuan, who protested political corruption by drowning himself in 278 B.C.

old days, you don't talk about sex, period. That was mortifying for my mother. As teenagers, we were [also] mortified. Of course as we grew older we understood my father and we said, "Too bad he wasn't born later. He would have made an excellent hippie or beatnik." Then he had this numerology business [in] which he thought number nine was the greatest. Stillwell is good or Churchill is good because they have nine letters in their names. You add it up, subtract it, minus it, multiply it, any way to get a number nine if they're for our side. That's why my father's nickname, and he was very proud to go by that name, was Mister Nine of Chinatown.

This hurt my mother quite a bit simply because people in those days were so conservative and here my father was a beatnik. But still she was very proud. She always went out with her head high. Nobody dared say anything bad in front of her. She was brought up that the father or husband is the figurehead. She would not let anyone degrade my father, especially in front of us, the children. Before she died, she told me, "No matter how bad your father is, you must respect him as your father." She knew that we were all suffering from his eccentric behaviors. Besides talking about [the] number nine, teaching someone how to have sex (or should I say, how to have boys or girls), he wrote a lot of poetry that was anticommunist. As a matter of fact, he even published a book on anticommunism—all the bad things that happened to the people, their suffering, and how they were tortured. We heard about it all the time because every Double Ten or Double Seven,[8] when they had a Rice Bowl parade, or [in] any parade in Chinatown, he always, with his own money and his own work, put up a float and sprouted anticommunist slogans. So those things bothered my mother, especially after 1945, when the Second World War was won, until 1949, when they started the Communist thing[9] and my mother passed away. Those four years were very hard on her. She knew that it was hard on us because we were just teenagers. And teenagers going to high school are always afraid of kids making fun of you. But she said, "No matter how bad your father seems to you, you must respect him as a father."

---

8. During the war years, parades were held in Chinatown to celebrate Double Ten, the day when the Qing dynasty was overthrown and the Republic of China was founded (October 10, 1911), and Double Seven, the day that Japan invaded China at Marco Polo Bridge (July 7, 1937).

9. Lorena is referring to the Communist takeover of China in 1949.

"She Tried to Do Her Share for the War Effort"

[Do you remember the extent of your mother's involvement during the war years?] When the Japanese invaded China, she was very concerned and wanted to help. She knew she could not go back [to China] because of her family here. (She was the only one that sent money home to her mother, father, and her husband's family.) So she tried to do her share for the war effort. She went to protest the sending of scrap metals to Japan in 1938.[10] (I have a picture of her and Arthur. She's holding a sign and parading.)[11] She was active in the Women's Auxiliary Club in Chinatown, called the Foo Nui Wooi.[12] They use to make those red-white-and-blue ribbons and wrap it around a little Chinese coin with the hole in the middle. They sold it for about ten cents each. They collected this money and gave it to the Six Companies.[13] It was supposed to be for the war effort, to feed the hungry people in China. She always attended the Rice Bowl parades and helped to carry that big flag with money pouring in.[14] And whenever there was a little tin to put your change in for war relief, she would put in her quarters. We were not desperately poor, but we really couldn't afford the extra twenty-five cents.

Because my mother was active in the Women's Auxiliary and my sister was too, I remember going and helping to make the coins to sell. I also remember from my sister's shop, I would run down Grant Avenue (lower Grant Avenue used to be full of gift shops just like now but at that time it was mostly run by Japanese), we would run up to the front door there and yell in our best English, "*Don't buy, lady, Japanese store!*" And then the Japanese ladies would come chasing us with their brooms. We would be running back to Clay Street. We were against the Japanese because they had invaded China. I remember some Catholic lady visiting the sick in the hospital gave me a dolly once. I turned it over and looked at it. Made in Japan. Gave it back to her. "I don't want it!" So we were very anti-Japanese as children.

When America entered the conflict in 1941, she [Lai Yee Guey] was

---

10. See page 438, note 5.

11. See Yung, *Unbound Feet*, p. 243.

12. Also known as the Women's War Zone Refugee Relief Committee, the Foo Nui Wooi (Funühui) was organized by the Chinese War Relief Association as a women's auxiliary with the primary purpose of mobilizing women to collect clothing and supplies for refugees in China and participate in the various parades and demonstrations.

13. See page 426, note 2.

14. See page 447, note 15.

all for America, hoping that the Americans would conquer the Japanese so that China would be free from the Japanese occupation. She was kind of frustrated because everybody was going to work in the defense area.[15] She wanted to go but she knew she couldn't because she did not know how to speak English. Besides, her family needed her. So I guess she sort of fantasized about how she would get into war work. She was sewing for about four Chinese stores at that time, besides the ladies who came up to have their gowns made for occasions like weddings and their own [future] funerals. I remember her telling one of the store owners that she was not going to work for them anymore, she was going to try and get a job for the defense department. So they said, "What can you do?" She said, "Well, I can make parachutes." So she fantasized that she could make parachutes as her contribution to the war effort.

She thought the only way she could help the war effort was to buy war bonds. She saved to buy war bonds because she believed in the American system a lot. She used to say that [if] worse came to worst, Roosevelt would provide social security. She believed that the American government [unlike the Chinese government] was not corrupt, that the government did help the people. So any time there was a war bond drive, she would always buy a thirty-seven-and-a-half-dollar-for-a-fifty-dollar bond. I remember her taking me to Union Square to see the submarine. In order to see that, you had to buy a war bond to get in or some war stamps. So I remember buying my ten-cent stamps and she quietly bought an eighteen-and-seventy-five-cents-for-a-twenty-five-dollar war bond. Then we went down to see the submarines.

[Do you remember Victory Day (August 14, 1945)?] Oh yes! I was fourteen or so. It came about four o'clock. The siren went off at the Ferry Building. We use to have the siren go off every day at twelve and at four-thirty. But this one rang off at four and for a long time. Then the bells of St. Mary's started chiming away. We turned on the radio to listen. Because my mother was educated, she read the Chinese papers all the time. She knew that the war was near an end. So when she heard all the siren and stuff, she said, "The war's ended." So Pat took us out in this little old Studebaker. There was no gas cap on his gas tank and we didn't know it. And firecrackers were going. The firecracker papers [on the ground]

---

15. During World War II, six major shipyards in the San Francisco Bay Area employed more than five thousand Chinese Americans, including five hundred women. See stories about shipyard workers Jade Snow Wong (pages 473–78) and May Lew Gee (pages 479–85).

Lai Yee Guey proudly holding the American flag and marching in the parade on V-J Day.
(Courtesy of Lorena How)

were at least twelve inch[es] thick. All over San Francisco—confetti, fire-cracker papers. Came home and, "Aiya, no gas cap!" It's a wonder we didn't all die. A few days later Chinatown held a huge parade, and we have a picture of her [Lai Yee Guey] proudly holding an American flag.[16]

"You Could Call Her a Feminist"

It was not only the war effort but I remember she contributed to any-thing the Chinese community did for Chinese women. She was very ac-tive in the Y[WCA], not in terms of going to meetings and having things done, but anytime there was a donation [drive] or anything concerning the Y, she was there. I remember her giving her share of money to build the Y building on Clay Street.[17] When they had the grand opening, they

16. As another example of Lai Yee Guey's faith in America, Lorena said she was among the first to apply for U.S. citizenship when the exam was offered in the Chinese language to those who had been in the country for more than twenty years. Her citizenship papers, unfortunately, did not arrive until two days after she died.

17. See page 238, note 7.

invited her to the dedication. She also donated to the Red Cross. She thought the Red Cross was good and the Y was good. I think you could call her a feminist. Although she was not outspoken, she would contribute to any women's cause.

As one of the few educated women at the time, she did a lot of letter writing for friends. While she sewed at home, the ladies would come up to the house, usually around two-thirty or so. Then the house was quiet and everyone had gone to school. They would tell her to read a letter. "Got a letter from home. What does it say?" My mother would always say, "Don't have to read it; it's bound to be asking for money." But she would read the letter and they would ask her to answer it. They would give her a piece of paper and she would write it out, address the envelope, and tell them to go to the post office. She did that not only for the Chinese women, but some of the men were not that well educated either.

There used to be a place called *nui gwoon*, the girls' residence that took in abused women. She knew the names of those Cameron House ladies, so she was able to refer women who were abused to them. She referred women to doctors for abortions, [to Cameron House] to get out of prostitution, and things like that. She listened to their stories and made suggestions about what they could do. Some things were your decision. Some things just had to be done, so she would refer you to the right people to get it done. She was more of a feminist without going out and shouting "chauvinist pig!"

[Did your parents favor the sons over the daughters?] One of my mother's last instructions were, "When I pass away, you keep the house. Don't sell it until after your father dies because no one will take care of him. When you sell it, I want you to divide it equally between your brothers and sisters. I'm not like one of those *tong saan poh* [recent immigrant women from China]—for boys only." So she was very modern in that sense. She didn't believe in having sons only and taking the daughter-in-law to live with her. She always told my brothers, "You guys, if you can support a wife, get married. I don't want you to come home and take care of *me*."

[Lai Yee Guey passed away in 1949 of high blood pressure.] Her last instructions were, "You can believe in Jesus if you want. I believe in mine. So when I go, I want you to *baai san* for me." So although at that time I was very religious [Catholic] and I thought that was a conflict of interest, I justified it by saying that I was not doing this to honor her as a god but as an ancestor. So I have carried on the ancestral worship.

When we go out to the cemetery, we bring the chicken and she gets all her stuff.

(SOURCE: Lorena How, interview with Sandy Lee, May 1, 1982, San Francisco)

Lai Yee Guey obviously had a positive influence on Lorena, who, despite being born with a defective heart, lived a full life. She traveled to more places than most people and was never afraid to try anything new or different. She went shooting for deer and braved the kickback of a rifle. She also went deep sea fishing and caught a swordfish weighing over a hundred pounds. (The proof was mounted on her living room wall.)

For a sickly, eighty-five pound woman, what Lorena accomplished in her lifetime is amazing. After her mother passed away, she started her own bookkeeping and income tax service, going on to graduate from San Francisco State College with a major in laboratory technology and a minor in Native American studies. When she encountered discrimination at Franklin Hospital, where she worked as a lab technician, she told her boss off and got a better job at the Veteran's Administration Hospital doing research. In 1968 she defied the odds and survived a massive heart attack, which forced her into early retirement at age thirty-six.

As my sister Sandy remarked, "I think Lorena feels she is living on borrowed time and must make the most of it." Following in her mother's footsteps, Lorena continued to give generously of her time, helping countless old ladies and immigrants with their taxes, medical problems, and translation. Except when she was too sick to move, she never said no to anyone. When asked why she didn't just take it easy, she said, "Well, someone has to do it. Besides, I'm making marks for heaven." Lorena How passed away on April 24, 1998, at the age of sixty-six. The last thing she told Sandy to tell me was how much she appreciated my write-up of her mother's story.

Giving Voice to Chinese American Women

Oral History Methodology

From the beginning, oral history has been central in my efforts to reclaim my history as a Chinese American woman and integrate that history into our collective memory as a multicultural nation. Given the paucity of writings by Chinese women themselves and their invisibility or distortions in the public record, I have relied on oral history to help me reconstruct their lives and express their worldviews in all my work, from *Island* to *Chinese Women of America, Unbound Feet,* and now, *Unbound Voices.*[1] Oral history allows ordinary folks like my subjects to speak for themselves, fill in historiographical gaps, and challenge stereotypes, as well as validate their lives. For too long Chinese women have silently borne the maligned images imposed upon them by the dominant culture—the exotic China Doll, erotic Suzy Wong, and diabolical Dragon Lady. They have rarely been asked to speak for themselves about their lives, their aspirations, struggles, and accomplishments. I felt it was time that America begin to listen to their herstories and I wanted to be the conduit that would make this happen.

What were some of the difficulties and rewards in conducting oral histories with Chinese American women? How did I go about giving voice to these women, and what did I learn in the process about oral history

An earlier version of this article appeared in *Frontiers: A Journal of Women Studies* 19, no. 3 (1998): 130–56.

1. Him Mark Lai, Genny Lim, and Judy Yung, *Island: Poetry and History of Chinese Immigrants on Angel Island, 1910–1940* (Seattle: University of Washington Press,

methodology, ethics, memory, narrative form, and analysis that may be useful and applicable to other oral history projects? Let me begin by saying that every good oral historian knows that planning and preparation are crucial ingredients to a fruitful harvest.[2] Moreover, oral histories cannot stand alone as evidence but need to be substantiated and contextualized with archival research. Conversely, historical data alone, devoid of human voices and stories, would be equally incomplete, a skeleton without any flesh. Combined, these two approaches to research allowed me to paint a fuller picture of Chinese American women's history.

Thus, as I began my research, poring over manuscript censuses, immigration documents, and microfilmed newspapers for any information on Chinese American women, I simultaneously mapped out the purpose and scope of my oral history project and lined up women to interview. I knew I wanted full profiles of the women, from their birth and childhood to adulthood, and broad coverage of different aspects of their lives, including immigration, work, family, and community. I also wanted to explore how race, class, and gender dynamics as well as culture, personality, and history have shaped their lives. Most important, I wanted to hear explicitly and implicitly what life in America has meant to them. I came up with a consent form and two lists of questions that covered these topics, one for immigrant women and the second for American-born women (see below).[3] As expected, I never got to ask all the questions on the list, but they served to lend focus and structure to my interviews and helped me stay on track in covering the essential topics. Within this structure I tried to be flexible about allowing the women I interviewed to pursue their own interests and story lines. At the same

---

[1980], 1991), and Judy Yung, *Chinese Women in America: A Pictorial History* (Seattle: University of Washington Press, 1986) and *Unbound Feet: A Social History of Chinese Women in San Francisco* (Berkeley: University of California Press, 1995).

2. The following works on oral history were especially useful to me: Willa K. Baum, *Oral History for the Local Historical Society* (Walnut Creek, Calif.: Alta Mira Press, [1967], 1995); Sherna Gluck, "What's So Special about Women? Women's Oral History," in *Frontiers: A Journal of Women Studies* 2, no. 2 (summer 1977): 3–17, 110–13 (appendix); Ronald J. Grele, *Envelopes of Sound: The Art of Oral History* (New York: Praeger, 1991); Sherna Gluck and Daphne Patai, eds., *Women's Words: The Feminist Practice of Oral History* (New York: Routledge, 1991); and Valerie Raleigh Yow, *Recording Oral History: A Practical Guide for Social Scientists* (Thousand Oaks, Calif.: Sage, 1994).

3. The consent form and interview questions were based on University of California's Human Subjects Protocol and suggestions from Sherna Gluck's article, "What's So Special about Women?" pp. 110–13.

time, I looked for opportunities to follow up on unexpected turns in the conversations that might lead to new information and insights into their history.

Being an insider, a Chinese American woman born and raised in San Francisco and bilingual in Chinese and English, had its advantages. It also helped that I was from a working-class background and was regarded in the community as a respectable scholar. Thus, it was relatively easy for me to find both immigrant and American-born Chinese women to interview, to establish trust and rapport with them in their familiar surroundings (usually their homes), and to ask them personal questions about gender roles and relations, sexuality, discrimination, and social change in their lives. However, there were also disadvantages to being an insider. My interviewees tended to omit information or gloss over details, assuming that I already knew them, or hide their true feelings and views for fear of my disapproval or further disclosure.

How did I find the women I interviewed? Most of them were either relatives or longtime acquaintances of mine, referrals from friends and organizations I contacted, or names I came across in my research. For example, I interviewed my own mother, aunts, and cousins. I found *sau saang gwa* (grass widows in China whose husbands lived overseas) through my contacts in the Overseas Chinese Affairs Office in Guangdong Province, and WACs by writing the Chinatown Post of Veterans of Foreign Wars. I was less successful finding ex-prostitutes and *mui tsai*, probably because no one wanted to be identified as such or there were few women still alive to talk about that experience. In one instance, after a great deal of trouble, I finally tracked down the author of an oral history paper on a *mui tsai* that I had found in a university library, only to be told she wanted to hold on to her grandmother's story and develop it into a book someday. Although I had developed a long list of women who had been involved in the war effort from the Chinese-language newspapers, I had a difficult time finding anyone to interview. When I finally located the three Chinese women leading a parade in the front cover photo of *Unbound Feet*, all three declined to be interviewed, saying that they had been coaxed into participating in the parade to welcome Madame Chiang Kai-shek to San Francisco in 1941 and that they really had nothing to add about women's contributions to the war effort. Even when I found an interview that had been done with one of the key leaders, she seemed reluctant to talk about that period of her life or to take credit for her many long hours of volunteer work. I suspect this reluctance has something to do with Chinese women's socialized behavior to be self-effacing, to downplay their political activities and emphasize instead their role in the family.[4]

Ultimately, I interviewed thirty-three of the forty-eight women cited in *Unbound Feet*.[5] Six of the interviews were conducted in Cantonese Chinese. Each interview took about two hours. In a few instances, I went back for a second interview. I always brought a gift with me, usually something sweet to eat, as is customary when you visit a Chinese home. I tried to engage in casual conversation, inquiring about the family members or remarking on the surroundings, to take the tension out of being interviewed. Before actually starting the interview, I would ask permission to tape the interview, explaining that I wanted to record their story as accurately as possible. Although I wish I had videotaped them, it was easier and less intrusive to do audio recordings. In hindsight, I regret that I did not take immediate notes about the surroundings, my impressions of each interviewee, and the ways we interacted, because my memory usually failed me when it came time to write up the interview, sometimes months later. I made my goals clear to them from the start: to learn about the experiences of Chinese women like themselves so that I could record them as history lessons for future generations.

I chose to pose my questions in chronological order to allow for a life history flow, beginning with where and when they were born, their family background, their childhood, and so forth. Although feminist scholars now recommend an interactive, dialogical approach, in which the interviewer and narrator are on an equal par, exchanging views and sharing research goals and analyses,[6] I preferred to play the role of the

---

4. A number of feminist scholars have noted that women often remember the past in different ways than men, that women are less likely to put themselves at the center of public events or boast of their personal accomplishments. See Joan Sangster, "Telling Our Stories: Feminist Debates and the Use of Oral History," in *The Oral History Reader*, ed. Robert Perks and Alistair Thomson (London: Routledge, 1998), p. 89.

5. The remaining fifteen interviews cited in *Unbound Feet* were conducted by staff of the Survey of Race Relations research project in the 1920s, the Chinese Historical Society of America in the 1970s, and the Chinese Women of America Research Project in the early 1980s.

6. See Ruth Frankenberg, *White Women, Race Matters: The Social Construction of Whiteness* (Minneapolis: University of Minnesota Press, 1993), chap. 2; Ann Oakley, "Interviewing Women: A Contradiction in Terms," in *Doing Feminist Research*, ed. Helen Roberts (London: Routledge & Kegan Paul, 1981), pp. 30–61; and Kristina Minister, "A Feminist Frame for the Oral History Interview," in Gluck and Patai (eds.), *Women's Words*, pp. 27–41.

attentive listener, an approach that seemed more effective with the Chinese women I interviewed, all of whom were my seniors. However, I never hesitated to give my opinions when asked. At times I would ask if my analysis made sense to them—that the lives of Chinese women changed dramatically in the early twentieth century, partly due to the influential roles of Christian organizations, Chinese nationalism, and economic conditions. Interestingly enough, regardless of their own religious and political views, most women agreed with my assessment, bringing forth different examples to support it.

Sometimes I would inadvertently hit a raw spot. During one interview a woman broke down in tears when I brought up the subject of her brother. Evidently, he had been kidnapped while visiting China and the family was unable to send the ransom money in time. He died tragically. In another instance, a woman began talking about how as a baby she was left at the doorstep of a mission home then immediately regretted having revealed the secret. Both times, I stopped the interview and waited for the women to regain their composure before continuing. Whenever I encountered uncomfortable lapses into silence, I tried to hold my tongue, but in most cases further prodding and probing on my part did more to elicit responses than waiting it out. At the end of the interview, I always asked to see family photographs, scrapbooks, writings, and any memorabilia. This is how I found many of the photographs and unpublished writings that are included in *Unbound Feet* and *Unbound Voices*. It was also at the conclusion of the interview that I would ask the person to sign the consent form. By then, they knew what had been covered in the interview and whether they could trust me with their stories. No one ever refused to give her consent.

Because of time constraints I decided to take the shortcut of doing index summaries instead of full transcripts of all the interviews. This process involves listening to the interview and, with the help of a transcriber, summarizing its contents by topic in the order in which the conversation evolved. Along the way I would transcribe verbatim any portion of an interview I thought I might quote later. Because I intended *Unbound Feet* to be a synthesis of Chinese American women's history based on a variety of primary and secondary sources, I could not include anyone's full life story, interesting and significant though it might be. Instead I selected excerpts from different interviews to make certain interpretative points about their collective history. In the process of interspersing my analysis with excerpts from the interviews, it was inevitable that I would end up cutting people off and omitting the natural flow of the interviews.

With this book, *Unbound Voices*, I wanted to use the oral histories differently. My intention was to bring together a diverse range of individual life stories and reproduce them as fully as possible without any interruption on my part. By so doing, I hoped to remove my partiality and allow a range of voices and viewpoints to emerge.[7] I began by reviewing all the interviews used in *Unbound Feet* for possible inclusion in this second volume. In my selection I tried to strike a balance in terms of generation, class, and coverage of topics. In addition, I wanted the oral histories to complement and not duplicate the contents and perspectives of the writings—letters, poems, essays, speeches, and editorials—that were to be included as well. I finally settled on twelve interviews, which included a *sau saang gwa*, immigrant wives and second-generation daughters, social activists and labor organizers, a shipyard worker and a WAC. Together, their voices were to represent the lived experiences of Chinese women in San Francisco from the turn of the century through World War II.

I was particularly attracted to strong women who were articulate, candid, and vibrant storytellers, such as Kwong King You, the *sau saang gwa* whom I interviewed in China (pages 113–23), and Lorena How, whose mother was active in the war effort (pages 496–510). In many ways Kwong King You represents the other half of the story of transnational migration, that of the many wives left behind in China by Chinese immigrants in America—a story that has seldom been told. How can a woman wait forty years for a man, who in the meantime has remarried, and not feel bitter about her fate? As I explain in the introduction to her story, women such as Kwong King You who became virtual widows because of restrictive immigration laws and patriarchal practices found ways to cope with the long separations. In exchange for a life of widowhood, they enjoyed economic comforts and social prestige in the village, though only as long as they remained faithful to their husbands overseas.

Like Kwong King You, Lorena How was a born storyteller and needed little prodding to relate her mother Lai Yee Guey's story. I was mesmerized by her tales, most of which had to do with her mother's strong personality, talents, and religious beliefs and Lorena's close relationship to her. By sharing her memories of her mother with us, Lorena offers us

---

7. As Robert Berkhofer notes, "The more nearly the artifact or text is reproduced as a whole, the less chance there is that the editor's or other intervener's selection and interpretation will enter the mimetic process" (*Beyond the Great Story: History as Text and Discourse* [Cambridge, Mass.: Harvard University Press, 1995], p. 148).

personal insights into Chinese American women's history, culture, and family life, and at the same time passes on to us precious lessons that took her a lifetime to learn. Although saddled with work, child care, and housework responsibilities, Lai Yee Guey always found the necessary resources to care for Lorena, who was born with a congenital heart defect, and to give to community causes. Through her teaching and example, Lorena grew up with an appreciation for her cultural heritage, a tolerance for difference, and a commitment to help others.

Although the task was somewhat onerous, I did not mind going back to transcribe and edit the twelve interviews. It gave me a chance to listen more carefully to each interview, do a closer transcription and translation, analyze the subtexts and silences, organize the text, and shape the story as I saw fit.[8] To allow for a narrative flow and to minimize interruptions, I deliberately eliminated most of my questions, except where they help clarify the answers, as well as any redundancies and false starts. If the interview was in English, I would rearrange segments of the taped interview for clarity and an organized flow, but never change the actual words used. If the interview was in Chinese, I had more flexibility with the choice of words and sentence structure in the translation. I tried to stay true to the meaning of the spoken word, but I usually had to sacrifice the manner of speech and the full impact of Chinese colloquialisms, proverbs, and metaphors in the process. For example, such translated phrases as "A bamboo door should be paired with a bamboo door, a wooden door with a wooden door" and "If your head has enough hair, you can put up with a lot of fleas" just do not carry the same powerful meaning and flavor as does the original Chinese.[9]

Rather than interject my voice into the stories, I use footnotes to clarify cultural and historical references as well as to note any discrepancies or contradictions in what was said. Keeping in mind that all forms of recorded history are biased and need to be critically evaluated, I looked for internal coherence and contradictions in the responses of my sub-

---

8. This process is in keeping with the practice of listening to the silences, the meta-statements, and the logic of the narrative for different levels of meaning. See Grele, *Envelopes of Sound*; Kathryn Anderson and Dana C. Jack, "Learning to Listen: Interview Techniques and Analyses," in Gluck and Patai (eds.), *Women's Words*, pp. 11–26; and Frankenberg, *White Women, Race Matters*, pp. 35–42.

9. The first phrase is taken from my mother's interview (p. 90) in reference to class compatibility in arranged marriages. The second saying comes from the interview with *sau saang gwa* Kwong King You (p. 119) and means that if a man is wealthy enough, he can have as many wives as he wants.

jects.[10] Whenever necessary I corroborated what I was told with other interviews and documentary evidence within the context of the broader social history. For example, my mother at one point said she was detained at the Angel Island Immigration Station. But she arrived in 1941, after the station was destroyed in a fire, so this would not have been possible. When I checked her immigration file at the National Archives, I discovered that she was detained at temporary facilities at 801 Silver Avenue in San Francisco. Evidently, she had heard me talk so much about Angel Island in conjunction with my earlier research that she had assumed she must have been detained there as well. As Alessandro Portelli notes in *The Death of Luigi Trastulli and Other Stories*, "Memory is not a passive depository of facts, but an active process of creation of meanings. . . . These changes reveal the narrators' effort to make sense of the past and to give a form to their lives, and set the interview and the narrative in their historical context."[11] My mother had shifted the place of her detention in order to give meaning to a crucial event in her life in relation to Chinese American history.

To add context and meaning, I preface each interview with an introduction that provides biographical background on the person, the circumstances of the interview, and an analysis of the individual's testimony. For example, in the case of Kwong King You, I discuss how I came to interview her in China, my impressions and interactions with her, and why she was willing to wait a lifetime for her husband to return home even though she knew he had remarried in the United States. In the introduction to Lorena How's interview, I explain the special friendship and rapport she had with my sister Sandy, who interviewed her, provide some basic biographical information on both Lorena and her mother, Lai Yee Guey, and note the unexpected pearls that came out of the interview, such as the powerful story of a mother's devotion to a disabled daughter as she taught her how to stand up for herself.

---

10. I always keep in mind what my colleague Paul Skenazy and oral historian Valerie Yow have to say on this subject: "Oral history is always reliable, always unreliable. It does not provide an account of an event so much as the experience, recollected, of an event" (Paul Skenazy, "Oral History: Some Guidelines and Comments," unpublished essay). In *Recording Oral History*, Yow reminds us that diaries, letters, and official documents can be just as biased as oral histories. She writes, "History is what the people who lived it make of it and what the others who observe the participants or listen to them or study their records make of it" (p. 22).

11. Alessandro Portelli, *The Death of Luigi Trastulli and Other Stories: Form and Meaning in Oral History* (Albany: State University of New York Press, 1991), p. 52.

After I completed each interview, I would send a copy to the interviewee or a family member for corrections and permission to publish. For those narrators who did not read English, I had to rely on the cooperation and judgment of their children. I was relieved to know that, except for a few minor corrections, everyone seemed satisfied with my rendering of their life story. I plan to eventually transcribe all the interviews, send them to the parties involved for approval, and deposit the tape recordings and transcripts in the Bancroft Library at the University of California, Berkeley.

To be self-reflexive about the process, I admit I went into the interviews with my own biases and agenda, which inevitably slanted the outcome of the interviews.[12] For example, in my line of questioning I tended to overemphasize racism and sexism. This became obvious when I went back to listen and transcribe the interviews. I just would not accept "no discrimination" for an answer but pursued the question in different guises: "Growing up, were you treated differently from your brothers? Were you treated differently at work because you were Chinese or female? Did the white staff at Angel Island mistreat you in any way? Did you see any evidence of discrimination in the shipyards? Did you ever wish you were not female?" Listening to the recordings later, I came to the conclusion that there were different degrees of discrimination and that most women did not experience blatant racism or sexism. And if they had encountered subtle forms of discrimination, they might choose to suppress it. For example, shipyard worker May Lew Gee told me, "I have never really experienced discrimination. If there was, it didn't bother me because . . . I've never let it deter me from doing anything."[13] Others made it clear that certain situations did not spell discrimination, as I seemed to suspect. In my interview with labor organizer Sue Ko Lee, I remember pressing her to admit that there was a gender division of labor in the National Dollar Stores sewing factory where she worked and that the male-dominated jobs drew higher pay. Why else was it that all the cutters were men? Exasperated with my persistence, she finally said,

---

12. Here I am reminded of what Ruth Frankenberg says in *White Women, Race Matters*: "An interview is not, in any simple sense, the telling of a life so much as it is an incomplete story angled toward my questions and each woman's ever-changing sense of self and of how the world works" (p. 41). Similarly, Paul Skenazy notes in his essay on oral history guidelines, "Oral history is an oblique reflection of the meeting of interviewer and interviewee. The material of the oral history is shaped by who it is delivered to and what that person chooses to hear, ask more about, respond to with face and body."

13. May Lee Gee, interview with author, July 16, 1994, Pacifica, California.

"Well, because the women can't do that type of work. They have to lift
these heavy bolts of material and push those knives through material piled
that high on the table (*raises her arm about six inches above the table*).
Like white muslin, starched, do you know how heavy those are? The cut-
ter would have to lift that and put it on the machine. It's heavy!"[14]

Quite obviously, most of my subjects did not like dwelling on the negative aspects of their lives, preferring instead to focus on the positive.
Immigrant women chose to emphasize how they overcame hardships for
the sake of their children. In their views and experiences, the cultural
baggage they brought from China sustained more than constrained their
lives in America. My great-aunt Wong See Chan, for example, stuck to
a bad marriage in keeping with her father's admonition not to disgrace
the Wong family name by divorcing her husband. Not only did her
strong sense of honor give her the strength to endure the marriage, but
it also helped her withstand the Great Depression (pages 356–64). Many
second-generation women talked to me about the "good old days" growing up in Chinatown and their positive interactions with white Americans. Contrary to Marcus Hansen's acculturation theory, second-generation women I interviewed did not simply reject and replace the old
Chinese ways with Western values and practices.[15] Rather, they operated
within a broad continuum of responses to cultural conflict and discrimination in America—from acquiescing to accommodating to rebelling.

Upon reflection, I know the power to shape my interviewees' stories
resided with me.[16] After all, I was the one who got to choose the storyteller, ask the questions, edit their answers, decide what to include and
exclude in the final story, as well as interpret the story. For example, as
an atheist and feminist I tended to downplay the role of religion and emphasize social agency in the lives of my subjects. Yet many of the women
I interviewed clearly relied heavily on Christianity or Chinese folk religion to help them survive and overcome hardships. My mother, who is
a devout Baptist, took every opportunity in her interview to *gin jing,* or
give testimony to her faith in God, although you would not know it from
reading her story in *Unbound Voices.* At one point in the interview, when
I asked her whether she got along with her co-workers in the sewing fac-

---

14. Sue Ko Lee, interview with author, October 26, 1989, El Cerrito, California.
15. According to Marcus Hansen, the first generation holds on to their culture, the second generation rejects the old for the new, and the third generation reclaims its cultural
heritage. See Marcus Hansen, *The Problem of the Third Generation Immigrant* (Rock Island, Ill.: Augustana Historical Society, 1938).
16. For a discussion of how power is tipped in favor of the interviewer, see Yow, *Recording Oral History,* pp. 105–9; and Frankenberg, *White Women, Race Matters,* pp. 29–42.

tory where she worked, she told me the story about how she went to pray in the bathroom one day after an argument broke out. When she came out of the bathroom, one worker had quit of her own accord and peace had been restored. "Even the boss said I was powerful," she said as she broke out into her favorite religious hymn.[17] Other women I interviewed, such as Law Shee Low, said they depended on *tin wong* (king in heaven) to get them through the hard times (pages 211–23). While I did not totally ignore the important role religion played in their lives, I often chose to highlight acts of agency by reading between the lines. Kwong King You said she accepted her fate as a *sau saang gwa*, but she also sought to be economically self-sufficient by becoming a midwife. My mother relied on prayer to help her through times of adversity, but she also went to relatives and social agencies for help when things got out of hand. Immigrant wives I interviewed were indeed the obedient wives they said they were, but I could also see that they often wore the pants in the house.

Ultimately, my subjects had their say, but it was I who shaped, interpreted, and presented their life stories. The decisions I made as to what to include or exclude in their stories were greatly influenced by my narrative goal to show how women responded to racial and gender discrimination in effecting social change in their lives. Considering that my interviewees approved the final story, I believe I have done an honorable job of staying faithful to their voices and to the substance of their testimonies.

Listening to Chinese American women tell their stories has always been a humbling, vicarious, and learning experience for me. Feminists may consider their lives oppressive, but the women themselves see only fulfillment. Karl Marx once said, "Men [and women] make their own history . . . but they do not make it under circumstances chosen by themselves."[18] Chinese women have always had to be inventive in order to survive, adapt, and contribute to the well-being of their families, community, and country. My job as an oral historian has been to record and give voice to their life stories, to lend context and significance to their history so that we as a nation might learn to bridge our differences and come to terms with our collective past—how we got to be the way we are and how we can make things better. It is for this purpose that I have dedicated myself to collecting oral histories of Chinese American women.

17. Jew Law Ying, interview with author in Chinese, September 7, 1982, San Francisco.

18. Karl Marx, "The Eighteenth Brumaire of Louis Bonaparte," in *The Marx-Engels Reader*, ed. Robert C. Tucker (New York: W. W. Norton, 1972), p. 437. I am indebted to Ann Lane for this citation.

CHINESE WOMEN IN SAN FRANCISCO

Consent Form

After being provided with a description of this research project and its benefits and possible risks, I consent to be interviewed and agree to the following use of my interview (please check):

_____ Use of tape recording and transcript by Judy Yung only
_____ Use of tape recording and transcript by other researchers
_____ Use my true identity
_____ Do not use my true identity
_____ Other stipulations:

I understand that information from this interview may be used in Judy Yung's research and its eventual publication on Chinese women in San Francisco, but only under the above provisos. Should I decide to withdraw from this study at any time, I will write to Prof. Judy Yung at Oakes College, University of California, Santa Cruz, CA 95064, at which time the interview tape and transcript will be destroyed.

Print Name: _____
Name: _____ Date: _____
Agreed:_____ Date: _____

CHINESE WOMEN IN SAN FRANCISCO

Interview Questions — Immigrant Women

LIFE IN CHINA

1. Where and when were you born? How large was your family? What did your parents do for a living?
2. Describe your daily life and living conditions (responsibilities at home, schooling, work, and social life).
3. How were you regarded and treated as a female in China as compared to a male (relationship with parents, gender roles, responsibilities at home, education preparatory to adulthood, freedom of movement, sex education and conduct, work choice and wages, choice of marital partner and marital role, social life, political and legal rights)?

IMMIGRATION TO THE UNITED STATES

4. When did you come to the United States (age and year)? Why and how (immigration status)? With whom?
5. Describe the voyage and the immigration process upon arrival.
6. What were your expectations and initial impressions of life in the United States?

LIFE AFTER ARRIVAL

7. What was life like after you settled down in San Francisco? Describe your living conditions, schooling, occupation, family life, and social activities.
8. If married in the United States, how did you meet your husband and decide to marry him? If married in China and separated for a period of time, how did the separation affect you and your marriage?
9. Describe your role as a wife, mother, and homemaker relative to your husband. Who controlled reproduction? What were your household, religious, and cultural duties? Who was responsible for child care and rearing? Who held the purse strings? What difficulties, if any, did you experience? How were you able to resolve them?
10. What kind of work did you do for a living? How did you like the job? Describe the wages and working conditions. How did it compare to your husband's? What difficulties, if any, did you experience? How were you able to resolve them?
11. Describe your social and political life as compared to your husband's (organizations, social activities, political involvement, interactions with other races).

12. How were you regarded in the community where you lived? Did you experience any discrimination because you were Chinese or a woman? How did you deal with it?

13. What, if any, differences were there in being a woman in China and the United States?

OBSERVATIONS OF LIFE IN SAN FRANCISCO, 1900–1945

14. What was life like for Chinese women in San Francisco during this period? Was there any more footbinding or prostitution? When did women start going out and why? What kind of educational and work opportunities were available to them? What kind of organizations did they belong to? How involved were women in politics?

15. How were the Chinese regarded and treated by other races? How were Chinese women regarded and treated?

16. Who were some of the prominent women then?

17. My thesis is that 1900–1945 was a liberating period for Chinese American women. Do you agree or disagree? If you agree, what do you think were the causes?

18. Which historical events had the greatest impact on you and other Chinese women (1911 Revolution, World War I, May Fourth Movement, World's Fair in 1915 and 1939, Immigration Act of 1924, Communist-Nationalist civil war, Great Depression, National Dollar Stores strike in 1938, World War II)?

19. How influential were Christianity and Chinese nationalism on the lives of Chinese women in San Francisco? How about the women's emancipation movement in China and the women's suffrage movement in the United States?

REFLECTIONS

20. Have your expectations of life in America been fulfilled? Any regrets?

21. How have you raised your children differently from the way you were raised? Are you satisfied with the outcome of your children?

22. What things do you cherish most about America? What things, if any, do you not like about America?

23. Do you have any favorite family stories you can share with me?

24. Do you have any photographs, letters, writings, or memorabilia I can use in my book?

CHINESE WOMEN IN SAN FRANCISCO

Interview Questions—Second Generation

FAMILY BACKGROUND, CHILDHOOD, YOUTH

1. Describe your parents' background (year and place of birth, life in China, educational background, occupation, immigration, life in the United States).
2. Where and when were you born? How large was your family?
3. Describe your daily life and living conditions growing up (responsibilities at home, schooling, social life).
4. How were you regarded and treated as a daughter compared to your brothers (relationship with parents, gender roles, responsibilities at home, education preparatory to adulthood, freedom of movement, sex education and conduct, social life)?
5. How much education did you receive? How did you choose your major or field of study? Did you experience any difficulties in school? How were you able to resolve them?
6. If you worked, what kind of jobs did you have? How did you find the jobs? Describe the wages and working conditions.
7. Describe your social life (organizations, social activities, interracial interactions).
8. What did your parents expect of you? Did you experience any generation gap or cultural conflict at home? How were you able to resolve them?
9. What were your aspirations? Who were your role models? Who influenced you the most (parents, friends, school, church, popular culture)?
10. Did you experience any discrimination because you were Chinese or female? How did you deal with it?

ADULTHOOD

11. What did you do for a living? How did you find the jobs? Describe the wages and working conditions. What difficulties, if any, did you experience? How were you able to resolve them?
12. How did you meet and marry your husband? In your relationship to him, would you regard yourself as his superior, subordinate, or equal? What was the division of responsibilities? What difficulties did you experience in your marriage, and how were you able to resolve them?

13. How many children did you have? Did you practice birth control? What were the conditions during childbirth? Who raised the children? How did you raise them differently than the way you were raised? What cultural traditions did you try to continue? Did you have any difficulties as a mother, and how were you able to resolve them?

14. Describe your social and political life as compared to your husband's (organizations, social activities, political involvement, interactions with other races).

15. How were you regarded in the community where you lived? Did you experience any discrimination because you were Chinese or female? How did you deal with it?

OBSERVATIONS OF LIFE IN SAN FRANCISCO, 1900–1945

16. What was life like for Chinese immigrant women as compared to second-generation women during this period? What kind of educational and work opportunities were available to them? How involved were they in community activities or politics?

17. How were Chinese regarded and treated by other races? How were Chinese women regarded and treated?

18. Who were some of the prominent women then?

19. My thesis is that 1900–1945 was a liberating period for Chinese American women. Do you agree or disagree? If you agree, what do you think were the causes?

20. Which historical events had the greatest impact on you and other Chinese women (1906 earthquake, 1911 Revolution, World War I, May Fourth Movement, World's Fair in 1915 and 1939, Immigration Act of 1924, Communist-Nationalist civil war, Great Depression, National Dollar Stores strike in 1938, World War II)?

21. How influential were Christianity and Chinese nationalism in the lives of Chinese women in San Francisco? How about the women's emancipation movement in China and the women's suffrage movement in the United States?

22. What was the impact of social institutions on the self-perceptions of second-generation women (public school, Chinese school, religious organization, women's organization, popular culture)?

23. Do you have any favorite family stories you can share with me?

24. Do you have any photographs, letters, writings, or memorabilia I can use in my book?

Chinese Glossary

Ah Fook　亞福
ah gung (grandfather)　亞公
Ah Kum　亞琴
ah mo (grandmother)　亞姆
Alliance of Guangdong Girls Schools　廣東女校運動大同盟
Baai Chat Je (Festival of the Seven Maidens)　拜七姐
baai nin (to pay respects at Chinese New Year)　拜年
baai san (to worship gods)　拜神
baak yim (mischievous)　百厭
Baat Yuet Sap Ng (Mid-Autumn Festival)　八月十五
bailan (a vernacular rhyming narrative used in Cantonese opera)　白欖
Bak Heong　逼鄉
Baohuanghui　保皇會
Baosi　褒姒
Bock Ma Hong Hospital　白馬行醫院
bok choy (Chinese leafy vegetable)　白菜
Canton (Guangzhou)　廣州
cha siu won ton (ravioli with roast pork)　火燒雲吞
Chan Chow Yung　陳秋容
Chan Gee Duk　陳志德
Chan Gee Geen　陳志堅
Chan Gum　陳金
Chan Hon Fun　陳翰芬

Changsha   長沙
Chaozhou   潮州
Che Ruoshui   車若水
"Cheelai (Qilai)"   《起來》
Chen Junqi   陳君綺
Cheng Xingnan   程星男
cheong saam (Chinese dress)   長衫
cheung hei (long winded)   長氣
Chew, Rose   伍秋梅
Chiang Kai-shek   蔣介石
Chin Foo   陳富
Chin Gway   陳貴
Chin Hong Dai   陳康大
Chin Lung   陳龍
Chin Mee Ngon   陳美顏
Chin Quong   陳元光
Chin Shee   陳氏
Chin Sou   陳壽
Chin Suey Kum   陳瑞琴
Chin Suey Ngon   陳瑞顏
Chin Wah   陳華
Chin Wing   陳榮
Chinese Hospital   東華醫院
Chinese Six Companies (Chinese Consolidated Benevolent Association)
    中華總會館
Chinese Students Association   中國學生會
Chinese Times   《金山時報》
Chinese War Relief Association   旅美華僑統一義捐救國總會
Chinese Women's Jeleab Association   旅美中國女界自立會
Chinese Women's Patriotic Club   婦女拒日救國會
Chinese Workers Mutual Aid Association   加省華工合作會
Chinese World   《世界日報》
Ching Ming   清明
Chinn, Thomas W.   陳參盛
choi! ("for fortune's sake!")   彩！
chone choy (Chinese green onion)   蔥菜
chop suey won ton (ravioli with mixed vegetables)   雜碎雲吞
Chung, Margaret   張瑪珠
Chung Mei Home   中美學校
Chung Sai Yat Po   《中西日報》

Chung Wah Chinese Language School　中華中文學校
Chungking (Chongqing)　重慶
Chungshan (Zhongshan) District　中山縣
Cixi, Empress　慈禧太后
da do dai gwok jue yi! ("down with imperialism!")　打倒帝國主義
Da Jiu (Feast of the Hungry Ghosts)　打醮
Daai Fau (San Francisco)　大埠
daap sik gwoon (boardinghouse)　搭食館
Dai Chek Hom village　大赤坎村
Daji　妲己
Dangui Theater　丹桂戲院
Deng Huifang　鄧蕙芳
Deng Yingchao　鄧穎超
dim sum (Chinese dumplings and pastries)　點心
Double Ten　雙十節
Doumen District　斗門縣
Doumen Overseas Chinese Affairs Office　斗門縣僑務辦公室
Dow Moon Market　斗門墟
Dowager, Empress　慈禧太后
Dragon Boat Festival　端午節
Du Qingchi　杜清池
Eng, Marietta Chong　張惠英
faan gwai jai (foreign devil boys)　番鬼仔
faan gwai lo (foreign devils)　番鬼佬
faan woon (rice bowl)　飯碗
Fang Zhenwu　方振武
Far East Company　遠東公司
Fat Shan (Foshan)　佛山
Festival of the Cowherd and Weaving Maiden　牛郎織女節〔七姐誕〕
Festival of the Hungry Ghosts　孟蘭節
foh yuk (roast pork)　火肉
Fong, Alice　方玉屏
Fong, B. S.　廣炳舜
Fong Ching　馮正初
Fong Chow　方佩文
Fong, Emily Lee　李彩瓊
Fong, Marian　方玉清
Fong, Martha　方玉娟
Fong, Mickey　方雪球
Foo Nui Wooi　婦女會

Foo Wing　富榮

Fucha, King　夫差皇帝

Fun, Alice Sue　蘇翠嵐

Funü Jiuguohui　婦女救國會

Funü Ju-Ri Jiuguohui　婦女拒日救國會

Funü Xinyunhui　婦女新運會

Funü Zhanqu Nanmin Chouzhenhui　婦女戰區難民籌賑會

gai (chicken)　雞

gai jook (rice gruel with chicken)　雞粥

gam saan haak (guest of Gold Mountain)　金山客

gam saan jong (Gold Mountain firm)　金山莊

gam saan poh (wife of a Gold Mountain man)　金山婆

gam saan siu ye (son of a Gold Mountain man)　金山少爺

gan (catty, equivalent to one and one-third pounds)　斤

Gee, Maggie　朱美嬌

Gee, May Lew　劉彩美

Gin, Gladys Ng　伍玉娥

gin jing (to give testimony)　見証

Golden Star Radio　金星廣播電台

Goon Yum　觀音

Goujian, King　勾踐皇帝

Guangdong Province　廣東省

Guangdong Women's Liberation Society　廣東婦女解放協會

Guangmin　《光明》

Guangxu　光緒

Guangzhou (Canton)　廣州

Guomindang　中國國民黨

gwa fun (a cut-up melon)　瓜分

gwok chi (day of national humiliation)　國恥

Hakka　客家

Han Shizhong　韓世忠

Hankow (Hankou)　漢口

har yuk won ton (ravioli with shrimp)　蝦肉雲吞

Haw Lon Yin Street　荷蘭園街

He Xiangning　何香凝

Heilongjiang　黑龍江

Heong Ma　鄉媽

Heungshan (Xiangshan) District　香山縣

Hin Bin village　田邊村

Hip Wo Chinese Language School　協和中文學校

Hip Yee Tong 協義堂

ho pei hei (a good temperament) 好脾氣

hoi nin (to start a new year) 開年

Hong Kong 香港

Hong Xiannü 紅線女

Hong Xiuquan 洪秀全

Hong Xuanjiao 洪宣嬌

Hop Sing Tong 合勝堂

How, Lorena 陳瑞球

Hoy, William 謝開

Hua Mulan 花木蘭

Huanghuagang 黃花崗

Huaren Shiyehui 華人失業會

Huie, Penny Chan 陳娉嬅

huiguan (organization of people from same region in China) 會館

Hung Sin Nui 紅線女

Jai Naam Chaam On (Jinan Massacre) 濟南慘案

jam cha (to serve tea) 斟茶

Jan, Flora Belle 鄭容金

Jang, Ruth Chan 陳月紅

Jew Hin Gwin 趙天炯

Jew Jin Dai 趙轉娣

Jew Jun Hei 趙振喜

Jew Law Ying 趙羅英

Jew Ngan Bun 趙雁賓

Jew Shee 趙氏

Jew Sing Haw 趙成賀

Jew Sing Jun 趙成振

Jew Sing Lurt 趙成律

Jew Siu Ping 趙少平

Jew Sun 趙申

Jew Wun Jee 趙煥珠

Jew Yee Yuet 趙以越

Jian On (Jing'an) 井岸

Jinan Massacre 濟南慘案

Jom Gong 湛江

jook (rice gruel) 粥

joy geen ("see you again") 再見

jue lung (pig's cage) 豬籠

jung (zhongzi) (glutinous rice dumpling) 粽

Kaiping District   開平縣

Kang Youwei   康有為

Kang-Ri   抗日

Kau Ma   巧媽

Kee Mo village   乾霧村

Kuan Yin   觀音

Kuang Su   光緒

Kuen Shek   權石

Kuomintang (Guomindang)   中國國民黨

Kwan, Florence Chinn   陳奇馨

Kwan Sung Tao   關頌韜

Kwong Fook Sang   廣福生

Kwong King You   鄺瓊瑤

Kwong Shee   鄺氏

Kwong Tak Tong   廣德堂

Lai, Him Mark   麥禮謙

lai si (lucky money in red envelope)   利是

Lai Yee Guey   黎如桂

Lau Shee   劉氏

Law Shee Low   劉羅氏

Lee, Charles Goodall   李肇榮

Lee, Chingwah   李華清

Lee, Clara   陳意妙

Lee, Hazel Ying   李月英

Lee, Jane Kwong   鄺連真

Lee Jew Hing   李祖慶

Lee, Lim P.   李泮霖

Lee, Rose Hum   譚金美

Lee Shee   李氏

Lee, Sue Ko   蕭修

Lee Yee Oi   李以愛

Lei Ok village   李屋村

Leong, B. Y.   梁秉彝

Leong, Charles   梁普禮

Leong Jew Shee   梁趙氏

Leong Kum Kew   梁琴嬌

Leong Shee   梁氏

Leong Yee (Shee)   梁余氏

Lew Hing   劉興

Lew, Rose   劉溢銀

li (Chinese mile, equivalent to one-third mile)　里

Li Ruzhen　李汝珍

Liang Hongyu　梁紅玉

"Lianzhen Ju Ji"　《蓮真劇集》

Lik Kei village　瀝歧村

Lin Hi　蓮弟

ling gok (a knuckle-rap on the head)　菱角

Lingnan　嶺南

Liu Qunxian　劉群先

Liu Yilan　劉義蘭

Liu Yonglian　劉詠蓮

lo fan (white foreigner)　老番

lo mo (mother)　老母

Loo Lin　盧蓮

Look Hoy Hung Hotel　陸海通旅館

Louie, Fong, Kwong Family Association　溯源堂

Low Fung Drama Club　蘆烽話劇社

Lowe, Eva　陳君綺

Lowe, Lawrence　蔡淪溟

Lowe, Rolland　蔡流輪

Lu Zhinang　盧枝楠

Lugouqiao　蘆溝橋

Lü-Mei Huaqiao Tongyi Yijuan Jiuguo Zonghui　旅美華僑統一義捐救國總會

Lü-Mei Zhongguo Nüjie Zilihui　旅美中國女界自立會

Lung Do　隆都

Ma Zhanshan　馬占山

Macao　澳門

mah jongg (Chinese game played with tiles)　麻將

Mai Zhouyi　麥灼儀

Man Jung　孟宗

Man Yun　曼雲

Manchu　滿族

Manchuria　東北〔東三省〕

"March of the Volunteers"　《義勇軍進行曲》

Marco Polo Bridge　蘆溝橋

mau (mou) (Chinese acre, equivalent to .15 acre)　畝

May Fourth Movement　五四運動

Meiguo Huaqiao Ju-Ri Jiuguo Houyuanhui　美國華僑拒日救國后援會

Meixi　妹喜

Mid-Autumn Festival　中秋節

Ming dynasty　明朝

mo (sister-in-law)　姆

mo min (no face or humiliated)　無面

Mong Shan village　岡山村

mui tsai (domestic slavegirl)　妹仔

Mukden Incident　瀋陽事變

Nam Shan (Nanshan) village　南山村

Nanhai District　南海縣

Nanking (Nanjing)　南京

National Dollar Stores　中興公司

Ng Poon Chew　伍盤照

ng yuet jit (Dragon Boat Festival)　五月節〔端午節〕

Ngau Bing Tong village　牛洴塘村

1911 Revolution　辛亥革命

Nineteenth Route Army　十九路軍

Northern Expedition　北伐

nui gwoon (girls' residence)　女館

Oi Wa Tong　愛和堂

ok (a mean temperament)　惡

On Leung Tong　安良堂

Onyett, Helen Pon　陳玉珠

op duey won ton (ravioli with roast duck)　鴨腿雲吞

Ow Muck Gay　區麥基

Ow, Rose Yuen　阮妹

Pai Shan village　排山村

Panyu (Punyu) District　番禺縣

Pearl River Delta　珠江三角洲

Peidao School　培道書院

Peking (Beijing)　北京

People's Hospital　人民醫院

Qing dynasty　清朝

Qiu Jin　秋瑾

Qu Yuan　屈原

Rice Bowl Movement　一碗飯運動

sai dei (wash the floors)　洗地

Sai Gai Yat Po　《世界日報》

sai yi (wash the clothes)　洗衣

sam jup won ton (ravioli with curry, ketchup, and roast pork)　三汁雲吞

Sam Yup Association　三邑總會館

Sang Wo　生和

Sap Baat Gwok (eighteen countries, or the Emporium)　十八國

sau saang gwa (a widow with a living husband, or grass widow)　守生寡

Schulze, Tye Leung　梁亞娣

See Ji Hou village　獅子頭村

Sek Jue village　石嘴村

seung tau gung (older man who assists the groom)　上頭公

seung tau poh (older woman who assists the bride)　上頭婆

Shamian　沙面

Shantung (Shandong) Province　山東省

Shanghai　上海

Shanghai Trunk Company　上海洋箱公司

Shantou　汕頭

Shee　氏

Shekki (Shiqi)　石岐

Shenyang (Mukden)　瀋陽

Shoong, Joe　周崧

Shunde District　順德縣

si man (genteel)　斯文

Sieh King King (Xue Jinqin)　薛錦琴

Silwing P. C. Au　區兆榮

Sin Dung village　仙洞村

Sing Kee　生記

Siu Chek Hom village　小赤坎村

Siu How Chung village　小濠涌村

Song dynasty　宋朝

Soong Ai-ling (Song Ailing)　宋靄齡

Soong Ching-ling (Song Qingling)　宋慶齡

Soong Mei-ling (Song Meiling)　宋美齡

Soong, T. V.　宋子文

Square and Circle Club　方圓社

Sue Hing Benevolent Association　肇慶總會館

Sui Sin Far (Edith Maude Eaton)　水仙花

suk (uncle, or father's younger brother)　叔

sum (aunt, or wife of father's younger brother)　嬸

Sum Tum village　深氹村

Sunning District　新寧縣

Sunwui (Xinhui) District　新會縣

Sun Yat-sen　孫逸仙〔孫中山〕

sung (vegetable or meat dishes)　餸

Taam, T. T.   譚祖鈿
Taierzhuang   台兒莊
Taiping Rebellion   太平天國起義
Taiwan   台灣
Tan Bokui   譚伯逵
Tang dynasty   唐朝
Tape, Joseph   趙洽
Tientsin (Tianjin)   天津
tin san (god in heaven)   天神
tin wong (king in heaven)   天王
to hau sui (to spit)   吐口水
Toishan (Taishan) District   台山縣
Tom Bak Fong   譚碧芳
Tom Bak Heong   譚碧香
Tom Bak Jing   譚碧貞
Tom Bak Kay   譚碧琦
Tom Choy Bun   譚才彬
Tom Fat Kwong   譚發光
Tom Fat Ming   譚發明
Tom Fat Tin   譚發鈿
Tom Fat Woon   譚發煥
Tom Fat Yuet   譚發悅
Tom Gim Wah   譚劍華
Tom Hin Biew   譚庭標
Tom Kwong Yuan   譚光遠
Tom Leung   譚良
Tom Mai Ming   譚買明
Tom Ngun Dai   譚銀娣
Tom See Heong   譚思鄉
Tom Share Dew   譚社資
Tom Share Gow   譚社教
Tom Wing   譚榮
Tom Yeen Kau   譚賢巧
Tom Yip Ghin   譚業建
Tom Yip Jing   譚業精
Tom Yip Keung   譚業強
Tom Yip Pooh   譚業培
Tom Yip Sou   譚業修
Tom Yip Yee   譚業餘
Tom Yuk Wai   譚裕威

tong (secret society)　堂號

Tong, Thomas　唐憲才

tong saan poh (a recent immigrant woman from China)　唐山婆

Tongmenghui　中國同盟會

True Light Seminary　真光學校

True Sunshine Chinese Language School　聖公會中文學校

Tsai Ting-kai　蔡廷鍇

Tse Kai Yuen　謝己原

Tung Chee　同治

Twenty-four Acts of Filial Piety　《二十四孝》

United Guangdong Women's Society　廣東女界聯合會

Wah Ching　華清

Wang Jianzu　王建祖

War of Resistance against Japan　抗日戰爭

White Crane Cave　白鶴洞

Wing Hung Cheong　永同昌

wo xin chang dan (to sleep on firewood and taste gall)　臥薪嘗膽

Women's New Life Movement　婦女新生活運動

Women's War Zone Refugee Relief Committee　婦女戰區難民籌賑會

won ton (Chinese ravioli)　雲吞

Wong Ah So　黃亞蘇

Wong, Anna May　黃柳霜

Wong Cheong　王祥

Wong, Esther　黃玉燕

wong gar (imperial family or federal government)　皇家

Wong, Jade Snow　黃玉雪

Wong Jeet Mun　黃捷文

Wong Leung Do　黃梁都

Wong See Chan　陳黃氏

Wong Shee　黃氏

Wong, Virginia　黃桂燕

Wu Minchi　吳敏墀

Wuhan　武漢

Xiangshan District　香山縣

Xiangzhou　香洲

Xiao Chaoqui　蕭朝貴

Xie Kuangshi　謝匡時

Xie Xingchou　謝星壽

Xinhui District　新會縣

Xuantong　宣統

Index

Text: 10/13 Sabon
Display: Sabon
Composition: Integrated Composition Systems
Printing and binding: Edwards Brothers

OTHER BOOKS BY JUDY YUNG

Unbound Feet: A Social History of Chinese Women in San Francisco
(California, 1995)

Chinese Women of America: A Pictorial History (1986)

*Island: Poetry and History of Chinese Immigrants on Angel Island,
1910–1940* (1980), coauthored with Him Mark Lai and Genny Lim